MW00632837

PAULINE DOGMATICS

PAULINE DOGMATICS

The Triumph of God's Love

Douglas A. Campbell

WILLIAM B. EERDMANS PUBLISHING COMPANY

GRAND RAPIDS, MICHIGAN

Wm. B. Eerdmans Publishing Co.
4035 Park East Court SE, Grand Rapids, Michigan 49546
www.eerdmans.com

Published 2020
Printed in the United States of America

26 25 24 23 22 21 20   1 2 3 4 5 6 7

ISBN 978-0-8028-7564-8

Library of Congress Cataloging-in-Publication Data

Names: Campbell, Douglas A. (Douglas Atchison), 1961– author.
Title: Pauline dogmatics : the triumph of God's love / Douglas A. Campbell.
Description: Grand Rapids, Michigan : William B. Eerdmans Publishing
   Company, 2019. | Includes bibliographical references and index. |
   Summary: "Douglas Campbell here offers a Pauline Dogmatics that moves to
   how Paul saw God revealed in Jesus and culminates in emphasizing the
   implications of Paul's gospel in his world and today"—Provided by
   publisher.
Identifiers: LCCN 2019026588 | ISBN 9780802875648 (hardcover)
Subjects: LCSH: Bible. Epistles of Paul—Theology. | Bible. Epistles of
   Paul—Criticism, interpretation, etc. | Love—Biblical teaching.
Classification: LCC BS2651 .C284 2019 | DDC 227/.06—dc23
LC record available at https://lccn.loc.gov/2019026588

To Rachel

. . . I would walk five hundred miles
And I would walk five hundred more
Just to be the man who walks a thousand miles
To fall down at your door.

"I'm Gonna Be,"
The Proclaimers
Sunshine on Leith (1988)

CONTENTS

ACKNOWLEDGMENTS

I owe my students a great deal in relation to this project: those of official standing at Duke (students such as Jon DePue, Chauncey Diego, Jonny Tuttle, Jacob Breeze, Andrew Rillera, and Ethan Taylor), those still in touch from my past posts in New Zealand and the UK (people such as Andy Goodliff), and those of less official standing whom I have met in cyberspace and elsewhere (people such as Michael Hardin, along with his friends and students). I don't classify Chris Tilling as a student, but he has certainly been a constant source of support, not to mention of sheer joy, in relation both to this and to other projects. Classes in the spring of 2016 and fall of 2018 have also patiently interacted with this material; I am so grateful for your help. I hope you enjoy it, learn from it, and go well beyond it. It is also a particular delight for me to acknowledge the help of Tom Kleingartner. No one has read or interacted with this work more thoroughly than he has (thirty-six pages of handwritten notes on the subject of universalism alone!), and I appreciate his support, dedication, and insights very much indeed.

I have benefited greatly from my learned and helpful colleagues at Duke, who have returned many anguished emailed requests for guidance with considered and elegant responses and references, in particular, Jeremy Begbie, Luke Bretherton, Chuck Campbell, Stephen Chapman, Mark Chaves, Curtis Freeman, Stephen Gunter, Stanley Hauerwas, Willie Jennings (now at Yale), Randy Maddox, Thea Portier-Young, Warren Smith, and Norman Wirzba. Testament to their virtue is the fact that though they must have regarded some of this material's applications as rather alarming, their generosity was not impeded. Some other old and dear friends and colleagues have chipped in with sage advice as well, especially John Stenhouse and Christian Smith.

I continue to benefit from my ongoing journey through Barth's *Dogmatics* with various friends and companions on that road—the "Barth and Beer" group that meets every Friday for discussion of the week's textual morsel, so Alan, David, Jeff, and more recently, Jack, Andrew, Colby, Jon, and Ethan. And I benefit from those truly learned Barthians who have gone before me and shown me the way: my great friend Alan Torrance, whom I continue to regard as the most brilliant living theological mind I have the honor to be in contact with; his father, James; and his uncle T. F.—and I now need to add the third generation here, notably Andrew, although David is breathing down his neck. How grateful I am for these theological mentors and advisers, and how they have opened up the riches of "the Christian thing" to me, helping me to grasp the momentous issues stirring Paul's ancient texts, issues that can barely be detected, let alone resolved, without being given eyes that can see them from people such as these.

All of the staff at Eerdmans have, as usual, been friendly, supportive, and professional, for which I am grateful, as has the indefatigable and indefatigably cheerful Judith Heyhoe, my in-house editor at Duke. Craig Noll provided a great deal of clarity and encouragement through the final stages, which was much appreciated. Ethan Taylor's assistance during the final proofreading and indexing stages can only be described as heroic. And I have been supported as well by the professional, devoted, and happy staff at the National Humanities Center, where I was fortunate enough to spend a paradisiacal year 2017–18, funded in part by a Duke Endowment scholarship. The manuscript was completed during a summer in Heidelberg at the invitation of my host-professor and much-admired colleague and friend Peter Lampe, where I was supported by the Von Humboldt Foundation. My thanks to you all for your support and for your care.

ABBREVIATIONS

Beyond   Tilling, Chris, ed. *Beyond Old and New Perspectives on Paul: Reflections on the Work of Douglas Campbell*. Eugene, OR: Cascade, 2014.

Deliverance Campbell, Douglas A. *The Deliverance of God: An Apocalyptic Rereading of Justification in Paul*. Grand Rapids: Eerdmans, 2009.

Framing   Campbell, Douglas. *Framing Paul: An Epistolary Biography*. Grand Rapids: Eerdmans, 2014.

Journey   Campbell, Douglas. *Paul: An Apostle's Journey*. Grand Rapids: Eerdmans, 2018.

Quest   Campbell, Douglas. *The Quest for Paul's Gospel: A Suggested Strategy*. London: T&T Clark, 2005.

AB   Anchor Bible

ABD   *Anchor Bible Dictionary*

BDAG   Danker, Arndt, Bauer, and Gingrich, *Greek-English Lexicon of the New Testament and Other Early Christian Literature*

BJRL   *Bulletin of the John Rylands University Library of Manchester*

BZNW   Beihefte zur Zeitschrift für die neutestamentliche Wissenschaft

CBQ   *Catholic Biblical Quarterly*

CEB   Common English Bible

EJPR   *European Journal for the Philosophy of Religion*

HBT   *Horizons in Biblical Theology*

HTR   *Harvard Theological Review*

IJST   *International Journal of Systematic Theology*

Int   *Interpretation*

JBL   *Journal of Biblical Literature*

JSNT	*Journal for the Study of the New Testament*
JSNTSup	Journal for the Study of the New Testament Supplement Series
JSPL	*Journal for the Study of Paul and His Letters*
JTI	*Journal of Theological Interpretation*
JTS	*Journal of Theological Studies*
LCL	Loeb Classical Library
NIGTC	New International Greek Testament Commentary
NIV	New International Version
NRSV	New Revised Standard Version
NTS	*New Testament Studies*
ProEccl	*Pro Ecclesia*
SBLDS	Society of Biblical Literature Dissertation Series
SJT	*Scottish Journal of Theology*
SNTS	Society for New Testament Studies
TDNT	*Theological Dictionary of the New Testament*
WUNT	Wissenschaftliche Untersuchungen zur Neuen Testament
ZNW	*Zeitschrift für die neutestamentliche Wissenschaft*

INTRODUCTION

Richard Longenecker, my wise doctoral supervisor, once quoted the famous adage to me that to write anything two factors usually have to be in place: one has to love one's subject and to hate what everyone else is saying about it. I have to admit that these factors do hold in the main for my relationship with Paul's theology. I love Paul and have always been passionate about his theological description. But I have a lot of problems with the way he is usually described, both within the church and within the modern academy. So this book provides that sweetest of opportunities. It lays out my basic account of Paul's deepest and most important theological convictions, their ideal coordination, and the further steps we need to take to bring those convictions into a constructive conversation with our modern locations. It is the heart of the matter.

Key Conversation Partners

If in what follows I am basically trying to explore the shape of Paul's think-ing—its inner orchestration—then we need to ask and try to answer certain sorts of questions: what topics and subjects and issues do we need to think about? And, equally important, in what order? Elsewhere I describe this in-terpretative dimension in Paul as his "systematic frame."[1] And it seems fair to suggest that this discussion of what is in essence Paul's theology will be assisted significantly if we know something about theology itself. We can learn a great

---

1. See especially ch. 7 in my *Deliverance*, especially 221–46. This chapter lays out the relationships between this particular interpretative dimension and all the other dimensions relevant within any comprehensive reading of Paul. Ultimately it describes and coordinates six "levels" and five "frames."

deal from listening to the outstanding theological minds who have spent a considerable amount of time working through just these questions of coordination, and at rather more depth than most biblical interpreters generally do. However, since space is limited, I tend to lean primarily on my favorite theologian in this area for guidance, Karl Barth, described appositely by T. F. Torrance, himself no mean Christian thinker, as the Einstein of the theologians.[2] It needs to be appreciated immediately that Barth is a useful guide to Paul partly because he was such a faithful Paulinist. Barth often led seminars on biblical texts, as well as on specialized theological subjects and issues, and he began his career with a famous commentary on Romans, forged on the anvil of ten years' work as a pastor at Safenwil in Switzerland (1911–21). The climax of his career, the *Church Dogmatics*, was written to underwrite preaching, and this work quotes the Bible an estimated quarter of a million times. So I suggest that an accurate account of Paul reads him in quite a Barthian way primarily because Barth was in many respects a faithful interpreter of Paul. Moreover, Barth was far more attuned to his own modernizing categories and impulses than many modernizing exegetes are. But we need to go beyond Barth and to build on him. By his own admission, he didn't get everything right.

To build on Barth, and especially in the context of the United States of America, I have been drawn especially to the work of my colleague and friend Stanley Hauerwas. In my view, Hauerwas is an ideal Barth extension kit, especially for American readers (meaning readers located in the USA). He stretches Barthian categories beyond interwar contexts and European nation-state politics into a postwar setting and a politics salted with the critical purviews of the peace-church tradition (something Hauerwas learned primarily from John Howard Yoder). But critical conversations about Christian formation and community are also inaugurated by Hauerwas with giants such as Alasdair MacIntyre. Barth, pressed through Hauerwas and his key conversation partners, yields a richer, more integrated account of Christian community and of Christian discipleship, which is ultimately what Paul's Trinitarian and participatory thinking demands.[3] My learned readers will

---

2. By Barth I mean primarily the mature Barth of the *Church Dogmatics*, which was written from 1932 to 1967.

3. Hauerwas, a generous scholar, constantly acknowledges debts to Yoder and to MacIntyre, whom he knew and knows personally. (His relationship with Yoder has been complicated by Yoder's history of sexual abuse; Hauerwas addresses this issue with typical candor in his lecture "In Defense of 'Our Respectable Culture': Trying to Make Sense of John Howard Yoder.") Barth is an often unnoticed but key influence

detect here, then, where I have seen that Paul is not merely Barthian but Hauerwasian.

But in a sense these conversations will get us to the end only of part 2. Part 3, on mission, and part 4, on navigating Judaism and, by implication, race and inclusion, show where I have tried to respond to the broader conversation over the last decade or so at Duke Divinity School. Gifted thinkers there of all manner and persuasion have forced me to think hard about how Paul and Pauline theology can be brought to bear constructively on problems such as the colonial critique of mission, the insensitivity of the church through most of its history to the dignity of women and of non-European races, and the current crisis unfolding in our churches over gender construction. Drawing on the insights of many of my colleagues, parts 3 and 4 try to craft a Pauline response to these challenges, freely utilizing, perhaps shockingly to some, the help we can get from theology, ethics, church history, homiletics, and pastoral studies. But it is important to appreciate further that the Divinity School is part of a formidable university and thus privy to many of the important conversations swirling around there between the usual detritus and muddiness of modern academic discourse. Duke prides itself on its "secret sauce," as its current provost, Sally Kornbluth, puts it, which is to say, on its interdisciplinarity, and so I have frequently found myself benefiting from fascinating insights supplied from well beyond the traditional conversation partners for New Testament scholars.[4] My readers will consequently find appeals in what follows to—among other things—the theory of relativity, brain science and affect theory, recent insights into gender construction and sexual behavior, sociological work on the nature of the person and on institutions, sociological and mathematical work on networking, and various practices of restorative justice that have been rediscovered in recent decades over against modern state-sponsored approaches to conflict resolution. And these conversations are

---

on his thinking, along with Thomas Aquinas, Thomas's critical classical antecedent Aristotle, and Ludwig Wittgenstein—although Barth's influence is now tracked insightfully by David B. Hunsicker in *The Making of Stanley Hauerwas: Bridging Barth and Postliberalism* (Downers Grove, IL: IVP Academic, 2019).

4. I will occasionally retain the phrase "New Testament" to refer to an academic discipline, but I prefer to use the phrase "Apostolic Writings" (AW) to designate the actual collection of texts usually known by the name "New Testament," a suggestion originally by Paul M. van Buren. See his *Discerning the Way: A Theology of Jewish-Christian Reality* (New York: Seabury Press, 1980), 123–24. I worry that the phrase "New Testament" is Marcionite, both in origin and implications. See Wolfgang Kinzig, "Καινὴ διαθήκη: The Title of the New Testament in the Second and Third Centuries."

not introduced lightly. I contend that New Testament scholars need to attend to the important insights unfolding rapidly around us in other disciplines in the university, and not merely in the Divinity School, that shed light on the basic assumptions informing so much of our own interpretative work. To neglect these conversations is to be impoverished in our understanding of the complex reality that is ultimately interconnected and within which all our analyses are taking place, although such conversations must always, of course, take place with the appropriate methodological controls. Space dictates that several of these conversations in what follows are the proverbial gesture, but they are gestures that I hope others will take up with further, deeper engagements. Many Pauline scholars have been talking largely with themselves for far too long.

But Duke has challenged me in a further important way, one that affects this book at a fundamental level. I have clearly spent the last fifteen years teaching (and even occasionally preaching) in its Divinity School as against in a fundamentally secular, state-funded university, and this context is explicitly confessional. So my basic task has been to train the Christian leaders of the next generation and not simply to try to write clever books and articles. I have consequently had to think hard about formation, about practical theology, and about activism, and I have seen new things in Paul as a result of this effort. Insofar as Paul was a theologian, he was a *practical* theologian. Many would not presumably disagree with this observation, but fewer might be facing what it entails. I am learning that we should feel the pressure of Paul's texts—not to mention of his example—to stop talking quite so much about him and to go out and to act more like him.

I sometimes wonder what Paul would make of the conferences at which scores of highly learned people sit around and debate for hours tiny semantic nuances in his preserved writings. I expect he might be patient with this exercise for a while, but then at some point I'm pretty sure that he would jump up—possibly wielding a whip—and shout: "For goodness sake! Haven't you read what my writings actually *say*? You're not meant to be sitting around *debating* them. You are meant to be out there *doing* what they tell you to do— meeting people and fostering Christian communities in service to your Lord. Get off your backsides and get moving!" Doubtless this challenge would be accompanied by the sounds of tables being overturned and piles of pristine books crashing to the floor.

There is such a thing as a scholar-activist, and I venture to suggest that scholars of Paul should by and large be scholar-activists. If we are not, then we are royally missing the point, and I suspect that our interpretations of Paul will suffer as well. So my readers will probably detect here not merely a

Barthian foundation and a Hauerwasian ecclesial and political extension but a particular set of anticolonial concerns more broadly familiar from Duke Divinity School, along with a commitment to concrete engagement and action.

The Ten-Letter Pauline Canon

It will not take my readers long to realize that I have used what scholars often refer to as the *ten-letter canon*. I judge the letter we know now as Ephesians, as well as Colossians and 2 Thessalonians, to be authentic. They join the seven-letter canon comprising Romans, 1 and 2 Corinthians, Galatians, Philippians, 1 Thessalonians, and Philemon, and these judgments are potentially quite significant. The following theological account of Paul is deliberately attentive to what I will generally denote as Ephesians, assisted by the insights of Colossians and 2 Thessalonians.[5] A rather different theology of Paul emerges when this canon is used, although arguably one closer to the way he was first read. Paul ends up being highly "Irenaean" and deeply orthodox. The extent of this reorientation surprised me at times, but I also found it clarifying, constructive, and at times quite profound. I would hope (and indeed pray) that any seminars working through this account of Paul would find it the same. The reasons underlying these authorial decisions are laid out in my *Framing*.[6] I argue there as well that 1 and 2 Timothy and Titus are demonstrably not by Paul. These letters, however, shed fascinating light on the critical context for Paul's interpretation that unfolded through the second century CE and on how his early, and fundamentally orthodox, disciples read him. I treat this material

---

5. I argue in my *Framing* that Ephesians is authentic, but only if it was in fact the letter that Col 4:16 notes was written to the Laodiceans. Ephesian addressees, which appear only late in the MS tradition, are an implausible ascription. If the letter was originally addressed to Ephesus, I would judge pseudonymity to be more likely than authenticity. But the earliest indications suggest a Laodicean address, which is eminently workable in historical terms. However, it is unfortunately unlikely that the church will rename the letter Laodiceans, as it should. So to avoid confusion I will continue to refer in what follows to Ephesians.

6. *Framing Paul: An Epistolary Biography* (Grand Rapids: Eerdmans, 2014). For those concerned about the general absence of Acts data here, I would respond that (1) authorship decisions must be made prior to any consideration of Acts data, since the letters are potentially primary sources, and Acts is, at least initially, secondary; and (2) I will publish my research into the Acts data shortly, which should address many of the questions now arising in this relation.

at the end of this book, when we turn to consider how Paul has been appropriated by the church, not always constructively, and how our Bibles contain considerable wisdom concerning how to read him helpfully. How important the voice and insights of the Pastor are, that faithful early follower of Paul and guardian of his reputation!

"Justification"

The Pastor's wisdom, along with other canonical insights into Paul's construal—especially from James—informs much of my approach to the data in Paul that is often arranged in terms of something called justification. Scholars sometimes refer to this arrangement as the Lutheran reading of Paul, in dependence on a famous essay by Krister Stendahl.[7] But this reference has the disadvantages that it is too hard on many Lutherans, as well as on much that Luther wrote himself. In the past I have often referred to this material with more neutral acronyms such as JF ("justification by faith") theory or some such. Whatever we call it, when this system is introduced, it prefaces and thereby frames the material I expound here, and so ends up controlling it. Hence I worry that this approach undermines a great deal that Paul has to say to us. It is really another systematic theology that enfolds the one I am developing here, and if we use it, we end up with another gospel that is really no gospel at all (note Gal 1:6–7). I have examined this material closely for many years and come to the conclusion that it is a massive theological misinterpretation resting on a few subtle and fragile mistakes at the textual level. Reread in more historical and critical terms, the relevant texts can be repositioned in a very different dogmatic location from their usual dominant role—something I do here.

This approach was introduced in my *Quest* and argued at length in my *Deliverance*, and then further summarized and defended in *Beyond*. But those analyses left the positive task largely incomplete. Readers of Paul wanting to move beyond justification still need to know what a Paul read in alternative "nonjustification" terms looks like. So this book fills that gap. It is in large measure an extended argument showing how much we can learn from Paul when we do not utilize justification dogmatically in first position, and how when we resist it we can thereby preserve his deepest and most important insights into the God acting among us in Jesus Christ through the power of the Holy Spirit. A kinder, gentler Paul results.

7. Stendahl, "The Apostle Paul and the Introspective Conscience of the West."

Beyond Paul

It will be increasingly clear by this point that this book is not just about Paul, appropriating him in a historical mode. It has been written for Christian leaders who live in the twenty-first century. So to be useful to them it needs to articulate where we also need to go beyond Paul. Here three interpretative techniques will be especially useful.

First, to bring Paul into a constructive conversation with modern churches, we will need to grasp the key parts of his thinking and then learn to develop a nose for those recommendations and texts that, read in a historicizing mode, contribute less constructively to his current application. Learned Germans in the past called this *Sachkritik* ("sense/subject interpretation"). The heart of the matter—the *Sache*—once it has been grasped, should be pressed clearly in relation to any statements that are not quite aligned with it. Now I do not think this approach is particularly helpful if we decide what the *Sache* is for ourselves, which was Barth's problem with Bultmann's use of the technique.[8] But since the church has already recognized for some time that the absolute heart of the matter is the triune God revealed in Jesus, it seems that the pressing of *this Sache* is not only helpful but mandatory. So in the following account *Sachkritik* will mean pressing Paul's Trinitarian and Christocentric claims over against any instructions that do not seem to be grounded particularly securely in those realities—places, that is, where Paul must reinterpret Paul.[9] This technique,

8. See Karl Barth's celebrated letter to Bultmann in which he discussed *Sachkritik* and its correct basis. This letter is accessible—along with the broader conversation—in *Karl Barth—Rudolf Bultmann: Letters, 1922-1966*, ed. Bernd Jaspert and trans. G. W. Bromiley (Grand Rapids: Eerdmans, 1981 [1971]), 108. Barth famously described his relationship with Bultmann in this letter as facing the difficulties attendant on any attempted meeting of an elephant and a whale. More important for our present concerns, however, is Barth's evident acceptance of the hermeneutical program of *Sachkritik* but his firm designation of the *Sache* as *Christ*, and not as Bultmann's anthropological commitments. Thus, although *Sachkritik* is usually associated with Bultmann—and frequently damned by that association and/or its anthropological presuppositions—it is also appropriate to Barth, suitably and very differently understood. I gesture in this interpretative direction in "The Witness to Paul's Gospel of Galatians 3.28" (*Quest*, ch. 5, 95–111). Note that this particular methodological commitment will also influence the contours of any demythologizing program. Barth demythologizes the Bible, but in very different ways from Bultmann.

9. Some have purportedly characterized this move rather unfairly, claiming in such instances that this knows Paul better than he himself does, which would of course be objectionable, but it is not the case. It is a matter of discovering tensions within Paul's

besides being an education into the theological method, will prove helpful as we think about how Paul's dynamic thinking can help us today. He did write his letters a very long time ago, in a different language, to people living in a society that was vastly different from ours. We need to grasp Paul very clearly, but then go beyond him, by standing on his shoulders.

Second, we will also, like all modern readers, *demythologize* Paul where we have to. Paul thought in ancient terms and sometimes assumed things that we know now are not the case. So, for example, he thought about planets very differently from how modern persons do. For him, they were semi-animate entities orbiting around the earth, but we know that they are in fact (generally) vast and distant balls of rock or gas orbiting around stars. The modern person informed by modern science just has a better grip on things here. So we will have to feel for the places where we have to update Paul a little, although, again, without losing our grasp on those central truths about God that lie at the heart of everything, whether of his activity, ours, or even of an accurate conception of science in general.[10]

A third technique has also become apparent as this book has developed— what I call *amplification*. Paul gets a lot right, which is probably a good thing because his conceptuality stands at the heart of the church. But he clearly stands at the very beginning of the church's reflections. As such, we will have frequent cause to recognize where he articulates a critical insight into the God acting in Jesus Christ, through the Spirit, that the church then developed, and that we in turn must continue to appropriate in as deep and precise a way as we can. We must *amplify* many of Paul's insights. In this fashion we again step beyond the strict boundaries of his original conceptuality, but we do so here in a way that is in direct continuity with it. He was usually on the right path, and in this fashion we simply travel further down the pathway, and it is frequently quite fascinating to see where we end up when we do so.[11]

In short, I will in what follows try to grasp the heart of Paul's theology

thought when it is historically reconstructed and of privileging one line of thinking over another, especially when one line is better grounded theologically. A more conventional and presumably acceptable way of putting this would be to say that here Scripture interprets Scripture. (Note also that no one is either an infallible writer, producing material without blemish, tension, or contradiction, or an infallible interpreter of his or her own material.)

10. Although Bultmann's name is primarily associated with demythologizing, with the technique usefully introduced in his collection of essays *New Testament and Mythology and Other Basic Writings*, the following analysis will, as noted in the previous footnote, be closer to Barth's approach.

11. I address in more detail the key methodological question arising here in the

because he was talking with great insight at a critical moment about the God revealed in Jesus with whom we are all involved. But I will go on to craft this theology for the modern period—without reducing it to modern thinking—by probing for the places where possible inconsistencies can be helpfully exposed and dealt with, where it needs to have scientific claims inserted and recognized, and where his insights need to be pressed further and amplified. We will move, then, from Paul to Pauline theology—from Paul's dogmatics to a Pauline dogmatics[12]—in a way that has both historical integrity and contemporary impact. For authentic Pauline theology is a marvelous thing. I live for the day when the church will grasp it more clearly, preach it more widely, and follow it more devotedly.

Further Reading

There is no substitute for reading Barth's work, and for reading his *Dogmatics* in particular. But an insightful and deeply learned introduction to his work is supplied by Eberhard Busch, who has also written the definitive account of his life. A more recent, delightfully learned entry into this crowded market now comes from the hands of Keith Johnson.

The key works by Hauerwas are widely regarded as *The Peaceable Kingdom, A Community of Character,* and *With the Grain of the Universe.* In addition, he has written scores of important essays that must be added to these texts, many of which I will reference in what follows.

Jennings broaches the question of the scholar-activist in his short essay "To Be a Christian Intellectual." It is available online in slightly different forms in two different places. Hauerwas's work constantly emphasizes engagement and practical theology as well.

Bibliography

Barth, Karl. *Church Dogmatics.* Edited by T. F. Torrance and G. W. Bromiley. 4 vols. in 13 parts. Edinburgh: T&T Clark, 1956–96 (1932–67).

---

following chapter and also point there to more resources for understanding this commitment fully.

12. "A" because other plausible constructions are also possible.

Bultmann, Rudolf. *New Testament and Mythology and Other Basic Writings.* Translated and edited by Schubert M. Ogden. Minneapolis: Fortress, 1984.

Busch, Eberhard. *The Great Passion: An Introduction to Karl Barth's Theology.* Translated by Geoffrey Bromiley. Grand Rapids: Eerdmans, 2004.

———. *Karl Barth: His Life from Letters and Autobiographical Texts.* Translated by J. Bowden. 2nd rev. ed. London: SCM, 1976.

Hauerwas, Stanley. *A Community of Character: Toward a Constructive Christian Social Ethic.* Notre Dame, IN: University of Notre Dame Press, 1981.

———. *The Peaceable Kingdom: A Primer in Christian Ethics.* Notre Dame, IN: University of Notre Dame Press, 1983.

———. *With the Grain of the Universe: The Church's Witness and Natural Theology: Being the Gifford Lectures Delivered at the University of St Andrews in 2001.* Grand Rapids: Brazos, 2001.

Jennings, Willie. "Willie Jennings: To Be a Christian Intellectual." *Yale Divinity School*, October 30, 2015. https://divinity.yale.edu/news/willie-jennings-be -christian-intellectual.

Johnson, Keith L. *The Essential Karl Barth: A Reader and Commentary.* Grand Rapids: Baker Academic, 2019.

Kinzig, Wolfgang. "Καινὴ διαθήκη: The Title of the New Testament in the Second and Third Centuries." *JTS* 45 (1994): 519–44.

PART 1

Resurrection

CHAPTER 1

Jesus

The Question of God

This book, like a lot of books written by and addressed to Christians and other followers of Jesus—although by no means excluding anyone else from entering into the conversation—is an extended instance of God-talk. It talks about God and wants to do so accurately, or "in truth" as the Bible sometimes puts it. But if this is the case, an important question must be addressed immediately. How do we know what God is like? If we don't *know* God, we will probably not be able to talk *about* God with any accuracy, and so we will end up, as Barth puts it wryly, talking about ourselves in a loud voice, which is unlikely to be much help to anyone. Any discussion of Paul, who is our principal conversation partner in what follows, raises this question immediately and acutely. His texts are nothing more than extended and at times quite authoritative instances of God-talk. How do we know that his talk of God is true? How do we know that our derivative talk of God is true? (How do we know that *any* talk of God is true?) Paul gives clear answers to these most important of questions, although not perhaps in the way we might at first expect.

In the spring of 51 CE Paul wrote the following statement to a group of fractious converts living in Corinth:[1]

> For us there is one God, the Father,
> from whom everything has its existence, and we exist for him,

---

1. This particular set of claims is justified in my detailed critical analysis of Paul's biography on the basis of his letters, *Framing*, especially by ch. 2, 37–121 ("The Epistolary Backbone: Romans and the Corinthian Correspondence").

and there is one Lord, Jesus Christ,
through whom everything exists, and we exist through him.

(1 Cor 8:6)[2]

In the part of this ancient letter that we now know as chapter 8, Paul is addressing a point of conflict at Corinth involving eating meat that in Jewish eyes was polluting. It had not been properly drained of blood, and it was often being consumed in a hired dining booth that was far too close to pagan temples and their images—a doubly disgusting practice. Members of the Corinthian church who had Jewish sensibilities were deeply offended by fellow church members who were doing all this.

Paul bases his instructions in chapters 8–10 about how to handle this situation on the claims I just quoted. They are the foundation stone for his unfolding argument. And it is clear from the immediate context that Paul is not using the word "lord" here in its generic ancient sense of someone in a superior social position, namely, a ruler or master or aristocrat. In this general sense we might even call our own modern managers and deans "lords." Paul is quoting here, in a highly distinctive way, the key Jewish confession concerning God, which was drawn from chapter 6 in the book of Deuteronomy. "Hear, O Israel: the LORD is our God, the LORD alone." Jews refer to this verse as the Shema, the Hebrew for "hear," which begins the verse, and the pious recited it every day. But 1 Cor 8:6 does something very challenging with this confession. Paul *distributes* the Shema *between* "God the Father" and "the Lord Jesus," all the while holding on, somewhat extraordinarily, to the unity of God. There is one divinity, although within this unity, there is someone called God the

2. Translations are usually either my own or modifications of the NIV (which I use because it remains a literal, not a paraphrastic, translation, and because my Doctorvater, Richard Longenecker, was closely involved with producing it). Note also that the use of masculine pronouns must not be understood as suggesting biological maleness or culturally constructed masculinity for God the Father. The English language is notoriously limited in this relation, and a much-needed pronominal flexibility is as yet too unstandardized to be employed. In part to compensate for the destructive bias unleashed tacitly by this situation, in what follows I will use feminine pronouns for the Spirit. There is also biblical precedent for this in the divine figure of Wisdom, who is gendered female by way of the Hebrew *hokmah*; see Prov 1:20–3:26. Jesus was a male, but I argue later that this fact must not be emphasized, otherwise the theological implications are catastrophic. His full personhood, understood in a manner that is necessarily inclusive of all sex and gender-construction, is critical.

Father and someone called the Lord Jesus, two titles Paul uses a lot.[3] This move is then emphasized as Paul speaks of Jesus sustaining the creation, which is an activity that the Jewish Scriptures reserve for God. It is clear, then, that whatever other questions we might now have, Paul is using "lord" in the specialized Jewish sense of a substitute name for God.[4] Furthermore, he is applying it to Jesus. And it follows from this observation, simply and shockingly, that Jesus is God for both Paul and the Corinthians. God is not reducible to Jesus, but God is not imaginable now without Jesus. Jesus is, as Richard Bauckham puts it carefully, part of the divine identity.[5]

It seems, then, that our critical opening question about God has just been answered, and it is one of the most important questions that we will ever ask. It is clear that Jesus will reveal God definitively and decisively *as* God. He *is* God—a momentous assertion! So to look at Jesus and to see what he is like is to look at God and to see what he is like. God is not reducible to Jesus, but if Jesus is God and if God is one, as Paul also affirms here in continuity with virtually the entirety of the Jewish tradition, then the rest of God will not be fundamentally different from Jesus. Other parts of God (so to speak) might be distinguishable from Jesus, but they will not and will never be separable from Jesus, to reach ahead to some useful Trinitarian categories. And we must not deny this claim, with its shockingly counterintuitive dimensions, or we lose everything.

Without affirming the absolute oneness of Jesus with God—his complete unity—we lose our grip on where God has chosen to be revealed fully and completely: namely, in Jesus. If Jesus is not God "all the way down," then we are still lost in our own world with all its fantasies and illusions; we have no

3. Paul uses "Lord" predominantly and ubiquitously of Jesus; he uses this signifier upward of 250x. He uses the signifier "Father" less frequently but still commonly of God—39x.

4. When God's name appeared in the Jewish Scriptures, it was too holy to be printed or spoken, so when the texts were read out loud another name was substituted for it—the more innocuous *adonai*. The Greek translators of the Jewish Scriptures then used the Greek equivalent *kyrios* in these locations.

5. See Bauckham's important essay "Paul's Christology of Divine Identity," in *Jesus and the God of Israel*, 182–232; also *God Crucified: Monotheism and Christology in the New Testament* (Carlisle: Paternoster, 1998), repr. as "God Crucified" in *Jesus and the God of Israel*, 1–59. N. T. Wright discusses this text in similar terms rather earlier than Bauckham: see his *The Climax of the Covenant: Christ and the Law in Pauline Theology* (Edinburgh: T&T Clark, 1991), 120–36. See also a similar case to Bauckham's in relation to Rom 10:13 by C. Kavin Rowe, "Romans 10:13: What Is the Name of the Lord?"

direct contact with God. We are hemmed in by our limited creaturely existence, now further corrupted by sin, and we do not know what God is really like. We are reduced, the theologians would say, to analogies, which means to inevitable and largely uncontrolled gaps in our understanding of what God is really like. God is *like* a sunset, but in what sense? Is he warm? or glowing? or fading? Clearly, none of this is quite right. God is like a mother, but in what exact sense again? Does he wear my mother's distinctive clothes or directly biologically breast-feed us or speak in a southern drawl about picking us up from soccer? Again, clearly none of this is directly applicable, although we sense that something insightful is going on. But if we want to press on these claims and be really precise, we don't know quite how to do so. This limitation arises because we are trying to understand a transcendent being who is fundamentally different from us, as creator to our createdness, by way of limited, emphatically nontranscendent things that this being has made, which are by the nature of the case different from him. There is a gap here that we just can't bridge *unless God has graciously bridged it from his side of the divide and become one of us and lived among us.* What a gift! So we should really avoid mitigating or avoiding this gift or watering it down in any way, which means to avoid adding other potential candidates alongside in any sort of equality. God is definitively known only in Jesus. This is where *God* is present with us *fully*, and nowhere else—not in a book, a tradition, a piece of land, a building, or even in a particular people (unless, that is, he has taken up residence in one of them fully). We worship and pray to none of these things; we worship and pray to Jesus because Jesus is God, and so we know God fully and completely only as we know Jesus.

I labor this point a little because it is so central, so simple, so quickly introduced and understood, *and so easily and rapidly abandoned* (note Gal 1:6). We must affirm the insight that Jesus is Lord, along with all its entailments, and protect it, vigilantly resisting all other candidates for this status. (People, and especially Christians, seem to love to avoid, to marginalize, and to obscure God's gift of God's very being to us in Jesus for all sorts of odd reasons.)[6] In sum, from this moment on, as I frequently tell my students, the answer to ev-

---

6. This cluster of insights is presented with superb clarity by an essay on Athansias and Arius by Alasdair I. C. Heron, "*Homoousios* with the Father." Note that Heron's position on Arius is now dated and should be corrected with reference to J. Warren Smith, "'Arian' Foundationalism or 'Athanasian' Apocalypticism: A Patristic Assessment"; however, Heron's account of the underlying epistemological and methodological issues remains unsurpassed.

ery question I ask in class, at least in some sense, is "Jesus." Accurate God-talk is Jesus-talk. And God-talk that is not in some very direct sense Jesus-talk is probably *not* God-talk. Jesus is the key piece of information concerning God, in the light of which all other God-talk must be evaluated, which includes everything in this book and everything that Paul wrote. But we also risk getting a little ahead of ourselves here.

The claim by Paul that Jesus is Lord challenges us and not merely the Corinthians with a further, related question of equal importance. In fact, we cannot go on any further with our discussion until we have grappled with it and done so in a deeply personal way. We need to decide right away whether what Paul is saying here is really true. There is a sense in which we can understand his position, which is shared by many other members of the church. The rationale for the centrality of Jesus as definitively identified with, and hence revealing of, God is clear. We grasp the importance of the claim that Jesus is Lord. But how do we know that this claim is actually true?

The Question of Truth

When Paul says Jesus is God, he is clearly making an extraordinarily important claim, one that is so important that all others tend to pale into insignificance beside it. I can imagine writing a book about this claim and continuing to urge its significance some time after it has been made—two millennia to be precise—if it is true. Paul would ultimately be describing a very different reality from the one that many people inhabit on a daily basis, and yet it would be a determinative reality; it would be the one that really matters. God has been definitively revealed, in full, without reservation, in a person—specifically in a Jew who walked the earth in the early first century and was executed by the Romans around 30 CE. But he was then raised from the dead and enthroned on high, from where he rules the cosmos beside his divine Father, right now (to anticipate a few of our later findings).[7] An entirely new approach to life is necessary if the claim concerning Jesus's lordship is correct, one alert to the resurrecting power of Jesus working away within history. The way we explain Paul must follow accordingly. We will analyze him in relation to this hidden,

---

7. This statement presupposes certain claims about the reality of a person walking the earth, Jesus, raising interesting, contested, and quite subtle questions vis-à-vis putative historical work. We will address these issues shortly, beginning a closer engagement from the end of ch. 3 ("A God of Love").

dynamic, determinative reality that is the divine Jesus. Paul's description will have visible and invisible dimensions, with the invisible dimension powerfully shaping and informing the visible. If Jesus is Lord, then he is the Lord of everything and he affects everything. Even an accurate historical account of Paul would, strictly speaking, have to take account of this multidimensional and partly hidden situation—if what he is saying here is true.

But if what he is saying is not true, then a very different book would be required. One could write a book on Paul as a matter of purely antiquarian interest, but we would have to explain him in terms he did not himself share. We would supply some alternative account of his extraordinary and—to put matters plainly—rather unhinged claims about reality, such as the idea that people are in some invisible but quite concrete way affected by a God identified with a person who is dead. People are locked away under state supervision for saying less. A description of Paul in these terms would be a much more visible and one-dimensional affair, and the sort of history it recounted would be very different. (And, to be frank, if this is the case, I would be writing about something more relevant and important than this ancient and somewhat deluded figure—and I wouldn't be a Christian either.)

So we need to ask whether this claim is true. Is it true to claim that Jesus is really God? If he is, then the implications are worth addressing carefully, and our description of those implications will be overtly theological. God will be at work, hopefully both then and now, in Paul's lifetime and in our own. But if Jesus is not God, then Paul, I, and not a few of my friends are of all people to be pitied. So how do we judge the truth of this claim that the brightest minds of humankind have struggled with in one form or another from the dawn of civilization?

Here Paul gives us a clue, and somewhat in opposition to the brightest minds in history. "Where is the sage? Where is the academic? Where is the intellectual of this age? Has God not shown the wisdom of this world to be stupid?" (1 Cor 1:20). Following Paul's lead here, I would suggest that we do not decide the truth of this question for ourselves. That is, I suggest that the most dedicated intellectual—or emotional or meditative or spiritual—journey will not make the slightest bit of difference to its resolution, although many in the past have gone astray at just this moment by supposing that it will. Paul goes on to say shortly after the passage we have just cited that God has chosen the foolish, the weak, the low-born, and the despised of the world to be followers of Jesus, and God has apparently made this choice by way of Paul's declaration that a person, Jesus, who was crucified, is now in fact the Lord. The motley Christians just denoted by Paul are convinced that this declaration is true, although Paul is quick to deny that this conviction even had anything to do with a particularly skillful presentation by him. There was no extended eloquence on Paul's part, merely the activity of the Holy Spirit. According to Paul, however, that very same Spirit searched the depths of God, and then she revealed the secret of Jesus's true identity to these lowly Corinthians (1 Cor 1:21–2:16). But how exactly does this information help us to decide our pressing question?

We need to be very careful at this moment. It is unlikely that we should be convinced that what Paul was claiming about the lordship of the risen Jesus is true simply because we have read that he and his Corinthian converts thought that it was true. Reading these things only tells us that Paul and the Corinthians believed that they were true, which is interesting but does not decide the question for us. But we have learned that Paul did not think that they worked these things out for themselves. It seems, then, that he would not approve of us trying to work them out for ourselves either, even if this includes us reading what he wrote to the Corinthians and believing that. That is not what happened either to him or to them.[8]

Paul attributes the cause of the conviction about the lordship of Jesus to the call of God the Father and the activity of the divine Spirit,[9] and here we see a third divine actor taking the stage in addition to the Father and his Son. Some of the Corinthians had responded to these promptings, which were mediated by Paul's timorous presence and proclamation. But the underlying causality, according to Paul, was divine action. By recognizing this aspect of the situation, we have returned to our original question armed with slightly more information, although we have not yet answered it.

We can see that once again Paul has made some dramatic claims concerning divine activity. Spurning the contributions of the intellectuals and academics of his day, he has attributed certain important events within visible history—here the conversion of the Corinthians—to the hidden workings of

8. Similarly, these things are not true simply because we have read them in an authoritative text like the Bible. We can learn about them from the Bible and then have these meanings affirmed and corroborated by God. That is, the Bible can *mediate* these key truths, as can other Christians, messianic Jews (if we are fortunate enough to know any), the proclamation of the church, the sacraments, and even, on one celebrated occasion, the mouth of a donkey. But these truths are not true in any of these situations because of these forms of mediation. God utilizes them, in effect, and speaks through and with them.

9. See, in addition to 1 Cor 2:1–16, Rom 5:5; 8:9–11; 1 Cor 12:13; 2 Cor 1:22; 3:17–18; 5:5; Gal 3:2–3; 4:6; Eph 1:13–14; 4:30; 1 Thess 1:5–6; 4:8.

God. They learned about God, he says, because God somehow spoke to them. and in so doing they became convinced of God's presence in Jesus. So we now need to ask ourselves again whether we believe that these things are true or not, and if we do, whether this belief is credible and reliable.

At this critical moment I suggest that it will be helpful to reach outside Paul to another important Christian thinker who has done the modern church an immeasurable service at just this moment, and someone with whom we will frequently be in dialogue during the course of this book: the Swiss theologian Karl Barth. Like no other theologian, Barth understands how modern people place this question, and in placing it often get it horribly wrong. Dismayed by the political wreckage that surrounded him in Europe—two world wars fought with one another by historically Christian powers, along with the hard-heartedness of his middle- and upper-class parishioners to the plight of their factory workers—Barth detected an underlying theological crisis that we will constantly revisit. He saw that modern Protestant theology had taken the route Paul rejected in his letter to the Corinthians: the high road of educated sagacity and public eloquence that sought to establish the reality and nature of God through human inquiry, beginning with doubt and then trying to construct some definition of the truth that led to God. What was needed was a return to the simple truth known so well by previous epochs in the church: the acknowledgment that the truth of God rests in the hands of God and not in the hands of humanity. God *reveals* the truth, and people *respond* to it (thereby constituting the church), so the theological journey begins *after* the fact of belief and reflects back upon it, studying, even as it prays to and worships the truth that has been revealed. Unsurprisingly, this claim on Barth's part elicited a great deal of mockery from the academic institutions it sought to correct, as Paul's similar claims did in his own day.[10] But Barth was right.

At the root of the truth attested by the church in every age and in every person is the simple recognition that God is at work revealing his nature and purpose, and that this nature and purpose are so definitively revealed in the figure of Jesus that we must acknowledge the truth that this crucified figure was and is God and hence God in person, although, as we have just seen, Paul spoke in biblical language here of Jesus as Lord. This truth then lies at the heart of everything else because God lies at the heart of everything else, and we now know just what God is like. And we know this truth about God because

10. Modern academic institutions, especially universities, are keen to protect their claim to be the cultural and social arbiters of truth.

it has been revealed to us by God.[11] The truth has revealed the truth. And in retrospect, this makes perfect sense. With God's shockingly unexpected identity revealed to us in Jesus, we see that we have no accurate notion of God in ourselves with which to measure a claim about God and God's nature and thereby to determine whether it speaks of God. God is foreign to our limited creaturely and sinfully distorted nature. Our previous statements are shown to be deluded. And we have learned that Jesus is God the only way we could—*because God has told us that.* "I am fully in this person" has been spoken to us at some point in some way by God, and we have believed it. In essence, then, Barth grasped with particular clarity that the truth at the base of the church rests on revelation—a particular revelation by God about the person Jesus, who is God, and hence one that is particular both in mode and in content.

This claim by Barth resonates strongly with Paul's account in 1 Corinthians concerning how the Corinthians came to believe and, equally important, with Paul's account in Gal 1:15–16 of how he himself became convinced of the identity of Jesus.

> When God, the one who set me apart from my mother's womb,
> and who called me by means of his benefaction,
> was pleased to reveal his Son to me
> so that I should proclaim the good news about him among the pagan
>   nations,
> I did not consult with flesh and blood. (NIV modified)

Paul uses the language of revelation here, and it comes up at other important points in his letters.[12] In Greek the language of revelation speaks of

---

11. One could add that because God, the center of all reality (i.e., of all that is), reveals the truth to us, we can see that what is—what exists or is and so has "being"—and truth are united here together in the tightest possible relationship. The importance of this insight can perhaps be better appreciated by placing this claim in reverse. We are not separating the source of all being and life (technically ontology) from truth (technically epistemology). These things are not divided but united. The Gospel of John put this point rather more poetically when it quotes Jesus saying, "I am the way, the truth, *and* the life" (14:6).

12. See Paul's use of the language of revealing and revelation (Greek *apokalypsis* or *apokalyptō*), in addition to 1 Cor 1:20–2:16, in Rom 1:17 (probably resumed by 3:21–22, although a different verb is used); 16:25 (a text whose authenticity is disputed because of its appearance in several different places in the manuscript tradition but on balance, I would suggest, is authentic); 2 Cor 12:1 and 7 (which is probably not directly relevant

unveiling something. To unveil is *apokalyptein*, and an unveiling is an *apokalypsis*, from which we get our words "apocalypse" and "apocalyptic." These have slidden a bit in the meaning, however, which is not surprising after two thousand years of usage. Apocalypses for us denote fiery cataclysmic events analogous to the coming day of judgment, which is why Francis Ford Coppola called his incendiary film about the horrors of the Vietnam War *Apocalypse Now* (1979). However, scholars would refer to these notions in Paul's day as "eschatology," using the Greek for "end," *eschaton*. And at this particular moment in our discussion it is important to be precise. We will need to move back to the ancient Greek usage and to recover its emphasis on revelation. Apocalyptic language in this sense will help us to talk accurately about the centrality of divine revelation for understanding Paul, and for understanding the truth affirmed by the church in general, whether in its messianic Jewish or Christian variations. Jesus is the Lord, and hence part of the divine identity. This is the focal point of the church's truth. And its truth rests on revelation. This is the particular content of revelation—that Jesus *is* Lord—and the church knows it because this particular truth has been revealed to it. In short, the Lord has revealed the truth to us about the Lord. For Paul, this revelation took place, he tells us, on the road to Damascus.[13] Moreover, this is not a revelation taking place within some broader category or group of revelations. It is *the* revelation to us of Jesus as Lord. Scholars who want to emphasize this critical element in Paul's thought, as I do, call it "apocalyptic," and its importance is about to become even more apparent.[14]

---

to his revelation of Christ on the road to Damascus but speaks of a similar, highly charged experience); Gal 1:12, 16; 3:23 (2:2 occupying a place similar to 2 Cor 12:1 and 7 above); and Eph 1:17; 3:3, 5. See also the closely related notion of a divine secret hidden in heaven that has now been disclosed—Greek *mystērion*, or "mystery": Rom 16:25–27; 1 Cor 4:1; Eph 1:9; 3:1–13 [3x]; 5:32; 6:19–20; Col 1:25–27; 2:2–3; and 4:3.

13. Strictly speaking, Paul tells us it took place near Damascus; the book of Acts, speaking of the same event, tells us three times that it took place on the road to Damascus as he was journeying there (9:3–9; 22:6–11; 26:12–18). Journeys, roads, and the way (*hē hodos*, which can denote a geographic way, whether a road or a river or, analogically, an ethical way of life) are all key elements in Luke's theological program.

14. I say this partly because a misrepresentation of apocalyptic approaches to Paul is sadly widespread. So let me clarify here that I am using this descriptor in the first instance as I have defined it here, to denote revelation, which is a fair reading of the term. Moreover, that this is a valid and useful thing to say about Paul is confirmed by the way he uses these words himself in Gal 1:15–16 and in other strategic locations to describe the revelation by which he was turned to the Lord Jesus.

As Barth saw with special clarity, when we press on this revealed truth a little harder, we find a triune God. There are three actors at work in this revelation: God the Father, Jesus the Son and Lord, and the Holy Spirit.[15] These actors are all distinguishable from one another. They clearly each have freedom or agency, and they act on us and in relation to one another. But they are also part of a single God. Their distinguishable but mutual activity helps us to grasp how effective this revelation is.

God the Father sent his Son, Jesus, into our desperate human condition, this being another issue we will consider shortly. As a person, Jesus had a particular body and lived in a specific time and place. He was a Jew, and God filled out every detail of his life with divine existence. Jesus walked and ate and breathed in the dusty hills of Galilee and the eastern Mediterranean coastlands, in the hills of Samaria, and in the trans-Jordan and Judea. This is the person where God dwelled in all his fullness.[16] But for this incarnate God to

---

The term "apocalyptic" can suggest other things, and important signifiers usually can. The great patriarchs of apocalyptic readings of Paul in modern NT scholarship are Ernst Käsemann and J. Louis (Lou) Martyn, and their use of the signifier, it should be noted, tends to mean "eschatological." Hence they often use the term in a different sense from the one I am utilizing at this moment. I will in fact shortly endorse this meaning too, and this account of Paul's theology, when we begin to describe the sense in which Jesus followers are resurrected. But for now the accent is on the closely related but distinguishable notion of revelation.

15. Paul does not speak that often in terms of overtly Trinitarian dynamics; the presence of a triune God rests more on widespread inferences from divine activity in relation to two actors, although the pairs vary (Father-Son, Father-Spirit, Son-Spirit). But triune activity is apparent, at the least, in Rom 8, and the entire chapter needs to be taken into account; arguably, more briefly, in 14:17–18 and 15:15–19, 30 (and my thanks to Scott Hafemann for pointing out to me the relevance of this last passage for Trinitarian dynamics in Paul); and in 1 Cor 2; 12:4–6; 2 Cor 13:13; and Eph 4:3–6.

16. I have not spent much time up to this point in our discussion emphasizing Jesus's full humanity in Paul because this is generally not so contested by modern scholars (presumably because their methodology tends toward Socinianism). Suffice it for now to note that his humanity is strongly affirmed by Paul—although not with the geographic details that I have just supplied here from the Gospels! Hays demonstrates how a surprisingly complete story of Jesus can be assembled from Paul's letters, which includes a healthy emphasis on his human life, which, as the church would later say, unfolded between his incarnation and his resurrection; "The Story of God's Son." Paul's complete account of Jesus extends both before and after these events. Paul's emphases on Jesus's humanity will emerge strongly first in his discussion of Jesus's death in ch. 6, and then in his development of a virtue ethic rooted in Jesus, which is described in part 2, especially chs. 11–15.

be directly comprehensible—and in a sense touchable—by us, in our modern locations, millennia later, as we walk and eat and breathe in very distant lands, we need God to come to us in those later and distant locations and to reveal Jesus to us. Just like the Corinthians, who were living in ancient Corinth in the 40s and 50s CE, many hundreds of miles to the west of Judea and some time after Jesus's ascension, we need the presence of God with us where we are if we are to appreciate what God has given us. It is helpful to think about how the Holy Spirit answers this particular need.[17]

To affirm a revelation of the truth that Jesus is Lord as a revelation of God to us is consequently and necessarily to affirm a threefold activity by God in three different places: the Father sending Jesus into the world (i.e., sending him here from some other place); Jesus being sent into the world, specifically to Galilee and Samaria and Judea; and the Spirit revealing this to us wherever we are. That this cluster of insights really is the heart of the matter is attested by the manner in which the church's later creeds focus on it. The last time the church visibly gathered as a whole and agreed unanimously on its key truths, it affirmed the disclosure of God fully in the person of Jesus Christ and defined

---

17. Things cannot be left here. Further reflection suggests that each divine person is constantly accompanied by the other two divine figures within the Trinity. It is as if they are holding hands all the time. To be in relationship with one is therefore immediately to be in relationship with the other two. They are distinguishable from one another, and hence one can take the lead (so to speak) in a particular situation, but they are never separable from one another, and thus to speak of one divine person is necessarily to speak *at the same moment* of the other two. It follows that where the Spirit is at work, we must recognize Jesus himself is at work as well, along with their Father. And so *Jesus* was also at work in Corinth, revealing himself, and his Father was immediately present revealing as well.

These realizations are not just a matter of doctrinal fussiness. They keep the Spirit tightly and concretely connected with the Father and the Son. We must not, that is, fall into tritheism, splitting the Father, Son, and Holy Spirit apart from one another so that they operate separately—a denial of the unity, or oneness, of God. (Sometimes this error is spoken of as "the heresy of the third article [of the creed].") Serious mistakes follow from tritheism, including, Barth would warn, the entire disastrous modern neo-Protestant project! However, wariness of falling into this abyss has led to a cautious posture toward pneumatology on the part of many theologians, although de-emphasizing the Spirit and thereby collapsing into a functional bitheism is ultimately just as dangerous and inappropriate as separating the Spirit from the other figures in the Trinity. Studies of the Spirit—theological books, essays, and NT studies investigating the historical and textual data more closely—are listed in ch. 7.

the parameters of that affirmation carefully. Many of the details and implications needed to be teased out, although they were all implicit in the claim that Jesus is Lord. So my claims here are located firmly within the ecumenical foundation of the church in the Nicene-Chalcedonian confessions, which were formulated in the 300s and 400s CE.[18] The church has always agreed that the absolute heart of its witness is the claim that Jesus is Lord. Everything else is illuminated by this claim, including the realization that he has been sent by his Father and is attested to by his Spirit. But a caveat is now worth quickly noting.

I am not suggesting that Paul operated with a full-fledged *doctrine* of the Trinity. He was not an explicit advocate of Nicene-Chalcedonian theology in all its subtlety. The church's finest minds took several centuries to articulate the precise contours of the initial claim that Jesus is Lord, and these contours needed to be articulated precisely because to lack precision is invariably to go badly astray in some way over time. Although Paul lived well in advance of these discussions with all their careful definitions, however, he did live out of the God that those definitions ultimately described accurately in triune terms. So a triune reality was pressing in upon him constantly, as it is constantly pressing in upon us. Consequently, Paul was involved with the Trinity. He simply did not have a fully articulated doctrine or dogma concerning the Trinity. His linguistic description, we might say, lagged behind a reality that later creedal articulations grasped more precisely.[19] But Paul did not understand how his digestive system worked either. In 1937 Hans Adolf Krebs would discover the citric acid pathway—the Krebs cycle—which is one of the key biochemical pathways for the digestion of food. But the cycle worked happily away whenever Paul ate his food in 50 CE, and nobody would deny that it did so. The theory of the Krebs cycle formulated two thousand years later describes accurately what took place in Paul's gut every day, and no one would seriously

18. The four key councils were in Nicaea in 325 CE, in Constantinople in 381, in Ephesus in 431, and in Chalcedon in 451. The statements of the creeds should not be viewed as inspired, because they contain their difficulties, but they are, shall we say, programmatically directive. At bottom, they mediate the truth. An interesting conversation with Scripture unfolded around them that also needs to be taken into consideration during any deeper investigation; see Christopher A. Beeley and Mark E. Weedman, eds., *The Bible in Early Trinitarian Theology*.

19. I am not saying here that history is basically a smoothly progressive sweep from lower to higher truths. The church can effect degrees of progress when things are going well. But it seems that things can also go backward. Nevertheless, the great ecumenical councils were, although not perfect, moments of real insight that need to be retained and defended at all costs.

suggest that the later discovery of the biochemical pathway entailed that Paul didn't digest his food properly.

I will therefore refer in what follows to the God Paul obeyed as the Trinity and will explicate much that he recommended in fundamentally Trinitarian terms—because this is what God as revealed in Jesus through the Spirit is really like: triune. To deny this would be to deny our central truth claims, along with some fairly obvious pointers from Paul's texts. But here I mean only that the identity and nature of God is triune. I do not mean to suggest that Paul's linguistic articulations possess exactly the same meaning and precision as the later creeds. (Having said this, I am nevertheless frequently astonished by Paul's insights. I suspect he was an extraordinary genius.)

A number of questions tend to arise at this moment but we should think first about how we as modern interpreters of Paul have now been positioned in relation to Paul himself. What sorts of books should we write about him?

Modern interpreters who themselves have responded positively to the divine revelation that Jesus is Lord within their communities and traditions, as I have, can now recognize in Paul's words to the Corinthians a description of the same process and the same God at work. As we have already seen, Paul wrote quite clearly of a process of revelation proceeding from God the Father and unfolding through the work of the divine Spirit ultimately in relation to the Lord Jesus. Paul, the Corinthians, and we modern Jesus followers are all what we are, convinced of the lordship of Christ, because the Lord has revealed this truth to us. (We will later discuss in more detail the more proximate and practical means God uses to reveal divine truths and realities—the question of mediation.)[20] Paul's convictions, the convictions of his converts, and our own convictions reach out across the centuries to touch one another within the single embrace of the one God who is at work in all these places in three persons. We all confess these truths together and witness and attest to them.[21] But it follows from this that a parting of the ways will probably take place from this moment in any analysis of Paul.

My description will proceed as if what Paul is saying is fundamentally true. The risen Jesus really was at work in his life. Consequently, the reality my discus-

---

20. See ch. 3 ("A God of Love"), and then part 2, ch. 10 ("Leaders").

21. These related practices will be discussed further in ch. 3 as well, alongside the modality of mediation. There we will see that, among other things, they affirm the fundamentally revelational mode of truth that I have been articulating here in conversation with Paul and Barth. Note also how this confession stands in an emphatically nonindividualistic way in the midst of a community that stretches through time.

sion presupposes will be no flat or merely externally visible affair. Paul's situation was alive with critical invisible dynamics that had something to do with a living God who was definitively revealed by Jesus. This book, guided by Paul, will search for this hidden but life-giving pulse within all reality. This viewpoint also shapes its ideal implicit reader and underlies my inclusive use of confessional language. If this is all true, and centrally so, then I ought to speak as if it is and write primarily to people located in the same conceptual space. I am, after all, by my own admission, merely responding here, at length and after some years of reflection, to an act of divine disclosure that has already taken place and into which I have been gathered. It would be both inauthentic and disingenuous if I denied it.

Others will not share this conviction and my subsequent account of reality, as well as, ultimately, my view of history.[22] I do not think their position is correct or that their own account of reality, along with any attendant historical analysis, is an especially complete one, but I understand this posture and wish its practitioners well—and if they are able to read a bit further and to tolerate my different point of view for a while, then I will be delighted. Moreover, I certainly intend to listen to them, deeply, and not just to talk to them.[23] But underneath it all, we will not be giving the same account of the truth or the same account of reality.

With this critical realization in place at the outset, we need to turn immediately to consider how to hang onto it in the face of some subtle potential subversions. In certain key respects the rest of this book is a running battle to preserve this truth faithfully and to resist being drawn away from it to other tempting but ultimately fatal positions. We will grasp how it unfolds into dynamic accounts of ecclesial formation, mission, and inclusion (see parts 2–4). But the road ahead is surrounded on all sides by proverbial snares. Nevertheless, we can enlist some important support for this struggle when we recognize that falsehood tends to choose the same basic strategy. It is extremely clever. But we can defend ourselves against it if we can recognize it as it comes into view, a moment when Barth will once again prove inordinately helpful. Frequently, the subversion of revelation merely masquerades as a new argument as it repeatedly utilizes a very old deception.

22. Tricky issues surround this important claim, although Murray A. Rae will prove an adept guide through them; see his *History and Hermeneutics*. They are also discussed in more detail in ch. 3.

23. As will become apparent in due course, especially in our later discussion of mission, my stance necessitates respecting and learning from the different viewpoints of others.

Theses

- The first and absolutely critical questions we need to answer concern the evaluation of our "God-talk," since both Paul and we are constantly involved with this—(1) What is God like? and (2) How do we know when our talk of God is accurate, which is also to know when it is not?
- The central insight into the nature of God, widely attested by Paul, is "Jesus is Lord."
- This statement affirms the full divinity of Jesus. Jesus *is* God.
- Jesus as God now measures the truth of all other God-talk. True God-talk must now in some demonstrable sense be Jesus-talk.
- This truth is affirmed in the Nicene-Chalcedonian creeds, attesting to its centrality for the measurement of all other God-talk.
- Most will experience this disclosure as shocking—the definitive dwelling of God in God's fullness in the lowly human person of Jesus. We almost certainly did not anticipate this.
- It follows that our previous notions of God were distorted and deluded.
- This affirms that we had to learn of the truth about God in Jesus *as God told it to us.*
- We must then speak of a revelation or apocalypse (Gk *apokalypsis*), and in two senses: (1) this revelation is of this particular truth—the thing revealed, and (2) this particular truth is known because it has been specifically revealed by God—the thing has been revealed.
- This use of the signifier "apocalyptic" to denote revelation differs from the way other important advocates of an apocalyptic approach to Paul frequently use it to denote eschatology. Both are legitimate lexicographically and simply need to be recognized in context.
- The Holy Spirit reveals it, as does the Father.
- The nature of God revealed within this revelation is triune.
- We recognize this truth in both Paul and the Corinthians, and we affirm it together with them, in continuity with the rest of the orthodox and confessing church.
- Both present reality and past reality (i.e., history) are seen to be informed fundamentally by a revealing and triune God.
- Paul does not use a fully developed account or doctrine of the Trinity.
- But Paul was gripped *by* the Trinity!

Key Scriptural References

Of primary importance: 1 Cor 8:4–6 (Jesus is Lord in the full, Jewish sense of God). Also Gal 1:15–16.

Of lesser, but still considerable, importance: 1 Cor 1:20 (Paul's rejection of the intellectuals of his day); 1:21–2:16 (a full and very important account of the disclosure of God's truth through a triune revelation); and 2 Cor 13:13 (a famous compact Trinitarian statement by Paul in the form of a blessing).

Further texts speaking of the divinity of God the Father, the Son/Jesus the Lord, and the divine Spirit, are listed in nn. 9 and 15. Revelation texts are listed in n. 12.

Key Reading

Superb introductions to the orthodox stance on theological epistemology being advocated here are three essays below by Alan J. Torrance (reading any one of these carefully should establish the issues and the approach); Heron's essay is also critical.

One of the best accounts ever penned of Paul's revelatory, unconditional epistemology is Lou Martyn's "Epistemology at the Turn of the Ages."

The basic case vis-à-vis the divine lordship of Jesus in Paul is introduced with typical incisiveness by Richard Bauckham in "Paul's Christology of Divine Identity," which can be accessed in his essay collection below on 182–232.

Further Reading

Two excellent studies broaching some of the dynamics implicit in the relationships between God, the Trinity, and the interpretation of Scripture are by David S. Yeago, "The New Testament and the Nicene Dogma," and by C. Kavin Rowe, "Biblical Pressure and Trinitarian Hermeneutics."

Key discussions of Jesus's divine identity in the NT are provided by Richard Bauckham and Larry Hurtado. An important recent step forward here has also been taken by Chris Tilling.

Finally, there is ultimately no substitute for reading Karl Barth himself, and especially for working through his magnum opus, *Church Dogmatics* (hereafter *CD*); the issue here is addressed especially in I/1. I recommend forming a coffee group to study twenty pages or so of the *Dogmatics* a week and swearing a blood covenant to persevere. The point is not to finish his work so much as to let one's mind be constantly reshaped by his subtle but profound engagements with the Bible and with the theological classics in the church's tradition, under the ever-present pressure of God as revealed definitively in Jesus Christ. (The one drawback to this practice is that most other Christian prose will increasingly seem tawdry by comparison.)

Bibliography

Barth, Karl. *Church Dogmatics*. Edited by T. F. Torrance and G. W. Bromiley. 4 vols. in 13 parts. Edinburgh: T&T Clark, 1956–96 (1932–67).

Bauckham, Richard. *Jesus and the God of Israel: God Crucified and Other Studies on the New Testament's Christology of Divine Identity*. Grand Rapids: Eerdmans, 2008.

Beeley, Christopher A., and Mark E. Weedman, eds. *The Bible in Early Trinitarian Theology*. Studies in Early Christianity. Washington DC: Catholic University of America Press, 2018.

Hays, Richard B. "The Story of God's Son: The Identity of Jesus in the Letters of Paul." Pages 180–99 in *Seeking the Identity of Jesus: A Pilgrimage*. Edited by Richard B. Hays and Beverly R. Gaventa. Grand Rapids: Eerdmans, 2008.

Heron, A. I. C. "*Homoousios* with the Father." Pages 58–87 in *The Incarnation: Ecumenical Studies in the Nicene-Constantinopolitan Creed, A.D. 381*. Edited by Thomas F. Torrance. Edinburgh: Handsel Press, 1981.

Hurtado, Larry W. *One God, One Lord: Early Christian Devotion and Ancient Jewish Monotheism*. 2nd ed. London: T&T Clark, 1998 (1988).

Martyn, J. Louis. "Epistemology at the Turn of the Ages." Pages 89–110 in *Theological Issues in the Letters of Paul*. Nashville: Abingdon, 1997.

Rae, Murray A. *History and Hermeneutics*. London: T&T Clark, 2005.

Rowe, C. Kavin. "Biblical Pressure and Trinitarian Hermeneutics." *ProEccl* 11 (2002): 295–312.

———. "For Future Generations: Worshiping Jesus and the Integration of the Theological Disciplines." *ProEccl* 17, no. 2 (2008): 186–209.

———. "Romans 10:13: What Is the Name of the Lord?" *HBT* 22 (2000): 135–73.

Smith, J. Warren. "'Arian' Foundationalism or 'Athanasian' Apocalypticism: A Patristic Assessment." Pages 78–95 in *Beyond Old and New Perspectives in Paul*. Edited by Chris Tilling. Eugene, OR: Cascade, 2014.

Tilling, Chris. *Paul's Divine Christology*. WUNT 2.232. Tübingen: Mohr Siebeck, 2012.

Torrance, Alan J. "*Auditus Fidei:* Where and How Does God Speak? Faith, Reason, and the Question of Criteria." Pages 27–52 in *Reason and the Reasons of Faith.* Edited by Paul J. Griffiths and Reinhardt Hütter. New York: T&T Clark, 2005.

———. "Jesus in Christian Doctrine." Pages 200–219 in *The Cambridge Companion to Jesus.* Edited by Markus Bockmuehl. Cambridge: Cambridge University Press, 2001.

———. "The Trinity." Pages 72–91 in *The Cambridge Companion to Karl Barth.* Edited by John Webster. Cambridge: Cambridge University Press, 2000.

Yeago, David S. "The New Testament and the Nicene Dogma: A Contribution to the Recovery of Theological Exegesis." *ProEccl* 3 (1994): 152–64.

CHAPTER 2

Vigilance

Avoiding "but . . ."

When I make claims to my students about the nature of the church's truth like those I made in the previous chapter, I usually encounter a polite "but . . ." from some of them. I completely understand people who say "but . . ."; however, I invariably go on to argue quite firmly that the introduction of a "but" here will subvert the entire basis of our truth, and therefore it needs to be avoided at all costs. Jesus's followers need to learn not to say "but" at this moment. Indeed, this "but . . ." needs to be repented of. The desire for an independent starting point for truth was, it should be recalled, the sin that led to the expulsion of humanity from the garden of Eden and to the arrival of death. For better and for worse, that desire also defines what has been called the epistemological "project of the Enlightenment." To say "but . . ." to the basis of truth in the revelation of God in the person of Jesus is not just a slip in epistemology—the sort of thing that might bother students in a divinity school but few others. It is a critical sin that results ultimately in the erosion of pretty much everything else that is important. It is to say "but . . ." to God, and as the Bible clearly teaches, this is never a good thing. I am not talking about doubt, which is not ideal but is a rather different phenomenon. We will talk about an appropriate response to doubt later. I am addressing the more brazen phenomenon of unbelief: the objection that the account I have just supplied is not truth or not the right account of where truth for the followers of Jesus should begin. But in order to appreciate fully and clearly why we should resist saying "but . . . ," we will need to explore our Pauline account of the truth in a little more detail.

I suggested in the previous chapter that we are grounded in the truth because we have responded positively to the divine disclosure that Jesus is Lord. In doing so, we have joined hands across the ages in witness with Paul and his converts (something we will talk more about shortly). We have, as he puts it, become convinced of this truth in our hearts and have confessed it with our lips (Rom 10:9–10). Paul tells us elsewhere that he was originally confronted very directly with the risen Jesus near Damascus (Gal 1:15–17; 1 Cor 9:1; 15:8). We probably had an experience more like the Corinthians, involving preaching and a teacher and the work of the Spirit. Our revelation was "mediated," and even Paul most likely had key mediations from people like Ananias. But whether like him or them (and I did meet a person once who had been visited by Jesus in the night, but he is the only such one I have ever met), God revealed the deep things of God to us and we said, "Amen; I acknowledge that this is true." So we know that Jesus is Lord because, at bottom, the Lord has spoken this truth to us.[1] But certain aspects of this arrangement probably make us nervous.

Clearly, we do not control this starting point for truth. It controls us, and I suspect that this is the point where the temptation to subvert the entire approach first tends to slither in.

The revealed truth about the nature of God in Jesus is a gift from God to us, and this particular gift is one over which we have absolutely no jurisdiction. We can respond to it, but we can't control it. God had to initiate the giving of this gift. Moreover, although the basic building blocks of our key truth claims might have been present beforehand—knowledge of the person of Jesus and of his crucifixion, the Jewish notion of God as the Lord, and so on—the convictions that these things had to be combined together and that, as such, they were and are true had to be supplied by God. They were whispered into our hearts by the Holy Spirit, even as they were confessed by disciples gathered together, perhaps for worship or for prayer. And this situation of complete giftedness seems to make us uneasy. It is as if we fear losing the truth, since we had no control over getting it, although this objection doesn't make a lot of sense once we think about it. The situation isn't reversible. Just because we give something to someone does not entail that we can necessarily take it back— think of having a baby. But perhaps something else is going on here as well.

The very giftedness of this truth, which comes all the way down to us, levels us all permanently and irrevocably in relation to one another. Everyone acknowledging this truth is placed on the same plane. None of us could

---

1. We could describe this starting point for truth more technically by saying that the deepest and most basic claims by the church are self-authenticating. The claims themselves are not self-authenticating. But they are claims about a God, and that God is authenticating them actively and personally.

access for ourselves the most important truth about reality, so humanity is radically equalized by this arrival, technically, in its incapacity. The gift of the truth about Jesus as Lord tells us that we all needed this gift and had nothing to contribute to it in advance. We are, then, in effect, all revealed by it to be equally stupid in and of ourselves. Presumably many Christians have found this suggestion a little offensive. Surely we can add to this process meaningfully? Surely some of us sense things in a slightly higher and deeper way and so make some contribution to our basic situation? (Is there no justice?!)

We do not, says Paul, reach this truth under our own steam, perhaps pointing by way of illustration to his own example of extreme educational effort and pious devotion, which nevertheless led him in a deeply destructive direction—to attempt to destroy the very people who were confessing the truth that he himself so desperately needed (Gal 1:13–14; Phil 3:4–6). But I wonder whether this arrangement ultimately is not quite a relief.

Jesus's followers no longer have to be the smartest people in the room—or at least to know or to read the smartest people in the room—in order to rest assured that their basic claims are impregnable. They are impregnable even if they are the weakest and silliest people in the room because the truth they rest on rests in turn on the prior activity of God. The result of all this could be—and even should be—a rather humbler, quieter presence, although, at just the same time, a deeply confident one.

But if the room is a seminar space in a modern university, it might very well be filled with Christianity's cultured despisers, or even with clever Christians who might not have fully engaged with their own fundamental ignorance. It is here that we encounter our first real trap in the form of an offer that, if it is accepted, can break apart our entire position. I call it "the truth gambit."

The Truth Gambit

Truth questions are tricky and have very far-reaching consequences, so we need to pay careful attention here. They tend to be debated with others who have different points of view. So discussions of the truth are very like a chess match—a very important chess match. Like Antonius Block, the tortured knight in Ingmar Bergman's classic film *The Seventh Seal*, we are playing chess with the devil. If we win, we will escape with our lives. If we lose, we will be dragged off with our companions in the dance of death. Moreover, as is usual in chess, much will depend on avoiding a mistake with our opening moves. Among other things, we must recognize the traps being set for us by our cunning opponent. We might be offered a piece in an apparently weak move only to find, on taking the piece, that we have been drawn into a disordered and ultimately untenable defensive system. We would have been deceived by a gambit. Our generic university seminar is offering up such a cunning and deadly gambit to us now.

Someone listening to my revelational confession in a seminar room might respond—and usually does: "How do you know that your claim 'Jesus is Lord' is true?" He or she might go on to say: "You are claiming that this is self-authenticating—that God just reveals this and in effect makes this true. But I need more than this. I need to know how you know that this is valid—that this revelation is really taking place. After all, I haven't had it. How do we know that God is real and that this revelation has happened? How do we judge this whole situation to be true?"

Although we hear it all the time, this challenge is a trap; it beckons before us like an open doorway into the smoothly reasonable discussions of the academy and beyond. It is so common that I want to spend some time in the rest of this chapter unpacking it and then supplying several important reasons why we should resist it, standing firm within the revelation of Jesus by Jesus.[2]

Our questioner is really posing a question about *truth criteria,* asking us to introduce another set to evaluate the one that we already have.

Everyone measures the truth of claims and statements in the light of truth criteria. Such criteria are rules and procedures that help us to ascertain the validity of individual claims. Every time we ask whether X is true, we presuppose a measurement of truth that judges the case. Those criteria stand over case X as its superior, bringing it before the bar of truth or falsehood, evaluating it. "How do we know that a cat is on the mat?" "How do we know that hydrogen gas is explosive?" "How do we know that the planet is warming up?" And so on. The truth criteria we use to evaluate different questions stack up in the order of their importance, and it follows that one set will be the king of the hill. These will be our highest, or, rather better, our deepest truth and our ultimate truth criteria.[3]

---

2. An ambiguous genitive construction in Gal 1:12 springs to mind here where it is hard to determine whether Paul is suggesting that "the proclamation [gospel] proclaimed by me . . . was [received and taught] by a revelation [*apokalypsis*] *of* Jesus Christ [*Iēsou Christou*]" or ". . . *from* Jesus Christ." Assuming repeated readings of the letter, however, it might be that he intended that both meanings were ultimately to be detected.

3. Strictly speaking, even this insight into truth claims and into what we might

Now we have just spent quite a bit of time reflecting on the fact that the basic truth criterion for the church is the lordship of Jesus, which is to say, the God whom Jesus embodies with complete fullness. And I have emphasized that we know this about Jesus because it has been revealed by the Lord to those who follow Jesus. So this truth claim is active and essentially reveals itself. God in person present with us is the truth, which is our central truth criterion as well. *Everything else now needs to be measured against this truth criterion*, and it is clearly an extraordinary one. The center of all truth is a crucified Jew who was resurrected on the third day, and all God-talk, and really everything else besides, has to be measured against it, which is really to say, brought in subjection to it. And we know this truth because this God has revealed it to us—that God is present most directly in this person and in the events and activities associated with his life. Hence our truth criterion is alive and active on its own behalf!

However, people who are not responding overtly to the disclosures of God in these terms understandably reject this criterion as the ultimate measure of truth. They bring different measurements to bear on every question, including on this one. Consequently, the questioner in our university seminar (a woman, let us assume), is asking us to place our claim about Jesus, and hence our truth criterion, underneath hers to be measured—an entirely reasonable procedure from her point of view, but an entirely fatal one from ours. She wants to measure my truth by her truth criterion and to encourage me to do the same. It is here that the gambit is offered *and must be firmly declined.*

If we do this—if we accept this request and, in effect, start playing this game—then we place another truth criterion over the top of God to judge God, who is our truth. Hence this move turns out to be a denial that God is the ultimate truth. God is merely *a* truth and no longer the supreme truth, which is to say, *the* truth. We have thereby abandoned our initial position that God is our truth criterion and by doing so, we are really saying that God is not God. God isn't synonymous with the truth, because there is another truth out there that is bigger and better than God, which really doesn't seem like a good idea, once we think about it. God is not *the* truth?! As a friend put it to me once, by making this move, abandoning the living God as the ultimate source of truth, we have not just shot ourselves in the foot; we have shot ourselves in the head.

---

call truth games will be derived by messianic Jews like Paul and Christians like me retrospectively, after the realization that Jesus is Lord and in the light of that realization. We will see how others have their own lordships, even, and perhaps especially, in epistemological terms.

We have done so, moreover, in defiance of what God has chosen to do for us. We have stepped back from God's gracious personal involvement as the truth in our own situation and have accepted the idea that an alternative approach to the truth—an approach more palatable to a seminar room—should be superior to it. We have said, in effect, "Thanks for the revelation, God—very helpful as far as it went—but we need something a little more secure and intelligible than that now." Perhaps we added, "Your approach just doesn't seem clever enough." God's mode of dispensing truth has thereby been demoted to second place—which, as we have just seen, denies what it is entirely—and we have turned to some other mode of our own invention.

The Bible prohibits this move in one of its most obvious variations in the first warnings of the Ten Commandments, and an important connection to the phenomenon of idolatry is also made apparent here, along with the appalling consequences of lapsing into this situation.[4] We are to have no other gods before our Lord God, which is to say, no other gods beside the God who has revealed himself to us as the Lord, the Lord who delivered the Hebrews from Egypt and who lives in the resurrected Lord Jesus. Moreover, we are not to try to image this God. The imaging of God is the province strictly of God; the depiction of God is in the hands of God and of God alone. To try to image God for ourselves, thereby to construct an idol, is consequently to take control of the imaging process for ourselves in defiance of God's self-presentation and of God's lordship over God's own presentation, an awful sin with awful consequences.[5] Hence idolatry is included in this account of the truth as its sinful complement and should be vigilantly avoided.

The misuse of God's name prohibited in the third commandment overlaps with these issues as well. God's name is to be applied correctly, with truthful speech, in worship, in response to God's self-disclosure, and not incorrectly, haphazardly, or lewdly. (See Exod 20:2–7; Deut 5:6–11.)

A more technical name for the procedure whereby we elevate our own truth criteria over the truth that is God, ultimately to judge God's truth or falsity, is "foundationalism," which denotes here our provision of a different foundation for truth from the one that God has laid for us in Jesus, and hence a structure that we ultimately build for ourselves. Foundationalism has a more

---

4. The warning implicit in the first of the Ten Commandments is especially pointed at this moment.

5. In the Tanakh these are ultimately the invasion of the land, the capture of the capital, the destruction of the temple, and the exile of the people, at which moment one wonders what the modern equivalents might be.

technical, although related, meaning in modern philosophical discussion, referring primarily to the desire of many thinkers post-Descartes to construct
an indubitable basis for knowledge—a foundation in this specific sense.[6] So
clearly there is some overlap here. Any such philosophical attempt to construct a perfect foundation for all thought and knowledge is indeed a form of
foundationalism. In the light of the revelation of the Trinity, however, we can
see that this exercise in human hubris exists in many more forms than philosophical foundationalism alone, and each of these needs to be identified and
resisted. Especially since the Enlightenment, Christians have often themselves
employed this way of reasoning—for example, by trying to prove the truthfulness of the Bible on the basis of historical records, reason, appeal to universal
moral intuitions, or the like, before explaining what the Bible teaches (an effort
labeled "evidentialist apologetics"). Yet, every such effort is also, at bottom, an
exercise in idolatry. To build a foundation for the truth ourselves is to reject the
truth and to build our own version of the truth, which we then make the judge
of all truth, and so the lord of truth, at which moment in effect we bow down
before it and proclaim it as our new lord. So epistemological foundationalism,
however sophisticated, is, at bottom, nothing more than another golden calf.

And we don't need to do any of this. We are Christians,[7] located by the
work of God within the central truth that explains all of reality. We are in
the truth already. Why step outside of this circle into a place where we no
longer belong? Why accept being a non-Christian for the sake of argument?
We don't help either ourselves or our interlocutors if we do so. We lose our
Christian identity and embrace an artificial alternative, and in the process our

6. Philosophers tend to use the term "foundationalism" in modern discussions
of epistemology primarily in the Internalist camp as against the Externalist. However,
both Internalists and Externalists would be accused by Barth on theological grounds
of being foundationalists in more general terms, because both camps work with truth
criteria that they have derived in some fashion for themselves, the differences between
the two camps being over the specific nature, location, and reach of those deriva-
tions. Sufficient orientation to the in-house philosophical debates for our purposes
is provided by Ted Poston ("Foundationalism" and "Internalism and Externalism in
Epistemology"), by Ali Hasan and Richard Fumerton ("Foundationalist Theories of
Epistemic Justification"), and by George Pappas ("Internalist vs. Externalist Conceptions of Epistemic Justification").

7. Or messianic Jews, of course. In what follows, the terms "church" and "community" include both Christians, in the sense of converts to Jesus from paganism (like
me!), and messianic Jews.

interlocutors lose contact with an authentic Christian. And we have launched an infinite regress as well!

Perhaps we succeed in finding another truth criterion that can judge our key claims, and we start to derive a sober evaluation. But once we pause and think about this step, we need to ask ourselves how we know that this latest criterion is true. We will need *another* criterion to judge it, so our search will begin again. And we will need another one after that, and another one after that, and so on, indefinitely. Do we really want to roll a stone up a hill and watch it roll down again *forever?!* In fact, everyone stops somewhere, at which point we see that everyone ultimately will rest his or her truth claims on truth criteria that are self-authenticating (a point that Aristotle made some time ago in *Posterior Analytics* 1.3).[8] No one can prove that his or her ultimate criteria for the truth are true. We cannot demonstrate that the truth is true. So we are quite entitled to start with the revelation that Jesus is Lord and to claim that this is self-authenticating—and God could hardly be a more convincing place to locate self-authentication![9]

I imagine that the acceptance of this gambit is now starting to look like a bad idea. It will subtly but irrevocably generate all sorts of subversions within our basic truth position. But there are other even more troubling reasons for avoiding accepting the truth gambit. Three in particular are worth pondering carefully. We see in them especially clearly how a mistake at the beginning of our game of chess with the devil leads quickly to the church's dance with death. Significant real-world consequences have followed in the history of the church from the acceptance of this gambit. It is not just an intellectual pitfall. Compromise at this moment releases what we can call the three horsemen of the foundationalist apocalypse.[10]

---

8. As noted by Poston, and by Hasan and Fumerton.

9. Note, however, that we do not start by appealing to this prior argument that all claims are ultimately self-authenticating, which would itself be a prior claim that in some way had to be self-authenticating! The problem of an infinite regress becomes apparent in due course, which means that we can use this observation defensively and Socratically, not foundationally. If someone challenges us for resting on self-authenticating claims, we can retort, "You do this too, so I don't really see what the problem is." We don't use this as a positive argument for our own position up front. That position rests (of course) on revelation.

10. I am using the signifier "apocalypse" here in its more popular sense to refer to a terrible, fiery day of judgment as spoken of by texts like the book of Revelation. Biblical scholars would refer to this as eschatology. The story of sinister horses and horsemen begins in earnest in the Bible in the book of Zechariah (1:8–11;

The Three Horsemen

When Jesus's followers have accepted what I earlier referred to as the truth gambit, thereby undermining the basis of their own truths claims about Jesus by adopting another set of truth criteria by which to measure their own claims, they have gone off and built their own foundation. But besides being a bad move simply in terms of irreverence for the God who is the truth, *these new foundations invariably collapse on closer scrutiny.* Certainly they have to date. To my knowledge, no universally demonstrable criteria for truth have ever been derived that successfully withstand philosophical scrutiny, whether by Christians, Jews, or non-Christians. The history of ideas is a litany of magnificent failures. My brilliant professor in undergraduate ethics, Jim Flynn, was particularly impressed by Plato's magnificent failure, and if Plato couldn't do it, who can? This is not to deny the presence of insights and fragments of truth and occasional bursts of inspiration within the accumulated thinking of humanity, but I am not aware of an independently and objectively derived and demonstrated truth criterion that leads us successfully to God or, for that matter, to much else. The cacophony of the university attests daily to this fact. Hence the ultimate result of accepting this gambit and making this move has succeeded only in creating a twisted demonic variation on the goal of our original project, namely, atheism, the first horseman of the foundationalist apocalypse.

If Christians think that they can prove the existence of God acting in Jesus independently of God's revelation of Godself, using some higher truth or argument or position that everyone acknowledges, they pay a heavy price. These attempts might be convincing to the faithful, but they tend to collapse under the withering scrutiny of modern philosophers. And a culture that has been told loudly that God can be proved but has found that God cannot be proved then feels justified in turning decisively away from God. The only thing that seems to have been proved is that God does not exist.[11] God is rejected as an unproved hypothesis without anyone confronting the place where that God has in fact chosen to become known, which

---

6:1–8), and recurs in Rev 6:2–8. So, we might say, the abandonment of apocalyptic (meaning by this the initial acceptance of the revelation of Jesus as Lord) leads to the apocalypse!

11. Strictly speaking, the existence of God has not been disproved either. But when people who do not believe, and who expect the existence of God to be demonstrated before they do, encounter repeated failures, they tend to draw this conclusion.

is personally, in Jesus. A key result flowing from the pretension that we can judge the truth about God for ourselves has consequently been the creation of a culture that confidently affirms God's impossibility and hard-heartedly resists the good news. We have reaped here what we have sown, and it is a bitter harvest.[12]

But not only do these magnificently pretentious truth systems designed to prove God's existence collapse under closer scrutiny, releasing a culture of atheism. They also tend to obstruct us from ever reaching the truth that really matters, which is Jesus. This obstruction is the second deadly horseman.

If we press on boldly with our foundationalist project, anxious that if our system collapses, then our faith does as well, we tend to end up—and arguably necessarily only ever end up—with "the god of the philosophers." This is because when we construct our foundation, we are invariably deriving some universal principle or dynamic from our own reality as our truth criterion and extrapolating or developing it in a way that will hopefully lead us to God. This key principle will have to be something very broad and universal and abstract. It must be known by everyone. So we will be reflecting on the inner nature of all reality in terms of an essence, or on the sense that we often judge things to be beautiful or not, or on the inner logic of history, or some such. But our conclusions will then be a long way away from the recognition that God was fully present in a Jewish person who was shamefully executed around 30 CE. We find and worship the God who is the essence of all reality or beauty or history or whatever else we managed to infer from, which is clearly rather different. And the further critical problem now emerges.

By supposing that this is the way to the church's truth, we then, in all good conscience, *oppose* those who try to approach it in other ways, including, and perhaps especially opposing, the poor people who simply claim that the crucified Jesus is Lord and attribute that claim to the Lord. (There is something offensive about this foolish claim to the fundamentally learned and intelligent approach of our alternative system.)[13] We are defending the way to the truth, which is perforce the only way. Are we not in the last remaining lifeboat on a stormy secular sea? Moreover, we have probably invested so

---

12. Michael J. Buckley traces out this sad theological, philosophical, and cultural trajectory with brilliant insight and detail. See his books *At the Origins of Modern Atheism* and *Denying and Disclosing God*.

13. As Paul notes in 1 Cor 1:22.

much time and effort in developing our magnificent system that we will be reluctant to abandon it, and if we think that our belief in God depends on this system, we will be very reluctant to abandon it. Perhaps our impressive careers within the institutions advocating this system even depend on our not abandoning it. But the end result of all this investment will be *the determined obstruction of the very truth that we are supposed to be reaching*—that God was fully present in Jesus and speaks this truth to the church in whatever way God wants to. Not only will our magnificent systems fail us then by proving untrue and generating atheism; they will block the way to the very objective that they are supposedly trying to establish. They will stand guard as authentic theologies barring the way to Jesus himself—a block that we have called the second horseman.[14]

The third horseman, however, is still more troubling. When we build our magnificent systems as we have just suggested, we will have to project some aspect of ourselves into God's location, and so we will probably isolate and extend something that we take to be especially impressive about our humanity or our situation.[15] *And these projections are never innocent.* They are projections by particular groups of people from specific cities, cultures, and locales, and usually by well-educated and self-confident male European leaders. The inevitable result of these projections is a subtle self-ratification of those leaders and their cultures. We cannot help affirming ourselves fundamentally with these systems. We build God in our own image (idolatry!). So we end up affirming our culture, and we thereby remove from judgment all those aspects of it that God might be speaking to us about when we grasp that he is revealed by a crucified Jew. When the truth about God is a gift, every aspect of our life is brought under its correction. When the truth about God is a projection, parts of our identity *are permanently reserved from judgment*, and the results can be horrific.

Barth grasped the truth about God, recovering the key insight that God had grasped him, as he worried about the church's compromises with wars

14. Arguably this problem could be characterized even more strongly. If a foundationalist system is being constructed, then later truth claims cannot and must not undermine or disrupt its opening claims or the entire structure must collapse into invalidity. So those later claims will be resisted and/or subordinated, *including Christology!* This problem will be noted time and again in what follows.

15. This process of projection is, as Barth put it, the one, monotonous, not-entirely-profound, but nevertheless true and helpful insight in post-Enlightenment modernity made by Ludwig Feuerbach.

and social cruelty in the early twentieth century. A particularly telling episode unfolded around him through the 1930s.

At this time, perhaps as many as 90 percent of German Protestant Christians—a devout, learned, church-attending nation—believed that Adolf Hitler was a leader sent to them by God to restore the pride of the German nation and to further its mission within broader Christendom. "God is using Hitler to make Germany great again." So they enthusiastically supported his political ambitions and even his leadership over the church. Subsequent events clearly revealed this support to be a catastrophic and tragic mistake. The regime supposed to last for a thousand years lasted for only twelve, and in that time it managed to inflict warfare across the globe, with millions of casualties and untold suffering.

During evil epochs like these—and they litter church history with distressing frequency—many Christian leaders have demonstrably accepted the truth gambit and strayed from the revelation that is Jesus, turning to philosophical or cultural projections of one sort or another. As Barth saw with particular clarity, however, these projections invariably cloak sinister political and cultural self-ratifications, ultimately involving the church in deep confusions and painful failures. Such churches become incapable, at bottom, of disentangling God from their own culture and politics, and so they often end up, in effect, dying for their flag in the name of God but in defiance of his real nature—the third horseman of the apocalypse.

We can probably see by now that the stakes in this chess game are high. We must be very wary of accepting a seemingly innocent but ultimately deadly truth gambit. For many reasons—principally the three horsemen of the foundationalist apocalypse, but also their earlier outriders[16]—we must resist any challenge to prove or to demonstrate that the claim Jesus is Lord is true on any other basis than its own. When we hear the claim "Jesus is Lord," we must

16. That is, the following problems: (1) God's supremacy and identity as the truth have effectively been denied; (2) God's own chosen method of establishing the truth has been rejected; (3) this is an entirely artificial and hence unnecessary procedure; and (4) this leads us only into an infinite regress. To these we then add the three horsemen: (5) any alternative truth criteria have inevitably proved unsustainable and collapsed, generating cultural atheism; (6) persistence in the erection of these alternative systems tends to block the way to an acceptance of the supreme truth that is the person of Jesus and related Trinitarian insight; and (7) any alternative system inevitably involves political and cultural self-ratifications, resulting in disastrous cultural compromises and widespread ethical failures on the part of the church.

learn to reject *and to repent of* adding the fatal word "but."[17] If we recognize the trap lurking here, however, we step back from the abyss.

But what of the doubters who, as we remarked earlier, might be sitting in the corner of the room? Someone might have responded a little less aggressively than our learned skeptical (or misguided Christian) interlocutor. Instead of demanding an "objective" and independent set of truth criteria with which to measure God, someone might simply have said, "I understand all this, but I struggle to respond with conviction to what I think God is saying to me about the lordship of Jesus. I don't want to step outside of the circle of revelation, but as I am standing here, I simply doubt it. I suppose I just lack faith."

This is an entirely understandable reaction to what is being suggested here—although it is not helped by the unleashing of atheism facilitated by the mistaken approach to the truth about God that we just noted—but I would suggest that it requires a very different sort of response from the vigilant rejection that was just recommended for the more blatant challenge. A constructive response to this problem must grow out of the community of Jesus followers, and in an entirely concrete fashion, so I need to ask my doubting readers to hold on until part 3 (although the community as that is described in part 2 should help here as well). Hopefully my answer will be worth waiting for.

If we have learned how to avoid compromising our basic truth claims by resisting the truth gambit offered deceptively to us by modernity, a gambit that, if accepted, unleashes the three horsemen of the foundationalist apocalypse,

---

17. A Pauline scholar might object to my argument at this point that Paul does appeal to natural theology in a foundational role in this sense so we have to find room for it, namely, in Rom 1:19–20 in the broader context of 1:18–3:20, which is Paul's first major argumentative unit in Romans. But I am firmly convinced that attributing this stated theological position to Paul is a major mistake on theological, argumentative, and exegetical grounds. I think his argument in this section is constructed Socratically, so these claims are part of an interlocutor's system (a case made in *Deliverance* and summarized in *Beyond*). Consequently, I line up here very much in Barth's camp over against Brunner in their infamous spat in 1934, and would support Barth's theological and political points with my exegetical suggestions. In the meantime, I would point out that this is really the only text in Paul that can be appealed to in this way, and this is far too slender a basis from which to launch foundationalism. *Perhaps* Rom 13:1–7 could be appealed to as well, but both these texts tend to stand or fall together. I do not think that Acts 17:22–31, when it is carefully read, is counter-evidence. C. Kavin Rowe, "The Grammar of Life," supplies an elegant, albeit quite technical, analysis of this important text that accords directly with my claims about Paul here.

then we now need to reflect more deeply on the God who has been revealed in Jesus. And as we do so, we will constantly be alert to temptations to step off the seemingly narrow pathway that leads to the God of Jesus, into foundationalist constructions that will ultimately lead us to ruin. Indeed, in many respects, the rest of this book will simply follow this pathway forward vigilantly, seeing where it leads and eschewing deceptive alternative paths, which lead off smoothly to the side only to end up in ruination.

Theses

> Because the truth about God is revealed, we have no control over it. This process tends to make us nervous.

> This process—or event—levels us all, revealing us all to be caught up, effectively, in a humanity-wide stupidity. For some of us, this is also offensive.

> We might be asked, "How do we know whether this truth is true?" The word "but" often begins such a question.

> Alert modern theologians call this foundationalism because we would thereby be constructing our own foundation on which basis to evaluate the truth about God.

> This use of foundationalism should be distinguished from the philosophical position of foundationalism, although the latter is a subset of the former.

> Foundationalism in the sense we are addressing here is a trap that must be avoided., We must reject immediately as illegitimate any demand that we evaluate the truth of God revealed in Jesus.

> Such a challenge asks us to erect another ultimate criterion for truth over the top of God, who is *the* truth.

> The Bible warns us, notably in the first of the Ten Commandments, to allow God to define and to reveal God.

> It prohibits the human construction of God's image, and hence any human control over the definition and disclosure of God, thereby articulating the connection between foundationalism and idolatry.

> Trying to create a foundation for the truth on any terms other than what God has given in his personal revelation of Christ is a bad idea in fact for all sorts of reasons:

   (1) As just noted, this denies that God is the ultimate truth and so denies that he is God. (God is *the* truth.)

(2) This rejects what God has done for us and to us through Jesus and the Spirit.

(3) This is artificial. We are adopting a nonbelieving viewpoint for the sake of argument, which neither we nor our interlocutors actually believe.

(4) This starts an infinite regress, resulting in an unstable foundation in any case.

(5) This foundation invariably proves untrue. This in turn releases atheism (the first horseman of the foundationalist apocalypse).

(6) This foundation nevertheless feels critical, so its advocates tend to remain attached to it and to go on to resist due attention to Christ, to the Trinity, and to their revelation up front (the second horseman). These last subjects can become a conclusion or even an appendix to theology rather than its correct foundation.

(7) Our false foundation invariably contains sinister political and social projections and self-ratifications (the third horseman). Cultural truths become inextricably confused with divine truths, with the result that we cannot, for example, distinguish reliably between our passion for God and our passion for our country—a point where the connection with idolatry becomes even clearer.

› Hence, when resting in the truth revealed to us by God that Jesus is Lord, we must at all costs and in every sense resist the use of the word "but. . . ." We must reject all Jesus-but theology!

› There is a more understandable role for doubt, when someone might accept that revelation is the basis of the truth about God but simply cannot recognize it in any existential or personal way. But this response is best addressed later on, in part 3, and also where appropriate in part 2, ultimately in practical, concrete, and relational terms.

Key Scriptural References

I have spent much of my career demonstrating that Rom 1:18–20 in its broader context is not an exception to the revelational claims made in the previous chapter in dependence on texts like 2 Cor 5:17. (See my *Deliverance* for more details. The arguments are anticipated by *Quest* and summarized and scrutinized by various scholars in *Beyond*.) Neither are Rom 13:1–7 or Acts 17:22–31 exceptions to this position. (On this last text, see Rowe's article below.)

Key Reading

Barth's experience of the German Christians during the 1930s is detailed on pages 216–53 in the definitive biography by his pupil and friend Eberhard Busch. This issue came to a sharp point in his famous exchange with Emil Brunner in 1934. Brunner's endorsement of natural theology in a foundationalist role led to an angry "Nein!" from Barth—a No!—seen in retrospect to be entirely correct in its repudiation of National Socialism.

The rise of modern atheism from the ashes of theological failure—ashes left over from the bonfire of vain epistemological compromise—is documented brilliantly by Michael Buckley, a Roman Catholic. Buckley's extended treatment published in 1987 is summarized in a briefer and more accessible book published in 2004.

Further Reading

Buckley's tale of Western theological and cultural declension is nicely complemented by Placher's documentation of the same process from a more Protestant point of view.

Feuerbach, the great theorist of religious projection, should at some point be read in his own right, especially by those who want to engage deeply with Karl Marx. His key work is the modestly titled *Principles of the Philosophy of the Future*. In the meantime, Barth's brief, amusingly arch summary on pages 520–27 in *Protestant Theology in the Nineteenth Century* is useful.

Bibliography

Barth, Karl. "No!" Pages 67–128 in *Natural Theology: Comprising "Nature and Grace" by Professor Dr. Emil Brunner and the Reply "No!" by Dr. Karl Barth*. Translated by Peter Fraenkel. Eugene, OR: Wipf & Stock, 2002.

———. *Protestant Theology in the Nineteenth Century: Its Background and History*. Translated by Brian Cozens and John Bowden. London: SCM Press, 1959.

Buckley, Michael J. *At the Origins of Modern Atheism*. New Haven: Yale University Press, 1987.

———. *Denying and Disclosing God: The Ambiguous Progress of Modern Atheism*. New Haven: Yale University Press, 2004.

Busch, Eberhard. *Karl Barth: His Life from Letters and Autobiographical Texts.* Translated by J. Bowden. 2nd rev. ed. London: SCM, 1976.

Feuerbach, Ludwig. *Principles of the Philosophy of the Future.* Translated by Manfred H. Vogel. Indianapolis: Bobbs-Merrill, 1966.

Hasan, Ali, and Richard Fumerton. "Foundationalist Theories of Epistemic Justification." In *The Stanford Encyclopedia of Philosophy* (Winter 2016 Edition). Edited by Edward N. Zalta. https://plato.stanford.edu/cgi-bin/encyclopedia/archinfo.cgi?entry=justep-foundational.

Pappas, George. "Internalist vs. Externalist Conceptions of Epistemic Justification." In *The Stanford Encyclopedia of Philosophy* (Fall 2017 Edition). Edited by Edward N. Zalta. https://plato.stanford.edu/cgi-bin/encyclopedia/archinfo.cgi?entry=justep-intext.

Placher, William C. *The Domestication of Transcendence: How Modern Thinking about God Went Wrong.* Louisville: Westminster John Knox, 1996.

Poston, Ted. "Foundationalism." *Internet Encyclopedia of Philosophy.* http://www.iep.utm.edu/found-ep/.

———. "Internalism and Externalism in Epistemology." *Internet Encyclopedia of Philosophy.* http://www.iep.utm.edu/int-ext/.

Rowe, C. Kavin. "The Grammar of Life: The Areopagus Speech and Pagan Tradition." *NTS* 57 (2011): 69–80.

CHAPTER 3

A God of Love

Personhood

We need now to press deeper into what Jesus as God is disclosing to us about God, and perhaps the first thing that impresses itself upon us as we do so is the realization that God is composed of persons. The God revealed through Jesus overflows with personhood. God the Father has sent his Son. And God the Spirit has drawn us through the Son back to her Father. God is intrinsically personal. Moreover, we learn from this in turn just what a person is—a useful thing to know, since we now realize that a fundamentally interpersonal God lies at the heart of all reality, and we are made in the image of this God.

A person is a *relational* entity. God the Father is defined *as* a father—that is to say, his identity as a person is bound up with his sending of his Son. Without the Son he is not the Father, which is to say, he would not be who he is. He is the Father because he has an only beloved Son, so his identity is constituted by his relationship with his Son. And exactly the same applies to the Son. He is the Son and the person of the Son because he has the Father. He is not who he is without his Father. That relationship constitutes him.[1] The

---

1. Zizioulas, an especially important advocate of this insight, is alert to it because of his deep immersion in the highly Trinitarian and relational thinking of the Cappadocians. Tallon helpfully describes how Zizioulas parses a healthy relationality facilitated by Christ and the Spirit, over against an unhealthy, sinful state: "Human *apo-stasis* and *dia-stasis* (separateness and individuality) become *ek-stasis* (communion, relatedness) and *hypo-stasis* (particularity, uniqueness), and thereby our fear of *dia-phora* (difference, otherness) becomes *ana-phora* (reference or movement towards outside creation)" (Luke B. Tallon, "Our Being Is in Becoming"; he is drawing here especially on John D. Zizioulas, *Communion and Otherness*).

same necessarily now applies to the Spirit. The Spirit is the Spirit of the Father and of the Son. Without her relationships with the Father and the Son, she is not the Spirit that she is.[2]

So we see that each person within the Trinity is constituted by relationships with the other members of the Trinity, from which we learn that to be a person is to be a fundamentally relational being—something created in, by, and for relationships with other people. We live as people by means of other people, and without them we lack full personhood. Never were truer words uttered then when John Donne wrote, "No man is an island." Speaking of islands. . . .

I am often struck by the diagrams of personal situations that people draw on the whiteboard of a classroom. If a student is illustrating a social situation or group, he or she often draws a scattering of small circles across the board with spaces of different distances between them. This depiction suggests that each person is a self-contained zone with a boundary, outside of which there is no fundamental need to venture. (See fig. 1.) Personhood exists in isolation, and society looks like a game of marbles. There is a gap between everyone that individuals presumably have to navigate carefully without compromising their personhood, which is separated off and even threatened by proximity to other people. But they have fallen here into a trap baited by Western spatial thinking with its mutually exclusive zones, something allied here with a Western conception of the person as a self-contained individual.

Instead of this approach, I encourage my students to diagram people with constellations of crossing lines like stars or flowers. (See fig. 2.) Every person is a radiation of different strokes, each one of which is a relationship with another person. We then see at a glance that these people are incomplete without their connections with other people—without other radiating stars. Society as a whole is a complex lacework or network. Moreover, the basic being of the person is extrinsic and radial. People are what they are in their links and connections with other people.

---

2. These insights can lead us to a particularly compelling account of the unity of the Trinity in terms of *perichorēsis*, along lines suggested by John Zizioulas. Paul's relational notion of unity or oneness is indicated by texts like 1 Cor 6:16; 8:6; Gal 3:28c; Eph 2:14–16; 4:3–6, 13; and 5:30–31. In several of these texts he uses a sexual metaphor informed by Gen 2:24, understanding sexual union as oneness or unification, as that text suggests. This usage denotes the unity of close relational intimacy, along with close bodily contact without any erasure of differentiation or individuated personhood, and supports a perichoretic account of the divine unity. This point is developed further in ch. 10.

Fig. 1. Persons as self-contained zones.

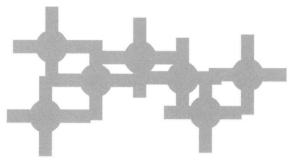

Fig. 2. Persons as constellations of intersecting relationships.

We can put things rather less prosaically than this if we think about our closest and most intimate relationships of love with someone else. I often invoke my relationship with my spouse at this point, since I am fortunate to enjoy a very happy one—a happy spouse and a happy relationship, although we can see now that these things are ultimately inseparable. We have been married for a long time—thirty-five years and counting. As a result, it is fairly obvious that where I go Rachel goes, and where Rachel goes I go. I am fundamentally incomplete without her and my relationship with her. A key part of who I am as a person, Douglas, is my relationship with her, and consequently she is a part of who I am and vice versa. When I speak, part of her is speaking. If Rachel dies, part of me, Douglas, dies; and if I die, part of Rachel would die. Rather more positively, insofar as she lives and enjoys life, I live and enjoy life, and vice versa. But what we see here particularly clearly holds for all our other relationships as well.

I am also a father, to Emile and Grace. My very identity as a person is constituted by these relationships too. I am what I am because of my parenthood of Emile and Grace, and they are part of me. So I take them with me wherever I go, and if I lose one of them, I lose a part of myself at the very deepest level as well. No wonder then that the American entertainment industry is obsessed with key family relationships. Recall that the climactic moment in the epic

Star Wars saga is really Darth Vader's declaration to Luke Skywalker: "*I* am your father!" This happens in episode 5. Fortunately, in the ensuing finale, the intrinsic relationality of personhood overcomes the dark side of the force, and Darth Vader rescues his son from death at the hands of the evil emperor.

We must let this revelation concerning the true nature of personhood sink down into our theological bones, since it will pervade all that follows. People are relational beings because the personal God that is the Trinity is a relational communion, and we are made in the image of God. But what are the immediate implications of this deep insight into the human condition?

Family

We are now in a position to grasp a stunning notion. At the heart of all reality lies an interpersonal and hence fundamentally *familial* God. We are involved with a divinity that is interpersonal in the most committed and relational fashion. So the closest analogies we have for this dynamic tend to be rooted in families—when these relationships are working at their healthiest. I am well aware that this caveat is often quite significant. Distorted and damaged families will emphatically not mediate these truths; instead, they often undermine, negate, and occlude them. Moreover, since families are composed of sinners, all families will fail in important respects to mediate these dynamics perfectly. Furthermore, other relationships can mediate these truths as well, such as close and faithful friends and confidantes. In no way should these mediations be excluded. I still suspect, however, that, given the way we seem to be presently constructed, what we might call covenantal families will predominantly mediate these truths, so a guarded use of this imagery is helpful. We can, with suitable caution and inclusiveness, deploy familial metaphors in order to understand what God is like, along with corresponding metaphors of friendship. It is no coincidence that Paul's favored metaphors for describing the reality that Jesus followers experience especially directly and clearly—despite how they are sometimes depicted—are fundamentally familial.[3]

3. The appropriate gender construction of couples and families will be discussed carefully in due course, but there are a lot of things that need to be in place before we can attempt an appropriately Pauline navigation of this complex and contested set of issues. So this third caveat needs to be borne in mind as well. Suffice it for now to say that Paul's language should be understood in thoroughly personal but not necessarily in gendered terms.

As we have already seen, God is God the *Father*, from which it follows that Jesus is the *Son*.[4] And the Spirit is identified as both the Spirit of God the Father and the Spirit of the Son. Moreover, "we all bear the image of his Son so that he is the firstborn of many brothers [Gk. *adelphoi*]" (Rom 8:29). Paul's most common designation for Jesus followers, by quite some margin, is "brothers." He uses it three times as often as his second most common title, "holy ones," and six times as often as his most widely quoted title, "believers."[5]

The implications of all this are simply staggering.

There has arguably been a predilection for describing God in much theology—and perhaps especially in reflections derived from Latin-speaking traditions—with categories that are fundamentally legal and political. God is viewed at bottom as a monarch or sovereign, and the key analogies for understanding his relationships, both internally and externally with us, are in terms of law and the state. However, careful attention to what God has actually revealed about his nature to us in Jesus, his Son, suggests that these reflections are inaccurate and possibly even quite misleading. They have their place, but only after due correction by the analogies that are primary. God is fundamentally familial and disposed toward us in this way as well—as our heavenly Father.

The implications of all this are, as I have just said, simply staggering. It is hard to know exactly what to talk about next, since so much has just been set in motion. But we should probably first press deeper into the exact nature of the family that is involved when God is at work. Sadly, our ofttimes fractured

---

4. This implication has been partly obscured by Paul's fondness for the title "Lord" for Jesus. But this predilection should not be taken to override or to obscure Jesus's underlying sonship. Paul does designate Jesus explicitly as Son on occasion and speaks of our sonship through him and also constantly places him in relation to his Father, thereby implying his sonship directly. So for Paul, Jesus is both Son and Lord, even if the weight of his explicit terminology falls on the latter. In just the same way, although I am most frequently referred to around the Divinity School as Doctor Campbell, and I do have a PhD, this title should not be taken to override my more fundamental relationships and identity as the husband of Rachel and the father of Emile and Grace. It is just that in the setting of the Divinity School my later title, received some time after my marriage, is situationally more appropriate. Just so, after Jesus's heavenly enthronement, he is spoken of by his devotees as Messiah and Lord. But he remains the Son of his Father as well. The relevant data is assembled in my essay "The Narrative Dimensions in Paul's Gospel," in *Quest*, especially n. 19, 83–84 (first published in Bruce W. Longenecker, *Narrative Dynamics in Paul*).

5. See "Narrative Dimensions."

human families may hinder us more than they help at this moment. We need to let God gently correct and restore our understanding and experience of family as we are involved with and healed by the divine family.

Love

If we have grasped the extent to which God is a fully familial God composed of persons who are what they are because of one another, then we are in a position to grasp another truth that is equally staggering. We know that the Father is the Father because of the Son, and that the Son is the Son because of the Father (and so forth). But what is the actual tenor of the relationship between this Father and this Son? Is it a formal sonship—a relationship primarily of obedience by the Son to his Father? ("The Father is obeyed by the Son.") Does it denote causality, if that notion has any meaning once we try to apply it to God? "The Father begets the Son" or "creates the Son"? Or is it something else?

It is highly significant here that Paul uses language drawn both from the story of Abraham and Isaac in Genesis and from the Bible's characterizations of the Israelite monarchy, especially of its founding figure, David, to suggest that the Son is God the Father's *beloved* Son.[6]

The Father dotes on the Son, we might say. The Son is the apple of his eye. And the Son loves his Father, which is why he does what the Father says, even when it involves what seem to us to be extraordinary demands. Here we can be helped, in their best moments, by the astonishing love that often does obtain within our families between spouses, and between parents and their children, situations where people can offer everything for one another. Such situations mediate the critical realization that the persons of the Trinity have a deep and profound love for one another, something that is then also apparent in the life of Jesus.[7] So as the author of 1 John puts it—characteristically a little more compactly than Paul, although doubtless the latter would have approved—"God is love" (4:8).

6. A basic orientation of these debates is supplied by my "Narrative Dimensions." In *Deliverance*, ch. 16, 639–76, I offer a more detailed case in relation to Paul's distinctive use of the word *hilastērion* in Rom 3:25.

7. I don't think the lexical defense of this insight famously offered by Jeremias, who appeals to Jesus's use of "Abba" for God, is as helpful as many might like it to be. See two incisive analyses by James Barr: "'Abba, Father' and the Familiarity of Jesus' Speech" and "Abbā Isn't 'Daddy.'"

This is a further exciting realization. At the heart of the universe is a play of love between the Father, the Son, and the Spirit.[8] But someone might ask how we actually know this.[9]

Paul says in a statement of near matchless importance—although he is echoing here a string of similar statements found elsewhere in this and other letters[10]—"God demonstrates his own love for us [in this]—that while we were still sinners, Christ died for us" (Rom 5:8). He goes on to say immediately in the verses that follow that it is this demonstration of love that eliminates any fear concerning a future angry judgment. We know now that God is just not like this. Hence, a scary future scenario of raging punishment is not merely now avoidable; it is false.[11] The nature of God is revealed definitively by the death of the Son on the cross for us at the behest of the Father and the Spirit. There the Father has offered up his beloved only Son to die for us, doing so, moreover, while we, the objects of this costly mission, were rebellious and hostile. Before any response had been offered, then, the Father undertook this ultimately costly act for us, which the Son obediently carried out. And this proves that the Father's love for us is utterly fundamental to his character,

8. Baxter Kruger's thoughtful account speaks of the great dance (*The Great Dance: The Christian Vision Revisited*).

9. I use the word "play" here advisedly and would want to emphasize, against other more doleful central emphases, the play and joy and fun that lie at the heart of the loving Trinitarian communion. But as Ethan Taylor, one of my students, pointed out to me, there is a danger of a pollyannaish account that highlights play while ignoring real pains and concerns, at which moment we are also perilously close to the Prosperity Gospel. Hence I would want to emphasize that any play not rooted in truthfulness and relational integrity will deceive us and ultimately turn into anything but real play. There is, however—speaking more positively—a connection evident here with traditions that emphasize the importance of *eudaimonia*, or beatitude. The latter would be defined here, however, in nonfoundational terms. This dynamic is elaborated further in part 2, ch. 15.

10. See also Rom 5:6; 8:35–39; 2 Cor 5:14–21; Gal 2:20; Eph 2:4–7; 3:14–19; 5:1–2, 25–32; 2 Thess 2:16–17.

11. Important questions still arise concerning judgment and anger, whether God's or ours, which, properly understood, are both compatible with love and necessary to it. When appropriate, relations of love involve anger and judgment. Any relationship that did not periodically include the latter would not be a relationship of love! These relational dimensions are addressed through part 2 as a Pauline virtue ethic is developed. Complementary questions also arise concerning Paul's internal consistency, which are addressed primarily in part 3, ch. 18.

and limitless, as is the Son's and their Spirit's. This God will stop at nothing in order to reach us and to heal us. God undertook this supremely painful action—the Father's sacrifice of his Son—to save a snarling and ungrateful humanity. Astonishing!

Paul is well aware that this divine dimension is nothing short of mind-blowing. So he even prays at one time that we will be granted the capacity to begin to grasp it with the help of the Spirit. Without this revelation, effected by God, we lack the ability to understand the enormity and power of the divine compassion. We are both too limited as creatures and too resistant as hostile sinners.

> For this reason I bend my knees to the Father [to ask]
> . . . that he might give to you from his glorious riches
> the capacity to be grasped by the Spirit in your inner person;
> and that Christ might dwell through a right understanding in your
> hearts,
> so that you might be rooted and founded in love;
> and that you—together with all the saints—
> might be able to grasp and to know the knowledge that surpasses
> knowing,
> namely, what the width and length and height and depth of the love of
> Christ is. (Eph 3:14–19)

Sometimes in my church we sing a jaunty chorus "Your love never fails, never gives up, never runs out on me,"[12] which I rather like. I wonder if we don't need to sing this or its equivalent every day, for most of the day, until this insight into the nature of God has sunk down into the depths of being. I offer this drastic expedient, knowing how some of my readers feel about choruses, only because it seems to be so difficult for the nature of God as love to penetrate into our thinking and to permeate the rest of our acting. We seem to resist this on every level. But we must allow the revelation that is Jesus dying for us while we were sinners to reshape our understanding of God on every level.

We have left an important question dangling from earlier phases in our discussion that should now be addressed. Someone is doubtless thinking at the moment, "It's all very well to speak of a personal God of love definitively revealed in Jesus, yada yada yada, but where exactly do we meet Jesus and this overpoweringly benevolent and kind God? I haven't met Jesus personally

12. "One Thing Remains," Jesus Culture, from the album *Come Away* (2010).

myself. So how do I get this deep internal conviction that he was God living among us, loving us, and dying for us? After all, he lived a long time ago."

Paul gives a pretty clear answer to this understandable query, although in some respects it is a little disconcerting.

Mediation

We meet God through people like him—that is to say, through the community, and especially through its designated leaders. And we learn from this phenomenon that Jesus's followers *mediate* God's revelations.

Clearly, God can and will act directly at times to carry out his plan. Paul was confronted by God in person on the road to Damascus. But this was a rare event, even for him, and as he got on with building communities, *he himself* was the means by which God came to people in cities and towns scattered around the Mediterranean coastline. "The Son of God, Jesus Christ, was proclaimed among you by me and Silas and Timothy" (2 Cor 1:19). God worked through Paul and his coworkers, attending them in addition by way of the Spirit. "I will not venture to speak of anything except what Christ has accomplished through me in leading the Gentiles to obey God by what I have said and done—by the power of signs and miracles, through the power of the Spirit" (Rom 15:18–19). Rather helpfully, this authentication by the Spirit allowed Paul to renounce complicated rhetorical approaches to presenting the good news about God.

> When I came to you [Corinthians],
> I did not come with eloquence or human wisdom
> as I proclaimed to you the testimony about God.
> For I resolved to know nothing while I was with you
> except Jesus Christ and him crucified.
> I came to you in weakness with great fear and trembling.
> My message and my preaching were not with wise and persuasive
>   words,
> but with a demonstration of the Spirit's power,
> so that your faith might not rest on human wisdom,
> but on God's power. (1 Cor 2:1–5)

The result of this divine authorization is that we see God constantly working through Paul and his fellow missionaries to reveal his truth and, ultimately, his plan. "We thank God continually because, when you received the word of

God, which you heard from us, you accepted it not as a human word, but as it actually is, the word of God, which is indeed at work in you who believe" (1 Thess 2:13).

What we see here, then, is Paul and his coworkers mediating God to other people. God communicates through Paul and other community leaders, and presumably through the average follower as well. This seems to be God's preferred way of acting and connecting. So all the theological information that we have been engaging with in this book up to this point has probably been mediated to us in this way.

Note, God is still in ultimate charge of the situation. God gets what God wants. God is still revealing Godself through all this definitively and decisively, although a difficult question arises at this moment that we should pause to consider. How can God ensure that his purposes work out while respecting our part in the situation? Are we not thereby necessarily reduced to mere instruments—the equivalent of rocks and stones, which would seem to override our very humanity?

The answer becomes apparent, as always, when we press more deeply into the great truth that is Jesus.

Correspondence

The church spent a great deal of time in the sixth and seventh centuries struggling with the question of how many "wills" Jesus possessed. During this period it pondered in particular the precise manner in which the human and the divine natures were combined together in one person, considering in particular Jesus's willing and acting. There had to be two wills willing within the single person of Jesus, otherwise he would not have combined the divine and human natures. Without this duality, the truth that he was God in person would have been voided. Jesus could not just be God willing away without a real human present (Docetism), nor could he just be a human willing away without God being really present (Nestorianism).[13] Both natures had to be fully present, including their willing. But there also had to be one thing willed, otherwise his unity as a person would have been broken and the unity of the divine and human natures in him would have fallen apart. The risk is that we have Jesus's human willing and his divine willing heading off in different directions!—and we would then have

13. For a brief definition of these heresies see "Docetism" at https://www.britannica.com/topic/Docetism; and "Nestorian" at https://www.britannica.com/topic/Nestorians.

two people. The identical challenges arise in relation to Jesus's activity as well. How does Jesus's activity relate to his divine activity so that only one person is ultimately acting? How does all this fit together? (*Can* it fit together?!)

Fortunately, Maximus the Confessor grasped the necessary solution with great clarity, as well as with great courage.[14] He realized that this theological needle could be threaded if we understand that the human will of Jesus corresponded perfectly to his divine will, notably in obedience.[15] If the human will of Jesus corresponded to the divine will constantly, obeying it, then the two wills, divine and human, combined together in a perfect, distinguishable, and yet indivisible unity. Their actual *willing* was completely unified—the willing of one person—although it derived constantly from two distinct wills, the divine and the human, willing together. These two wills move together, inseparably, like two ice dancers moving perfectly together on the ice. And the same realization could then be applied to Jesus's activity as well. The human nature in Jesus acted in perfect, obedient correspondence to the divine activity.

However, not only has a nasty christological conundrum just been resolved. A plausible explanation of mediation has become apparent. When other people are willing and acting in a way that corresponds to the willing and acting of God, in a dim echo of Jesus's perfect, constant, and devoted obedience, the correlation between divine and human action is real. Both divine and human activity are present *distinguishably*, but they are also at this moment of obedient correspondence present *inseparably*. The people involved are not being overridden. They are fully engaged, freely obeying. But they are also corresponding to the will of God. And it follows that human actors can thereby mediate the actions of God, although clearly they will struggle to correspond obediently in the way that Jesus did.[16]

---

14. Maximus the Confessor is usefully introduced at https://en.wikipedia.org/wiki/Maximus_the_Confessor.

15. Presumably the situation was also, under the right circumstances, reversible. The divine will could *condescend* to follow, to correspond to, and in a sense to obey the human will. Think here of a parent doing, out of delight and love, what a young child has decided that he or she wants to do, despite the inconvenience or pointlessness of the plan. But the primary mode of correspondence is the appropriate submission of the flawed human will to the divine in obedience.

16. Someone might object that totally fallen people cannot ever fully correspond in their actions to the divine will, and I certainly sympathize with this sentiment. But a proper consideration of Christology necessitates the view that fallen people can correspond perfectly to God's will, since Christ himself, who assumed the fullness of human flesh, did so. To claim that he had special assistance in this obedience under-

Paul is pointing toward this phenomenon—this blessed occurrence—when he writes things such as,

> Therefore, my dear friends, as you have always obeyed
> —not only in my presence, but now much more in my absence—
> continue to work out your own salvation with fear and trembling,
> for God is working through your willing and acting
> in order to fulfill his good purpose. (Phil 2:12–13 NIV modified)

The same correspondence is visible in an incisive statement in 1 Thessalonians about Paul's speech and the community's response; here the word of God and the word of Paul corresponded together and were recognized as such:

> We thank God continually because,
> when you received the word about God, which you heard from us,
> you accepted it not as a human word, but as it actually is,
> the word of God,
> which is at work in you who believe. (2:13)

It seems, then, that we can fully affirm that God does not override us when mediation takes place, while in the very fact that he is acting through us, we see that he is deeply concerned to involve us with his plans in every possible way.[17] Indeed, this mode of connecting is so pronounced it is almost as if God is hiding behind people, which prompts the question: why are people so central to God's disclosures? This is probably not the way that we would have set up the salvation of the world.

------

mines his full assumption of our humanity directly, and so this claim is best avoided. This line of thought makes possible our perfect correspondence, if only momentary, and the fact of our repeated sinning all the more egregious. An interesting connection is also evident at this moment with the Wesleyan doctrine of perfection. The claim that people can be perfectly righteous is a valid one. One should of course have realistic expectations about achieving this, without ever denying its ongoing possibility or our accountability when we fail.

17. That is, does this divine action overrule people so that they are reduced to the equivalent of robots or, in more biblical idiom, to lumps of clay? But if full play is given to human activity, which is so frequently sinful, then will this not impede God's activity? However, we need some other insights to be in place before we try to grasp this particular nettle, that is, the relationship between divine and human action. It is addressed in chs. 8 and 9.

Why Mediation?

One answer can be found in a passage that will guide much of our discussion in what follows:

> Christ Jesus . . .
> being in form of God,
> did not consider equivalence with God something to be grasped;
> rather, he emptied himself
> by taking the form of a servant,
> being made in human likeness.
> And being found in form as a person,
> he humbled himself to the point of death. (Phil 2:5–8)

God has already reached down as far as our human nature when he came to us in Jesus. Why did he do this?

At least part of the reason is so that the definitive encounter between God and humanity now takes place completely on humanity's terms. As a result, God does not overwhelm people. People are met where they are, as human beings, by someone who is exactly like them, who bears their very nature. And this act *respects* humanity. There is now no coercion in the relationship, whether physical or metaphysical. We are not overawed; we are not struck; we are not pushed and pulled around by an overtly superior being. God respects our humanity, including our free responsiveness, profoundly, by meeting us as an equal, which necessitates an incomprehensible lowering on God's part. And yet this mode of humble engagement makes perfect sense. God is a God of relating and a God of love. And a God of love would relate to us in the most gentle and noncoercive way possible. Loving relating is gentle, not coercive, and it entails equal relating. It follows from this remarkable insight into the nature of God that of course God the Father, the risen Jesus, and the Holy Spirit would delight in continuing to reach people through other people, gently and noncoercively, on their terms, walking alongside them, through other people. A relating and loving God is an incarnational God—incarnational *because* he is loving—and an incarnational God is also a mediating God. Such a God delights in using "vessels of clay." Hence the human mediation of God's truth simply continues the loving approach of the incarnation—although just to ensure that people understand that God is present, the Holy Spirit walks alongside these figures to authorize and to authenticate their occasionally stumbling words.

We will provide another compelling reason for mediation at the beginning of part 2, when we start to reflect on the community that God calls into being. And we will talk more about the fascinating missional implications of all this in part 3. But for now all we need to know is that God meets us shockingly and yet, on reflection, entirely unsurprisingly through people, and particularly through chosen leaders like Paul. So here we are, almost two thousand years later, reflecting on some of the words he wrote as he mediated God to his neighbors.

Having said this, it is important not to overspecify where and how God shows up. God is God, so God can show up wherever and however he wants to.[18] The Bible is filled with interesting variations on this phenomenon—a burning bush, a still quiet voice, a heavenly vision, a massive catch of fish, a shriveled gourd, a dream. Nevertheless in Paul's life we can detect an overt preference on God's part for showing up through people. This seems to be God's favorite mode of relating to us. It is the bread and butter of our relationship with God. If we seek God, then we must face the uncomfortable fact that God is hanging out with the people who are all around us, although some people are probably mediating God more effectively than others! Paul's life and letters attest clearly that God works through people all the time. Our God *loves* to relate through people. This is how a loving God operates.

It is now worth pausing briefly to note that this mode of disclosure—mediation—confirms the fact of revelation as those who mediate God's truth and reality to others *witness* to this truth and to this God.

Witness

Because the truth about God is both self-authenticating and yet mediated by people, the form this truth must take is witnessing, along with the allied practice of confessing. There is no common ground in relation to the truth to which God's representatives can appeal as they make their case for loyalty to the triune God whom Jesus has revealed to them. And as we now know well, any attempt to construct a common platform for discussion—a basis

---

18. Barth wisely observes in *CD* I/2 that a precise specification or expectation of where God can (and cannot) show up subtly conceals a way of controlling God's revelation and inserting prior conditions for its actuality, which amount to the reestablishment of foundationalism. Nevertheless, it seems theologically apposite to recognize a divine preference for using people.

held in common between those convinced by Jesus and following him and those who are not that would allow the former to prove God's existence (and so on)—unleashes a catastrophic erosion of that very foundation, even if that attempt is deeply well-intentioned and those consequences are not immediately apparent.[19] There is, as we will see later, a preexistent relationship with God in everyone, confessing or not, that could resonate on a deep, intuitive level with the truths being spoken by any of God's local representatives. But this resonance is tangled up with stubbornness, hostility, and constant collaboration with sheer evil. So there is no basis here for a clear discussion. No definitive organization can be given to the tangled and distorted thinking of people until the lordship of Jesus is restoring order and clarity to the entire situation. So God's representatives must simply state what they take to be the case, which is to say that *we* must speak of the truth that we know and experience and live out of. We must point to this truth and claim that it is *the* truth, and that if you come over to where we are, then you will know this as well. It is as if we are standing on the other side of a brick wall from a puzzled group of bystanders where we are pointing to a glorious sculpture and saying to those seeing nothing but a facade of bricks, "Climb up the ladder like I did; come over and you will see as we do. Trust me, it's worth the effort."

The human mediation that correlates to a revealing and self-authenticating God is consequently a group of witnesses who point to this truth and who are supposed to hold on to this truth under pressure, confessing it and resisting any pressure to recant. Indeed, it was pressure from hostile pagans that eventually led to the transition of the meaning of the Greek word for "witness," *martys*, to "martyr," meaning a "courageous witness even in and through a horribly inflicted death." But the early, more manageable meaning remains fundamental.

If we have grasped that the human mediation correlative to God's revelation is witness, and the allied truth that God mediates his revelation through this practice respectfully but effectively to the friends and families of his witnesses, then we should note that as witness takes place through time and

---

19. Stanley Hauerwas and Charles Pinches, "Witness," add the important insight here that any foundationalism consequently eliminates the church! The central need for a particular community to grasp and to communicate the truth about Jesus is essentially obviated if the truth about God becomes available to all abstractly and generally, merely through rational speculation, perhaps even by just an individual who is clever and reads the right books. Foundationalism is therefore profoundly anti-ecclesial and corrosive.

ultimately through the generations, it is necessary also to speak of some sort of tradition.

The truths about God to which witnesses attest are learned *and handed on* to subsequent witnesses, creating a tradition, which is to say, a group of people who stand together through space and time in relation to particular practices that include important and quite specific truth claims. And so Christians today stand in one of the largest and longest traditions in human history—a two-thousand-year-old transmission of the claim that Jesus is Lord, along with all that this confession entails. We stand within an unbroken line of witnesses and converts stretching back to the first witnesses—at this stage, messianic Jews—who knew Jesus, who attested among other things to his resurrection. Paul himself, a conspicuously early convert, knows well that he already stands within this tradition of witnesses. Here is what he attests to in 1 Cor 15:3–8:

> I delivered to you what I also received—
> that Christ died for our sins according to the Scriptures,
> and that he was buried,
> and that he was raised on the third day according to the Scriptures,
> and that he was seen by Cephas [and] then by the Twelve,
> then he was seen by upward of five hundred brothers all at once,
> of whom most remain alive until now although some have fallen
>   asleep,
> then he was seen by James, then by all the apostles,
> and last of all, as to one born unnaturally, he was seen by me.

It is critical to note that Paul prefaces this rehearsal of the truths of the nascent tradition by urging the Corinthians, in 15:1–2, to hold on to them firmly and accurately themselves, thereby joining the chain of witnesses, connecting what lies before with what will follow (and here the tradition stretches already from followers within Judaism to followers converted from paganism, later dubbed Christians).

> Brothers, I want you to know clearly
> the proclamation which I proclaimed to you,
> which you also received,
> on which you stand,
> through which you are saved
> (if you hold on to the teaching I proclaimed to you,
> and outside of which you have believed in vain).

In due course we will explore in more detail the wider, traditioned dimension within Paul's nurturing of his communities. Paul has much that he wants to impart beyond these verses. After all, he writes entire letters about what his converts need to know (and by ancient standards, they were *long*). At this moment, however, we need to turn to consider a little more closely the *form* that mediates this tradition, which is to say, we need to learn how to tell the story of Jesus properly.

Theses

- We learn a number of critical things from the revelation of God taking place in Jesus.
- A person is a relational being. That is, a person is "extrinsic," existing for, toward, and through others. We should therefore diagram people like flowers or stars, not like spheres or marbles.
- We learn of this fundamental relationality particularly because Paul speaks repeatedly of God as our "Father" and of Jesus as his "Son" (here less frequently explicitly, but often by implication), as well as, derivatively, of us as being adopted, possessing sonship, and being "brothers."
- It follows that the Spirit is relational as well.
- Family metaphors—as necessary, suitably healed—can now be seen to be fundamental to God's nature, as against legal and political metaphors. Metaphors drawn from deep friendship can also apply.
- These relationships are relationships of love.
- We know they are because while we were still hostile and sinful, the Father offered up his only beloved Son to die for us, and the Son obediently did so.
- So God is love in his inmost communal being, fundamentally and limitlessly. (The definitions of divine judgment and anger will flow from this basic reality.)
- God reveals in the incarnation that he takes great pains to respect our personhood by meeting us where we are, "on our level."
- The mediation of his revelations and relationship through other people now makes complete sense. It is a loving, respectful approach as an equal, although necessitating a great sacrifice on God's part.
- The mediation of God through people is a preferred mode, not a determinative one. (God can show up in whatever mode he chooses.) Human mediation extends the mode of engagement apparent in the incarnation.

▸ This mediation is possible because people can freely respond in perfect obedience to the divine will, at least momentarily, in a dim echo of the constant perfect correspondence of Jesus's human will to the divine will (this being Maximus the Confessor's solution to the challenge that Jesus's human willing and divine willing, and human acting and divine acting, threatened to separate, which would rupture his single personhood). When such correspondence happens, the divine will can be mediated accurately by way of obedient human activity.

▸ Those mediating the truth of God witness to it and confess it, because there is no common ground epistemologically for persuasion, and any attempt to establish one would be foundationalist folly. Mediators can only point to the truth they know and assure others of its existence.

▸ Witnesses pass on the key claims about God to other converts and witnesses in a tradition, which is now a great tradition stretching back for two thousand years, and out to many, many further witnesses.

▸ The attempt to construct an abstract, general, self-evident basis for the truth about God—foundationalism—eliminates the need for particular people in a tradition attesting to the truth that they have been personally enveloped by. The church seems unnecessary. People would supposedly reason to God self-evidently, abstractly, and individually. Hence, given that witness *is* God's mode for mediating revelation, foundationalism now reveals itself to be even more destructive than first thought.

Key Scriptural References

Romans 8, especially verses 1–32, is an especially rich text for the following key associations, the most direct statement being verse 32. A more compact arrangement of much the same material can be found in Gal 4:1–7.

Paul refers to God the Father 89x, which is his preferred designation for *theos* (God). He primarily refers to Jesus as Lord, although Jesus's sonship is implied in every designation of God as (his) Father. Paul explicitly refers to Jesus as Son 17x. But Paul also implies Jesus's sonship when he speaks of the adoption of converts, mentions their transfer into a state of sonship, or refers to them using the language of children or siblings, literally brothers, these last references being ubiquitous.

Romans 5:6–8 speaks of God's unconditional love for us as revealed by the death of the Son for us when we were still hostile to God. The christological basis for this insight into God's nature is unimpeachable and programmatic. This is what God is really like. (See also 1 John 4:8.)

See also, in this relation, Eph 3:14–19.

Paul frequently uses the language of gratuitous redemption from debt-slavery to convey God's unconditional benevolence. In this narrative sin is analogized in monetary terms as debt (see Anderson for the broader background to this metaphor; an insightful, although technical, application of financial imagery in Paul is supplied by Lang). Paul does not spend any time on whom the debt is owed to because that is not the point of the analogy for him. The debt *results* in death if it is not remedied (Rom 6:23). Death is the final payment owed by the debtor. But Jesus "pays the debt off" by way of his sacrificial death and shed blood, which function like a limitless fund of money, thereby remitting our obligations and liberating everyone from debt-slavery—which is to say, from death. Moreover, this remission is entirely unsolicited and gratuitous—an astonishingly costly act for him and an astonishingly expensive outlay for us *that speaks directly of God's great love for us*. See the redemption and remission of sins spoken of, in slightly different ways, in Rom 3:23–26; 1 Cor 6:20; Gal 1:4; Eph 1:6–7; and Col 1:14; 2:13; and presupposed by Rom 6:17–23. (This release from debt-slavery corresponds to release from jail or acquittal as well, that is, to "justification"; so 1 Cor 1:30; Gal 3:22–25.) We will delve deeper into the imagery and its function in part 2, chapter 11 ("Love Is All You Need"), as well as, to a certain extent, in chapter 12 ("Loving as Giving").

Human mediation of divine revelation is apparent in Rom 15:18–19; 1 Cor 2:1–5; 2 Cor 1:19; and 1 Thess 2:13–14. Its theological rationale is implicit in Phil 2:5–11.

Paul attests to witnessing, confessing, and the tradition, along with ample evidence of its truth, in 1 Cor 15:1–11. This material needs to be held together with, not placed in a zero-sum relationship with, revelatory claims like Gal 1:11–12. Revelation always has mediated content, but that content is not known to be true ultimately because of its mediators or other local, evidential claims, but because of divine revelation. Paul emphasizes the common mediation of the tradition in 1 Cor 15 and then polemically affirms the self-authentication in Gal 1. In the latter text he is also emphasizing his personal apostolic call from God to missionary work among the pagans; see my "Galatians."

Key Reading

John Zizioulas supplies a profound account of relational personhood in chapter 1 of *Being as Communion*, "Personhood and Being" (27–65). It is not easy reading, but it is worth the struggle.

James B. Torrance makes the critical programmatic observations about God's familial, not legal, nature clearly and tirelessly. See, among his many wonderful essays, "Covenant or Contract" and "The Contribution of John Mc-Leod Campbell." He draws here heavily on the thinking of John MacMurray.

My particular account of the language of "father" and "son" (etc.) in Paul is described briefly in my essay "The Story of Jesus in Romans and Galatians." (Key studies by Barr and Jeremias that could be usefully included as further reading are noted there.)

The practices of witness and confession are described brilliantly by Hauerwas and Pinches.

Further Reading

Barth's account of the person is highly relational. His systematic treatment of humanity can be found in *CD* III/2, but relational thinking is detectable in relation to God and humanity throughout *CD*. He was influenced by Martin Buber's classic relational text *I and Thou* (although the extent of this influence is debated).

Zizioulas's thought is helpfully expounded by Luke Tallon (see esp. 141–90, 223–27).

More accessible expositions of a relational account of personhood than Zizioulas's include C. S. Lewis's short essay published as *Beyond Personality*; Baxter Kruger's *The Great Dance*; William P. Young's remarkable homegrown theological novel *The Shack*; and Marty Folsom's three-book series *Face to Face*.

A fascinating account of a relational conception of personhood developed in conversation with sociology is supplied by Christian Smith.

Although the view of God and the persons constituting God here shares much with "the social Trinity," it should not be either confused with that view directly or reduced to it. The Trinity is social, as the thinkers associated with that view suggest, but we do not *copy* this God or *map* it for ourselves. We are drawn into an ontology composed of relational people that is consequently social. With this caveat, there is much to learn from writing on the social Trinity, which is accessibly introduced by Volf in his article "The Trinity Is Our Social Program." See also Moltmann's *The Trinity and the Kingdom of God*. Volf also intelligently resists the reduction of personhood to relationality alone (as we see, e.g., in Fiddes) in *Exclusion and Embrace*.

Alan Torrance discusses the centrality of love to God's nature in his essay "Is Love the Essence of God?"

Barth frequently leans heavily on a correspondence account of freedom, drawn ultimately from Maximus; see especially III/1 and III/2, but also IV/2. We will see later that III/3 expands his account of human agency beyond mere correspondence and obedience, as does II/2 more implicitly as it discusses the freedom of God in election. But human freedom understood as obedient correspondence seems to be his baseline.

Wesleyan perfection is discussed helpfully by Randy Maddox.

In *CD* I/2 Barth insightfully notes the importance of not overspecifying the locus of God's engagement with humanity, although the preferred locus for divine revelation is the Bible. I have broken with that decision here, in fear and trembling, emphasizing appointed human intermediaries like Paul. I am not excluding a scriptural mediation—by no means. But I do view it as less common and as secondary to the overwhelming primacy of God working through human relational interactions. Jesus did not write a book; he called disciples.

Bibliography

Anderson, Gary A. *Sin: A History*. New Haven: Yale University Press, 2009.

Barabási, Albert-László. *Linked: How Everything Is Connected to Everything Else and What It Means for Business, Science, and Everyday Life*. New York: Penguin/Plume, 2003.

Barr, James. "'Abba, Father' and the Familiarity of Jesus' Speech." *Theology* 91 (1988): 173–79.

———. "Abbā Isn't 'Daddy.'" *JTS* 39 (1988): 28–47.

Barth, Karl. *Church Dogmatics*. I/2; III/1; III/2; IV/2.

Buber, Martin. *I and Thou*. Translated by R. G. Smith. 2nd ed. New York: Scribners, 1958.

Campbell, Douglas A. "Galatians." In *The New Oxford Bible Commentary*. Edited by David Lincicum et al. Oxford: University Press, 2020.

———. "The Story of Jesus in Romans and Galatians." Pages 97–124 in *Narrative Dynamics in Paul: A Critical Assessment*. Edited by Bruce W. Longenecker. Louisville: Westminster John Knox, 2020.

Fiddes, Paul S. *Participating in God: A Pastoral Doctrine of the Trinity*. London: Dartman, Longman & Todd, 2000.

Folsom, Marty. *Face to Face*. Vol. 1: *Missing Love*; vol. 2: *Discovering Relational*; vol. 3: *Sharing God's Life*. Eugene, OR: Wipf & Stock, 2013–16.

Hauerwas, Stanley, with Charles Pinches. "Witness." Pages 37–63 in *Approaching the End: Eschatological Reflections on Church, Politics, and Life*. Grand Rapids: Eerdmans, 2013.

Kruger, C. Baxter. *The Great Dance: The Christian Vision Revisited*. Jackson, MS: Perichoresis Press, 2000.

Lang, T. J. "Disbursing the Account of God: Fiscal Terminology and the Economy of God in Colossians 1,24–25." *ZNW* 107 (2016): 116–36.

Lewis, C. S. *Beyond Personality: The Christian Idea of God*. London: Macmillan, 1945.

Longenecker, Bruce W., ed. *Narrative Dynamics in Paul: A Critical Assessment*. Louisville: Westminster John Knox, 2002.

Maddox, Randy. "A Change of Affections: The Development, Dynamics, and Dethronement of John Wesley's 'Heart Religion.'" Pages 3–31 in *"Heart Religion" in the Methodist Tradition and Related Movements*. Edited by Richard Steele. Metuchen, NJ: Scarecrow Press, 2001.

———. "Shaping the Virtuous Heart: The Abiding Mission of the Wesleys." *Circuit Rider* 29 (July/August 2005): 27–28.

Maddox, Randy, with Paul Chilcote. Introduction to *A Plain Account of Christian Perfection*, by John Wesley. Kansas City: Beacon Hill, 2015.

Moltmann, Jürgen. *The Trinity and the Kingdom of God*. London: SCM, 1981.

Smith, Christian. *What Is a Person? Rethinking Humanity, Social Life, and the Moral Good from the Person Up*. Chicago: University of Chicago Press, 2010.

Tallon, Luke B. "Our Being Is in Becoming: The Nature of Human Transformation in the Theology of Karl Barth, Joseph Ratzinger, and John Zizioulas." PhD diss., University of St Andrews, 2011. https://research-repository .st-andrews.ac.uk/bitstream/handle/10023/2572/LukeTallonPhDThesis.pdf ?sequence=6&isAllowed=y.

Torrance, Alan J. "Is Love the Essence of God?" Pages 114–37 in *Nothing Greater, Nothing Better: Theological Essays on the Love of God*. Edited by Kevin J. Vanhoozer. Grand Rapids: Eerdmans, 2001.

Torrance, James B. "The Contribution of McLeod Campbell to Scottish Theology." *SJT* 26 (1973): 295–311.

———. "Covenant or Contract: A Study of the Theological Background of Worship in Seventeenth-Century Scotland." *SJT* 23 (1970): 51–76.

Volf, Miroslav. *Exclusion and Embrace: A Theological Exploration of Identity, Otherness, and Reconciliation*. Nashville: Abingdon, 1996.

———. "'The Trinity Is Our Social Program': The Doctrine of the Trinity and the
Shape of Social Engagement." *Modern Theology* 14 (1998): 403–23.

Young, William P. *The Shack.* Newbury Park, CA: Windblown Media, 2007.

Zizioulas, John D. *Being as Communion: Studies in Personhood and the Church.*
New York: St. Vladimir's Seminary Press, 1985.

———. *Communion and Otherness: Further Studies in Personhood and the Church.*
Edited by Paul McPartlan. London: T&T Clark, 2006.

CHAPTER 4

A God of Story

Narrative

If we know that God's truth is almost invariably mediated to us through witnesses, then we are ready for another important question. What do they actually say? As Paul indicates in almost every word he wrote, witnesses do not limit themselves to the truth claims that Jesus is Lord and that God loves us, important as these are. They have much more to communicate, at which moment we have to make another key methodological move.

It will be hard to say much about what God is up to in Jesus without telling a story. Stories are generally the way people communicate with one another when they want to talk about other people acting in relation to one another, and about how they deal with various challenges over time. To speak of people is inevitably to tell a story. Consequently, the explication and development of the truth is always closely tied to a story, since God is so deeply personal, and the sharp-eyed will already have noted narrative fragments studding our three earlier chapters. To speak of a Father who loves us because he offers up his only beloved Son, and of a Son who loves us because he becomes one of us and obediently accepts death on a cross, is to utilize short stories. But we will need to start telling a broader story as we move on from our starting point in the key events, namely, the revelation of Jesus's lordship and the realization of his deep love for us. We will have to talk about the reach of this God through all of time, and we are particularly interested for the moment in God's actions in the past—both in the past of humanity as a whole, which we tend to designate "history," and in our own personal pasts, which, if we are converts, was a non-Christian journey. We need to tell the story of how God got us from there to here. But as we do so, we must recognize that another trap is concealed here and waiting to spring. There are two ways we can tell the story of God's activity in the past, which has now been brought to its key moment in Jesus: a right way and an emphatically wrong way, and if we can't recognize which is which, our very telling of the story will radically undermine what that story is trying to say.

A Narrative Trap

Underneath it all, the same trap lurks here as the one we described in chapter 2: a gambit asking us to leave the truth that has been revealed in Jesus and to join hands with some other set of truth criteria. To avoid it we must learn to tell any story preceding Jesus in the right way: *retrospectively,* or *backward.* This important dynamic is generated directly by the way we have learned the truth, through revelation. A revealed truth imposes a certain structure on stories that expand on that truth.

The difficulty we are navigating here is caused by the way that a commitment to revelation disrupts a common approach to storytelling. We have already spent some time emphasizing that Jesus is God in person and that this is our definitive and central truth. It is the truth that stands over all others and that, in the words of the Fourth Gospel, illuminates all others. It is the light that shines in the darkness. And it has broken into our minds just as it broke into Paul's and into the Corinthians' some time ago. But this starting point poses a problem for storytelling.

Stories have to begin somewhere, and they generally begin well before the key moment to which they build, and Jesus is obviously the key moment to which our story will build. As we have just seen, however, Jesus arrives in our story somewhat unexpectedly. He is a *revelation*, and we learn about him by way of revelation. He is a gift. So he simply arrives, suddenly, unannounced. He is a surprise. Before the arrival of God in person in Jesus, we did not possess *this* truth about the universe in all its fullness, and so we could not tell our story properly. *It was his arrival that told us where our story needed to go.* We probably did know *some* things, and possibly some quite important notions, before he came. Many of the Jews would put their hands up at this point. But neither we nor they knew *the* thing, and this is what really matters—that a humble artisan from Nazareth, who was eventually killed by the Romans, was the point where the divine and the created fully intersected. Extraordinary! So how do we tell a broader story about Jesus, in a way that leads up to him but does not compromise the fact that the truth about him is known only by revelation?

If we want to tell a true story about Jesus, whose truth has been revealed to us, then we need to begin with Jesus. We have to begin our story in the middle. I don't see any other alternatives. Jesus is the truth. We must therefore begin with his arrival as a fact and with our initial response to this arrival in confession and adoration, which is why this book began where it did, with the truth that is Jesus. The story about Jesus must begin with Jesus having already arrived.

Now this approach might feel a little awkward at first, but it's actually OK. We can begin stories wherever we want to. However, we still need to tell a story that will extend out through a sequence of events in time. We have to fill in the blanks (although we will never fill in all of them) and talk about what happened before Jesus, even as we try to fill out what will happen later. A story will be developed around Jesus.

It is here that things need to be articulated very carefully, in a certain way. How exactly do we tell the story of what happened before Jesus and what led up to him? There is only one way to proceed here. We must tell this story *retrospectively*, or *backward*. We can look back on what preceded Jesus, with our vision now clarified by his definitive light, and see what previously was not apparent to us. We move from the present to the past, and the past is then presented like a flashback in a movie. All sorts of truths were always there, in the past. But without the illumination of Jesus, they were not visible, or at least not fully so. "I was blind, but now I see" the famous hymn says quite accurately, not to mention, the Gospel of John (ch. 9). This is the right way to tell the broader story about God, and it was something Paul knew well.

In a telling passage written to the Philippians, Paul speaks of the extraordinary reevaluation that the arrival of Christ imposed on his life (see 3:2–11 and especially4b–8):

> If someone else thinks they have reasons to put confidence in the flesh,
> I have more:
> circumcised on the eighth day;
> of the people of Israel, of the tribe of Benjamin, a Hebrew of Hebrews;
> in regard to the law, a Pharisee;
> as for zeal, persecuting the church;
> as for righteousness based on the Torah, faultless.
> But whatever were gains to me I now consider loss for the sake of
>   Christ.
> What is more, I consider everything a loss

because of the surpassing worth of knowing Christ Jesus my Lord,
for whose sake I have lost all things.
I consider them excrement,
that I may gain Christ. (NIV modified)

Looking back on his past, Paul asserts confidently here that in any competition in terms of Jewish markers and practices, he wins. In the Olympic games of Judaism, Paul is the uncontested champion. He was circumcised correctly, on the eighth day, and is of impeccable ancestry, being descended from the tribe of Benjamin. He speaks the right languages, here "Hebrew."[1] Such is his zeal for God's Scriptures that he belongs to the Pharisees, a group that practices stringent application and accountability, and he militantly persecutes those who step too far outside the boundaries of the appropriately cleansed and pious people, which is to say, the Jews. *But now, in the light of Christ*, hence looking *back* on this previous life, *he counts everything that previously seemed to be a gain as a loss.* In comparison to Christ, these things are not absolutely negative in and of themselves, but just so we don't miss the point, Paul says that these badges of pride and gold-medal activities are—in relation to Christ—tantamount to excrement (Gk. *skybala*). From a gold medal to what the Irish lyrically call shyte.[2] That's a big reevaluation. Moreover, it is clearly being effected here retrospectively. The story of piety does not work forward for Paul. In his past, he was vigorously pursuing activities with some pride, but now that he is in a relationship with Christ, they are tantamount to a pile of stinking dung. The priority of his retrospective viewpoint could hardly be clearer.

If we appreciate that the correct way to tell our overarching story is backward, reconstructing the past in the light of the present, we need now to detect and to reject any suggestions that we tell our story forward. Once again, we must exercise constant vigilance.

---

1. Technically, he probably read the Scriptures in Hebrew and spoke Aramaic or Syriac, its contemporary linguistic descendant.

2. The point is not entirely blunted even if the translation of "excrement" should now be broadened to something more like rotting garbage. Ancient street garbage would have included a fair amount of excrement, along with urine, rotting food, and the occasional corpse. The modern translation "crap" would fit. But the meaning "shit" or its equivalent, with its shock value, remains most likely. See Daniel Wallace, "A Brief Word Study on Σκύβαλον," Bible.org, https://bible.org/article /brief-word-study-skuvbalon.

Dangerous Storytelling—Forward

If we tell our story forward, we fall again into foundationalism, and it is vital to appreciate this trap clearly.

If it is revealed at a particular point in space and time that Jesus is God in person, then it follows that prior to this revelation this truth was not known. To suggest that we did have a precise prior expectation of it to the point where we could correctly predict and identify the nature of his arrival is to deny that the later revelation took place and was a revelation, which are clearly very bad moves directly into error. If we are expecting Jesus in a tightly defined way, then we already know the truth about him before he arrives. Vague intuitions and inchoate expectations are one thing. But if we know the definitive truth about Jesus before Jesus is revealed, we must have found the truth somewhere else. And we would have measured the arrival of Jesus in the light of these truths that we found somewhere else, *recognizing* his arrival in their light, so we are immediately caught up here in foundationalism and all its problems. Our prior truth has now judged the truth, and the horsemen have been untethered.

Christians fall into temptation here all the time when they start talking about creation, Israel, history, and even their own journeys to conversion. So it is very important to be clear about this error and to guard against it. We must check stories about Jesus by asking what the basic purview of the plot in the story is. There is a simple test here that the right stories must pass.

A Test

Are the stories we are telling about Jesus *quest* stories, or are they more like *memoirs?*

In quests the characters know what they are seeking. The knights of the Round Table were seeking the Holy Grail. There is no mystery or critical disclosure here. The key parameters of the story are all known up front both by the characters in the story and by the reader. The interest in the story is generated by the technical difficulties the characters have fulfilling their quest. The knights don't know where the Holy Grail is, for example, and so they travel around a lot and try to find it. They have to battle various temptations, puzzles, and monsters to get there (like the notorious Knights who say Ni), which generates the conflict and interest in the quest.

The modern action novel is a variation on this construction. The military personnel and secret agents who generally star in these stories all know what they have to do. They must thwart the nefarious plots of their country's enemies, hopefully killing them in the process. So, again, this is no mystery. It is a fight between obvious protagonists with obvious goals in view. These heroes simply face difficult technical challenges accomplishing these goals—breaking into the CIA headquarters at Langley to steal a NOC list, or some such. Indeed, we need to know what the problem is so that we can worry about it and root for our heroes to solve it. "Save us from nuclear annihilation, Ethan Hunt; you can do it!"

But this is not the way to tell the broad story surrounding Jesus. If we place his arrival at the climactic moment in a quest, then we undermine that arrival as the definitive moment of revelation and truth for Christians, as we have just seen. Both the readers and the characters already know the key truths before he arrives and so lapse at this moment into an alternative set of truth criteria, thereby unleashing the horsemen of the foundationalist apocalypse. The story about the God revealed by Jesus as he acts through history is not a quest, and we betray that story when we recount it like a quest.

Memoirs, however, are much more explicitly retrospective. Their authors look back on their lives and select material to craft a biographical trajectory in the light of where they have ended up. Reflection yields the meaning. Hence the characters in the story, and usually the author himself or herself, do not know exactly where the story is going within the episodes that are being recounted. They tend to wander around a bit. It is the composition of the memoir itself that generates the key organizing insights. Looking back, those telling the story see a journey with a goal, and perhaps even the hand of God, which were not necessarily apparent with any clarity at the time of the episodes themselves.[3] Consequently we can—and should—tell the story of God acting in Jesus like a memoir. There is a very real sense in which the Gospels are memoirs.[4]

We could put this distinction a little more technically and distinguish between stories that are explicitly *telic* and those that are *epiphanic*.

---

3. Some of my colleagues are adept at this genre. See, e.g., Stanley Hauerwas, *Hannah's Child: A Theologian's Memoir*, Lauren Winner's three volumes *Girl Meets God*, *Mudhouse Sabbath*, and *Still*. So Hauerwas writes in the introduction to his memoir, "On Being Stanley Hauerwas," "I have written this memoir in an attempt to understand myself" (xi). He also refers helpfully here to Sven Birkerts, *The Art of Time in Memoir*.

4. See especially John 2:17, 22; and this retrospective approach is also one of the key implications of Luke's story about the disciples on the road to Emmaus in Luke 24:13–35.

The Greek for "end" or "goal" is *telos*. All stories have a *telos,* or goal, but I am using this word to suggest here that a story's goal is in view obviously from the beginning. Explicitly *telic* stories have their end in view from the start, and hence their key truth claims are also in view from the beginning. The characters are well aware of where things are going and why, and it is this sort of story that undermines Christian truth. People do not know that Jesus is the definitive revelation of God in person until this truth has been revealed to them, and telic stories that occlude this fact occlude that fundamental truth. *Epiphanic* stories, however, can capture this truth. *Epiphaneia* are appearances and, in the case of divinities, revelations. In the light of a definitive moment of revelation—an *epiphany*—the author grasps a trajectory that had until then been obscure or even completely hidden. The readers are made explicitly aware of this narrative arc as the past is reread retrospectively, in the light of the epiphany. The stories can still read in a *telic* way ultimately. The stories still go somewhere, but the characters within the story are not aware of this definitive truth prior to its arrival. They may have a partial grasp of the truth, but they lack the clarity of its final, epiphanic form. We, the readers, know things then that the characters in the story do not.[5]

In sum: we need to cleave faithfully and vigilantly to the practice of retrospective storytelling during our witnessing, which is constructed like a memoir, because of the subtle trap that lurks here for the unwary. If we tell this story in its other main fashion, forward, as a quest—and a quest story and a memoir story can look so similar—we unleash the horsemen of the apocalypse. And exactly the same retrospective approach applies to any evaluation of the historical claims implicit in the story of Jesus, a point where Paul has been much used against Jesus.

History

In the last chapter an important summary by Paul of the essential elements that Jesus's followers are called to witness to and to confess was quoted (1 Cor 15:3–8). Even in Paul's day, these elements constituted a rapidly forming tradition of truth claims to be grasped and passed on, and they can already be seen extending in various directions generating further important truth claims. Telling Jesus's story involves a first generation of witnesses to his resurrection. And his death and resurrection both fulfill the Jewish Scriptures, something

5. See Mark 1:1 and John 1:1–14.

doubtless apparent clearly only in retrospect. We know well by now that our understanding that this short story is true rests primarily on God rather than on those who transmit it to us. In our locations God attests to the divinity of his Son especially by the work of his Spirit. But another issue is present here that we need to recognize and to handle appropriately, or once again, we risk catastrophe. A *historical* dimension is implicit in this tradition that we should briefly address, because if modern historians are allowed to dominate its evaluation, the foundationalist horsemen will be unleashed once again.

> For what I received I passed on to you as of first importance:
> that the Messiah died for our sins according to the Scriptures,
> that he was buried,
> that he was raised on the third day according to the Scriptures,
> and that he appeared to Cephas, and then to the Twelve.
> After that, he appeared to more than five hundred of the brothers and
>   sisters at the same time,
> most of whom are still living, though some have fallen asleep.
> Then he appeared to James, then to all the apostles,
> and last of all he appeared to me also, as to one abnormally born.
>
> (1 Cor 15:3–8)

Paul transmits certain critical claims here about Jesus that are easily recognizable as things that could have happened to anyone—that he died and was buried. Such information tells us that in various key respects Jesus was a person like us. He lived and then died, and after he died, his lifeless body was placed in a tomb as it began to decompose. Paul follows these claims, however, with the rather more extraordinary claim that Jesus was raised from the dead, and so he understandably lists multiple appearances by the risen Jesus to various witnesses. But this detail suggests that the resurrected Jesus was still present within our human experience in some way, appearing, at least for a time, to these figures of flesh and blood. In short, these events are said here to have been *real*. They really took place. And since they took place in the past, they were *historical* in the broad sense of that word, which raises an additional truth question for us.

It is now both fair and appropriate to go back and to examine evidence from this period to confirm our key claims—to undertake a historical investigation. Such events leave marks that creatures of flesh and blood both produce and process. But we *evaluate* the lingering evidence from the past as confessing Jews and Christians, rooted in the truth that God was fully present in Jesus and that Jesus is related, inseparably, to his Father and his Spirit. And this location creates a presumption about reality—about the very nature of history. From this location we do not expect past events to be limited to what we see and hear and touch, or to the material and textual remainders of those events. The past as people have lived and experienced it is not all that is.[6] God can work there, and we believe he did work there. In fact, God made the entire situation in the first place. So we should not evaluate the past in the way that many modern historians do, when they bring a different, fundamentally secular account of broader reality to bear on it, and go on to pronounce certain things possible or impossible.[7] (Such judgments are often not, strictly speaking, historical at all, but are philosophical and even religious claims; they are claims built on various foundationalist projects.)

But we do nevertheless expect any material and textual remainders to attest to the truths of the gospel insofar as those intersected with the lived experiences of those who see, hear, feel, and touch. So the question still arises whether this attestation exists, as we expect it to. As God enters our situation, one of the results of his graceful condescension is a vulnerability to this sort of procedure. As God enters history, however gently, we expect an impact on history, however slight. So do we find it? Are the historical claims implicit in the tradition—understanding history appropriately—true insofar as the fragmentary preserved evidence points to this conclusion?

When we look at the evidence we find in Paul himself, most extensively in the text we just quoted, although in other places as well, we can confirm that the events in question did indeed take place. So the short answer is yes. A historical investigation conducted under the auspices of the triune God finds Paul listing ranks of witnesses to the risen Jesus, including himself, although

6. As Barth put this point succinctly, "Revelation is not a predicate of history, but history is a predicate of revelation" (*CD* I/2:64, quoted and discussed in Murray A. Rae, *History and Hermeneutics*, 28–30, 71–73).

7. Such a worldview is not really history; a secular account of the past does not arise from historical analysis. Historical analysis in these or any terms, which is to say, the reconstruction of the past, has to presuppose an overarching metaphysics in order to proceed making judgments about what did or did not happen—assumptions about the nature of humanity, agency, causality, time, and so on. And Jews and Christians who are historically investigating the origins of the church in the life, death, and resurrection of Jesus should not allow their investigations to be distorted by the introduction of an alternative, secular metaphysics. They already have a metaphysics rooted in the revelation of the triune God, in the light of which they can investigate the past historically.

acknowledging a degree of oddness about his own experience.[8] No less than six separate attestations are listed, which in and of itself is actually enough. The key historical elements in Paul's confession remain true. There really was a person called Jesus. He really died. And when he rose from the dead, many people saw him, including Paul.[9]

Thus assured that Paul passes the challenge of history, suitably conceived,[10] and armed with our vital insight into how to tell our story, epiphanically, or backward, we now need to try to do just this. What *is* the story of the past as that has been revealed by Jesus? Looking back, what do we now see and learn?

Election

At this moment we should recall that the God we see revealed in Jesus is what God is really like, deep down, which is to say at exactly the same moment that *this is what God has always been like.*[11] We now understand the past—and

8. We should not at any point entertain a methodological posture of doubt, distantly echoing Descartes, because this would be to step immediately outside of the circle of our revealed truth into an alternative location. (Descartes's posture, although extraordinarily influential, is arguably incoherent in any case.) We already know the truth, and we are turning to examine the historical evidence implicit in that truth. We *could* potentially doubt as a response to the evidence, after it has been evaluated in the light of an appropriate account of history, if it proved inadequate. But when we examine the evidence, we find it to be sufficient and so do not need to enter into these doubts either.

9. Moreover, there would be something faintly ludicrous about the suggestion to any of the witnesses listed or to Paul himself that the person who was raised and now enthroned as Lord was discontinuous from the person who was executed and buried. The person raised is certainly different because the one who died made-of-flesh was raised made-of-spirit (1 Cor 15:35–56). Indeed, such a person no longer dies! But Paul affirms most emphatically that it was Jesus who was raised.

10. A suitable conception is really the key point. To reiterate my earlier note: a broad account of history does not emerge from a consideration of evidence from the past; it is a metaphysic of reality that is, at least to some degree, imposed on the past, assisting with its evaluation. Jesus followers investigating the past already possess a metaphysic of reality and thus have no need to embrace another one. Furthermore, to do so would be a foundationalist move; the truth of God's incarnation in our human reality would thereby be subject to criteria not derived from that reality. Modern historians tend to mix strictly evidential and metaphysical claims together, necessitating a careful sorting of the wheat from the tares in this question.

11. The realization that Jesus is God entails this conclusion. Jesus as God defines

the very deepest past—in the light of this present, even as the future will be drawn into this truth as well.[12] Moreover, the present Jesus, who died for us while we were still sinners, reveals a Son, along with a Father and a Spirit, of limitless love. And so we now know, in particular, that a divine communion of love must have existed prior to the creation of the world. And we can see now *why God created the world in the first place.* The great story that structures all other stories is now apparent.[13]

God is a communion of persons living in love. And it seems to be the most natural thing in the world (so to speak!) that this communion, in its compassion and joy, wanted to create other people to share in this communion. Love overflows. It gives. So God overflows and gives life to other people to relate to and to love. Humanity is this chosen partner and so is destined for fellowship with God and always has been and always will be. This was the divine intention for humanity "prior to" its creation.[14] And this fellowship is still the ultimate goal of the cosmos with respect to humanity. We have been made as persons to share in the divine communion of persons, although without becoming divine. This is

---

God for us definitively. It we posit a change in God, perhaps injecting that notion of divinity before the incarnation, then we undermine this truth. Put differently, we have no grounds for positing such a change in God because we have no definitive access to God to verify such a change outside of this disclosure of Jesus. Theologians subsequent to Paul still had to parse Jesus's humanity carefully when thinking in these terms, since human nature was assumed. The divine person preexisting the incarnation and its assumption of human nature was the Son. Jesus's humanity, however, was not a person preexisting its union with the divine Son so that two persons, one divine and one human, merged together. It was *anhypostatic,* lacking full personhood in and of itself. But it gained full personhood in union with the divine nature, and so, as the theologians put it, was also *enhypostatic.* The result was the *hypostatic* union: one person, or one *hypostasis,* combining two natures, divine and human, without confusing, merging, or mixing these natures together. (If mixing happens, then the definitive revelation of the divine in and through Jesus is lost.) But they also remain inseparable, even as they remain distinct, because if they are at any point separated, then the definitive revelation of the divine through Jesus is lost once again.

12. Reconstructions of the future can suffer as much from foundationalist projections as stories about the past. But we are concentrating for the moment on our story of the past. The future will be parsed in ch. 18 ("The Triumph of Love").

13. Note that my reasoning here is a little different from the argument found in the work of some Pauline scholars concerning the evidence for Jesus's preexistence in Paul (not *as* Jesus). See further in the exegetical notes at the end of the chapter.

14. Time is created, so the use of "prior to" here is a metaphor.

plainly apparent.[15] So there is a very real sense in which God has created us to play with, not in the sense of toying with us, but in the sense of playing together with us. In a moment of near matchless insight, G. K. Chesterton once said, "The true object of all human life is play."[16] Later, James Cone, speaking of spirituals, said much the same thing: "The spiritual is more than dealing with trouble. It is a joyful experience, a vibrant affirmation of life and its possibilities. . . . The spiritual is the community in rhythm, swinging to the movement of life."[17] We were made so that God could have fun together with us—so that we could swing and move and dance to the movement of life. Remarkable!

It seems, then, that love seeks others to love and gives to others what they need—in this case, existence, and an existence created in and for fellowship, and ultimately for fun. At the heart of the divine identity is an overflowing relational reality. Relationships of love are outward facing, giving, and inclusive. It makes perfect sense that a God of love would create more people to love.

Paul's most succinct statement of God's purpose for humanity and for the cosmos is in Rom 8:29, which is one of the most important texts he ever wrote. This verse follows an infamous claim in verse 28, but a more sensitive translation can soften some of the difficulties.

15. Just to avoid all possibility of misunderstanding, I will avoid calling this process in Paul *theosis*. Chalcedonian categories allow us to parse this state that Paul envisages helpfully. We will share in the Son's resurrected *humanity*. This is joined in him to his divinity in the hypostatic union—but only in him. In the Son the two natures are inseparable but also distinguishable, and not to be mixed or confused together. Just so, we, as bearers of Jesus's resurrection humanity, will always be distinguishable from the divine nature and never mixed or confused with it. But we exist inseparably in relation to it with the intimacy of the hypostatic union—an extraordinary gift given originally in the condescension of the incarnation. How close has God drawn us? As close as this.

16. In context, Chesterton wrote: "It is not only possible to say a great deal in praise of play; it is really possible to say the highest things in praise of it. It might reasonably be maintained that the true object of all human life is play. Earth is a task garden; heaven is a playground. To be at last in such secure innocence that one can juggle with the universe and the stars, to be so good that one can treat everything as a joke—that may be, perhaps, the real end and final holiday of human souls" ("Oxford from Without," in *All Things Considered* [1908]; available at http://www.gutenberg.org/files/11505/11505-h/11505-h.htm#oxford_from_without).

17. James Cone, *The Spirituals and the Blues: An Interpretation*, 32–33. My thanks to Luke Bretherton for this reference. Chris Tilling also drew my attention to Lincoln Harvey's book that addresses the same delightful phenomenon from another angle, *A Brief Theology of Sport*.

> We know that [God the Father] works out everything
> for the good of those who love God—
> for those who are called according to his purpose.

Paul now gives an account of this purpose in verse 29:

> Because those whom he knew beforehand
> he also appointed to be conformed to the image of his Son
> so that he [the Son] might be the firstborn among many brothers.

We need to dwell on this statement for a moment, for this truth is as important as it gets. The secret of the universe and the point of the great narrative that encompasses us all is God's plan to draw us into a community imaged and formed by his resurrected Son. The risen Jesus will have primacy but also a rather extraordinary equality with those who surround him and look like him. Everyone in this community will therefore be a "brother," bearing the image of the Resurrected One. The grammar is masculine, although my advice for now is not to press this usage in a literal direction. It simply denotes our personhood, as we will see in more detail later on. Our destiny, then, is to be a "band of brothers,"[18] which is to say, "a family of siblings." This is God's great plan that lies at the heart of the cosmos. Its fulfillment is the story that enfolds us all, and it is the only story that really matters.

Just the same notion is expounded at length in the opening section of Ephesians. There Paul uses the form of a blessing—entirely appropriately, since it is a blessing—to convey the insight that fellowship with the triune God lies at the heart of the cosmos. Such is his enthusiasm that he articulates this notion in one sentence that runs on for twelve verses (vv. 3–14). This purpose existed "before the foundation of the world: that we should be holy and blameless before him, having been chosen in love" (v. 4). At the heart of the cosmos, its inception, its existence, and its future, lies the divine plan to create us and to enjoy us in fellowship. And this plan entailed initiating this relationship by creating us and then calling us and drawing us into communion in the loving movement often known as election, the Greek literally meaning "calling out," hence "summoning."

In the past I have summarized this great cosmic goal as "Trinitarian participation," abbreviating it as TP. I now also use the phrase "Trinitarian communion," abbreviated TC, which captures the intensely relational nature of the

18. William Shakespeare, *Henry V*, act 4, scene 3, lines 18–67.

situation. The goal of the cosmos, within which people stand at the very center, is communion with God. Furthermore, this communion is with a triune God who communes together within God, the Trinity. And it is effected by the triune God as Father, Son, and Spirit all work together to make it happen, drawing us into participation in their eternal play. Astonishing!

But clearly not everything has gone exactly according to plan. . . .

Theses

> ‣ We need now to tell a broader story about God's relationship with us as centered in Jesus—the point and the person where the divine is fully revealed.
> ‣ The story will stretch back into the past and forward into the future, but we will focus first on the narration of the past because problems often arise here.
> ‣ Our learning of the truth about Jesus and God by revelation has important consequences for how we construct the story of what preceded Jesus.
> ‣ Because the truth that Jesus is God incarnate is revealed, the climax of the story is unexpected.
> ‣ We begin then with *this* moment, perhaps in the immediate past and the present, and look back on what preceded it. We must therefore learn to compose the story leading up to Jesus as something that makes sense only in retrospect, or backward.
> ‣ This sort of story, whether broadly of human and/or Israel's history, or of our own personal history before conversion, is constructed like a memoir.
> ‣ Paul models this retrospective purview in Phil 3:2–11, especially verses 4b–8, although it is apparent in other texts like (correctly read) 2 Cor 5:16.
> ‣ If we do not recognize these consequences and instead construct this story forward or in an explicitly *telic* way, we fall into a trap and reactivate foundationalism.
> ‣ This is because a story told or constructed looking forward knows the goal of the story before it arrives. But this means that the truth is already known before Jesus arrives. This means in turn that Jesus himself is not the truth. That is, the truth was present prior to his arrival and could judge him and recognize him when he arrived—a foundationalist procedure.
> ‣ This sort of story is constructed like a quest, in contrast to the correct type of story, which is a retrospective memoir.
> ‣ We should note in passing that historical claims are implicit in the witness

85

of the tradition, meaning, claims that Jesus was real and that certain things really happened in the past.

> Such claims can therefore be investigated historically.

> But both history and historical investigation must also be understood retrospectively, in the light of the central claim that Jesus is Lord. This central claim suggests a particular, open view of history.

> Alternative conceptions of history and of historical investigation should also therefore be rejected as foundationalist, for example, systematic methodological doubt as recommended by Descartes.

> Any historical investigation of the earthly Jesus, undertaken in the light of the central truths revealed by him, with a clear understanding of what history really is, finds Paul's historical claims about Jesus's life, death, and resurrection in fact to be plausible, attested, and reliable.

> We do need to know God's goal or purpose or plan for reality, beginning in our past.

> But we should construct this story revelationally, or epiphanically, looking backward from the key revelation of God's nature and purpose in Jesus. This *telos* will orient the great story of the past leading up to Jesus that we ultimately need to tell.

> Because God is love, as revealed by Jesus, we can infer that he initiated his relationship with us in the first place by creating us, in the way that parents beget children in love.

> In other words, God's plan, revealed to us through Jesus, is to draw people into communion with him, a communion the triune God is and already enjoys.

> In that communion we bear the image of the Son, and thus we are all "brothers." (We will address the gendered grammar in this claim later.)

> This creation for fellowship and fun together with us was the divine plan for creation, existing from "before" the foundation of the world.

> We speak of this plan doctrinally as "election."

> Communion is the goal of the cosmos.

Key Scriptural References

Paul models a retrospective, or backward, account of the past in Phil 3:2–11, especially verses 4b–11. Numerous Pauline texts affirming this retrospective approach will be cited in due course. Both John 2:17 and 22 and Luke 24:13–35 support the position being advocated here in Paul.

Some scholars might want to introduce 2 Cor 5:16 into the discussion of history. Rudolf Bultmann famously argued that this verse indicated Paul's disinterest in what modern scholars call "the historical Jesus." (A nice summary of this debate is supplied by Rae.) Bultmann's view assumes that the prepositional phrase *kata sarka* (according to flesh) in 2 Cor 5:16 is taken attributively, as modifying the persons in view. "So then from now on we know no one in his or her fleshly identity. Even if we knew Jesus when he was fleshly, now, by way of contrast, we no longer know him in this sense." Bultmann thus concluded that Paul was not interested in "the historical Jesus." But the key prepositional phrases can also be read adverbially, modifying the verb of knowing that Paul applies to himself. "So then from now on we know no one in a fleshly way. If indeed we knew Jesus in a fleshly way, now, by way of contrast, we no longer know him in this way [i.e., from this viewpoint]." If this latter reading is correct, which probably seems the more likely, then Bultmann's claim fails. In fact, when pressed, Bultmann's attributive reading struggles to make complete sense of both key clauses. Paul *does* still know people made of flesh, even though this knowledge is secondary, and his knowledge of the risen Christ does not entail that he does *not* now know the Jesus who lived in the flesh. Such claims are both non sequiturs. Furthermore, Paul's statements in verses 14 and 15 presuppose the fleshly Christ and the importance of his crucifixion, something Bultmann's reading of verse 16 immediately goes on to deny. These difficulties are erased, however, if the prepositional phrases in verse 16 are functioning adverbially. It is then Paul's fleshly perspective or viewpoint that is left behind, not his actual knowledge of the people themselves. Understood in this way, the second claim—no longer knowing Christ in a fleshly way—contributes strongly to Paul's first claim—that anyone should now not be understood in a primarily fleshly fashion. Appearances notwithstanding, they are new creations! And it follows that 2 Cor 5:16 does not suggest any derogation of the earthly life of Jesus, although it is fair to suggest that Paul is primarily interested in the resurrected and ascended Jesus *because this is the Jesus who is alive*. That the risen Jesus lacks a prehistory for Paul in an earthly life and death is, nevertheless, a false inference. One of Martyn's first essays—"Epistemology at the Turn of the Ages"—is a classic case for the perspectival view. His definitive case shows how this text is actually a decisive affirmation of Paul's *retrospective viewpoint*.

The importance of Rom 8:29 as a statement of God's cosmic plan can hardly be overstated.

Paul speaks of election in more depth in Eph 1:3–14.

Other texts mentioning election in his letters include Col 3:12; 1 Thess 1:4; 5:9–10; and 2 Thess 2:13–14.

Note that Paul speaks not infrequently of an agent's exalted existence *prior to* the incarnation, and perhaps even of preexistence in a divine form; see especially Phil 2:6–7, but also Eph 1:4–5 and Col 1:15–17; the Son's role in creation is also explicit in 1 Cor 8:6; and texts involving "sending" the Son into the cosmos suggest the same, so Rom 8:3–4 and Gal 4:4–5, these being echoed by John 3:16–17 and 1 John 4:9–10, 14. So there is direct textual warrant in Paul for the preexistence of Jesus in some other form and for some type of election through him.

The precise status of the preexistent agent is difficult to determine, however. Most probably, Paul is utilizing Wisdom (see esp. 1 Cor 1:30; 2:7–8; 2 Cor 4:4, 6; Col 2:3). It is then hard to determine whether Wisdom should be understood in Arian or Athanasian terms (to use Heron's categories). Is Wisdom the first thing created, and hence of matchless importance within creation? Or is Wisdom divine and hence uncreated? The Jewish evidence is arguably ambiguous and in any case would have only speculative status. (See Prov 8:22–31; Wis 9:1–2, 9–10.) My suspicion is that Paul understands Wisdom not to be exactly equivalent to the Lord, since this is what he says in Phil 2:6, going on to say that Jesus nevertheless received lordship after his humble and relentlessly obedient self-emptying. Having said this, Paul is clear that divinity acts through and even pours out through Jesus in full measure: see 2 Cor 5:19 and Col 2:9.

My argument in this chapter has been a little different from these debates, namely, that the recognition of Jesus's divinity in relation to his lordship, which Paul affirms explicitly and unambiguously after Jesus's resurrection and heavenly enthronement (see Phil 2:9–11; also Rom 1:4; 10:9–13; etc.), combined with the revelation of Jesus's limitless compassion through his death for the sinful and ungodly (Rom 5:5–6), results in a solid theological *inference* to election in the terms I have described in this chapter, and hence to Jesus's divinity. A Pauline account of election must then be understood in fully Athanasian terms, and in the compassionate terms that Barth articulated, even though Paul's account of Jesus's preexistence and later divinity arguably has an adoptionist side, and his account of election is not always stated in universal terms.

Key Reading

A superb summary of the extended story of Jesus found in Paul is Richard Hays, "The Story of God's Son," which also touches briefly and accurately on the history question. I cover much of the same narrative ground in "The Story of Jesus." We will return to this material in more detail in part 2.

Further Reading

I have learned much about the importance of story or narrative for theology and Christian exposition more broadly, and for the interpretation of Paul more narrowly, from my colleagues at Duke Divinity School, especially from Stanley Hauerwas and Richard Hays. Narrative is ubiquitous in Hauerwas's work. Hays's famous doctoral dissertation, now published as *The Faith of Jesus Christ*, although overly informed by structuralism and its precursors in the analysis of European folk tales (the influences of which should by no means be dismissed but should be mitigated), introduces and establishes many of these concerns in relation to Gal 3–4. Hauerwas and Hays were both shaped by concerns at Yale, where the work of Hans Frei is especially noteworthy, with its famous exposure of the marginalization of narrative in much modern biblical analysis. (Rae helpfully summarizes the contributions and limitations of Frei's work in pages 39–44 in his *History and Hermeneutics*.)

A useful summary of the use of story explaining Paul is B. W. Longenecker's collection of essays. Stephen Fowl presents an elegant updating of the case in conversation with the key figure of Alasdair MacIntyre, whom we will further discuss later.

However, to be cognizant of story alone is not enough! It must be told in the right way (which Hays and Hauerwas do, Hauerwas at times in deeply personal terms). Barth's *Church Dogmatics* offers a constant lesson in the correct, retrospective telling of the right story of the past, from creation, and even "prior to" creation, through to Jesus and beyond, in a profoundly continuous narrative, but one always told in the light of the definitive but gratuitous and unexpected gift of God fully to us in Jesus.

A particular view of history must then result from this approach. A brief and highly insightful discussion of an appropriate view of history, in opposition to the false but regnant view as epitomized in the thinking of Ernst Troeltsch, is supplied by Nate Kerr (23–62). A typically clear account of the entire situation, exquisitely derived and argued, has been supplied by Murray Rae; it is hard to commend his book highly enough. A complementary analysis has been supplied more recently by Sam Adams, in specific conversation with N. T. (Tom) Wright. Wright's broader account of history needs further work, as does his description of the options in relation to resurrection, but his summary of the historical case in relation to 1 Cor 15:1–8 is on target (see 317–61, 382–84). A classic figure summarizing much of the skeptical case in this relation is Rudolf Bultmann; his two famous essays on the subject are listed below. Martyn's rejoinder is definitive.

Francis Watson has written two important books addressing many of these concerns helpfully: *Text, Church, and World* and *Text and Truth*.

The great constructive move on election is made by Karl Barth in *CD* II/2. When his correction to Calvin finally comes, it is difficult to resist the urge to sing and dance (a correction, it should be noted, Barth drew from Pauline texts, especially Eph 1:4–14, supported by Eph 3:10–12, Rom 8:29–30, and Col 1:15). It is also wonderfully expounded by John Flett in *The Witness of God*. We will shortly talk more about election in relation to human agency.

Bibliography

Adams, Samuel V. *The Reality of God and Historical Method: Apocalyptic Theology in Conversation with N. T. Wright*. Downers Grove, IL: InterVarsity, 2015.

Barth, Karl. *Church Dogmatics*. II/2.

Birkerts, Sven. *The Art of Time in Memoir: Then, Again*. St. Paul: Graywolf Press, 2008.

Bultmann, Rudolf. "Jesus and Paul." Pages 183–201 in *Existence and Faith*. Translated by Schubert M. Ogden. New York: Living Age Books, 1960.

———. "The Significance of the Historical Jesus for the Theology of Paul." Pages 220–46 in *Faith and Understanding*. Edited by R. W. Funk. Translated by L. P. Smith. Vol. 1. London: SCM Press, 1969.

Campbell, Douglas A. "The Story of Jesus in Romans and Galatians." Pages 97–124 in *Narrative Dynamics in Paul: A Critical Assessment*. Edited by Bruce W. Longenecker. Louisville: Westminster John Knox, 2002.

Flett, John. *The Witness of God: The Trinity, Missio Dei, Karl Barth, and the Nature of Christian Community*. Grand Rapids: Eerdmans, 2010.

Fowl, Stephen E. *The Story of Christ in the Ethics of Paul: An Analysis of the Function of the Hymnic Material in the Pauline Corpus*. Sheffield: JSOT Press, 1990.

Frei, Hans. *The Eclipse of Biblical Narrative: A Study of Eighteenth and Nineteenth Century Hermeneutics*. New Haven: Yale University Press, 1974.

Hauerwas, Stanley. *Hannah's Child: A Theologian's Memoir*. Grand Rapids: Eerdmans, 2012.

Hays, Richard B. *The Faith of Jesus Christ: The Narrative Substructure of Galatians 3:1–4:11*. 2nd ed. Grand Rapids: Eerdmans, 2002.

———. "The Story of God's Son: The Identity of Jesus in the Letters of Paul." Pages 180–99 in *Seeking the Identity of Jesus: A Pilgrimage*. Edited by Beverly Roberts Gaventa and Richard B. Hays. Grand Rapids: Eerdmans, 2008.

Kerr, Nathan. *Christ, History, and Apocalyptic: The Politics of Christian Mission.* London: SCM, 2009.

Longenecker, Bruce W., ed. *Narrative Dynamics in Paul: A Critical Assessment.* Louisville: Westminster John Knox, 2002.

Martyn, J. Louis. "Epistemology at the Turn of the Ages." Pages 89–100 in *Theological Issues in the Letters of Paul.* Nashville: Abingdon, 1997.

Rae, Murray A. *History and Hermeneutics.* London: T&T Clark, 2005.

Watson, Francis B. *Text and Truth: Redefining Biblical Theology.* Edinburgh: T&T Clark, 1997.

———. *Text, Church, and World: Biblical Interpretation in Theological Perspective.* Edinburgh: T&T Clark, 1994.

Winner, Lauren. *Girl Meets God: On the Path to a Spiritual Life.* Chapel Hill, NC: Algonquin Books, 2002.

———. *Mudhouse Sabbath: An Invitation to a Life of Spiritual Discipline.* Brewster, MA: Paraclete Press, 2003.

———. *Still: Notes on a Mid-faith Crisis.* New York: HarperCollins, 2012.

Wright, N. T. *Christian Origins and the Question of God.* Vol. 3: *The Resurrection of the Son of God.* Minneapolis: Fortress, 2003.

CHAPTER 5

Resurrection and Death

We have been just talking about God's plan for us, which is both disclosed by and focused on Jesus. We have done so (at least in part) because it is so important to grasp that God's purposes for us are positive, and it is this positive purpose that ultimately matters—our destiny of communion with each other and with the triune God in an interplay of profound interpersonal relating and loving. *But clearly something has gone wrong with the execution of this plan.* We are certainly not now bearing the image of the risen Jesus or enjoying unbroken communion with God and with one another. Even if we think we are experiencing a precious foretaste of this communion, the world around us spends much of its time ignoring and rejecting it, people acting toward one another with indifference and even savagery, and we need to think about this aspect of things now. We can see the full range and complexity of human sin at work in Paul's Corinthian community.[1]

Corinth

The church at Corinth was a mess. We can count fifteen distinguishable problems that Paul addresses in 1 Corinthians. (Technically, two of these aren't big problems yet, but they soon will be, as evidenced by 2 Corinthians.) Paul will spend a great deal of time over the next six months unscrambling this toxic tangle—a task complicated by the fact that his teaching was contributing to

1. I am reproducing here a short summary of the Corinthian situation that I developed for *Journey*, ch. 7, 91–102.

some of the tensions, especially by way of his hard line on sexual activity. And he himself arguably behaved with a degree of insensitivity. But there is much at Corinth that is not as it should be:

1. Partisanship (1:10–4:21; 16:10–18). The Corinthians have factionalized behind different leaders. Some follow Paul, some Cephas, and some a rival called Apollos. Some might even have formed their own "Christ party." Disrespect for rival leaders extends to their followers, so, at the end of the letter, Paul has to ask the Corinthians to respect Timothy and the leadership of the humble household of Stephanas.
2. Incest (5:1–13). A man is sleeping with "his father's wife."
3. Prostitution (6:12–21). Pagan society thought nothing of men visiting prostitutes, and some male Corinthian converts are continuing to do so.
4. Celibacy within marriage (7:1–7). By way of contrast, some marriage partners are withdrawing from sexual activity with their partners on "spiritual" grounds.
5. Some converts married to one another are asking about divorce (7:8–11, 39).
6. Some converts married to pagans are asking about divorce, or they are being asked about divorce by their pagan spouses (7:12–16).
7. Some engaged couples wish to marry (7:25–40). Their marriage arrangements have been on hold for reasons we will talk about when we address sex and gender in more detail (see chs. 25 and 26). They want to move forward in their relationships to the next step. Some widows also want to remarry.
8. Lawsuits (6:1–11). Some people in the church are litigating against one another. Second Corinthians might suggest that the problem was a theft (2 Cor 2:5–11; 7:11–13).
9. Contact with idolatry (8:1–11:1). Some Corinthians are happily eating meat that has been purchased secondhand from the meat market. This meat has come from animals that have been sacrificed in pagan temples by priests to idols, so converts who are Jewish or who have Jewish sensibilities find this food offensive. It is polluted and contains blood. In addition, some Corinthians are feasting in restaurants located on temple premises, and even attending pagan worship events with their processions and celebrations and feasts. Those converts who are more respectful of Jewish traditions are again outraged by these practices.

10. Some converts are offended by the abandoned way in which women are praying and prophesying (11:2–16). Their clothing is slipping off, so perhaps think of someone worshiping up at the front of the church today like a pole dancer.

11. The period of worship is chaotic (ch. 14). People are babbling in tongues and speaking on top of one another. Nothing is intelligible.

12. The communal meal is a bring-your-own rather than a potluck, and significant differences are apparent (11:17–34). Some poorer participants are going hungry; others are feasting and getting drunk.

13. Some people are denying the bodily resurrection both of Jesus and of his followers (ch. 15).

14. Paul notes that a large sum of money is supposed to be collected that will be sent to Jerusalem to firm up his relationships with the other leaders of the early church who are based there (16:1–4). This is not a big problem yet, but it will shortly become one.

15. Paul announces a change in his travel plans (16:5–9). He has canceled a direct visit to Corinth from Ephesus, substituting a route that will head directly to his churches in Macedonia, and then down through Greece to Corinth at the end. He was always going to visit Macedonia, but this new plan means that the Corinthians are losing their first visit from him when he would have looped through them up to Macedonia and back. They will see Paul later and just the once now. Again, this is not a big problem yet, but it will shortly escalate into one.

Preachers and teachers tend to moralize about the awful Corinthians. But this is to miss the point royally. The Corinthians are us, and we are the Corinthians. All of us are caught up in communities that are deeply sinful in multiple ways, large and small, and we all contribute actively to this relational damage, all of which is to say that God's plan for perfect fellowship and communion with us faces some sort of massive problem, and that problem is us. We are incapable of acting in a good way relationally. And it follows that God's plan for us to live in perfect communion has to be brought back on track, even rescued, so the story we tell about it will have to have a saving dimension. Scholars refer to this as a soteriology, drawing on *sōtēria*, the Greek word for "salvation." The overall story is bigger than a soteriology. God's plan is not solely focused on salvation from some predicament. As we already know, it is fundamentally positive. But it does have this saving aspect to it, and it has to.

It follows that there must be something that we need to be saved from; there needs to be some explanation of the difficulties we are now in. We will need to supply an account of "the problem" to flesh out this stage in our story more fully—the story of the problem to which God acting in Jesus is "the solution." And although we can appreciate that there is a problem in a superficial way simply by listing the sins that we are currently involved with, as we just have for the Corinthians, ultimately we need to supply a more precise account of what a sin is, and we need to speak more accurately about evil. We will need some deeper account of its mechanics. But we must construct our account of our problem carefully. It is a certain sort of story, hence, as usual, a trap will lurk here in the way that we tell it. We must avoid constructing a quest narrative in relation to our problems and their solution, which would work forward and launch foundationalism; instead, we must tell this story retrospectively, like a memoir.

Unleashing Foundationalism Again

When we start telling a story about a problem and its solution, it is so easy to use a straightforward sequence and thereby unwittingly fall back into foundationalism. We revisit here the same issue we faced when telling a story correctly about Jesus in any sense. Because Jesus arrives as a revelation and hence unexpectedly, in a way that cannot be anticipated, we had to learn to tell the story about him retrospectively, or backward. As in a memoir, we look back on our past in the light of the present flash of revelation, and things become clear in its light. We dubbed such a plot epiphanic. Conversely, if we ignore this dynamic and tell the story of Jesus forward, like a quest, aware all the time of what we are looking for, we surreptitiously introduce a set of truth criteria in advance of Jesus, and by introducing that set we undermine his ultimacy. We know the truth about him before he arrives, and it follows that Jesus himself is not then the truth, from which mistake disaster must ensue. In just this manner, when we begin to talk about "a problem" to which God acting in Jesus is "the solution," we might reinstate foundationalism. If we introduce our account of the problem first and work forward, rather than introducing the solution first and thinking backward to the implicit definition of the problem, we tell the wrong story and unleash the three horsemen.

Every detailed account of a problem contains an implicit account of a

solution. To define the problem *is* to define the solution. Absolutely fundamental truth claims are present in any definition of a problem.

- My problem at work is you, your attitude, and your inadequate skill set.
- Our problem is vast climate change caused by massive use of fossil fuels,
  which, ultimately, is causing the earth's atmosphere to heat up.
- The problem our society faces is inequality brought on by tax cuts for
  absurdly wealthy people and the financial starvation of welfare programs
  for the least advantaged among us.

Once we have stated the problem in each of these cases, it is clear what the
solution is. The problem defines "the space" where the solution must fit so that
the solution bolts onto the problem into the space already prepared for it, like
a tire onto a car wheel. The place for the solution and the exact shape of the
solution have already been prepared. "You are my problem at work." "Fossil
fuel use causes dangerous climate change." "Flat tax rates result in inequality
and diminished government revenue and related programs of redistribution."
("My problem is a flat tire.") All the critical analysis in these different dilemmas
has been done by the definition of the problem. Solving them just involves
enacting the solution that we already know.[2] And there is something very seductive about this way of working. It seems to be the right way of proceeding
in terms both of history and of rationality.

If history is a closed causal process, then we should be able to analyze a
problematic situation now and infer toward the necessary solution that we can
then effect. We will naturally think forward because history moves forward.
We will detect causes today so we can alter their outcomes tomorrow. And
isn't this just the way we think in any case? We struggle with a question that
becomes a problem that then resolves itself into a solution by dint of rational
inference. Don't we all reason in this fashion, forward? And doesn't reality
work this way as well? Well, yes and no, but preponderantly no, and in the
case of God, emphatically not.

As we have seen from the outset of this book, history is not open to
us in its fullness or subject to our control. God holds the complex inter-
relational process that is history in his hands and shapes history, so the

2. Defining a problem is, incidentally, rather different from posing a question.
Questions can be rather more vague and less definitive, although they still tend to
contain important truth claims as well. "What is wrong?" is a different type of statement
from "*This* is the problem."

truth about history must include both internal and external causes, and we can know what the most important external cause, God, is like and is doing only if God tells us. It doesn't matter how hard we scratch our heads here about what problems we face. We need God to inform us of certain key things. A problem-solution sequence that we are driving is not going to work.

Moreover, even if vast causal nexuses move forward, thereby influencing if not determining many subsequent events, it does not follow that our intellectual analysis of those nexuses does as well. A great deal of research suggests that our thinking about issues and problems is exponentially more complex than a simple process that works from problem to solution. We don't grasp a universal set of truth criteria, calmly derive a basic cosmic problem from them, and then reason toward an account of the gospel that will correspond to that problem and thereby save us.[3] Some would argue that we jump to solutions in moments of inspiration as entirely new paradigms are grasped or completely different accounts of reality are posited. There is no rational road from the deficiencies of Newtonian physics to the seminal truth that the key constant in the cosmos is the speed of light; there is an imaginative leap to an entirely different metaphor for how reality works.[4] So a simple rationalistic problem-to-solution story is naive, even from the point of view of modern science, and is doubly so for anyone on a theological journey. History isn't constructed in a neat sequence like this; our thinking isn't either, and to act as if they are is to unleash the horsemen of the foundationalist apocalypse. Problem-solution stories that attempt to explain what is wrong with reality by working forward in this order must be identified and avoided like the plague. Rather, we must cleave to our current practice and explain sin and evil in the light of the revelation of the solution that has already taken place, backward, as Paul himself knew well.[5] The nature and definition of the problem are known only as we reflect on their solution, a reflection we now turn to in more detail.

3. The opinion that we do is rational*istic*, not rational, and assumes that reality is constructed like an encyclopedia, with the whole being the sum of the parts, when it isn't.

4. One of the brilliant insights of Michael Polanyi. See especially his *Personal Knowledge: Towards a Post-Critical Philosophy*.

5. Few modern Pauline scholars have grasped this as clearly as E. P. Sanders, *Paul and Palestinian Judaism*, 434–35, 438–40, 442, 474–85.

Salvation in Two Acts

The way ahead is usefully set out again by Phil 2:5–11.[6] It summarizes lyrically how God has acted in Jesus to help us, recounting this story as a great drama with two acts.

The drama begins in verses 6–8 with act 1 describing how the Son, despite being in the form of God, emptied himself by becoming a person—a slave-like state in comparison to what he was before. He then humbled himself further by submitting to death—death, moreover, by the hideous method of crucifixion. This is the first act in the drama—a massive downward trajectory by the Son into the human condition, and ultimately into its bitterest depths of public humiliation, torture, and death.

Paul's depiction of Jesus continues in verses 9–11 with the second act. This act describes an equally dramatic lift of the Son up from death in resurrection, ultimately to heavenly exaltation. There Jesus receives the acclamation of everything as the Lord, the name above every other name, which belongs to God alone. So the upward trajectory that is the second act in Jesus's dramatic journey ends in triumph, rejoicing, and acclamation. Moreover, this account informs us that Jesus's lordship is not an isolated event but the climactic moment in a more extended drama. We will now concentrate for a moment on the

---

6. Scholars debate extensively the imagery Paul uses at this moment, as well as its precise dynamics, often because they fear an implicit adoptionism or some equivalent heresy. Was the Son tempted to usurp full divinity from the Father, from a slightly inferior position, before the incarnation (or some such)? My view is that it is easy to overread this passage. Unfortunately, we do not have the space here to work through it in detail. For the record, I would say that I am unconvinced that Adamic imagery is in play. There is an important set of influences from Isaiah, nicely laid out by Richard Bauckham in his essay "Paul's Christology of Divine Identity," in *Jesus and the God of Israel*, 182–232. The initial state of what I have been calling the Son, described in v. 6, draws, in my view, on Wisdom imagery, which is important in the letter and in Paul's context. Compare the description of Wisdom in Prov. 8:22–31 and Wis. 7:22–8:1 with the traces of Wisdom imagery used for the Torah in Rom 2:19–20. Significantly, in Rom 2 these claims are made by a figure representing Paul's opponents (see Rom 2:1–23; 6:1; 16:17–20), who were also, I suggest, active at much the same time at Philippi (see Phil 3:2, 18–19). If this is the case, Paul would have had a good localized reason for arguing that the wondrous features attributed by Torah-loving missionaries to their Scriptures were in fact the features of Jesus. I argue for this scenario in my *Deliverance*, ch. 13, and *Framing*, especially chs. 2 and 3. "You want Wisdom? You'll find it in Jesus, not in the Bible—although the Bible remains helpful." This is Paul's basic move.

event that just precedes his acclamation as Lord and his consequent universal rule over the cosmos, which is to say, on his resurrection. The resurrection is clearly a key part of God's solution to our current problem, and we will work back from it to grasp the problem in its light. (The resurrection is also clearly supposed to affect us in a way that Jesus's heavenly enthronement as Lord, i.e., as God, does not.)

Resurrection in Judaism

We can detect in Paul what amounts to a specific development and concretization of the widespread Jewish expectation of resurrection and entry into the age to come. Many Jews living in Paul's day talked about a coming age that would resolve all the problems and injustices of the present one. This is the hope that infuses the book of Daniel, as well as much related Jewish literature that didn't find its way into the Bible, and it gave great comfort to many Jews as they endured frightful persecutions and pressures in the centuries before the time of Jesus and Paul.[7] Predictably, as a theological position about future events, it had both proponents and critics. Some Jews thought the whole notion was unbiblical and rejected it, and it is quite hard to find in the Pentateuch. The Sadducees held that when someone died, that was it.[8] Even advocates of entering into the new age debated its specifics with one another vociferously and endlessly.[9]

Paul's particular Jewish faction, the Pharisees, supported the prospect of resurrection enthusiastically,[10] even if they too probably differed on the details. Hence Paul was trained in all the key texts and ideas before he encountered Jesus on the road to Damascus. As a result of this preparation, the right terminologies and conceptualities for Paul to articulate what had happened to Jesus lay just to hand. When Jesus revealed himself to Paul near Damascus,

---

7. We will talk about this Jewish literature more in ch. 18, when we discuss the probable shape and extent of this future age in more detail.

8. Hence Jesus's interesting debate with the Sadducees; see Matt 22:23–32.

9. Some believed that only the righteous would be resurrected to enjoy the blessings of this age; the wicked simply stayed dead. Others held that everyone would be resurrected to face a final evaluation before God's throne. Those judged worthy of entering the blessed new age would be granted entrance, while those judged unworthy would be condemned to a much more unpleasant location. We will explore the important implications of this debate for Paul's thought later as well.

10. As Acts rightly notes: see 23:6–8.

Paul knew that he was in the presence of resurrection. However, a resurrection had now happened, so Jesus gives definitive shape from this moment onward to Paul's broader Pharisaic expectations. Paul no longer possessed resurrection hopes and thoughts and reflections, we might say; he had a resurrected person to be guided by. So we see further precision emerging concerning all these expectations as Paul develops them in his letters.

Paul is completely confident that this resurrected figure enthroned in heaven really is Jesus. In a sense, he had an unfair advantage over most of us. Jesus appeared to Paul and identified himself quite clearly when Paul was hunting down his followers in and around Damascus. (As Acts 9:5 puts this: "Who are you, Lord?" "I am Jesus, whom you are persecuting.")[11] But any confusion or doubt is not apparent anywhere, so I suspect that he would have found the suggestion that the resurrected person he spoke of was not Jesus quite astonishing. Paul is clearly quite comfortable with the claim that the resurrected Jesus is Jesus, and again, those convinced that Jesus is God in person will not be troubled by this identification either.

I emphasize this somewhat obvious point because of the nervousness some people sometimes express to me at this moment concerning personal continuity. People seem to worry that a resurrected person will not be the same person as the one who died. "How can we guarantee this?" they tend to ask. I tend to reply: "Well, in a sense, we can't. We are not in control of this process. We can rest assured, however, that while Jesus was not exactly the same—and we must discuss his exact bodiliness at some point—he was clearly the same *person*. His identity had been reestablished by God in the act of resurrection, and I don't know whether it is either meaningful or useful to insist on anything else beyond this."

If we are relying on God to raise us from the dead, we have to trust that the resurrection will end up reconstituting us in a meaningful way, as it seems to have done for Jesus. What form this resurrection takes is not ultimately up to us, and we are not really in a position to make demands in advance of it concerning how it should happen. (We will be dead.) We should, I suspect, simply be grateful that it is going to happen at all. What exactly it will look like is a question that we can answer only by reflecting—as usual—on Jesus, the only person who has been resurrected in the way we're considering here. We certainly won't make any progress by worrying about it in advance and making various demands about what it should look like.

11. Paul speaks of this experience himself, without providing details of the conversation, in 1 Cor 9:1; 15:8 and Gal 1:12, 15–16. But it is clear that Jesus is in view.

With the resurrection firmly in place, we need to ask how this event has thrown light on the problem we have been facing since God's plan for perfect communion with us has clearly been derailed.

Resurrection and Death

Resurrection implies death. Only the dead are resurrected. To be resurrected is, then, by necessity to have already died. Resurrection is God's solution to the problem of death, a solution that only God can offer as the creator and author of life—and how thankful we should be that it is offered. As Paul says in Rom 5:17:

> For if, by the trespass of the one person, death reigned through that
>   one figure,
> how much more will those who receive God's abundant benefaction,
> namely, the gift of deliverance,[12]
> reign in life through the one person, Jesus Christ!

But we need now to face another closely related issue. God did not abolish death altogether with Jesus's resurrection. God refused to give death the final answer. But Jesus still died—the tragic climax of act 1 in the drama of Phil 2:5–11. So this death must have accomplished something as well. It too had a part to play. But what?

Paul's answer to this question goes back to the arrival of death within the cosmos as that dreadful story is told in the opening chapters of the Bible. Genesis 3 states famously that Adam's and Eve's transgressions led to death, and Paul reprises this story in Rom 5:12:

12. Here and elsewhere, when God's activity is in view, I will translate the Greek word *dikaiosynē*, normally rendered the "righteousness [of God]," as the "deliverance [of God]." Paul is alluding in these passages to Ps. 98:2–3, which he echoes strongly in the key text Rom 1:17, and this is a psalm of divine kingship in which the right or righteous act by God, Israel's king, in relation to an oppressed and struggling Israel, is to *deliver* and to liberate it from its troubles. This is exactly what Paul has in mind when describing God's act on our behalf through Jesus, as here. I make the case for this translation, building on Hays's work on Paul's intertextuality, in my *Deliverance*, ch. 17, 677–714, a chapter that has also appeared by itself elsewhere.

So then,
just as sin entered the world through one person,
and death through sin,
in this way death came to all people—
because all sinned.[13]

Death is connected to sin, and both now characterize our world. But Gen 3 presents death *as God's initial solution to sin*, a solution that Jesus's death as spoken of by Phil 2:6–8 in some sense endorses.

Death is God's solution to sin because it is God's judgment on sin. God judges sin by refusing to give it a future. God sets his divine face implacably against sin. It is judged *as* sin and as unworthy of continuation and hence of life. The causality in this judgment is significant, however. God does not actively inflict an event of death in an act of judgment on those who sin. The Father did not execute the Son and does not execute us either. The process is, in a sense, rather more passive than this.

God is the author of life. We were created by him from *nothing*, and without God we are nothing and collapse back into nothing. We are, as the theologians put it, contingent. All existence and continuation and life come from God, much as a computer receives its life by being plugged into a wall socket and drawing the energy afforded by electricity from that connection and ultimately from the power grid. If the computer turns away from the source of its life, perhaps becoming a little overconfident, unplugging itself and striking out on its own in a fit of self-conscious autonomy, it will at some point topple over and become inert and effectively dead. When its battery runs out, the consequences of its unplugging will become quite clear. Its sentience and "life" will cease. In like manner, when people turn away from the God of life, they bend themselves away from the source of their life and turn, however paradoxically and foolishly, toward their own extinction. To use a more biblical idiom, they are branches that have cut themselves off from the tree that holds them up and sustains them. This is how death works, along with the judgment implicit in it. Death is the consequence of sin *and* its necessary termination *and* hence its judgment.

In fact, we see this process of judgment playing out in death all the time. Every living thing that exists around us has a shelf life, and even the universe itself will one day collapse back onto itself. In the death of Jesus, however,

13. It is unnecessary to read this sentence as an anacoluthon or to deviate significantly from the way Paul uses these signifiers and phrases elsewhere.

who has become one of us, we see that this ubiquitous destiny is—to borrow a Barthian idiom—the divine "no" to our sinful condition. That twisted state cannot continue indefinitely. God absolutely refuses to give life to a cosmos that is contaminated with sin. Its existence must end. Death is God's judgment on things that have been contaminated by sin. It is the refusal to give life to those things that have turned from life to evil—and doubtless accompanied by a righteous anger against these things. Because it is right to get angry with sin. Indeed, if we don't, something is wrong. It is just that our definitions of sin and resulting angry reactions tend to be rather less precise than God's, and they result, furthermore, in less disciplined responses.

But someone might still query why God has to be so implacable when it comes to sin. Is it *so* serious? Must it ultimately be extinguished?

I am afraid so.

Those involved with sin tend to trivialize it. But there is nothing trivial about sin and about a cosmos that has been overrun by it, and it might be helpful to think momentarily here in terms of ancient purity and pollution practices. Paul grew up in a nation-state centered on an enormous temple complex. He originally lived a life as a Pharisee dedicated in large measure to maintaining temple purity and cleansing offending pollution. Unfortunately, these categories are not treated with much respect by modern cultures, so it is worth recalling that these ancient concerns are comparable in the modern world to epidemics and to contemporary obsessions with disease. Reframed in these terms, we see that question of purity and pollution has a truly frightening force.

The only appropriate response to an outbreak of a deadly and incurable virus is quarantine, at which moment issues of purity and pollution become matters of urgency and dread. Tragically, once a virus like Ebola has taken hold, it must be left to play out to its conclusion within those infected. They must be allowed to die, alone, and then be buried or incinerated. The spread of the virus to new victims must be prevented at all costs. Many a movie has played on this desperate struggle, although I imagine that personal involvement in such a procedure would be anything but entertaining. A plague must be contained. And in just this sense, God is implacably committed to the containment of sin within this world and this age, and to its ultimate termination, in death. The crippling and deadly virus of sin cannot be allowed to spread. Indeed, we are fortunate that God is so resolute in this opposition to something that we tend to treat rather too lightly.

Sin is evil. Viewed in its clearest incarnations—something it generally tries to avoid—it causes massive and unnecessary suffering. If anyone doubts this, a visit to the Jewish Holocaust Museum in Washington DC (or the equivalent experience elsewhere) will be a quick corrective. A world in which the virus of sin has been released experiences epidemics of baffling cruelty—in this instance, the fastidiously organized collection and transportation of designated ethnicities and deviants to slave labor camps, and their starvation, degradation, exploitation, and/or summary execution. This sort of world cannot be allowed to continue, and that which causes it cannot be allowed to live on indefinitely. If humanity carries this virus, then it too cannot be allowed to continue. It will die, and it must. And in this relation, it is depressing but important to recall the pervasiveness of sin within our cosmos as evidenced by the corresponding pervasiveness of death.

Everything living dies, which implies, on theological grounds, that everything is somehow contaminated by sin, while the very interweaving of death with our situations suggests the radical nature of our problem. Sin extends all the way across and all the way down. We are saturated with it—soaked in it. The only solution to this entire situation is to go through the termination of death and be resurrected beyond that. And at this moment we can grasp how God's act of resurrecting Jesus has resolved not just the directly correlative problem of death but the problem of sin as well—at least for him! Sin and the sinful condition have been terminated in death, and death has been "terminated" through resurrection. So God's plan is back on track. Sin's contamination has been quarantined, and the future of humanity has been reestablished in Jesus. He now lives in a new, sin-free state, beyond death—in a new world and a new age!

Furthermore, the paradox of death is resolved by resurrection. As we have just seen, death is in a certain sense correct and positive in its termination of the bad, to which it is the appropriate judgment. But it is negative in its termination of the good. That which is personal and good but intertwined with sin dies with it. Death has this painful side, as we all know. So it halts God's plan for perfect communion with those he creates and loves in spite of their corruption. Resurrection, however, taking place beyond death, can reconstitute that which is good and leave that which is bad terminated and hence contained forever within the old cosmos. The good that death forecloses on is retained as it is reconstituted by resurrection; the harm that death does is defeated and terminated.

We come now to an absolutely critical point.

Our Resurrection

All of Jesus's early followers probably had much the same hope as many of their Jewish contemporaries, with some additional variations centered on Jesus. Jesus had been resurrected, which was clearly exciting. Their beloved leader had been raised from the dead, his lordship had been declared, and his teachings had been vindicated. The cross did not have the last word. Furthermore, the expectation of an age to come with a bodily resurrection of all involved was clearly rock solid, so they could all look forward to some future day when this would happen. On that day God's plan would be definitively reestablished. Apart from all these important things happening to Jesus, however, and the attendant privilege of being part of his following and thereby guaranteed a bright future, the schema was otherwise unchanged. Jesus's resurrection was past, so he was now alive in the present. This was the odd part. However, the resurrection of his followers was still future, although their loyalty to him guaranteed that one day they would share in his blessed state. Eventually what had happened to Jesus would happen to his disciples. So in certain regards this was still a pretty standard view. God's cosmic solution was still future. *That* was when his plan would be finally reestablished—in that wonderful new age, the age to come. In the meantime, life was a matter of faith and hope.

Paul utterly disrupts this nice sequence, however, by claiming something quite extraordinary: *our* resurrection is, in some sense, *present as well*. The resurrection of Jesus's followers too has begun. Scholars like to use the phrase "inaugurated eschatology" (the noun here from Gk. *eschaton*) to describe this concept. The events of the end have been inaugurated, or initiated, although the sense remains that they are not yet complete.

Paul's claim raises a host of challenges. Before we deal with them, however, we need to be certain that he really was committed to this view. It is an absolutely critical point. But the evidence that he believed it is fairly overwhelming.

Paul affirms the present resurrection of Jesus's followers directly in 2 Cor 5:17, although he doesn't use the language of resurrection per se. He speaks of living in a manner structured by the age to come, which presupposes that a resurrection of sorts has taken place.

If someone is in Christ, he is a new creation.
The old has departed. Behold, he has become quite new.[14]

---

14. The preceding verse, 2 Cor 5:16, rightly understood, underscores this same message.

He concludes his letter to the Galatians with the same claim.

> Neither circumcision nor uncircumcision is anything
> but a new creation. (6:15)

Paul's most famous assertion of this fact is probably Gal 3:28, which is best read along with its two preceding verses. This text has rightly been called the Pauline Magna Carta. The claim of present resurrection is again not directly stated but lies right behind the extraordinary transformation Paul states here that his Galatian converts *presently* enjoy.

> All of you who are in Christ Jesus are, by means of that fidelity,[15] sons
>   of God.
> For you have been immersed into Christ;
> you have been clothed with Christ.
> There is no "Jew" or "pagan," no "slave" or "free," no "male and female."
> All of you who are in Christ Jesus are one and the same. (3:26–28)

Those who have been immersed and reclothed are something new, Paul says here. They are "sons of God" like Jesus, the Son of God, and no longer characterized by ethnicity (Jew or Greek/pagan), social status (slave or free), or gender (male or female). These claims confirm that something quite concrete happens to converts and that this new state lies beyond existing categories such as race, class, and even biology.[16] Hence this wording again affirms that an entry into the age to come has taken place in some sense right here and now. Christians have already been resurrected.

In Col 3:9–12 Paul repeats his belief that Christians live in a new situation beyond current structures, emphasizing how racial and ethnic divisions have been transcended:

> You have taken off your old self with its practices
> and have put on the new self,
> which is being renewed in knowledge in the image of its Creator.

---

15. This phrase is a reference back to a key motif in the previous argumentative stage. It refers primarily to Jesus's "fidelity" and not to ours. His coming has made our sonship possible—so Phil 2:6–8.

16. Incidentally, this wording also tells us that we should not understand being a "son of God" as a strong claim about gender; it is metaphoric.

Here there is no Gentile or Jew, circumcised or uncircumcised,
barbarian, Scythian, slave or free,
but Christ is all, and is in all.
Therefore, as God's chosen people, holy and dearly loved,
clothe yourselves
with compassion, kindness, humility, gentleness and patience.

This text confirms the reality of present resurrection for Jesus's followers on some level. We all now live beyond structures of race and class, and even of gender. What is going on?

We learn from this that the resurrection of Jesus is not just God's solution to death. *It is God's solution to sin*; and it is God's solution to sin for us *now*.

These claims are so important—and at times so subtly argued by Paul—that we will devote the following chapter entirely to their explanation.

Theses

- God's purposes for us are fundamentally positive, namely, the destiny of eternal fellowship in communion with God.
- However, it is clear that something has gone wrong with his great cosmic plan.
- We can clearly see this generalized problem in the Corinthian community, where Paul confronted a shopping list of problems—fifteen—although we should not distance ourselves from the Corinthians. They represent us.
- This sad reality implies that we have some sort of current problem, to which Jesus is the solution.
- So there has to be a saving aspect to what God does for us in Jesus—an act by means of which God's original plan for communion is brought back on track.
- However, we need a deeper explanation of sin and evil than a mere list of its instances.
- Nevertheless, a trap lurks here for the unwary that must be identified and avoided—a foundationalist account of the problem and its solution.
- Because Jesus is the definitive revelation of God, he is the definitive revelation of the solution to whatever problem we have, and we must therefore infer the nature of the problem backward, from his solution. He is the definitive revelation, that is, of the problem as well.

- We must, conversely, avoid working forward here like the plague, establishing a definition of the problem and then articulating Jesus's solution in its light. Such an approach reinstates foundationalism. The nature of the problem dictates the solution if we work forward, so truths put in place prior to Jesus's arrival will overrule his revelations—foundationalism.
- Working forward seems the right historical and rational way to proceed, but these sensibilities are inaccurate. History is not a closed causal nexus, and thinking is not a forward, step-like process.
- Paul's programmatic text Phil 2:5–11 is a useful guide for our next analytic steps as we think about the solution and its implicit account of the problem.
- In "act 2," as recounted in verses 9–11, Jesus is acclaimed and worshiped as Lord after he has been resurrected. He must be resurrected to be acclaimed as Lord.
- The conceptualities underlying this journey are Jewish expectations widespread in Paul's day of the age to come, especially resurrection.
- Resurrection solves a problem of death.
- Death itself is, however, God's initial response to the problem of sin and a resulting sinful cosmos.
- Death is, strictly speaking, the consequence of a person turning away from God and God's life. God's judgment is the passive judgment that refuses to gift life to a situation contaminated by sin.
- This response is right and necessary because a sinful situation cannot be allowed to continue. A sinful situation is *deeply* contaminated and dangerous and evil. We tend to minimize sin and ask for its continuance. God sees it clearly and maintains a judgment of impermanence against and on it. A cosmos that contains things like the Holocaust must end.
- But death and its terminations clearly also interrupt God's plan for eternal fellowship with those he creates and loves.
- Hence resurrection solves the problem of death, after death has solved the problem of sin. And God's plan is thereby reestablished—in the future, in the age to come.
- *But* according to Paul, Jesus's followers do not have to wait for an entirely future resurrection. He claims that they are to a degree *presently* resurrected, although we have yet to discover exactly how and why.

Key Scriptural References

Philippians 2:5–11 is one of Paul's most famous and important texts. (It is much discussed. I am unpersuaded that it is a preexisting hymn drawn from earlier church tradition: see Stephen Fowl's elegant analysis. I also suspect that Joachim Jeremias was correct, and that its underlying imagery, so widely debated, derives from the Hebrew text of Isa 53. He was not the first to suggest this connection, but he is perhaps this reading's most famous champion. Bauckham concurs. I *do* think that Paul himself may have composed this text, so it is a preformed text in a certain sense; it is a song from Paul originating in an act of worship.)

Hope in a future resurrection is attested for Jews in Scripture bordering on or written during the intertestamental period, that is, the time between the material contained in the Tanakh (OT), excepting Daniel, and the time of the materials in the New Testament, which I will refer to in what follows primarily as the Apostolic Writings, for reasons noted earlier (see Introduction, n. 4). The book of Daniel is consequently an especially important witness to this period. The Apocrypha contains more relevant material. Noncanonical Jewish texts known as apocalypses contain a great deal of this imagery as well.

Resurrection solves the problem of death, present since Adam: see Rom 5:17.

Death entered the cosmos after sin according to Gen 3, as corroborated by Phil 2:6–8 and Rom 5:12. It is God's (passive) judgment on sin and a situation contaminated by sin.

The present life of Christians as a new creation and hence resurrected is stated clearly in 2 Cor 5:17 and Gal 6:15. Important summaries of the transition through baptism to a resurrected life are Gal 3:26–28, 1 Cor 12:13, and Col 3:11.

Key Reading

The interpretation of the apocalypses is also much debated, but especially insightful accounts are provided by Martinus C. de Boer.

Further Reading

Barth's *Dogmatics* is a constant exercise in retrospective, christologically informed thinking. Significantly, when discussing salvation in part 4—what

Barth called the doctrine of reconciliation—in each of the three main treatments, he first discusses the positive, christologically revealed and grounded material and only then turns to discuss the sin that has been revealed in the light of this analysis in §§60, 65, and 70. However, a particularly crisp instance of this retrospective viewpoint, grounded in Paul, is his short essay on Rom 5:14. Barth's powerful analysis of death can be found largely in III/2. It is developed in terms of judgment in IV/1.

There is a long debate over the conceptual categories that Paul utilizes in order to speak of these things. I am persuaded that his language of flesh, curse, death, and resurrection is best explained by Jewish discussions of the future, which is to say, by Jewish eschatology, imagery often found in the apocalypses, hence my analysis here. This explanation is often credited to Albert Schweitzer, although it preceded him, as he acknowledges in his famous survey of previous Paul scholarship. Schweitzer is critical because this realization reoriented discussions of Paul's "in Christ" phrase and its implications toward Jewish categories and away from the pagan religious categories that had heretofore (mainly) been used to describe it. Analogies with the Greco-Roman mystery religions had been appealed to by scholars such as Boussett, offending those with canonical sensibilities, and Deissmann appealed also to mysticism, which is a famously nebulous notion.

Anathea Portier-Young has provided a compelling historical account of the historical background to the apocalypses.

An accessible presentation of the account of death that I am urging here— as God's "passive" response to sin and a sinful, contaminated reality, allowing them to run their course consequentially to extinction—can be found in Greg Boyd's two-volume treatment *Crucifixion of the Warrior God*, especially chapters 15 and 16, "Divine Aikido" and "Crime and Punishment" (2:767–850). I would not follow Boyd's program in every respect, but he has placed his finger here on a key insight.

Bibliography

Barth, Karl. *Christ and Adam: Man and Humanity in Romans 5*. Translated by T. Smail. New York: Collier, 1962.
———. *Church Dogmatics*. III/1; IV/1.
Bauckham, Richard. "Paul's Christology of Divine Identity." Pages 182–232 in *Jesus and the God of Israel: God Crucified and Other Studies on the New Testament's Christology of Divine Identity*. Grand Rapids: Eerdmans, 2008.

Bousset, W. *Kyrios Christos*. Translated by John E. Steely. 5th German ed. Nashville: Abingdon, 1970 (1964).

Boyd, Gregory A. *Crucifixion of the Warrior God: Interpreting the Old Testament's Violent Portraits of God in the Light of the Cross*. 2 vols. Minneapolis: Fortress, 2017.

Campbell, Douglas A. "An Echo of Scripture in Paul and Its Implications." Pages 367–91 in *The Word Leaps the Gap: Essays in Honor of Richard B. Hays*. Edited by J. Ross Wagner, C. Kavin Rowe, and A. Katherine Grieb. Grand Rapids: Eerdmans, 2008.

De Boer, Martinus C. *The Defeat of Death: Apocalyptic Eschatology in 1 Corinthians 15 and Romans 5*. JSNTSup 22. Sheffield: JSOT Press, 1988.

———. "Paul and Jewish Apocalyptic Eschatology." Pages 169–90 in *Apocalyptic and the New Testament: Essays in Honor of J. Louis Martyn*. Edited by Joel Marcus and Marion Soards. JSNTSup 24. Sheffield: Sheffield Academic, 1989.

Deissmann, G. A. *Saint Paul: A Study in Social and Religious History*. London: Hodder & Stoughton, 1912.

Fowl, Stephen E. 1990. *The Story of Christ in the Ethics of Paul: An Analysis of the Function of the Hymnic Material in the Pauline Corpus*. JSNTSup 36. Sheffield: JSOT Press, 1990.

Hays, Richard B. *Echoes of Scripture in the Letters of Paul*. New Haven: Yale University Press, 1989.

Jeremias, Joachim. "*pais theou*." *TDNT* 5:654–717.

Portier-Young, Anathea E. *Apocalypse against Empire: Theologies of Resistance in Early Judaism*. Grand Rapids: Eerdmans, 2011.

Sanders, E. P. *Paul and Palestinian Judaism: A Comparison of Patterns of Religions*. Minneapolis: Fortress, 1977.

Schweitzer, Albert. *The Mysticism of Paul the Apostle*. Translated by W. Montgomery. Baltimore: Johns Hopkins University Press, 1998 (1910).

———. *Paul and His Interpreters: A Critical History*. Translated by W. Montgomery. London: Adam & Charles Black, 1912.

CHAPTER 6

Resurrection and Sin

The Resurrected Mind

It is important to appreciate that we experience our present resurrection primarily as a new mind, and this mind is characterized, Paul asserts repeatedly, by *peace*.[1] So for example he says in Rom 8:6b, "The mind of spirit is life and peace." Our resurrected thinking possesses a new tranquility, although peace in the Bible is stronger and more active than mere tranquility. It is the state and the pursuit of *shalom*, which is a deep wholeness and enjoyment of life when it is ordered as it should be. The resurrected mind is at peace with God and with itself, while it pursues peace within its communities (Eph 4:3). This mind is led by the Spirit of God and walks obediently as a child of God (Rom 8:13–14). Hence despite the troubles he experienced with his converts and the concerns he shared, Paul's attitude toward himself is remarkably free from self-recrimination, from doubt, and even from a consciousness of sin. He speaks of this peace "guarding" his mind, protecting it with a peace that passes all comprehension (Phil 4:7). This peaceful mind is so important that Paul begins and closes every letter with the prayerful wish that his readers will be blessed with this peace as well.

It is important to appreciate this emphasis because Paul also speaks of a divided mind in conflict with itself—a mind that struggles to do the right thing. He uses two principal narratives to explain what is going on within and around this unhappy, unresurrected mind: the story of Adam in the garden of Eden, suitably reinterpreted; and a story revolving around what scholars often refer to as "the powers." For Paul and his contemporaries these were evil entities such as fallen angels and demons who populated the unseen world and

---

1. We will talk in much more detail about this new mind in part 2.

opposed God by seducing and bullying human beings into disobedience under the leadership of Satan. Both stories come up fairly frequently in Paul in highly strategic places, and the question of their interaction is one that must be faced.[2]

The Mind of Adam

Paul's longest description of the unresurrected mind can be found in Rom 7.[3] There he states that part of a human mind might recognize the goodness of God's divinely gifted instructions in the Torah, and even enjoy them: "In my inner person I delight in God's instructions." So things are not all bad. Nevertheless, these instructions will not be carried out. "I do not understand what I do. Because I do not practice what I want, but what I hate—this I do!" (7:15), an observation repeated many times through the paragraph that follows. The

2. The story of Adam (and Eve!) is used in Rom 5:12–21; 7:7–25 (and the story is also probably alluded to in 3:23); 1 Cor 15:21–28, 42–49; and 2 Cor 11:2. Genesis 1 is echoed by Gal 3:28 ("male and female"), and arguably by Col 3:11 as well. The powers are spoken of in Rom 8:38–39; 1 Cor 2:6–8; 15:23–28; Eph 1:20–23; 3:8–11; 6:11–12; Phil 2:9–11; Col 1:13, 16; 2:13–15. (In my view, the "elements" [Gk. *stoicheia*] refer to something a little different, although there is some overlap: see Gal 4:1–3, 8–11; Col 2:8–10, 20–23.) Satan is referred to in Rom 16:20; 1 Cor 5:5; 7:5; 2 Cor 2:11; 6:15 (as "Beliar"); 11:14; 12:7; Eph 2:2 ("the ruler of the power of the air"); 6:16 ("the evil one"); 1 Thess 2:18; and 2 Thess 2:9.

3. The precise identification of this mind has vexed commentators for millennia. As Richard N. Longenecker, *Paul, Apostle of Liberty*, elegantly notes, three main options have been advocated in the modern period: (1) a biographical reading supposing this was Paul's mind *before* he became an apostle, (2) a biographical reading supposing this was Paul's mind *after* he became an apostle, and (3) a "gnomic" reading, following the suggestion of W. G. Kümmel, that a more general account of humanity is in view. My own considered opinion is a variation on option 3 but more specific.

Paul is writing in this letter to Jesus followers in Rome, and he is trying to dissuade them from following an alternative gospel that advocates Jewish proselytism and full Torah-observance. Romans 7:7–25 occurs in the middle of a long argument presupposing baptismal transformation as the basis for ethics by way of life in the Spirit. Such people possess the mind of the resurrected Jesus and think and live accordingly. Romans 7, then, is a highly dramatized warning not to step from life in the Spirit *back* into a life in the Flesh, *which will happen if piety is oriented primarily by Torah and not by Christ and the Spirit*. To adopt the Torah as the key to ethics will necessitate this lapse into the world of the Flesh, and into the situation of the divided and agonized mind of Rom 7; such a move is clearly best avoided.

chapter explains this struggle by infusing this struggle with the story of Adam (and Eve) in the garden, suitably modified. Paul speaks specifically of the tenth commandment, which forbids coveting: "Do not desire. . . ." This command in its original biblical context prohibits any covetousness or lust for a neighbor's wife, male or female servant, ox, donkey, or anything else that belongs to the neighbor. But Paul goes on to observe that the divine prohibition against lust creates the desire to do these very things when an evil force that Paul here calls Sin, like the snake in the garden of Eden, *deceives* the human agent and generates all manner of covetousness. It thereby utilizes the presence of this prohibition to subvert it. "Sin, seizing the opportunity [afforded] through the commandment, worked every type of desire in me." The result of this deception is that he "does the thing he does not want to do" and is, conversely, unable "to do the thing I want to do," so that at present he is a slave to Sin, and in the future, like Adam, he will die.

Hence even the attempt by this person to obey a God-given command in the Torah leads to a cascade of wrongdoing. He sins repeatedly, and God's instructions are now seen to be a plaything of some evil force that lives within humanity, deceiving it, and ultimately selling it as a slave to wrongdoing. Paul's language is personal and also inclusive. *We* have been taken captive, enslaved to this entity called Sin, and now live trapped in a body that is doomed to die. Small wonder that this person cries out finally, "What a wretched person I am! Who will rescue me from this body of death!?"

I don't want to trivialize the point, but I can't help but think at this moment of the remarkable ineffectiveness of dieting programs—a statistical fact, I am told. Rigid regimens with constant instructions *not* to drink beer and wine, *not* to eat potato chips in a guacamole dip for starters and then move on to porterhouse steak, *not* to finish a three-course meal with blue cheese and port, and *not* to have a quick nightcap before bed will tend—on bitter experience—only to suggest that we do these very things. So Paul's observations certainly resonate with common human experience. But he supplies a powerful explanation for the presence of this painful experience, sharpening its depth and consequences beyond this psychological dynamic. We get the sense that some hostile force occupies human nature and both deceives and enslaves it—the human passions or lusts.[4] The result is an ongoing failure to

---

4. Desire is not always negative in Paul (see Phil 1:23; 1 Thess 2:17), but it frequently is, at which points it is best translated "lusts." Medieval commentators would speak of concupiscence. Although Paul's longest explication of the lusts is in Rom 7:7-25, where he dramatizes its operation as Sin, after reemphasizing the phenom-

do the right thing, and failing to obey God is eventually fatal. God will ultimately quarantine this situation within humanity descended from Adam and terminate it through death.

Paul's preferred summary term for this situation is "flesh," which translates the Greek *sarx* and should also be linked to the Hebrew *basar*. It is scattered through most of his writings with ninety-odd occurrences.[5] We learn from Rom 7 that a humanity of Flesh[6] is in the grip of something called Sin that overwhelms any ability to do the right thing, whether by deception or by force. Humanity's deadly plight is highlighted with special clarity by any attempt to obey God's commands—here, the notorious tenth commandment. Candid self-reflection on our inability to obey the tenth commandment will reveal instantly that people composed of Flesh are in a bad way. They can't actually

---

enon in 7:5–6, they recur in many other important places. He varies his vocabulary a little, speaking mainly of negative desires (*epithymia* 12x) but also of lust(s) (*pathē* 3x) and of negative passions (*pathēma* 2x; see BDAG def. 2). See Rom 1:24, 26 (no coincidence!); 6:12; 7:5, 7; 13:14; Gal 5:16, 24; Eph 2:3; 4:22; Col 3:5; and 1 Thess 4:5. The presence of the theme in Ephesians, Colossians, and 1 Thessalonians suggests it is not just a product of the localized contention unfolding in Romans, Galatians, and Phil 3 (i.e., Paul's engagement with the Teachers; see more details in my *Deliverance*, especially ch. 13, 469–518; *Framing*, ch. 3, 122–89; and *Journey*, chs. 10–11, 127–50).

The conceptual background for this notion is debated. It was ultimately a legacy of Greek philosophical thought, especially Stoicism, since the anthropology Paul is engaging with counterposes a rational, good, controlling mind to a lower, disordered, lustful element in human nature. Once introduced, biblical warrant was found in Gen 6:5 and 8:21. Platonic anthropology also had a role for disordered and evil desire but was tripartite (hence a countervailing emphasis on the *yetzer hatov* [good inclination] might indicate this influence). However, the view may have been mediated to Paul indirectly by way of the rabbis and their notion of the *yetzer hara* (evil inclination), or simply by certain general currents within Jewish thought in his day. See W. D. Davies's typically elegant treatment "The Old Enemy: The Flesh and Sin," ch. 2, 17–35, in *Paul and Rabbinic Judaism*. Martyn, using early work from Joel Marcus ("The Evil Inclination in the Epistle of James"), makes some use of the motif as well. It is readily apparent in Jewish texts like 4 Maccabees.

5. Only the Thessalonian letters do not use it.

6. I will capitalize "Flesh" when using it in Paul's distinct theological sense. There is a more neutral sense in which "flesh" simply denotes what we are currently made of without being especially pejorative—the prevailing sense of *basar* in the Jewish Scriptures. But Paul's account of humanity in terms of Flesh denotes our particular vulnerability to sin.

do what they want to do, even when God is asking them to. They end up doing the converse. Something is wrong, and at a very deep level.[7]

It is worth recalling now that the mind of Flesh is characterized by conflict—where there is enough moral awareness to generate this conflict, perhaps through the presence of a divine command in Scripture—and by hostility to God. When Paul describes the person of Flesh in Rom 7, as we have just seen, sinful desires, perhaps here better translated "lusts," exploit even God's righteous instructions, with the result that sins are multiplied. They thereby "wage war" on any good elements within the person and "enslave" the person as a whole to habitual wrongdoing. Any remaining "inner" part of a person that desires to do the right thing looks on helplessly at this outward wrongdoing, crying out for rescue like a pitiful slave (vv. 23, 14, 22, 24). The person currently exists in a hopelessly conflicted state. "I do not understand what I do but the good that I want to do I do not do, and the evil that I do not want to do—this I do" (paraphrasing parts of vv. 15–20). And this internal conflict extends to a posture of enmity toward God.

Repeated disobedience to God's instructions places a person in ongoing opposition to God. Such a person can hardly delight or please God, and one is reminded here of the proverbial rebellious teenager. Such figures are a stock item in modern culture, whether in books or movies, but their frequent comic exploitation belies the pain that actual rebellious children cause their families. Young adults who are off the rails and, despite love, support, and nurture, engage in self-destructive or vicious practices, are causes of horrible suffering to their parents, siblings, and friends, and Paul is naming this aspect of the fleshly dynamic here in two texts from Romans:

> For if, while we were God's enemies,
> we were reconciled to him through the death of his Son,
> how much more, having been reconciled,
> shall we be saved through his life! (5:10)

---

7. The seriousness of Paul's account of human wrongdoing here needs to be noted. If sin is just a series of bad choices that proceed from a fundamentally healthy nature, then Jesus needs to provide only a clear example of how to behave, along with some additional teaching about right acting. That he had to die, executing our *condition*, then resurrecting human nature *in a new form*, suggests that there was something irredeemably corrupt and contaminated in the old one. As some scholars would put it, our problem is *radical* (from the Latin *radix*, meaning "root"), suggesting that our problem goes down into the very roots of our nature.

And,

> The mind governed by the flesh is hostile to God;
> it does not submit to God's law,
> nor can it do so. (8:7)

God is grieved and hurt by this mindless and self-destructive hostility on the part of fleshly humanity to his instructions.

Hence it seems we are on to something when we counterpose the conflicted and struggling mind of Flesh to the resurrected mind of the person who lives through and in the Spirit and is characterized by a tranquil obedience to God, a harmonious internal life, and the pursuit of peace with others. Moreover, it seems highly likely that Paul grasped this contrast in retrospect, looking backward—and to a degree "sideways"—at his life in the Flesh. As Krister Stendahl argued in 1963, when Paul gives us an unmediated flash of insight into his previous life, he speaks of being "blameless" (*amemptos*; see Phil 3:6) in relation to a certain sort of righteousness achieved by way of Torah-observance. This is *not* the purview of Rom 7! Moreover, Paul's position that all sin, even those obeying the Torah, seems to be, at least in part, a reflection on the universality of death. If death is the consequence of sin, then the fact that all die (with one or two notable exceptions) entails that all have sinned. Any quick attempt to achieve ethical perfection alert to this position will then only confirm it. We lust, all of us, for *something*, however trivial. The point is not that God is then angry with us and sentences us to death. The point is that we want to behave rightly but that any attempt to do so, and especially when undertaken in the light of the most important set of moral directives available, the Torah, exposes our inadequacy almost immediately, from which it follows that we *do* sin and that we do therefore have a problem with death. Our sinful condition has somehow been cut off from the God of all goodness and life and will, one day, be terminated. And both pagans and Jews face this underlying problem intrinsic to the human—or, as Paul would say, the Adamic—condition. To slightly paraphrase some of Paul's most famous phrases in Romans:

> All sinned and lack the glorious image originally given to us by God.
>
> (3:23)

> [Therefore, now] through the Torah only a knowledge of sin comes.
>
> (3:20b)

But Paul does not leave things here, bad as they are. It is important to push still deeper into his explanation of what is going on in the cosmos where everyone is made of Flesh.

The Powers

Paul's analysis of wrongdoing does not end with a description of the lusts operating within the Flesh—operations that sometimes exploit even the Torah. He supplies a brief discussion of demonic forces at the end of Rom 8, which complements his earlier descriptions of the sinful lusts. Paul states resonantly at the end of Rom 8 that no angels, rulers, or any other power, whether occupying the heights or the depths, will be able to break the relationship between God and his community established by Jesus. Neither will they be able to sentence God's people to death. So beyond the operations of fleshly lust in Rom 7—its power, its sinister intelligence, and its bullying oppressions—lie the powers. In the Flesh, we battle evil forces *from both within and without*. Paul himself usually calls these dangerous powers (evil) heavenly rulers, although his precise nomenclature varies, and he frequently refers to their leader as Satan. So in Rom 8 we are opposed, but

> neither death nor life,
> neither heavenly messengers nor rulers,
> neither the present nor things to come,
> neither powers—neither height nor depth—nor anything else in all
>   creation
> will be able to separate us from the love of God
> that is in Christ Jesus our Lord. (vv. 38–39)

In the light of all this material, which appears throughout Paul's writings, it seems that the origin of sin did not lie directly in Adam. Evil forces achieved access to the world of humanity through Adam's stupidity and thereby threw God's earthly creation into disarray.[8] But they preexisted Adam's transgression.

---

8. It is hard to detect further information in Paul about the origin of evil angels. Perhaps Col 1:16 suggests Paul's dependence on the story of the Watchers to explain their origin, because they were originally created good (Col 1:16). This story traces the origins of evil to the union of the "sons of God" and the "daughters of humans," producing unnatural, monstrous offspring and knowledge of many evils (see Gen 6:1–4,

Evil lived outside of him and beyond him. It was not innate to his nature or to his situation. The evil powers achieved this entrance into the cosmos through deception and then occupied it, rather like an oppressive colonial invader. Sinful humanity now sins, in part, because it has been colonized, although Adam opened the door to this invasion and must take some responsibility for it (noting, in addition, that in 2 Cor 11:3 Paul blames Eve). As a result of this combination of stupidity and gullibility, humanity now lives browbeaten by powerful forces that seduce and exploit people and human structures to achieve evil ends, most obviously effecting the crucifixion of Jesus (1 Cor 2:6, 8).

This, then, is the problem of sin that humanity faces—life in a nature that is prone to lustful sinning from within and, from without, prone to constant assaults from deceptive and evil forces. Small wonder that God steadfastly maintains the judgment of termination. That judgment is a refusal to extend life permanently to a contaminated cosmos, resulting in an existence that is limited, declining through steady corruptibility to death. We know already, however, that resurrection will restore God's great plan for eternal fellowship with those who bear Jesus's image in the age to come. Death will not have the final answer, and sin will be quarantined and cut off as this age perishes. However, Paul has emphasized that the baptized possess a resurrected mind in the present. It is one of his most extraordinary, repeated, and important claims that the age to come and its eschatology have been inaugurated now. But *why*?

This is God's solution to sin where we are right now. The resurrected Jesus is the divine solution to death and to sin and to *present* sinning. Hallelujah!

---

as elaborated especially by Jubilees and Enoch, a notion also found at Qumran). This might suggest in turn explaining the origin of evil in Paul in terms of a "free will defense" in that specific location. The heavenly rulers or powers chose at some point to turn away from God. However, I would not myself appeal to that account of freedom, with its liberal presuppositions, or to that explanation ultimately of evil. On grounds of both ambiguity and theological inference, I would suggest making a further inference in terms of *Sachkritik* to an agnostic account closer to Barth's analysis of evil in terms of "the Not-ness," or sheer negation (*CD* III/3, §50). This view eschews the need to attribute an origin to evil, since causality and explanation presuppose the good created categories of rationality and order, which evil, in effect, lacks and attacks. Evil is at bottom negation, erosion, and absence. As such, it lacks coherence, origin, and rationale. And perhaps appeal could be made here to the creation narrative arguably threaded through the Tanakh of God's conquest of chaos, and of the monster of chaos, Leviathan. The battle with disorder presupposed by various texts is, I would suggest, an excellent complement to Paul's explanation of sin and evil at its most fundamental level. (These topics are treated in more detail in ch. 23.)

The Solution to Sin

There is a sense in which God could have waited to resolve our problems by resurrecting us only after we die and lifting us then into the age to come. This sequence would eliminate sin, exclude evil, and re-create the cosmos in the fellowship that it was destined for. But in the meantime it would leave us struggling away where we are, in the old cosmos. Jesus's resurrection would certainly give us hope. We would know that death will not have the last word, and the coming of the future age will be assured. But the gift to us now of a part of the age to come in the form of a re-created mind brings the re-creation of that age into our current situation. The result is that we can live and act in an obedient, peaceful, and loving way within the old age, immediately. Put a little more technically, we can say that under this arrangement, God gifts us with agency, which is to say, with the ability or capacity to act rightly, which previously we lacked. So we are not left alone. We are helped and supported—and in fact re-created—before the age to come arrives in all its fullness, in an act of great kindness on God's part (Gal 2:21).

There are two distinguishable but ultimately inseparable parts to this solution, however, that we now need to think about a little more deeply. First, Jesus assumes our nature of Flesh, executes it on the cross, then travels through death to resurrection life, rising in a new, cleansed, and liberated condition. So, as Paul puts it pithily in Rom 4:25, "He was delivered for our transgressions and raised for our deliverance." Second, we are somehow connected to his journey, concretely, so that the termination and resurrection he experienced are determinative for us as well. In particular, we gain access to the mind of the risen Jesus, which has been remade beyond the contamination of sin and the corruption of death.

We see Paul talking about all these aspects of the solution fairly frequently in his letters. We have already described Jesus's journey through death in the previous chapter. The only detail we need to add here is the evidence that his death was an execution of our contaminated Flesh. He entered into our condition—the technical term is that he *assumed* it—and so our Flesh died on the cross with him and was terminated there. "One on behalf of all died, therefore all died," Paul states in 2 Cor 5:14b, reiterating in verse 21a that "the one not knowing sin was made sin for us." Paul basically indicates this work of Jesus on our behalf whenever he says that Christ died "for us" (or in some subtle variation on this).[9] He also says that Jesus carries our burdens. So, sim-

---

9. Romans 4:25; 5:6, 8; 8:3–4, 32; 14:15; 1 Cor 8:11; 11:24; 15:3–4; 2 Cor 5:14–15; Gal 1:4; 3:13; Eph 5:2, 25–27; 1 Thess 5:10 (see also 1 Cor 6:20; 7:23).

ilarly, when we carry burdens, we "fulfill the Torah that is Christ"; we follow a burden-bearing God.[10] Paul summarizes these insights neatly in Rom 8:3:[11]

For what the Torah was powerless to do
because it was weakened by the Flesh,
God did
by sending his own Son
in the exact form of sinful Flesh
to atone for sin.

It is worth pausing at this moment to grasp what this burden-bearing tells us about God. God does the right thing in refusing to extend life indefinitely to a cosmos that is contaminated by evil. (Of course, we don't really make this judgment of God's actions for ourselves; we learn that this is a correct judgment from those actions.) This refusal to endorse the ongoing existence of sin is the divine judgment on sin. The Flesh must spiral into the consequences of its turn away from God and be extinguished. In short, it must be allowed to die. But even as this judgment is followed implacably, *God takes this burden directly upon himself.* So God initiates judgment, frames its nature, and also makes a pathway through it, bearing it for us. Hence, in the midst of this judgment, God's actions are fundamentally covenantal. They remain the committed, unconditional actions of love. In the depths of judgment God journeys with us and beyond us on our behalf because he loves us. And he then is raised to new life, in a new form, so that we too might live.

Theologians have given us some key terms to talk about this saving work precisely. It is *vicarious* in the sense that it is something Jesus does for us. We do not experience and suffer the cross as he does. We can even speak of *substitution* here in a certain sense. But it is *participatory* in equal measure. Jesus assumes our condition for us, takes it upon himself, and in so doing takes *us* upon himself, so that our sinful nature can die in him and thereby pass through into the new life that lies beyond death in his resurrection.[12] We have to be a part of what happens to him on some level,

10. Romans 15:1–3; Gal 6:2 (see also 5:13–14; 1 Cor 9:21).

11. Romans 4:25; 5:6, 8; 8:3–4, 32; 14:15; 1 Cor 8:11; 11:24; 15:3–4; 2 Cor 5:14–15; Gal 1:4; 3:13; Eph 5:2, 25–27; 1 Thess 5:10 (see also 1 Cor 6:20; 7:23).

12. So the meanings of "vicarious" and "substitutionary" cannot be construed to the exclusion of participation or Paul's position is not being represented properly, and the model itself *won't work.* We *must* participate in Christ's death and resurrection, in

or the whole thing just doesn't work—which leads us to consider briefly the second part of the solution in a little more detail.

We are part of Jesus's journey and new life. We are not resurrected entirely, and we will talk shortly about the tensions this apparent partiality generates; *but our resurrection has begun.* Paul is quite clear on this point. His favorite way of expressing it is by saying that we are "in Christ" (or some similar wording). He uses this expression upward of 160x in his letters, and often in highly strategic locations.[13] So at the end of Rom 6, 7, and 8, he writes:

---

some sense, if we are to be transformed and thereby gain the ethical capacity that we so desperately need.

13. Not all of these phrases are equally pregnant with theological meaning, but many are. The classic study was by G. A. Deissmann, *Saint Paul: A Study in Social and Religious History* (London: Hodder & Stoughton, 1912); but also critically important was W. Wrede, *Paul*, trans. Edward Lummis (Boston: American Unitarian Association, 1908); and Albert Schweitzer, *Paul and His Interpreters,* trans. W. Montgomery (New York: Schocken, 1964 [1912]); Albert Schweitzer, *The Mysticism of Paul the Apostle,* trans. W. Montgomery (Baltimore: Johns Hopkins University Press, 1998 [1931]).

The view was then picked up by English-speaking scholarship. See in particular James Stewart, *A Man in Christ: The Vital Elements of St. Paul's Religion* (London: Hodder & Stoughton, 1935); and Morna Hooker, "Interchange in Christ," *JTS* 22 (1971): 349–61; and "Interchange and Atonement," *BJRL* 60 (1978): 462–81.

A recent important and prolific advocate of the importance of participation is Michael J. Gorman; see his article "Romans: The First Christian Treatise on Theosis," and his four books *Cruciformity* (2001), *Inhabiting the Cruciform God* (2009), *The Death of the Messiah and the Birth of the New Covenant* (2014), and *Becoming the Gospel* (2015). His most important studies have now been gathered together and published as *Participating in Christ* (Grand Rapids: Baker Academic, 2019).

More recent treatments by other American scholars also include M. David Litwa, "2 Cor 3:18 and Its Implications for Theosis," *JTI* 2 (2008): 117–34; and *We Are Being Transformed: Deification in Paul's Soteriology,* BZNW 187 (Berlin: de Gruyter, 2012); Constantine R. Campbell, *Paul and Union with Christ: An Exegetical and Theological Study* (Grand Rapids: Zondervan, 2012); and Ben C. Blackwell, *Christosis: Pauline Soteriology in Light of Deification in Irenaeus and Cyril of Alexandria,* WUNT 2.314 (Tübingen: Mohr [Siebeck], 2011). Robert C. Tannehill provides an elegant summary in "Participation in Christ: A Central Theme in Pauline Soteriology," in *The Shape of the Gospel: New Testament Essays* (Eugene, OR: Cascade, 2007), 223–37. An important recent summary volume is *"In Christ" in Paul: Explorations in Paul's Theology of Union and Participation,* ed. Kevin J. Vanhoozer, Constantine R. Campbell, and Michael J. Thate, WUNT 2.384 (Tübingen: Mohr Siebeck, 2015).

For the wages of sin is death,
but the gift of God is eternal life
in Christ Jesus our Lord. (6:23)

What a wretched man I am!
Who will rescue me from this body that is subject to death?
Thanks be to God, who delivers me *through Jesus Christ our Lord*!
So then, I myself in my mind am a slave to God's Torah,
but in my sinful nature a slave to the Torah associated with sin.
Therefore, there is now no condemnation for those who are *in Christ
    Jesus,*
because *in Christ Jesus* the "Torah" of the Spirit who gives life
has set me free from the Torah associated with sin and death. (7:24–8:2)

For I am convinced that neither death nor life,
neither heavenly messengers nor rulers,
neither the present nor the future,
neither any powers—neither height nor depth—nor anything else in all
    creation,
will be able to separate us from the love of God
that is *in Christ Jesus our Lord.* (8:38–39)

Both the cosmic spread of God's work in Jesus and its creative depths are signaled by the way Paul opposes this life in Christ to life as it is shaped by Adam, something he articulates especially in 1 Cor 15.

But Christ has indeed been raised from the dead,
the firstfruits of those who have fallen asleep.
For since death came through a man,
the resurrection of the dead comes also through a man.
For as in Adam all die,
so *in Christ* all will be made alive. (vv. 20–22)

And later in the chapter:

It is written: "The first person Adam became a living being" [Gen. 2:7];

We will supply important further categories to understand Paul's conceptuality here in due course, largely in part 2, ch. 10.

the last Adam, a life-giving spirit.
The spiritual did not come first, but the natural, and after that the
spiritual.
The first person was of the dust of the earth; the second person is of
heaven.
As was the earthly person, so are those who are of the earth;
and as is the heavenly person, so also are those who are of heaven.
And just as we have borne the image of the earthly person,
so shall we bear the image of the heavenly person. (vv. 45–49)

One of Paul's most famous and compact statements of this identification with Jesus is made in Gal 2:19-20. If readers miss the strong sense in which Paul is claiming to be part of Jesus's death and resurrection, this text can be a little puzzling. Once that identification has been grasped, however, then Paul's dramatic claims make complete sense.

I have been crucified with Christ and I no longer live,
but Christ lives in me.
The life I now live in the body,
I live by means of believing—the believing of the Son of God,
who loved me and gave himself up for me. (NIV modified)[14]

Baptism

Baptism is an important marker for the vital matters that we are discussing here, provided it is correctly understood. I am not referring to the questions of whether it is efficacious in its own right, its exact technique, and so on, interesting as these inquiries are. The single point we need to grasp here is that baptism denotes a concrete transformation in the baptized, coding that transformation explicitly in terms of rising from the dead. Baptism enacts our death and resurrection in Jesus. Paul's most extensive treatment can be found, as is often the case, in the second major section of Romans, specifically in chapter 6, although we don't need to dive into too much detail here.

In Rom 6 Paul is appealing to the ritual as it was practiced in the early church, in which people were immersed under water. Moreover, it seems that

14. Believing is discussed extensively, and this Christocentric reading explained, in ch. 13.

converts took off their clothes beforehand, being immersed naked, and then clothed with new garments that were possibly a gift from the community. Most people in the ancient world owned only one set of clothes, the generally ragged and dirty set they were standing in, so a gift of clothing would have been clean and fresh and rather special.[15] But in Rom 6 Paul does not interpret this ritual in terms of cleansing, which water and clean clothes might first suggest. It *is* these things, but it is also more. The immersion is a participation in the death, burial, and resurrection of Jesus. "Are you ignorant that whoever has been immersed into Christ Jesus has been immersed into his death?" (6:3). To go under the water is to die with Christ and to be buried with him, while to rise out of the water is to be raised from the dead and to ascend with him to new life.

> We were therefore buried with him through immersion into death
> in order that, just as Christ was raised from the dead through the glory
>   of the Father,
> we too may live a new life.
> For if we have been united with him in a death like his,
> we will certainly also be united with him in a resurrection like his.
> For we know that our old self was crucified with him
> so that the body ruled by sin might be done away with,
> that we should no longer be slaves to sin—
> because the one who has died has been set free from sin. (6:4–7)

The ritual clearly denotes these concrete realities within the life of converts, and Paul is emphasizing these dimensions because the reality of Jesus's journey within their own lives is the basis of their new Christian behavior. They are to understand, Paul declares in verse 11, that to have been immersed "*is* to be dead on the one hand to sin, but living on the other hand to God in Christ Jesus." This new reality, enacted in baptism, is the ground of Paul's ethic.

Of course, there is an obvious sense in which converts are not yet fully resurrected. A future aspect of resurrection is still apparent. Paul notes this, among other places, in Rom 8.

> If [the Spirit of] Christ is in you,
> on the one hand, the body is dead because of sin,

---

15. See Gal 3:27.

but, on the other, the spirit is living because of God's righteous
    deliverance.[16]
Hence,
if the Spirit of the one who raised Jesus from the dead lives in you,
then the one who raised Christ Jesus from the dead
will also make your mortal bodily parts alive
by means of his Spirit dwelling in you. (vv. 10–11)

But this resurrection, although future in part, is not entirely so. Paul goes on
to speak of its present effect as well. This is the point of the first third of the
chapter.

Those who are led by the Spirit of God—these people—are sons of
    God. . . .
You *have* received a Spirit of sonship,
by means of whom we cry "Abba, Father." (8:14–15)

It is this cry in the present, in the Spirit, that guarantees a future fullness of
resurrection. At the very same moment, it is the Spirit, present alongside our
spirits, who allows us to live obedient lives now, a point Paul has emphasized
from verse 1 onward. We "walk" according to the Spirit he says in verse 4,
which is a Jewish expression for living obedient lives following the pathway
laid down by God's teachings. And shortly he adds, "The mind of the Spirit
is life and peace. . . . Therefore, we are obliged . . . to put the practices of the
body to death" (vv. 6, 13).

We might need to pause here in order to appreciate what radical moves
Paul has just made.

First, he has brought resurrection into the present, although, strictly
speaking, he didn't do this; God did it, and Paul recognized it.[17]

Second, he has thereby grasped that participation in Jesus has ethical
force. Those who live a new life in Jesus now, beyond death, also live beyond an
existence of Flesh, possessing the very different resurrected and reconstituted
mind of the Spirit. Their Flesh has been executed, and they live out of a new

16. The reasoning behind this translation was noted earlier.
17. I will talk later at length about the personal and communal journey Paul went
on, driven primarily by the Spirit, that led to these realizations; this is also extremely
important. But for now we need to grasp just the theological contours of Paul's astonishingly insightful and important realizations.

mind of peace and can act accordingly. The details and implications of this new reality will occupy our discussion now for quite some time.

Third, he has highlighted and, if it were possible, reinforced, the depth of God's love for us. More clearly than ever, we see in Jesus's death on our behalf, and in his resurrection on the third day following, just how much God cares for, and is involved with us. The one who must judge our sinful world has entered into that world and borne the appropriate judgment on that world for all of us himself.

Fourth, he has given us further critical reasons to resist telling the story of salvation forward and to stick resolutely to a retrospective, backward narration. It is clearer than ever at this moment why backward storytelling—the story of salvation as memoir—is so vital.

The Story of Addiction

We can now see, in view of Jesus's liberation of our minds from the Flesh and its entangling sinful dynamics, that our past is caught up in thinking that is corrupt. If we adopt a foundationalist approach, then, telling our story forward, not only do we roll over the top of the revelation that is Jesus, structuring his solution to a problem we must have defined for ourselves in advance, thereby defining the solution for ourselves as well; tangled up with sin, we set up an account of God in advance of God's definitive revelation to us. Our accounts will be seduced and deceived by the powers, and that can't be good! There is a relatively simple analogy for this situation that can help us.

We can now see that we are telling the story of Jesus, broadly speaking, in the way that addicts recount the stories of their recoveries. These are stories that make complete sense only when their tellers look backward on their past. They are stories that pivot on a definitive revelation—the step from full addiction to being clean, with its attendant clarity. And they are stories that emphatically do not make sense before these moments of clarification and reflection. Prior to these moments any storytelling tends to be self-serving and destructive.[18]

---

18. There is a fundamental analogy here. But there is also a danger in pressing this too far. First, many Jesus followers do not retrace the specific and frequently painful steps of the substance abuser in recovery, and those narratives of recovery need to retain their own particularity. Second, the moment of revelation need not be a memorable and literally single moment. It can be, but it can also be a journey with various important steps forward (and backward). Third, substance abuse is a variegated phenomenon affecting different people in differtent ways. Some people

Let us suppose that I have just made it through a successful rehab program. Supported by a generous and honest community—perhaps a local meeting of Alcoholics Anonymous—I have beaten my habit (although as experienced AA members would add, at least for now). And one of the most striking features of my recovery is my new ability to tell a truthful story about my past struggles.

I now begin my story confessionally, with the acknowledgment that I am at present free, although I can see that in and of myself, I am an addict. Then I recount my tragic former biography in these terms—how I fought a long battle with alcohol. I describe how alcohol effectively controlled me, leading to deeply destructive and tragic activity. Because of the constant need to find money to buy a drink, I damaged all my close relationships badly, lying to and stealing from those I loved. Fortunately, because of the 12-step program, the support and penetrating honesty of my buddy and my group, and a long period of time with my mind free of the abusive substance itself, I am seeking to rebuild the trust within the important relationships I have damaged. And I am beginning to see things clearly, as they really took place.

But of course I did not tell this story prior to entering rehab, when I was in the grip of my habit. Then I spoke very differently. I never said at that time, in the full throes of alcoholism, that I was an addict, out of control, and enslaved. I said the very opposite. "I am in control of my drinking and doing just what I want," I would assert; "In fact, I'm having the best time of my life. No one is getting badly hurt by my behavior. It's just harmless fun. And I can give it up any time I want to. I'm not like those sad alcoholics over there."

Of course, with a mind clarified by rehab and free from the distortions of the drug itself, this narrative is revealed to be utterly delusional. In many respects it is the very opposite of the truth, while its very dishonesty masks the deeply destructive activity that is going on in tandem with its callous legitimations. It is a false and deceptive account of my former life—although narrated from within the midst of that life. And converts are all in the same basic position as this substance abuser.

We can look back with minds being clarified by the Spirit and tell a more

---

are, to speak generally, inclined to abuse substances for fundamentally circumstantial reasons, which can be dire but are contingent. Others have particular addictive propensities in their brain chemistry, which means that the battle and the solution take on different dimensions.

honest story about our previous activity. We can see where our constant col-laboration with sin has led to destructive behavior, and where this activity has been intertwined with destructive thinking. And we confess now both the center of our lives and the key point of our developing clarity, namely, Jesus, and our commitment to letting his clarity penetrate more deeply into our distorted and twisted minds, aided by the Spirit, showing us, among other things, how destructive and broken we are.[19]

There is something in this whole contention that is very redolent of Au-gustine. We will have frequent cause in what follows to gauge the influence of this towering intellectual figure in the Christian West on Paul's interpretation. Here I am going to strongly affirm it. Although Augustine converted to Chris-tianity in 386 CE at the age of thirty-one, it was only later on, from 397, that we see the development of a deep sense of his own sinfulness. Then, around 400 CE, fourteen years after his conversion, he wrote one of the most famous accounts of sinfulness ever penned, *The Confessions*. My best friend from my teenage years, while training to be a banker and, like me, a new Christian at the time, told me that this book captured his own spiritual struggles at the time exactly. This sense of personal incapacity continued into Augustine's later reflections, when he trenchantly opposed the optimism of Pelagius and affirmed the centrality of God's activity. What we see here is the clarification that Augustine experienced as his mind was cleansed, and the resulting need on his part to retell and to redescribe the events that led up to his conversion and ministry—to provide an explicitly retrospective but also a far more accu-rate account of his past, of his conversion, and of his underlying nature. Any account of sin, in short, must be undertaken *in a confessional mode*. Looking back, in the light of Christ, we *confess* our previous actions to be sinful, and we generally know rather better than we did before just what to confess.

But the first Augustinian was of course Paul, and I suspect that he came face-to-face with his sin very early on in his apostolic career.[20] Paul is refresh-ingly honest about his past mistakes. Prior to the revelation of Jesus to him

19. As we will see later, we can tell the same sort of story more broadly about Jesus in relation to history and to his people; we are, after all, all substance abusers, or as the Bible puts it, sinners and idolaters. Without Jesus, we risk not getting this story right either.

20. Krister Stendahl wrote a classic essay on how the interpretation of Paul is overly influenced by Augustine and Luther—"Paul and the Introspective Conscience of the West." I agree with a great deal that he says but do still see similarities between Paul, Augustine, and Luther in this particular dynamic. Stendahl's broader case against their influence is not affected by this qualification.

on the road to Damascus, Paul, known to everyone then as Saul, was a deeply devout servant of God, but he understood that status to mean being prepared to kill on God's behalf—something that is still a mark of religious zeal in some parts of the world. Moreover, his targets at this time were Jesus followers.[21]

It is important to let the full gravity of this behavior sink in. Paul belonged to a religiously motivated death squad, to a terrorist cell. Like some terrorists, he was completely sold out for God and was clearly working hard to do God's work. But the revelation on the road to Damascus of God's very nature in the person of Jesus Christ revealed in the same moment the utter, total, and complete misdirection of his zeal. Instead of accelerating ahead of the pious crowd, winning the race for Jewish virtue, Paul was deeply and profoundly mistaken about God, God's nature, and God's purposes—so much so that he was zealously opposing God, fighting against the very God he thought that he was serving. This all became apparent no doubt when God was revealed to Paul in Jesus on the road to Damascus. From this event onward Paul's story changes dramatically, including his account of his past. The zealous Pharisee is a zealous *misdirected* Pharisee. The one viewing Jesus then in a merely "fleshly" or "human" way does so no longer but sees him as the very creator inaugurating the glories of the age to come (2 Cor 5:16–17).

This must have been a humbling moment, and I doubt that Paul ever forgot the way that his own zeal had misled him. He now realized that in and of himself he had nothing to offer God and was in fact deeply twisted in his understanding of his Lord. The God revealed in Jesus Christ judged his activity and exposed its corruption. And the result was a Paul who speaks very much like our substance abuser. He was now able to look back on his previous life with a mind clarified by this revelation and to see where his previous activity—which looked entirely reasonable, if not praiseworthy, at the time—was in fact profoundly distorted and destructive. Moreover, the story he now tells retrospectively, after the fact, is the correct one. It is the story clarified by the gift of truth in Jesus. As we have already noted, "Whatever I previously considered gain or advantageous, I now consider, in the light of Christ and in comparison to him, loss. Indeed, compared with the surpassing wonder of Christ I consider everything as mere excrement!" (Phil 3:7–8).

Every story that we tell about what precedes the arrival of Jesus in our sinful lives up to that arrival now needs to be told in this way. Moreover, we need to cleave to this practice faithfully and vigilantly because of the subtle trap that lurks here for the unwary—ourselves! If we tell this story in its other main

21. See 1 Cor 15:9; Gal 1:13; see also Acts 8:1, 3; 9:1–3.

fashion, forward—and they can look so similar—we unleash the horsemen of the foundationalist apocalypse and now realize *that we do so deliberately,* deceived by our Flesh. Consequently, we must learn to craft our stories epiphanically, and hence backward, *in a confessional mode,* like the testimony of the alcoholic emerging into sobriety. This is how Augustine learned to speak, and how Paul himself also learned to talk several centuries before him.

With this reinforcement of our retrospective purview on the past in place, we are ready to turn back to the question of the present. God has broken into our situation and has freed us from our twisted and addicted minds of Flesh so that we can begin to think more clearly about him and simply to respond more obediently to him. We have the mind of the resurrected Christ, Paul says (1 Cor 2:16). But important challenges arise as we make this claim, and we can go no further until they have been squarely faced and dealt with, and they are not inconsiderable.

Theses

▸ According to Paul, *we are* in some sense presently resurrected within Jesus.

▸ In particular, we have the mind of the risen Jesus and can live at peace.

▸ This contrasts with an unresurrected mind.

▸ Paul explains this contrasting, conflicted mind by using two stories: Gen 3 and the powers (i.e., fallen and evil heavenly rulers under the overall control of Satan).

▸ Romans 7 argues that the dynamics of Gen 3 are operative within when someone tries to obey Scriptures like the tenth commandment. Something he calls Sin here deceives us, leading to disobedience, and ultimately it enslaves us, leading to repeated disobedience.

▸ This disobedience must incur the judgment of death.

▸ It is a state Paul denotes as Flesh.

▸ Hence the mind of the Flesh is characterized by conflict, both internally and toward God.

▸ Sin is most likely a dramatization of the presence and evil suggestions of the "desires," or "lusts," present in the Flesh since Adam.

▸ Romans 8 suggests that the powers also assault human nature from without. These evil beings, possibly fallen angels, led by Satan, constantly attempt to deceive and to attack humanity.

▸ God solves this situation for us presently, in two ways.

> First, Jesus takes up our condition of Flesh, executes it, then is raised from the dead in a new form, liberated from Sin's lusts and free from a world where the powers roam.

> Paul speaks clearly of what Jesus has done for us here in assuming our sinful Flesh, and he speaks in addition of how Jesus carries our burdens.

> This judges our sinful condition by terminating it and provides a new form for humanity that is free from infiltration and occupation by sinful lusts.

> Second, we are concretely joined or connected to Jesus's journey in some way, so that we possess a resurrected mind now.

> Paul's favorite expression for this connection is that we are "in Christ." But he also speaks of how we are caught up in a new creation that is superior to Adam's and is spiritual as against earthly.

> This resurrection must, to some degree, be present. As such, and only as such, it has ethical force.

> This all speaks of the divine love for us clearly as well, although to a near incomprehensible level. God judges sin, refusing to extend life to it, but he also takes that judgment upon himself and bears it in order to create a pathway out of it.

> The claim that we are concretely transformed in Jesus is expressed by the ritual of baptism; see especially Rom 6:1–11.

> The difficulties of thinking clearly with a mind of Flesh reinforce the importance of telling any story of salvation backward, or retrospectively.

> The account of our past telling the story forward is like the accounts substance abusers like alcoholics provide while they are still involved with substance abuse—in the case noted here, with alcohol; they are deeply distorted.

> Only with a clarified mind, looking back, can the story approach accuracy.

> Augustine attests to this approach to appropriate storytelling with his famous retelling of his conversion in *Confessions*.

> We can detect this posture in Paul too—a profound lack of confidence in the insights he had before he was called to follow Jesus on the road to Damascus.

> He probably learned about the misguided nature of his past fleshly life when he reflected on the evil of his persecution of Jesus's followers prior to his call.

Key Scriptural References

Paul's underlying explanation of sinning in terms of Gen 3 (i.e., the story of Adam and Eve in the garden), developing into an account of humanity imprisoned within the Flesh and its sinful lusts, is anticipated by Rom 5:12–21, especially verse 12, and articulated at length by Rom 7:7–25. The implications of 2 Cor 11:3 should also be noted. The role of the powers, attacking from without, then becomes apparent in Rom 8:31–39. We will nuance this interior/exterior analysis in due course; see especially chapter 23, although the move there in terms of *Sachkritik* is set up by chapter 7 and its analysis of time.

Second Corinthians 5:14 in context (vv. 14–21) is a key description of Jesus's vicarious work. Romans 4:25 and 8:3–4 are important and useful references in this relation too. Romans 4:25 speaks very clearly—in a probable echo of Isa 53—of Christ bearing our sin to death and terminating it there, and of his being resurrected to make the liberation of a new life free from sin possible for us as well. Christ's burden-bearing is succinctly spoken of in Gal 6:2, although Rom 8:3–4 also implies this directly.

The "in Christ" motif is ubiquitous in Paul. Examples are Rom 6:23; 7:24–8:2; 8:38–39; also 1 Cor 15:21–22, 45–49.

Paul's most extended account of baptism is supplied by Rom 6; the main claims are all made in verses 1–11.

Philippians 3:2–11 speaks clearly and most significantly of Paul's retrospective purview on his past.

The sheer deceptiveness of the Flesh was probably realized for Paul personally after his call on the road to Damascus exposed the misguided nature of his zealous persecution of Jesus followers. That activity is mentioned in 1 Cor 15:9 and Gal 1:13; see also Acts 8:1, 3; 9:1–3.

This turn can also be inferred from the shift from Paul persecuting Jesus followers to becoming a zealous advocate of the gospel. That activity is mentioned in 1 Cor 15:9 and Gal 1:13; see also Acts 8:1, 3; 9:1–3.

The hostile mind of the Flesh is noted in Rom 5:10 and 8:7. This contrasts with the peaceful resurrected mind; see Rom 8:6b and Phil 4:7.

Key Reading

A superb updating and development of the motif of the powers in particular conversation with Paul, and spanning both European/post-European and African contexts, is supplied by Robert Moses.

Further Reading

Barth's rich account of the work of Christ can be found largely in *CD* IV/1 and IV/2. Volume IV/1 describes the descent of Jesus into our humanity and his bearing of judgment on our behalf; vol. IV/2 describes the other side of Jesus's work. His incarnation begins an assumption of humanity that lifts it up further, in the resurrection, into a new, transformed life, enthroning it on high with God. In Christ we also ascend.

The whole notion of atonement in Paul—a word itself that needs to be used *very* carefully—is poorly handled, in my experience, by scholars and preachers alike, partly because it is usually derived from an incorrect, foundationalist account of Paul's gospel. We have emphatically rejected that broad approach here and are pursuing an orthodox and Christocentric account, of which, rather sadly, there are very few trustworthy summaries. Background motifs are discussed with delightful erudition by Stephen Chapman, although they need to be used very carefully when deployed in relation to Paul, under the control of Christology, and not vice versa. Colin Gunton makes useful preliminary remarks. My account of Paul links hands here with a classic critique by Gustaf Aulén of the usual approach, assisted by the church fathers. This critique requires supplementation but is on the right track.

Some of the scholars who emphasize participation in Paul were listed in note 13. This critical category will be deepened in the chapters that follow, especially 8, 9, and 10.

Accounts of baptism are ten a penny, but theologically perceptive accounts of baptism are rather rarer; see, however, powerful theological essays by Curtis Freeman ("One Lord, One Faith, One Baptism," chapter 9 in *Contesting Catholicity*), and Emmanuel Katongole.

The standard analysis of the powers is a three-volume treatment by Walter Wink. A classic application of the powers to the US context is provided by William Stringfellow (who greatly impressed Barth on his visit to the US). Having noted this important work, however, I would add that it must be utilized with caution. The appeal to "structures" as vehicles for the powers risks sliding into a revolutionary discourse that demonizes particular groups of people, and often in an undifferentiated binary fashion, which is *not* a Pauline analytic. Chuck Campbell provides an insightful and critical corrective to frequent popular use of this material by insisting on an explanatory threshold; condemnation of the powers must not step across into a blanket condemnation of people (see his *Word before the Powers* below, esp. 91–92; Paul makes much the same point in 2 Cor 10:5). The underlying theological justification for this vital insight will be emphasized here shortly, and its practical outworking developed more in part 3, when we begin to discuss mission in more detail.

Bibliography

Augustine. *The Confessions*. Translated by H. Chadwick. Oxford: Oxford University Press, 1992.

Aulén, Gustaf. *Christus Victor*. London: SPCK, 1953.

Barth, Karl. *Christ and Adam: Man and Humanity in Romans 5*. Translated by Tom A. Smail. New York: Collier, 1962.

———. *Church Dogmatics*. III/1; III/2; IV/1; IV/2.

Campbell, Charles. *The Word before the Powers: An Ethic of Preaching*. Louisville: Westminster John Knox, 2002.

Campbell, Douglas A. *The Quest for Paul's Gospel: A Suggested Strategy*. London: T&T Clark, 2005.

Chapman, Stephen. "God's Reconciling Work: Atonement in the Old Testament." Pages 95–114 in *T&T Clark Companion on the Atonement*. Edited by Adam J. Johnson. New York: T&T Clark, 2019.

Davies, W. D. *Paul and Rabbinic Judaism: Some Rabbinic Elements in Pauline Theology*. 4th ed. Philadelphia: Fortress, 1980 (1948).

Freeman, Curtis. *Contesting Catholicity: Theology for Other Baptists*. Waco, TX: Baylor University Press, 2014.

Gorman, Michael J. *Becoming the Gospel: Paul, Participation, and Mission*. Grand Rapids: Eerdmans, 2015.

———. *Cruciformity: Paul's Narrative Spirituality of the Cross*. Grand Rapids: Eerdmans, 2001.

———. *The Death of the Messiah and the Birth of the New Covenant: A (Not So) New Model of the Atonement*. Eugene, OR: Cascade, 2014.

———. *Inhabiting the Cruciform God: Kenosis, Justification, and Theosis in Paul's Narrative Soteriology*. Grand Rapids: Eerdmans, 2009.

———. "Romans: The First Christian Treatise on Theosis." *JTI* 5 (2011): 13–34.

Gunton, Colin. *The Actuality of the Atonement: A Study of Metaphor, Rationality, and the Christian Tradition*. Edinburgh: T&T Clark, 1998.

Katongole, Emmanuel. "Greeting: Beyond Racial Reconciliation." Pages 68–81 in *The Blackwell Companion to Christian Ethics*. Edited by Stanley Hauerwas and Samuel Wells. Oxford: Blackwell, 2006.

Longenecker, Richard N. *Paul, Apostle of Liberty*. 2nd ed. Grand Rapids: Eerdmans, 2015.

Marcus, Joel. "The Evil Inclination in the Epistle of James." *CBQ* 44 (1982): 606–21.

Martin, Dale B. "Paul without Passion: On Paul's Rejection of Desire in Sex and Marriage." Pages 65–76 in *Sex and the Single Savior: Gender and Sexuality in Biblical Interpretation*. Louisville: Westminster John Knox, 2006.

Martyn, J. Louis. *Galatians: A New Translation, with Introduction and Commentary*. AB 33A. New York: Doubleday, 1997.

Moses, Robert Ewusie. *Practices of Power: Revisiting the Principalities and Powers in the Pauline Letters*. Minneapolis: Fortress, 2014.

Stringfellow, William. *An Ethic for Christians and Other Aliens in a Strange Land*. Waco, TX: Word, 1973.

Wink, Walter. *Engaging the Powers: Discernment and Resistance in a World of Domination*. Philadelphia: Fortress, 1992.

———. *Naming the Powers: The Language of Power in the New Testament*. Philadelphia: Fortress, 1984.

———. *Unmasking the Powers: The Invisible Forces That Determine Human Existence*. Philadelphia: Fortress, 1986.

CHAPTER 7

Defending Resurrection

Partial Resurrection in Philippians

The challenges we must now face emerge as we think about the fact that our current state is *partially* resurrected. This puzzling partiality is clear if we draw a quick summary of our present situation from Paul's letter to the Philippians.

Paul's main concern in Philippians is captured by the verse that begins the famous passage that has informed much of our discussion thus far: "Think this among yourselves, which is also in Christ Jesus," Paul writes in 2:5, going on in verses 6–8 to describe Jesus's self-effacement in the incarnation and the crucifixion. This emphasis in verse 5 on the centrality of the mind of Jesus to right behavior is then found in many other places in the letter. Paul details in 4:7 how "the peace of Christ, which exceeds [that of] every mind, will guard your hearts and your thoughts in Christ Jesus." We infer from elsewhere that this peace is derived by way of "fellowship with the Spirit" (2:1), as well as through "fellowship with [Jesus's] sufferings," "conformity to his death," and "knowing the power of his resurrection" (3:10). It is apparent, then, that Paul constantly urges his Philippian converts to live out of the mind of Jesus, available through the Spirit, expecting this factor to concretely change a congregation that seems to be threatened with internal fracture. "I beg Euodia and I beg Syntyche to think the same way in the Lord," he writes revealingly in 4:2. By way of contrast, he points to the practical embodiment of the humble and sacrificial mind of Jesus present in Epaphroditus, Timothy, and himself (2:19–30; 3:17).

As a result of these pointers, we can see that most of the ethical admonitions Paul writes to the Philippians will be eviscerated if we overlook the reality of the present resurrected mind of Jesus within them, available through the work of the Spirit. But—and herein lies the rub—it is also clear that something still has to happen. The Philippians, along with Paul himself, "eagerly await a savior, the Lord Jesus Christ," who, appearing from heaven one day, "will transform our lowly bodies, conforming them to his glorious body by the working of his power" (3:20–21). Meanwhile, Paul labors away in his present body, which is so obviously vulnerable to suffering and death (1:20, 22, 24). Fortunately, his present experience of resurrection, even if it is partial, allows him to be impressively unconcerned by the prospect of imminent execution. If he dies, he will be with Jesus in an even more intimate way than he is now and will thereby leave behind this body of Flesh with all its troubles (1:21, 23). But in the meantime, he still has a body of Flesh with all its troubles, which includes the fracturing Philippian community.

If we combine these data with what we have already assembled, we end up with an interesting picture. The baptized, according to Paul, presently exist in two ways simultaneously. We are made of Flesh—a sorry situation, the difficulties of which we have already briefly outlined. We live in vulnerable, mortal bodies that die, largely because we think fleshly thoughts and sin. *At the same time*, we possess a resurrected *mind* from Jesus and the Spirit. This is a very different mind from the mind of the Flesh, being attuned to the concerns of God and at peace in following those. It is a sharing in Jesus's resurrected and reconstituted mind that has left its struggles well behind (so this is quite a gift). On one occasion, Paul describes its construction out of "spirit" (thereby leaving us with a few further puzzles to solve in due course).[1] Meanwhile, we await the loss of our bodies of Flesh, along with the mind, and the receipt of a glorious new spiritual body.[2] We lose our bodies and minds of Flesh either when we die or when Jesus returns in glory, whichever happens first.

Paul elaborates in some of his other letters on the distinctive characteristics of this awkward interim period in which those with a resurrected mind await a resurrected body. It is a place of some tension.

He speaks at times of the constriction he feels, including "the daily pressure that is my anxiety for all [my] congregations" (2 Cor 11:28). And he references the "agony" of living in a fleshly, not a spiritual, body: "We groan, longing to be

1. First Corinthians 15:35–50; see especially vv. 42b–44: "The body that is sown is perishable, it is raised imperishable; it is sown in dishonor, it is raised in glory; it is sown in weakness, it is raised in power; it is sown a natural body, it is raised a spiritual body." But see also Rom 8:16; 1 Thess 5:23.

2. Paul also speaks of an "inner" and an "outer" person in this relation in 2 Cor 4:16 (and possibly in Eph 3:16 as well). He uses the same phraseology in Rom 7:22, 23, and 25, although I am not sure that in that context it means the same thing. There it seems to be describing the divisions within a person made of Flesh. The fleshly, inner mind is positive, but it is in thrall to "members" that are enslaved to lusts. That is, I don't think this terminology is used systematically by Paul. It is a semantic resource—"Hellenistic street psychology"—that he deploys as he needs to.

clothed with our dwelling from heaven" (2 Cor 5:2), a pain that all of creation shares (Rom 8:22–25). However, Paul denotes the vulnerabilities and struggles of this situation most frequently by speaking of "weakness" (Gk. *astheneia*).[3] Fortunately, the Spirit is a "deposit," or "down payment" (2 Cor 1:22; 5:5; Eph 1:13–14; 4:30), who brings gifts and virtues in the present (Rom 12:3–8; 1 Cor 12 and 14; Gal 5:22–23), thereby guaranteeing the perfected state that lies ahead. We have already seen Rom 8:9–11 speak of this guarantee. Hence, despite all the struggles, the presence of the Spirit now, in love, peace, and joy, brings "hope." Paul cannot exactly *see* all these resurrected realities, and certainly cannot yet see "the glorious freedom of the children of God" (8:21). This freedom will become apparent only after we have been liberated from our slavery to mortality on the great day of Jesus's return. All of creation is waiting for this moment— this flash of cosmic revelation—but it isn't here yet. So Paul perseveres through the present faithfully, in hope. "For in hope we were saved; and hope that is visible isn't hope, for who hopes for something visible? But when we hope for something which we can't see, we wait for it with perseverance" (8:24).[4]

Paul's basic position can be depicted as follows:

		Death or Jesus's
The past:	*Conversion and the present:*	*second coming:*
Fleshly mind	....	X (terminated)
Fleshly body	....	X (terminated)
	Spiritual mind	
		Spiritual body...

Meanwhile:
Suffering, pressure, vulnerability, weakness
Deposit of the Spirit, bringing virtues and gifts
Hope
Training, discipline (etc.)

We can probably see by this point how critical the power and reality of life in the resurrected Jesus are for Paul, right where we are, here and now. This gift is present by way of our new, resurrected minds. This is the heart of his ethic. It frees us from sin's grip.

---

3. We will develop a particular aspect of weakness much more in part 2—the necessary vulnerability that an incarnational approach to initiating relationships incurs, which Paul develops especially in his correspondence with Corinth (1 Cor 1:26–31; 2:1–5; 4:9–13; 2 Cor 1:3–11; 4:7–12; 11:21b–12:10; 13:3–4). But weakness is not reducible to this dynamic: see Rom 8:26–27.

4. See also especially 1 Cor 13:7, 13; Gal 5:5–6; Eph 1:15–20; Col 1:3–5; 1 Thess 1:3; 5:8.

Beyond Western Dualisms

It might be helpful to note at this moment that the intrusion of some common but profoundly problematic Western categories into our thinking might limit our grip on Paul's position here, especially as we try to think about the nature of this new, resurrected mind of spirit that he thinks we all possess. This is possibly a much more dramatic and significant dimension than we modern Westerners might tend to conceive of.[5]

Insofar as we are modern Westerners, we tend to view thoughts as separate from acts. We think, and then, in the light of this thought, we act. Moreover, we think in our heads, internally, and then go on to act "out there" in the world, through our bodies. "I think I should have my second cup of tea around about now. . . . But I should really finish editing this chapter first . . . but I can't be bothered, and it can wait. I am going to indulge myself." And so I rise from my chair, leave my office, go to the kitchen, and act; I make my cup of tea and sip it guiltily, in a classic instance of a thought-act sequence—except that every event here *is* an act, and several are not in a particularly ordered and rational sequence! That is, the distinction between thoughts and acts is clearly a strange notion once one reflects upon it. (Do thoughts float around in our heads like ghosts?) Thoughts *are* acts. (For this reason I will generally prefer the translation "believing" to "faith" when Paul uses this language [the root of both words is Gk. *pist-*], for "believing" suggests a more dynamic activity.)

But we modern Westerners also tend to operate with a being-act distinction that is equally odd. We often view being or existence in terms of static substances, and activity as something substances might do in addition to sitting still, or as something done to them by another substance. Reality viewed in these terms is a bit like a pool table. Hard balls of substance roll around in predictable lines after they have been struck by another ball of substance, making other little balls go in further lines, hopefully to disappear from view in a pocket. (This account is clearly influenced heavily in our day, and perhaps most perfectly exemplified, by the physics of Isaac Newton.) Balls of different colors "naturally" want to be at rest and don't do anything until something else does something *to* them. They don't do anything by themselves. Substances are static; dynamics are extraneous to being. Movement is something that happens

---

5. Gunton traces these incoherent but widely influential distinctions to the alienations and relational collapses of post-Enlightenment thinking; see his *Act and Being: Towards a Theology of the Divine Attributes*, along with his earlier work *Enlightenment and Alienation: An Essay toward a Trinitarian Theology*.

to substances. They don't move by themselves, which is really to suggest that they don't act.

But reality is not like this—not at all. The God revealed by Jesus, who walked faithfully to the cross, gives the lie to this modern Western perspective immediately, although I suspect that not a few modern physicists and environmentalists would support this correction as well, simply on the basis of their own research. God *acts* to become a human, who then journeys to the cross, and this is what he *is*, not to mention, who he is. He is as he acts, and relationships are obviously involved here as well. We learn here that *being, or existence, is active*. It is in movement in and of itself. *Reality is fundamentally dynamic.*[6]

We can now complete the circle. Thinking is acting; being is acting; and thinking is also being, which is to say, a new, dynamic, active sort of existence. To think differently is to act differently and consequently to be different. So it follows that when we recognize that we possess the mind of Jesus, we recognize that we possess an entirely new type of existence. Our new beliefs are not some small zone mainly comprising thoughts and a few pieces of information that reside somewhere in a person's brain that do not change what we actually are anywhere else, at least directly, but that we hope will eventually cause other things to happen by way of acts. Rather, *they denote a comprehensive claim about what a person actually is and what he or she does*, at which moment Paul's astonishing statement toward the end of Romans is now intelligible: "Everything that is not 'through believing' is sin" (14:23b).[7] Everything that does not proceed from the mind of Jesus within us by way of the Spirit—a mind that is, at least in large measure, an ongoing dynamic bundle of believing, acting, and existence—must by definition belong to the old world of the Flesh and consequently be sinful. To have the mind of Christ, with all its new beliefs, is to be a new person, as Paul said and as we noted a short time ago. We are a new creation.

But we now need to introduce a further correction to probable Western distortions that can sneak in at this moment.

We have pushed past the false convictions that thinking is separate from acting, and acting from being and existence. To have a new mind is to think differently, which is also to act differently, and this new acting is a new way of existing. But we now need to push past any notion that these wonderful new

---

6. For this reason I often use the word "dynamic(s)" in this book. When thinking about the shape or nature of active being—a being in motion, so to speak—we are basically describing dynamics. More old-fashioned, and regrettably misleading, discussions might speak instead of "properties" or "attributes."

7. The phrase "through believing" that is used here is an echo of Hab 2:4.

minds, with all their activities, are restricted to rationality and cognition, as many modern Western readers might also suppose. Another prejudicial Western dichotomy may have led us astray here too, between "rational" thoughts and emotions.

Scholars are increasingly beginning to realize that thinking without emotion is dead. Passions are intertwined with more rational thoughts, so to speak, so that human thinking is best understood as a complex synthesis of "affects" and other processes. Excitement, reasoning, logic, inference, anxiety, subliminal information, drives, and a large number of other things all intertwine and interact during our thinking, *and have to*. Thought is impossible without emotion. It has no reason to do anything, and it generally doesn't. For the body to act further, affects must be activated—by factors such as interest, fear, or anxiety—and then things happen. (Speaking precisely, we would say that thought *itself* will not take place unless an affect directs the attention of the mind to a certain set of stimuli.) And the new mind created by the risen Jesus is no different.

Believing for Paul, as for us, is caught up with emotions, although appropriately. It is a thinking that rejoices, although rejoicing in the right things, not the wrong ones. We tend to think of "joy" as an emotion or feeling, but to rejoice is actually to think something. If you doubt this, just try quickly to do some rejoicing without thought. So Paul speaks in biblical language in this relation of our hearts, a word he uses about fifty times, denoting how we feel within our broader thinking. And at the end of his letter to the Romans we can now understand why he prays for the Holy Spirit to gift Christians with hope, joy, and peace, in their thinking or believing (15:13). The new mind of Christians with all its new beliefs and thoughts is a hopeful, joyful, and peaceful way of thinking, so it is indeed a new mind for many of us, including all its properly ordered emotional dimensions. It is joyful and peaceful as it constantly does the right thing in a way that it couldn't before.

In what follows, we must be sensitive to connections between believing and what we might call emotions. Believing is not just a matter of thinking, narrowly construed. It is an entire mental landscape encompassing activities like reasoning, data processing, communicating, chattering, engaging, rejecting, worrying, exulting, moaning, glorying, enjoying, and relaxing.[8] But with

8. I am not going to supply an account here of the way that this new mind interacts with and through its embodiment in the Flesh; it will suffice to note that the new mind *is* embodied in our old bodies of Flesh and *does* act through them, although we will receive new spiritual bodies in due course. This account of the mind will be significantly developed when we discuss imitation in relation to "the second personal" perspective in part 2, ch. 10.

all these clarifications, we have arguably just made especially acute the challenge we face in this entire relation.

We clearly live in a state of *partial* resurrection, and things can get very difficult from this moment, especially for Paul's modern readers. We need to ask whether this gospel, which claims that we are presently resurrected in Jesus, at least in our minds, is fundamentally intelligible. Or is it simply insane, as Festus exclaimed rather understandably in Acts 26:24 (see also 2 Cor 5:13)? *The validity of Paul's entire gospel depends on whether we can respond plausibly to this challenge.*

Plausibility: Reality as Musical

Paul's claim that people are fundamentally resurrected in their minds and located in a new creation—minds bundling together activity, a new existence, and rightly ordered emotions—is strongly counterintuitive. Someone might object immediately that Paul's claim that a resurrected mind is present in Jesus followers is simply implausible in the face of so much sin and general nonsense. It cannot be the case that we have access to an unfettered ethical existence; such a claim is make-believe. We are surrounded by all sorts of tawdry transgression and sheer awfulness. The world is a mess. The news provides daily examples of pain, suffering, and unmitigated evil, in which Jesus followers also share. It seems clear, then, that we must wait for a future, perfected state to arrive on some blessed future day, along with a problem-free resurrected mind, because all we can see at the moment, including ourselves, is comprehensively and deeply fallen.

In a related way, someone might object that the suggestion that a resurrected mind is present, capable of obeying God peacefully and without difficulty, is functionally libertine. The claim that we possess a resurrected mind implies that Christians no longer sin; the sinful mind has been driven out. And this idea too is clearly implausible. Just go to a church and hang out there for a while! So, in something of an irony, this claim concerning a new, sinless mind leads, it is said, to a highly unethical situation in which Christians overlook the fact that they sin, and go on to sin both frequently and egregiously. "We do sin, and to deny that we do so is dangerous, so the resurrected mind be damned! It *can't* be the case, and it *shouldn't* be the case."

In short, someone might feel that the obvious fact of sin makes the presence of a resurrected mind in the baptized implausible, while someone else might fear that the supposed presence of a resurrected mind in the baptized implies sinlessness, which is not a little dangerous, so the presence of that cleansed and purified mind must once again be denied.

Fortunately, a solution to these particular anxieties lies just to hand. Zero-sum thinking lies at their base, and once we identify and move past it, they fade away. We can have a spiritual mind fully present *and* have a mind of Flesh present in full measure, at the same time, as well. This basic realization will not solve all our difficulties because some tough queries in relation to bodiliness still lie ahead of us, but it will solve some important challenges.

People shaped by modern Western culture tend to think about entities as occupying discrete, mutually exclusive spaces. Like oil and water in a bottle, different things (so we expect) separate out from one another and occupy different layers within broader reality. Things don't mix together.[9] Moreover, modern Westerners are biased toward visual, ocular metaphors. When we think of accessing reality, we imagine looking at it with our eyes, and so we tend to imagine things that are, again, mutually exclusive. We see tables sitting next to chairs and on carpets, and they don't move through one another.[10] This is how we visually construct our worlds. But if we insert these metaphors unselfconsciously into Paul's claims about simultaneity, then we will inevitably find them difficult and will probably want to reject them out of hand. When Paul says that we inhabit the world of the Flesh, a world we can see all around us, then we immediately feel that this world is mutually exclusive of anything else. To claim that a world of spirit is present as well as the world of the Flesh is basically impossible. The oil of the spirit cannot be present within the water of the world. We can conceive of this situation only if we carve out a little space within our fleshly world into which the Spirit can move, at which point we generate some further nasty problems.[11] Hence Paul's claim that a spiritual world is present within and around us, offering to determine all our activities over against their determination by the Flesh that we can see, is powerfully counterintuitive.

But these difficulties will be alleviated if we switch to some more appropriate metaphors. Paul himself locates the visual dimension firmly in the Flesh. As he said to the Corinthians at one point, "Fix your eyes on what is not visible, not on what is visible, because the visible is temporary, but the invisible

9. See here especially Thomas F. Torrance, *Space, Time, and Resurrection*.

10. In addition to Torrance's study just noted, see Richard Rorty's classic *Philosophy and the Mirror of Nature* (Princeton: Princeton University Press, 1979). A useful constructive complement to his discussion is Michael Polanyi's reliance on the metaphor of touch, most compactly found in his *The Tacit Dimension*.

11. For example, Which part of us *is* a space into which the Spirit can move?

is permanent" (2 Cor 4:18). Following his cue, then, let us try to think about this situation sonically, using music, with our ears, instead of optically, visually, and with our eyes. Reality is better conceptualized musically. This will enable us to think about things and realities and spaces in ways that are both more accurate and not mutually exclusive.

Imagine that instead of responding with some rationalization to the cynical and ethically anxious students who have voiced these concerns, I simply click on a link and start to play a song by Zao through the classroom's loud speakers. I crank up the volume a bit. "Praise the War Machine" floods the seminar space—the music (with due apologies to death metal and its subtle satirization here) of the Flesh. "We shall destroy the earth. Rebuild it. None shall inherit it." Then, while Zao is in full voice, I take my iPhone and flick to Bach's "Air on a G String" in iTunes and begin to play it, quite softly. I can just catch the extraordinarily placid and delicate resonances of the strings as they move through their interlacements of pizzicato and bowing—the music of heaven (at least for those who love Bach). Then I begin to slowly turn down the volume on Zao. As the death metal fades—perhaps we catch "Carry us off in your claws"—Bach's music begins to become audible. I turn down Zao's music still further and turn up Bach a little more. The "Air" can now be heard easily all over the room and begins to dominate Zao, although the pulse of the death metal can just be heard in the background. Then I explain the metaphor to my doubting but intrigued students.

There is nowhere in the room that lacks, or ever lacked, the music of both pieces. Every single part of the space that we occupy together is touched by Zao and by Bach at any given moment. Both pieces of music were fully present, within and alongside one another, and yet completely distinct from one another. Moreover, even when the volume of one piece was so high that the other was drowned out, we knew that the music was still there. Both pieces were present. It was just that we couldn't hear one because our senses were dominated by the other.

Just so, Paul's suggestion that we live in two dimensions simultaneously makes rather more sense when it is conceptualized sonically and musically. The music of the Flesh might dominate some, but this does not in any way prevent the music of the Spirit from being fully present and accessible. Both arrangements occupy exactly the same space in all their fullness. We live with the music of the world and the music of heaven playing in the same location all the time. Moreover, if the existence of the music of heaven is doubted, it might simply be that the volume on the music of the world is turned up too high. Perhaps, if it is reduced, the Spirit's music will emerge—a gentle, delicate music present there all along that we were unable to hear. The problem is not the music itself, then, but our deafness and lack of attention. And the real question for our doubter might actually be—as it has always been—"Where do I go to hear God?"

The same realization should allay any related concerns that the presence of a resurrected mind could dangerously displace the ongoing reality that is sinfulness, perhaps leading to a denial of actual sinfulness and a resulting ironic plunge into libertinism. Just as the resurrected mind of the Spirit can coexist quietly in and behind the jarring music of the Flesh, so too that realization indicates how sinfulness can still be fully present alongside the resurrected mind. To affirm the presence of the resurrected mind is by no means to collapse into some potentially libertine denial of the Flesh. We are, in Luther's important phrase, *simul iustus et peccator*, "at once righteous and sinful," a notion that is worth grasping and holding on to because, rightly understood, it is so insightful.[12]

We currently live in a duality (as against an outright dual*ism*, a challenge we will face in an especially sharp form momentarily). In effect, we possess two minds at any given moment, along with a dragging and vulnerable body of Flesh. We are located in two different, fully overlapping, existences. But Paul is very clear that we should be living out of just the one, the mind of the Spirit—if necessary, beating our bodies of Flesh into submission (1 Cor 9:24–27). It is, as McSwain's recent analysis makes clear, an *asymmetrical* duality. The relationship between *iustus* and *peccator* in the person is not equal or balanced. The presence of righteousness by way of Christ is vastly more important and dominant than the reality of the Flesh, hence the duality is

---

12. One of Luther's famous additional emphases was that the baptized person is not only *simul iustus et peccator*, that is, simultaneously righteous and sinful, but *totally* so (*totus*). Jeff McSwain has recently explored the importance of this claim to Barth (*"Simul" Sanctification: Barth's Hidden Vision for Human Transformation*), arguing for an even wider application in his thought than has heretofore been seen, notably to his Christology. While making this case, McSwain develops a number of distinctions that will assist readers of Paul as they detect the presence of a certain sort of *simul* in his thinking, as here. (I am assuming that the *simul* is writ large on Paul's Christian anthropology, as both the opening argument in this chapter and the arguments in the last subsection have demonstrated.) McSwain uses Chalcedonian categories to point to the key difference between the "duality" that the *simul* denotes (with the two dimensions being different and distinguishable but not separable, just as the divine and human natures are present in Christ) and an outright "dualism" that would comprise two natures or dimensions that are different and separable. The former antithesis is theologically grounded and insightful, while the latter antithesis is unwarranted and destructive.

profoundly asymmetrical. (Paul's cognizance of this point is apparent in texts like Rom 5:15–17.)[13]

We have just responded to a powerful challenge to the intelligibility of Paul's theology posed by the visible pervasiveness of sin, along with the strongly counterintuitive suggestion that our unseen, indwelling, resurrected mind of spirit is determinative. However, eschewing spatial, zero-sum categories in favor of sonic and musical dynamics can alleviate these particular doubts. Unfortunately, however, the dualist demon has by no means yet been slain. We need now to face a perennial challenge in relation to the interpretation of Paul that departs from much the same point in Paul's thinking as the earlier challenge of unbelief on grounds of incredulity, namely, Gnosticism. We must know exactly what this challenge consists of, where it comes from, and how to deal with it, because it crops up, whether explicitly or more slyly, "functionally," all the time, and it is deadly to the flourishing of a truly Pauline theology.

The Challenge of Gnosticism

Gnostics were a particular difficulty for the early church during the second century, although they have resurged subsequently at various points down to our own day, often in thinly disguised variations. And it seems that Paul himself was facing at least a quasi-Gnostic challenge at Corinth as early as

---

13. Having drawn broadly on Luther's (and Barth's) use of this analytic, I would also inject a note of caution into Luther's more detailed construal of Paul in its light. Luther views Christians as characterized by an awful ongoing conflict between the two dimensions of spirit and Flesh, a conflict he held that Rom 7:7–25 described. Christians are *totally* characterized by *both* dimensions, and they war with one another. I would suggest, however, that this is not a completely accurate reading of Paul. The two dimensions certainly conflict with one another in his thinking; see Gal 5:17. The Flesh is also hostile toward God; so Rom 5:10; 8:7. There is also a totality of influence. But the conflict is, as was said earlier, profoundly asymmetrical. Paul frequently portrays this fight—perhaps a little hyperbolically—as over. The Flesh is dead, having been crucified; so Gal 5:24; 6:14. Hence the life of the baptized, provided it is lived out of the correct place, namely, the reality of the Spirit, is one of peace; so Gal 5:16, 18, 22–23 (and Rom 8:6). Paul clearly believes that his converts can live consistently out of that dimension, so to speak, as Christ did. They can lapse into the Flesh and frequently do, but that dimension is not necessarily present and fully determinative. Romans 7:7–25 consequently describes the life of those who attempt to live in the Flesh. The Flesh is the primary location of conflict, struggle, and agony.

52 CE. But what are Gnostics, and why are they a problem, and such a recurrent one?[14]

There is something persuasively simple and affirming about their position. Gnostics—to cut a long story short—view the resurrection as applying only to a part of the person, usually the soul or spirit. The rest of our present location, including our bodies, is viewed as contaminating garbage and so relegated to a zone of irrelevance, if not of direct pollution. So Gnostics believe in the goodness of just a tiny piece of a person. That "fragment of light" (or some such) has been trapped. God's plan is to release it—to help it to escape from where it is presently—so it can rejoin the rest of the spirits, wherever they are. Gnostics are all about escape from where we are in all its breadth, complexity, and tawdriness. They just want to downplay and ignore the Flesh in favor of our better side—a highly persuasive appeal!

The affinity between Gnosticism and Paul's claim that we currently possess a resurrected mind is readily apparent. Gnostics, in a way, just strip down Paul's gospel to this claim. They double down on the present reality of resurrection in our minds or spirits. We have it all now! In this way, the ongoing, counterintuitive nature of the claim that we indwell two realities at once is defused; we live in the one. The other is not a fundamental reality but a fundamental illusion, or at least irrelevant. Moreover, we live out of the happy, elevated, free place now, appearances notwithstanding!

But in fact Gnostics pay some heavy prices for this bold simplification. The initial difficulties they run into are primarily ethical.[15] Their position generates either a frightfully harsh ethic or a frightfully lax one and thereby condemns itself both as a viable practical system and as a genuine interpretation of Paul.

If the resurrected soul is imprisoned in the body, ascetic Gnostics might discipline the body harshly, perhaps embracing highly restrictive dietary practices and banning sexual activity altogether. Such a regimen is meant to keep the body's

---

14. Descriptions of Gnosticism in the past have trusted too much the highly polemical accounts of the figures later received as church fathers who attacked them. Historians now recognize that the Gnostics were diverse, and perhaps even rather orthodox at times. The underlying *issues* remain the same, however.

15. There are theological challenges as well. Gnostics don't want to attribute our contaminating locations, laden with evil, to God, but if they then attribute them to some other power, they basically collapse into Manichaeanism, which viewed the universe as a battle between two supreme deities, one good and one evil. The single sovereign God of Jews and Christians is thereby impugned, and another evil power is elevated to the rank of a deity—a well-intentioned but ultimately terrible act of idolatry. It is as if Jesus bowed down to Satan on the mountaintop.

ghastly grip on the soul under control. This type of Gnosticism was stringently legalistic and so lived a long way away from Paul's flexible and relational ethic.

But this was probably less destructive than libertine forms of Gnosticism, which regarded many bodily activities as matters of indifference. Since all that matters to these types of disciples—if they can be called that—is the resurrected spirit and the appropriate "knowledge" of this, a life of shameless dissipation can result. "Now we can just ignore all these temporary structures and categories playing out through our fleshly bodies that will be so decisively transcended on the last day." Some of the Corinthians seem to have thought this way and plunged into a rampant enjoyment of eating, drinking, and radical sexual practices.[16] "Wow. This Christian lifestyle *is great*. We get saved *and* we get to have a great time waiting for the end." In fact they seem to have quoted the maxim "Food for the stomach and the stomach for food," which results in pretty flexible behavior when it is applied to certain other organs. They also seem to have employed the even more exciting slogan "Everything is legitimate!"[17]

Both these views tend to translate into a stunning ethical indifference to the needs of others. Since they concern only "irrelevant" bodily activities, problems in relation to food, water, land, work, sex, illness, and even violence can be treated as matters of indifference. *But what important ethical issue does not at some point involve a body?!* There is no actual ethic operative in this system, and certainly not an ethic of love. So there are very real dangers here. In the name of resurrection and transcendence, Paul's gospel has been lost almost without a trace, and a ghastly legalistic *askēsis*, or set of bodily disciplines, substituted for it, at least where it has not unleashed an effluvium of pagan excesses and inhuman indifference. Small wonder that many of Paul's readers take fright at this. But if Gnosticism appears inherently unlikely, we must still fashion an effective rejoinder grounded in Paul's deepest insights. Moreover, we cannot simply reject it; we must *refute* it, and we must do so carefully. In their enthusiasm to reject Gnosticism, Christians have often affirmed contrary positions that have led to equally if not more unhealthy alternatives. We must be sure that the cure we offer is not worse than the disease.[18]

---

16. A brief account of these connections is supplied under the heading "Christian Intellectualism [at Corinth]," in my book *Journey.*

17. First Corinthians 6:13; 6:12. This may even have been a slogan the Corinthians derived from Paul's teaching concerning various Jewish rules, especially in relation to food, that he regarded as irrelevant to pagan converts.

18. A common countermove is to affirm immediately the goodness of creation, equating creation directly with where we are currently located, which does meet the

Beyond Gnosticism

An earnest but unwittingly Gnosticizing student might protest: "How can we really say that God is involved with all this temporary stuff? Food, and clothing (as we know it), and even time, are going to be radically transcended. So why does God care about all this? Surely he doesn't!" There is a sense that God's deep involvement with what is transitory and impermanent is somehow out of place.

But we need to grasp clearly at the outset that this Gnosticizing application of eschatology—not uncommon, *quelle horreur*—is a straightforward non sequitur. It simply does not follow from the fact that aspects of our current existence are temporary and ultimately being transcended that they do not matter—a common inference, but a false one. Doctors and nurses still work hard to heal people, despite the knowledge that one day their patients will all die. *Everything* positive we do to people made of declining Flesh is temporary. But we still do it! Temporary things involving people still matter. And God is the same way. Temporary things still matter to him as well.[19] And there are lots of good reasons for repudiating any allied Gnostic attempt to divide our present existence into a spiritual zone that matters and a material one that doesn't.

There is no such zoning in our lives. Everything matters, all the time, at least in some sense. We see indelible proof of this in the incarnation.[20]

Gnostic challenge. Everything about us matters, it is said—and this is true—because the good God has created is good and in this exact way—and this is where we can run into problems. Paul's emphasis on the way the resurrection transcends our current situation will have to be repudiated as well, and this transcendence arguably underlies his ethics, as well as, ultimately, his cosmology and his doctrine of election. Jesus's role in these critical areas will be curtailed. And all these prices will be paid in the name of a quick response to Gnosticism. At bottom, this strategy trades away Jesus's lordship because of concerns about dualism, which seems like a bad idea; it is a foundationalist defense. So we will not use this argument. (These contentions are developed in ch. 24, "Rethinking Creation," under the rubric "The Abyss of Tertullianism.")

We will engage deeply with the definition of creation from Paul's point of view in part 4, as our understanding of his ethic is being fully developed. Suffice it to say that Paul must ultimately be understood in terms of an implicit supralapsarianism, which is not foundationalist. The countermove to Gnosticism I am rejecting here commits him unhelpfully to infralapsarianism, which is foundationalist.

19. We should recall here also the point just made that sin damages people.

20. I am echoing here an ancient anti-Gnostic theological move first developed by Irenaeus. Paul Blowers summarizes it helpfully in his *Drama of the Divine Economy: Creator and Creation in Early Christian Theology and Piety*, 85–90.

When Jesus assumed a human body of Flesh, *everything* was assumed. The previous chapter emphasized how Jesus did fully assume our current nature made of Flesh. Nothing was left behind. We appreciate now that every *detail* was assumed. He lived a life in all its particularity and specificity, speaking certain words in a certain language in a particular place among particular people (and so on). Every hair on his head mattered.[21] But it follows directly that every hair on ours does as well. We learn from Jesus's assumption of our entire existence, that is, that there is no part of human life where God is not fully engaged. It might be transformed in due course, and even radically changed, but for the present it matters, and one suspects that this is, at least in part, because the good is inextricably tangled up with everything else.[22] So every aspect of life must feel the pressure of God's presence and activity.

But we learn all this, second and in any case, from God's lordship. The grammar of the God whom Paul worships and obeys includes at its heart the affirmation that God is the ruler and sustainer of all that is. There is therefore no area of life as we know it that lies outside of God's concern and involvement. None. Everything must be subject to the God who made and rules and redeems everything; all must remain open to his commands.[23]

This broad commitment to the here and now is confirmed by the deep involvement of Paul's communities with practices that are bodily—things like appropriate sexual practices, shared food and clothing, healing, deliverance, and nonviolent peacemaking. (We will discuss all these in detail later on in part 2.) And these practices are all directly involved with our present bodies and with the world of the Flesh. Having said this, Paul's concretely engaged communities are reflecting here only the concretely engaged actions of the Son. No quiet or hidden corner of life is uninteresting either to God or to those whom he has called when we think about the church. Everything we are and do matters.

21. Here we must also continue to resist the ancient family of heresies that denied Jesus's full humanity—Docetism and the like. The Greek verb *dokein* means "to seem" or "to appear," suggesting in this context that Jesus was primarily divine and only appeared to be human. The complete unity of the divine and human within the person of Jesus, implicit in the claim that Jesus is Lord, necessitates this resistance. Not to have a human Jesus is in fact not to have access through him to the divine either.

22. Many of Jesus's parables also include this "mixture." The most familiar is probably his story of the wheat and the tares (Matt 13:24–30). But see also the saying about leaven (Matt 13:33 // Luke 13:20–21) and possibly also about salt (Matt 5:13).

23. To deny this openness is, ironically, to lapse into what T. F. Torrance perceptively calls "functional Marcionism"; see his *Space, Time, and Resurrection*, 64. This important insight is revisited frequently in what follows.

Complementing this insight into the importance of positive bodily practices is the sense of damage that negative activity inflicts on others. Whenever we fail to obey the promptings of the Spirit and turn, irrationally and foolishly, to our own sinful actions, we inflict pain on ourselves and on others. Evil is unleashed to this degree within the creative dimensions operating within our present locations, and disorder and pain ensue, which should all clearly be avoided. Damaging people is wrong; it is not simply irrelevant.

At this moment we should be able to see quite clearly, then, that the problem with Gnosticism and all its variations is not that it emphasizes the spiritual dimension within the community too much—that our inaugurated eschatology is too inaugurated—but that it misunderstands the extent to which this dimension is involved with our current situation, and especially with our bodies.[24] The complete intersection of the two dimensions that we live in has been obscured. Our situation has been oversimplified. Jesus came in a body and was resurrected with a body. He expects us to act through our bodies in relation to other people as the church—and how else could we act?!

In short, we can continue to affirm strongly that allowing zones of irrelevance within our lives in Gnostic terms on the grounds that only our resurrected minds matter would be a violation, in particular, of our doctrine of God and of our understanding of Jesus, both as he was incarnate and is the Lord, and it is harder to imagine stronger countervailing considerations than these. But this allowance would also misunderstand how our current activity, in bodily ways, affects those around us, for good or for ill. (And it risks embracing a simple non sequitur; the temporary, despite being temporary, is still freighted with significance.) The Gnostic challenge, then, seems to have been well met.

However, one nagging vulnerability remains within Paul's thinking that can open him up to Gnostic misinterpretation again, which will require a more extensive rebuttal, although our engagement here will ultimately stand us in good stead.

The Intermediate State

Paul expected Jesus to return at any moment, when he expected to receive a wonderful new resurrection body made of spirit, which he describes in some

---

24. It is as if a gap is posited between the sphere of redemption and the sphere we currently occupy, with the former circle somehow being smaller than the latter. It is this "gap" that begets Gnosticism, so in resisting this restriction on resurrection, we resist Gnosticism very directly.

detail in 1 Cor 15:35–50, as we noted earlier. And we probably should have roughly the same expectation as well. But in the event Jesus does not return before we die, another question comes up. *What happens to us then?* In particular, we need to ask about the relationship between our resurrected mind, which we have now, and our resurrected body of spirit, which we hope to get later, when Jesus returns. This might seem like a purely academic worry that we could on practical grounds bypass for the moment. The main thing is that it will happen one day, right? However, quite important issues turn out to be at stake. Further reflection suggests that we are forced here into a nasty conundrum, and Gnosticism will raise its head again if we end up embracing one horn of this dilemma.

There are two basic scenarios, but each of them leads to a problem. On the one hand, we could die and then cease to exist until our complete resurrection, soul and body, on the day of Jesus's return. At that vital moment we would be entirely reconstituted. Now this would not presumably bother us. Paul euphemistically calls this "being asleep," but that metaphor would be applied with reference to the complete lack of consciousness associated with death.[25] In fact, we would "wake up" on the last day as if from a deep anesthetic, not remembering that a great deal of time might have passed—something of a Rip Van Winkle moment—because we would not actually have been in existence at all. But a potential problem is lurking here.

Clearly we would not have spent the intervening time with God, in the arms of Jesus. Moreover, death would thereby have intervened decisively into our relationship with God. And the resurrection mind would basically have died too. The break in relationship would not have proved permanent, but death would have been temporarily victorious. God's desire to commune with us would have been thwarted for a time, and in Paul's case for almost two thousand years so far. So God's lordship would have been called into question, along with the efficacy of his resurrecting act in Jesus. If death can interrupt our relationship with God in this way, then there is something quite weak about it, along with the one who is establishing it, and the resurrection into the new age would be reversible, and Paul really doesn't seem to think this is the case. Whatever else we say about God in Paul, we must say that God is the victor through Jesus, even over death, and that he has gripped hold of us now, and nothing else has the power to break that relationship (Rom 8:38–39). There is no going back on the resurrection.

Perhaps we can get around this difficulty, however, simply by supposing,

---

25. First Corinthians 15:6, 18, 20, 51; 1 Thess 4:14; 5:10. The issue is introduced tidily by David Aune's essay "Anthropological Duality in the Eschatology of 2 Cor 4:16–5:10."

on the other hand, that we do go to be with God and to rest in the arms of Jesus after we die, but before we receive our new bodies on the last day. That final event—that consummation—will lie ahead of us, but we will wait for it safely tucked up in the folds of Jesus's robes, perhaps in the way that the poor man Lazarus was being carried around after his death by Abraham (Luke 16:19–31). We would be asleep in the other sense, then, that we would still exist, and time would pass quickly at times, but we would also experience periods of wakefulness and communion with Jesus.[26] Scholars sometimes refer to this temporary existence of our spirits with Jesus after death but before full bodily resurrection as "the intermediate state."[27] We live in this state until the last day when—with a blast—we receive our wonderful new bodies and become fully alive and operational again (out of bed and, presumably, running around fully awake, embracing the day). And this scenario does explain a number of Paul's texts, especially his firm expectation that death will not separate him from God. If death arrives imminently, perhaps at the hands of some venal Roman official, he will go straightaway to rest in the arms of Jesus (so Phil 1:21, 23). But there is another potential problem here.

If we go to be with Jesus after we die, living in a real, authentic relationship with him prior to the receipt of a new body, we must exist in some soulish state as a spirit and so rather like a ghost. Part of us floats off to be with Jesus while it waits for the other part to be added later on. But if we really live with Jesus after death in this soulish state, sleeping in the ancient sense of that happy activity, it seems that we don't really need a body to be added later on at all. If we are already with him, sleeping and waking off and on in his arms, then this is the goal of the entire process. We are living with Jesus! *And* we have thereby opened the door again to Gnosticism. It seems we have conceded that only souls or spirits really matter. Bodies are unnecessary and can be treated accordingly, with horrific asceticism or with an equally horrific libertinism, while God's interest in what our bodies do seems to be strictly limited.

But someone might insist against this foolish Gnostic inference that we will still need a body to be fully alive. Our soulish existence isn't complete until

---

26. The modern conception of sleep is very different from premodern conceptions. The invention of artificial light has altered a sleep pattern that the rest of humanity otherwise experienced, in particular, very long hours in bed during the winter months, often with *two* periods of sleep, each roughly four hours in duration, interspersed with several hours of wakeful but bed-related activity (reading, writing, conversation, story-telling, sex, prayer, etc.). This realization alters the force of Paul's metaphor.

27. See especially 2 Cor 5:1–10 and Phil 1:21–26. See also Rev 6:9–11.

we get a body. However, if that is the case, then we haven't actually, fully, as ourselves, gone off to be with Jesus after our death, and death has broken our relationship with God. We are, in effect, extinguished, any previous experience of the resurrection having been snuffed out, as we wait for our reconstitution as persons on the last day. That is, we are back to scenario 1, with all its problems in relation to God's questionable lordship and capacity to save, along with the apparent fragility of our resurrected relationship with him.

It seems, then, that we are on the horns of a real dilemma here. If we can't live with Jesus fully as a soul but need to wait for a new body, which we will receive on the last day, this leaves us with a broken relationship with God for a while. Both God's lordship over death and the reality of his resurrecting act in Jesus are thereby impugned. If we can live and be with Jesus effectively as a soul or spirit immediately after we die, it follows that we don't need a body, and Paul's thought collapses into a destructive Gnostic dualism.

I suspect that Paul and a lot of other thinkers in his day did not worry about these issues too much. After all, they had a lot of other things to be getting on with. Paul himself seems to affirm the intermediate state, going on to affirm scenario 1 as well(!). When he dies, he will fall asleep in the arms of Jesus as a soul or spirit, but he will get a new body eventually. This view seems particularly clear in Philippians, as we have already briefly seen. He desires to depart and to be with Christ after death immediately in 1:21–26; but he also looks forward in 3:20–21 to the receipt of his glorious new body when Christ returns. He has a new soul or spirit in the meantime, and it is tightly intertwined with the divine Spirit. Indeed, it is his indwelling by this Spirit that makes him especially confident that he will, one day, be fully resurrected, in soul, mind, and body (Rom 8:1–14). It seems clear, then, that a certain sort of dualism is present here in Paul's thinking about the person, although he does not press it in destructive directions.

This conclusion will not suffice for us, however, because Paul's later interpreters had no reason not to press him to his necessary conclusions. So Paul seems to have left this problem for us to work out later on. That is, *Gnosticism flows legitimately from a key set of claims within Paul.* His commitment to an intermediate state necessarily commits him to the concession that human existence with Jesus is possible without a body. We simply have to think about the implications of his position here a little harder, his Gnostic readers might say, and then introduce a particular *Sachkritik*, overriding Paul's explicit commitments to embodied human existence in the light of what he says elsewhere, and yet this direction is, as we know well by now, highly destructive.[28]

28. F. B. Watson notes the legitimacy of this connection in a lively essay "Resurrec-

I consider myself enormously fortunate to live after 1915 because only then was the source of our difficulty fully revealed, along with its solution. This is of course some time after Paul himself, so we will have to work out in due course how to interpret him constructively. But the first thing we need to do is to grasp our problem precisely, along with its necessary solution. After we have done this, we will turn back to Paul.

Time as a Field

The difficulty in this whole relation is being caused by a false conception of time. The problem of the intermediate state is arising because time is being treated as a fixed, linear constant. It is being treated like a "line" that both God and we travel along. (Alternatively, it travels slowly and steadily past us all, like a river.) Neither God nor we can shift around on this line beyond our regular fixed movement as a point along it. We cannot reach behind the point where we are into the past or jump forward into the future. Time is inexorable, and we are locked into the present, a single moment that moves along steadily and remorselessly. A line of time stretches out behind us and before us—zones that are forever inaccessible to us.

The result of this view of time is that we will probably die at a point ahead of us on the line, whether near or far, while the last day must take place still further away, down at the end of the line. And a long gap now opens up, created by the piece of time that will need to elapse between these two events. This piece is the stretch of linear time that is yet to unfold between our death and the final day. It is this particular piece of the timeline that creates the tension or pressure that we are currently struggling with. It *separates* our deaths at particular points on the line from the full bodily resurrection of all, which takes place at the end of the timeline.

We don't want to be separated from God now or at any point in the future. In this moment and from henceforward, we expect to be in relationship with God somehow, otherwise our relationship is broken. We therefore resist this gap. But we have to wait until we get our new bodies, at the end of the timeline, to be complete. So the gap reasserts itself. A piece of time still has to pass. And we already know that conundrums lie in both directions, whichever aspect of the situation we choose to emphasize, while it is clearly impossible

---

tion and the Limits of Paulinism." (Sadly, Watson fails to press on to develop a coherent Trinitarian response, but to recognize an issue in the first place is half the battle.)

to hold them together coherently when they are mapped in these terms. They are separated from one another on the timeline by a considerable distance. We might say, then, that an unavoidable piece of time on the timeline in between personal death and the end of the age is causing this problem.

In 1915, however, Albert Einstein published his celebrated equations demonstrating that reality is constructed rather differently from this naive viewpoint. Time is in fact not a constant or a line that moves along steadily; rather, it is a *field* just like our experience of space. And all the physical fields interact with one another relationally and dynamically. People exist in a space-time continuum. The one constant in the universe—so the only thing approaching a line in form or notion—was, Einstein proved, the speed of light.

This view of time as a field is hard to detect at our local level, where Newton's equations, based on a false view of reality presupposing time as a constant, nevertheless predict movement (and much else) very well. At vast distances of interstellar dimensions, however, it quickly becomes apparent that Newton's account is false and Einstein's is correct. Time is a field that *bends* in the vicinity of large masses like stars. It interacts and shifts in relation to mass and other things, just as space does (hence the phenomenon of gravity as well). Consequently, space travelers experience time at different speeds from people living on earth, something that gives the lie to any sense in which time is a line or a constant. Time changes as its field bends in the vicinity of large objects. (The film *Interstellar* [2014], directed by Christopher Nolan, articulates this notion rather nicely, while Nolan's earlier picture, *Inception* [2010], explores some of the implications more playfully, folding different times into one another.)[29] In the light of this realization, we must now return to our initial problem and reconceptualize it.

We are still "presently" caught up in the field of time, experiencing it as a movement from past to present to future. In terms of our experience it *feels*

---

29. Time is apparently a particular concern of Nolan's, and he explores a linear reversal in an earlier, very watchable, film *Memento* (2001), although this is less helpful for those wanting pointers about Einstein. Having said this, *Memento* helps us to understand the impossibility of us living without the structure of time. Without it, human life as we know and experience it now would be effectively impossible. A famous aphorism puts the same point slightly differently: "Time is what keeps everything from happening at once," which is commonly attributed to Einstein but more probably originated from the character Tubby in legendary science-fiction writer Ray Cummings's short story "The Time Professor" (*Argosy All-Story Weekly*, January 8, 1921). This, at any rate, is its earliest attested use; see Paul J. Nahin, *Time Machines: Time Travel in Physics, Metaphysics, and Science Fiction*, 2nd ed. (New York: Springer-Verlag, 1999), 98.

like a line. But *God is not part of this temporal experience.* He is not governed by a timeline (and neither in fact are we; we are "moving" through a field). Consequently, he is not waiting for the cosmic clock to expire so that he can transform everyone who is still standing around at that point and resurrect everyone else finally at that point on the timeline. He is not subject to time and is certainly not affected by time as a constant. Time is something he created and governs. It gives us a structure within which we can exist, but it hardly structures God. There is a sense, then, in which we must think about God as being "above" the field of time. And there is a related sense in which we must think about all of time as being "present" to God. Barth speaks of God living in the perfection of time, with all past, present, and future, which amounts to much the same thing.[30]

It follows from all this that the end of history, when God transforms and resurrects everyone at that moment on the timeline, in effect cutting it off and ending it, no longer makes much sense as some particular future day in relation to which the cosmic clock is ticking, and toward which the line of time is slowly moving. It is not a point at the end of a timeline, any more than the new heaven and earth is another space somewhere next to our present one. Any day is simply a particular plot on the space-time continuum, while the continuum itself has no obvious end. It is more like a vast sphere—an expanding sphere, some suggest—and spheres do not have an obvious beginning and ending on their surface. They are, precisely, a continuum.

However, the sphere *itself* does, as a whole, "begin" and "end," which suggests that God's transforming and resurrecting action will not take place on a day at some supposed end of a line of time as much as *to* time in its entirety. Just as time itself began one day, so to speak, the whole sphere of space-time will be transformed and resurrected one day as well. Time *itself* will be resurrected and transformed, just as space will be, and it is important to grasp this last point. We all look forward to a new creation. And we all have no trouble expecting our spaces to be transformed. Jews in Paul's day thought this too. All of space will be changed and displaced by a radically new space. The new heaven and the new earth will not be a nice new space added onto the one we are already in. It will involve the comprehensive transformation of all our space. But it follows directly from this that the structure that is the field of time will be transformed as well. All of old time will be changed and displaced by perfect time, which is to say that the space-time continuum will be resurrected in its entirety.

30. *CD* III/2, §47, "Man in His Time."

It would be fun to pause here a little longer and to think about all this, but it would also be too time-consuming. We have to cut to the chase (although we will have to revisit some of the important implications of this insight later on, in part 4). What does all this have to do with our struggles in relation to death, resurrection, and the intermediate state in Paul?

Given the reality of a space-time continuum and the resurrection of the entire continuum, we still have some mind-bending thinking to do, but at least our problem here has been solved. This problem, because it presupposes a temporal linearity, now basically disappears. It seems that when people die, they leave our space-time continuum and go to live with God in the perfection of time, and consequently in a sense "above" our time. They enter another type of time altogether—the perfect resurrected time that transforms the entirety of our time but that we have not yet experienced because we are still located in that old time. There in the new, perfect time, I imagine they dwell with their new bodies, which are of course present to them but unrealized for us, because we still live in the space-time continuum that has "not yet" been transformed as a whole. Basically, the dead enter another time, in the sense of another dimension, and one very unlike our own. They enter what we tend to think about as our future. They enter our resurrected and perfected time, doing so "immediately."[31]

We see this change in Jesus himself, however, who was resurrected in a fully embodied and perfected state. So at least we see in him the concrete instantiation of what we are when we die. We catch a glimpse of perfect time. And Paul knows this. In Colossians he exclaims with extraordinary insight: "You are dead and your life has been hidden with Christ in God. When Christ is made manifest—your life!—then you also will be made manifest with him in glory" (3:3–4). This entry into another time, where a new embodiment takes place, *eliminates the intermediate state,* when souls have to waft around waiting for their resurrection bodies. We will never exist in a disembodied, intermediate state. There is no gap.

We tend to think about this fully embodied resurrection as "future." We cannot "see" bones being raised from the ground and clothed with a stunning new existence. However, this is because we are caught within our fallen structures that include time. This is where we live. But none of this applies either to God or to our transformed state. God is experiencing the perfection of the space-time continuum, which is where we are headed. Moreover, as we

---

31. Strictly speaking, all those who die and are resurrected enter that perfect time *at the same time.* Resurrection is simultaneous.

already know, this time-bending action by God is not really difficult, because he created it. So there are no gaps here, no partial actions on his part. Everything holds together.

I suggest, in short, that there will be no separation between death and a fully embodied resurrection in the presence of God, but the dead will enjoy that fullness in another place and another time, so to speak, as they are resurrected there. We who are left behind experience this situation differently. It feels future to us because we have not seen it take place, except in Jesus. But this is a deceptive intuition derived from our experience of time as a constant.

On the other side of the coin—the arrival of the end of the age—we can now see that the last day and its resurrection will come all around us, in the past, the present, and the future, "when" it comes. The perfect time of God will overwhelm and transform the fallen time that we are living in. So, just as we can think of God's arrival as happening all through existing space, we ought to think about it happening all through time as well. Both these fields will be transformed. To ask "when" this will happen is consequently to ask a meaningless question. We are in time and structured by its categories, so we cannot ask a temporal question *of* time. "When is something going to happen to time?" This is the same understandable but incoherent question as asking "where" space is, or where heaven is going to be located outside of it. We simply run here into a limit on our human capacity to analogize helpfully, which is why physicists often rely on mathematics to try to map what is involved in the bafflingly counterintuitive but elegant dynamics that structure our existence.

It seems, then, that we have resolved our nasty dilemma concerning the intermediate state by grasping that its difficulties were created artificially—although understandably—by presupposing a false notion of time, namely, of time as a fixed constant. But we have raised further questions. Most important, we need to know how to move forward interpreting Paul on these questions.

Paul and Future Time

I think Paul's stated positions give us permission to interpret him generously, in terms of an accurate understanding of time, which can resolve the tensions generated by his account of resurrection. I am clearly demythologizing him here, introducing later, more scientific concepts into his thinking, displacing the less accurate ones that are there, but not without his permission, which is to draw on *Sachkritik* as well. Paul is explicitly committed to (1) our departure after death, if this "precedes" Jesus's return, to be with him; and (2) our receipt of a future, glorious body at the end of all things. And he is explicitly committed to denials of the two problems that occur here.

He is no Gnostic, making numerous exhortations in present bodily terms. We see this first in the resurrected Jesus, so this position is nonnegotiable. Hence we cannot accept the soulish, proto-Gnostic implications of the intermediate state. Paul believed in embodiment. But Paul is equally committed to the unbreakability of our present relationship with God, into which nothing can intervene—not death or life, the present or the future, and so on. So we cannot commit to an "interval" imposed on us by our deaths, as we wait for new bodies, which Paul is expecting to be provided on the last day. And in fact, in this famous text, Paul comes very close to giving us permission to think about how time cannot break our relationship with God.

If *death* cannot separate us from God, then *time* cannot separate us from God. These amount to the same thing. Moreover, Paul even says so explicitly: "neither the present nor the future . . . can separate us from God" (Rom 8:38–39). Again, then, time cannot separate us from God. Moreover, Paul is committed to a christological understanding of creation, which means, in the end of the day, a relational and accurate understanding of created structures, including of time.[32] Time is something that God, through Jesus, made. Consequently, we are entitled to understand time in a way that does not control God and does not separate us from God, which means abandoning any view of it as a constant. We are fortunate, then, that for the last hundred years we have been able to adopt a more accurate, modern view of it as an interactive field, resulting in the elimination of the problems generated at both ends of the intermediate state, and we have also learned how to think more accurately about God living in another, perfect temporal dimension. Consequently, this seems to be a supremely useful instance of demythologizing, a method that can have a bad reputation but that here seems quite constructive.

Obviously, Paul himself did not understand this view of time. Presumably, he simply lived with the tensions, although he may not have noticed them, being focused on other matters. But we are fortunate because Einstein allows us to see that these tensions are fundamentally ephemeral or artificial. They are not actually real, and the adoption of a more accurate understanding of time allows us to dispense with the tensions. And with this rebuttal we can continue to affirm the plausibility of Paul's claim that we presently possess a resurrected, spiritual mind, despite lacking a corresponding spiritual body. There are no good reasons for resisting this claim or for collapsing into Gnosticism, even as

32. We will talk about creation much more in part 4.

we contemplate our deaths "before" the return of Christ, so now we can return to our positive descriptive task.

We now need to spend a little bit more time exploring the nature and significance of this incredible (yet credible) gift that is the mind of the resurrected Jesus. We have been gifted with the capacity to act rightly. So now we need to think much harder about how exactly we do this. As we do so, we encounter a critical but much-contested dimension of discipleship as Paul understands it.

Theses

> Paul's gospel claims that present resurrection is real but partial. The baptized possess resurrected minds while they wait for the receipt of a resurrected body at the second coming of Jesus (Phil 3:20–21).

> Meanwhile, they feel pressure and anxiety and experience vulnerability but have hope. They must discipline the body of Flesh, and they have the "deposit" of the Spirit, who brings virtues and gifts.

> People located in modernity, and especially in Western (i.e., post-European) modernity can be hampered in their grip on Paul's claim here if they unwittingly endorse certain widespread conceptual dichotomies.

> Modern people often tend to split thoughts apart from acts as if they are two quite different things—a thought-act binary. But thinking *is* an activity. To have a new thinking mind is to be acting in a new way.

> We must also push past a being-act dichotomy. A new way of acting *is* a new existence or being.

> Believing, for someone like Paul, also includes what many modern people would separate again—rational thoughts and emotional states like peace and joy. To have the mind of Christ is to have the emotions of Christ as well—his peace and joy (etc.).

> Some very basic questions of plausibility arise here now that need to be addressed.

> The claim that the resurrected mind of the Spirit is fully present can be resisted initially on grounds that there is too much obvious sin, even in those supposedly resurrected, for their claim to be resurrected to remain plausible. Concomitantly, it is ethically dangerous for sinful people to suppose that they are fully resurrected and are no longer sinning.

> These concerns dissipate when it is grasped that reality can be analogized musically, with two completely different pieces of music coexisting simultaneously "in the same space."

▸ Luther's notion of Christian anthropology as *simul iustus et peccator*—also much used by Barth—is helpful here as well, suitably adjusted.

▸ Hence, the presence of a resurrected mind does not displace the mind of Flesh, although it is more important. The baptized comprise an asymmetrical duality.

▸ A further significant challenge arises at this moment—whether Paul's claim is vulnerable to Gnosticism, which endorses a dangerous separation between (1) the present body and other material things and (2) a realm of spirit. This view tends to unleash either horrific asceticism or an equally horrific libertinism.

▸ The incarnation suggests directly that God takes our present situation with complete seriousness in all its fullness and all its details.

▸ Jesus's lordship suggests the same.

▸ The many concrete activities undertaken by the church as Paul describes it suggest the same. (See more in part 2.)

▸ That something temporary does not matter ethically is also a straightforward non sequitur.

▸ Hence there are no "zones" in our current location that lie outside God's involvement and rule. Gnosticism must be repudiated.

▸ However, a further challenge is apparent in Paul's thinking that could yet again open the door to Gnosticism. If death occurs before the second coming of Christ, and hence before a general bodily resurrection, what happens between these two events? If we explain this situation in terms of a complete death of annihilation, followed by a full resurrection at the second coming, we allow death—and time—to temporarily but decisively rupture the relationship of partial resurrection between God and us. If we posit a soulish existence "asleep" with Christ between these two events, we admit the possibility of real authentic existence without a body, thereby creating a justification for Gnosticism in the heart of Paul's thought.

▸ Fortunately, since Einstein's revolutionary discoveries, we have learned that time is not a constant but a field that interacts with space in a space-time continuum. Time is not a linear, fixed, static line or movement, and it is this latter (false) construct that causes the foregoing conundrum.

▸ God lives in the perfection of time. So "one day" all of time itself will be resurrected.

▸ Presumably, the dead leave our space-time continuum—our dimension— and are resurrected in his perfect dimension bodily. This feels future to us, but it is an entrance into the perfection of time. There is consequently no intermediate state. That idea is an implication of a false, linear view of time.

➤ Paul did not of course argue this point of view, but some of his positions give us permission to extrapolate from his stated positions to this more mature solution—a judicious combination of demythologizing in relation to his false view of time as a constant, and *Sachkritik*, as we press the implications of some of his other claims more fully. In particular, he states that nothing, including death and presumably also therefore time, can separate us from the love of God in Christ Jesus, while maintaining that human life is embodied.

➤ We conclude overall that there are no good objections to Paul's claim that the baptized are indeed presently partially resurrected with a new mind. This claim *is* plausible and does *not* entail Gnosticism.

Key Scriptural References

Our summary sketch of the present nature of Christians—who have bodies and minds of Flesh, who possess the mind of Christ and the Spirit as well, but who nevertheless await a spiritual body at the *parousia* (i.e., the second coming) of Jesus—was derived from data in Philippians; see espcially 1:20–24; 2:1, 5; 3:10, 20–21; 4:7. But see also Rom 7:1–8:13 and 1 Thess 5:23.

Caution about visual evidence is stated by Paul in 2 Cor 4:18.

The intermediate state is denoted in 2 Cor 5:1–10 and Phil 1:21–26.

That death cannot separate us from God is stated famously in Rom 8:35–39.

The spiritual body is anticipated most concretely and described in detail in 1 Cor 15:35–57, but see also 2 Cor 5:1–10.

Key Reading

A useful description of the basic data generating the problem (or not) of the intermediate state is supplied by David Aune.

Barth was very sensitive to the problems caused by linear time and developed a wonderfully lucid account of God's time in terms of its perfection in III/2, §47. Nevertheless, he ought to be supplemented directly here by the work of his brilliant pupil T. F. Torrance, specifically his seminal *Space, Time, and Resurrection*.

Further Reading

The work of Colin Gunton and Stanley Hauerwas is a constant education regarding the dangers of thought-act and being-act distinctions, as well as the joys of thinking beyond those limitations. I have not listed specific references to Hauerwas's work because for him it is a mentality rather than a specific topic, as it should be. For Gunton, see especially his *Act and Being* and his earlier *Enlightenment and Alienation*. Barth is largely immune to such distinctions, and working through his material is a constant education beyond such distorting categories as well.

Jeremy Begbie's contributions concerning musical analogies for theology are both seminal and especially helpful for understanding the anthropology generated by existence in Christ in terms of two mutually indwelling but asymmetrical and opposed dimensions. Of particular importance to the claims in this chapter is his brilliant essay "Room of One's Own? Music, Space, and Freedom" (*A Peculiar Orthodoxy*, 145–80). The peculiar capacity of music to instantiate and thereby to illustrate a fully interpenetrated mutual presence or indwelling was drawn originally by Begbie from the work of Viktor Zuckerkandl.

Intriguingly, Barth thinks very musically and often appeals directly to musical analogies. Those reading him who have not detected their dependence on ocular metaphors and zero-sum conceptions of space may miss the highly dynamic way he understands key realities, especially the Trinity. Hence Barth's emphasis on the Son is often taken to imply a Christomonism and an impoverished pneumatology. But Barth's dynamic understanding of being entails that where the Son is present, the Father and the Spirit are always dynamically present and fully involved as well, something a careful reading of his texts will generally go on to corroborate. (He is also fully cognizant of the dangers of collapsing into modalism.) And Jeff McSwain, in particular dependence on Barth, helpfully explores the importance of Luther's view of Christians as *simul iustus et peccator*. Luther's usage can be found in his collected works, the Weimar Ausgabe, 56:347, lines 3–4, 7, and 56:442, line 17.

Richard Rorty points to the unwarranted and often highly distorting dominance of visual metaphors in Western philosophy. And Michael Polanyi relies much more informatively on the metaphor of touch. My frequent use of "grasp" and related tactile metaphors of understanding is a constant reference to this way of thinking.

A quick overview of Gnosticism can be found in Pearson's introductory treatment, "What Is Gnosticism?," in *Ancient Gnosticism*, 7–19. Helpful remarks are also made by Blowers in *Drama*, 78–90, segueing into an analysis of Irenaeus. It is also important to recall that scholars such as Williams dispute the very existence of the category "Gnosticism."

Once linear time has been identified and abandoned in favor of the treatment of time as a field, the Pauline texts—and other biblical passages dependent on linear time—must clearly be demythologized. At this moment, Bultmann's treatment is both exemplary and somewhat misguided.

Analogies and illustrations drawn from science fiction can be quite helpful here. A charming introduction to this relationship is Stephen May, *Stardust and Ashes*.

The importance, nature, and roles of the Holy Spirit in Paul have begun to emerge into prominence in this chapter.

Excellent book-length introductions to the Spirit include Heron, Holmes, Smail, and Thiselton; an important treatment is Rogers. Two essays well worth consulting are Wainwright's excellent introductory essay "The Holy Spirit" and Hauerwas's rather repentant account "How to Be Caught by the Holy Spirit."

Fee's detailed study *God's Empowering Presence* is seminal for the discussion of the Spirit in Paul. He should be supplemented by Levison and Rabens. (Missionally oriented studies will be noted later.)

An interesting debate has been unfolding lately within Pauline studies over Paul's conceptuality. Some have argued that Paul's thinking about the Spirit is tightly allied with his understanding of a notion of spirit per se that was ultimately drawn from Stoicism (see, for example, Engberg-Pedersen). In that tradition, spirit (Gk. *pneuma*) is—speaking very summarily—one of the key features of the cosmos; a mixture of air and fire, it gives life to all living things in relation to the proportions of air and fire present and structures the cosmos and everything in it. It is tensile, somewhat like air, but also warm.

There is arguably some support for this position in Paul's account of the resurrection body in 1 Cor 15:35–54. He might be envisioning resurrected bodies made of spirit there, although not necessarily to be confused thereby with the Holy Spirit.

Others have argued that this pagan conceptuality is not determinative for Paul's account of the Holy Spirit, or even not present at all (Fee, Levison), finding it somewhat threatening. Paul's understanding was drawn from Jewish tradition and the account in Jewish Scriptures of the Spirit in essentially vitalistic but also personal terms, and in relation to eschatology (Dunn making a vital earlier contribution here).

Rabens's work is an excellent guide through this debate, offering both learned and constructive conclusions.

The former NT scholars all argue largely in historical-critical mode, which has both value and limitations.

David Bentley Hart reminds us, in a short, typically delightful and pugnacious essay ("The Spiritual Was More Substantial than the Material for the Ancients"), that an understanding of being in terms of spirit, notwithstanding any philosophical origins, is not necessarily problematic for sound theological thinking. And resisting this conceptuality may even betray suspiciously modernizing and destructive tendencies. To this opinion we may add that any Stoic conceptualities may simply be a further instance of contextualization, something Paul, like any good missionary, does frequently. (Benefaction, for example, is another pagan discourse he appropriates frequently; this feature of his thinking is assessed several times in what follows, benefaction being specifically engaged in ch. 12.) Furthermore, speaking theologically, the divine Spirit *must* ultimately be construed fundamentally as a person, on grounds both of the unity or oneness of God and of a presence distinct from both the Father and the Son. All analogies are then simply subject to this criterion, and Paul either grasps this dimly or should have his discussions of the Spirit amplified in these terms, whether in terms of originally Jewish, intertestamental, or pagan analogies.

Bibliography

Aune, David. "Anthropological Duality in the Eschatology of 2 Cor 4:16–5:10." Pages 215–39 in *Paul: Beyond the Judaism/Hellenism Divide*. Edited by T. Engberg-Pedersen. Louisville: Westminster/John Knox, 2001.

Barth, Karl. *Church Dogmatics*. III/2.

Begbie, Jeremy. *Music, Modernity, and God: Essays in Listening*. Oxford: Oxford University Press, 2014.

———. *A Peculiar Orthodoxy: Reflections on Theology and the Arts*. Grand Rapids: Baker Academic, 2018.

———. *Resounding Truth: Christian Wisdom in the World of Music*. Grand Rapids: Baker, 2007.

———. *Theology, Music, and Time*. Cambridge: Cambridge University Press, 2000.

Blowers, Paul M. *Drama of the Divine Economy: Creator and Creation in Early Christian Theology and Piety*. Oxford: Oxford University Press, 2012.

Bultmann, Rudolf. *Jesus Christ and Mythology*. New York: Charles Scribner's Sons, 1958.

————. *New Testament and Mythology, and Other Basic Writings.* Translated by S. Ogden. Minneapolis: Fortress, 1984.

Dunn, James D. G. *Baptism in the Holy Spirit: A Re-examination of the New Testament Teaching on the Gift of the Spirit in Relation to Pentecostalism Today.* London: SCM, 1970.

Engberg-Pedersen, Troels. *Cosmology and Self in the Apostle Paul: The Material Spirit.* Oxford: Oxford University Press, 2010.

Fee, Gordon. *God's Empowering Presence: The Holy Spirit in the Letters of Paul.* Peabody, MA: Hendrickson, 1994.

————. *Paul, the Spirit, and the People of God.* Peabody, MA: Hendrickson, 1996.

Gunton, Colin E. *Act and Being: Towards a Theology of the Divine Attributes.* London: SCM, 2002.

————. *Enlightenment and Alienation: An Essay toward a Trinitarian Theology.* Eugene, OR: Cascade, 2006.

Hart, David Bentley. "The Spiritual Was More Substantial than the Material for the Ancients." *Church Life Journal*, July 26, 2018. http://churchlife .nd.edu/2018/07/26/the-spiritual-was-more-substantial-than-the-fleshly-for -the-ancients/#.

Hauerwas, Stanley. "How to Be Caught by the Holy Spirit." In *ABC Religion and Theology*, November 14, 2013. https://www.abc.net.au/religion/how-to-be -caught-by-the-holy-spirit/10099524.

Heron, A. I. C. *The Holy Spirit: The Holy Spirit in the Bible, in the History of Christian Thought, and in Recent Theology.* London: Marshall, Morgan & Scott, 1983.

Holmes, Christopher R. J. *The Holy Spirit.* Grand Rapids: Zondervan, 2015.

Levison, John R. *Filled with the Spirit.* Grand Rapids: Eerdmans, 2009.

————. *Inspired: The Holy Spirit and the Mind of Faith.* Grand Rapids: Eerdmans, 2013.

May, Stephen. *Stardust and Ashes: Science Fiction in Christian Perspective.* London: SPCK, 1998.

McSwain, Jeff. *"Simul" Sanctification: Barth's Hidden Vision for Human Transformation.* Eugene, OR: Pickwick, 2018.

Pearson, Birger A. *Ancient Gnosticism: Traditions and Literature.* Minneapolis: Fortress, 2007.

Polanyi, Michael. *Personal Knowledge: Towards a Post-critical Philosophy.* New York: Routledge & Kegan Paul, 1958.

————. *The Tacit Dimension.* New York: Doubleday, 1966.

Rabens, Volker. *The Holy Spirit and Ethics in Paul: Transformation and Empowering for Religious-Ethical Life.* 2nd rev. ed. Minneapolis: Fortress, 2014.

———. "*Pneuma* and the Beholding of God: Reading Paul in the Context of Philonic Mystical Traditions." Pages 293–329 in *The Holy Spirit, Inspiration, and the Cultures of Antiquity*. Edited by Jörg Frey and John R. Levison. Berlin: de Gruyter, 2014.

Rogers, Eugene F. *After the Spirit: A Constructive Pneumatology from Resources outside the Modern West*. Grand Rapids: Eerdmans, 2005.

Rorty, Richard. *Philosophy and the Mirror of Nature*. Princeton: Princeton University Press, 1979.

Smail, Thomas A. *The Giving Gift: The Holy Spirit in Person*. London: Hodder & Stoughton, 1988.

Thiselton, Anthony C. *A Shorter Guide to the Holy Spirit: Bible, Doctrine, Experience*. Grand Rapids: Eerdmans, 2016.

Torrance, Thomas F. *Space, Time, and Resurrection*. Edinburgh: Handsel Press, 1976.

Wainwright, Geoffrey. "The Holy Spirit." Pages 273–96 in *The Cambridge Companion to Christian Doctrine*. Edited by Colin E. Gunton. Cambridge: Cambridge University Press, 1997.

Watson, F. B. "Resurrection and the Limits of Paulinism." Pages 452–71 in *The Word Leaps the Gap: Essays on Scripture and Theology in Honor of Richard B. Hays*. Edited by J. Ross Wagner, C. Kavin Rowe, and A. Katherine Grieb. Grand Rapids: Eerdmans, 2008.

Williams, K. *Rethinking "Gnosticism": An Argument for Dismantling a Dubious Category*. Princeton: Princeton University Press, 1996.

CHAPTER 8

Election

A Horrible Dilemma

We know already that we are caught up into God's great plan and purpose for the cosmos. We have learned, moreover, that our death and resurrection in Jesus have brought this plan back on track after it was derailed by our sinful lusts and by the evil powers who have infiltrated our world. The plan is now rolling steadily on, as it was always meant to. So Rom 8:29 states programmatically,

> Those whom he knew beforehand
> he also appointed to be conformed to the image of his Son
> so that he [the Son] might be the firstborn among many siblings.

The technical term for God's overarching activity here, which bends the future of the cosmos to his purpose, is "election." But talk of election tends to make people very nervous, and in some respects it does have a nasty track record. After mentioning this word, students I am teaching often rush off like horses stampeding away from the smell of a mountain lion, unaware that their panicked flight is heading toward a gorge. We must confront this challenge too, then, as we seek to deepen our understanding of Paul's thinking.

Many students tend to think immediately of God's electing influence upon us as some hard, causal, mechanical, or chemical process like an oven baking a piece of clay, and a straightforward literal reading of various biblical passages can reinforce this notion, including a well-known argument in Romans, namely, 9:6–24. They then immediately start to worry about the people who have been left outside of God's electing purposes, apparently having reliable information in advance of judgment day about who has been left out. If these poor folk have been hardened like the proverbial clay, then God seems to be behaving like something of a monster, and I actually agree with this concern. A God who creates people destined for annihilation at best and enduring torture at worst is a monster. At the same moment as they are worrying about those predestined inflexibly and rather cruelly for the lake of fire, my stampeding students also worry that their freedom has been irreducibly compromised. The causal process the electing God is directing toward humanity has apparently baked all the freedom out of his subjects, which seems highly counterintuitive, not to mention detrimental to even the most basic ethics. Are we accountable actors or in reality just metaphysically complex lumps of clay? (Paul supposedly tells us at this moment in Rom 9:20–21, rather unhelpfully, not to answer back to God.)

We are obviously running into some conceptual obstacles here that are blocking the pathway to a smooth acquisition and deployment of the notion of our chosen and elected destiny of Trinitarian communion. In fact, we are struggling with a classic theological challenge: the relationship between divine and human activity or, as the technicians often put it, between divine and human agency. It is as if, on the one side, we have God's activity directed toward us and, on the other, we have our acting, and these notions seem to compete with one another. It feels as if it is either God's election (i.e., his agency) or our agency. To the degree that God acts, we cannot act; and insofar as we act, God cannot act. It is a zero-sum relationship that creates an awful dilemma.

We need God to act so that he can be God and generally act as the Lord. God runs things. He has to act ultimately in a sovereign and all-powerful way. How is his plan going to be carried out if he can't? If he isn't acting, why would we talk about him and get involved with him in the first place? But we need to be able to act as well, or there is something very odd about everything down at our level. Where we live, we seem to act all the time. This is part of what we are as human beings. And God even seems to *want* us to act for much of the time, especially by loving him with all our heart, soul, mind, and strength. However, if God is acting, isn't this cutting into our acting? And if we are acting, is this not cutting into God's acting? We need both these things to be completely true, and yet it looks as though they can't both be true at the same time.

It seems, then, that we have to resolve this basic dilemma, or Paul's contention that we are being caught up meaningfully within the triune God's great plan for a final communion together, bearing the image of the risen Son, doesn't make sense. Either our activity within God's plan, as he works to carry it out, is meaningless, or the plan—which is to say, God—isn't relevant. Both options are clearly pretty horrendous.

However, there is a solution. All our difficulties here are being caused, I would suggest, by a basic theological mistake. The conceptualizing that is being done at this moment, especially about the way God acts on us, is *uncontrolled* and *projected*. In other words, we have slipped once more into foundationalism. We are making things up for ourselves. We are *analogizing* about very deep dynamics in relation to God and reality in an undisciplined and ultimately inaccurate way, grabbing notions and metaphors from around us—from our history and culture and from a naive approach to reality—and supposing that they explain accurately both God and us, instead of letting God supply the key analogies through the prism of Christ. This is what is getting us into trouble, as it usually does. In fact, this is the way in which foundationalism can reenter Christian thinking and subvert it, infecting a particular issue or area within a broader, healthy body (i.e., a body of thinking that is basically oriented by Jesus) and spreading contamination outward from that point. To deal with this diseased theologizing, we must return to strictly christological analogizing and cut out the offending foundationalist tumor. Some theological surgery is necessary!

In this specific relation, we are almost certainly thinking about God's electing activity in terms of an automatic, or "hard," causal analogy. God acts on us the way we shape or cut an inanimate object like a piece of wood or the way we boil water. And these analogies will cause legitimate concerns because they must block human activity, and it will be particularly nasty when it is combined with the conviction that at least some folk are not going to be saved. We are reasoning that this hard causal process on God's part exists in a zero-sum relationship with human activity—and this sort of causality does. To be caused in an automatic, or even mechanical, way is not to be free to this extent. A lump of wood does not act freely. The more an automatic election, the less freedom, so any maximal commitment to election in this sense must erase human freedom, which then reduces much of the Bible's advice and our own experience to nonsense (although the practical effect of this inference will often be the moral repudiation of any notion of election).

At the heart of this problem, then, is the uncontrolled projection of an analogy, that is to say, the projection of a theory about causality, narrating it a certain way, into the deepest regions of divine and human interaction, with the resulting generation of some nasty consequences. We are assuming that God acts on us—or, put differently, that divine agency is to be understood—like a person boiling a kettle of water to make a cup of coffee, or in more biblical parlance, like a potter shaping a clay cup. And it follows that we may well clear up our difficulties if we reconceptualize these areas with more theological discipline. Knowing what we already know about God as he has been revealed by Christ, can we think through these notions more accurately and thereby avoid generating this conundrum?

I think we can.

Rethinking Election

First of all, we need to resist the separation of election as a divine activity toward us from what we already know about God and his relationship with us through Jesus here and now. This is critical. We shouldn't start imagining what God was doing, electing, before the foundation of the world, as if we really know anything about this topic. We weren't there. The only thing we know is what we know now, which is revealed definitively by God with us, namely, Jesus, who was sent by his Father to save us while we were yet sinners. This event and this person tell us definitively about how God acts toward us and on us. And it has become apparent to us from this information that God loves us and therefore that he has loved us from before the foundation of the world. (God does not change!) Moreover, if we grip this truth strongly, we are in a very fortunate position. We can now go on to appreciate that *some critical insights are present in the doctrine of election*—some truths about God that are precious and affirming—provided it is understood in the right, suitably controlled, way. Election, then, is not just not a problem. Rightly understood, it is a blessing. Election tells us about some of the key features of God's love for us. Three closely related things are actually implicit in God's action on our behalf before we even existed. Election tells us that God's love *initiates*, that God's love *gives*, and that God's love is *creative*.

Think about parenting again for a moment (with the necessary caveat that we picture it in the healthiest form we know of). In a dim echo of God's great act of creation, parents "elect" to have children. They *initiate* this process. The children are not consulted! Parents then *give life to* their children. Children are conceived, carried, born, and nurtured. And this act is deeply and fundamentally *creative*. New things spring into being—in this case, most marvelous of all, people. Moreover, in the entire history of the human race (Adam and Eve excepted), it has never been otherwise. This *life-giving*, at its best, is a decision of love. It is not otherwise with God. We see from the story of God's initial love for us, then, in place before we existed as more than a plan, that love has these key dynamics. It initiates and gives and creates to such a degree that it fosters life so that others not yet born *can share in its joy*. A loving communion seeks other partners to join it, and a divine communion calls those partners generously into existence. Just these dynamics unfolded as God initiated a relationship with us, gifted us with life, and thereby created us and called us into being—as we were elected. A fabulous gift.

In view of God's intertwining of election and its gracious initiatives with love, we must now abandon the idea that such a God would elect anyone to be lost eternally to the annihilation of death or, worse still, to endure eternally in a place of pain. It makes no sense to restrict God's loving election in any way; this is literally nonsense. "I love you and am going to call you into being with the initial purpose of communing with you, but ultimately so that you can die or, perhaps better, endure eternal torment." Everything that has been called into being or created—that has been gifted with life—has been elected, and everything elected has been elected from and for love. It has been elected for companionship and communion. There is only one election, and it is good and kind. We will want to inquire in due course about the eventual fate of those apparently not included.[1] But before doing so, we must grasp the insight firmly that a loving election must be single and universal in intent. Its scope corresponds to creation, and it is incoherent if it doesn't.[2] There is only one electing purpose—the summons to everyone to love and to sport with the Lord our God within an entire creation that is loved by God and called into being for this purpose and for this alone. This is the electing purpose visible in Jesus and effected by Jesus. and there can be no other. Double predestination be damned!

In view of all this, we must also abandon any understanding of God's influence upon us in a hard causal way. It is not a chemical or mechanical or any other automatic process. God is in a loving relationship with us. It would be absolute nonsense to reduce this relationship to the impersonal relationship we can observe between us and rocks and stones and chemicals—to inanimate objects and processes. We must think instead of our deepest and most important relationships—hopefully of our friendships and of some of our key family relationships—if we want to begin to grasp how God acts on us. These relationships influence us, even as we influence those we are in relationship with. My spouse is a huge influence on my life. Much that happens in my life happens because she causes it, and vice versa. This influence on me is central and primary. In fact, it is doubtless the most powerful causal influence in my life, in addition to God's (although I suspect that they are often working

1. The subject of ch. 18, "The Triumph of Love."
2. Barth's recovery here of Paul's original insight is extremely important; see *CD* II/2, supplemented powerfully by IV/3.2.

together). But this is a *personal* influence on me—powerful, to be sure, but by no means mechanical or automatic. God's influence on us, in election, is consequently rather like this. It too is a personal, relational influence; indeed, it is *the* relational influence. It is powerful—massively powerful—but not automatic or mechanical. It has causal force, but only in the sense that an enormously influential and loving relationship does. God's influence upon us is a great wave of loving relating that preceded us, that created us, gifting us with life, and that constantly seeks to enfold us, irrevocably. It is the most powerful causal force in the universe![3]

So we must banish reductionist metaphors for divine agency from our heads and carefully reinterpret any scriptural texts that use them, bearing in mind that the Scriptures are probably speaking metaphorically and poetically at these moments to describe something very difficult and revealed decisively only with the coming of Jesus. We are not *literally* a lump of clay that God kneads. He loves us, and that love is a powerful force. So he shapes us from uninspiring and useless lumps of mud into the equivalent of beautiful crafted vessels suited for his purposes—and he does so within a complex relational process involving summoning, chiding, waiting, liberating, guiding, gifting, and blessing. This deeply personal journey together is perhaps ultimately as irresistible as a potter's shaping of a vessel (this being the question we wrestle with in ch. 18), but it is by no means *reducible* to that relationship. It is a complex journey in love, particular to each one of us, and oriented toward an ultimate destiny of eternal communion.

In short, we can see now that the love of God operative in election, before we were born, has these fundamentally generous dynamics—initiating, giving, and creating. And it acts on us relationally because it has destined us for personal relationship. But election names some other critical things that we now need to turn to consider.

Election as Covenantal

Election also introduces the critical insight that God's love, and hence all authentic love, is *unconditional* and *irrevocable* in its relationships with those whom it has called into existence (Rom 11:29). We see decisive evidence of this level of commitment in the Father's and the Spirit's selfless sacrifice of their Son

---

3. We will expand our understanding of this "relational causality" a great deal and in a rather fascinating way shortly in part 2.

for a humanity that was still hostile and vicious, and in the Son's acceptance of a cruel death for the same (5:6–10). This commitment speaks of the incomprehensible benevolence of God toward us that reaches out and pays the ultimate price prior to any response on our part and hence irrespective of whether we respond or not. We have seen, that is, that the gift of life to us through Jesus was not conditioned by any response on our part. A response was certainly expected, if not dreamed of and hoped for. But it was not a necessary condition for the entire process to begin—for the relationship to be called into being and then rescued after it had fallen among thieves. "God releases the *un*godly" Paul says pithily in Rom 4:5, making exactly the same point.

We need to let this insight into God sink down into our bones. Whether we respond or not, God is utterly committed to us. God died for us before we satisfied any conditions. So God is clearly prepared to do anything to reach us and to save us, irrespective of how we are behaving. And this deeply committed love for us was in place before the foundation of the world. God created us from nothing, before we could satisfy any conditions then either, and consequently remains committed to us even if we fail to satisfy them in due course, which is why he later died for us. And this commitment is consequently an essential part of God's elected relationship with us. We learn, that is, that our relationship with God, initiated in election, is fundamentally unconditional and irrevocable. It is unbreakable and irreversible. It is in place permanently, all the way from and through eternity. And a useful word to describe this aspect of our elected relationship with God is *covenantal*.

The signifier "covenantal" is much used in scholarship today and often means rather different things for different people. But I think we should retain it in spite of this semantic confusion because, properly understood, it tells us something so important. Election is covenantal in the sense that God's loving relationship with us is irrevocable. God's commitment to us will outlast time itself.

We must immediately add that God initiates these relationships in the expectation of a full response of obedience, and we will spend a great deal of time in what follows describing the details of this response. In essence, God asks for a response to his love characterized by all our hearts, all our minds, all our souls, and all our strength. But we must not lose sight of the covenantal aspect of election. *God does not withdraw the relationship if this response is inadequate or absent.* If he did, he would not be the God that he is. Hence the hand of God remains extended to a recalcitrant and obstinate people (Rom 10:21, citing Isa 65:2).

Parents may again be a useful if dim reflection of this dynamic. Parents are always parents, irrespective of the actual behavior of their children, although they invariably possess strong expectations concerning how they should be-have. I will never not be the father of my children Emile and Grace, no matter how much I am tempted to walk away on occasion by certain events and ep-isodes that shall remain unspecified here. And I will take that identity to the grave, if not beyond. My expectations remain in place, but my covenantal rela-tionship is more fundamental and enduring. (I would add quickly that I trust that *they* will never walk away from me either, despite the things that I have done; we live in a bilateral covenantal arrangement—a set of unconditional covenants running in both directions.) But God is vastly more committed to us than I am to my family. My parenting is nothing but a blurred exemplar of the fact that God is always our loving God in covenant with us and will be this, if necessary, in spite of everything we do and say.

In short, God is at heart covenantal (in this sense), and we gather the priceless further insight from this fact that *the universe is constructed cove-nantally*. We just saw that covenantal relationships of love initiate life, which is to say, they foster life. But we see now that *they also provide the framework that sustains life*. People are nurtured by covenantal relationships, which are relationships that are put in place unconditionally and that hold irrevocably. People flourish within covenants and languish outside of them.

These are profoundly important insights into the character of God and into the relationship that God has with us. They are also important insights, at one step removed, into how people should relate to one another, and we will develop them more fully in the parts that follow.[4] For the moment, however, we should pause to note that, as a result of all this, election is a deeply *pastoral* doctrine, which is exactly how Paul deploys it in his most famous discussion of the subject.

Election as Pastoral

God's election comforts us in our afflictions because it assures us in the midst of any sufferings that God loves us and is actively working things out. God is on our side. God is "for us," as Paul puts it (and as Barth also never tired of saying, although he tended to use the Latin, *pro nobis*). We might not see this love now—appearances can be truly frightening—but these are the underlying historical and cosmic facts that we know to be true because this is the nature

---

4. So, for example, we will press them later on when we consider the practice of marriage, in chs. 24 and 25.

of the electing and loving God as revealed by Jesus. Romans 8:28 consequently turns out to be a critical thesis statement for the glorious and positive if counterintuitive affirmations that follow through the end of the chapter:

> We *know* that [God the Father] works everything out ultimately for a
>   good purpose
> for benefit of those who love God—
> for those who are called according to his purpose . . .

—Paul introducing here, up front in a thesis statement, the pastoral function of the notion, going on to ground it appropriately—

> . . . *because* those God foreknew
> he also predestined to be conformed to the image of his Son,
> that he might be the firstborn among many brothers and sisters.
> And those he predestined, he also called;
> those he called, he also released;
> those he released, he also glorified. (8:29–30 NIV modified)

God's electing plan, in place before the foundation of the world, has now been crisply stated. But where does Paul go with this thought?—toward anxieties about the erasure of our own agency? toward concerns about those who are now automatically being designated for hell? Absolutely not! He *comforts* his auditors in absolutely every conceivable difficult circumstance—and quite a number are specified.

> What, then, shall we say in response to these things?
> If God is for us, who can be against us?
> He who did not spare his own Son, but gave him up for us all
> —how will he not also, along with him, graciously give us all things?
> Who will bring any charge against those whom God has chosen?
> It is God who releases.
> Who then is the one who condemns?
> No one.
> Christ Jesus who died—more than that, who was raised to life—
> is at the right hand of God and is also interceding for us.
> Who shall separate us from the love of Christ?
> Shall trouble or hardship or persecution or famine
> or nakedness or danger or sword?

As it is written:
"For your sake we face death all day long;
we are considered as sheep to be slaughtered."
No, in all these things we are more than conquerors through him who
    loved us.
For I am convinced that neither death nor life,
neither heavenly messengers nor rulers,
neither the present nor things to come,
neither powers—neither height nor depth—nor anything else in all
    creation
will be able to separate us from the love of God
that is in Christ Jesus our Lord. (8:31–39 NIV modified)

It seems almost impertinent to add anything at this moment, but there is one
further thing we should address now, however briefly.

Human Activity

Someone might still ask, "What is true human activity? What does it actually
consist of (so to speak)? You haven't answered *that* question yet with your
kinder, gentler account of God's activity on us! As far as I can tell, he might
be nicer, but he can still *effectively* override us and reduce us to the status of
puppets, appearances notwithstanding, and who wants a bar of that?!"

This challenge, which is often heard when discussing election, raises the
whole complex and important issue of our human agency, which is of course
the other side of the relationship. But the exploration of this question is best
handled as we consider ethics, which presupposes learning and the development, as a result, of a detailed account of agency, and this is the subject
of part 2 following, comprising seven chapters. We must basically be patient
then (although we will not have to wait for long). Having said this, it is worth
putting a brief marker in place here concerning the reality and the significance
of our agency, even if we don't fully understand it yet, doing so, however,
somewhat ironically, by way of the doctrine of election, which is so often held
to override it.

We learn from a correct account of election that God wants us to be free
actors in a very real sense and so gifts us with agency for the simple reason
that a loving relationship without some sort of freedom is meaningless. God
has chosen us from before the foundation of the world to live in loving com-

munion with him. And there is clearly no such thing as a loving relationship with someone who does not possess the freedom or capacity to respond to love with love. Love is free, by definition, in some sense. We respond freely in love to God—or we are meant to. Consequently, God's electing love of us to communion *entails* our freedom! And it follows that both God and Paul are very strongly committed to freedom, as am I. Robots cannot love. Neither, to use a more biblical idiom, can rocks or stones. But people can love because they are free to do so. Our freedom, however we understand it precisely (and this is an important and subtle matter that is addressed shortly), is guaranteed.

If this is all reasonably clear, it is worth pausing now to consider two of the main ways that people have wandered away from the Pauline path at this moment—what we might dub the Scylla and Charybdis of a virtue ethic, which I am just about to describe. Here, the errors about relating divine and human activity that we have just engaged with can creep back into our thinking, derailing either the need for further responsive activity, including discipleship, or the need for God to be closely involved with it. But these confusions must be resisted. Zero-sum thinking in relation to personal agents, whether God or us or both parties acting together, must be continuously and trenchantly repudiated! Our insights into God's loving election setting us free to respond to him as we ought to must be pressed home.

Hyper-Augustinianism

If election is understood mechanistically, someone might attach this notion to grace and argue that God has *given* us *everything* we need in the act of electing us. God simply acts decisively upon us, albeit generously. This gift would then operate in spite of anything we do, and anything we might do should be excluded. Indeed, if we had to act, we would to that degree undermine what God has given us. Grace and human activity operate here in a zero-sum relationship, so, if we take the side of God, we would go on to attack any endorsements of a need for human activity in the name of grace.

A particular reading of Augustine can cause readers of Paul trouble in this respect, so that the assertion of any need for agency or even learning in response to grace is dubbed "Pelagianism"! I don't think this is a complete reading of Augustine, who was a complex thinker and shifted significantly in his thinking over time. But an extreme account of some of his positions can be advocated in this way and in his name, and at this moment his influence—however misrepresented—*must* be resisted. We can speak of a hyper-Augustinian view, then, that eliminates any role for human agency in discipleship, the long-term results of which are serious. The whole process of formation is neglected if not opposed by hyper-Augustinians, and the end result is a church without discipleship. How good is this church likely to be? And how Pauline will it look?

Fortunately, we have already exposed the error at work in this view and corrected it. God's election is certainly unconditional, but in the sense that a covenantal relationship is. It will never be withdrawn and will ultimately prevail. In the meantime, however, it respects human agency carefully, as seen most clearly in God's incarnation to meet us. Moreover, as we will see in much more detail shortly, among those who respond to it, it enhances human freedom. Those who learn actively and wholeheartedly to live out of their new location in Christ can grow dramatically in their capacity to act in good ways. Relational election nurtures human agency and freedom; it does not stifle it. It summons us to ongoing and deeper responsiveness, which is to say, to learning, and many of Augustine's writings contain a great deal of wisdom about this process.[5] Nevertheless, any exclusion of human activity in response to God's initiative in his name, in a type of hyper-Augustinianism, must be vigilantly opposed and rejected. *This* type of unconditionality undermines the heart of the life of discipleship.

However, a further mistake is, as is often the case, a swing to the opposite and complementary error. Whereas hyper-Augustinians emphasize election and grace to the exclusion of human agency, misconceiving both divine and human agency in the process, Pelagians share the same basic misunderstanding but emphasize human agency on the other side of the supposed divide, and so go on to override divine election, with equally destructive results.[6]

Pelagianism

If the relationship between divine and human agency—which is to say, between election and our free responding—is not properly understood, those

---

5. See Jennifer Herdt, "Augustine: Disordered Loves and the Problem of Pride," in *Putting on Virtue*, 45–71. Her account draws on Augustine's *City of God, On Christian Doctrine, On the Lord's Sermon on the Mount, Confessions, The Trinity*, and *Soliloquies*.

6. An underlying ethical anxiety often propels this move, but theological work founded on anxiety is invariably misdirected. We will also address this anxiety and its appropriate (as against its inappropriate) mollification when we distinguish between an "intrinsic" and an "extrinsic" approach to ethics in ch. 15.

who take the side of the human actor rather than the electing God, like Pelagius (or, to be charitable, by some of his less-nuanced followers, rather than the great exegete himself), must oppose divine activity. If what really matters are human acting and ethics and all the accountability that go with these, then the causal process of election must be eliminated. Human actions and their attendant learning and growth must characterize the entirety of the divine-human relationship or, in less extreme versions, most of it, creating a functional Pelagianism. But the result of this well-intentioned move is, once again, shipwreck, and it will be very instructive to note here just how.

This move strips the electing and covenantal frame of learning away completely, setting a disastrous set of consequences in train. Instead of locating the progress of disciples and their acquisition and description of freedom *within* a strong relational and covenantal frame, the relationship *itself*, as well as its first establishment and underlying maintenance, is drawn into a notion of human action and progress. And this *replaces* the unconditional covenant, with all its insights into God's initiating and sustaining love, with a conditional arrangement, which is an unmitigated theological disaster! God's loving, unconditional covenant with us is erased, which is quite a loss!

If Jesus followers have to act in a certain way not only to advance in their lives ethically but to relate to God in the first place, a fundamental displacement takes place in the whole relationship between God and humankind. It follows that this relationship must have had conditions inserted into it. God will not relate to people kindly until they have acted in a certain way. Only after certain things have been done will a relationship be entered into at all, and certainly for one of any benevolence. (Recall that we are in this awkward position because we have stripped election out of the picture, so we have no story now of God initiating his relationship with us—of making the first move before we move toward him, and thereby establishing our relationship together.) This viewpoint consequently shifts the covenant of salvation into a profoundly different mode, namely, a contract. And once we are structuring the relationship between God and humanity in terms of a contract, we are talking about a different God altogether.

Contracts are underpinned by justice and oriented by conditions. *If* people agree to do A, *then* someone else, in a contractual relationship with them, agrees to do B. So if A is not forthcoming, neither is B. For a very long time, human culture has organized many of its interactions in this way. The Code of Hammurabi, promulgated from around 1750 BCE, devotes a lot of its space to specifying contractual obligations. And modern societies are cocooned in a massive tangle of legal structures, regulations, laws, and contracts. However, the result of inserting this legal arrangement of complex human society into the relationship between God and us is devastating.

This move restricts God's love to the inside of a contractual arrangement. God will love us *only if* we fulfill the conditions that he stipulates for us to enter into a relationship of this nature with him, and outside of this relationship, his love does not apply! Many Protestants who think in this way claim that we can activate this contract by believing—which is rather harder than they realize, as we will see shortly.[7] But assuming for the sake of argument that this is how we get into a proper relationship with God, then and only then will God love us. God loves only believers. Everyone else relates to God in terms of justice, and things are probably not going to work out well for them, even in terms of justice, because everyone is supposed to embrace the gospel contract. So nonbelievers are almost certainly going to fall under the harsh side of God's justice, and retribution and punishment await.[8]

It is probably evident already that we have effectively destroyed the story about God that we have been articulating so carefully up to this moment. This God is not fundamentally characterized by love. He is fundamentally characterized by retribution, and he has to be conditioned into loving someone. He loves only converts, and everyone else is screwed, to put things bluntly. Moreover, *he doesn't really love converts either.*

Contractual love is not really love. Love is not conditional. It is *unconditional!* It is covenantal and irrevocable. It is unbending. I love my kids, and they will always be my kids. It doesn't matter what they do. They are not my children because they have fulfilled some parent-child contract, which will be abrogated if they fail to measure up. (I have expectations to be sure, but they are not structured by a contract.) And I am a very pale imitation of the God who sent his beloved only Son to die for us while we were still hostile to him.

---

7. In ch. 13, which addresses believing.

8. This theory will struggle with any strong account of human sinfulness too. Any greatly reduced capacity to act well makes any unassisted fulfillment of God's contractual demands difficult if not impossible, and we now face a horrible dilemma. If we hold on to humanity's incapacity, emphasizing its deep sinfulness, God is a monster for holding us accountable to the terms of a contract that we could never fulfill. He is just playing games with us before he executes us. Alternatively, we might cheerfully emphasize our capacity to do the good, but thereby greatly trivialize the seriousness of our situation, which is in fact deeply incapacitated by sin. Moreover, in emphasizing how good we are already, we lose the importance of what Jesus does for us when he gifts us with a new nature. We don't really know what to do with the atonement, and we certainly don't know what to do with the resurrection. Jesus becomes an example of good behavior to us, but little more.

Hence, the contractual account of God that the followers of Pelagius are forced to introduce because of their overriding emphasis on human activity strips out God's love. They have thereby rejected one of the most important insights that Jesus gives us into the character of God. And they have thereby abandoned our key truth—that Jesus is the one point where God has come to us, fully entered into our situation so there can be no confusion and no excuses, and revealed what he is really like. Indeed, we can see now how Pelagius's disciples have just accepted a gambit from the devil and unleashed the horsemen of the foundationalist apocalypse. They have activated foundationalism. They have imposed a truth drawn from their own locations onto God and controlled the information that God supplies them with through Jesus in those terms, and we don't have to look very far to find where they have drawn this imagery from. Contractual imagery is the language of law and commerce, and it is generally upheld—as the code of the ancient Babylonian king Hammurabi suggests—by the state. Consequently, it is clear that Pelagians have created God in their own political and legal image—and thereby also blocked any reconstruction of politics in God's covenantal and familial image, so the damage just goes on and on. Instead of supposing that God relates to humanity in a hard, automatic, causal fashion, Pelagians suppose that God relates to us in a conditional and legal way (and it is hard to know which is worse).

In sum, the Pelagian overriding of God's unconditional and loving election of humanity in the name of human agency, and an accompanying—and quite legitimate—need for learning and pedagogy, thereby conditionalizing that relationship, is clearly a very bad idea and must be resisted at all costs. We must hang on to the critical insight that our relationship with God rests on election. He initiated our relationship, sustains it, and will consummate it. *Within* this relationship we are, however, summoned to learn and to move forward, and to do so stringently.[9] Pelagians, we might say, are right from

9. There is a conditional element to this learning, as there always is, although it is not a *contractual* conditionality. It is simply *consequential*. For example, if I hold a blowtorch to my leg, then it will get burned. I don't have a contract with the blowtorch, but this is a conditional arrangement. If I fulfill the condition (which is the application of the blowtorch to my leg), then the consequence will be horrible damage to my leg, and probably also a profound learning experience. But if you agree to see me only after I hold a blowtorch to my leg, then we do have a contract—one additional to the damage I will inflict by fulfilling the condition of blow-torching my leg. (I would add that our relationship is unlikely to proceed unless I become peculiarly desperate to see you.)

Learning has this sort of consequential conditionality, although hopefully a slightly less painful one than this illustration. Only if we learn to do X will we be

this point on.[10] It follows that human agency, along with learning, should be embraced wholeheartedly, and any hyper-Augustinianism must be avoided with as much vigilance as Pelagianism is. We must carefully avoid the Scylla of Pelagianism, but in sailing around its shoals, neither must we allow ourselves to be sucked into the whirlpool that is the hyper-Augustinian Charybdis.

Conclusions

In closing this chapter, then, it is clear that we can and must wholeheartedly affirm God's election. Proper theological thinking, with our metaphors and conceptuality disciplined by what we already know about God as that has been revealed through Jesus, has saved us from a nasty theological dilemma, which turned out to be constructed out of our own fearful imaginings, here operative as projections. Election, rightly understood, speaks of God's love for us. It is a love that calls us into being in the first place. It initiates its relationship with us, gifting us with life, and creating new life as it does so. God's election is nothing more—or less!—than God's love for us before we exist. And it remains committed to us, unconditionally and irrevocably, hence covenantally, through thick and thin. Consequently, there is no sinister decision on God's part prior to the foundation of the world that anyone must ultimately be excluded. The divine plan is for everyone to be created for eternal play with the triune God. The loving purpose and activity is universal.

---

free to do X; moreover, if Y and Z presuppose X, then we will be free to learn to do Y and Z only if we have first learned X. This is all true. Learning is conditional. But this conditional learning process is clearly not a contract that could structure our entire relationship with God. It is a consequential conditionality and hence a qualitatively different kind of conditionality from a legal form. And it is nested within relationships that are emphatically not contractual, as a child's learning is nested within an overarching relationship with parents. We will develop these insights in ch. 9.

10. As Stanley Hauerwas quips in one of his famous aphorisms, "Once you're a Christian, you can't be Pelagian enough." He is being characteristically provocative, but underlying the startling claim is, as always, a serious theological insight. People who have been saved are supposed to be fully engaged in their discipleship, as we have already noted, and as the most important commandment in the Jewish Scriptures, endorsed by Jesus, directly suggests. We are all supposed to be striving with *all* of our willing, as well as with all of our thinking, feeling, and any additional acting—*with the entirety of our being*—to love God. So, insofar as Pelagius was frustrated by a lack of commitment to discipleship, and ultimately of commitment to following hard after God, and emphasized in his work a full human commitment to this relationship, he was right.

As such, however, election is clearly a relationship with us. So this is how it influences us "causally." It is a vast wave of divine love resonating through all our relationships and ultimately into our unique journey together toward the cosmic destiny of communion. There is no overriding of our activity in response, then—far from it. This election has created us precisely so that we *can* respond. It *establishes* our freedom.

We will have more to say about the exact nature of human freedom momentarily. But a relational and covenantal account of authentic freedom will inform everything that follows—and what follows is the realization in our midst now of the plan God hatched before the foundation of the world: that everyone should bear the image of the risen Jesus and should live in communion with him, along with the other figures in the triune God, in communion. It is time to turn from our anxieties about God, to God's actual plan and its outworking in our lives.

Theses

> God's plan—"election"—involves God acting on us in accordance with his good purpose before we existed to call us into existence, to transform us, and to gather us into communion.
> This plan generates the age-old theological challenge of relating election and human freedom.
> In fact, however, we are asking here about the relationship between divine activity or agency, here operating in election, and human activity and agency.
> These agencies are often viewed as competitive with one another—as existing in a zero-sum relation to one another.
> This conception leads to an awful dilemma.
> An emphasis on divine agency in these terms overrules human activity. It also suggests a monstrous God, who creates people only to damn them.
> An emphasis on human agency eliminates God's sovereignty, purposes, and electing initiative and hence, ultimately, his relevance.
> The underlying difficulty, however, is being caused by faulty analogizing.
> It is *foundationalist*—the projection of cultural analogies into the realm of divine agency, here the projection of an automatic, "hard," and perhaps even mechanical understanding of causality into God's activity toward us.
> A hard account of divine causality operative through election would exclude human agency. God would treat us and act on us like a lump of clay in the hands of a potter.

- We need to discipline our analogies concerning election and divine causality (and also, in due course, concerning freedom) in relation to the definitive information we have had revealed to us through Jesus.
- Consequently, election needs to be understood in a loving way.
- It can be seen in this light that it refers to God's initiative, which is also creative and giving. Love initiates and, in God, creates and gifts life to us, so that God might share the triune communion with humanity.
- It is therefore single and inclusive; everyone created has been destined in love for divine communion.
- There is no double predestination. This doctrine should itself be damned.
- It follows that God does not act on us in any automatic, causal way. Such action would hardly create a loving relationship. It would in fact be nonsense.
- God created us for fellowship, which cannot be offered by the equivalent of rocks.
- Consequently, God acts on us relationally and personally. We thus experience a relational causality, the exact mechanics of which will be elucidated shortly.
- Scriptural images must be interpreted to elucidate aspects of this relationship, never to undermine or to obscure it.
- The establishment of the relationship of love between God and humanity is also unconditional and irrevocable. It is irreversible and unbreakable.
- Election is in this sense "covenantal."
- Covenants, with their establishment through the divine initiative and with the irrevocable commitment of God to them, are the right context for all human flourishing.
- Election, rightly understood, is consequently a deeply pastoral doctrine, which is how Paul uses it in his most extensive description, in Rom 8:28–39.
- It follows, finally, that people must possess agency, or freedom.
- For us to fulfill our destiny as God's covenant partners, we must be able to respond to him in love, and hence freely.
- Election therefore—contrary to popular opinion—*establishes* human agency.
- A detailed account of our freedom should nevertheless emerge from our account of Christian ethics, which presupposes Christian learning and hence our agency—the subject of part 2.
- Hyper-Augustinianism must clearly be vigilantly and resolutely opposed. Human freedom is critical.

- ‣ Pelagians, conversely, wish to emphasize human activity and so exclude divine agency and election (again, misunderstanding the overarching relationship between God and humanity competitively).
- ‣ But Pelagianism necessarily reduces the entire relationship between God and humanity to a legally conditional arrangement that then functions like a contract. This relationship is initiated or, at the least, appropriated by human activity. Election is excluded.
- ‣ This too is theologically destructive. God's fundamental attribute is now retributive justice; God has to be conditioned into loving people, although conditional love is actually not love at all. This view conceals the information about God revealed to us through Jesus, and especially through his death on behalf of a hostile humanity; and it reintroduces foundationalism, here specifically as a political and legal form, the contract, and projects it onto God.
- ‣ Pelagianism is therefore a combination of positions and problems that undermine the correct account of God and salvation, substituting in its place what amounts to a completely different account of God and the gospel.
- ‣ Pelagianism must be vigilantly and resolutely opposed.
- ‣ Once the covenant is established, however, a "Pelagian" emphasis on a wholehearted human effort to follow and to love God is appropriate.

Key Scriptural References

We already know the key election and love texts (Rom 8:29!), although Rom 8 has been emphasized here more broadly (esp. vv. 29–39), and verse 28 is also significant. Barth also appealed, quite correctly, to Eph 1:4 in context.

God's irrevocable love for us is implicit in the important statement of his irrevocable love for Israel, made in Rom 11:28–29. See also Rom 10:21, citing Isa 65:2. His love for us "while we were yet sinners/ungodly" (Rom 5:6) is also again critical; see also the famous claim of Rom 4:5.

Romans 9:6–24 is the classic location for "hard" double predestination. This text needs to be interpreted very carefully and, if necessary, in terms of *Sachkritik*. (I don't think it does as much damage as it is often held to. My reading of it is forthcoming in my theological reading of Romans.)[11]

---

11. *Romans: A Theological Reading*, Commentaries for Christian Formation (Grand Rapids: Eerdmans, forthcoming).

Key Reading

Much that is said here depends on Barth's insights in *CD* II/2 (God's freedom in election).

Further Reading

The nature of God's activity in relation to us is elaborated much more fully in the following chapter, where we begin to elaborate an account of human agency. One of Barth's most insightful discussions can be found in *CD* III/3.

We have met the critical notion of covenant but have now linked it more clearly with a contrasting and highly destructive notion of contract. This distinction is articulated most helpfully, as was said before, by two key essays by James B. Torrance.

Bibliography

Barth, Karl. *Church Dogmatics*. II/2; III/3.
Torrance, James B. "The Contribution of McLeod Campbell to Scottish Theology." *SJT* 26 (1973): 295–311.
———. "Covenant or Contract?: A Study of the Theological Background of Worship in Seventeenth-Century Scotland." *SJT* 23 (1970): 51–76.

PART 2

Formation

CHAPTER 9

A Learning Community

What Happens Next?

We have learned many things through part 1: first and foremost, that God's intention from before the foundation of the world was to call people into existence, to give them life, and then to fellowship with them as a communion of persons, ultimately to delight in them and to enjoy them. This is the secret that lies at the heart of the universe. We have also learned that something has gone wrong. A great dislocation in this communion has taken place so that God's unfolding creation has become pervasively contaminated with sin. Nevertheless, God has acted decisively—in person!—to deliver us from our deathly contamination and to set us back on the pathway to life. We have been resurrected, at least in our minds, a claim that is plausible when we avoid applying distorting Western categories to it. We have also learned how to avoid crippling our ongoing journey by misunderstanding the way God's electing actions relate to ours. God influences us as a loving creator and parent, initiating his relationship with us, gifting us with life, creating us, and then committing to us in an irrevocable covenant.

A simple but important question now arises. What happens next? It's easy to feel at this moment a bit like a group of hikers who have come over a pass in the mountains late in the day and stand dwarfed and immobilized in front of a sunset that stretches from horizon to horizon. This stunning scenery is all very well—I give thanks for it and admire it—but how does it relate to us where we are on the ground right now?

As always, we should go back to first principles (so to speak),[1] and I

---

1. Thinking about God's plan as definitively revealed through Jesus and the Spirit is not, strictly speaking, to consider a set of "principles." Principles suggest something

will try to do so here and to construct a chain of important theological inferences.

We have learned already that God has reestablished his plan, which is the goal of fellowship with us all. God is a personal God and desires to commune with us as persons. Our next step then surely consists of getting on with effecting this plan. But what does this look like?

As Aristotle said helpfully when pondering just this question for himself, "The means is the end." Basically, he meant that if we are heading for perfect goodness, then we get there by being as good as we can from the beginning. We don't head for goodness by *not* being good. That would be bad!—and presumably unhelpful. Rather, the end of goodness is also the means, in an insight that is reversible, the means being the end. Beyond Aristotle, however, we have learned by way of revelation that our specific end—our good—is to commune with God and with one another. It follows, then, that if we are heading for a good communion, *we get there by pursuing a good communion here and now.* The end of good communion, imprinted by the Trinity, is also our means. It's as simple—and as difficult—as this.

We can probably see immediately that effecting this communion will now break down into two closely related but distinguishable activities. We should deepen the communion of those who are already acknowledging and living explicitly out of it. And we should try to reach people who are currently turned away from God, drawing them back into the communion with God and with one another for which they have always been destined. God calls us into communion, he always has and always will, and so those who have broken this fellowship will be called, ceaselessly, back into it, while the broken people currently indwelling it will be tirelessly encouraged to further abandon their brokenness. Hence, at bottom, when we think about what God's sweeping cosmic vision looks like concretely, on the ground, as we are actively involved with it now, we can see that God is in the business of *nurturing and founding* (further) *communities.* So clearly we need to start exploring these two closely related processes in more detail.

In fact, these investigations will occupy us in one way or another for the rest of this book. We will begin with a consideration of the nurture of our existing community here (part 2) and then turn to consider how they are founded (part 3). This analysis then devolves into a further consideration of how new

---

abstract. God's plan, along with its execution, is quite specific and concrete. It revolves around particular realities, which are, in some ways, the very opposite of principles. When I use the expression, then, it is a figure of speech.

communities flourish into an appropriate diversity (part 4), by which point we can conclude our discussion because we will have plenty to be getting on with.[2]

To tackle the first of our programmatic questions here: How are Christian communities nurtured? This inquiry is much the same as asking, What is church all about? Fine minds have a spent a lot of time pondering this question!

In fact, however, we have already learned the answer to this question, although in very broad and fundamental terms. God has revealed to us from the depths of his nature that a person is a relational being. People are their relationships. So a community of people is necessarily *a relational phenomenon*, and consequently the church is *all about its relationships*. Relationships are what matter, and they are relationships of love. Some important and very basic clarifications flow straightaway from this realization.

A Pauline understanding of community is not a bounded entity. It is not a walled compound with a group of people inside an explicit boundary who are rather different from the great mass milling around outside. It is not a circle on a board. It is not a discrete space set off from other spaces. It is not contained. It should certainly not be conceptualized as a building, which is what the word "church" tends to evoke for many of us today, perhaps along with regular Sunday gatherings there, which is why I have been cautious about using it. It is not "steepled," as I heard someone put it the other day. People are irreducibly and fundamentally relational, whether they are explicit Jesus followers or not. Hence a community of disciples is, at bottom, a *network*. This is how we need to think about things moving forward.

Communities are a lacework, a lattice, a web. There might be shifts in density, in a manner of speaking, where relationships connect with those who do not confess Jesus as Lord as against with those who do—or there might not be.[3] But all talk of internal versus external relationality is misplaced, as is all mention of borders and boundaries. These sorts of spatial metaphors will mislead us. There is just relationality with all those with whom we come into contact, although that relationality can operate in slightly different ways.

2. This claim might seem to be counterintuitive at first, but my rationale is as follows. In order to undertake mission appropriately, we will first need to be deeply grounded in what we might call Christian relationality; we will need to be schooled in it so that Christian relating to outsiders takes place appropriately, not inappropriately. Consequently, I suggest it is better in dogmatic terms for an account of Christian mission to follow after an analysis of the Christian community and its ethic.

3. We will really need to speak here in due course of hubs or clusters in accordance with network theory. See on all this Barabási's useful introduction *Linked: How Everything Is Connected to Everything Else and What It Means for Business, Science, and Everyday Life*.

But we are going to need a little more specificity than this as we try to move forward. Clearly, we need further information about relationality—about both when it is flourishing and when it is not. And if we were sociologists analyzing the relationality of a human family or network, we would probably ask two basic questions.

We would ask about how the family is *arranged*. Its relationships would all be functioning within forms and structures, and we would want to know what those are. As we settle into months of participant-observation, watching live cameras and recorded film and taking notes, we would try to find answers to questions such as, Who is in charge? Who makes most of the decisions? Or more likely, who makes which decisions? Which roles do which family members fulfill? We would want to ask who earns the money, who does the cleaning, who cooks, who shops (and for what), what recreation is and for whom, who educates, who books the holidays, who communicates the most, and about what, and so on. These arrangements would constitute the structure within which the relationships played out, so the way the relationships operate is tightly bound up with them.

I hesitate to recommend a dose of reality TV, but a little of its occasionally nasty banality might just be helpful at this moment. We might be taking a group of attractive but immature young adults to an exotic location and hoping that a deep romantic attachment between two will emerge from the maelstrom of competition and exposure, or taking a range of people and dropping them on a tropical island and asking them to survive, or we could be locking eight people in a house together for a couple of months to see what happens as they get bored and short of food. Their relationality would be profoundly shaped by these scenarios—by these forms or structures.

But we would also, in addition, spend some time pondering the *quality or nature of the relationality itself* in our object of study. This would not be separable from the forms and structures within which it operated, but it would be distinguishable. Recall again why we might watch *The Bachelor* or *Survivor*. The relational dynamics in these programs, which frequently get pretty vicious, are the real attraction. So we would scan the accumulating evidence about our family or network and ask, Are the relationships considerate, impatient, insulting, encouraging, kind, oblivious, and so on? Of course, if it's a real family, there will be moments characterized by all of these dynamics (note the Kardashians!), but the preponderant dynamics will matter most. Is the family relating in a way that is fundamentally caring and good-humored, or detached and frequently disparaging? After long months of careful surveillance, we would have built up a sense of how the relationships in the family work—how they are textured. Like listening to a note or musical sound, we would sense what their basic tenor was, although to convey our information to others helpfully, we would almost certainly have to rely on narrative.

Much the same applies, I would suggest, to our analysis of a Pauline community. We need first to explore the structure of the community. What arrangement of communal relationships—strictly speaking, of a particular cluster or hub within a broader network—best fosters an appropriate loving relationality? Who should do what? What are the key roles? How many are there? And so on. After working all this out, we would need to turn and try to discover more about the nature of the relationality involved—about the tenor of its relations—bearing in mind that the structure is devoted to fostering appropriate relationality, although we already know some critical things about the relationality involved.

We spoke in part 1 of the loving relationships that we are called to in triune communion. When reflecting on election, we also spoke of initiating, gifting life, and creating, as well as—briefly—of the unconditional, covenantal nature of loving relationships. These qualities link up with familial dynamics, provided those are correctly understood, recalling once again the caveat that not all families mediate God's relationality well. Friendships will be in play here too. But clearly we need to deepen and to "thicken" these basic insights here. Our earlier analysis of the dynamics of Trinitarian ethics was fairly generalized, and we need to think now about how loving and covenantal relationships work out more practically, concretely, and specifically, on the ground, looking as always to the concrete embodiment and exemplification of Jesus. And this in turn means that much of what follows will be oriented by a story about Jesus.

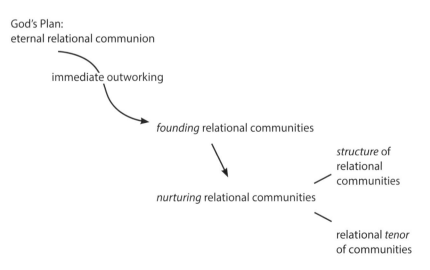

God's Plan:
eternal relational communion

immediate outworking

founding relational communities

structure of
relational
communities

nurturing relational communities

relational tenor
of communities

We begin with the question of structure. Once we know how God intends to arrange a right relationality among us, by way of Paul's extensive advice on the subject, it will be easier to think about how exactly that relationality ought to unfold in terms of its tenor or quality. If we don't proceed in this way, our account of relationality risks becoming somewhat abstract and disembodied, which we need to avoid at all costs. Pauline communities are concrete. They comprise real people acting in practical ways toward one another. And this feature will also help us to generate a clear answer to the question of human agency or freedom.

It is very easy to wander off at this moment in various unhelpful directions, misled again by inappropriate analogizing, which we need to resist as we journey deeper into our account of appropriate community. I am now going to make some important bridging connections that will feel very unfamiliar to many people who work on Paul, and yet they are connections, I would wager, that would have felt entirely familiar to Paul himself. These will set up our discussion of structure that follows.

Learning

It turns out that Pauline communities are all about *learning*, and ultimately about learning in a particular way—a mediated way, we will be unsurprised to find. It might not be exaggerating too much to say that much of the Protestant tradition has lost its way badly at just this moment, although I am not ultimately going to let Catholics or the Orthodox off the hook here either. Paul's communities are laboratories of relationality. They are designed to teach and to enhance the right sort of relating.

It is clear from almost every word Paul wrote that he expected the participants in his communities to learn things. That is why he wrote his letters. His letters presuppose that people would read them and then somehow modify their behavior. They would stop doing things that were wrong and start doing more things that were right. Someone at Corinth was to stop sleeping with his mother; someone else was supposed to refrain from taking a church member to court; a group of women was to stop prophesying in such a frenzied fashion that their hair became unkempt and their clothing began to slip. All were to behave more respectfully and inclusively at their eucharistic dinners and to love one another, abandoning keeping records of wrongs. And so on. Moreover, insofar as Paul's letters shed light on the rest of the things he did—his initial preaching missions, follow-up visits, and occasional dispatches of coworkers and friends—we see the same thing. All these events and figures assume that community members will act in response, improving their behavior, and this voluntary progression is really just what we otherwise call education or learning. On one level, it's as simple as this. Appropriate Pauline communities are communities learning about relationality and should be structured accordingly.

This initial impression that we have much to learn is reinforced when we reflect again on our destiny, remade in the image of the risen Jesus and living in eternal communion with him, the Father, and the Spirit in an irrevocable covenant of love. Clearly we are not there yet! But equally clearly, we should not stop trying to get there. This future is good—indeed, it is the definition of perfect goodness—and we ought to try to be good right where we are, here and now, or we are merely lapsing deeper into what is wrong. The way to the perfect good is to participate in goodness as best we can and to grow from this point onward.

In addition to this helpful Aristotelean insight that we have already noted—and bearing in mind that Aristotle and Paul differ greatly over the nature of goodness—the supremely and perfectly good God has been kind enough to break into our present situation and to remake us where we are, summoning us to live out of his reality at the same moment, and we ought to respond to this invitation. Trinitarian communion has started, although it has not yet been perfected in our lives, and so we should strive in the meantime with all our might and main to indwell it. We should, as one of the most important texts in Bible says, "Love the Lord our God with all our hearts, and with all our minds, and with all our souls, and with all our strength," and try to learn to do this better, since clearly we aren't doing it perfectly yet.

Jesus followers in the past have sometimes balked at emphasizing this learning process for various reasons that we will touch on shortly, but perhaps mainly because they forget that such learning is enfolded by a relationship. Once this is recalled, a lot of difficulties we might have with the notion of learning tend to melt away.

The relationship that frames any learning is, as we have already seen, elected. It is unconditional. It is established as a gift. And it is unbreakable. Nothing we do can ultimately distract it from its irrevocably loving goal. Having said this, like all covenants, this relationship is laden with expectations, and in our case, with expectations of learning. A covenant of love expects and hopes that its covenant partners will respond lovingly, freely, and wholeheartedly, and will learn to do so better and better. In fact, covenants have enormously high expectations. Agents who establish covenants expect a covenantal response! What good parents, who have called their children into being, do not frame their relationship with a covenant and then unload a truckload of expectations onto their children?! What person approaching a marriage, freely and joyously, does not nevertheless have a string of expectations of their spouse? What person does not expect a certain response from their best friend? We even expect great things of our dogs! Relationships are filled with expectations, and the deeper and more covenantal the relationship, the deeper and more comprehensive the expectations. Hence, in our case, as we respond to a covenantal God who is pulling us back into fellowship after we have gone astray, we have a great deal to learn as we begin to meet his covenantal expectations, and probably in two rather different senses.

First, we have a great deal that we need to *un*learn. It is already apparent at this relatively early stage in the book's argument how confused we are about God and how far we have gone astray as we think about truth and related matters like salvation. We desperately need the clarifications of God to simplify and to steady our minds on the truth, and to close the doors that repeatedly open onto falsehood. What confusions are we going to encounter now as we start talking about ethics, the church, the cosmos, practical ethics, and our individual lives?! We are all over the place. We must learn to resist the seductions of the Flesh and the deceptions of the powers. There is so much that needs to be repented of. To follow Jesus is in many respects a great unlearning, a comprehensive turning away from all the practices of the Flesh that damage, oppress, and destroy, from their most trivial instances up to our great excesses and addictions. In this respect, it is a momentous simplification.

But it is also clear that complementing this negative learning is an equally expansive positive education, one that vastly overshadows it as a glorious future outshines a tawdry past. We have, second, to learn a great deal as we press deeper into God.

We are in a new relationship, and our partners are exceptionally fascinating. We are living with the creator and sustainer of the cosmos. The secrets of the universe are lying at our fingertips, and this relationship is in place. It is here. (It has always been here.) It is whole and perfect right at this moment because the perfect God *is* in relationship with us. And yet there is so much more to learn, so we are summoned to learn in the sense that we must go deeper. Within this relationship there are untold things to find and to treasure, to detect and to adopt. Learning about God is a bit like exploring the ocean. We might presently be snorkeling in the shallows, discovering the delights of coral reefs and tropical fish. But it would be a significant mistake to think that this is all that the ocean contains. There are deep, dark trenches teeming with luminous and fascinating life-forms, as well as distant stretches of coastline with glorious flora and fauna we have never experienced. We see here, then, both the unconditional givenness of our relationship with God *and* the corresponding task of further growth and development.

Learning Is Freedom

We can now deepen our developing understanding of human agency significantly as we press in to our need for learning, noting that this is also a helpful place to introduce the loaded term "freedom." What we have just learned, once we reflect on it, is that *learning is freedom* and *freedom is learning*.

Admittedly, when God pulled us back on track, into communion, in his great act of resurrection, he delivered freedom to us in what Isaiah Berlin in a classic essay on the subject called negative freedom, or "freedom from," which is not quite the same thing as an understanding of freedom in terms of learning, although it is related to it. God set us free through Jesus *from* the forces and debilitations that had been constraining us. Our minds were liberated then, and we will be set free *from* our deteriorating fleshly bodies in due course (so Rom 8:18–23). These liberational acts were a critical precondition for our positive learning now. Without freedom from the things constraining and crippling us, we were not in a position to go forward.

But this was only the start. We are now becoming free in what Berlin called a positive sense, which is a different type of freedom. (To distinguish these two types, it will be helpful at times to speak of negative freedom as liberation, and of positive freedom as freedom proper.) Positive freedom describes how we are free to do things that we couldn't do before in a way that Berlin describes with some (although not complete) accuracy as "freedom to."[4]

This is an important but rather countercultural insight. Freedom in this sense is not any one thing at all, and it is certainly not an abstraction, value,

---

4. It is important to note that we are very soon going to develop a very different account of what positive freedom is from Berlin's. He was strongly committed to the classic liberal understanding of freedom as a space within which we make choices, which is an analysis that will shortly be severely criticized. If we displace his liberal account of positive freedom with a Christian understanding, however, *and* nuance his understanding of negative freedom, then his distinction between negative and positive freedom remains helpful.

or ideal that exists by itself. It correlates with the actions that we freely do, with our bodies, within our relationships, so it is a thousand and one things. Each action we freely undertake is an act characterized by freedom. And here is the critical point: Freedom in this sense *grows*, or at least, it *can* grow *if it learns*. As I learn new things, I am free to do things that I couldn't do before. Most important, when we relate to someone in love, we presuppose freedom, which is to say, loving freely, and as we learn to relate in love *better*, whether initiating or responding or doing any one of other countless loving things, *our freedom grows and increases*. So positive freedom—at least at first blush—is, properly understood, all about *capacity*, and our capacity should grow as we learn various things, in particular, to love well.

Ancient philosophers know all about these dynamics. They commonly used a craft image to talk about this and related matters, an analogy that has its limitations as well as its helpful side, but at the moment it can assist us. If I don't discipline myself to throw clay and to shape it on a wheel, then I'm not free to create beautiful clay pots and cups. I also need to know how to fire up and to stoke a kiln, how to source and preserve good clay, and of course how to mix, apply, and bake glazes, and so on. In fact, these relationships were so obvious to ancient thinkers that they spent most of their time concentrating on the interesting part of the situation, which was what training was needed to be free to do certain important things that couldn't be done before. Training to be a good potter was obvious. But what training was required to be a good philosopher? a good politician? or even just a good person? Those were tougher questions, and shortly we have to answer the question, What must we do to become a better disciple? No learning meant no further freedom to do X or Y, and X or Y could be pretty important. This was what mattered.[5]

We need now to add a further important dimension to our developing understanding of learning and freedom. Freedom, in the positive, increas-

---

5. One of the great delights in human life is mastering a skill, because we can then move forward to act creatively in a distant resonance of the great creator. Skills that have been learned are seldom applied—and in most cases cannot be applied—*exactly* as they were learned. They are flexible and transferable, and there are a lot of them. The result is that we can often combine and use our newly acquired skills to do things that bear a resemblance to what has been done before but that are in other respects new. Learning allows us to be creative. The carpenter who has learned how to skillfully use hammers and nails, screws, planes, saws, and lathes is in a position—is free—to construct a house that is obviously a house but has as yet, in this precise form, never been built before.

ing, incremental sense of learning, requires structures to grow in relation to, and is in fact inconceivable without these underlying, preexisting forms. Our liberal culture—as we will see in more detail shortly—might be tempted to denote these structures as limiting our freedom. Anything that encroaches on or blocks our freedom is often thought to be a bad thing and emphatically not an aspect of freedom itself; it intrudes on our "space." But this is to be deceived by the liberal account of freedom. Free behavior is acting, and acting always takes place in relation to something. By acting in relation to structures, many other acts are closed off—but so what? *Structures allow further free acts that we couldn't do before.* They *facilitate* them. This is so obvious that we tend not to notice it. But it is ultimately very important.

If I sit in a plane, I can't sit on the grass or drive a car to Memphis or be in a café. I am "limited" by sitting in the plane. A liberal might complain at this moment that my freedom has been horribly compromised. But if I let my abstract ideology of freedom be limited by getting into a plane, I can take off and fly around in the sky. And if I wasn't sitting in the structure that is the aircraft—assuming for the moment that it can fly—I couldn't fly. I would not be free to do this (and I can, if I want, fly to Memphis in any case).

If I sit in a room and learn ancient Greek, there are a myriad things that I can't do at that moment—what economists would call the opportunity cost of learning Greek. I can't run, watch a movie, or eat a burger. But if I sit in a room for long enough and learn sufficient ancient Greek, then I can read books written in ancient Greek, including a number of letters by Paul. Moreover, I need the preexisting structure that is a pedagogical tradition concerning ancient Greek so that I can begin to learn Greek within it. I need a textbook and teachers and now can even utilize the occasional YouTube clip. I need an entire *structure* that orchestrates and conveys a complex arrangement of information and knowledge in such a way that I can respond and gradually learn it, and this structure is considerable. It includes all sorts of texts like dictionaries, encyclopedias, grammars, and many, many texts themselves written in ancient Greek, texts surrounded by a great cloud of commentators and analysts. And this all entails schools, classrooms, registries, examinations, publishers, printing presses, emporia, libraries, reviews, editors, and so on. Without this vast structure, I could not acquire the capacity to do this important thing. I would not be free to act in this way—to read Paul in the language he wrote. I could not learn Greek.

In the light of all these considerations, it can now be seen especially clearly that, far from being mutually destructive and problematic, *election and freedom are mutually correlative and enhancing dynamics*, which is something we need to dwell on and to internalize because it is so culturally counterintuitive, and yet it is so important.

Musical analogies are, as usual, helpful. I could strike a piano randomly or make notes with my voice haphazardly, but I would not be making music. Beautiful and striking music is composed. It is a predetermined choreography of sounds—a structure—that takes a great deal of skill to craft. (As I review this chapter, I am listening to Rodriguez's *Searching for Sugar Man*, and then thinking of following that up with—on the recommendation of Jeremy Begbie—Mahler's *Auferstehungs-Sinfonie*, levels of skill and beauty that I am simply in awe of. I hasten to add that after this uncharacteristic venture into orchestral music, I will return to my playlist of hard-rock classics from the '70s and '80s, which I maintain is also characterized by awe-inspiring skill and beauty.) So, if I go on to sing in a choir, I sing a score that has been prepared for me, as do those all around me. This score, along with the skill of the composer, has created the activities I am now involved with, provided that I obediently respond in the terms that have been prescribed. I am participating in a complex structure. And I must sing my scripted part and correspond to the score, and I need to do so freely. I do not *have* to sing, and I do not have to sing *this*. But if I do respond in free obedience to the structure that is the music, in concert with the free obedience of all those around me, I get to participate in and to experience the full searing majesty of something like Benjamin Britten's *War Requiem*—or, as in my youth, the pop and pizzazz of *Joseph's Amazing Technicolour Dreamcoat*. By doing so—by freely obeying the musical script set before me, along with the coordinate actions of others, along with all the apparatus of a performance, including venue, audience, scores, and a conductor—I have become more than I was. I have freely entered into activities that I did not create for myself, and could not. Thus the composer's elected activities, the composer's music, the very orchestration of the choir, the music, and the event, and my free obedience, in concert with the free obedience of all those around me, have actually created something new for us all. This elected structure has facilitated our freedom together to make beautiful music.

We can put all this crisply by saying that freedom grows as our learning grows, and we learn as we respond to the opportunities to do things that structures provide us with. And we don't create those structures, although hopefully we will contribute to them. They are a gift. They preexist our learning. They are elected! And they are filled with practices and patterns and people transmitting these patterns—with things learned by their guardians from those who were guardians before them—so they have a history.

One way of speaking of these all-important preexisting structures is in terms of "traditions." This word can sound a little negative to some, but it is really nothing more than the recognition that human beings cannot act without these vast, complex, preexisting patterns and arrangements. A more trendy designation is "discourses," which can also be pejorative, but there is in fact nothing innately and necessarily negative about a discourse either. When an intellectual structure is in view, we can also speak of a paradigm. And some people prefer simply to speak of "structures," although this designation can apply to a very large number of rather different entities besides the types of structures that are in view here, so this particular usage needs to be apparent.

If this is all reasonably clear, then we need to pause to consider how our modern culture can betray us at this moment, undercutting the arrangement and the definitions that have just been warranted with a certain sort of well-intentioned silliness.

Liberal Freedom

I have lived in the United States of America for fifteen years now, after living for fairly long periods of time in four other countries, and never have I heard a country go on as much about freedom and have as little idea of what it really is. But the situation is really worse than mere confusion. The prevailing US definition of freedom *cripples* real freedom. Having said this, it is only fair to note that when it comes to notions of freedom, America is only the loudest voice in the room. One of the dominant cultural narratives pervading many modern European and post-European states pivots around a false notion of freedom. And although it resonates with our experiences as people in some respects, if it is embraced in its totality, it generates all sorts of theological problems.[6] So if we are to move forward constructively, we must undertake some further disciplined reflections on the nature of true freedom, and we must learn to recognize and to repudiate its cultural counterfeit, here as offered by liberalism.

Unlike most philosophical traditions, the liberal account of the person and attendant account of society is extraordinarily widespread in our modern world. Even in states that do not possess smoothly functioning, Western-style

---

6. Its seductive qualities are not that surprising because it grew out of Christian culture. It is a quasi-Christian notion, then, a semblance of the truth. But it now threatens to deceive more than it informs, which is a sure sign that the powers are at work.

democracies, a liberal version of the political and legal order tends to be acknowledged, and it can admittedly be a very big step forward from despotism. The vast majority of constitutions in the world today are constructed in these terms, probably because the position's development went hand in hand with the industrial revolution and the rise to global dominance of Western Europe and its offspring. The liberal states in Europe actively exported this viewpoint, especially Napoleonic France, and it underpinned the key European colony as well, namely, the United States.[7] At the heart of liberalism is a passionate account of freedom, although it breaks into two principal dimensions that we have already met. The first is nicely identified by the notion of "freedom from," or negative freedom—the dimension of freedom that we have been calling liberation. We will treat it here first, turning shortly to positive freedom, or "freedom to."

The first liberal democracies emerged, as we just intimated, from monarchies during the eighteenth century—the United States in 1776, and France in 1789—and they justified that emergence largely on the grounds that an unelected government was an unacceptable imposition on human freedom.[8] People of suitable quality were citizens, and they necessarily possessed the right to choose their own activities free from the debilitating depredations of a state that might extort and confiscate their wealth, in part through unjust taxation, and provide nothing in return, enforcing that predatory behavior, if necessary, with arbitrary arrest, imprisonment, and punishment. However, rather than holding on to the insight that relationships should be intrinsically free and loving—or at least respectful—and not characterized by bullying and coercion, liberals tend to think about "freedom from" as a *space* that individuals need to be able to live in, where they can operate unconstrained by *anything*. To be free in the sense of liberated is to be free from any relationships at all, a position that arguably resolves definitively the problem of tyrannical intrusion by a government or by any other entity. However, several other intellectual notions underpin this ultimately rather curious notion, allied with a final, more self-serving claim.

7. A bureaucratic dimension is operative here as well. Modern, complex states depended on large bureaucracies, and these, working in combination with governments, depended on a mushrooming framework of regulations and laws. It became assumed that modern bureaucratic societies could function in this way and no other. The original model for this state was Prussian.

8. Citizens can bind themselves only to limitation, consenting to restrictions on their activities; they can choose to give some of their freedom away. Hence the only legitimate form of government is democratic.

The broader universe is generally being understood here by liberals in the zero-sum terms that we have spent a lot of time refuting in previous chapters, and the tradition's key thinkers did live in the heyday of the hard sciences. Reality was just a game of billiards, consisting of atoms running in predictable lines into one another, as suggested by Newton. Or it was a vast, complicated watch crafted by the great watchmaker in the sky, as suggested by Newton's theological equivalents. That is, liberalism tends to assume a cosmos within which causal factors are automatic and so necessarily limit freedom as choice. *Any* causality acting on us must in that very influence constrain us. Causality is always automatic, and frequently mechanical. Hence to be caused in any way is not to be free to that extent. It follows from this line of thought that our freedom is the part of our reality that is set apart from causality and protected from it (although this need to divide reality into two fundamentally different worlds has caused liberal intellectuals a lot of problems). Freedom must exist, for those thinking in these terms, in some sort of uncaused space of its own. And the arrival of anything else in that space must, by definition, cramp the freedom of its occupant.

It is probably clear by now why various Americans spend a great deal of time resisting government activity on the grounds that this is necessarily and inevitably a reduction of their freedom, and human rights discourses can be drawn into this way of thinking as well. Where I have a right, I basically have a free space that no one else is allowed to interfere with or to enter, and by this, some American rights activists seem to mean that when you cross the line into their zone, they are morally entitled to shoot you. Such actions on your part have necessarily compromised their freedom. But at this moment we stumble upon another critical ingredient in the liberal definition of freedom, and one that has been embraced by Americans with particular zeal. The free space we inhabit includes our property, characterized as "private," and the modern rhetoric of freedom consequently turns out to include land, its produce, and ultimately money.[9]

If freedom is a key value within society, both culturally and politically, which means, at least in the first instance, a space or zone that is free from

9. As noted perceptively by Joan Lockwood O'Donovan; see her essay "The Poverty of Christ and Non-proprietary Community." However, it should be appreciated that her criticisms apply principally to classical definitions of rights informed by property. Modern rights discourses can be fashioned in less individualistic directions, Franklin D. Roosevelt's Second Bill of Rights, proposed in 1944, being a nice illustration. Modern liberalism is also complex, and different forms attach greater and lesser degrees of importance to rights.

interference from anyone else, then my own land and the produce of my land belong to me necessarily and to no one else. This is the basic morality of the situation, so any acquisition by someone or something else of my property—of that which I possess, in my space—must be justified, and justified while it runs the gauntlet of limiting my freedom. If it isn't, it is theft! (This viewpoint handily underpinned the Enclosure movement, which drove untold small farmers both from their feudally designated land and from any commons in the UK to make way for the more lucrative and cost-effective farming of sheep.)[10] Moreover, this morality applies necessarily to money as well. The resulting visceral resistance to government "intrusion" in the form of taxation and the like, along with any other unlawful acquisition of that which is mine through obviously wrong actions like theft, is written deeply into American identity, and entirely understandably. The United States of America's foundational narrative is a story, as we have noted, of freedom from inept and tyrannical intrusion—and who doesn't want to be free from the folly of King George III?! To be American is to be free, and to be free *in this sense*. The immediate cost paid, however, is the focal overlooking of all the structures and relationships that make any property and/or produce actually possible.

In sum, negative freedom is a space that we occupy that is free *from* the influence of anyone or anything else, and to allow *any* unacknowledged intrusion into this zone evokes a deep hostility to its tyrannies. But we need now to introduce the second major type of freedom that liberals advocate, which Berlin called positive freedom, or "freedom to." It flows rather naturally out of the first.

If negative freedom is existence unconstrained by causality, including by any input from other people, then it must operate in a rather individualistic way, within the zone of freedom that we hope society will establish and protect around every person. As such, the seat of its powers will actually need to be in our heads, although this suited the boffins of the liberal tradition nicely, who rated their powers of reasoning very highly. Zones of freedom surround individuals, in relation to which they can think freely with their minds that are unconstrained by causality per se and hence operate "freely," in terms of other processes like logic. Moreover, everybody in a society spends most of their life acting, which is to say, doing things that they think they are determining

10. The process was complex, and scholars differ over whether it was fundamentally positive, negative, or something in between. See https://en.wikipedia.org/wiki/Enclosure. Certain constituencies, however, suffered greatly. The Highland Clearances created vast displacements. See https://en.wikipedia.org/wiki/Highland_Clearances.

to do for themselves, hence freely; this holds irrespective of whether one is a liberal or not. But it follows from all this that positive freedom for a liberal, which is to say, the freedom to do things, *will be what the individual chooses to do in and of him- or herself, having made a "decision" to do so, without external consultation or influence.* A spatial analogy tends to return here; such freedom is being conceptualized as a space that I can move in, in any direction I want to, rather like a basketball player in the middle of the court is free to dribble the ball forward, sideways, backward, or in some serpentine variation on all of these movements. All of which is to say that people will *choose* between different options perhaps by weighing their benefits and consequences rationally, or perhaps simply because they prefer one option over another as a matter of taste. I would add as a quick aside that taste is generally indefensible but quite important. I can't explain why I simply adore New World Sauvignon Blancs but find most bottles of Müller Thurgau and Riesling thoroughly objectionable and not worth drinking, let alone paying for. I am not sure, however, that this defines my freedom in a fundamental way. Yet many people seem to think we exercise our freedom most vibrantly when we stroll down a supermarket lane and pluck one breakfast cereal off the shelf as against another. It is a triumphant realization of my freedom when one day, for the first time, I pick Frosties instead of a packet of oatmeal—or a Pinot Grigio instead of my trusted customary Sauvignon. At any rate, freedom, in this cultural account, is intrinsically connected with choice, and choice signals the presence of different options. Without options to choose from, there is no freedom.

Since the conceptualization of positive freedom is bound up tightly with options—and with consumer products!—it is, again, highly individualized. Only individuals can make choices in this way. And this all results in an approach to acting that is oriented very strongly by our "wills." Wills are a strange notion, but we have to infer their existence if we are thinking in this way. Because freedom must operate in relation to different options, it follows that there must be some faculty in us that operates over these choices that simply wills one option as against another and so prompts our acting. We must then have "free will," meaning that we have the capacity to choose between different alternatives. Freedom is located somewhere antecedent to these decisions. As a result, many modern people, almost certainly unaware that they are repeating liberal talking-points, speak about their freedom as if it is just a matter of their possession of free will. Moreover, people exercise their wills and their freedom in the end of the day by making choices, and often simply because they choose to—because they just want to. Choices must be unconstrained and free from any outside influences! So people "volunteer" for themselves and by themselves what they want to do. Anything else would be tyranny! "You can't tell me what I want or don't want." And this conception has led to a long and very unhealthy intellectual trend in Western thinking called voluntarism. Voluntarism *isolates* willing (i.e., acting, along with freedom) from any other relational connections and defines it strictly in relation to choices between options made by individuals—choices between different lines of movement in their space, so to speak, that individuals volunteer.

Combining negative freedom (i.e., freedom as a space) and positive freedom (i.e., freedom as choosing), we can see that ultimate freedom for some of these advocates is not unlike a Mad Max movie fantasy (and I recommend in particular the most recent effort at time of writing, starring Charlize Theron—*Fury Road* [2015]). Max is ultimately free when he possesses a fast, all-terrain vehicle, with plenty of fuel, which he can drive in any direction he wants to around the massive, flat, Australian desert. A cliff, a pile of rocks, or another vehicle in the way all limit his choices and hence constitute infringements on his liberty, but otherwise his endless driving, by himself, is the acme of freedom. (Ironically, the movie's protagonists in *Mad Max 4* begin by striking out in a dramatic bid for personal freedom but ultimately realize that no true freedom is possible without water and community.)

With this quick description of liberal freedom in place—essentially in terms of a zone of freedom from all external influences around the individual, since those are viewed as determining and tyrannical, allowing the freedom to grasp whatever option he or she chooses—we can turn to theological evaluation. There are insights present within these notions, and we will return to them in a few moments of theological retrieval. But to absolutize and to abstract them into fundamental principles at the heart of what it is to be human and to be a society unleashes some deeply destructive consequences.

The notion that people are truly free from tyranny when they are free from any outside influence launches a damaging and self-defeating ethical and political program. It absolutizes a non- and even an antirelational account of the person—the individual—which entails the elimination on ideological grounds of the very influences that a person needs in order to be a healthy and good person! A clearer case of the baby going out with the bathwater is harder to imagine. (It also reifies a clumsily reductionist account of causality, encouraging the thought that all causality is automatic and hence, in effect, coercive; relational causality is not.)

Admittedly, liberals were aware that people live in groups all the time. So they argued that relationships are permissible, provided that they are based on *consent*. The two freedoms basically combine here again into the notion that I may choose to enter into a relationship with someone, or choose to let them enter into a relationship with me, thereby allowing them entry into my zone of freedom to constrain me, but the relationship is only valid on this basis—the giving of my consent. But this view unleashes conditionality and contractualism into the heart of all human relationships, and we have already seen some of the damage that this can do.

It is of course quite right for liberals to point to the unacceptability of tyrannical and abusive relationships and to the unacceptability of coercion. Forcing people to act is profoundly disrespectful to their personhood, and liberals are right to protest against this. But Jesus followers learn this same truth from the incarnation and from the loving relationality that God destined us for and draws us into. Loving relationships do not coerce. Love is offered and received freely. And we learned from God, furthermore, that the solution to abusive and broken relationships is courageous interventions to restore and heal relationships, along with the provision of nurturance in covenant by those who love us, not no relationships at all or occasional relationships carefully limited by contracts and conditions. These will heal nothing and no one.

But if the liberal account of negative freedom, or freedom from, is problematic, its account of positive freedom, or freedom to, doubles down on the damage. Few suggestions are more destructive than the notion that true human freedom consists of choosing between options, largely on the basis of a "will," and in a way that is necessarily unconstrained by outside influences. In the first instance, this pulls freedom out of its appropriate location, in concrete, particular, personal relationships, where it operates within those relationships, usually either initiating or responding. Healthy freedom, understood in these relational terms, has a unidirectional quality. It chooses to initiate or to respond *but it does not choose between equal options*. And the relationship *itself* is not one of a number of options that its participants choose between. If we introduce choice into relational situations in the sense of the freedom to make selections between different options, then we can damage those relationships horribly.

Let's think for a moment about how a marriage relationship or a close friendship is going to unfold, depending on whether a covenantal or a classic liberal account of freedom is in play. In a self-consciously covenantal marriage or friendship, the participants will celebrate the way that their love is freely initiated and responded to. They will delight in the interplay that is their relationship, one that is freely given and freely received. There is no coercion or force in this relationship. It is, precisely, free, from beginning to end, and from top to bottom. The *marriage* is free, as is *friendship*, and "freedom" denotes some key aspects of its love.

A marriage or friendship intertwined with a liberal account of freedom might unfold very differently, however. Perhaps influenced by the belief that freedom is a space around the individual free from influence from anything or anyone else, a spouse might feel that marriage is a restriction on freedom. This might even have been symbolized by the groom's wearing of a ball and chain at his bachelor's party the night before the ceremony—prison awaits![11] And this attitude make sense. After marriage, choice is clearly delimited. A married man cannot simply will or do what he wants to, and he cannot just choose what he wants to any more, so marriage *is* a sacrifice of liberal freedom. But perhaps if another tempting opportunity comes along, in the name of freedom, a participant might decide to leave the marriage, to dissolve it, and to move on to another relationship. Such marriage dissolution would be a blow on behalf of freedom! Or someone might simply decide to move on, as Lynyrd Skynyrd's immortal signature song, "Free Bird," puts it:

> If I leave here tomorrow
> Would you still remember me?
> For I must be traveling on, now
> Cause there's too many places I've got to see.
> But, if I stayed here with you, girl
> Things just couldn't be the same
> Cause I'm as free as a bird now
> And this bird you cannot change.
>
> (Chorus)
> And this bird you cannot change.
> And this bird you cannot change.
> Lord knows, I can't change.[12]

Needless to say, this viewpoint is short-sighted (although it is a great song). True freedom has meaning only when it operates in a covenantal relationship, where it characterizes one aspect of the commitment and love that ground that relationship. By destroying their covenantal relationship, participants have only destroyed their freedom. Yet this is exactly how the liberal definition of freedom, in terms of individual space and choice, encourages

---

11. A common saying when a male leaves a group of male friends to return home or to his girlfriend is "back to the ball and chain!"
12. https://genius.com/Lynyrd-skynyrd-free-bird-lyrics.

us to think.[13] (Please let me emphasize at this moment that I am speaking of loving and flourishing marriages, not troubled relationships, where love and freedom can be so damaged that dissolution is arguably a step forward for all the parties concerned. Navigating actual marriages can be a far cry from reflecting on healthy ones.)

There's such a fundamental mistake here that it is baffling how it can persist in our popular imaginations. We know well by now that love is not coerced or coercive—with the exception of extreme circumstances where protective restraint is required—and that it is profoundly free. Love that is not freely given and freely received would not be love. But if the basis of a relationship is shifted to choice, it is necessarily shifted away from love, *and undermines it*. We do not *choose* those whom we love. We love them! And this means that there is a great compulsion about our relationship! It is not physically and abusively coercive, but it is a powerful thing—a tide of emotional and psychological longing and affection and curiosity and passion. We commonly say that we *fall* in love. In the first great high of love, the thought of enduring a long separation from the one we love feels like the pangs of death! My relationship with my wife, Rachel, began freely. But it was not a choice between different options. I did not walk into church one day and look around and say, "I think I'll choose Rachel today to be my wife, although I could equally well choose Mary or Joan or Cynthia. In fact, I might just choose Sybil. Or I might not. So many options, so little time." What nonsense! I didn't pick Rachel off the pew the way someone picks a lump of garlic from the supermarket's bin of options. I was compelled to marry her, in love! Free, yes, but a choice, in the sense of a random pick between different options? no—definitely not! And the same applies to God.

We don't *choose* to respond to God in the sense that we have option A, obey God, and option B, don't obey God, and our freedom consists in the way we hover above this choice and decide which way to go. God is not an option. We have been created to love God with all our hearts, souls, minds, and strength, and to do so freely, without coercion. And this is where our true freedom resides, *in* this relationship, where it stays freely, and where it can grow as we learn to love God more and more. The "option" of choosing not to love God is not a step proceeding from freedom, nor would it be a step into freedom and away from the unacceptable divine constraints on our free zone.

---

13. And money is not far behind. The prenuptial contract now removes money from the covenantal obligations of marriage, thereby subordinating covenantal vows and relationships to prior accumulations of property!

It would be a step that proceeds ultimately from evil and steps into evil, which is to say, into sin, decay, and an ultimate enslavement to death. It would be an abuse of our God-given capacity to love God freely, as well as a betrayal, and an act of ultimate stupidity.[14]

But with these realizations, the theological damage introduced by a liberal account of positive freedom has not yet ended. An emphasis on freedom as a choice between different options, unconstrained by outside influences, *also destroys any traditioned process of formation* (which is why we are discussing it here). This account of freedom is hostile to traditions, and hence to learning, since all learning presupposes tradition. Such traditions, with their accumulations of learning and knowledge and wisdom, and their influences from teachers and from other guardians of the tradition who know more than the learner, along with their relational patterns of attentiveness and subordination, tend to be viewed as unacceptable impositions on the freedom of the individual, who finds the deepest roots of choice within himself or herself! Learning, it is said, should begin with the learner, not with those who know more and who are deeper within the tradition. People should guide their own learning. To be free and to make the right choice ultimately entails only that a person "know thyself" (and presumably this is why so much of modernity is characterized by an obsessive quest for identity). Hence a more perfect recipe for *avoiding* learning, along with all the freedom that learning entails, would be hard to imagine. Understanding freedom as a type of consumer preference then risks sliding into even more damaging postures.

Inveterate consumers might begin to think that preference precedes truth and might be encouraged in this perversion by market-oriented news outlets and social media. Classical liberals would be horrified by the current profession of many citizens of modern democracies that the truth is chosen, and that they will choose as they see fit. They would implore such dilettantes to employ their reason and their integrity to seek hard after what is actually true—to address things like evidence and valid argumentation. But their system has no strong reasons for enjoining these virtues upon modern liberals (virtues that

14. It follows from these realizations, moreover, that God did not construct our created situation so that it contained a trip wire in every person, namely, his or her faculty of free will. Creation was not a minefield waiting for a single wrong choice—for one false step—to trigger a spiral of corruption and death. Creation was founded in a strong, healthy, loving covenant, bound by commitment and hedged with kindness and concern. And sinful humanity wrenched itself away from that covenant, abusing its goodness, and unnaturally turned itself toward damage and pain!

classical liberals may have taken for granted from their Christian tradition), and liberal rationalism is no match for the powerful narratives and emoting of modern consumer society—for that tradition. Hence, as this paradigm bottoms out, it is possible to detect a widespread cultural slide into narcissism, because "the only thing that really matters is me and my preferences"—a mentality that modern capitalism both cultivates assiduously and manipulates.

I have been saying for some time now in this book that we do not choose the truth; it chooses us (and it "chooses" us in the right, loving way, of course, not as one option among many but in a covenantal commitment of election). Furthermore, truth is objective. Nothing we do or say can change it. Truth exists whether we like it or not. But it is a personal truth, and so it comes to us with expectations that we must learn, and it is enfolded in and mediated by a tradition. True freedom is found only as we submit ourselves to this tradition, patiently, obediently, learning to do the things that we were destined for since before the foundation of the world, having been set free through Christ from those things that were really constraining and enslaving us, namely, sin, corruption, and death.[15] And it is now clearly vital to hold on to these realizations and to resist being drawn off the right path by the siren call of liberalism.[16] If liberalism's well-meaning definitions of freedom are embraced, both negative and positive, the entire Pauline project will be impeded and eventually destroyed. But I am confident that we have now been warned sufficiently well. With the common but dreadful misunderstandings of freedom offered to us seductively by liberals identified and charted—charted not so that we can find them but so that we can recognize them at a great distance and sail safely around them—we now need to think about the process of appropriate formation more deeply. We have realized that God is all about forming and nurturing communities, and communities are all about relating, ultimately and primarily, in love. Moreover, they are all about learning to relate in love better than they currently do, since it is self-evident that most Jesus followers need to do some work here. This learning is what true freedom is all about. But how *exactly* does it take place? And what are the implications for how community should best be structured? These are the vital questions we turn to in the next chapter, the answers to which will ground all our further growth in freedom.

15. We will also learn to innovate and to initiate in love.

16. I refer here *not* to the current media construction of liberalism in the United States but to classic philosophical and political liberalism. (The media who often charge their opponents with being "liberals" are in fact themselves usually classic philosophical liberals, with all the strengths and weaknesses of that tradition in play.)

Theses

- Communion is the goal of the cosmos.
- In the quest for the good, the end is the means; we pursue the perfect good by being as good as we can here and now.
- We therefore pursue perfect communion here and now (aware that the basis for this pursuit is that this communion has first pursued us).
- Pursuing this communion entails founding and nurturing communities.
- Communities are composed of people, and people, we learned from the Trinity, are primarily relational.
- A community of Jesus followers is therefore primarily a relational entity. Everything else is secondary.
- Communities are not bounded entities but networks.
- Relational communities can be analyzed in more detail in terms of (1) their structure or arrangement and (2) their relational quality and tenor.
- There is something of a parting of the ways in the church tradition at this moment. One way correctly grasps and emphasizes that Pauline communities are communities of relational learning; the other tends to resist and to obscure this insight.
- In one respect, this realization is strongly intuitive. We are clearly not perfected yet; we therefore have to make progress, and we do so by learning to be better messianic Jews or Christians.
- In saying this, we need to be clear, however, that an unconditional relationship of electing love frames this process.
- This relationship contains extensive expectations, as the analogy of good parents and children suggests.
- We must learn negatively. There are many things we must learn not to do, or to unlearn. In this respect we must simplify.
- We must learn positively. There are depths in our relationship with God that we can dive into forever.
- This learning constitutes growth in freedom as we learn to do things—here, most important, to be better covenant partners with God—which is an increase in our freedom in terms of capacity.
- Various misconceptions can lead us to oppose or to misunderstand this learning process.
- It is clear, however, that structures are necessary to facilitate the freedom to do certain acts. These restrict. But without structures, the freedom to do the things presupposing these structures is impossible.

- We see here, by way of learning, what true freedom is, and how it presupposes election in the sense of preexisting forms and structures.
- Liberal and hence fundamentally spatial notions of freedom can be offended by structures and their restrictions, but this response serves only to expose the shortcomings of liberalism.
- Liberalism provides the dominant account of freedom in European and post-European states.
- Liberalism values freedom highly and offers a particular account of it, but it is deeply destructive if its definition are adopted by Jesus followers wholesale.
- Liberalism contains two main aspects that we have already met: in Berlin's parlance, negative liberty, or freedom from; and positive liberty, or freedom to.
- Liberals are especially sensitive to tyrannical impositions.
- There is a valid insight here: it is not appropriate for people to be bullied or coerced.
- Liberals are also unhappy about any undue influence on the person from causality, which is generally construed as automatic if not mechanical, and therefore exclusive of human freedom.
- They therefore insist on a "space" or "zone" of freedom around the individual that is free from any influence.
- The uncaused and free space of individuals is anchored by their minds and their rationality.
- It includes their property, which is private.
- Positive freedom is exercised in this space. It is the freedom to do what the individual chooses to do, usually by way of deciding between different options (i.e., voluntarism).
- Positive freedom therefore presupposes a faculty of free willing that precedes and initiates these choices.
- This definition of freedom contains insights but is theologically destructive if pressed.
- Negative freedom denies the need and legitimacy of relationships, thereby denying the very thing that gifts personhood and learning, which results in a growth in positive freedom.
- Recognizing the ubiquity of relationships, it allows people to engage relationally on the basis of the individual's consent.
- However, this framework introduces conditionality and contractual dynamics into the heart of all relating, which undermines their healthiest form, which is loving and covenantal (i.e., unconditional).

- ‣ The introduction of choice into relationships also displaces their loving and covenantal nature.
- ‣ There is a valid insight here, namely, that relationships of love are free. Love is offered and received freely.
- ‣ However, it is a grave error to suppose that this sort of freedom means a choice between options. Love does not choose between options—far from it! Love compels us to love our beloved.
- ‣ Hence it is inappropriate, also destructive, for a liberal to suggest that we can choose to obey God, in a way that we consider this as one of two or more options. This is an abuse of freedom.
- ‣ God did not create us with a dangerous proclivity to sin rooted in our very natures. We were created free but not free in the sense of being able to choose between options—in this case, between a good and an evil action.
- ‣ The account of freedom in terms of choice is heavily reinforced by modern consumerism, which reinforces the legitimacy of our own internal preferences.
- ‣ But this account undermines the legitimacy of traditions and of learning from others who know more than we do.
- ‣ It also suggests that the truth is a preference, thereby eliminating its objectivity and the hard work and the virtues sometimes needed to acquire it.
- ‣ It even encourages sheer narcissism. The identity of modern individuals rests in the exercise of their preferences and is violated if those preferences are denied or challenged.
- ‣ We must therefore trenchantly reject and resist a false liberal account of freedom, whether in terms of freedom from any causal influence from outside of the individual, especially traditioned or relational influence, or in terms of freedom to do things anchored in a faculty of will that merely decides to act on the basis of internal preferences, choosing one option over another.

Key Scriptural References

All of Paul's writings presuppose the possibility of growth in goodness and so are relevant here in a generalized way.

Paul speaks not infrequently of growth in human terms. Converts are babies, infants, or ascending to maturity. See especially 1 Cor 3:1–3; 13:11–12; and Eph 4:14–15. (The birth imagery in Gal 4:19, as well as the infancy imagery used in 1 Thess 2:7, is not necessarily relevant here.)

Key Reading

An important argument was made in this chapter that communities need to grow into the fullness of their relationships with the triune God that they have been placed within. They are communities of learning. Put slightly more technically, I am tracing out a connection between an orthodox account of God and a certain sort of virtue ethic—defining this term rather loosely—and I am unaware of many studies that articulate this connection well in relation to Paul. One excellent analysis, however, by a former doctoral student of mine, now revised and published, is Colin Miller's *The Practice of the Body of Christ*. In my view this book ought to receive rather more attention than it currently does.

The connections between Barth and a quite tightly defined virtue ethic are made constantly in general terms within the work of Stanley Hauerwas. Hauerwas's key works are *A Community of Character* and *The Peaceable Kingdom*, along with his collection coauthored with Charles Pinches, *Christians among the Virtues*, and his 2000–2001 Gifford Lectures, published as *With the Grain of the Universe*. In the lectures Hauerwas generously but perceptively criticizes Barth for lacking a full account of Christian formation. Not all of this material needs to be read to grasp Hauerwas's basic approach, but it is well worth reading some of it carefully. An accessible point of entry into his thinking is (with Will Willimon) *Resident Aliens*.

An insightful introduction to the discussion of freedom is provided by Richard Bauckham. Jeremy Begbie provides a very neat critique of liberal, spatial accounts of freedom, using helpful musical analogies to lead his readers to a more accurate understanding in his brilliant essay "Room of One's Own."

Further Reading

The basis of the claims in this chapter concerning the centrality and relational nature of appropriate community is the cluster of insights we have already met from Barth and Zizioulas, and from James and Alan Torrance: the priority of revelation; the importance of election; God's election as focused on communion; God's personhood, and hence ours, as relational; and God's relations as loving and unconditionally covenantal. So I will not reproduce the details of those earlier discussions and readings here. It follows that communities should not be understood in a bounded spatial way but as clusters or hubs within relational networks. Networks are introduced in a fascinating way by Albert-László Barabási.

These insights all combine into emphases moving forward on founding and nurturing communities, although our detailed analysis should continue with questions of community nurture before turning to questions in relation to their founding. A key dimension in community nurture is their development or learning, at which moment we make contact with the important tradition of virtue ethics, as noted in the Key Reading above.

A lot of scholars have been awakened to the importance of Christian formation and virtue by the work of Alasdair MacIntyre. This was the case for me to a certain extent. The principal influence on me, however, was Hauerwas, who was also influenced strongly in this relation by Yoder and the emphasis on community in the Peace Church tradition. In this chapter, however, I have undertaken a completely different theological justification for formation from MacIntyre, and my subsequent account will continue to differ from his in key respects. MacIntyre is a foundationalist, a position I clearly want to avoid. I have also avoided using Aristotelean categories in a seminal role. Neither MacIntyre nor Aristotle develops an eschatological virtue ethic! Having said this, there is always much to learn from MacIntyre's stunningly learned mind (and from Aristotle's). I use some Aristotelean moves, suitably warranted.

Another important figure bridging from Barth through virtue ethics, and moving beyond MacIntyre's limitations, ultimately in conversation with social anthropology, is Michael Banner. The grounding in Barth is not overtly stated but is present in the important methodological chapter that begins his *Ethics of Everyday Life* ("Moral Theology, Moral Philosophy, Social Anthropology, and the State We Are In: On (the Lack of) Everyday Ethics," 6–34).

Further contributions helpful for understanding a virtue ethic, along with Paul's possible relationship to its variations, are listed at the end of the next chapter.

The notion of freedom or agency is always intertwined significantly with these sorts of discussions, and this chapter picks up and deepens the previous chapter's analysis of divine and human agency—with the emphasis there on the divine—while the following chapter continues this conversation.

I have been influenced in my understanding of agency by the relational and pragmatic thinking of John Macmurray, who tightly links together human action, freedom, and embodiment and vigilantly opposes all abstract accounts of human agency. Our agency and activity are an embodied and experienced fact before they are anything else. This seems to me to be quite correct and deeply helpful. Macmurray goes on to undertake brilliant Socratic deconstructions of the main ancient and modern accounts of freedom where they embrace abstraction, demonstrating their invariable collapse into self-referential incoherence. I am following Macmurray's lead here, to a large degree, by letting an account of human agency emerge from incontestable practicalities like infant learning, as those are corroborated by basic theological warrants. These insights will also lead to a conversation about formation that differs from classic virtue ethics, as we will see in more detail momentarily. Macmurray's key works are, like Hauerwas, his Gifford lectures, in his case delivered in 1952–54 and published as *The Self as Agent* and *Persons in Relation*.

Barth treats agency a great deal. His usual account tends to emphasize freedom in the sense of an obedient and willing correspondence to God's will. Barth is working here from Christology, and ultimately in dependence on thinkers like Maximus the Confessor, who parsed the relationship between Jesus's divine and human willing in these terms. This account can be found in III/1, III/2, and IV/2. But there is a more creative dimension to Barth's account of human agency. This develops the agency of humanity beyond mere correspondence to the divine will in the direction of initiative and creativity, although within its appointed—and necessary!—limits. He supplies a brilliant analysis in these terms within his broader treatment of providence in III/3 (see esp. 95–107).

A pithy but deeply insightful critique of classic liberalism from a Christian perspective is supplied by Stanley Hauerwas in *After Christendom*. His criticisms of non-Christian accounts of justice and freedom in chapters 2 and 3 (45–68 and 69–92) are particularly telling. I supply a brief complementary analysis of liberal categories in my *Deliverance of God*, especially 295–309. Joan Lockwood O'Donovan's critique of the Catholic (specifically Jesuit) origins of human rights discourses is also deeply perceptive.

Bibliography

Banner, Michael. *The Ethics of Everyday Life: Moral Theology, Social Anthropology, and the Imagination of the Human.* Oxford: Oxford University Press, 2014.

Barabási, Albert-László. *Linked: How Everything Is Connected to Everything Else and What It Means for Business, Science, and Everyday Life.* New York: Penguin/Plume, 2003.

Barth, Karl. *Church Dogmatics.* III/1; III/2; III/3; IV/2.

Bauckham, Richard. "Freedom in Contemporary Context." Pages 26–49 in *God and the Crisis of Freedom: Biblical and Contemporary Perspectives.* Louisville: Westminster John Knox, 2002.

Begbie, Jeremy. "Room of One's Own? Music, Space, and Freedom." Pages 141–75 in *Music, Modernity, and God: Essays in Listening*. Oxford: Oxford University Press, 2013.

Berlin, Isaiah. *Two Concepts of Liberty*. Oxford: Clarendon, 1958.

Campbell, Douglas A. *The Deliverance of God: An Apocalyptic Rereading of Justification in Paul*. Grand Rapids: Eerdmans, 2009, ch. 9, 284–309, esp. 301–9 and endnotes.

Hauerwas, Stanley. *After Christendom: How the Church Is to Behave If Freedom, Justice, and a Christian Nation Are Bad Ideas*. Nashville: Abingdon, 1991.

———. *A Community of Character: Toward a Constructive Christian Social Ethic*. Notre Dame, IN: University of Notre Dame Press, 1981.

———. *The Peaceable Kingdom: A Primer in Christian Ethics*. Notre Dame, IN: University of Notre Dame Press, 1983.

———. *With the Grain of the Universe: The Church's Witness and Natural Theology: Being the Gifford Lectures Delivered at the University of St Andrews in 2001*. Grand Rapids: Brazos, 2001.

Hauerwas, Stanley, with Charles Pinches. *Christians among the Virtues: Theological Conversations with Ancient and Modern Ethics*. Notre Dame, IN: University of Notre Dame Press, 1997.

Hauerwas, Stanley, with Will Willimon. *Resident Aliens: Life in the Christian Colony*. Nashville: Abingdon, 1989.

Lakoff, George. *Whose Freedom? The Battle over America's Most Important Idea*. New York: Farrar, Straus, & Giroux, 2006.

Lockwood O'Donovan, Joan. "The Poverty of Christ and Non-proprietary Community." Pages 191–200 in *The Doctrine of God and Theological Ethics*. Edited by Alan J. Torrance and Michael Banner. London: T&T Clark, 2006.

MacIntyre, Alasdair C. *After Virtue: A Study in Moral Theory*. 3rd ed. Notre Dame, IN: University of Notre Dame Press, 2007.

———. *Three Rival Versions of Moral Enquiry: Encyclopaedia, Genealogy, and Tradition*. Notre Dame, IN: University of Notre Dame Press, 1990.

———. *Whose Justice? Which Rationality?* Notre Dame, IN: University of Notre Dame Press, 1989.

Macmurray, John. *Persons in Relation*. London: Faber & Faber, 1961.

———. *The Self as Agent*. London: Faber & Faber, 1957.

Miller, Colin. *The Practice of the Body of Christ: Human Agency in Pauline Theology after MacIntyre*. Princeton Theological Monograph Series 200. Eugene, OR: Pickwick, 2014.

CHAPTER 10

Leaders

Imitation

Several important realizations flow from the basic insight that communities of Jesus followers are communities of learning. As we saw earlier in chapter 3, God delights to work through people, mediating his presence and purposes. And we now appreciate more deeply just how important this realization is. It seems likely, moreover, that some people are going to know more than others, and to mediate God more clearly and consistently than others as learning takes place, so there are inevitably going to be two categories of people in these communities (or, more precisely, two roles): teachers and students. People will be at different points on the learning curve. A basic stratification will be apparent. And we will need to learn, in particular, from those who are positioned a little further along the learning curve than we are.[1] Moreover, as Plato noted some time ago, it is best if leadership and virtue coincide.

The technical term for the resulting communal arrangement of those who know more and teach, and those who know less and learn, is one that self-respecting humanities scholars generally flee from in terror—elitism. But it is nothing to be afraid of. As sociologists have long known, elitism names the construction of every human community we are a part of. All groups have leaders and followers. Every human group is hierarchical in some way, whether we are speaking of families, classrooms, playgrounds, factories, faculties, churches, governments, or tribes. Hence, although intellectual resistance

---

1. This "hierarchy" shouldn't be overstated. Everyone mediates God to some degree, and everyone can do so with clarity—and can also block that mediation suddenly by some deeply foolish act. Within these parameters, however, some stratification seems probable.

to this notion is widespread, one wonders whether this is not rather like standing on the beach and defying the tide to come in. Elitism is ubiquitous, which is also to say in the same breath, that leaders and leadership are ubiquitous. The really useful questions we need to ask at this moment are not whether elitism exists or what the way to eliminate it is as much as what specific mode of instruction leaders should employ and students should submit to, what sort of leaders we should have, and how we should relate to them. Just because we know we should have teachers and should learn something doesn't tell us how they should teach and how we best learn.

Once again, we begin from first principles. We have already grasped that we are our relationships. They make us who we are. But if who we are is bound up with those we are relating to, it simply follows that these relationships must shape us as well. They are not just the place where we live and exist. We don't relate in a static and unchangeable way. Our relationships are dynamic, and it follows directly that our relationships change us. Because we are who we relate to, we *become* who we relate to. The people I care for and respect and admire and am in a direct relationship with the most—they change me. We might summarize this point more technically by saying that a relational ontology entails a relational pedagogy.

In fact, this shaping process is unfolding all around us all the time—so much so that we usually don't notice it. Our environments, and especially our personal environments, constantly affect us, and dramatically, which is why we might need to be rather more careful than we normally are about what is in them. A nice example of the astonishing degree to which people relate to and emotionally resonate with one another can be found in a famous longitudinal study conducted in the United States. Originally a research exercise investigating the high incidence of heart disease, data were collated for a population of 5,209 people living in Framingham, MA, beginning in 1948.[2] Scientists wanted to know whether heart disease was genetic or environmental and, if the latter, which factors in the environment affected it (diet, exercise, climate, etc.). The data collected were so detailed, however, that social psychologists were able

---

2. See James H. Fowler and Nicholas A. Christakis, "Dynamic Spread of Happiness in a Large Social Network: Longitudinal Analysis over Twenty Years in the Framingham Heart Study," *British Medical Journal*, December 4, 2008 (*BMJ* 2008;337:a2338), available at http://www.bmj.com/content/bmj/337/bmj.a2338.full.pdf. The results of this study, and its implications for the way people resonate with one another, are summarized accessibly in the PBS program *This Emotional Life*, presented by Daniel Gilbert, dir. Richard Hutton (2010).

to map the emotional well-being of many of the participants as well, and they found something remarkable. People were *incredibly* sensitive to one another's emotional states. An increase in happiness within one person could be traced radiating out significantly through three degrees of separation, losing just a certain percentage of its effect at each step (roughly 10 percent). As a result, a significant 40 percent increase in one person's happiness would increase the happiness of someone who was a friend of their friend's friend by 10 percent. Needless to say, the distant friend-of-a-friend-of-our-friend had no idea what had just happened three relational steps away from that person, and may not even have known the original happy person at all! Yet that figure had had their well-being measurably and significantly changed by the original happy person and by their community and its networks of relationships.

People are extremely sensitive to one another. They respond to minute shifts in emotion, often without even registering the fact consciously. These responses then radiate through their relational networks to four degrees of separation and beyond. Our relationships change us to a degree we find it hard to imagine, although the data are quite clear.

Followers of Jesus want to be intentional about their learning, however. We don't want to be shaped randomly by our environments; we want to make genuine and wholehearted progress in our ability to relate to one another and to God. And the obvious thing to do here is to attend to our leaders. We have just grasped that the key players in our communities will be our leaders, namely, those who mediate God to us most effectively, which is to say, those who have learned to do so, are a little ahead of us on the relational growth curve, and have been called and equipped by God to do so. As we relate to these leaders, we have the opportunity to become more like them in the sense that they are mediating Jesus. We can, like them, learn to set aside the entrapments and practices of sin and to practice healthy and loving ways of relating. But we still need to take one more important explanatory step.

We know that we are shaped primarily by our relationships. We know that we resonate with those around us (and with those around those around us, and with those around them). And we want to be shaped by the most mature relationships around us—by our relationships with our communal leaders. But how *exactly* do those relationships shape us?

Paul provides us with a further important clue in relation to this critical question, one he shares with the rest of the New Testament and with much of the tradition besides, although it has fallen sadly, and even disastrously, out of favor in the modern period. We learn to be like our leaders—to relate like them in ways that are more loving and covenantal—*as we copy them.* Learning is *imitative*. Stating this point slightly more technically, we could say that the heart of the appropriate community is *mimēsis*, the Greek term for copying or imitation.[3] To learn how to relate well from leaders who are following Jesus assiduously is to be more like them, and the quickest and easiest way to do so is not so much to read a book about them or by them or to receive a set of formal instructions from them—although these can help in a pinch—as to copy them directly and personally. Effective learning is basically all about sitting at the feet of those who relate better than we do, and learning from these sages how to do this through imitation (which is why, incidentally, "electronic campuses" are so misconceived, whether for seminary education or for Sunday gatherings). We learn by walking in the footsteps of our teachers as they walk on ahead of us. And this is not rocket science. Any parent of teenagers already knows that teens don't do what you say; they do what you do. And Paul knew it too.

Paul states explicitly on several occasions, and then everywhere implies, that his converts should copy their leaders. We are called to imitate. In fact, we imitate one another all the time. But Paul is of course especially concerned to have people imitate him! Exhortations to imitate both him and his trusted followers stud his letters.

> I am writing this not to shame you but to warn you as my dear
> children.
> Even if you had ten thousand guardians in Christ, you do not have
> many fathers,
> for in Christ Jesus I became your father through the gospel.
> Therefore I urge you to imitate me.
> For this reason I have sent to you Timothy,
> my son whom I love, who is faithful in the Lord.
> He will remind you of my way of life in Christ Jesus,
> which agrees with what I teach everywhere in every church.
>
> (1 Cor 4:14–17)[4]

3. Mimesis and imitation get developed ultimately in various different ways, for example, within aesthetics, which we won't be that interested in here. Our interest is minimal and basic: people imitate one another.

4. See also 1 Cor 11:1; Gal 4:12; Eph 5:1–2; Phil 2:5–11; 3:17–4:1, 8–9; 1 Thess 1:6–10; 2:14; and 2 Thess 3:6–12. It is worth noting, in addition, that Paul generally wants to be present with his converts when they get into trouble so he can model and exemplify the way forward, although his difficult relationship with Corinth is a partial exception to this practice.

These contentions all seem to connect together plausibly. But there is a sense in which the whole situation is "black-boxed." We know both intuitively and theologically that we are shaped by our relationships with one another, and so we should imitate one another and should especially imitate those who mediate Christ better than we do. But it would be nice if we could push deeper into the actual mechanisms underlying this powerful process, which as yet seem to lie out of view. And we are deeply fortunate to be located where we are as we consider this question, looking back on twenty-five years of astonishing progress in our understanding of the human brain, because this provides us with a particularly compelling answer to our query.

The Second Personal

Research on the human mind and brain, which has accelerated exponentially in the last three decades, is able to shed new light on some of the actual processes underlying the evident effectiveness of imitation. In a field known as the second personal, scholars have become aware of the profoundly interactive and relational formation of the person.[5] The development of newborns in relation to their primary caregivers has especially proved particularly illuminating.

Close study of this relationship has revealed that newborns develop as they receive and mentally imprint information from the faces, bodies, tone, and voices of their primary caregivers, usually their mothers.[6] One of the earliest and most important imprints is the activation of the newborn's affect system, which is its basic array of integrated emotional and mental states that identify and motivate all subsequent action. This activation takes place as the newborn mimics and reflects the detailed facial pattern on their caregiver's face, whether interest and excitement (brows slightly furrowed in concentration), delight and enjoyment (mouth relaxed, open, and smiling; eyes relaxed and slightly hooded), or one of the many more negative affects like anger or

5. The field is well introduced in the Pinsent and Stump (eds.) 2013 issue of the *European Journal of Philosophy and Religion* dedicated to the second personal. Eastman's *Paul and the Personal* should be the point of departure for further work in this entire area in relation to Paul.

6. Nicely accessible in the following YouTube clip released by developmental psychologist Edward Tronick: https://www.youtube.com/watch?time_continue=6&v=KRy4uAbQaao. It is also interesting to note Macmurray's prophetic affirmation of the importance of this relationship in 1950.

anxiety. (There are nine affects in total.)[7] Affects are gradually correlated with incoming sensory data into short scripts or stories that guide human action, and human formation is in certain respects nothing more than the development of a massive repertoire of such scripts, which are nested into one another and often highly diverse between different cultures.[8] At bottom, however, all this development—this growth into a functioning person within a particular culture—can take place only as long as the relationship between the primary caregiver and the newborn continues and deepens through infancy and then on through childhood and adolescence, the caregiver being assisted along the way by other key relationships. Scripts are learned from other people in constant relationship, face-to-face. Hence human relationships *precede* individuation, and they support and nourish it.

As a result of this complex interactive process, infants learn to participate in various types of relationship: dyadic, in which two people relate face-to-face; and dyadic relationships characterized by joint attention, when two people together relate to some object, this relationship being a primary way in which caregivers teach their infants about the world. Growth in dyadic relating is followed in due course by triadic relationships, when two people contemplate another person.

During all these processes the knowledge in one person's mind—a mind inseparably embodied and thus communicating through numerous bodily cues such as gesture, movement, and tone, but especially through the face, and then also through language as that is acquired—is transmitted to the person in relation resulting in a "simulacrum" of that knowledge in the recipient's mind. But brain processes of recognition exist whereby the simulacrum of someone else's knowledge, significantly reproduced, is nevertheless known to be different from the knowledge that the recipient already possesses. Mental events, pictures, stories, associated feelings, implicit actions, and information are thereby shared and yet remain distinct. Hence as we learn, we literally have

7. Affects are actually an assembly of mental, emotional, and biophysiological dynamics. Particular rates and intensities of nerve firing correlate with particular mental feelings, facial expressions, and additional bodily correlations. The pioneer in the field was Silvan Tomkins. The importance of facial expressions, however, was first noted by Darwin. See his *The Expression of the Emotions in Man and Animals* (London: John Murray, 1872; repr. Cambridge: Cambridge University Press, 2013).

8. I know no one who articulates the key scripts in the United States better than George Lakoff. His expertise in cognitive linguistics also allows him to anchor scripts in key embodied metaphors, although he does not link his work with affect theory.

the mind of someone else in our mind, so that we share the same construction, with all its depth and complexity and effects, and yet we know that it is not "our" mind. And at this moment we can see that the entire complex learning process, as yet not *fully* understood, is nevertheless radically interpersonal, leading to the characterization of groups of people as fundamentally "intersubjective."[9] Other people are both within us and outside of us simultaneously and have to be so that humanity can learn and act and live as it seems designed to. In this sense we even participate in one another, both becoming and not becoming each other. Other people around us, with whom we are in relationship, are neither a separate object nor collapsed into our subjectivity, although they are positioned in both these locations. Hard subject-object relations that have so characterized post-Enlightenment thinking are, in any relationship to people, obsolete. *Human identity and formation is irreducibly interactive and relational.*

In the light of the powerful processes of reflection, largely unnoticed, but taking place all around us, face to face, body to body, and mind to mind, we can now well understand how the happy moods of certain people in Framingham radiated outward through their networks of relationships to affect people at three degrees of relational distance. The deeply intersubjective space that was the Framingham community resonated with shifts in happiness, just as it would have resonated with shifts in other moods as well. The people living in Framingham participated in one another. Moreover, we can also understand now how imitative learning is so deeply embedded in human history, even when its processes have been barely understood. It is wired into our development, and its powerful ongoing effects can be seen all around us every day. So Paul intuitively affirms our radically relational constitution and the importance of the resulting imitative learning process.

We are now in the happy position of being able to significantly deepen our earlier account of transformation in Christ as Paul describes it.

Revisiting Participation—and Pneumatology

Paul's preferred reference to our transformation through Jesus is, as we first noted in chapter 6, being "in Christ" or some closely equivalent phrase. This notion was clearly very important to him, occurring in various critical theses and summaries, as well as throughout the arguments of his letters. But it is so

9. Stump gives a nice account of this process in the special issue of *EJPR*.

compressed, and the common Greek preposition *en* (usually translated by the equally bland English "in") is so flexible that scholars have struggled to nail down Paul's meaning precisely. What does it really mean to say that we are no longer "in Adam" but are now "in Christ," especially when Paul also speaks of Christ (and Sin!) being "in us"? But if we correlate Paul's claim here concerning some sort of existence in Christ, as well as, less frequently, the notions of being in the Spirit and in Adam, with the overtly relational way in which he expects people to copy him and his coworkers, we can detect an underlying intersubjective and relational dynamic that the second personal explains neatly.

We know now that people learn from one another as they receive, imprint, and respond to simulacra—that is, reproductions—of the mental and affective states of other people with whom they are relating and, in a sense, resonating with.[10] If my spouse, Rachel, is looking at me and talking with me, I am receiving into myself some corresponding construction of what she is thinking and feeling and acting in relation to. If she and I are both looking at a fabulous painting of the Yorkshire countryside by David Hockney, we are sharing overlapping thoughts and experiences and feelings concerning his extraordinary art—a dyadic relationship characterized by joint attention. If she and I are discussing our children over the breakfast table, we are sharing a construct that our children possess as well—their concerns and moods and intentions and thoughts and aims; we are in a triadic relationship. The mapping will never be exact, *but it will be close* and *it will be enough*. We understand one another—and hopefully our children—and so continue to communicate with one another and to relate together and to live happily together. And in fact just the same process of sharing allows us to work through experiences of difficulty and problems that one of us might have inflicted on the other, generally unawares. Just as we enter into the interests and enjoy-

10. So, as Pinsent argues in the special issue of *EJPR*, this is not a classic Aristotelean account of learning by way of habituation. This is a fundamentally relational and interpersonal account of the acquisition of virtues, which he argues is present in Aquinas. Because of the grounding of learning and the virtues in a relationship, one particularly serious sin, which Aquinas calls in traditional terms a mortal sin, can sever the relationship and cut off the virtues instantly, something that is impossible for habituating learners. Conversely, all the virtues are immediately and fully present for imitation and embodiment once the virtuous person is present, notably Jesus himself, along with those mediating Jesus, and so they are acquired fundamentally as a gift. Moreover, they are introduced to us directly, hence, in Aquinas's terminology, they are infused. (Note that if we can categorize Aquinas as a virtue ethicist, in these terms, then we should also probably categorize Paul as a virtue ethicist in these terms.)

ment of one another, we enter into the pain we have caused, internalize it, and respond accordingly.

Because of this constant and profound sharing, what we are is radically affected by who we are relating to. They, in the sense of their simulacra, are literally in our minds, which are embodied, as we are in theirs. We know which simulacra are theirs and which are really ours, but even those that are not ours are still literally in us. In just this sense, then, it seems that the mind of Jesus is present within Paul because of their deep connection and relationship. Jesus is present to him and in him but in distinction from him. They are one, but one in this interconnected, resonating, relational sense—and Paul is following hard after Jesus's internal presence! The phrase "in Christ" captures this situation nicely (and especially when it is qualified by Paul's proximate references to his own agency).[11]

We can understand now, moreover, how Paul can speak of oneness, or unity, in fundamentally relational terms that seem to stretch to include multiple people, who do not lose their distinctiveness but are also a unity in some powerful sense. God is one, but is God the Father; and the Lord is one, but is the Lord Jesus. Both are also one God in their inseparable relationship with one another and sharing in one another.[12] Similarly, a man who has left his father and mother and cleaved to his wife in marital and sexual union is one

11. Susan Eastman points correctly to the highly indicative statements in Gal 2:19–20: "I myself, through the Torah, died in relation to the Torah, with the result that I lived in relation to God. I have been crucified with Christ. It is no longer I who live, but Christ lives in me. And the life that I live now in my fleshly body, I live by way of believing—the believing of the Son of God, who loved me and delivered himself up for me." It is difficult if not impossible to make sense of Paul's switches in agency and identity here unless the profoundly intersubjective notions of the second personal are introduced—at which moment he makes perfect sense! See her essay "The Saving Relation: Union with Christ in Galatians 2," ch. 6 in *Paul and the Person*, 151–75.

12. A direct overlap is apparent here between this understanding of Trinitarian unity in relational terms explained by the second personal and the classic orthodox account of divine unity in terms of *perichorēsis*. Often translated incorrectly but helpfully in terms of the divine dance together, this Greek word actually denotes "a standing within one another," which is an impressively exact grasp of personal relationality and intersubjectivity, wherein a person is both external and internal to someone else, inseparably but distinctly. The doctrine is expounded neatly by Colin Gunton, *The One, the Three, and the Many: God, Creation, and the Culture of Modernity*, especially 155–79; and Thomas F. Torrance, *The Christian Doctrine of God: One Being, Three Persons*, 203–34; although their accounts can now be helpfully augmented by the second personal.

with her. They are profoundly intertwined relationally, as one, with many simulacra, putting things prosaically, from the one existing in the other, and yet
they are distinct. And in just the same way, Paul envisages his teaching taking
place imitatively through coworkers. Jesus is in Paul, and Paul is in Timothy,
along with Jesus (the latter indwelling being rather more important). So the
Corinthians can experience Jesus through Timothy and should imitate him.
In just the same sense, Paul always works in groups, in a relational team. He
is never alone. Jesus is mediated within the team to one another, and through
them to others. This inherently relational interplay also explains Paul's application of a body metaphor to his communities in an analogy we will develop
in more detail later on. People in Paul's day thought of bodies in highly relational ways, as porous and interconnected entities, so this metaphor deepens
his investment in a unified relationality.

A delightful role for the Holy Spirit is apparent in all this as well. In an
intersubjective, interpersonal community she can assist the formation of the
mind of Jesus within the minds of people such as Paul *without ever overriding
or dominating their own thinking and acting.* An important connection with
the doctrine of mediation is evident here too.[13] If we are presented with people
strongly committed to the presence of Jesus's mind within them already—people like Paul and Timothy—then we receive the simulacra of Jesus's mind in
ourselves as we engage with and resonate with these local leaders. The Spirit
can then use our imperfect mediations of Jesus to one another to correct us.
But although the mind of Jesus is in us, it is not ours—we know we are distinct
from it—so we are not coerced or overridden. We are invited to respond to this
most intimate of invitations, which I hope we do with all our hearts, minds,
souls, and strength. The Spirit thereby leads us to Jesus through one another,
and both together lead us on to the Father.[14]

If this is all beginning to come into focus, it is worthwhile pausing for a
moment to gather up the threads of our discussion. We have now completed
another important chain of theological insights:

13. This also explains the apparent preference by the Spirit to work through embodied agents, which is to say, through other people. This is overtly apparent in Paul's
letters and in Acts. Several points of contact are apparent at this moment with Rogers's
important book on pneumatology *After the Spirit.*

14. How profound it is to be caught up in the triune God! The Father with the
Spirit gifts the Son to humanity. (This follows the initial gift to the Son of humanity by
the Father and the Spirit.) The Father with the Son gifts humanity with the Spirit. And
the Spirit with the Son gifts humanity back to the Father.

1. At the heart of Christianity is community, the community of the divine communion and God's summons to us to join it.
2. At the heart of community is interpersonal relating to the point that we can see that this is what a person is, a relational entity.
3. At the heart of relating is—once our incapacity has been healed—a learning process, a process that also leads to our growth in freedom.
4. And at the heart of learning is our copying of leaders, which is to say, our imitation of those who are better at relating than we are and who thereby mediate Jesus to us, assisted by the Spirit.

This reasoning all nicely confirms a phenomenon that is very widespread within human culture and history and that we can now see is arguably, if not providentially, wired into our very biology. People copy one another and resonate with one another intersubjectively to the point that they are "in" one another, and yet always distinct. Just so, followers of Jesus are in one another and, insofar as they mediate Jesus, Jesus is in us and we are in him.

We couldn't sign off on the validity of this social and biological phenomenon without good theological reasons for doing so. But we have those, and so we can enthusiastically embrace the burgeoning literature that attests to the importance of imitation and its many mechanisms and modes, including increasingly powerful insights from recent research on the brain and its formation through intersubjectivity. We are learning rapidly today that imitation is an enormously powerful engine of change that bears an intimate relationship with the construction of our brains and the rest of our bodies and results in a directly relational pedagogy that many of us badly need to acknowledge and to recover.

Ancient Philosophical Practice

By grasping the importance of mimesis in Paul, we have, on one level, merely circled back to the sense in which the early followers of Jesus organized themselves like a group of ancient philosophers, because this is how ancient Greek philosophers organized their learning. And so we can now profit from exploring this tradition in a little more detail.

Many modern thinkers have lost their way in all this. But ancient philosophers knew well that the best way to influence the moral formation of people was to live with small groups of students who were led and shaped by a teacher, a pedagogical approach that we see figuring forth clearly in Paul, although with important additional variations. It is unlikely that Paul learned about this mode of learning from Greek philosophers directly, although he could have. He taught in Greek cities for decades, and he was a very smart guy. But an indirect influence from the philosophers is detectable on both him and Jesus, as on many other Jews in their day.

Paul lived and taught in the first half of the first century CE. Prior to his revelation on the road to Damascus, he had been trained as a Pharisee, the Pharisees being just one of a number of Jewish groups around this time who operated sociologically very much like students of an ancient Greek philosophy. Pharisees followed teachers, rabbis, to whom they attached themselves as students or disciples. They devoted themselves to the interpretation and application of key texts, sometimes in self-contained groups and conventicles, guided by their teachers. They ate together and met regularly for prayers, for meals, and for further textual explication and discussion, building gathering places to do so ("synagogues," the Greek literally meaning "[places for] gathering together"). Interpretative disputes, which tend to arise when important texts are read and applied, then led to divergences between different teachers and their traditions. Pharisaic tradition distinguished in particular, in its earliest days, between the followers of Hillel and the followers of Shammai.

Very little of this sort of thing is recognizable from earlier Jewish history and its sacred texts. Readers will search most of the Tanakh (i.e., the Jewish Scriptures) in vain for much evidence of these arrangements. The textuality of Judaism in the Jewish Scriptures is largely priestly. Yet all of this later activity is recognizable in broadly Greek terms as a Jewish version of ancient Greek philosophical practice.

For centuries, Greek philosophers had been gathering small circles of disciples and meeting together to dine, to drink, and to discuss things, and some had been sufficiently well organized to set up schools in key cities, usually in Athens, namely, the followers of Plato, Aristotle, and, a little later on, Zeno the Stoic. Others were not so well organized or preferred not to be, and wandered itinerantly. Unsurprisingly, however, they struggled to pass on their teachings quite so effectively, although they still managed to accomplish a lot. The notorious Cynics fell into this category. (One famous Cynic, despising the trappings of civilization, lived in a barrel.) The formal Athenian schools had been shut down prior to Jesus's and Paul's day by the arrival of the Romans in the second century BCE, but by this time the underlying practices of Greek philosophy were deeply embedded in the broader culture. Hence the majority of Greek and, later, of Hellenistic philosophers were organized in this way, although modern people would regard much of this as religious in addition to philosophical. These groups taught about god or the gods and the importance of correct behavior and ethics, they met in houses or small meeting places, not temples, often to study texts rather than to adore and pray to images, and they exhorted their students to follow a comprehensive way of life.

Judea had been subject to direct political influence from the time of Alexander the Great, who reigned 336–323 BCE, with cultural influence significantly preceding Alexander's time. So we know that these teaching practices were quite well established by the time of the first major confrontation between Judaism and its Hellenistic overlords in the second century BCE (from the 160s). John the Baptist, Jesus, and Paul were at work almost two hundred years later. It is no surprise, then, to find even atypical Jewish figures from outside the mainstream like John the Baptist and Jesus gathering groups of disciples around them in the early first century CE and teaching weekly in synagogues when they were not instructing their disciples and other followers on a daily basis. The Greek philosophical model had well and truly taken hold, although in distinctive Jewish variations.[15] And we are fortunate that it did so. Discipleship and its imitation are the mother of effective progress in anyone's basic way of life, as we have just learned.

Unsurprisingly, however, Paul added some critical additional twists to this originally Greek model that had been filtered to him through Judaism. He both uses and modifies the philosophical emphasis on learning imitatively from teachers.

Qualifications

Paul frames leadership in the church in a very helpful way. It is not a question of leaders leading and shaping students, period, which would imply a highly authoritarian situation. Some church movements in the past have thought that it was, which has resulted in astonishing abuses of power and aberrations in formation. However, as we might already expect, leaders of Pauline communities only mediate the character of God, revealed most clearly in Jesus himself, so just as these leaders possess authority, they are also under authority, constant reminders of which are built into the communities.

Any community that worships regularly acknowledges, among other things, that God is God and people are people. Things are kept in perspective. Moreover, any community regularly celebrating the Lord's Supper and

---

15. Some scholars would consequently want to speak here of "hybridity."

baptism acknowledges that these two dramatically different agents, God and humankind, have come together perfectly in only one person. Many traditions, including the Jewish, also tend to spend some time in their communal meetings on confession, and my recommendation is that local teachers don't just take the lead in this practice liturgically, reciting generalized requests for forgiveness loudly and enthusiastically, but model this personally, confessing actual faults. It takes a certain sort of community to do this, and a certain sort of leader, but I have been fortunate to attend such a church for a time. We would have a part of the weekly service set aside for personal sharing that often invited the public acknowledgment of wrongdoing—something I have made use of myself. Those who don't attend this sort of church might like to think of—or even attend—a meeting of Alcoholics Anonymous or Al-Anon, where communal confession is built into the warp and woof of the program as well. Worshiping and confessional gatherings are constantly modeling the fallibility of their own leadership, and I see all these practices at work in Paul's communities.

Paul's account of leadership is more complex than this, and we will plumb its depths in due course. But for now we are emphasizing the explicit fallibility of its leaders. They are not perfect and don't expect to be. In addition to their fallibility, however, there is another delightfully destabilizing dimension to community leadership as Paul understands it.

Benefaction

In several passages Paul links Christian leadership to the ancient language of benefaction, or giving.[16] In his letter addressed to the "holy ones" at Rome, the majority of whom did not know him or his teaching, Paul states,

> For by the gift given me I say to every one of you:
> Do not think of yourself more highly than you ought,
> but rather think of yourself with sober judgment,
> in accordance with the understanding God has distributed to each of
> you.
> For just as each of us has one body with many members,
> and these members do not all have the same function,
> so in Christ we, though many, form one body,

16. See Rom 12:3–8; 1 Cor 11:4–6; 12; 13:1–3; 14; 1 Thess 5:19–22.

and each member belongs to all the others.
We have different gifts, according to the gift given to each of us.
If your gift is prophesying, then prophesy in accordance with your
    understanding;
if it is serving, then serve;
if it is teaching, then teach;
if it is to encourage, then give encouragement;
if it is giving, then give generously;
if it is to lead, do it diligently;
if it is to show mercy, do it cheerfully. (12:3–8 NIV modified)

Paul is using language here drawn from the ancient economy of giving—which we will explore in more detail in a later chapter—to talk about Christian leadership, and the implications are intriguing. Ancient economies were not structured exactly like modern economies. A great deal of activity revolved around a certain sort of giving that classicists refer to as *euergetism* (lit. "good activity"). We might speak of this giving today as philanthropy or charity work. In the ancient world, elite figures, who monopolized the lion's share of the resources in their societies, gave vast amounts of money and other gifts such as food to their clouds of clients, donated animals to temples for slaughter and public sale, and even built enormous public buildings at their own expense.

In like manner, Paul frames community leadership in Rom 12 and elsewhere in terms of God's generous gift-giving. Like an ancient benefactor, God distributes different gifts of leadership as the community, described as a body, needs them, and Paul specifically mentions here prophecy, serving, teaching, encouraging, giving, managing, and "showing mercy" (which is probably a particular ability to help the marginalized). It is interesting to envisage a community led by leaders with these particular activities and to think about what imitating these sorts of leaders might look like. (How do our churches measure up?) But Paul's explicit point in context is that God's act of distribution in this way grounds these leaders in humility. If the basic capacity to lead has been given, then there are no grounds for boasting or self-aggrandizement. Comparison is pointless, since the gifts are both donated and diverse, an important point to make, since ancient society was deeply competitive. Certainly these leaders should strive to carry out their duties with all their hearts, souls, minds, and strength. They should grow. But they are developing something that in the first instance they have merely received. "What do you have that you did not receive? And if you did receive it, why do you boast as though you did not?" Paul says accurately in 1 Cor 4:7. Community leadership is not a competition. But this observation does not end Paul's contributions to the qualification of leadership.

Something quite astonishing lies within Paul's description of God's diverse gifts of leadership, although modern eyes might spot this more quickly than ancient or medieval readers. By benefacting leadership in this way, God is not respecting the usual channels of leadership as they were customarily established in society, channels carved by genealogy, wealth, and education. Ancient society thought that leaders were born, not made. They were born to the right families, from which would flow wealth, success, and acclaim—the traditional marks of leaders. But Paul is describing a very different process. Leaders in Pauline communities are designated by the gift of God, which seems to be given indiscriminately of anything else. *Anyone* could be a leader of a Pauline assembly. Leaders could be drawn from any walk of life and any social stratum, a phenomenon that would be enormously beneficial to the community, but it could also be enormously disruptive.

On the one hand, this opens up community leadership to everyone. Elite and well-born families were a tiny percentage of society as a whole in Paul's day. The leaders in the Roman Senate were a thousandth of a percent of the population as a whole—a mere 0.001 percent! Drawing the leaders of the empire from this pool of talent was going to massively constrict the options, especially when it was a little too inbred. The leaders in Paul's movement could be drawn from 100 percent of the available options, and church history would attest to the results. Astonishingly clever and able Christian leaders came to lead the church from all walks of life—poor, middling, and elite—although most Christian traditions still foolishly followed convention and drew only from males. As time passed, they also became increasingly susceptible to drawing leaders from elite families. Nevertheless, Paul's basic system of radically redistributed leaders reverberated away in the Scriptures, and the Holy Spirit still distributed gifts of leadership within the community diversely, as she pleased.[17] So occasional bursts of indiscriminate leadership, usually regional, are frequently apparent. The church fathers were all men, but they were frequently brilliant and able. Equally brilliant and able women occasionally guided the church as well, especially later on in northern European regions,

---

17. Recalling here that I am using feminine pronouns to refer to the Spirit, and masculine to refer to "the Father" and "the Son," partly to indicate that God is fully personal but not gendered. A charming version of much the same practice is William P. (Paul) Young's *The Shack*, although he uses the feminine gender for both "the Father" and "the Spirit."

where a combination of factors made this phenomenon more socially acceptable. (Few leaders in the history of the church have been able to compete, for example, with the wisdom of Hildegard of Bingen.)

On the other hand, the designation of leaders in countercultural terms is potentially provocative. Precisely because leaders are being drawn from all walks of life in violation of existing cultural expectations, community disruption could occur. "*They* are leaders?! I don't think so. No one from that family has ever led anything before!" Culturally designated leaders can clash with nonconformist leaders—another recurring phenomenon in church history. We won't dig down into this aspect of Paul's communities just yet; it was a particular feature of his community in Corinth.[18] But we can note a hint of this disruption in Paul's brief plea at the end of 1 Corinthians in 16:15–16 for the church to respect someone called Stephanas. Stephanas's household was the first to convert to Paul in the region of Achaia, the region where Corinth was.

> You know that the household members of Stephanas were the first
>   converts in Achaia,
> and they have devoted themselves to the service of the Lord's people.
> I urge you, brothers and sisters,
> to submit to such people
> and to everyone who *joins in the work* and *labors at it.*

Paul codes Stephanas's role here carefully. In Paul's original Greek, Stephanas is a "fellow-worker" and "laborer" with Paul. This description confirms the information we get from Acts, which says that Paul met Prisca and Aquila around this time, who were handworkers as well (18:2–3). So we can deduce that Paul was following his usual evangelistic practice in Corinth and working as a humble artisan when Stephanas and his household converted. We will explore Paul's fascinating missionary methods more carefully in due course. It must suffice for now to appreciate that Stephanas was almost certainly the head of a household of handworkers or artisans.

Handworkers were pretty unimportant in ancient society. They were badly educated, horribly poor, and had to work from dawn to dusk with their hands

---

18. Another factor will need to be introduced before we do so, and it complicates the situation still further. Not only are Christian leaders being gifted in defiance of cultural convention, but the leadership they exercise defies cultural convention as well. Christian leaders don't lead in the same way as other leaders. "You're not a leader, and it's pretty obvious in what you look like and in the way that you 'lead'!"

to eke out a living. The upper classes despised them because they were just one step above slaves and beggars. Anyone who had to work with their own hands for a living was a social nonentity, and no one with any class would do anything that was manual. (For this reason the upper classes refused to learn certain art forms such as painting and sculpture, and even the playing of instruments.) So Stephanas and his family would have lived in a tiny two-story apartment combining a shop, a workroom, and a living space, where the parents, their children, and any hangers-on made their wares and tried to sell them—a far cry from some of the spacious villas we can still see the remains of in Corinth and in various similar ancient cities today. Yet Paul asks his Corinthian community, which seems to have included a number of relatively wealthy members who lounged around in such villas, *to submit* to Stephanas. Stephanas is a designated leader in the community, in part because he was the first adult male to convert to the new religious movement. He is now not merely a worker and a laborer but a coworker and colaborer with Paul in God's work, and the Spirit has gifted him accordingly.

We can surmise that the community benefited from Stephanas's expertise and gifts. His range of contacts through a massive, underprivileged urban class of artisans would be an opportunity for evangelism, and he would have known just how to relate to this group because he was one of them. Perhaps the majority of the church ultimately came from this constituency. And although we lack the information to be specific, we can be confident that Stephanas was gifted in certain ways as well. We don't know whether he was a prophet, a servant, a teacher, an encourager, a giver, a gifted administrator and manager, or someone with a particular supply of mercy for those who were suffering. But we know that he had one or more of these gifts.

However, we could have predicted that Stephanas's leadership was bound to cause problems if anyone from higher up the social ladder was converted, as happened to be the case in Corinth. The high-status members of that community had to cavil at Stephanas's undeserved and distasteful elevation. They would have felt humiliated and utterly disinclined to respect this leadership. Moreover, in typical Greek fashion, they would have recruited their own supporters within the community to echo these opinions and to agitate against him. A political contest for community control conducted in brutally secular terms ensued!

We see here then, in a nutshell, both the promise and the problem posed by Paul's account of leadership in terms of a Spirit-led benefaction. It is all very well to enjoy, from a modern vantage point, this radical distribution of leadership by the Spirit. Those leading a community—its elite—could be drawn from any walk of life and then equipped to fulfill some leadership role.

How refreshing! And how profoundly challenging! This system is so welcome in theory and so difficult to navigate in practice.

A Key Summary

It might be helpful at this point to step back and to observe that despite the plethora of gifts that community leaders could be endowed with, certain roles seem to be especially critical. They are articulated most crisply in the letter we know as Ephesians. The four types of leaders that Paul names in Eph 4:11 are so significant they will basically structure the remainder of this book.[19] (Again, I am being a little schematic.)

Ephesians 4 is one of Paul's classic statements of the way God gifts the Christian community with various leaders. It ends in verses 7–12 with a short and deeply insightful enumeration.

> But to each one of us a gift has been given as Christ has apportioned it.
> This is why it says:
> "When he ascended on high,
> he took many captives
> and gave gifts to his people."
> (What does "he ascended" mean
> except that he also descended to the lower, earthly regions?
> He who descended is the very one who ascended higher than all the
>   heavens,
> in order to complete the whole universe.)
> So Christ himself gave:
> the apostles first,
> then the prophets,
> then the evangelists,
> and then the pastors who are teachers,
> to equip his people,
> to do works of service,
> and to build up the body of Christ.

19. I have been thinking hard about Eph 4:11 since hearing a talk on the priesthood of all believers by Alan Hirsch that emphasized this text. I take his additional point that Paul's approach to leadership was nonstipendiary and will briefly discuss that issue in part 4 when the Pastor introduces the phenomenon of a paid, hence professional, clergy.

It is clear from Paul's writings that community leaders come in many shapes and forms. According to Rom 12, as we saw earlier, some prophesy, some serve, some teach, some encourage, some give, some administer, and some show mercy (vv. 6–8). According to 1 Cor 12–14, some also evidence spectacular charismatic gifts of insight and healing, some live extraordinarily self-sacrificial lives,[20] being prepared even to offer themselves up in martyrdom (1 Cor 13:3). But it is equally clear from a consideration of the basic shape of Paul's thinking about community that the four types of leaders identified in Eph 4:11 are especially important: what Paul calls apostles, prophets, evangelists, and teachers. Any Pauline network of communities—thinking here, like Ephesians, of the church as a whole, and not merely of a particular community—will need these four roles in order to function at all. They are the sine qua non of a Pauline community, although they fall into a distinctive arrangement. We already know that a Pauline community can be considered from two points of view: its formation, or establishment, and its subsequent nurture and formation. These two different phases cast light on the four types of leadership that Paul names in Eph 4:11.

The establishment of communities is clearly the work of what Paul calls apostles and what most of us today would probably call missionaries. The apostolic gift is really just the missionary gift, and I will devote part 3 of this book to Paul's account of what missionaries should look like. Apostles are missionaries, but missionaries should also be apostles, we might say. Paul has a detailed and insightful account of how apostles should operate when they first arrive and try to make converts.

Among other things, however, we will learn from part 3 that apostles arrive, establish communities, and then leave! The ongoing nurture of the community is the work of the remaining three types of leaders. Communities continue to be formed and grow primarily through the work of their teachers, their prophets, and their evangelists.

Paul doesn't tell us very much directly about evangelists, but I think we can make some useful inferences about them. He tells us a lot about apostles, who founded communities cross-culturally. So I suspect that evangelists are gifted with the knack of converting people as well but are simply not called to venture out cross-culturally, like a missionary, to plant churches among foreign people.[21] They are supposed to operate locally, continuing to grow the community that

---

20. See 12:1–31; 13:1–3; 14.

21. Note that the sense of distance suggested by work in a foreign territory need not just be limited to geography; crossing class and race (and other) barriers can involve reaching across important distances in sociological terms.

they are in, in their familiar local networks and surroundings, where they have the knack of converting people. It follows from this surmise that evangelistic practice can be inferred from Paul's apostolic practice, minus some of the cross-cultural challenges. The way Paul evangelized a local community as an apostle will be very much the way local evangelists are supposed to operate there as well. So we will fold our account of an evangelist into our account of Paul's cross-cultural evangelism as a missionary or apostle, which will be undertaken in part 3. This realization simplifies things, as does a further realization.

The church has frequently distinguished between pastors—in the Greek literally "shepherds"—and teachers. Pastors, as their name suggests, care for people and look after them. But literal shepherds *guide* their sheep, herding them along in the right direction, which is a teaching role. Moreover, no other list of leadership gifts in Paul's preserved writings mentions being a shepherd or pastor in isolation. We can explain this omission by realizing that the Greek syntax linking "shepherd" and "teacher" in Eph 4:11 is not *enumerative*, specifying different roles (although it could be this on formal grammatical grounds), but, for the foregoing reasons, *explicative*. The word "shepherd" specifies or explains what sort of teacher Paul is talking about and, to ancient ears, familiar with thinking of teachers as guides we live with and imitate, this would have been quite appropriate. Teachers were supposed to be kind and caring—but also authoritative—like shepherds. This is what Paul is getting at (and this is why I talk about four, not five, basic types of church leader in what follows).

The kind and caring teacher is the leadership role that we are focusing on right now, in part 2. This might seem a little out of sequence at first (shouldn't we start with how communities are formed and then go on to consider how they are nurtured?), but, as we observed earlier on, we need to be formed in basic relational practices deeply before we can export those both locally and cross-culturally. Hence we have just spent some time working out that the community is nurtured and formed by leaders who are copied, and who in turn personally guide their students. It is these figures, the community's teachers, who are imitated, and who are consequently the key to their deepening moral formation, and we will go on to spend some time in what follows working out just what virtues and practices they should evidence. Teachers are the key to moral formation, to community development, and consequently they are at the center of the discussion of part 2, just as apostles and evangelists are at the center of part 3.[22] But what of our fourth remaining role, the importance of which Paul specifies repeatedly—the prophet?

22. I am assuming here as well that apostles can teach.

After we have thought long and hard about how apostles and teachers are supposed to nurture Pauline communities and to grow them in a virtuous life, and how they are supposed to found them sensitively and noncoercively in the first place, with evangelists continuing that work, we will in fact encounter a third major dimension within Paul's church practice. The founding and nurturing of communities was also a flowering into a certain sort of variety. Paul's network of churches evidenced a shocking diversity in some of its practices. Things previously thought sacrosanct were no longer compulsory, things previously thought unclean were sometimes permitted, and he fought hard to preserve this diversity. It is here that the work of discernment within Pauline community becomes strikingly apparent. The establishment of Pauline communities and their subsequent growth involved a *navigation* of various subtle differences in behavior, and this is where prophetic leaders must *discern* what is of God and what isn't. The work of prophets in the early church wasn't limited to this function—they seem to evidence many of the more overt acts of the Spirit too—but I view this practice of discernment as especially critical for the healthy development of a Pauline type of network.

Certain new things can be undertaken and embraced. God approves of them, perhaps unexpectedly. But other things that have been practiced or that we are tempted to practice must be rejected. So we see here the work of Paul as a prophet and learn that the apostle must be a prophet. But we learn simultaneously what a Pauline prophet is, and that communities need them to flourish. The story of the apostle as a prophet, and of the nature of prophecy, along with all its challenges, is consequently the story of part 4. We will trace there the way that Paul navigated diversity within the early church—something we hope that he got right, because if he didn't, then the basic rationale for Christianity collapses!

Following this fairly detailed discussion, and a little like Reformed discussions of Jesus in terms of his threefold office of prophet, priest, and king, the rest of this book will discuss Paul's theology largely in terms of the apostle as a teacher (in part 2 here), as an evangelist (in part 3), and as a prophet (part 4).[23] These are the four critical leadership roles that Pauline communities particularly need. But before moving on to a deeper discussion of Paul's teaching ministry, we need to add one final and highly significant detail.

23. The final part of the book briefly discusses in ch. 29 Paul's contested legacy, which is represented canonically by the anonymous author of 1 and 2 Timothy and Titus, whom we will call the Pastor.

The four different groups of leaders in Paul's programmatic statement in Eph 4:11 are all enumerated in the plural, as they are in all the passages that discuss community leaders. There are apostle*s*, prophet*s*, evangelist*s*, and teacher*s*. The point is obvious but fundamental. Paul's writings, not to mention his powerful intellect, tend to bend our discussions of his thinking in an individualistic direction. We are drawn magnetically to think about the apostle Paul by himself. We envisage Paul walking the dusty roads of the ancient Mediterranean coastline, writing letters, founding communities in small hot workshops. But Paul never thinks of either himself or community leadership in these terms. He is individu*ated*, with personal gifts and roles, and at times he is clearly dominant, but he is never an individu*al*. Paul's own communities were always founded by more than one person. "For the Son of God, Jesus Christ, who was preached among you by us—by me and Silas and Timothy—was not 'Yes' and 'No,' but in him it has always been 'Yes'" (2 Cor 1:19). He invariably traveled with friends and coworkers and was supported by a veritable cloud of the same.

> Epaphras, my fellow prisoner in Christ Jesus, sends you greetings.
> And so do Mark,
> Aristarchus,
> Demas, and
> Luke, my fellow workers. (Phlm 23–24)[24]

Paul always operated in groups, with coworkers.[25] Hence, despite the personal dominance of Paul himself, we must hold on tightly to the collective, interpersonal activity underlying everything that follows. At the risk of sounding like a sporting cliché, we have to say that just as there is no "I" in team, there is no isolated "P" there either. Community leadership for Paul, whether at a community's founding or during its ongoing nurturance, was always a team effort, something that has the further virtue of allowing a more effective and accurate mediation of the mind of Jesus.

---

24. Insofar as we can tell, Epaphras was a local convert (Col 1:7–8; 4:12–13); Aristarchus was a key missionary coworker (Col 4:10; Acts 20:4; 27:2); Mark was a missionary associate as well, now reconciled to the fold (Acts 13:13; 15:37–41); and Demas and Luke seem to have been friends.

25. It seems likely that some of Paul's key missionary coworkers would have been called apostles, just as he casually acknowledges the apostolic status of Junia and Andronicus in Rom 16:7. They were apparently a missionary couple rather like Prisca and Aquila (Rom 16:3–4).

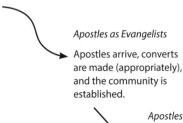

Apostles as Evangelists

Apostles arrive, converts are made (appropriately), and the community is established.

Apostles as (shepherding) Teachers and Prophets

The Apostles nurture the community, and navigate its particular diverse formation.

Presumably they continue to evangelize as and when they can too.

The Apostles leave

The community is grown by its own *Evangelists*.

It is nurtured and guided by its *Teachers* and *Prophets*.

Other diverse and more specialized leadership roles and gifts emerge, e.g., service, encouragement, giving, organizing, and showing mercy.

Theses

- The existence of communities of learning implies that some people know more than other people.
- The former will be—broadly speaking—in the role of teachers and leaders; the latter, in the role of students and followers.
- God mediates his character and practices primarily through teachers, although also through students if and as he determines.
- This means that all Pauline communities have an elite structure, with leaders (like all human communities).
- This observation generates questions, initially, concerning the mode of appropriate learning. What sort of leaders are appropriate? How should we relate to them?
- In view of the relational ontology of people, as revealed by Trinitarian personhood, relationships make us who we are and so, unless they are static, we expect them to shape us and to form us as well.

‣ This theological truth is corroborated by empirical data concerning the astonishing interactiveness of people—their sensitivity to those around them.

‣ But interaction in Pauline communities is intentional.

‣ There, students copy their leaders. They imitate.

‣ Research on the human brain and infant development, undertaken in the last two decades in particular, suggests the "wiring" of human beings in astonishingly powerful and resonant ways to learn relationally, and basically by way of imitation.

‣ People's minds, including feelings (i.e., affects) and potential actions, are present to and in one another concretely, although also in a way that is distinguishable.

‣ This is apparent from birth, as newborns are taught by their primary caregivers, through imitation, affective resonance, and an intersubjective sharing of understandings.

‣ This pattern of growth explains how people can mediate the mind of Jesus to one another.

‣ The assistance of the Holy Spirit is also central.

‣ Relational and mediated learning allows the Spirit to present Jesus to people in a noncoercive way *and* to moderate that presentation in a noncoercive fashion.

‣ This relationally intersubjective experience of Jesus seems to underlie Paul's key summary phrase "in Christ."

‣ This relational reality also allows us to explain how overtly participatory claims by Paul such as being in Christ combine with highly relational emphases in his letters on unity (in God, in the community, and in marriage), with learning through imitation, with missionary work in constant and irreducibly plural terms (i.e., in teams), and with the conception of the community as a body (from an ancient point of view), which was porous and relational.

‣ These relational insights into formation lay intuitively at the heart of much ancient philosophical practice.

‣ They were mediated to Jews in Jesus's and Paul's day by the Hellenization of Judea, which took place from the 300s BCE.

‣ Pharisees used this technique.

‣ However, leadership by teachers of Pauline communities—and of many other Jewish and messianic Jewish groups—is qualified in a way that ancient virtue ethics was not.

- Such leaders are not and never will be perfect.
- Worship of the one true God incarnate only in Jesus constantly reminds us of this imperfection, as does confession.
- The Spirit gifts leadership capacities to various figures within the community.
- Paul uses the language of ancient benefaction to describe this "euergetism."
- Hence community leadership should not be boastful, for all leadership is a gift of the Spirit.
- This indiscriminate benefaction overrides cultural qualifications and expectations of leadership.
- This origin of leaders generates the benefit of a much wider pool of talent for leaders than traditional narrow elite practices would allow (i.e., a small pool characterized by birth, education, and wealth).
- This generates a corresponding challenge, however, as those not regarded as culturally qualified to lead are gifted with leadership by the Spirit—a challenge apparent in Paul's day especially at Corinth, and in the example of the artisan leader Stephanas.
- Paul's descriptions of community leadership activities are diverse. However, four main types of leader are designated in Eph 4:11, which are clearly critical to his entire approach to community: apostles, prophets, evangelists, and teachers.
- The word "pastor" or "shepherd" in 4:11 is best read as explaining the nature of Christian teachers rather than as enumerating a separate, fifth type of leader.
- An apostle evidences all three of the other leadership types and enacts them cross-culturally, in missionary work. Communities are established or founded (the apostle as evangelist and, if cross-culturally, as missionary) and then nurtured and formed (the apostle as teacher), and their ethical differences are navigated (the apostle as prophet).
- After the apostles leave a community, local leaders take up the roles of evangelist, teacher, and prophet.
- Other less common leadership roles also emerge as those are called for—roles of service, encouragement, giving, management, showing mercy, and so on.
- We learn from Paul's apostolic work of community formation what a pastoral teacher is like—the story of the rest of part 2 here.
- We learn from his apostolic work establishing communities what an evangelist is like and how this activity must be undertaken appropriately—the story of part 3 following.

- We learn from his navigation and defense of ethical diversity in relation to messianic Jews and Christians what a prophet is like—the story of much of part 4 following.
- Church leadership is also always plural. Communities are formed and led by teams.

Key Scriptural References

Imitation is a frequent theme in Paul. First Corinthians 4:14–17 was cited at the outset of this chapter and basically says everything that needs to be said. (See also 1 Cor 11:1; Gal 4:12; Eph 5:1–2; Phil 2:5–11; 3:17–4:1, 8–9; 1 Thess 1:6–10; 2:14; 2 Thess 3:6–12.)

Paul's "in Christ" terminology was summarized in chapter 6. The key references there should be revisited.

Clearly Eph 4:11 is an important text for detailing leadership—verses 4–16 are especially relevant.

Other lists and treatments of various leadership gifts can be found in Rom 12:3–8; 1 Cor 11:4–6; 12; 13:1–3; 14; 1 Thess 5:19–22. (Benefaction language is evident there, although it is by no means limited to these passages. This language is most pronounced in Paul in 2 Cor 8 and 9, although it is not applied there to the Spirit's gifts of leadership.)

Key Reading

Eastman has written a programmatic book on Paul's anthropology in conversation with ancient and modern neuroscientific accounts of the person, *Paul and the Person*, which includes significant insights from the second-personal perspective. She also contributes to an important 2013 issue of the *European Journal for Philosophy of Religion* edited by Stump and Pinsent that is entirely dedicated to the second personal. The contributions of Stump and Pinsent to the issue are also especially noteworthy. Pinsent argues that a Thomist account of the acquisition of virtue is illuminated by the second personal and stands over against an Aristotelean account in terms of habituation, which is rooted in a craft analogy. Stump provides a compact account of the mental reproduction by people of the minds of one another both in identity and in difference. All three figures provide a wealth of references to the relevant neuroscientific and behavioral research.

Further Reading

Somewhat indicatively, there are no programmatic treatments from Barth's *CD* to list on formation (at least to my knowledge), bearing out Hauerwas's key concern with Barth's project. Barth does talk of formation from time to time, however; his writings are by no means barren in this respect. His development of personhood in (critical) dependence on the thought of Martin Buber and his emphasis on I-Thou relationships is especially relevant.

The sociological notion of elitism is usefully introduced, albeit in a very different context, by Anthony Giddens.

The reliance here on a relational conception of personhood goes back to chapter 3 and the insights noted there of John Zizioulas. (Relevant writings are listed there as well.) I suggest developing its pedagogical and formational dimension by way of "the second personal," as noted above. Marty Folsom's practically oriented trilogy is also a useful and insightful guide from this point.

The notion of mimesis has been developed by many scholars in many ways beyond the mere imitation of people, but I am using it here in the limited sense. Morrison provides a useful overview of its broader development.

Girard and those influenced by him speak much of mimesis. Their approach is usefully introduced by Garrels. Again, I am using mimesis in a rather more limited way than the Girardians do, although there is some overlap.

I would want to add a suitable use of affect theory to the deployment of the second personal by Eastman, Stump, Pinsent, and others. Indeed, it is hard to emphasize too much the explanatory power of all of this fascinating material—the second personal, affect theory, and Lakoff's work on scripts and metaphor, all of which are closely intertwined. Affect theory originated with Tomkins (whose life and work are introduced with suitable panache by Gladwell, although Gladwell's application of the theory is confused). It is neatly introduced by Moore (125–63) and, with more depth, by Nathanson. This material should also be combined with the work on scripts and root metaphors undertaken by Lakoff.

Virtue ethics is neatly introduced by Rosalind Hursthouse and Glen Pettigrove. They unsurprisingly identify a basic commitment to ethics construed as virtue as one of the two key hallmarks of a virtue ethic. (This contrasts with a commitment to ethics understood in terms of deontology or rules—Gk. *deon* is "duty"—or in terms of happiness acquired by way of utilitarian or consequentialist calculations.) The other hallmark is a commitment to a mentality, or mind, that can make situational and practical judgments about the right thing to do, and also do so with the right motives—practical reason, practical morality, or *phronēsis*. Paul certainly evidences these two key notions. The subordinate issue arising, however, debated by virtue ethicists a great deal and less by the other two main approaches, is *how* this mind is formed. Paul has a particular answer informed by relational considerations and not mere habituation. So he would be a distinctive variation within virtue ethics from this point onward, although Pinsent argues that Aquinas is fundamentally similar.

An influential figure in the recovery of the importance and the basic sociology of the Greek philosophical tradition is Pierre Hadot. An elegant development of his project is C. Kavin Rowe's most recent book. Jennifer Herdt's analysis of the virtue of magnanimity is exemplary. Harrington and Keenan provide an introductory engagement with virtue ethics in relation to Paul.

The Hellenization of Judea and of the Jewish people was one of the great intellectual realizations of Martin Hengel. The broader story can be found in any basic history of the intertestamental period. Cohen's is accessible.

The key recent work in Pauline studies on gifts and benefaction is by John Barclay; we will use this important text later. He was preceded by, among others, James Harrison.

Gorman's most recent work on Paul should be especially noted here; it is a significant contribution in this general area of participation and ethics by an important Pauline scholar.

Bibliography

Barclay, John M. G. "Manna and the Circulation of Grace: A Study of 2 Corinthians 8:1–15." Pages 409–26 in *The Word Leaps the Gap: Essays on Scripture and Theology in Honor of Richard B. Hays*. Edited by J. Ross Wagner, C. Kavin Rowe, and A. Katherine Grieb. Grand Rapids: Eerdmans, 2008.

———. *Paul and the Gift*. Grand Rapids: Eerdmans, 2015.

Buber, Martin. *I and Thou*. 2nd ed. Translated by R. G. Smith. New York: Scribners, 1958.

Cohen, Shaye D. *From the Maccabees to the Mishnah*. 3rd ed. Louisville: Westminster John Knox, 2014.

Darwin, Charles. *The Expression of the Emotions in Man and Animals*. Chicago: University of Chicago Press, 1965 (1872).

Eastman, Susan Grove. *Paul and the Person: Reframing Paul's Anthropology*. Grand Rapids: Eerdmans, 2017.

———. "Philippians 2:6–11: Incarnation as Mimetic Participation." *JSPL* 1 (2010): 1–22.

————. "The Shadow Side of Second-Person Engagement: Sin in Paul's Letter to the Romans." *EJPR* 5 (2013): 125–44.

Galinksy, Ellen. "Trusting Relationships Are Central to Children's Learning—Lessons from Edward Tronick." *Huffington Post*, December 1, 2011. https://www .huffingtonpost.com/ellen-galinsky/trusting-relationships-ar_b_1123524.html.

Garrels, Scott R., ed. *Mimesis and Science: Empirical Research on Imitation and the Mimetic Theory of Culture and Religion.* East Lansing: Michigan State University Press, 2011.

Giddens, Anthony. "Elites in the British Class Structure." Pages 1–21 in *Elites and Powers in British Society.* Edited by A. Giddens and P. Stanworth. Cambridge: Cambridge University Press, 1974.

Gladwell, Malcolm. *Blink: The Power of Thinking without Thinking.* New York: Little, Brown, 2005.

Gorman, Michael. *Becoming the Gospel: Paul, Participation, and Mission.* Grand Rapids: Eerdmans, 2015.

Gunton, Colin. *The One, the Three, and the Many: God, Creation, and the Culture of Modernity.* Cambridge: Cambridge University Press, 1993.

Hadot, Pierre. *Philosophy as a Way of Life.* Translated by Michael Chase. Oxford: Blackwell, 1995.

Harrington, Daniel, and James Keenan. *Paul and Virtue Ethics.* Lanham, MD: Rowman & Littlefield, 2010.

Harrison, James R. *Paul's Language of Grace in Its Graeco-Roman Context.* Tübingen: Mohr Siebeck, 2003.

Hengel, M. *Judaism and Hellenism: Studies in Palestine during the Early Hellenistic Period.* London: SCM, 1974.

Herdt, Jennifer A. *Putting on Virtue: The Legacy of the Splendid Vices.* Chicago: University of Chicago Press, 2008.

Hursthouse, Rosalind, and Glen Pettigrove. "Virtue Ethics." In *The Stanford Encyclopedia of Philosophy* (Winter 2016 Edition). Edited by Edward N. Zalta. https://plato.stanford.edu/archives/win2016/entries/ethics-virtue/.

Lakoff, George. *Moral Politics: How Liberals and Conservatives Think.* 3rd ed. Chicago: University of Chicago Press, 2016.

Moore, David B., and John M. McDonald. *Transforming Conflict in Workplaces and Other Communities.* Sydney: Transformative Justice Australia, 2000.

Morrison, Karl F. *The Mimetic Tradition of Reform in the West.* Princeton: Princeton University Press, 1982.

Nathanson, Donald L. *Shame and Pride: Affect, Sex, and the Birth of the Self.* New York: W. W. Norton, 1992.

Pinsent, Andrew. "The Non-Aristotelean Virtue of Truth from the Second-Person Perspective." *EJPR* 5 (2013): 87–104.

———. *The Second-Person Perspective in Aquinas's Ethics: Virtues and Gifts.* London: Routledge, 2012.

Pinsent, Andrew, with Eleanore Stump, eds. *The Second Personal in the Philosophy of Religion.* Special Issue: *EJPR* 5 (2013).

Rogers, Eugene F. *After the Spirit: A Constructive Pneumatology from Resources outside the Modern West.* Grand Rapids: Eerdmans, 2005.

Rowe, C. Kavin. *One True Life: The Stoics and Early Christians as Rival Traditions.* New Haven: Yale University Press, 2016.

Stump, Eleanore. "Omnipresence, Indwelling, and the Second-Personal." *EJPR* 5 (2013): 29–54.

———. *Wandering in Darkness: Narrative and the Problem of Suffering.* Oxford: Oxford University Press, 2010.

Tomkins, Silvan S. *Affect Imagery Consciousness: The Complete Edition.* 4 vols. Philadelphia: Springer, 1962–92.

Torrance, Thomas F. *The Christian Doctrine of God: One Being, Three Persons.* Edinburgh: T&T Clark, 1996.

CHAPTER 11

Love Is All You Need

Making Sense of Paul's Ethics

We turn now from the question of structure—how best to arrange a Pauline learning community—to the question of its relational tenor—what exactly its relationality should look like. And Paul provides us with an initial challenge here because his letters are loaded with ethical instructions, but his various commands, arguments, and admonitions do not fall obviously into a neat arrangement. He doesn't use the four cardinal virtues that many ancient virtue ethicists used. He was a Jew, so he uses biblical idioms, but these come and go, and at times he seems to give wildly divergent recommendations about Scripture.[1] Moreover, he is clearly not overtly tradtioned. He can write long lists of good actions, along with corresponding, even lengthier lists of bad ones, but the content of these lists varies quite considerably.[2] So we must ask whether there is any order here—any underlying detectable rationale. Another return to first principles may shed light on what Paul is up to.

---

1. We will consider further these variations later. They give us an important clue concerning the basic structure of his ethics.

2. See 2 Cor 6:6–7 (purity, knowledge, patience, kindness, sincere love, truthful speech); 8:7; Gal 5:22–23 (love, joy, peace, patience, kindness, goodness, faithfulness, gentleness, self-control); Phil 4:8–9 (whatever is truthful, honorable, right, pure, pleasing, commendable, virtuous, praiseworthy); Col 3:12–15 (compassion, kindness, humility, meekness, patience, forgiveness, love, peace, thankfulness). These lists can then be contrasted with lists of vices: Rom 1:29–32 (although this extraordinarily bombastic list might be partly tongue-in-cheek); 13:13; 1 Cor 5:11; 6:9–10; 2 Cor 12:20–21; Gal 5:19–21; Eph 4:31; 5:3–5; Col 3:5–8.

We already know that we are being drawn into the triune communion, which it is our destiny to enjoy eternally. Our community, by way of our resurrected minds and the Spirit, is participating in the relationality of the Trinity. This reality is pressing down upon us. (Doubtless it can do so directly, although we have also learned that there is a detectable preference on God's part for working through other people and, in particular, through community leaders and teachers, who are supposed to be mediating the relationality of the triune God to us.) Moreover, because these are personal relationships, we have found that they are best described by using stories or narratives. It follows from this, then, that we should search for some sort of narrative structure underneath Paul's ethical instructions. Furthermore, that story should be the story that unfolds around Jesus, who definitively and concretely reveals as a human being what Trinitarian relationality is all about. It can be mediated through Paul and others, but those communications will, precisely, be a mediation of Jesus's life as explained by a narrative. In short, a story about Jesus, in the immediate setting of his Trinitarian relationships with his Father and his Spirit, should supply the content for everything else that Paul says about the relational tenor of his communities. This, at least, is what we hope we will find.

But we have good grounds for optimism. We already know that Paul tells a story about Jesus, and he certainly talks about Jesus a lot. And in two places Paul speaks of the sense in which Jesus is his Torah, a cryptic phrase that probably means that Jesus himself is the sacred teaching Paul now obeys and learns from, in the way that he previously studied and enacted the Jewish Scriptures and their sacred teachings (see 1 Cor 9:21; Gal 6:2).[3] It seems, then, that a story of Jesus might very well be doing some important work in Paul's thinking and writing about ethics. So we need to return to the narrative that we described in chapters 3–6 and press on it for the sorts of details that might undergird a comprehensive account in Paul of right relationality.[4]

3. Hays provides a nice analysis of Gal 6:2 in essentially these terms: "Christology and Ethics in Galatians: The Law of Christ." It is hard to improve upon W. D. Davies's account of the nature of Torah for Jews as their sacred teachings and instructions in "Law in First-Century Judaism" and "Reflections on Tradition: The 'Abot Revisited."

4. The story of Jesus is actually surprisingly frequent and extended in Paul—surprising because for much of the modern period scholars have seen fit to deny this. But see especially Richard B. Hays, "The Story of God's Son: The Identity of Jesus in the Letters of Paul." See also several contributions by Michael Gorman: *Cruciformity*, ch. 5; *Inhabiting the Cruciform God*, ch. 1; and "Paul and the Cruciform Way of God." See also my essay "Narrative Dimensions."

A Story about Jesus

Paul not infrequently alludes to episodes from an implicit story about Jesus, and sometimes he even spells it out in full. The basic plot feels pretty stripped down when it is placed next to the Gospels, a brevity Paul even seems to be quite proud of. He exclaims with some passion at one point to the Corinthians that when he arrived in their city and announced the good news, he preached about the cross and very little else (1 Cor 2:1–2, 4–5). There are no good reasons for thinking that this was unusual, and Gal 3:1 seems to confirm this focus.

> When I came among you, brothers and sisters,
> I came proclaiming publically the divine secret,
> and not with a surfeit of eloquence or education.
> For I resolved not to depict anything among you
> except Jesus Christ, and this one crucified! . . .
> My teaching and my proclamation were not in persuasive words of wisdom
> but through a demonstration of the Spirit and of power
> so that your believing might not be through the wisdom of a person
> but through the power of God! (1 Cor 2:1–5)

> Stupid Galatian provincials! Who has bewitched you?!—
> those to whom Christ was visibly inscribed as crucified! (Gal 3:1)

Paul is here not speaking strictly literally. He did not arrive and speak about the pieces of wood on which Jesus was executed. He is making a metonymic statement in which the part stands for the whole. The motif of the cross signifies the broader story of Jesus's death, so it presupposes who died and what happened immediately afterward.[5] But Paul is clearly focusing the content of his preaching on a story about Jesus's crucifixion, as we have seen already in 1 Cor 15:3–5 as well:

> For what I received I passed on to you as of first importance:
> that Christ died for our sins according to the Scriptures,
> that he was buried,
> that he was raised on the third day according to the Scriptures,
> and that he appeared to Cephas, and then to the Twelve.

---

5. Paul also speaks of "the blood," "the wood/tree," "the obedience," "the faithfulness," and "the death" of Jesus in the same way. These data are analyzed in ch. 13.

So what does this compact story of Jesus, which we suspect is so common to Paul's thinking and speaking, tell us about relationality?

We already well know the answer to this question.[6]

A Story of Love

The story about Jesus centered on the cross is a story of love. To speak of a God acting definitively in Jesus as he goes to the cross is immediately to grasp that God is love and to a degree that we find hard to fathom. This God was prepared to die for us—the critical import of Rom 5:6–10. The Father and the Spirit delivered up their beloved only Son for us to a horrible death, and the Son obediently accepted this fate, sacrificing himself for our sakes. And they did so *while we were yet sinful and hostile.* There is no greater love than this—a love, it should be emphasized, that was revealed ultimately in the ghastly event of the cross and that must never as a result be reduced to mere sentimentality.[7] Jesus loved us enough to die hideously for us when we stood on the side of those who executed him. Love is this sort of action, and it characterizes our God all the way down.

Data drawn from other letters, however, can now deepen this account of the divine love. God's loving action through Jesus on our behalf has several different facets, nicely summarized and grouped together by the opening to Ephesians but found in more scattered locations in several other places.[8]

---

6. See ch. 3.

7. The legitimate concern of both Stanley Hauerwas and Hays. See Hauerwas, "Love's Not All You Need," in *Vision and Virtue: Essays in Christian Ethical Reflection* (Notre Dame, IN: University of Notre Dame Press, 1981 [1974]), 111–26; and Richard Hays, *The Moral Vision of the New Testament*, 5. However, the best antidote to the sentimentalization of love by modern culture, a definite abuse of love, is, I suspect, not abandonment but right use. A resolutely christological location also speaks to Augustine's legitimate concern that love must be rightly ordered. The love that matters is the love of God and the love we share with God; it is *this* love and no other. People can love all manner of things, and such love is not necessarily appropriate but is frequently downright evil. Another way of putting this is to say that love cannot be abstracted or separated from the love of God as revealed in Jesus. An abstracted or separated love is not love but some artificial counterfeit.

8. As noted in ch. 3, financial imagery is deployed in relation to the atonement and related events in Rom 3:23–26; 1 Cor 6:20; Gal 1:4; Eph 1:6–7; and Col 1:14; 2:13; and presupposed by Rom 6:17–23. Release from debt-slavery in the sense of release from jail is probably also referenced in Gal 3:22–25.

Debt Release

As noted earlier, in chapter 3,[9] Paul analogizes our problematic situation in the Flesh, mired in sin and transgressions, as many in his day did, in financial terms.[10] Our sins are viewed as debts, which steadily accumulate. Moreover, death is the "payment" that we ultimately have to make on our debt mountain (Rom 6:23). However, we are liberated from this debt and its consequences by God through his gift of resurrection. Through Christ and the Spirit we receive life instead of death. God thereby forgives us our debt (2 Cor 5:19), releasing us from its deadly consequences. Furthermore, God does this utterly gratuitously (2 Cor 5:14; Gal 2:21).[11] This release is a gift, proffered to us freely, without charge or cost or legal conditions (although it is of course freighted with the appropriate relational expectations). Nevertheless this gift costs God a great deal. Jesus must die for us to make this happen, and the Father and the Spirit must sacrifice their only beloved child to do so as well.[12] Hence the only way to make sense of this story of this great and gracious gift is to grasp that it is underpinned by God's near-incomprehensible benevolence for us. We have been gifted with life instead of death, and gifted while we were still viciously hostile to the giver. God loves us.

But God's loving generosity toward us through Jesus is only just beginning.

Adoption into Filial Status

Having had the consequences of our sin debts erased, being released thereby from nothing less than death, we are now adopted *into God's family*. Our status thereby shifts from that of slaves to "sons," so that family metaphors now

9. The discussion can be found under Key Scriptural References.

10. An insight now especially associated with the work of Gary A. Anderson; see his *Sin: A History*.

11. See also Rom 3:24.

12. It is a significant mistake to press the language of payment beyond these parameters, supposing that God is the one who oversees this debt and then demands the ultimate payment of death for it to himself in essentially retributive terms. Paul never actually says this. The language of debt is metaphorical, and the context allows us to grasp which connotations are in view. Paul means only that, as he explains most clearly in Rom 6, we are gifted with life instead of the appropriate consequence for sins of death. Other texts confirm that our future death is not an event endorsed by God but God's enemy. Death must be *defeated*; see Rom 8:33–39; 1 Cor 15:54–55.

become central to our understanding of God's being and ways and our relationship with him.[13] We are God's children, which is what we were always destined for.

> God sent his Son . . .
> so that we might receive adoption.[14]
> And because you are [now] sons,
> God sent the Spirit of his Son into your hearts
> crying "*Abba!* Father!"
> So then you are no longer a slave but a son,
> and if you are a son, then you are also an heir—an heir through
> Christ![15] (Gal 4:4–7)

We can see here, in fact, that we are not simply adopted; this new status as children of God has two further significant implications.

Inheritance and Resurrection

As adopted children of God, we now stand to inherit what God has promised, and stored up for, his children, an offer first apparent in his promises made to Abraham and the Jews, who were adopted long ago (Rom 4:13–14, 16). But we are all now God's appointed heirs and are included within these promises to Israel made initially to Abraham. Moreover, it is especially clear from Paul's development of these promises in Rom 4 that we will inherit rather more than mere money. We will receive eternal and imperishable life in the age to come, a glorious age from which sin and death will be banished. And we will of course

13. Rom 8:12–23; 2 Cor 6:18; Gal 3:26; 4:4–7; Eph 1:5.

14. It is helpful to reinsert the sense of Gal 3:26–29 here: For all of you who are in Christ Jesus are sons of God by means of the believing we have just been talking about. For some of you have been immersed into Christ, you have been clothed in Christ. There is no Jew or pagan; there is no slave or free person; there is no "male and female." For all of you who are in Christ Jesus are one and the same. And since you come from Christ, you are Abraham's seed, and so you are heirs in accordance with the promises made to him.

15. On internal grounds, I am following the most likely variation among the various possibilities for the end of this verse present in the manuscript tradition: DIACU. See the minuscules 81, 630, and the Sahidic (Coptic) version.

be resurrected from the dead and gifted with glorious new bodies of spirit in order to participate in it—quite an inheritance![16]

Gifts and the Indwelling of the Holy Spirit

In the meantime, as we wait for the dawning of the new age, we are gifted with the very presence of God within us by way of the Holy Spirit, who acts as a down payment guaranteeing our future inheritance—so here Paul is using financial imagery again.[17] And we are given further gifts to encourage each other with during this stressful time—miraculous gifts of prophecy, glossolalia, discernment, healing, service, generosity, and so on.[18] As we wait for our inheritance, then, we enjoy the continued generosity and benefactions of a deeply involved and benevolent patroness.

Let's quickly string these distinguishable episodes together into one continuous story and try to grasp what it is suggesting.

The Story in toto

Let us suppose you are a poor, benighted student, struggling with an enormous debt-load that, it turns out (thanks to the indifference of your parents, the government, and the loan agencies), you can never in fact repay. Interest payments mount, the sum owed increases, and soon you face not only the humiliation of bankruptcy but arrest and imprisonent. Moreover, like many of the poor in the United States, you lack the solvency to post bail or even to raise bond money, and thus you have to submit to incarceration awaiting trial, while you watch your more well-heeled college companions walk free.

One day, however, you wake to the sound of the cell door being unlocked. "You are free to go," your jailer announces. This happy news naturally elicits some suspicion, for it is beyond the realm of possibility. And yet your lawyer is waiting smiling at the jail exit, waving some paper that proves the entirety of your debt has been paid off. It is gone. But more is to come, your lawyer says. Another sheaf of papers proves that your unknown benefactor has also adopted you as a child, with full legal rights from this moment onward.

---

16. Rom 8:17–21; 1 Cor 15:50–57; Gal 3:18, 29; 4:1–7, 30–31; Eph 1:18; 3:6; Col 1:12; 3:24.
17. Rom 8:9–11, 23; 2 Cor 1:21–22; 5:5; Eph 1:13–14; 4:30.
18. Rom 12:3–8; 1 Cor 12:1–31; 13:1–3; 14:1–33a, 37–40; Eph 4:4–16.

You read deeper into the adoption document, where still more surprises are waiting.

You have been written into your benefactor's will, fully and completely, so that on her death, you stand to inherit an extraordinary fortune. There is so much money stored up waiting for you that you will instantly go onto the Forbes Rich List. The amount is beyond imagining. And yet there is more. Your lawyer gestures toward the limousine sitting in the parking space outside the jail door. A liveried driver awaits, who sweeps open the car door and says, "Your private jet is waiting, and we are scheduled to fly you to Hawaii to your month-long, all-expenses-paid vacation in the Royal Hawaiian Hotel on the beachfront at Waikiki." You gasp but then recover your wits and point out that this all sounds very nice, but won't you be a little lonely? "Your family and closest friends will all be there as well, all expenses paid as well of course," your driver replies.

You are feeling somewhat overwhelmed but go on to ask the obvious question, "Who did this, and why?"

Your lawyer explains. "It turns out that you have a long-lost and bereft aunt who has loved your parents, and loved you, since from before the day you were born, but she has been rejected by the family and has had no opportunity to show you how much she loves you until now. Up until now you have been taught that she is a ghastly, miserly hag. So you remain a little suspicious."

"Yes," you reply. "I've heard about this aunt and the internet company she owns. Surely she could just be throwing me a bone from her vast resources. I mean, I appreciate it, but it's not necessarily the way you think it is."

"Oh yes it is," your lawyer answers. "Your aunt—and my client—has liquidated her fortune and spent every last cent on this arrangement for you. Last night she moved out of her mansion and into a trailer so that enough money would be available after its sale for your limousine and for the purchase of your plane and your holiday and your inheritance. She has given everything up for you in one final last attempt to break through your family's hostility. She really, really loves you."

You pause and then say, "So, let's make her trailer our first stop on the way to the airport." You then add, "I'm horribly ashamed to think we have driven her to such lengths to reach out to us, but there's no time to waste on recriminations. Clearly she adores me. I want to meet her and find out all about her and take her on my holiday. Heck, I want her living down the hallway from me for the rest of my life. There's a lot of catching up to do!"

In just the same way—although in ancient pagan legal idiom—we should be able to see that all of the episodes we just enumerated in Paul's story of how

God relates to us speak of his unconditional and limitless love for us. God rescues us from our enslavement to the debt of sin, releasing us from its deadly repayment plan freely and fully, while we didn't even want him to, and he did so at the ultimate personal cost to himself. The consequences of that debt were taken on himself, and he died so that we might live. God then adopted us as children and members of his divine family. As a result of this, God promised us a full inheritance in due course, as is proper for heirs, and in this case, it is nothing less than a triumph over death in eternal and glorious life. And while we wait in the interim, God gifts us with his very self, in the Spirit, as a down payment, guaranteeing this promised future gift and distributing other helpful benefactions to us as we need them. Blessing upon blessing, and gift upon gift. God loves us!

The Sufficiency of Love?

It seems clear, then, that love is absolutely central to the nature of God, to God's very personhood as revealed by Jesus, and consequently to our communities. We are rooted in love, flourish in love, and are called to love. So it is entirely unsurprising to find Paul affirming its primacy quite explicitly: "These three remain: faith, hope and love. But the greatest of these is love" (1 Cor 13:13). But this very centrality raises a further important question. Can love undergird all that we need for ethics, as Augustine sometimes suggests?[19] Is love comprehensive enough to carry Paul's entire ethic, a position sometimes dubbed "agapeism"?

19. See, among other locations, *City of God* 15.23 (virtue is "rightly ordered love"); *On Christian Doctrine* 1.27–28 ("But living a just and holy life requires one to be capable of an objective and impartial evaluation of things: to love things, that is to say, in the right order, so that you do not love what is not to be loved, or fail to love what is to be loved, or have a greater love for what should be loved less, or an equal love for things that should be loved less or more, or a lesser or greater love for things that should be loved equally"); and *On the Morals of the Catholic Church* 15.25 ("I hold that virtue is nothing other than perfect love of God. Now, when it is said that virtue has a fourfold division, as I understand it, this is said according to the various movements of love. . . . We may, therefore, define these virtues as follows: temperance is love preserving itself entire and incorrupt for God; courage is love readily bearing all things for the sake of God; justice is love serving only God, and therefore ruling well everything else that is subject to the human person; prudence is love discerning well between what helps it toward God and what hinders it"). See also his homily 7 on 1 John, in which he famously says, "Love God and do what you will."

It is highly suggestive that in 1 Cor 13, the chapter we just quoted from, Paul elaborates in verses 4–7 what love looks like, and in doing so utilizes several other virtues.

Love is patient,
love is kind.
It does not envy,
it does not boast,
it is not proud.
It does not dishonor others,
it is not self-seeking,
it is not easily angered,
it keeps no record of wrongs.
Love does not delight in evil but rejoices with the truth.
It always protects,
always trusts,
always hopes,
always perseveres.

We see here at a glance that love operates in particular situations in different specific ways. Love is patient when a relationship of love is frustrated and tested—say, when we are managing a new puppy or a grumpy toddler. It is kind in situations requiring involvement, perhaps a sick spouse or a stubborn student. Love avoids sinful acts like envy, boastfulness, pride, mockery, self-aggrandizement, rage, and the reductions of all human relationships to contractual terms. In doing so, it is presumably also the converse of these things as it acts in ways that are content, humble, encouraging, self-controlled, and covenantal. Love abhors evil, which is to say, actions that are unloving or destructive to love, and in this vein it holds fast to the truth. It is also protective but is fundamentally trusting of others, thinking and expecting the best of them, and so is hopeful. Hence it keeps no record of wrongs and is also trusting, not jealous, and it is fundamentally expectant about the future, not anxious and negative.

This is a panoply of specific virtues, although all are derived by Paul from love. One thus feels the force of Augustine's point. There does seem to be a sense in which everything can be related back to love, and thereby to the loving relationality of the Trinity as revealed by Jesus. And we can even see that John Lennon opined the same quite correctly a little later, in 1967: "Love is all you need."[20] But in 1 Cor 13 Paul nevertheless articulates love in different ways as he presupposes different specific settings. And these observations invite us to view the other virtues as more specific instantiations of love as particular circumstances suggest. Hence Pauline communities clearly need to know what love looks like in practical terms and in various different circumstances. Love, we might say, needs to be parsed out in more detail. And at this moment we need to ask whether we have quite enough as yet to work with. Up to this point a story of Jesus centered on the cross has been emphasized, since this speaks so directly of God's great love for us. But we now need to add one or two further key episodes to this basic plot so that it can provide further "parsed" guidance to us about love. And it is here that scholars have long recognized the importance of Phil 2:6–11.

Four Moments in the Story of Jesus

Philippians 2:6–11 is one of the most profound passages Paul ever wrote, hence its frequent occurrence in our discussions before this point. And in a couple of important ways it supplements the story of the cross, burial, and resurrection, which we have detected in 1 Corinthians and Galatians.

> 6 [Christ Jesus] being in the form of God
> did not consider equivalence with God something to be grasped
> 7a but emptied himself,
> 7b taking the form of a slave,
> 7c becoming the exact likeness of people,
> 7d and being found in form as a person
> 8 he humbled himself,
> becoming submissive to the very point of death–
> death on a gallows!
> 9 Therefore God lifted him up
> and gifted to him the name that is above every name
> 10 so that at the name of Jesus
> every knee in heaven and on earth and under the earth should bow
> 11 and every tongue confess
> that Jesus Christ is LORD
> to the glory of God the Father.

20. A. J. Torrance argues the same persuasively in his essay "Is Love the Essence of God?"

This elegant paragraph still focuses on Jesus's death and resurrection, but these are the fulcrum on which a slightly longer plot pivots. There are additions to both ends of the story of the cross, so to speak—to what precedes, and to what follows it.

The cross is now the culmination of a great trajectory of descent that speaks of Jesus's obedience in the midst of this humiliation. Most scholars rightly detect two stages of descent. First, a preexistent person (v. 6), living in some highly exalted form,[21] becomes a human being (v. 7a–c), which is a slavish state compared to what preceded it, a descent the church later spoke of as the incarnation. Then, second, in this human state, as Jesus, he submits further to death, and to a horrifically humiliating death—the death in fact of a disobedient slave (vv. 7d–8). We have already read about the last part of this descent elsewhere in Paul, namely, the crucifixion, and the element of Jesus's great obedience implicit there is explicit here. But we see now that the descent involved was much greater than a merely human submission to a humiliating death. The person who died descended first into the human condition in a first step of humiliation, going on to submit, consistently but horribly, to death on a cross. This first great descent from the heavens seems to be part of Paul's story leading up to the cross.[22]

But we also see clearly in Phil 2:9–11 how Jesus's great trajectory of submissive humility is reversed by God the Father's lifting of Jesus beyond his resurrection up into a highly exalted place in the trajectory the church later spoke of as the ascension. There he receives the title of Lord (v. 9), universal worship (v. 10), and divine acclamation (v. 11), although these acts are directed toward God the Father as well. Jesus is not just resurrected then, appearing to his followers after this, as suggested by 1 Cor 15:4–8. He is enthroned in heaven as Messiah and Lord, from where he presumably reigns even now.[23] Indeed, it is this event that explains Jesus's messiahship. He has been enthroned as

21. Its details are debated. But I would suggest two fairly well-established identifications. The Preexistent One is Wisdom, and the Preexistent One is also in some sense the Father's Son. Paul applies the narrative of Abraham and Isaac to Jesus's death (Gen 22), suggesting that God the Father did not spare "his only beloved son." This wording speaks of a preexistent relationship of parent and child. Since Wisdom is figured in the Jewish Scriptures as a child sporting with God during creation, these two identifications inform one another easily and richly (see Prov. 8:22–31; Wis 9:1–2, 9–10). Other Pauline texts suggesting the Son's equation with preexistent Wisdom include 1 Cor 8:6; 2 Cor 4:6; and Col 1:15–17; and perhaps also Rom 10:6–7, which resonates with Bar 3:29–30.

22. Second Corinthians 8:9 confirms this descent very clearly, while other texts just noted confirm the Son's role in creation, thereby implying his preexistence.

23. See Rom 1:4.

Israel's king in heaven, permanently (the event that so excited the author of the letter "to the Hebrews"), this status being signaled by a royal anointing (so also Rom 1:3–4).

We see here, in short, four critical narrative moments in the extended story of Jesus that Paul both articulates and alludes to so centrally and repeatedly:

1. We see in the incarnation, and then in the cross, that loving involves *giving*, if necessary of oneself, to the point of *self-sacrificing*.
2. We see in the immediate journey to the cross that loving involves *obedience* and *faithfulness*.
3. In what the cross and then the resurrection accomplish, we see that loving involves *peacemaking*, as these events reconcile, heal, and transform the broken cosmos.
4. And as we see Jesus entering into a new, resurrected, heavenly life with his Father and his Spirit, we see that loving involves *enjoying*, celebrating, and delighting.

With this additional information, all the narrative elements in relation to Jesus essential for a more extended ethical discussion are in place. Information from elsewhere in Paul can fill out the story with a few more details, but we have what we need.[24]

The rest of the letter to the Philippians does add a footnote to this story about Jesus, although this need not hold us up for long here. In 3:20–21 we read that both Paul and the Philippians are waiting for something more. One day their savior, Jesus, will appear from heaven and transform their lowly bodies of Flesh into glorious bodies like his.[25] In the meantime, the Philippians are

24. Hays notes how we learn from other texts scattered through Paul's letters that Jesus was descended from David (Rom 1:3), was born of a woman (!) (see 1 Cor 11:12), was a Jew (Gal 4:4), had brothers (Gal 1:19; 1 Cor 9:5), was a teacher (1 Cor 7:10–11; 2 Cor 9:14), and instituted the Lord's Supper (1 Cor 11:23–25, thereby suggesting, among other things, that he anticipated his death); see Hays's essay "The Story of God's Son." Death by crucifixion implies that the Romans executed Jesus, but 1 Thess 2:14–15 suggests that some Judeans were also hostile to him. Maximalist and minimalist positions exist when it comes to ascertaining the presence of unmarked Jesus traditions in other Pauline texts: see Rom 8:15–16; 12:17; 13:8; Gal 4:6; 5:14; 1 Thess 4:15–17. Hence it does seem wise to err here on the side of caution and not use these data too aggressively as evidence that Paul knew the Jesus tradition, and Jesus primarily as a teacher.

25. I am not going to make extensive use of the scenarios depicting Jesus coming in future judgment, because (1) it hasn't happened yet and (2) it is critical to subject these

"working out their salvation," even as "God is working in them" (2:12–13) "to complete the good work that has already begun" (1:6). So during this waiting period they are to do things like pray to God (4:6–7) and worship him by means of the Holy Spirit (3:3). In other words, the implicit waiting period in Paul's story about Jesus, after the ascension but before his final glorious return, is a period of time characterized by his rule and by life in the Spirit, at which moment we link hands with the statement in 1 Corinthians that we began this chapter with. *We* have now been located in this story, as part of its penultimate chapter, in an explicit relation to both Jesus and his Spirit (since Paul expects signs and wonders to take place in confirmation of the truth of the rest of the story when it is told by his witnesses).[26]

Duly noting our rather complicated involvement in the part of the story between the ascension and the second coming, we now need to work through each of the four key dynamics in Jesus's life in more detail, and after we have done so, we will find that we have explained most of the things that Paul has to say about right behavior and ethics. It is all about love, *and* it is all about Jesus.

Theses

‣ We are now addressing the relational tenor of a Pauline community as against its structure.

‣ People are living under the impress of the Trinity and its particular, interpersonal relationships.

‣ We expect any account of these relationships to take a narrative form.

‣ We expect, moreover, a narrative of Jesus to do most of the explanatory work in Paul.

‣ Revisiting the story of Jesus in Paul as stated by texts like 1 Cor 15:1–3, it is clearly centered on the cross, meaning specifically the events of Easter: Jesus's crucifixion, burial, and resurrection.

‣ Carefully examined, this is a story of divine love, and in several respects.

‣ Jesus freely releases us from the "debt" of our sins, dying and rising for us, thereby releasing us from the deadly repayment that otherwise needs to be made.

---

scenarios to Pauline *Sachkritik* (which we will do shortly when discussing peacemaking). Because scenarios of future judgment are so susceptible to undisciplined cultural and political projection, extreme caution is in order.

26. See also Rom 15:18–19.

- › God the Father adopts us in Jesus as children.
- › As children, we are also now heirs and are promised a rich inheritance—life in the age to come, beyond death.
- › While we wait for our inheritance, the Spirit dwells with us as a "down payment" and guarantee of the reality of this future promise, distributing further gifts and benefactions to us as we have the need.
- › We must ask now whether love, which is clearly so central to God and to the story of Jesus, can explain everything important about ethics—"agapeism."
- › First Corinthians 13 suggests "yes" in a broad sense, but it also articulates how a loving relationality takes on various more specific forms in different circumstances.
- › Returning to Jesus's story, articulated most clearly in Phil 2:6–11, we can now detect *four* moments when loving activity takes place in a specific way that we can explore further.
- › First, in the incarnation and then in the cross, we see God's great generosity, surrendering up the Son, the Son surrendering himself. We see here that loving involves giving—if necessary, self-sacrificially.
- › Second, in the journey to the cross, we see that the Son obeys God steadfastly, submitting to his wishes; loving thus involves obedience, submission, and faithfulness.
- › Third, in the state that cross and resurrection effect, we see that loving leads to peacemaking, reconciliation, and transformation.
- › Fourth, in Jesus's resurrected and ascended state at the right hand of God, acclaimed and in glory, we see that loving involves celebrating, enjoying, and delighting.
- › It should be noted that the story has not finished yet. Jesus will return one day, at which moment his followers will receive a complete transformation. In the meantime we wait under his rule, strengthened, guided, and comforted by his Spirit.
- › However, we will address this dimension within Christian living later. We will address immediately the four, more detailed instantiations of Jesus's love revealed by Phil 2:6–11—the instantiations we are to learn and to practice now as we wait.
- › After explicating each of these four loving dynamics in more detail, we will have explained the bulk of Paul's ethical advice in terms of its fundamental content—and given ourselves several major ethical challenges!

Key Scriptural References

Telling the story of Jesus as it is found in Paul relies on texts we have already met: 1 Cor 2:1–5 and Gal 3:1 emphasize its focus on the cross. And Phil 2:6–11 anchors a slightly longer story extending from the incarnation through the ascension.

An absolutely critical, and much briefer, love text in Paul, much used in our discussion already, is Rom 5:6–10.

Paul's most famous love text—and one of the most famous texts ever written—is 1 Cor 13 (I quote vv. 4–7 above).

God's action through Jesus and the Spirit on our behalf is narrated with financial analogies in many texts; see especially Rom 3:23–26; 1 Cor 6:20; Gal 1:4; Eph 1:6–7; and Col 1:14; 2:13; and see also the very important explanation that culminates in Rom 6:20–23.

For adoption, see Rom 8:12–23; 2 Cor 6:18; Gal 3:26; 4:4–7; Eph 1:5.

For the promises and the inheritance, see Rom 4:13–22; 9:6–9; Gal 3:6–4:7; 4:21–31.

Benefactions are treated more fully in the following chapter.

Key Reading

Richard Hays's essay "The Story of God's Son" is exemplary.

Further Reading

Barth describes love especially in *CD* IV/2. His description of Jesus as a person for others in II/2 should not be overlooked, however; and the root of divine love as shown in election is also described in II/2. He describes hope in IV/3.2. (He treats death extensively in III/2.)

I discuss the story of Jesus in my essay "Narrative Dimensions"; Gorman has analyzed this story numerous times.

The financial analogy for God's loving salvation of us through Jesus and the Spirit, initiated by redemption from the debt of sin, is set up by Anderson's seminal work *Sin: A History*. A pristine application of this imagery to a (very difficult) Pauline text is made by Lang.

The centrality of love to a Christian ethic—largely because it is so central to the God Christians know—is nicely explicated by Alan Torrance's essay "Is

Love the Essence of God?" (the answer: "yes"). A rather charming book-length treatment is Norman Wirzba's *Way of Love*.

Theologians sometimes discuss the relation between self-love and the love of others. Do we have to love ourselves in order to love others, or not? In my view, a fully relational ontology of persons blunts the edge of this particular discussion. Nevertheless, see O'Donovan's treatment of the question in Augustine. Barth also engages with the question briefly.

Bibliography

Anderson, Gary A. *Sin: A History*. New Haven: Yale University Press, 2009.

Barth, Karl. *Church Dogmatics*. II/2; III/2; IV/2; IV/3.2.

Campbell, Douglas A. "The Narrative Dimensions in Paul's Gospel." In *Quest*, esp. n. 19, 83–84.

Davies, W. D. "Law in First-Century Judaism" and "Reflections on Tradition: The 'Abot Revisited." Pages 3–48 in *Jewish and Pauline Studies*. London: SPCK, 1984.

Gorman, Michael. *Cruciformity: Paul's Narrative Spirituality of the Cross*. Grand Rapids: Eerdmans, 2001.

———. *Inhabiting the Cruciform God: Kenosis, Justification, and Theosis in Paul's Narrative Soteriology*. Grand Rapids: Eerdmans, 2009.

———. "Paul and the Cruciform Way of God in Christ." *Journal of Moral Theology* 2 (2013): 64–83.

Hays, Richard B. "Christology and Ethics in Galatians: The Law of Christ." *CBQ* 49 (1987): 268–90.

———. "The Story of God's Son: The Identity of Jesus in the Letters of Paul." Pages 180–99 in *Seeking the Identity of Jesus: A Pilgrimage*. Edited by Richard B. Hays and Beverly R. Gaventa. Grand Rapids: Eerdmans, 2008.

Lang, T. J. "Disbursing the Account of God: Fiscal Terminology and the Economy of God in Colossians 1,24–25." *ZNW* 107 (2016): 116–36.

O'Donovan, Oliver. *The Problem of Self-Love in St. Augustine*. New Haven: Yale University Press, 1980.

Torrance, Alan J. "Is Love the Essence of God?" Pages 114–47 in *Nothing Greater, Nothing Better: Theological Essays on the Love of God*. Edited by Kevin J. Vanhoozer. Grand Rapids: Eerdmans, 2001.

Wirzba, Norman. *Way of Love: Recovering the Heart of Christianity*. New York: HarperOne, 2016.

CHAPTER 12

Loving as Giving

Paul's Emphasis on Grace

Each of Paul's letters begins with a blessing upon his audience of "grace" (Gk. *charis*).[1] So, for example, even when writing to the fractious and problematic Corinthians, he begins by saying, "Grace to you, along with peace, from God our Father and from the Lord Jesus Christ" (1 Cor 1:3).[2] And this blessing concludes every letter as well.[3] Paul actually writes this blessing personally, "in his own hand," to authenticate it in the way that we sign our names to checks and contracts. So a grace blessing is literally his signature statement. (The rest of the text would have been written by a scribe.)

We learn about this distinctive signature from Colossians and 2 Thessalonians. The Colossian community had been founded by proxy and so had not yet met Paul. So he writes at the end of a letter addressing problems already arising in that community,

> I, Paul, write this greeting in my own hand.
> Remember my chains.
> Grace be with you. (Col. 4:18)

And at the end of 2 Thessalonians he responds to some confusion in that gathering about which messages were coming from him and which were coming from imposters (see 2:1–3).

1. Except Galatians, which indicates the depth of the crisis in that relationship.
2. Strictly speaking, this is a performative utterance, bestowing the grace in the act of speaking this sentence.
3. Including Galatians, perhaps indicating a degree of hope after the letter itself has been read and processed.

I, Paul, write this greeting in my own hand,
which is the distinguishing mark in all my letters.
This is how I write:
the grace of our Lord Jesus Christ be with you all. (3:17–18)

But besides opening and closing his letters, "grace" occurs in numerous other places within Paul's exhortations and arguments in the body of each letter, occurring especially densely in Rom 5 and 2 Cor 8 and 9. Clearly, then, it is one of his favorite notions. But what exactly does it refer to? When some of my students talk about grace, I get the sense that it is an ethereal gas that floats down from God affecting various people (or not) as they breathe it in (or don't).[4]

The actual word "grace" (Gk. *charis*) is relatively rare in the Jewish Scriptures, but the practice of *giving* was ubiquitous in ancient society. Moreover, when we consider the various pagan and Jewish sources that explain or presuppose giving, we see that it is not a motif or a notion (or a gas) as much as a complex social practice that was intertwined with quite concrete activity. And once we realize this, we see that numerous other words in Paul point toward this activity as well. But we need to tread carefully.

In the first instance we need to appreciate that ancient practices of giving were very different from our own. They were a vastly more important part of the culture, for starters, being one of the key practices that structured and held an ancient Hellenistic city together. Once we have grasped this complex discourse, we will then need to ask, second, whether Paul is simply lifting this practice into a central explanatory role for the gospel in toto, or whether he is utilizing it but also modifying and shifting it appropriately under the influence of theological insights. (Hopefully the latter, if he is half the theologian I think he is.) As we try to answer these questions, it will be best to begin with the generalized practice, describing it and then considering how Paul tweaked its meaning in eccesial directions.[5]

---

4. Wainwright presciently notes the use of God's attribute of grace inappropriately as a substitute for an impoverished pneumatology in his essay "The Holy Spirit."

5. Jews were as involved with giving practices as the pagans who surrounded them, and so the discourse can be seen imprinting Jewish sources from Paul's day in various ways. John M. G. Barclay's elegant and learned treatment is the current point of departure for the question (*Paul and the Gift*).

Giving

Ancient society was unequal, and especially in its cities. Roughly speaking, the top 1.5 percent of the population controlled about 20 percent of any city's resources, while the next rung down the urban social ladder, comprising 10 percent of the population, controlled the next 20 percent of resources. That's 11.5 percent of the population in charge of 40 percent of its resources, and ancient cities didn't have many! Between 80 and 90 percent of any city lived just on, or below, the subsistence level. Moreover, there was no extensive Christianization process in place, with its patient generation of a politics of compassion. Nobody recognized any need for organized support for the poor and disadvantaged in the way that the Victorians did, along with the new German nation, bequeathing us the modern European notion of a welfare state. As a result, ancient cities functioned in a rather different way from modern ones. They were much more of a dog-eat-dog environment. But they still worked, in large measure because of their massive social networks based on benefaction and patronage. This practice coordinated great networks of people together and also placated large numbers of the poor, in effect by throwing them red meat—although the system did have its disadvantages.

People living in ancient cities generally grouped together in hierarchical patron-client networks, within which patrons dispensed of their largesse to their clients, and their clients responded with expected types of support. *Benefaction* flowed down from the wealthy at the top to those below them who were less fortunate but loyal, eliciting various sorts of culturally prescribed responses. And this benefaction could be quite concrete, including gifts of food, clothing, and other resources. This pattern of the wealthy donating and giving to worthy and loyal recipients overflowed into larger urban situations as well. The extremely wealthy donated entire buildings and events to the cities. They would build temples, archways, monuments, gateways, and theaters at their own expense. And they would fund the religious festivals, at which vast numbers of animals would be slaughtered and roasted, with the meat being distributed to the eager attendees. The precious gift of roasted meat—an enormous privilege—would buy the quietude of the masses, as for once their stomachs would be filled.

These gifts, though, were never anonymous! Buildings would have their benefactors' names inscribed beautifully and prominently upon them, memorializing their generosity and wealth. And festivals and other public gatherings made similar acknowledgments, allocating to the wealthy the most prestigious place in a procession or the best seating. Theaters sometimes even had dedicated carved marble couches, suitably inscribed, permanently reserved for their patrons—the equivalent of a corporate box at a modern sport stadium. (Plus ça change!) Sometimes these seats were even right up behind the stage. The parade of wealthy patrons would then be as much of a show as the drama of the games playing out just down below.

In short, many of the key structures in an ancient Hellenistic city, whether buildings, monuments, or events, were funded by the benefaction of the wealthy in a practice scholars often refer to as euergetism (from Gk. *euergeteō*, lit. "do good"). Euergetism was expected of the rich. It was a practice that was deeply embedded in the culture of the *polis*, and without it many of the key features of that urban culture collapsed. However, various appropriate responses by those benefiting from this largesse were equally deeply embedded in these cities, so something of a social contract is detectable. The wealthy would spend, and spend big, and those benefiting directly would be loyal to their benefactors, while the great unwashed, living far below these giddy social heights, would enjoy their entertainment, eat their free food, and not riot.

When we turn to consider how Paul is deploying "grace," we need first to navigate the fact that the word could denote two closely related but distinguishable things. It could denote (1) a gift, which was generally from a superior person, who had resources, to an inferior one, who lacked them. When it is used in this sense, *charis* can be translated helpfully as "benefaction." But it could also denote (2) the personal disposition on the part of the giver or benefactor to make such a gift. Unfortunately, it is difficult to find an appropriate translation for this disposition today because our modern social structure is so different. But "grace" in this sense basically denotes the *favor* with which a superior could view an inferior in the ancient world, with the result that giving of some sort followed. We should think then of a superior who is willing to bestow benefits on someone—to bless and to resource and to give to his or her inferiors. Modern words like kindness, generosity, goodness, favor, blessing, and even magnanimity capture this second sense. Significantly, the word "grace" does not really capture either of these two ancient senses very precisely.

Because of these two closely related meanings, we always have to ask whether the gift or the disposition is in view when Paul uses *charis*. Is he talking about the event and act and even "item" of generosity, which is, almost invariably, the gift of Jesus himself? Or is Paul addressing God's generosity and kindness, his innate desire and inclination to give? It is a pleasant interpretative conundrum to be caught in.

Having noted this initial issue, we can nevertheless see here at a glance why the language of benefaction was so helpful to Paul. The coming of Jesus, both to get God's cosmic plan for communion back on track and to fulfill it, is a gift. We have been gifted with this rescue and regathered into the greatest gift of all, which is God's great plan for the cosmos: communion with him. And this gift of God's very self to us, and in extraordinarily humbling circumstances, immediately speaks of a God who overflows with generosity and kindness—with grace in the second sense, denoting a fundamentally benevolent posture and disposition. Moreover, we already know well what the virtuous root of this giving is, although it is well worth reemphasizing it.

God loves us. Consequently, he calls us into being, destines us for loving fellowship, and rescues us when we stupidly and brazenly wander away. Giving and gifts are consequently a deeply natural part of this basic relationship of love. They are aspects of love in action. On one level, it's as simple as this. Who loves someone and doesn't want to give them everything they need (note, everything they *need*, not everything they *want*)? I know parents who would gladly donate their own organs, even their very lives, to save their children if they had to. We sacrifice everything for those we love, when we love genuinely. So it is entirely understandable that Paul grasps the pervasive social practice denoted by *charis* to communicate the gospel. Any pagan walking the streets would straightaway understand some critical things about this God acting in Jesus when Paul began talking about God's "grace." He or she would know that this God was donating generously—that he was a gift-giving God—and that Jesus was the ultimate gift from God to us.[6]

But we need to think now about the countercultural pressure that Paul places on this practice. Just as the language of giving helps Paul to explain the gift of Jesus, along with his disclosure of the giving God who provides this gift, he sanitizes and corrects the surrounding practice of giving. A more biblical way of putting this change would be to say that he sanctifies the language of grace. But how does he do this exactly, and why did he have to?

We can distinguish four ways in which Paul is using "grace" language to move his converts well beyond surrounding pagan practices of giving that are helpful but ultimately inadequate for expressing the full generosity—the full grace—of the God revealed in Jesus.[7]

---

6. Barclay develops his own specialized terminology for analyzing benefaction; it is described briefly in the subsection Key Reading at the end of this chapter.

7. This is also a nice example of Paul "navigating" a pagan structure and its relationality, something we will devote some time to understanding in detail in part 4.

Self-Sacrificing

A programmatic statement by Paul about the gracious benefaction of the Son gives us an important clue about the first countercultural move Paul makes. "He [the Son] was rich, but for your sakes became poor, so that by means of his poverty you might become rich" (2 Cor 8:9). Because the giving of God is rooted in God's great love for those he gives to, God is prepared to sacrifice himself within the giving process. Jesus abandoned a comfortable life as God (wherever God is exactly) and assumed the human condition, which was a slavish condition compared to his original enjoyment of sheer divinity. Eventually, this step led to him enduring an awful death.[8] God impoverished himself in the incarnation, Paul says here, in order ultimately to enrich us. Giving here is deeply and fundamentally *self-sacrificing*.

This recommendation would have rather shocked the well-heeled members of the Corinthian church. Surrounding pagan practices of giving were never supposed to hurt the givers. People with resources gave to those who had none when they desired to, as well as, as we will see momentarily, when they could expect a suitable return. But this very differential marked out their superiority. Their ability to give without suffering loss demonstrated their importance. Their largesse was an ongoing social statement of their superiority. Patrons were considered great people if they had "a busy doorway," which was the case when queues of clients were seeking their benefaction. The more clients and the busier their doorways, the more their importance was publicly recognized and their status was acknowledged and elevated. A quiet doorway indicated an insignificant person. Certainly the clients benefited from this arrangement, but the notion that the givers should give to the point that they hurt themselves in the process was unthinkable. The main point of the practice was to enhance the ongoing recognition of the magnanimity of the givers. The ancient system of giving was supposed to maintain the situation of giving and receiving, with all its massive differentials of class and status, not to undermine it.

Yet in 2 Cor 8:9 Paul points out that relocating the practice of giving into the electing and covenantal relationships of love that characterize God and his communities introduces a self-negating dynamic that may well ultimately subvert the very differential on which giving is based, and yet it is inescapable. God is a generous God to the point of *complete self-sacrifice*—generous, then, in his very being, which now defines the true nature of giving. He is this way because he is loving, and love redefines pagan giving, pressing it to enter into the realm of self-sacrifice.

8. So Phil 2:6–11 and related texts.

Surrounding paganism would have recoiled from its extent and its corresponding demands, revealing that it was not a giving that was always or primarily located in love.[9] Giving among the followers of Jesus was—and it is still supposed to be.

Lavish[10]

The propensity to give of the God who gives through the gift of his Son is incalculable, and he does give; he gives us *everything*. He gives of his very self. Moreover, we have been gifted with existence and life in the first place, ultimately so that we might be gifted with Trinitarian communion. So *the entire universe is a gift rooted in a giving God* (at which moment we reemphasize the importance of election, properly understood). And we can probably see now why speaking of mere "kindness" or "generosity" or "magnanimity" doesn't really cut it unless the disclosures of Jesus are pushing the boundaries of this language beyond their cultural limits. God's giving is vast and lavish. It overflows. It exceeds our capacity to even imagine it, at which moment I am reminded again of Paul's prayer in Ephesians for us to be given the capacity to begin to understand God's love when it so exceeds our ability to do so. The same applies to grace. And this generosity is again in marked contrast to the carefully measured portions of grace that pagan benefactors generally gave their clients. Pagan grace was measured and limited, even stingy. God's grace is immeasurable, unlimited, and unimaginably abundant!

In fact, we have already seen Paul cashing out this aspect of God's grace in his use of financial imagery to describe God's love. Characteristically, the economy of God contrasts qualitatively and quantitatively with the economy of the Flesh. Whereas the Flesh, contaminated by sin, is committed to the remorseless *repayment* of this debt through death, God *gives*, and *gives abundantly*. The gift is lavish, not proportional. It is as if God's heavenly bank is packed to overflowing—gushing with money that is pouring out upon us.[11] Our sin-debts are repaid, but we are also promised an inheritance and are further blessed with gifts in the meantime!

9. In Barclay's terminology, the *self-sacrificing* nature of the gift of Jesus in Paul reinforces God's *singularity*, or motive.

10. Barclay's term for this feature of Christian giving is "super-abundant."

11. This is the solution offered by T. J. Lang to the otherwise deeply puzzling statement by Paul in Col 1:24–25, as noted in the previous chapter. The contrasting economy of God's giving is also especially apparent in Rom 5:15–21.

Undeserved[12]

Ancient givers were highly sensitive to the reputations of those to whom they were giving, and it was a widespread belief that those receiving gifts should be worthy of them. People did not give gifts to the undeserving. Rather like the views of some politicians in the United States today, welfare payments funded by the money of others that has been gathered by taxation should not be given, they believed, to poor people who lack character. The "lazy" ought not to receive these payments. Similarly, only those of good character received gifts in the ancient world, whether of food, trinkets, jobs, or recommendations. To give to worthy clients enhanced the reputation of the giver. Worthy, upstanding clients were "congruous" with the worth of the giver. They reflected well on the character of their patron and so were judged appropriate for funding. They met these conditions. The unworthy were not, and did not.

This is an important aspect of Paul's use of gift language that many acknowledge in theory but seem to frequently lose sight of in practice—on a "heart level" as many sitting in the pews might say. When God gives to his children, especially through that greatest of gifts that is his Son, he gives *irrespective of their initial character*. Those who lack character, known in the Bible as sinners, receive this gift, which is an important claim, because according to Paul everyone is a sinner. If God gives only to those who already possess a good character, we are all doomed!

This, then, is another significantly countercultural emphasis within Paul's broader use of giving language, in addition to the realization that God gives to the point of complete self-sacrifice, giving lavishingly and abundantly, beyond all measures of proportionality or appropriateness. God is no respecter of persons, we might say, and not just in terms of status but in terms of character.[13] God's giving is incongruous in the sense that it is not symmetrical with those who merit it; he gives to the undeserving. Similarly, his giving is unconditioned. It does not require its recipients to demonstrate their moral rectitude in advance of receiving the gift of Jesus—to fulfill what are in effect prior

---

12. John Barclay goes on to emphasize a third countercultural dimension within Paul's use of the language of giving and gift, which he calls "incongruity." Barclay distinguishes between the incongruity of God's choice of unimpressive people and the lack of initial conditions attaching to this choice, which he denotes by using the word "unconditioned." I cannot detect a deep difference between these two descriptors. They seem to me to be pointing toward the same very important dynamic.

13. See Rom 2:11; Gal 2:6; Eph 6:9; Col 3:25; see also Acts 10:34; 1 Pet 1:17; Jas 2:1.

conditions in terms of good acts demonstrating good character—in order to receive him. As Paul puts this point on one occasion:

> Do not be deceived:
> Neither the sexually immoral nor idolaters nor adulterers nor the
>   effeminate
> nor thieves nor the greedy nor drunkards nor slanderers nor swindlers
> will inherit the kingdom of God.
> And that is what some of you were. (1 Cor 6:9b–11)

We see here once again how the great love of God revealed through Jesus has pushed the ancient cultural parameters of giving out in an important new direction. God's loving giving has an indiscriminate and open dynamic, which is highly significant. Among other things, it allows Paul to be shockingly inclusive in those to whom he offers God's gift. The normally despised—and slightly feared—people on the street have been offered the gift of God in Jesus, and some have responded to this offer—although one or two have brought certain street practices into the community, which is not a good thing. Divine welfare is to be distributed with a complete disregard initially for the moral quality of the recipients (and we then learn that we are actually all in this position). Clearly, moreover, there was an entirely practical pay-off from this realization for evangelism. No one had to satisfy prior conditions to be offered a place in the community. The socially despised were welcome.

But this factor raises another important aspect of the practice of giving where we need to thread an important needle.

Expectations

Ancient givers *always* had expectations of an appropriate response to their gifts,[14] which is unsurprising. Gifts and giving are embedded social practices, surrounded by a thicket of relationships with all their complicated notions of interaction, reciprocity, and responsibility. As soon as we put a present, gift-wrapped, beneath a Christmas tree for somebody, expectations are set in motion—although these will doubtless be rather different from the expectations set in motion if we provide someone down on their luck with a job or write a glowing reference for an academic protégé (and so forth). Expectations will

---

14. And most modern givers too, I would suggest, contra Derrida.

even differ depending on whether our Christmas gift is designated for our four-year-old grandchild, our ten-year-old dog, or our twenty-seven-year-old daughter. But expectations will still always be present.

In ancient society, as we have briefly seen already, such expectations were structured largely by the principal relationships within which giving took place, between patrons and clients, although we should not discount internal family relationships from patterns of giving and gifts. Ancient patrons gave all manner of things to their clients. But these gifts always came, as the saying goes, with strings attached. Patrons had firm expectations of the appropriate responses from their clients: words of praise and thanks, if not of fulsome flattery; political support, perhaps by daubing slogans on city walls, and by voting (where eligible), and cheering and applauding in meetings; suitable public inscriptions and engravings and even statues; and so forth. Not to respond appropriately was unthinkable.

In the light of this critical part of the ancient practice of giving, John Barclay is concerned to emphasize in his landmark study that Paul's use of the language of giving and gift does not minimize or even erase the importance of people responding to God. Moreover, in this respect, Paul is *not* being counter-cultural. Here Barclay cleverly uses the ancient language of giving, recovered from beneath later layers of historical and theological development, to resist any hyper-Augustinian reading of Paul, which is often done in the name of grace. Properly understood, grace, far from erasing a human response, expects a response—and with the whole heart, mind, soul, and strength! Grace is supposed to *elicit* ethics and moral growth. God's giving and God's gift call these things forth from his communities, and by now, I trust, we are well aware of these important dynamics. They are front and center. God is not interested in inert covenant partners. Those created in love and destined for love are called also *to respond* in love.

But this concern to resist any minimizing of human agency in the name of grace, which I fully support, can sometimes lead interpreters to overlook another point at which Paul's usage of the language of giving is distinctly countercultural. There is a trap beckoning here that we need to recognize and to avoid, although it is one that we have already met.

Unconditionality

We have already seen that it is possible to extend the *pedagogical* conditionality of the relationship established by God's gift of Jesus, along with all its expectations—which are fine—into the *soteriological* realm, which is to say, into the framing relationship itself—which is not fine. The result of this subtle overextension is God's eventual termination of his relationship with us if his expectations for moral growth are not met. According to people who think in this way, Paul might be quite countercultural in his expectation that God's gift is given *initially* without respect for the morality of the recipient. But if the *continuation* of the relationship rests upon suitable progress being made, the overarching relationship slides here over into conditionality *and is fundamentally redefined*. Ultimately, salvation is conferred only on those who have gone on to progress morally and thus have met God's expectations. In Barclay's terminology, the initially incongruous recipients of God's favor and gift are supposed to become congruous later on, as they grow into newly moral people, and if they don't. . . . In this view, incongruity and an unconditioned relationship clearly do not continue all the way through and all the way down for God. Something else takes over, namely, the contractual and conditional expectations of pagan culture, as well as of Judaism in its less kindly expressions.

There is something quite reasonable about this expectation of a necessary response. It is very much the case that the gift of God is given to elicit a comprehensive moral response and further growth. We must affirm this expectation (and we have!). But any extension of this expectation into soteriology effectively conditionalizes the entire relationship, at which moment, as we have already seen, some of Paul's most central claims about God's act in Jesus are undermined. God's basic relationship with us in Jesus would ultimately depend on our fulfillment of these moral conditions—on our growth into "congruity," which is to say, into righteousness—which would necessarily mean that God does not ultimately love us unconditionally and irrevocably. A relationship that is not unconditional in and of itself, and not irrevocable, as this one would be, with all its expectations of progress, is not ultimately a relationship of love. Love has expectations to be sure, but it is not itself dependent on those expectations. Expectations *arise from* love; *they do not limit it!*[15]

I would suggest, then, that Paul, in his handling of expectations, is being countercultural in his original ancient setting in a fourth way. God's giving is self-sacrificial and costly, lavish and superabundant, undeserved and incongruous, expectant and circular (this last not being countercultural)—*and irrevocable*. If expectations are not met, however disappointing, this fact will *not* terminate the relationship. And this arrangement is very different from

15. So the motivation, or singularity, of God's giving, in love, would ultimately be undermined, which is one of Paul's and Barclay's key emphases.

the vast majority of surrounding giving, which was, in effect, conditional.[16] If the right responses were not forthcoming, then the giving was terminated. To demand "congruity" of one's recipients ultimately is immediately to conditionalize any gift.[17] So this commitment to unconditionality, or irrevocability, guards us from any spiral into Pelagianism, with all its unhappy entailments.[18]

In sum: God's giving is self-sacrificial; it is lavish; it alights upon the worthy and the unworthy indiscriminately. It nevertheless expects a wholehearted response, but it also remains unconditional, which is to say, irrevocable. And above all, in the light of these five dynamics, we can see now that the language of gift and giving, suitably corrected, identifies an absolutely critical dynamic within God. Our God is a *giving* God all the way down, as seen in the greatest gift imaginable, which really exceeds our ability even to imagine it—Jesus. And God is this way because he is *loving* all the way down. To love is to give (and to initiate that giving). But it follows that the practice of grace now identifies a critical dynamic within all true and healthy relating.

16. Judaism in Paul's day displayed different positions here, which Barclay charts.

17. Barclay resists using "unconditional" to characterize giving and the gift of Jesus in Paul, apparently worrying that it will override human agency. I would hope by now, however, that such a concern is groundless. We can affirm the unconditional nature of the relationship given to us by God through the greatest of all gifts, Jesus, and its corresponding incongruous and unconditioned features. These all amount to the same thing. But this enhances, rather than eliminates, human agency. And it also applies the strongest possible considerations for ethical behavior, although we will see more in this relation shortly.

18. This set of realizations does lead us to an important challenge, however. Does Paul's God in fact have just these sorts of limits? Certainly, many of his texts might suggest he does, along with, somewhat distressingly, many of his modern readers. If so, scholars like Barclay might be right to resist my suggestion that God's relationship with humanity is unconditional. If Paul's God eventually throws a lot of people under the bus, then perhaps his relationship with us is far from unconditional. But I would say immediately that Paul's most important insights into the nature of God, mediated by Jesus, and particularly by his death on our behalf, push directly against this implication. Texts like Rom 5:6–10 stand in the gap here. Nevertheless, an observable tension does lie in his texts that we will have to resolve in due course. But it is best to do this later, after our account of ethics is complete here in part 2, along with our analysis of the best way to approach the Other, the missionary question addressed in part 3. It must suffice for now to say that I am confident that the use of the word "unconditional" to describe the basic nature of our relationship with God will remain. The gift of God to us that is Jesus guarantees this, and, if I am right, then this remains the fourth important countercultural move we can detect in Paul's use of gift language.

Like the God who gives extravagantly, and most extravagantly in Jesus, his followers are to give to one another, and we see from Paul's communities that in fact they did. Furthermore, just as Jesus himself was a gift that was real and powerful and solid—something embodied—their gifts were quite concrete. They gave food and money to one another, and probably also clothes as well. And they helped each other in further deeply practical ways.

Food

Second Thessalonians 3:10 is especially clear: "If someone does not want to work, then he shall not eat." If participants work, they can provide bread for a communal meal, bread being the staple of the ancient urban diet. If they don't, "shirking instead of working," they are to be excluded from community's meal.

Significantly, this looks like a daily rather than a weekly meal.[19] Exclusion from a weekly meal could hardly have been a serious matter. Exclusion from a daily meal would have been a rather more compelling consideration. So it seems that at least some of the early Pauline communities had daily meals that provided food to those who—legitimately—could not provide any for themselves. And this assumption goes some way toward explaining Paul's irritation with various Corinthians who, apparently, to display their wealth and social superiority, brought food and drink with them to their communal meeting and then proceeded to consume it to excess in the presence of other, poorer church members without sharing it. This was an acceptable Hellenistic dining practice—a "bring-your-own" as against a full "potluck" meal—but it clearly violated the body of Christ, which was being both remembered and participated in at that very moment through the Eucharist (1 Cor 11:17–34). The Thessalonian data, then, add the information that this stinginess and corresponding humiliation of the hungry were taking place daily.[20]

In short, it seems clear that Paul's communities were eating together and sharing their food together, a practice that is significant when many members of ancient cities were living hand-to-mouth, and many other people were

19. This conclusion accords with the evidence of Acts 2:42 and 46, and with Luke 24:30; and arguably also with the evidence of the Lord's Prayer, if this had a eucharistic setting (see Luke 11:3 // Matt 6:11).

20. It is hard to tell whether the larger Corinthian church met in its entirety every day, but perhaps many of its members gathered together daily in the house of Gaius; see Rom 16:23.

hungry. The daily communal gathering was, as a result, a very practical affair, meeting a major need directly—the need for food.[21]

In view of this, it is not surprising to find Paul making similarly strong recommendations to share money.

Money

The programmatic statement about grace that lies at the heart of our discussion here, 2 Cor 8:9, is embedded within a long promotion of a particular issue. Four of Paul's letters attest to a plan to collect a large sum of money from his communities to give to the poor members of the early church in Jerusalem. This collection was an important gesture of unity between the pagan converts in Paul's churches and the Jewish communities who were loyal to Jesus and lived in Judea (Rom 15:25–28). It was also a token of appreciation for the great gift that the Judean people had given to the rest of humanity in the figure of the Jew Jesus, although many other Jewish gifts could be acknowledged as well, like the Jewish Scriptures.[22]

Galatians 2:10 indicates, albeit subtly, that the plan began in an important meeting between the key leaders of the early church in Jerusalem in the winter of 49–50 CE.[23] Romans was written in the spring of 52 CE, by which time the collection had been completed, about two and a half years later after its announcement. At this moment, a large posse of friends and supporters of Paul was about to head to Jerusalem with thick money belts under their tunics, and presumably also with stout staves in their hands (Rom 16:21; Acts 20:2b–4). But in between these dates, Paul's relationship with one of the key donors, the church at Corinth, which contained a number of reasonably wealthy converts, had spiraled into serious trouble.

This was partly Paul's fault. He dropped a bomb on them in the letter we know as 1 Corinthians, which was written in the spring of 51 CE. He somewhat naively concluded this frequently caustic letter with instructions to carry on collecting money for the Jerusalem collection (1 Cor 16:3–4). As many of

21. This gathering was also the setting for the "Lord's meal" (*kyriakon deipnon*). We will develop a very brief account of the sacraments in ch. 17.

22. Rom 15:27 speaks of spiritual gifts from the Jews to the pagan converts, in the plural.

23. See especially Gal 2:1–10, explicated by Acts 15:4–29, although the conference should actually be located in Acts 18:22.

us know, when members of a congregation get unhappy with their pastor, their wallets close. So we see Paul in 2 Corinthians expending a great deal of effort restoring his fractured relationship with the Corinthians, and within that broader repair a long subsection is devoted to restarting the stalled fundraising for the collection.[24] It is in this subsection, 2 Cor 8–9, that we find an especially concentrated cluster of grace language and an especially extended analysis of Christian giving. We don't need to trace through all of the complexities of Paul's arguments here.[25] We have already picked out the key theological presupposition—the great gift of God himself to us in Jesus, and the great underlying generosity of God that this gift discloses, a gift and a propensity to give rooted in love (see 2 Cor 8:9). But Paul's discussion contains one further detail that is worth noting. He writes,

> Our desire is not that others might be relieved while you are hard
>   pressed,
> but that there might be equality [Gk. *isotēs*].
> At the present time your plenty will supply what they need,
> so that in turn their plenty will supply what you need.
> The goal is equality, as it is written:
> "The one who gathered much did not have too much,
> and the one who gathered little did not have too little."[26] (2 Cor 8:13–15)

This is a novel application of Exod 16:18. Other Jews in Paul's day supplied other explanations for the phenomenon of "equality" after the daily gathering by the Israelites of manna in the desert. Paul implies here, however, that the equality occurred when those Israelites who had gathered more manna than they needed *gave their surpluses to those who had not collected enough*, resulting in a happy "isomorphism" (*isotēs*), which is to say, in an equivalence. As Paul quickly points out, any giving away of a surplus can then rely on reciprocity. Those living in a community acting generously in this way will have their needs supplied in due course, should those arise. "When I have more

---

24. Details of the chronology can be found in my *Framing*, chs. 2 and 3, 37–189, and more briefly in *Journey*, ch. 9 (see the subsection "Wooing Corinth").

25. A typically elegant analysis of the first phase of this discussion is John Barclay's essay "Manna and the Circulation of Grace."

26. Paul quotes here from Exod 16:18, which occurs in the middle of the story of the Israelites' daily collection of manna during their sojourn in the wilderness; see Barclay, "Manna and the Circulation of Grace."

than enough and you have needs, I give to you; and when you have more than enough and I don't, you give to me." So self-sacrifice will not actually even be harmful. The donation of a surplus will be reciprocated if necessary. *But the practice is clearly redistributive.*

I live currently in a country where this redistributive approach to money is often labeled socialist, which is a dog whistle, as some of the pundits put it, for "communist," a word that conjures up in turn the Cold War and the horrors of the USSR (i.e., Communist and Soviet horrors both real and imagined). A visceral response against it is thereby guaranteed. On one occasion, I even heard Oprah react in this way! (She blurted out that the Danish approach to healthcare was "socialized medicine.")[27] However, Paul's account of giving, which is redistributive, is simply unimpeachable. It is grounded in the nature of God, revealed most clearly in the gift of Jesus. And Paul reinforces it in 2 Cor 8:15 with a scriptural analysis, suitably shaped, as the Corinthians are reengaging with their great act of giving for the poor among the Jewish brothers and sisters living in Jerusalem. Consequently, there is no avoidance of redistributive dynamics, whatever we call them, and we certainly should not use what we might choose to call them as an excuse for avoiding them.

Communal giving is concrete, so it involves money, and it can involve gifts of large sums of money. Occasionally this money is directed toward the undeserving—the incongruous; moreover, this giving is deliberately redistributive. Those who have much are called, like the Israelites in the desert, and like Jesus himself, to give of their riches and surpluses, and so, in a sense, to leave them, to resource those who have less. Giving is self-sacrificial if that is necessary. But community members can give in this costly way in part because they are cradled by a generous network that will support them in any future needs that they might ultimately have. And ultimately, they are sustained by an extravagantly generous God.

Paul's discussion of the great collection in 2 Corinthians does not exhaust his comments on money. They pop up throughout his letters, just as money tends to pop up through our daily lives at all sorts of points. Much comes back to money. But Paul attests in one other place to his approach in a particularly striking way.[28]

---

27. Oprah's interlocutors replied immediately that the Danish simply called it "civilized."

28. See also various comments about Paul's manner of arrival into a community, "working with his own hands" and so not receiving money (1 Cor 4:12; 1 Thess 2:9; 2 Thess 3:7–9) and his nuanced approach to receiving monetary gifts, which raised

In a rare instance of his personal writing intruding into a letter outside of his signature, Paul affirms his commitment to covering any financial loss generated by the errant slave Onesimus, or (so we could translate this Latin name, which means "useful") Handy. "I, Paul, am writing this with my own hand: I will pay it back—not to mention that you owe me your very self!" (Phlm 19). Paul drops a heavy hint here about how he sees the spiritual finances of the community operating, but the monetary commitment on his part is real. Slaves who fled to seek interventions into their troubled relationships from some friend of their owners technically caused financial loss as their labor was removed. Compounding this loss, Handy might also have been a little light-fingered. (Col 3:25 is possibly a subtle hint here.) But Paul stands surety for this deeply underprivileged and socially untrustworthy, not to mention unimportant, person. Clearly, then, when it came to money, Paul practiced what he preached. He gave as he needed to, and probably beyond what seemed comfortable. This pledge is made from prison.

Having said all this, the concrete benefactions made by a community in Paul's day did not stop at money.

Clothing

I strongly suspect that the early church provided clothes for people. Most ancient people possessed only one set of clothes, which may have been worn and dirty, and were often deeply inadequate in cold and wet weather. It seems telling, then, that the baptismal slogans that we find scattered through some of Paul's letters speak of putting on Christ as one puts on new clothes (see esp. Gal 3:27; Col 3:12). Although modern commentators, most of whom have serried dressers and even walk-in closets filled with clothes, concentrate on the metaphorical meaning of this phraseology, which is valid, I suspect that this act was literal as well. After converts' old and dirty clothes were stripped off, they went under the water naked and then emerged to be clothed in new garments, a gift of the community and thereby of Christ. These fresh new clothes powerfully suggested a new identity for the baptized figure although, in addition to their new identity, these new Jesus followers were probably a little cleaner and warmer—and more fragrant—than they

---

delicate cultural issues in the ancient world (1 Cor 9:3–14; 2 Cor 11:7–10; 12:14–18; Phil 4:10–20). But this advice is best treated in our later discussion of Paul's missionary practice, in part 3.

had been before. Perhaps significantly, when the Christian community of Cirta, an ancient township located in modern Tunisia, was raided during the great persecution of Diocletian, vast quantities of clothing were noted (and they were disproportionately female), along with the more predictable eucharistic vessels and books.[29]

We will insert an important caveat here in due course, but for now we simply need to ask whether our modern churches care for their members' concrete needs?[30] Do we provide the modern equivalents to the ancient provision of food, money, and clothing, namely, food, money, clothing, *housing*, *education*, and *jobs*?! I suspect that Paul would be both angered and ashamed of our customary tepid efforts here, and of our ceaseless theological prevarications justifying the same.

Healing

Paul's communities were overtly "charismatic" or "Pentecostal," by which I mean that the Spirit was working explicitly and obviously within them, including in signs and wonders.[31] Some of these events were doubtless healings, which allows us to see that Paul's communities were filling another important niche in ancient culture quite concretely.[32]

Ancient society lacked the inventions of modern medicine, and hence, in particular, access to its inoculations, antibiotics, and the discovery of the usual causes of infection. Plagues were not uncommon, and early mortality was widespread. Presumably much like mortality rates in the poorest parts

29. This charming example of early church demographics, revealed during the Diocletian persecution of the Christian community in Cirta (located in what is now Tunisia), is documented in Ramsay MacMullen and Eugene N. Lane, eds., *Paganism and Christianity, 100-425 C.E.*, 247-60. The court documents record (249), among other things, the presence at the church of 98 tunics (82 women's, 16 men's) and 60 pairs of shoes (47 women's, 13 men's), a female/male ratio of 4.4 to 1. In addition, there were 38 women's veils.

30. See part 3, where the abandonment of cultural capital during missionary work, and part 4, where the resulting interactions between missionaries and their new partners, results in new insights into what exactly are "needs" and what are merely "wants."

31. See Rom 15:18-19; 1 Cor 2:4-5; 2 Cor 12:12; probably also Gal 3:5; see also Acts 14:3; 15:12; and 19:11-12.

32. We will discuss this aspect of Paul's teaching in more detail shortly when we consider his missionary approach in part 3.

of the developing world today, most deaths took place during or shortly after childbirth (perhaps 100-150 deaths per 1000 in the first year, followed by the same number up to the age of five).[33] But even in adulthood, death could be quick and sudden. The most common killers were infections, which were rife: drinking water and food were often contaminated, and sanitation was poor. So there was a huge appetite in ancient society for healing.

High-quality healing in the ancient world, however, was expensive, involving a stay in an Asclepion, which was something of a cross between a private hospital and an exclusive health spa. Hopefully the god would reveal the source of the malady, along with the cure in a dream to the spa's resident, who would enact it and then be cured, and these spas boasted a very high success rate. (Success, however, was assisted by the fact that they only admitted—at the god's instruction—certain people for healing.) But most folk could not afford such pampering, and so they appealed to street healers, where healing shaded imperceptibly into magic. Illnesses were often thought to be caused by demonic forces or by curses from an enemy, so the purchase of protective amulets or the performance of defensive spells from these less reputable healers might suffice to produce a cure. And all of this clearly cost money as well.

Paul's communities spoke directly to these concrete needs in at least three different ways.

First, they offered healing in the power of the Spirit—and for free! They did not obviously guarantee healing to everyone, but everyone could certainly ask, and there is plenty of evidence that healings took place. A great deal of Paul's theology is based on this phenomenon.[34]

Second, they offered deliverance in the power of the Spirit. also for free. This category must probably be understood now to include those facing mental challenges, as well as those struggling more directly with evil forces—an important group then to experience healing. (The distinction between mental illness and demon possession was first made by physicians like Paracelsus in the late 1400s and early 1500s.)

Third, healing would have been assisted in a highly practical way simply by offering a community of support. Many diseases can be fought off if the sufferers are kept warm and well fed and are given water. But pagans were often frightened of diseases and fled from their sufferers, abandoning the ill

33. See http://www.who.int/pmnch/media/press_materials/fs/fs_mdg4_child mortality/en/.
34. See the texts referring to signs and wonders noted above.

to their fate when basic nursing could have saved them. Church communities, by way of contrast, seem to have behaved in a far more engaged and even self-sacrificial fashion, something apparent later in the history of the church, during the great plagues in the empire. There is evidence that some Christians nursed those who were sick and thereby saved many, although these caregivers themselves became sick and occasionally died (a place where an openness to martyrdom is important).[35] We cannot tell whether Paul's communities were overtly committed to this activity. But certainly any such behavior would have accorded directly with their ethos. I mention this here simply to point out that the healthcare offered for free by the community was not confined to miraculous interventions by the Spirit. Quite practical support could be offered as well.

In my experience, most Christians I know today are generally well disposed toward healthcare in a general sense, and many of my friends are directly involved in delivering it professionally. However, I live in the United States, and this healthcare is anything but free. Paul's communities—which were desperately poor in many respects by our own standards—nevertheless offered as much free healthcare to surrounding pagans as their resources and the work of the Spirit allowed, because such actions spoke directly of their deeply committed and unconditionally loving God, who heals freely. Do our modern communities send the same message?

It seems overall, then, that grace in the early church was no mere cipher or symbol. It was a reality. It named, first, the concrete benefaction that was Jesus himself, along with the extravagant generosity of the God who sent him. But in accordance with this understanding, it named further practices of generosity. The community gifted food, money, possibly clothing, and healing to its needy members. And we can see from all this activity that Pauline communities are supposed to be communities of grace. They should be committed to the *self-sacrificial, lavish, incongruous,* and *expectant* resourcing of those in need, within relationships that are nevertheless fundamentally and ultimately *irrevocable.* That this resourcing is redistributive goes without saying. The generosity of these communities should be so obvious, exuberant, and extreme that only a God generous enough to sacrifice his only Son for an evil humanity can explain it, while, when it is, it testifies in the strongest possible terms to the reality of that God of grace.

---

35. This kind of sacrificial care was brought to my attention in Rodney Stark's idiosyncratic but fascinating book *The Rise of Christianity.*

Theses

> The language of "grace"—Greek *charis*—occurs frequently in Paul. A grace wish begins and ends almost every letter, penned in the latter instances by Paul's own hand. The language occurs with special density in Rom 5 and 2 Cor 8 and 9.

> The language is part of a complex ancient Greco-Roman practice—patronage and *euergetism*.

> Ancient cities relied on their wealthy elites to freely fund buildings and events.

> Elites were also benefactors, presiding over complex networks of clients.

> So Paul is, in part, "contextualizing" when he uses this language of grace; he is drawing on language familiar to his unschooled pagan converts to express important truths (although Jews shared in this practice and evidence various theological deployments of it as well; but Paul's engagements with Judaism and Jews are assessed later, esp. in part 4).

> Grace denotes two closely related things: (1) a gift or benefaction and (2) the generous disposition, usually of a superior, to give—beneficence, generosity, or some such (this sense is very difficult to translate).

> So gift language in Paul can denote the great gift that is Jesus, and it can denote the deeply generous nature of the giving God who lies behind this gift.

> Paul also corrects the surrounding language and practice of gift and giving in the light of the great gift that is Jesus and the giving God whom he reveals.

> First, God's giving acting in Jesus is deeply self-sacrificing. Pagan giving was self-affirming and had no intention of impoverishing the giver.

> Second, God's giving and gifts are lavish.[36]

> Third, God graciously gives to those who do not appear to deserve it or who are unworthy.[37]

> Grace, nevertheless, has strong expectations of a comprehensive response—of a journey toward congruity. Paul is not being countercultural here. Gifts always come with expectations, and God's gift to us in Jesus is no exception.[38]

---

36. Barclay's term here is "superabundant."

37. Barclay calls this "incongruity" and also speaks of the "unconditioned" nature of this giving.

38. This is a key part of Barclay's agenda. In a recovery of the original language

▸ Nevertheless, it is important not to let this expectation of an appropriate response extend to a redefinition of the overarching relationship between God and humanity so that its continuation is premised on an appropriate response being undertaken.

▸ Pagan relationships involving gifts were almost certainly conditional, which is to say, breakable if certain expectations were not met. If an appropriate response was not forthcoming, the relationship would be terminated.

▸ God's gracious gift, however, was (and is) not. It is elective, unconditional, and irrevocable. To allow any failure to achieve the appropriate response to undermine or terminate the relationship would be to slip from a covenant to a contract. Paul, however, resists this slippage. The relationship framing God's gift and God's giving is irrevocable. God's relationship with us remains, if necessary, incongruous and unconditioned.

▸ This is the fourth countercultural aspect in Paul's language of gift and giving.[39]

▸ Drawing these countercultural aspects of God's gift of Christ together— self-sacrifice, superabundance, and incongruity, along with their irrevocability (i.e., their covenantal and unconditional basis)—we can see that Paul deploys them to speak above all of *God's great love for us*.[40]

▸ God's gift of Jesus is embodied and "concrete." Acts and practices of grace by Jesus followers are therefore supposed to be embodied and concrete as well, and they were in Paul's communities.

▸ Second Thessalonians 3:10 suggests that the Thessalonian community had a daily communal meal. This represented a gift of food.

▸ The communities also gave money.

▸ The most obvious example of a financial gift is the great collection that Paul took up from his churches for the poor in the church at Jerusalem. This collection was announced at the Jerusalem Conference in the winter of 49–50 CE (see Gal 2:10) and taken to Jerusalem in person in the spring of 52 (see Rom 15:25–28).

---

of giving, he emphasizes, against some later theological readings that we have already dubbed hyper-Augustinian, that Paul's account of grace is not "efficacious" or "noncircular," as parts of subsequent church tradition later unhelpfully developed the notion.

39. Barclay's treatment unfortunately fails to identify this critical distinction within the discourse, the theological implications of which are far-reaching.

40. Barclay denotes this "singularity." He adds that such love also "initiates" giving, as has already been noted here at length; see especially ch. 3.

‣ A smaller instance of this costly financial giving is Paul's personal pledge to pay any debts incurred by the errant slave Handy (Onesimus; see Phlm 19)—a pledge made from a prison.

‣ Baptismal texts like Gal 3:27 and Col 3:12 might imply that Paul's communities gifted converts with new clothes. Some evidence from later church history—especially from Cirta during the Diocletian persecution—suggests that the communities gave away a great deal of clothing.

‣ Healing in the ancient world was desperately needed. The wealthy could afford to go to an Asclepion, provided the god admitted them for healing. The poor turned more to street magic.

‣ However, Pauline communities provided (1) free healing, (2) free healing of mental illness as/and deliverance from demonic influence, and (3) probably, if later church history is any guide, free nursing, this last sometimes being at great personal cost.

‣ Community giving, in sum, reflecting the love of God that gave us Jesus, as well as the Jesus who gave himself, is concrete and generous to the point (if necessary) of costliness.

Key Scriptural References

Colossians 4:18 and 2 Thess 3:17 attest to Paul's personally signed wish for grace and peace. The wish itself is present at the beginning and end of every letter (except at the beginning of Galatians).

Second Corinthians 8:9 is a key statement describing God's grace enacted in Jesus.

Grace language is especially concentrated in Rom 5 and in 2 Cor 8 and 9.

The irrevocability of God's relationship with us is stated in Rom 11:29.

Second Thessalonians 3:10 suggests that the Thessalonian community met together daily for a shared free meal.

The most overt instance of giving money is the great collection that Paul organized from among his pagan churches for the poor in the community in Jerusalem. Its origins are subtly noted in Gal 2:10.

Its continuation is apparent in 1 Cor 16:3–4; 2 Cor 8–9; and Rom 15:25–28.

Second Corinthians 8:15, quoting Exod 16:18, presupposes the explicit redistribution of community resources.

Philemon 19 attests directly to Paul's own commitment to alleviating the financial burdens of others, especially of those under duress, here the errant slave Handy/Onesimus.

The baptismal texts Gal 3:27 and Col 3:12 suggest that converts received new clothes at baptism.

First Corinthians 2:4–5 speaks of the reality of signs and wonders in Paul's work. (See also Rom 15:18–19; 2 Cor 12:12; Gal 3:5.)

Key Reading

Barclay's *Paul and the Gift* is now the point of departure for all future scholarly discussion of grace in Paul—and of much else besides—but it is complex and challenging. The best way into his work on benefaction is by way of his short essay "Manna and the Circulation of Grace."

The importance of practical giving by the early Christians in their challenging urban environments is snappily portrayed in various ways by Stark in *The Rise of Christianity*. This book, which must be used with caution, is deeply innovative.

Further Reading

An accessible and insightful analysis of giving and grace in theological terms is Miroslav Volf's *Free of Charge*.

The charming example of early church demographics and the interest of communities in clothing, as revealed during the Diocletian persecution of the Christian community in Cirta (located in what is now Tunisia), are documented in the MacMullen and Lane edited volume *Paganism and Christianity, 100–425 C.E.: A Sourcebook* (247–60).

In order to understand Paul fully, it is important to build up and then continually deepen an understanding of life in a Hellenistic city within the early Roman empire. A good way into this whole area is through Stambaugh and Balch, *The New Testament in Its Social Environment*. Meeks, *First Urban Christians*, and Stark, *The Rise of Christianity*, are also excellent appetizers, asking all the right questions and supplying not a few useful answers. See also Jerome Carcopino, *Daily Life in Ancient Rome*. (And dipping into a well-researched popular work doesn't hurt; Robert Harris's series on Republican Rome, focused on Cicero, is quite charming.)

Meal practices in the early church are discussed enthusiastically and informatively by Hal Taussig's study *In the Beginning Was the Meal*.

John Perkins is an important voice in the current construction of Christian community, thinking in the practical and concrete ways that, I am suggesting here, Paul does as well. Perkins has authored or coauthored a series of informative books that frequently include emphases on redistribution: *Let Justice Roll Down*; *With Justice for All: A Strategy for Community Development*; *Beyond Charity: The Call to Christian Community Development*; (with Wayne Gordon and Randall Frame) *Leadership Revolution: Developing the Vision and Practice of Freedom and Justice*; and (with Wayne Gordon) *Making Neighborhoods Whole: A Handbook for Community Development*.

Bibliography

Barclay, John M. G. "Manna and the Circulation of Grace: A Study of 2 Corinthians 8:1–15." Pages 409–26 in *The Word Leaps the Gap: Essays on Scripture and Theology in Honor of Richard B. Hays*. Edited by J. Ross Wagner, C. Kavin Rowe, and A. Katherine Grieb. Grand Rapids: Eerdmans, 2008.

———. *Paul and the Gift*. Grand Rapids: Eerdmans, 2015.

Carcopino, Jerome. *Daily Life in Ancient Rome*. Edited by Henry T. Rowell. Translated by E. O. Lorimer. London: Penguin, 1941.

Gordon, Wayne, and John Perkins. *Making Neighborhoods Whole: A Handbook for Community Development*. Downers Grove, IL: InterVarsity, 2013.

Harris, Robert. *Dictator*. London: Penguin Random House, 2015.

———. *Imperium: A Novel of Ancient Rome*. New York: Pocket, 2006.

———. *Lustrum*. London: Hutchinson, 2009.

———. *Pompeii*. New York: Ballantine, 2003.

MacMullen, Ramsay, and Eugene N. Lane, eds. *Paganism and Christianity, 100–425 C.E.: A Sourcebook*. Minneapolis: Fortress, 1992.

Meeks, Wayne A. *The First Urban Christians: The Social World of the Apostle Paul*. New Haven: Yale University Press, 1983.

Perkins, John. *Beyond Charity: The Call to Christian Community Development*. Grand Rapids: Baker Books, 1993.

———. *Let Justice Roll Down*. Grand Rapids: Baker, 2014.

———. *With Justice for All: A Strategy for Community Development*. 3rd ed. Ventura, CA: Regal Books, 2007.

Perkins, John, and Wayne Gordon, with Randall Frame. *Leadership Revolution: Developing the Vision and Practice of Freedom and Justice*. Ventura, CA: Regal Books, 2012.

Stambaugh, John E., and David L. Balch. *The New Testament in Its Social Environment*. Philadelphia: Westminster, 1986.

Stark, Rodney. *The Rise of Christianity: A Sociologist Reconsiders History*. Princeton: Princeton University Press, 1996.

Taussig, Hal. *In the Beginning Was the Meal: Social Experimentation and Early Christian Identity*. Minneapolis: Fortress, 2009.

Volf, Miroslav. *Free of Charge: Giving and Forgiving in a Culture Stripped of Grace*. Grand Rapids: Zondervan, 2009.

Wainwright, Geoffrey. "The Holy Spirit." Pages 273–96 in *The Cambridge Companion to Christian Doctrine*. Edited by Colin E. Gunton. Cambridge: Cambridge University Press, 1997.

CHAPTER 13

Loving as Faithfulness

The Faith of Christ

We come now to the second main moment in Paul's story of Jesus, which was his faithful walk to the cross.

Paul speaks of submission, and hence of obedience, when describing in Phil 2 this part of Jesus's life:

> . . . being found in form as a person,
> he humbled himself,
> becoming submissive to the very point of death—
> death on a gallows! (2:7–8)

Jesus steadfastly obeyed the will of his Father and the Spirit and accepted the humiliation of taking shape as a human being, and the further humiliation of death—and a shameful execution at that, Paul exclaims. Paul also references Jesus's obedience in Romans (5:19), and links this virtue with faithfulness at the front and the back end of that letter (1:5; 16:26), which makes it clear that Jesus's obedience means essentially the same thing as his faithfulness when it comes to the cross. To carry out a difficult task is both to obey the command to do it and to be faithful to that task and to the one who has commanded it.[1] And this is the place from which we need to develop our understanding of faithfulness,

---

1. Faithfulness is always an element within obedience, but it can be deployed more widely as well, not necessarily in relation to carrying out some task or duty. Someone can be a faithful servant, which is an obedient servant, and vice versa; but this is not the same thing as being a faithful friend or spouse. A faithful friend or spouse in certain circumstances might *not* be obedient, just because they are faithful.

including the implicit notions of believing (because faithfulness involves key beliefs), trust, and hope. It is also from here that we see how obedience and faithfulness are aspects of love. Love when faced with a task acts in obedience and faithfulness. Hence this narrative moment within the broader story of Jesus unveils a great deal of important behavior. But as we seek to describe it in more detail, we need to ask first just how to handle a distinctive and rather famous cluster of "faith" texts in Paul.

The "Faith of Christ" Debate

A vigorous debate has been unfolding over the last thirty years or so in English-speaking scholarship over whether Paul speaks in several phrases of the faith of Christ or, alternatively, of faith in Christ.[2] The disputed phrases mainly occur in Romans and Galatians and use the Greek noun *pistis,* which can mean "faith," "faithfulness," "fidelity," "trust," "belief," or even "the thing believed" (i.e., an argument or proof or a token of trustworthiness like a ring or a handshake).[3] In Greek the disputed phrases combine the noun *pistis* (in any syntactic case) with the noun *Christos* (in the genitive case). This so-called genitive construction can mean many things and so requires careful analysis. The reading "faith *in* Christ" is known as an objective genitive because here Christ is the *object* of (someone's) faith;[4] Jesus is understood as the object of a follower's believing; the faith is in him. The other reading, "the faith *of* Christ," is known as a subjective genitive because here Christ is the *subject* of the faith; he is the one exercising the faith or faithfulness.

The disputed data in Paul are quite sparse, and opinions are strongly held on both sides of the question. But I have long been convinced that Paul is speaking in these texts about Jesus's own faith (i.e., here Paul uses a subjective genitive).

---

2. A solid introduction to the situation, and the beginnings of a good case, is Morna Hooker, "ΠΙΣΤΙΣ ΧΡΙΣΤΟΥ."

3. Scholars generally refer to Rom 3:22, 26; Gal 2:16 (2x), 20; 3:22 (taking 3:26, following the majority manuscript reading, to be a coordinate construction and hence a "false positive"); Phil 3:9a. Various unmodified instances of faith in context are then immediately affected as well, e.g., Rom 3:25 and 26. Ephesians 4:13 ought to play a rather larger role in the debate, along with 3:12. Moreover, 2 Cor 4:13 is critical but tends to be overlooked.

4. The verb "believe" in Greek at the time did not generally take a direct object noun in the genitive case; it was more commonly followed by a prepositional phrase.

The phrases are all part of a group of similar texts that discuss faith a lot, frequently doing so by quoting or alluding to Hab 2:4, which was a very important scriptural verse for Paul. The discussions spread mainly through Rom 1:16–5:1; ch. 10, and Gal 2:15–3:29. In these passages Paul quotes Hab 2:4 twice and alludes to it around twenty times. This programmatic text reads, "The righteous [person] *through faith* will live." So it seems that Paul is getting a lot of his faith language in these passages from this text, whatever he means by it. He is "echoing" Hab 2:4, as Richard Hays would say. The important question now arises concerning whom Paul understands the original scriptural text to refer to. And I would suggest that various subtle clues indicate that Paul is using this Scripture as *a messianic proof-text* that prophetically predicts Jesus's death and resurrection.[5] It points to Christ. With this reference in mind, we would translate it as, "the Righteous One through faithfulness will live."

"The Righteous One" was a title that the early church used to denote Jesus, probably in ultimate dependence on Isa 53, which they read as another prophecy of his death.[6] The "faithfulness" in Hab 2:4 refers to Jesus's heroic obedience and faithfulness to the point of death. And "life" refers to the way God the Father and the Holy Spirit gifted Jesus with resurrection life after his faithful and obedient self-sacrifice. Read in this way, the Scriptures, by way principally of this Scripture, predict that, after a period of great endurance that led ultimately to his death on the cross, God gifted his Son, the Messiah, with resurrection and life—the exact story, in other words, that Paul tells about Jesus in Phil 2:6–11, as well as more briefly elsewhere. It is this

---

5. I supply arguments for this reading in relation to Rom 3:22 in particular in "The Faithfulness of Jesus Christ in Romans 3:22." I argue the case in relation to the rest of the disputed genitives in Romans, Galatians, and Philippians in *Deliverance*. Much of the detailed interaction with other scholarship can be found in the relevant endnotes. The elucidation of Paul's use of *pistis* in Gal 3:15–26 is, I would suggest, especially decisive. I build here particularly on the seminal work of Hays in *The Faith of Jesus Christ*. As noted below, I use a new angle of approach in my more recent essays (one closer to Hooker's). I would also be more confident now about the relevance and decisiveness of the evidence in Ephesians (see esp. 2:8; 3:12; 4:13). Ephesians is emphatic that the baptized possess a new mind characterized by a certain sort of faith, *and* that the mind of faith is gifted to us through the Spirit by way of the faithful mind of Christ. Much of the letter is then devoted to the articulation of just exactly what this new mind ought to believe. Markus Barth's older Anchor Bible commentary, *Ephesians*, is sensitive to the importance of the faith of Christ for Paul in that letter.

6. It is even placed on Paul's own lips by the author of the book of Acts in 22:14; see also Acts 3:14 and 1 John 2:1.

underlying story of Jesus's faithfulness that several of Paul's discussions of faith allude to by way of this scriptural text, which uses the phrase "through faith [Gk. *pistis*])." But this periodic allusion by Paul to Jesus's faithfulness, death, and resurrection functions as part of a larger argument, although so much Pauline interpretation goes astray at this moment—by failing to grasp the presence of Jesus's faith in Paul's argument, going on to misconstrue his broader contention—that we need to spend some time grasping just how this argument worked. And the best way to do so is by first stepping back and asking why Paul felt the need to deploy it in the letters that he did, principally in Romans and Galatians, with some cryptic flurries in Ephesians and Philippians.

Paul's "Enemies"

Paul never writes things without a local, practical reason for doing so; he doesn't write to self-reflect, in a fashion many modern writers anachronistically hold to be self-evident. Moreover, as F. C. Baur, the great founder of modern critical Pauline scholarship, observed some time ago, practical problems generally arose when third parties arrived and stirred the pot. Almost all of Paul's letters address interlopers and troublemakers (at least as Paul views them!). And this is very much the case here. When he wrote Romans, Galatians, and Philippians, the letters that emphasize faith the most, he was having a broader debate about access to the age to come and to its resurrection life. It seems that Paul and certain "enemies," as he calls them on one occasion (Phil 3:18),[7] had rather different ideas on how faithful people obtained this access. So what was at stake between them was the bedrock question of salvation. Are you in or out?! The enemies were circulating through Paul's communities, mainly during the second half of 51 CE, and trying to shift his converts to a rather different version of the gospel (see Gal 1:6–9; 5:7–12). They were sheep-stealers! They were not necessarily nasty people and may have been motivated by the best of intentions (although Paul doesn't think so).[8] But they didn't like Paul and caused him a lot of problems. Basically, they didn't trust his account of salvation. They thought it was completely bogus and that he was an apostate,

7. Strictly speaking, they are enemies of the cross of Christ. But enemies of Christ and of his cross, as Paul understands it, tend to be his enemies as well. We discuss their agenda in more detail in part 4, ch. 27 ("Beyond Colonialism").

8. Paul casts aspersions on their motives in Gal 6:12–13.

so his converts had to be rescued from him for their own good. If they stayed with Paul, they were doomed.[9]

Paul couldn't always be on hand to oppose these sheep-stealers, so he did what any right-thinking person in his position in the ancient world would do. He wrote letters and sent them with trusted emissaries to settle his converts down and to refute the arguments of his enemies. His letters to the Galatians, the Philippians, and the Romans have these opposing figures particularly in view, which is where we find the texts and arguments alluding to Hab 2:4, as well as to other scriptural texts that undergird his gospel.

Paul's enemies were an early type of Pelagian. Their account of how to access the age to come was conditional. They were deeply legalistic in their approach (and possibly here atypically for Jews in Paul's day).[10] Certain things had to be done, specifically, works and deeds informed by the Torah, especially circumcision. So Paul's pagan converts had to convert again and become messianic Jews. Moreover, it follows that the pious must be insecure until the day of judgment, uncertain whether or not they have been saved. Have you done enough good deeds? Have you acted well or wickedly? Are you a sheep or a goat? Hopefully, God would pronounce them innocent of all wrongdoing on that day and hence worthy of entry into heaven as they stood nervously before his throne.

Clearly, this is rather an anxious approach to salvation that opens up a space for these enemies of Paul's gospel to insist on the fulfillment of all sorts of conditions in the meantime that could help their listeners to be more confident about a positive outcome. Perhaps think of these figures then as analogous in

9. Exact details of this biographical scenario are argued in *Framing*, ch. 2; a briefer and rather racier overview is supplied by *Journey*, part 2.

10. E. P. Sanders argues that hardly any Jews in the late Second Temple period thought about salvation and God in legalistic terms; see both his *Paul and Palestinian Judaism* and *Judaism: Practice and Belief, 63 BCE–66 CE*. The diversity of Judaism, along with one or two overtly conditional texts (notably 4 Ezra), stands against this strong conclusion, however, as Barclay, among others, has argued (see his *Paul and the Gift*, 194–328). But granting exceptions does not undermine a weakened but still significant judgment that *many* Jews in Paul's day were not legalistic, as they have frequently been portrayed by modern Christian scholars. Paul's enemies were legalistic, but in this respect they were not necessarily representative of broader Judaism. And there was probably a degree of unintentionality about even their legalism. In their insistence on circumcision and Torah-observance for Paul's male converts, they may not even have been aware that they were activating a fundamentally conditional soteriology. But Paul spotted it!

our day to some particularly harsh, militant evangelists. (Not all evangelists by any means are militant and harsh, but historically some have been.) "If you want to be saved, you must be baptized, and I mean by your own free choice, as an adult, and be fully immersed! If you have not been baptized, fulfilling its requirements to the letter, then your salvation is in doubt! You are risking hellfire on the day of judgment. God will pronounce you 'out!' not 'in!'" Paul's enemies were making similar demands, although in relation to Jewish practices like circumcision. "You must be circumcised, assuming that you pagan men are not, if you want to be saved! If you aren't, you will be held accountable, judged, and damned. You then need to keep the rest of the Jewish Torah as well, which I will now teach you. . . ."

Unsurprisingly, Paul pushes back strongly on this insecure and highly conditional approach that his enemies are peddling through his congregations, which would basically change them into communities of legalistic, and highly anxious, messianic Jews. (Paul has nothing against messianic Jews, by the way,[11] but he doesn't think that his pagan converts need to be turned into them.) One way he resists this program is by appealing to faithfulness, although his argument is subtle.

He begins, as we have seen, by emphasizing Jesus's martyrological fidelity. This faithfulness included certain beliefs and believing. Such fidelity was in fact the rock-like, unwavering believing that underpinned Jesus's acceptance of death on a cross. It was a believing that was steadfast in its conviction that death would not be the end. So it involved constant trust and hope. Resurrection would follow whatever horrors evil men would throw at him, and it would overthrow death itself. God (the Father) would sustain and deliver him. Hebrews 11 famously talks about this type of believing as well, which was very familiar to Jews in Paul's day—and still is—and Paul's account of Abraham in Rom 4:17–23 is very similar again.[12] It is a remarkable, enduring faithfulness, which maintains the confession that the Lord is God, the only Lord, and hence the Lord over death, as suffering and execution approach. As a result, we would gloss the sense of "believing" in play here with more specific words like "steadfastness," "endurance," "perseverance," and "faithfulness" or "fidelity." And as Phil 2:8 notes, this believing also involves "submission" to the will of the

---

11. A position discussed at length in part 4. Paul also does not seem to have regarded Judaism as fundamentally legalistic; see especially Rom 9:11, 12, 16; 11:6.

12. See especially vv. 16b–23, where Abraham's faith is a heroic unwavering belief in God's capacity to give the life of a son to Sarah's effectively dead womb and to his effectively dead loins, which I discuss in *Deliverance*; as does Daniel Kirk.

Father, which is to say, "obedience." In this moment in his life Jesus is faithfully obeying the will of his Father with extraordinary courage and strength.

With this basic plot concerning Jesus in place, Paul goes on to point in his broader argument to the existence of faith within his followers as well. References to Jesus's faith tend to occur either in or near a short sequence that extends to our faith. So, for example, we read in Rom 3:22a:

> The deliverance of God has been revealed
> *through* the steadfast faith of Jesus Christ
> *to* all who have faith.

This faith series is replicated in various other texts such as Rom 1:17, Gal 2:15–16, and 3:22, and probably also Phil 3:9. It is important to appreciate, then, that Paul's argument in no sense excludes personal faith as its critics sometimes fear—far from it. His argument depends on it. Paul is confident that all the converts in his threatened congregations are following Jesus, which means confessing the truth concerning his resurrection and his lordship. They believe as exemplified in a text such as Rom 10:9:

> When you confess with your mouth that Jesus is Lord,
> and believe in your heart that God [the Father] raised him from the
>   dead,
> then you are saved.

Moreover, Paul's converts are clearly supposed to hang on to this confession through thick and thin—whatever the cosmos or the powers can throw at them (Rom 8:14–39). They are to keep confessing that Jesus is Lord.

But at this moment we can see that people who believe in the way Paul has just suggested, faithfully confessing Jesus's resurrection and lordship and walking forward obediently through trials and tribulations toward a glorious but unseen future, *are following the faith of Jesus himself on the way to the cross.* These two stories are basically the same, which is to say, these two particular ethical activities are effectively identical. Both parties, Christ and all the messianic Jews and Christians following him, are believing steadfastly in the unseen realities that determine their lives but that lie ahead of them. At bottom, they are both believing faithfully in God as they await resurrection beyond death, and trusting and hoping through thick and thin that this will be the case. And for this reason God's deliverance is revealed *through* faith—the faith of Jesus—*to* those who have faith—the faith of his followers.

However, Jesus and his followers are clearly located at different points in the story. Jesus has already gone on to resurrection and glorification. His story of difficulty has concluded, as the Scripture from Hab 2:4 predicted. He lives now in glory. But the story of his followers has clearly not yet concluded. We are still in the first half of the narrative, walking forward faithfully. Resurrection still lies ahead of us, after death. Will it still come then? Should we listen to the threats of the enemies? Do we need to be worried about the day of judgment, and whether or not we will be admitted to the delights of the resurrected in heaven? Is there something else we have to do now? Or are we locked into salvation already?

Paul now makes his clinching move. Because we are walking faithfully, sharing in Christ's faith, we know that we are *guaranteed* the second half of the story.

Resurrection and glorification must await us too. Jesus has already received this second part of his story, so to speak, and we are presently sharing the first part of his life, so we are guaranteed the receipt of his resurrected life as well. We are part of the first stage in Jesus's journey, connected to it, thinking here particularly of his faith, so the arrival of the second is inevitable. Our shared faith testifies to this certainty.

It is as if we are traveling up an incredibly long escalator, rising up through the center of a hotel for many stories. Jesus is already at the top. We can see him ahead! He has stepped off, and his glorious presence illumines the final level, where the escalator arrives. We aren't quite there yet; we are still some way back down the escalator rising up behind him. But we can see from his arrival up ahead that our arrival is inevitable. *We are on the same escalator!* We are joined concretely to something that is already there. We are connected to him by strips and sheets of metal and by a chain of steel steps rising up around and ahead of us. If we just stand firm and hold on tight, the final level arrives for us too in a moment.

The underlying assumption on Paul's part that many of his later interpreters miss here that helps all this to make sense is his strong commitment to the presence of the resurrected mind of Jesus in all his followers. We have the mind of Christ, mediated through the community and guaranteed by the Holy Spirit. We have therefore been immersed into Jesus, into his death and his resurrection, even if we are not yet perfectly raised. (We are waiting now for the loss of our lives of Flesh and the receipt of a body of spirit.) This present indwelling reality is absolutely central to everything Paul says about the Christian life. So for us to have faith is automatically for Paul to think of how that is rooted in Jesus's faith. Our faith is a gift and a fruit of the Spirit of Jesus.

It follows that we are a part of Jesus's life trajectory, released now from our debt of transgressions and from its looming repayment of death, and destined for the age to come. We are *connected through Jesus to our future*.

The results of this realization are quite practical, and it still helps us in certain situations today. We need have no fear when any teachers come around our churches, as they did in Paul's day, and threaten us with possible exclusion from resurrection life on the day of judgment because we are not doing certain things properly. We know simply by observing the fact of our own faith that we are already guaranteed entry into the age to come. We are already concretely and so obviously saved. And this is a reasonably easy thing to test. Do we believe that Jesus is Lord and that God raised him from the dead? If we do, then we believe; we have faith (although we do need to hold on to this faithfully). And if we have faith, believing and confessing the Lord Jesus, and walking forward faithfully, we are joined to Jesus, echoing his faith, and we are guaranteed future life already. "Examine yourselves to see whether you are in a state of faith; test yourselves. Do you not realize that Christ Jesus is in you—unless, of course, you fail the test?!" (2 Cor 13:5). The brief argument in this text makes sense only if we share our minds with Christ and our believing with his. To have "faith" is to have Christ Jesus in us and so to pass the test and to be on track for glory.

At this point, then, one foot is already in the age to come—our minds— and the one whom we share in, the preeminently faithful one, is already there fully, so our other foot is about to lift off the ground behind us. We are heading for heaven, and we don't need to fear any future exclusion because we haven't fulfilled certain key conditions. Clearly, we have done enough already.

It is a brilliant argument, undergirded by Scripture but grounded also in spiritual realities and in a profound theological coherence. But note carefully how it is actually functioning. It is critical to grasp what this argument is trying to do, and what it is *not* doing.

It is vital to appreciate, first, that Paul's argument for assurance really works only if our faith is grounded in concrete participation in Jesus and his faith. Indeed, I'm not sure it works at all if it isn't. But we *do* have the mind of Jesus by way of the Spirit. We *are* thereby concretely linked to him and explained by his story. This is what makes the argument sure and certain. Since we really do participate in Jesus, this position is invulnerable. Our faith shows that we are literally joined to him in some sense, so we are joined to his future resurrection. We really are locked in and need fear nothing that lies ahead (Rom 8:14–39!).[13]

13. We could then, strictly speaking, substitute any other virtue for faith, and

It follows, however, and most importantly, that *we don't generate this believing for ourselves*. We respond to the gift of Jesus's believing presented to us through his Spirit. So we rest in the love of the God who has chosen us from before the foundation of the world and is at work in our lives. Our believing and our faithfulness are gifts (Eph 2:8–10). They are a figuring forth of the life of Jesus in our lives. We still have to respond, of course, but we don't have to produce faith for ourselves, ginning it up from within us—we don't have to choose in some sense to believe—which would throw all the onus on us at the critical moment. Faith arises out of our relationship with the preeminently faithful one (intersubjectively, a modern student of the second personal would say).

And at this moment we can see, drawing all these motifs and contentions together, that Paul has provided an argument in terms of faith for *assurance*. Steadfast believing is evidence that God is at work in our lives and that we are destined for glory. It proves that we are saved already. It can give us confidence that we are to live as God calls us to live and not to waver. And it follows, furthermore, that faith is not the way we *appropriate* God's salvation; it is not the means by which we gain entrance to the community; it is not something we do for ourselves. To say that it is would be to radically misappropriate and mischaracterize faith in Paul. Faith is evidence of a life in Christ that has already been established by the Holy Spirit and by our participation in Jesus. As we have just seen, Paul's argument depends on this prior establishment.

It is worth noting, finally, that certain specific beliefs provide particularly strong and obvious evidence for the presence of Jesus's believing in the minds of his followers—confessional beliefs like Jesus's lordship and belief in the resurrection life to come. Here we echo Jesus's unwavering belief in his Father and the promises made by him of life after death. But these obvious beliefs merely indicate the presence of the whole new mind of Christ that believes many things. So faith must not be restricted to these particular beliefs—to this particular

---

Paul's argument would work just as well, although he would want it to be connected with scriptural texts. The fact that faith occurs so helpfully in Gen 15:6, Isa 28:16, and Hab 2:4 makes it impossible for Paul to resist running the argument in this believing variation against his Bible-thumping opponents. But we shouldn't be misled by this fact into supposing that the participatory argument is formally limited to faith. That Jesus loves and that we love too as part of his love suggest just the same resurrected destiny as our shared faith does, as do our shared giving, hope, peace, obedience, wisdom, and any other virtue we might care to mention. We simply have to evidence the character of Christ in our lives to be able to point to our connection with him and his resurrection. So this argument, we might say, does not live by faith alone.

circle of faith—important as they are, a realization opening up an inviting path that we need now to push down further. That is, we have really yet to mine the importance of faith in Paul as a virtue. There is a sense in which its use in this particular argumentative context makes it seem both more important and more tightly defined than it really is. We can now set this cluster of faith texts to one side, at least for the moment, and see what light the other faith texts in Paul shed on its dynamics.

From Faith to Belief

We began this discussion with the *obedience* of Jesus, as evidenced in the second key moment of his story—his obedience to the will of his Father and his Spirit that he suffer death, a humiliating death on a gibbet as a condemned criminal, as Phil 2:8 notes. It was this obedience that overcame a humanity imprisoned within Adam and a broken existence dominated by the Flesh, Paul wrote in Rom 5:19, so it was by no means unimportant. But obedience to an important task in the role of a servant or slave, through the passage of time, and especially under duress at the level Jesus experienced it, is *faithfulness*. Hence it is no surprise to see Paul speak of a faithful Jesus in several other places in his writings, while he also equates the two notions at times directly.

The sort of faithfulness that Jesus evidenced, however, must have included both trust and hope, to an exemplary degree. Jesus, we may assume, walked to his death assured that his Father and his Spirit would sustain and rescue him, granting him his promised inheritance and eternal communion with them. And as a Jew of his time, so we may assume, he thought that this would take place through resurrection, which events subsequently fulfilled. These convictions imply a steadfast faithfulness underpinned to a large degree by trust and hope.

Paul confirms this constellation of virtues when he gives a detailed description of Abraham's faith in Rom 4:17–21:

> He trusted in the God who makes the dead live
> and calls that which is not into being;
> against hope in hope he believed that he would become the father of
>   many nations
> according to what was said to him: "this will be your seed";
> and not weakening in trust—
> he knew his body had died being around a hundred years old,

and the death of the womb of Sarah—
he did not waver in unbelief in relation to the promise of God,
but having been strengthened in trust,
gave glory to God,
being fully convinced that he was powerful enough to do what had
    been promised.

Commentators frequently gloss over this long passage in Paul quickly. It seems far too forbidding to be a description of the faith whereby converts will be saved. But when we grasp the centrality of Jesus's faith for Paul, we can recognize here a patriarchal anticipation of his heroic walk to the cross, which was characterized by these exemplary virtues exactly. Jesus's faithfulness was deeply infused with trust in his God, with hope for the future, and as Paul portrays things, it fulfilled the great story of faithfulness that lay at the inception of Israel in its founding father Abraham.[14]

But we also see in this portrait of faith how trust and hope, along with obedience and faithfulness, all connect indelibly with beliefs and believing. To be obedient, faithful, trusting, and hopeful are all particular constellations of beliefs. As Paul says quite clearly in Rom 4, Abraham trusted that God would do certain things—that God would grant him an heir; he held these promises to be true, which is to say, he *believed* them; and he held on to them over time, as Jesus doubtless did as well (see 2 Cor 4:13), thereby *hoping*.[15] To trust is to believe certain things about a person, here God, and if those things concern future promises, it is also to hope. Trust, hope, and believing are all inextricably intertwined together. But fidelity and obedience are not far from view as well, especially when, as in Jesus's case, a terrible challenge has been set before him that he is being asked to complete.

Paul will slide between these closely related meanings, as we have done for some of the preceding analysis, but it is entirely fair for him to do so. They all name different aspects of a tightly connected cluster of actions that we can summarize with the broader notion of *faith*. Moreover, Jesus's followers are clearly called in Paul's view to walk in the footsteps of the faith of Christ and

14. This theme will be developed in a later chapter, when Paul's account of Israel is discussed.

15. The presence of Jesus's actual believing in Paul is subtle, but I would argue it is implicitly and indelibly present; see my "2 Corinthians 4:13: Evidence in Paul That Christ Believes," *JBL* 128 (2009): 337–56. Also important here is Richard Hays, "Christ Prays the Psalms: Israel's Psalter as Matrix of Early Christianity."

to embody faith as well, as best they can, most especially by way of possessing his mind of faith. But before we move on to our next analytic challenge in relation to faith, it is worth pausing for a moment to dwell on hope. This virtue is frequently identified by Paul and placed alongside faith and love, and with good reason.[16]

Hope

Sociologists have long made a distinction between the various needs that underlie new religious movements. We have already discussed the way in which Pauline communities met what sociologists would call relative needs under the rubric of loving as giving. They resourced their members when they lacked basic material resources that other members of society around them possessed, so they addressed deprivations that were evident relative to one another. But these communities also met an absolute need. No member of ancient society could escape mortality, so the promise of salvation and the enjoyment of the blessings of the age to come was a gift that spoke to everyone, regardless of a person's social and actual capital. And this broad appeal is very important. Communities need to speak to all walks of life. Paul befriended high and low— people like Sergius Paulus, a former praetor, and Lydia, a former slave.[17] This contrast reminds us that Paul's communities addressed the enduring problem of human history encompassing us all, namely, our mortality. *The church provides hope in the face of death.*

Most funerals are difficult. The funeral of someone who has died an untimely death is awful, but a secular funeral is a terrible thing. It has no hope. The rupture of important relationships is seen as irrevocable and lasting. The grief is truly bitter. What a gift it is, then, to be present in these situations, even if silently, in hope, representing the goodness of God and the victory of Jesus over death. We ourselves might be (or have been) condemned to a period we experience as a long separation from a loved one. But we live in the firm expectation of being reunited one glorious day. We have hope.

This is a precious gift to offer a society that avoids its date with mortality assiduously, desperately prolonging its days with staggering technological investments. A headline in the newspaper *The Onion* announced appositely on January 27, 1997: "World Death Rate Holding Steady at 100 Percent." It went

16. See especially 1 Cor 13:13; Gal 5:5; Eph 1:15–20; Col 1:3–5; 1 Thess 1:3; 5:8.
17. We will discuss these conversions further in part 3.

on to comment that, "despite the enormous efforts of doctors, rescue work-ers and other medical professionals worldwide, the global death rate remains constant at 100 percent."[18] Death, however, is not something to be feared but a doorway to a better, perfected place. It is the necessary prelude to our complete bodily resurrection. But only hope grounded in Jesus allows us to offer this narrative to the rest of society, a group that so desperately needs it. And this hope springs from love.

We hope because of what the God who loved us has done for us. He loved us enough to die for us, so we know that this hope is firm. And he loved us enough to open up a doorway for us into another world, within which relationships will be healed and permanent. Our loved ones will never be lost in perpetuity. Love will continue. Our firm expectations about the future concerning rising beyond death are consequently grounded in love and are expectant about love. Love and hope are tightly tied together. It is a great gift to be able to be fundamentally realistic about the chal-lenges of history and the failures of people and yet cast over these clear-sighted perceptions, like a canopy, a great and fundamental optimism. We are grasped and held firm by the one who loves us deeply and irrevocably and who has conquered death! We can firmly anticipate a happy reunion one day!

In 1 Thessalonians Paul addresses the issue of grief. Either some converts have become concerned about the question of death in a general sense or, more likely, someone has died, and the community has been suddenly con-fronted by its awful impact. Paul probably expected Jesus to return during his lifetime, and at this stage in his missionary work, might have been expecting Jesus to return in a matter of months. So Paul may have overlooked the need to provide teaching to his pagan converts about what death entailed. He now addresses this oversight, offering what is basically a pretty standard Jewish position, at least for a Pharisee. If someone died, that person would not miss out on the resurrection. You don't have to be alive to experience transforma-tion when Jesus returns, along with the beginning of the big party in the sky. You can be resurrected in a new body and then be caught up with everyone who is still alive.[19] In a little more detail:

The Thessalonians have introduced the issue to Paul, to which he responds in the latter stages of his letter:

18. For those unfamiliar with American culture and confused by the foregoing, *The Onion* is satirical.

19. The awkward difficulties implicit here were addressed in part 1, ch. 7.

> Brothers and sisters, we do not want you to be uninformed
> about those who sleep in death,
> so that you do not grieve like the rest of mankind,
> who have no hope. (1 Thess 4:13)

Paul replies first with an admirably compact christological thesis.

> For we believe that Jesus died and rose again,
> and so we believe that God will bring with Jesus
> those who have fallen asleep in him. (4:14)

A more technical discussion follows:

> According to the Lord's word, we tell you
> that we who are still alive,
> who are left until the coming of the Lord,
> will certainly not precede those who have fallen asleep.
> For the Lord himself will come down from heaven,
> with a loud command, with the voice of the archangel
> and with the trumpet call of God,
> and the dead in Christ will rise first. (4:15–16)

The party now begins:

> After that, we who are still alive and are left
> will be caught up together with them in the clouds
> to meet the Lord in the air.
> And so we will be with the Lord forever.
> Therefore encourage one another with these words. (4:17–18)

And this really is an encouraging truth. Not only will we pass through death if we die before Jesus's return (as has been the case for some time now), but we will join together with those who have died before us or, in the opposite case, with those whom we have left behind. The creeds therefore speak of "the communion of the saints," a prosaic phrase that points toward an utterly wonderful event. We will meet our loved ones who have died. We will meet some enemies too, quite possibly, but let's not allow that awkward thought to interrupt our contemplation of the wonderful prospect of being reunited with those loved ones we have lost. Death is not definitive. A funeral of a follower of Jesus is a statement, in part, that death is temporary. It points toward a long wait—a wait that can be painful and grievous, to be sure. *But it is not permanent.* Hallelujah!

And with this quick detour through hope complete, we need now to consider how faith—along with its implicit disposition of hope—is related to love.

Love and Faith

Is faith a different kind of action altogether from love, thereby disproving Augustine's contention that I endorsed here earlier on, that all right activity comes back to love? Or is faith in all these different respects in fact, underneath it all, tightly connected to love?

I would suggest that, properly understood, all the different types of faith that we have just enumerated are responses of love to certain specific circumstances. Faith names how love should act when it is faced with a task, and especially a difficult one, as well as when it is simply presented with a relationship of ongoing love. The loving response in these situations is, respectively, to be obedient and faithful, and then trusting, hopeful, and understanding (i.e., believing). In a little more detail:

When Jesus responds obediently to the will of his Father, he is acting out of love. He obeys because he loves, and we obey because we love. When someone we love asks us to do something (something that is not utterly unreasonable or self-destructive), we respond and obey, and we delight to do so. To love is frequently to obey. Moreover, when we are asked to do something hard or challenging by someone we love, we obey faithfully; we endure; we carry out our assigned task, again, because we love. We delight to be faithfully obedient to those we love. And we delight simply to be faithful to those we love. Love entails faithfulness. Do we betray those we love?! Hell no, to paraphrase one of Paul's pithy Greek phrases. Love and faithfulness belong together like love and marriage and a horse and carriage. Love is covenantal.

And when we are living in a mature relationship of love, as part of that love we trust in the one we are relating to, and we hope. Sadly, we may not always be able to trust or to invest hope in a relationship with someone we love—say, with a struggling teenager. But a mature and healthy love relationship is characterized by trust and by hope, as both Jesus and Abraham have supremely modeled for us. And with that said, we come now to belief.

This is a particularly interesting aspect of this question. I am going to suggest that love and believing are tightly coordinated, but we will need to spend a little more time tracing out the contours of this relationship because a correct understanding of believing is so important for an accurate grasp of Paul's thinking.

A certain type of Protestant often reduces the content of faith to being convinced of the truth of particular propositions about God—to believing a few key things such as "Jesus is Lord." And believing things like this is true and important. But to reduce believing to this activity is a horrible distortion. True believing within a community of Jesus followers is a comprehensive believing about God and all things related to God, because every aspect is ultimately oriented by love. True believing, in other words, is theology and is, moreover, a never-ending theological journey. We should seek ever deeper and broader beliefs about God because God is the one we love.

Protestants who restrict believing to assent or conviction about certain propositions are a little like a marriage partner who sits alone at home and says, "You know, the really critical thing here is that I believe that my spouse exists and that she runs the local mayor's office. She also solved some really big problems that the city faced last year with water quality; we all owe her one for that. But that's it. This is absolutely all I have to think about her. It's the only thing I have to do, actually, to be in this marriage." We might be tempted to probe for the presence of some further appropriate thoughts concerning this relationship.

"Is it important to love your spouse at all? Do you think it's worthwhile actually living together and interacting, so thinking about what your spouse is doing and is interested in, and what you are bringing to the table? Is it of any value that you enjoy your spouse or trust her or are faithful to her or feel strongly about her? Should you talk to her?" Our solitary figure replies, "Absolutely not. These are unnecessary add-ons. The only beliefs that matter here are the facts I mentioned first. I am entirely content with my marriage living alone and knowing nothing else about my partner beyond those, and thinking nothing else beyond them."

I suspect we would find this relationship a little odd, and it is just the same with believing in Paul. Believing is a characterization of an entirely new mind and hence encompasses every aspect of relating, and that relating is, at its heart, loving (or it is meant to be). To grasp believing as Paul understands it is to connect it organically with love, while to fail to do so is to have misunderstood it. (This curious restriction to a minimal, essentially propositional set of beliefs comes from a misreading of Paul's "faith of Christ" texts and a misunderstanding of his broader arguments in those texts.) And love will ask us to deepen our understanding of the God who loves us and with whom we are supposed to fall ever more deeply in love. Moreover, this process of growing in love will clearly involve *knowing* this God—grasping accurately who God is and what God is like. Hence *theology is vital to the life of Jesus's followers* because a deepening knowledge of and accuracy about God is central to our love for God.

I hope we have already learned well by now that our existence as followers of Jesus is rooted in God. It derives from God and is lived in its best moments in correspondence to God. So who God is, which is also to say, how God acts, is absolutely fundamental to who we are and how we act, especially as we seek to love God. Everything we are and do—and we are what we do—is bound up with the identity of God. All our loving relationships flow from and to this God. But this identity is invisible. It is real, but it is, as Paul puts it, unseen. It is always ever mediated to us only through the imperfect members of our communities and our obviously fallible leaders. So we are heavily reliant on our new minds and their convictions, their truths, about this God with whom we are involved. This believing will structure all our godly acting and obeying. Consequently, it is very, very important.

It is difficult to correspond to, to obey, and ultimately to love an unseen person whom we don't actually know very well or grasp very clearly—whom we have inaccurate beliefs about. This would be a little bit like trying to live happily in a marriage in which I think I am involved with a Hispanic woman born and raised in Mexico who is passionately committed to the plight of undocumented immigrants, and who lost her parents early on in life to a drive-by shooting by a drug cartel. But in reality—and the psychological mechanisms here are complex, so I won't go into them—I am married to a white, culturally conservative lady, born and raised in Oklahoma, who likes Pekinese dogs and paints water color pictures, and who has a massive expense account from her father, who is in the oil business. How effective and happy will my marriage be if I persist in thinking—and thereby structure all my acting—in terms of the former construct when I am in fact married to the latter person? Things are not going to go well. And it is like this with theology.

Theology is the linguistic outworking in truth of our developing love affair with the God revealed in Jesus. And, what could be more important than this growth?! The more this outworking advances, the more nearly and closely we will know our beloved as our beloved really is, and the better our situation will be simply in its own terms and as the basis for our relationships with others. But the more we will also sense what this beloved asks us to do, and the more we will hopefully detect when what we are doing is straying from our beloved's concerns. For this reason we can detect an important theological dimension within Paul's account of appropriate believing that we ought to emphasize strongly. Paul is always pushing his converts deeper in their understanding of God, a task we should continue to pursue.

In sum: love believes things about God and pursues further knowledge and truth passionately to know more about the beloved. That knowledge includes the knowledge that the loving God resurrected Jesus and will resurrect us, so our love should issue forth in trust and in hope. When this God speaks to us and asks us to do something, our loving becomes obedience. And when we obey under duress—in trust and hope as well—our loving obedience is best spoken of as faithfulness. Paul knew all this well. As he put it, "Love . . . always trusts, always hopes, always perseveres" (1 Cor 13:7b), although these are a tall order for mere humans of Flesh. So we are fortunate indeed that the faith of Jesus is always present to us, summoning us to imitate these virtues that he himself possesses perfectly and gifts to us generously.

With these important realizations in place, one final aspect of faith in Paul needs to be clarified because otherwise it can cause confusion.

Faith and Love

Faith in Paul primarily names particular loving actions in certain circumstances, which we have spent some time detailing—fidelity, obedience, hope, and so on. But we saw earlier on that Paul also constructs an argument for assurance in terms of faith by presupposing that the followers of Jesus possess his mind, a revolutionary if strongly counterintuitive claim he is nevertheless quite explicit about at times (Rom 12:2; 1 Cor 2:16).[20] It follows from this that there is a sense in which every action in Jesus's mind, also ours, is a believing of some sort. So Paul can occasionally use "faith" or "belief" in this more comprehensive sense, essentially metonymically, to denote the presence of the mind of Christ within his followers in its totality. Paul's astonishing statement toward the end of Romans is now intelligible: "Everything that is not 'through believing' is sin" (14:23b), meaning everything that is not proceeding from the

---

20. In addition to Rom 12:2 and 1 Cor 2:16, see Rom 8:5–8, 12–13; 15:5; Eph 4:23; Phil 2:5; and Col 3:10. We will note some other lines of data in Paul later on that will corroborate this important claim, while our opening discussion of 2 Cor 5:17 in ch. 1, along with related texts, points directly to this as well. First Corinthians 7:19 is arguably a strong indirect confirmation of this claim in Paul as well.

mind of Christ is sin.[21] We simply need to recognize when Paul is using faith language in this broader, as against one of its narrower, senses. And a further potential confusion can now be avoided.

The specific actions of faith, modeled on the faith of Jesus, are particular loving responses. Love enfolds them and gives rise to them, we might say. So someone who loves, in certain circumstances, is obedient or faithful or trusting and hopeful, as his or her central relationship of love demands. Love comes first. However, when Paul speaks of faith as a metonym for our possession of the entirety of the mind of Christ, thinking here presumably especially of its dynamic bundle of believing—of its new existence—he can say, quite correctly, that its activities will *be* loving. The mind of Christ is a mind of love, so insofar as it is a mind of faith, it will love, and the roles of faith and love here seem to be reversed (and in a way they are). So Paul can say in Gal 5:6 that "in Christ Jesus neither circumcision nor uncircumcision has any value. The only thing that counts is faith expressing itself through love." But this a semantic trick of the light, we might say. Faith here names the form or structure through which Jesus's followers act, which is the mind of the resurrected Christ gifted by the Spirit and mediated by the community. The content of this mind—the actual dynamics of its believing—is love. And that love will, a little paradoxically, act in such a way that on occasion, as the circumstances demand, it will act in faith!

Excursus: Faith Alone?

Now someone could say—and usually does—that Paul's main argument about faith in Romans and Galatians is rather different from the way I have presented it here: "*If* you believe that Jesus was resurrected and is the Lord, *then* you will be saved—and that's all you have to do. (And otherwise you are damned.)" Certainly this is how I hear the argument made, and it is plastered all over evangelistic tracts and tools like the Roman Road and the Four Spiritual Laws. But one problem in this claim is immediately apparent to those of us who have been schooled in the deceptions of liberalism.

The underlying assumption here is that people can choose to believe. This is an act of their "free will," and it is so important to the argument's advocates that I even see it sometimes as part of the name of local Baptist congregations—"The Mount Horeb Road Free Will Baptist Chapel" and so on. (It's

---

21. The phrase "through believing" is an echo of Hab 2:4!

really impressive to have a major theological error written into the actual name of your church!) But people don't just choose to believe things. This is a liberal fantasy. *They can't!* We *respond* in a *relationship* with believing. We can't just believe things are true because we decide to. Truth is a judgment that we make about certain states of affairs that are presented to us, and that to a certain extent force themselves upon us. We assent. We don't just choose to believe certain things and not to believe others (which sounds like consumers are getting their shopping habits horribly confused with their truth habits). You can offer me a million dollars if I will only believe that three green Martians are sitting on the railing outside my office window having a cup of coffee together. But I can't believe this, no matter how much I clench my teeth and try to choose to do so. We just can't choose our beliefs. Things have to impress us *as* true.

So how am I supposed to choose to believe that Jesus is resurrected on high to the right hand of God, where he sits enthroned and rules as Lord?! It's not exactly obvious. Sadly, I have met several people who want to believe in God, even in a rather reduced sense, and they just don't. They can't, and it tortures them. So there is actually something rather cruel about this reading of Paul's gospel. It asks people to get saved, offering something supposedly easy, but it turns out that the key condition is impossible—a classic bait-and-switch play.

Advocates of this argument could come back at me at this moment, however. They might say that since it's so difficult, God helps us to believe. The Holy Spirit gifts us with belief.

But this rejoinder should be repudiated.

Of course the Holy Spirit gifts us with belief! I'm going to agree with this, as should any right-thinking theologian. We get *all* our virtues from the character of Jesus figuring forth in our resurrected minds as those are worked in us by God, which is to say by the Holy Spirit, and as we respond obediently. This is true. *But,* if we take this (true) qualifier seriously, *it changes the entire argument,* and this is the problem. Salvation is now no longer up to us and to our decision of faith; it's up to the Holy Spirit and whom she decides to offer faith to. We are talking about election, then, not about individual believing. So we are really having a different discussion entirely. Indeed, this reading of Paul's argument is now very close to mine. And there don't seem to be any good reasons for resisting going the whole way and emphasizing Jesus as well as the Holy Spirit. After all, where the Holy Spirit is, Jesus is as well, unless we want to endorse one of the major Trinitarian heresies. God is one. What gift of character and personal action from the Holy Spirit to us is not going to be a gift that is grounded in Jesus?! It follows, then, that if the Holy Spirit offers us faith, we are being offered that through the faith of Jesus, and there is no point in limiting that gift to anything less than the full mind of Christ. In other words, this caveat has conceded so much it has ended up agreeing in all its essentials with me, which is not, presumably, what this objector wanted to do.

So I regard this attempted defense as inadequate, and the original reading is not off the hook. The construal of Paul's argument in terms of grasping salvation by belief alone asks for the impossible. No one is going to get saved this way. But there are other very important reasons for resisting the introduction of this reading. To mention just a few more: introducing this argument at this moment, in this way, in relation to this theological motif and its particular cluster of texts in Paul, *dislocates his entire theological system.*

We have already come across the dislocations in question. If we insert this argument into Paul's thought as a whole, we introduce the topic of *soteriology* (which comes from Gk. *sōtēria,* "salvation") and link it to an act of faith on our part (assuming for the sake of argument that we can actually do so in the way the argument's advocates expect us to). But this link ties salvation to a conditional arrangement in the full-blooded legal sense, at which moment we make salvation into a contract again. If and only if we believe will we be saved; God will then undertake to save us. If we fail to fulfill this condition, however, then he won't. Salvation is consequently conditional upon belief, which, of course, is a big problem.

We have just contradicted, in a massive way, the story we have been telling for chapter after chapter about God based upon Jesus dying for us while we were yet sinners. The God of love and of loving election is now sitting uncomfortably alongside a God of justice, retribution, and punishment. The God of limitless forgiveness has been placed next to the God who endorses the death penalty to the point that he executes his own Son. This is a contradiction, and a big one. Is Paul really this confused? Are there what amount to two radically different conceptions of God jostling within his thinking? But things are about to get even worse. We have also reintroduced *foundationalism.*

The story we tell about getting saved through faith alone must now start with the individual in the pre-Christian state journeying toward salvation, hopefully to make the right decision about God. If people are going to get saved by believing certain things, then we need to give them the right reasons to believe, which means that a lot of important information about God is going to have to be present before the critical decision gets made, in that pre-Christian state. We need to get the individual to the point of decision and hopefully get him or her to make the right decision. The argument's advocates generally appeal to natural theology here, as they have to, and to the one text in Paul that might suggest that this is the case, Rom 1:19–20. And they will develop an account of broader non-Christian reality in terms of attempted justification by works. Setting the interpretation of Rom 1 aside for the moment, let's look at what has just happened in broader theological terms.

We have launched foundationalism, although this should not be too surprising. Any contractual account of salvation is necessarily foundationalist. It must begin with the individual (a woman, let us assume) who is thinking about taking up the contract, and it must give her a reason to do so in the pre-Christian state. These reasons must be true, so important theological work must be done before she becomes a Christian, and it cannot be revised after she has become a Christian because then the basis of the decision to become a Christian would be undermined! So contractual salvation is necessarily foundationalist. But we know well by now what happens next. The horsemen are unleashed, and this entire system will eventually collapse. Its initial truth claims will prove untrue; it will block the way to sound Christian thinking done on the basis of Jesus and his clear revelations of the real nature of God; and it will reify sinister political and cultural positions, writing them into the cosmos as the will of God, after which it lacks the tools to scrutinize them (see the second horseman). And so on. Our entire theological account will, in short, have been undone. Paul's gospel will collapse into two different gospels, one profoundly Trinitarian and unconditional, and the other, harshly retributive (and also functionally monotheist, although we don't need to go into this implication just now). And inherently and profoundly supersessionist consequences have just been unleashed as well; Christianity arises here in fundamental distinction from Judaism, and out of that benighted religion's deficiencies.

I sometimes summarize this situation in terms of the famous proverb that is often linked to Richard III and his death at the battle of Bosworth Hill (partly by way of Shakespeare's dramatization).

> For want of a nail, a shoe was lost;
> for want of a shoe, a horse was lost;
> for want of a horse, a rider was lost;
> for want of a rider, a battle was lost;
> for want of a battle, a kingdom was lost;
> and all for the want of a horseshoe nail.

The nail, in this particular case, is a judgment about the meaning of the word "belief" (Gk. *pistis*) in half a dozen passages in Paul. If this is misconstrued, being applied to the individual instead of to Jesus, and in voluntarist terms, we end up with the wrong argument—salvation by faith alone. If this argument is then introduced into Paul's broader thinking, it frames it, conditionally, contractually, and foundationally, and ultimately destroys it. The nail of a misconstrued word in an ambiguous phrase thereby leads to the fall of a theological kingdom, and hence my concern to bang the nail in properly here at the end of the chapter!

The widespread use of this (false) argument in Paul has produced a lot of very insecure Christians (while it has also alienated a lot of very pious Jews). I am always saddened and a bit astonished when I ask my classes if they are confident that they are saved. After all, I do teach in a divinity school. Most of my students hesitate to put their hands up. I usually go on to suggest that they rethink Paul's argument about faith in participatory terms and take their existing believing in Jesus's lordship—which they generally have—as evidence of the work of God in their lives already. The presence of the character of Jesus within their thinking and acting before he was resurrected is a cast-iron guarantee of their salvation. It is evidence that God is already indelibly and undeniably at work in them, and this comment seems to greatly comfort everyone. I then often go on to say that they need to stop worrying about their own salvation, in a fundamentally introverted and individualistic way, and turn outward to worry about those who are not yet responding to God as they ought to. Our adage should be, "Don't import anxiety; export joy!"

I suggest, in short, that we badly need to avoid define believing in Jesus in terms of (1) something we basically do for ourselves in order to (2) gain access to Christian realities (i.e., "get saved"), rather than as Paul himself uses it: as a marker of our existing inclusion in Jesus that has already taken place through the prior work of God. For Paul, believing is all about assurance, and not about appropriation. It means we are saved, not that we are about to be saved. Those who believe have proved that they are saved already; they do not need to fulfill any conditions in order to be saved. It is the result of salvation and not its instrument.

It follows, furthermore, that believing belongs within Paul's ethics, not within soteriology, which is why it has been treated here, in part 2, as a part of formation. It is one of the great errors of Protestantism to prefer the soteriological position all too frequently, dislocating faithfulness from its proper place in ethics and its proper grounding in the work of Jesus and the Spirit—a decision that has set up many a problem for further Protestant thinking downstream from this mistake. A rationalistic individualism, contractualism, and foundationalism are all thereby unleashed, not to mention an intrinsic and rather vicious supersessionism, and all in the name of Paul's gospel! Fortunately, we have used quite Protestant claims and positions to resist this catastrophe. An emphasis on Jesus's own believing springs straight out of Calvin's emphasis on Jesus as our representative. Jesus first assumes our humanity, entering fully into its depths of suffering and its need for faithful obedience.[22] Having done so, he then lifts us up to God the Father. (Clearly an overlap with the thinking of Hebrews is apparent here as well.) In just this sense, Jesus assumes our need to believe, does so on our behalf, and then opens up the way for us into the presence of his Father in the heavenly places. The way forward for Pauline interpretation—at this juncture[23]—is through Calvin.

Theses

> - The best way into Paul's broader treatment of faith is through the debate whether certain phrases speak of faith *in* Christ or of the faith *of* Christ, that is, respectively, an objective or a subjective reading of the genitive construction here.
> - I am convinced that these phrases all begin by speaking of the faith of Jesus himself. (See also Heb 11.) They allude to Hab 2:4, which is best read as a messianic proof-text and hence as referring to Jesus: "The Righteous One through faithfulness will live."
> - As such, they play an important role in a broader argument for assurance, rooted in participation.
> - Paul discusses faith in an especially concentrated way in parts of his letters to Galatia, Philippi, and Rome. Faith here has a special argumentative function as he combats his enemies. These figures were probably zealous but misguided messianic Jews, whom he calls his enemies in Phil 3:18.
> - Some of Paul's converts were being frightened by the conditional theology of the enemies. They were being told that they needed to obey the Jewish Torah—to convert to Judaism fully, with any uncircumcised men getting circumcised—or they would face the wrath of God on judgment day and be excluded from the blessings of the age to come.
> - One of Paul's key counterarguments appeals to the already-existing reality of faith in the lives of these converts. They already confessed that Jesus

22. Nicely described by James B. Torrance in his essay "The Vicarious Humanity of Christ."

23. Corrections to Calvin, like Barth's reformulation of the doctrine of election in *CD* II/2, remain critical as well of course.

was Lord, believing that God had raised him from the dead and would raise them in due course, and they held on to this belief steadfastly, along with its hope.

> Jesus had believed in this way, trusting in his Father to resurrect him from death after his suffering and execution.

> But if his converts were faithfully confessing and believing in this way too, then they were part of the first part of this trajectory and, in effect, locked into it. Hence their blessed destiny was certain, and they could ignore the legalistic demands of the earnest but misguided interlopers unsettling them in Galatia, Philippi, and Rome.

> Paul presupposes here—as we have already seen at length in part 1—that Jesus's followers possess a new mind—a new set of thoughts, beliefs, acts, and related emotions, which they have had gifted to them through Jesus. This possession entails that they are connected to Jesus—bolted onto him! Their resurrection is therefore guaranteed, as they are bolted onto his.

> Often Paul's account of believing is limited to correct confession. This is a serious mistake.

> Believing, properly understood in Paul, in relation to the preeminently faithful and believing one, Christ, refers to a number of things.

> It can refer to the need for love to act in an ongoing way, faithfully, patiently, perseveringly.

> In a loving relationship that has made a reasonable request, a loving response will also be a faithful response that is obedient and even submissive.

> But faith can also refer to beliefs narrowly (i.e., holding particular truths to be true, especially about God).

> However, it is important to recognize the theological aspect of believing. Having correct beliefs about the person (or persons) whom one loves is an important part of relating to them. So *increasingly* accurate beliefs are to be pursued. Inaccurate beliefs can be a very great hindrance to the healthy development of a relationship.

> Faith can also refer to trust, which shades into hope.

> This declaration speaks to absolute as against relative deprivation among potential converts. Everyone, whether rich or poor, faces an acute problem in death.

> But we hope because we are loved by God, and we hope for the perfection of love as those who are dead are raised and reunited. Hence God's love grounds and informs hope, especially in relation to death.

> All of these activities—faithfulness, obedience, correct beliefs, trust, and

hope—are specific instantiations in certain circumstances of love—so 1 Cor 13:7b (etc.).

- ➤ Faith in Paul, however, can *also* refer to the presence of the entire new mind of Jesus in his followers, with all its thinking and acting. This sort of faith (i.e., the mind of Jesus within us) puts itself into action through love (Gal 5:6).
- ➤ A different reading of the texts that speak cryptically of either *faith in* or *the faith of* Christ—that is, taking the former reading—undermines Paul's argument for assurance in terms of faith and therefore seems inadvisable.
- ➤ There would be few or no guarantees of future blessedness, since any believing would be up to us.
- ➤ This position tends to presuppose a voluntarist account of believing: we just choose to believe. But this is impossible. People cannot simply choose to believe certain things are true, or not.
- ➤ If appeal is made to the Holy Spirit eliciting belief, then we have moved to an entirely different system. In effect, the truth of the view that our faith is derived from Jesus's has been conceded.
- ➤ Any insistence on the need for the individual non-Christian to choose to believe also turns salvation back into a contract, generating tensions with Paul's broader thinking in a number of directions. In particular, the God of love revealed by Jesus is negated and overlaid by a God of retributive justice. Rationalistic individualism and foundationalism are unleashed, as is supersessionism. So endorsing this position—which appeals to uncritical modern liberals—again seems inadvisable.

Key Scriptural References

The standard "faith of Christ" texts are Rom 3:22, 26; Gal 2:16 [2x], 20; 3:22; and Phil 3:9. Also important are Eph 3:12 and 4:13. In this relation, Heb 11 is well worth consulting. Second Corinthians 4:13 implicitly but unavoidably affirms the motif of Jesus's believing for Paul (i.e., using the verb *pisteuō*, "believe," in relation to Jesus, and not just the noun *pistis*).

Romans 4:16b–23 is a critical exposition of the steadfast believing, trusting, hoping, and faithfulness Paul has in mind in his argument with his enemies. It applies in context to Abraham, but it presupposes Jesus's similar behavior.

The key "mind of Christ" texts are Rom 12:2 and 1 Cor 2:16. The resurrected mind is also implicit in the programmatic text this book began with: 2 Cor 5:17.

First Thessalonians 4:13–18 is a nice compact treatment of community hope in the face of death. The connections between love and hope are also articulated with inspiring insight in Rom 8:14–39.

First Corinthians 13:7 connects love to believing, trust, and fidelity, showing how love in specific circumstances acts as faith.

The comprehensive use of faith by Paul is apparent in Rom 14:23, summarizing here our possession of the mind of Jesus; see also 2 Cor 13:5.

Galatians 5:6 is succinct and clear about the organic relation in Paul's mind between the new believing mind and loving activity. Romans 15:13 indicates that believing includes hope, joy, and peace.

Key Reading

A christological understanding of faith in Paul has been championed in my generation most obviously and effectively by the work of Richard Hays. Hays's main work on the faith of Christ is his doctoral dissertation, republished with a new introduction, and an important SBL exchange in 2002 with J. D. G. Dunn. Hays analyzes the way that the motif of faith functions within the story Paul tells about Israel in Gal 3:15–4:5, pointing out that it has agency and is therefore best understood in relation to Jesus, and not to our decision-making. I revisit and summarize his arguments in *Deliverance*, 866–75.

I have done a fair bit of work on this debate as well, although my faithful readers should note that my angle of approach to this question has shifted a little in my most recent essays (i.e., in my articles noted below that were published in 2015).

Further Reading

Markus Barth makes an important contribution in relation to the data concerning the faith of Christ in Ephesians. His father, Karl Barth, was criticized for emphasizing Jesus's faithfulness in actual translation and so pulled back a little from that specific emphasis. But the careful reader will still find it from time to time in his *Dogmatics*, while the participatory emphasis is present throughout his thinking, although perhaps most obviously in IV/2. He describes hope in IV/3.2, and he treats death extensively in III/2.

Hooker's 1988 presidential address to SNTS marked a certain surge to prominence by the debate at the time. (It was published in 1989.)

J. B. Torrance provides an elegant, brief account of the vicarious humanity of Christ in the thought of Calvin. This theological—and deeply biblical—position lies behind the emphasis here on Jesus's own believing.

In my *Deliverance* I analyze Rom 4, emphasizing the frequently neglected subsection verses 16b–23. The text speaks at length of believing as steadfast fidelity, in the context of Abraham's unwavering believing in God's promise of an heir to him in his old age. A more accessible exposition of this text in these terms can be found in Daniel Kirk's *Unlocking Romans*.

More literature criticizing the traditional view of faith and in support of the view I am urging here can be found listed in chapter 27. Bird and Sprinkle have assembled various essays on both sides of the question in a useful reader, which includes an essay of mine summarizing the contentions of my first half-dozen studies on the question in relation mainly to data in Rom 1:16–17 and 3:21–26.

Bibliography

Barth, Karl. *Church Dogmatics*. III/2; IV/2; IV/3.2.

Barth, Markus. *Ephesians: A New Translation, with Introduction and Commentary*. 2 vols. AB 34. New Haven: Yale University Press, 1974.

Bird, Michael F., and Preston M. Sprinkle, eds. *The Faith of Jesus Christ: Exegetical, Biblical, and Theological Studies*. Peabody, MA: Hendrickson, 2009.

Campbell, Douglas. "Faith." Pages 327–36 in *The Oxford Encyclopedia of the Bible and Theology*. Vol. 1: *ABR–JUS*, edited by Samuel E. Balentine et al. Oxford: Oxford University Press, 2015.

———. "The Faithfulness of Jesus Christ in Romans 3:22." Pages 57–71 in *The Faith of Jesus Christ: Exegetical, Biblical, and Theological Studies*. Edited by Michael Bird and Preston M. Sprinkle. Peabody, MA: Hendrickson, 2009.

———. "Participation and Faith in Paul." Pages 37–60 in *"In Christ" in Paul: Explorations in Paul's Theology of Union and Participation*. Edited by Michael J. Thate, Kevin J. Vanhoozer, and Constantine R. Campbell. WUNT 2.384. Tübingen: Mohr Siebeck, 2015.

Hays, Richard B. "Christ Prays the Psalms: Israel's Psalter as Matrix of Early Christianity." Pages 101–18 in *The Conversion of the Imagination: Paul as Interpreter of Israel's Scripture*. Grand Rapids: Eerdmans, 2005.

———. *Echoes of Scripture in the Letters of Paul*. New Haven: Yale University Press, 1989.

———. *The Faith of Jesus Christ: The Narrative Substructure of Galatians 3:1–4:11.* 2nd ed. Grand Rapids: Eerdmans, 2002.

Hooker, Morna D. "ΠΙΣΤΙΣ ΧΡΙΣΤΟΥ." *NTS* 35 (1989): 321–42.

Kirk, Daniel J. R. *Unlocking Romans: Resurrection and the Justification of God.* Grand Rapids: Eerdmans, 2008.

Torrance, James B. "The Vicarious Humanity of Christ." Pages 127–47 in *The Incarnation: Ecumenical Studies in the Nicene-Constantinopolitan Creed, A.D. 381.* Edited by T. F. Torrance. Edinburgh: Handsel Press, 1981.

CHAPTER 14

Loving as Peacemaking

Christians and Conflict

One of the most desperate needs of the world today is for peacemaking. Our globe is riven by conflict, also with the further conflict generated by foolish and clumsy attempts at resolving clashes that have already taken place. Peacemaking is difficult, skilled work, and to this task the church since its inception has been called. Surely, then, the world can look to the church for the leaders and tools it needs to resolve its cascades of bitter disputes?[1]

Of course it can't! The church is widely and rightly seen as an entity that is deeply proficient at *generating* conflict. It finds and creates conflicts where secular folk simply look on agog. "The name of God is blasphemed among the pagans because of us."[2] Some Christian identities are even rooted in oppositional thinking, which is to say, in fundamental definitional conflict with others, including with other Christians. I worry that many Christians are held in check, restrained from unleashing deadly violence on one another, only by a secular state. (Note the sad reversal here of Paul's viewpoint in 1 Cor 6:1–11.)[3] We must turn from our deadly misconceptions, from our deluded politics and

---

1. Another version of this chapter appeared as "Paul the Peacemaker and the Ministry of Restorative Justice" in *Practicing with Paul: Reflections on Paul and the Practices of Ministry, in Honor of Susan G. Eastman*, ed. P. R. Burroughs (Eugene, OR: Cascade, 2018), 211–30.

2. Drawing here on Paul's rather caustic comment in Rom 2:24, which draws in turn on Isa 52:5 and Ezek 36:22.

3. We cannot make recourse to communal adjudications of wrongdoing but must rely on secular institutions because they are so much more constructive and measured than our own approaches.

priorities, and from our shameful divisions and instead relearn the patient skills of peacemaking. And here we can follow Paul's deeply costly practices of ecumenism and reconciliation, along with the restorative lead that some of his communities took under his guidance. Peace was one of his key emphases. Like grace, it opened and closed every letter, and it structured much else in his practice besides.[4]

Paul's Diplomatic Career

I worry, however, that Paul has been rather misrepresented in this respect. If we approach Paul through a particular Reformational lens, perhaps as an early Luther, and read him in terms of his fiery letter to the Galatians, we tend to build confrontation into the heart of his leadership. "Here I stand," he shouts, to the rest of the leaders of the early church, as well as to posterity. Now I agree that Paul stood firm on occasion. But this was in very particular circumstances. When the basis of his missionary work was under threat, he defended it, and all Jesus followers have to act similarly on occasion. When certain issues are being attacked, we are called to stand firm—in the practice of witness. But otherwise we are called to walk alongside those brothers and sisters who disagree with us. So perhaps we ought to think of Paul as a little less like Martin Luther and a little more like Martin Luther King. King was not an aggressive person. He was fun-loving and was initially uninterested in class and race relations, until he received what was in effect a divine call, mirroring Paul here again. He was passionate, but he could compromise. Hence he is remembered as both a courageous advocate of racial reconciliation and an ambassador of peaceful methods of protest.[5] Perhaps Paul was less of a Luther and more of an MLK. It is, at least, an interesting thought experiment to imagine that he was the latter and to see where this leads us.

Galatians is frequently presented as a battle cry, and in certain respects it is. The basic truths of the gospel are not to be compromised. But when we press deeper into the events that led up to this letter's composition, we find a strenuously diplomatic and reconciling effort on Paul's part, one that we see continuing well after this incendiary letter was sent. In Galatians Paul describes his relationship with several other key leaders in the early church

---

4. Peace characterized the resurrected mind—something that is quite significant. But we have already spent some time on this, in chs. 5 and 6.

5. See Stephen B. Oates, *Let the Trumpet Sound: A Life of Martin Luther King, Jr.* This being said, aspects of King's life were deplorable and should not be unacknowledged.

who were based in Jerusalem—the brothers of Jesus and Jesus's original core of disciples, led by James, Peter, and John (see Gal 1:11–2:14). This group led the messianic Jewish wing of the early church, which was originally the dominant group (an interesting situation we will explore in more depth in part 4). Paul recounts two visits to Jerusalem to meet with these leaders, one more than two years after his call, and the other more than sixteen years later. He also briefly describes a confrontation with Peter in Syrian Antioch. But things will be clearer if we rearrange these events from their rhetorical order in Galatians into their probable historical order.[6]

Paul was converted some time in 34 CE (or perhaps very late in 33). He visited Jerusalem as a Jesus follower for the first time late in 36 CE and stayed for about a fortnight. He met Peter and James at this time. Then he worked independently of the Jerusalem leaders, mainly around the coastlands of the Aegean Sea, so quite some distance away, until a series of arguments broke out in Syrian Antioch that he had to travel back and deal with late in 49 CE. However, everyone involved in the argument at Antioch realized that they had to go up to Jerusalem for a major consultation to sort things out, since the origins of the conflict lay there, and this meeting took place over the winter of 49–50 CE. In Galatians Paul presents it as ending well, with a shake of the hand by all the key players.

We know already that at this important Jerusalem conclave Paul promised to gather a large sum of money from his churches and to send it to Jerusalem to assist their ministry among the poor—a *charis*, or gift. He was kept busy keeping this collection on track—especially at Corinth—through the rest of 50 CE and during the early part of 51. His two letters written to Corinth in 51 open windows on various stages in its progress. Then the crisis in Galatia broke later in the same year. We learn from Galatians that hostile teachers were traveling through his communities in Galatia, trying to undermine his gospel there. Paul is uncertain in this letter of their exact relationship with the messianic leaders based in Jerusalem, and so another visit to the holy city looms to work this out. Had the Jerusalem agreement collapsed? Or were these hostile teachers traveling under a false flag, claiming the support of the apostles when they actually lacked it?

The rival teachers whom Paul addresses in Galatians weren't messing around. They arrived in Corinth, where Paul was working at the time, and proceeded to take him to court at the highest local level, before the Roman governor. Their intention seems to have been to have Paul executed after the successful prosecution of a capital case. From their point of view, this would

---

6. Further details can be found in my *Framing*, especially ch. 2.

have put a stop to Paul's blasphemous activities quickly and emphatically. We learn about this nasty episode especially from Philippians, which was written while Paul was imprisoned awaiting this trial during the winter of 51–52 CE.

In the spring we then learn from his extraordinary letter to the Romans that Paul won his case—as he expected to in Philippians—and that he is now planning to return again to Jerusalem with the money that he has collected, although he is not expecting an especially warm welcome.

> I urge you, brothers and sisters,
> by our Lord Jesus Christ and by the love of the Spirit,
> to join me in my struggle by praying to God for me.
> Pray that I may be kept safe from the unbelievers in Judea
> and that the contribution I take to Jerusalem
> may be favorably received by the Lord's people there,
> so that I may come to you with joy, by God's will,
> and in your company be refreshed. (Rom 15:30–32)

The pathos of this prayer is palpable. Paul has spent over two years collecting a massive sum of money, often at considerable personal cost, that he is now delivering, as promised, to the messianic Jewish community in Judea. But he asks for prayer because he might be killed on arrival. Moreover, he is not sure whether his offering will now be accepted by the church.

Rather sadly, the book of Acts confirms that Paul's anxieties were well-founded. Acts tells us how Paul ran into serious trouble in Judea, although he was not killed there. He was arrested by the Romans after a riotous disturbance in the temple and subjected to a series of imprisonments and trials that immobilized him for years until, after a harrowing sea journey and a further long incarceration, he was finally executed at Rome.

Now this is a dramatic tale. But I am not as interested here in the content of these events as much as the effort they involved. *Look at what Paul has done.* Think briefly about the lengths he has just gone to.

He has broken off his missionary work, to which he has been called by God, to make the long journey to Jerusalem twice, the second time at great personal risk, by way of Syrian Antioch. Think of walking hundreds of miles on foot through dangerous territory. He has then undertaken complex negotiations with the Jerusalem leadership concerning his disconcertingly radical missionary work, in the teeth of trenchant opposition to his program. He has raised money, written letters, and crafted a joint declaration; he has challenged, interpreted, and cajoled. He has traveled and argued and prayed. And he has done so as it has become increasingly obvious that his involvement in these activities will lead to a death sentence. (These experiences of Paul explain why I toy with the idea that he was a bit like Martin Luther King.)

This is an extraordinary level of commitment to ecumenicity. How many of us, faced with opposition from other Christians, would be willing to travel, fund-raise, write letters, and endure risk at this level in order to preserve unity with figures who hate us so much that some of them are trying to have us executed? Paul's reconciling efforts within the early church put most of us to shame. At least in doing so, however, they model the lengths to which the leaders of the church should be prepared to go as they try to hold on to its visible unity. This is the cost we should be prepared to pay to promote peace within the church. It is something of an understatement, then, when Paul writes, "Labor to guard the unity of the Spirit through the bond of peace" (Eph 4:3). When we plug in Paul's own story, we know just how much force we need to give to the word "labor" here, although this should not really surprise us.

We see here once again the life of Jesus figuring forth within Paul, although in this respect in its third significant "moment." In the two previous chapters we identified Jesus's love for us being enacted through his giving and his faithfulness, which were seen most clearly, respectively, in his incarnation and related self-offering at the cross and in his faithful obedience to that fate. But here we are brought face-to-face with the cross itself, followed by the resurrection, and with what those events together achieved. Much of the analysis of these pivotal events has already taken place in part 1, so our findings need only to be summarized quickly here.

We have learned that through his loving assumption of the broken human condition, namely, the Flesh, its termination on the cross, and his resurrection in a new spiritual state on the third day, Jesus has wrenched God's great plan for the cosmos back on track. Our wounds and brokenness have been healed, and our destiny of supreme relationality has been reclaimed, which entails that our relationships themselves have been restored. In a word, we would say that through these momentous events, Jesus has brought us *peace*. He has mended the shattered cosmos, healed its divisions, and brought its people together in a way that reestablishes God's primordial plan to gather all people together in one family—one communion—imaged and united by Jesus himself. And he has achieved this, as we saw in his first and second moments, through great giving and self-sacrifice, and great steadfastness and faithfulness. So our recent observations that Paul trenchantly, and ultimately *martyrologically*, worked for peace, which is to say, for functioning, evident, relational wholeness in the early church, make perfect sense. He is instantiating Jesus closely once more, following in his footsteps, here to make peace, however costly that process might eventually prove to be.

Restorative Justice at Corinth

The lessons we can learn from Paul about peacemaking do not stop with his example of dedicated, patient, determined work preserving church unity. We also find some highly practical advice in his writings about how to actually go about this. That is, we might accept that we desperately need peacemaking within our communities, as well as between them, and be committed to pursuing that at great personal cost, exhorting our leaders to follow in the footsteps of Jesus and do the same. But we might not know how to go about effecting this peace. Fortunately, a *restorative* practice is detectable unfolding through Paul's letters to Corinth.

In 1 Corinthians Paul lays out a series of sins that he wants the Corinthians to deal with, and there is quite a list.[7] In 2 Cor 7, however, written some weeks later, he is able to praise the Corinthians for addressing something well—not everything, but something. They have reacted with grief, repentance, and zeal to demonstrate that they are pure in a particular matter in which someone has committed a crime against someone else. (Paul's language here has a legal cast.)

> See what this godly sorrow has produced in you:
> what earnestness, what eagerness to clear yourselves,
> what indignation, what alarm, what longing, what concern,
> what readiness to see justice done.
> At every point you have proved yourselves to be innocent in this
>   matter.
> So even though I wrote to you,
> it was neither on account of the one who did the wrong
> nor on account of the injured party,
> but rather that before God you could see for yourselves
> how devoted to us you are.
> By all this we are encouraged. (7:11–13)

It is clear here that the Corinthians have acted communally against a person who has done something wrong. However, we also see in chapter 2 of the

---

7. See *Journey*, ch. 7, reproduced here in ch. 5.

same letter that someone who has caused grief has now suffered enough from the grief inflicted on him by the majority. He is to be forgiven and encouraged, not overwhelmed.

> If anyone has caused grief,
> he has not so much grieved me
> as he has grieved all of you to some extent—
> not to put it too severely.
> The punishment inflicted on him by the majority is sufficient.
> Now instead, you ought to forgive and comfort him,
> so that he will not be overwhelmed by excessive sorrow.
> I urge you, therefore, to reaffirm your love for him. (2:5–8)

Reading between the lines of all this material, we can see that, most likely, the offender of 1 Cor 6 has been addressed by the community's court as Paul recommended in 1 Cor 6:1–11, and the offense was most probably a theft. However, this "case" has been fully resolved. So Paul is able to praise the Corinthians in 2 Cor 7 for their zeal and cooperation in this matter—something he cannot do for every item on his agenda. But Paul is also advocating forgiveness and support for the offender. Indeed, he urges these actions in the letter in chapter 2, well before he describes the successful outcome of the case in chapter 7, arguing that to fail to extend forgiveness to an offender would be to fall prey to a satanic deception. So to fail to restore relational wholeness after an offense is to sin!

> Another reason I wrote you was to see if you would stand the test
> and be obedient in everything.
> Anyone you forgive, I also forgive.
> And what I have forgiven—
> if there was anything to forgive—
> I have forgiven in the sight of Christ for your sake,
> in order that Satan might not outwit us.
> For we are not unaware of his schemes. (2:9–11)

This whole situation looks to me very like a traditional communal resolution of a dispute that tends to be known now as restorative justice. Modern Western institutionalized justice, which is essentially punitive, has largely lost touch with the methods of conflict resolution that traditional societies practiced in ancient village and tribal settings—literally around campfires. But these are now being recovered as advocates are recognizing their superiority to modern procedures for addressing the harm caused by disputes and conflicts.

Every approach to conflict resolution presupposes a narrative about the world. It supplies an account of the nature of wrongdoing and of what to do about it, in two complementary stories. And because of the ubiquity of conflict, along with its costliness, societies are deeply committed to the practices that their key narratives legitimize. However, arguably the modern Western narrative—in which we invest billions of dollars, endless years of people's lives, and vast institutions—has gone somewhat astray. The ancient tribal narrative is closer to the story of wrongdoing and its correction, rooted in revelation and resurrection, that has thus far been informing our analysis of Paul.

The slightly divergent practices grouped together under the rubric of restorative justice—victim-offender conferences, talking circles, family group conferences, and so on—presuppose a fundamentally relational and covenantal account of reality, and they affirm the importance and dignity of every member of a community. When a dispute takes place or a conflict evolves, resolution in traditional terms tends to be envisaged as a process of communal healing and restoration that all who have been harmed must participate in, in order to move forward. Everyone must have a voice. This process does not appeal to a third neutral actor—to some sort of state—to inflict pain on a key perpetrator and then assume that this process solves the problem. Framed by an unconditional commitment to all involved, the relationships that have been strained and torn must be mended or "restored," just as a tapestry that has been slashed by a knife must have its threads patiently knotted and resewn. Furthermore, ancient communities knew that this work must ultimately take place face-to-face.

Victims, in particular, must be allowed to speak their story in a secure space if they want to, thereby recovering their dignity and moving beyond their fear, as they voice their anguish directly to those who have harmed them. This can be a deeply healing process.[8] More than anything else, victims generally need those who have hurt them to experience directly from them—from their story and from all the emotions set in motion by it—the pain that they have had inflicted on them. And they need to see this deep emotional resonance taking place in those who have hurt them. Once this has happened, people who have been victimized are generally satisfied and are able to move forward. (This deep-seated desire for emotional communication is no sur-

---

8. Healing cannot be guaranteed. But this is the nature of human interaction in any case. Those harmed must respond to the invitation to address the harm in this potentially painful, but ultimately restorative fashion.

prise in view of the intersubjective construction of our identities, which we discussed earlier.)

But this process is generally transformational for people who have committed offenses as well. As offenders experience the pain they have inflicted on others as a result of their actions, face-to-face, in the frequently harrowing stories told by the people who have been hurt, they are placed in the ultimate learning situation. Often crimes are thoughtless actions. There is little forethought and minimal appreciation of their consequences. But an appropriate restorative process brings the devastating consequences of an action home with full force. Only a psychopath can remain unaffected by the expressed anguish of a victim.[9] Those who have committed an offense are generally deeply affected and transformed by this process. They learn to be ashamed of their criminal activities in an appropriate instance of shaming. And they invariably want to respond to their victims in ways that demonstrate their good faith in the future, making restitution.

We can see in this brief description that restorative justice processes, which are in large measure a recovery of traditional communal practices, integrate smoothly with the basic truths of Paul's ethics as they arise out of the story of Jesus. They presuppose more clearly than perhaps anything we have discussed so far how a relational God working through Jesus is powerfully committed to the healing and restoration of torn and damaged relationships.[10] So it is no surprise to see these practices at work in Paul's communities, especially in the troubled community in Corinth, where conflict was especially severe. But it is worth pausing for a moment here to consider a relational notion of repair that Jesus modeled in the cross and that Paul clearly emulated closely, and its particular healing of shame.

Loving as Healing Shame

Ancient society was exquisitely hierarchical, and like most such societies, it operated with deeply entrenched codes of honor and shame. A tiny fraction

9. Psychopaths and sociopaths should be carefully screened out by preconference analysis, since their participation in restorative processes can be ineffective or damaging. Having said this, psychopaths are not necessarily criminals, despite their frequent portrayal.

10. Punitive practices—the infliction of pain, often by the state, on people who have committed offences—cannot heal relational damage; rather, in effect, they double the pain. See my "Mass Incarceration: Pauline Problems and Pauline Solutions."

of the population were "winners," possessing high status and honor—and even then often only temporarily—while the vast majority were arrayed beneath them in descending ranks of inferiority. Honor is a complex cultural code. But while shame is a code as well, it is also one of the nine basic biophysiological affects that we have already come across in relation to the second personal in chapter 10 and it is a deeply unpleasant one.[11] The affects, including the negative states, are important evolutionary adaptations. They have enabled not merely the survival of our species but its unparalleled and extraordinary success. However, the constant triggering of the negative affects by our cultural locations can be destructive. We need the negative affects, but we cannot live in them permanently—this is like living in a vat of emotional acid—and our particular concern here is with shame.

Shame has an impact on our faces and bodies. The specific markers of shame are disordered thoughts, a reddened face, a hanging head that averts the eyes, and a sagging posture. Internally, this affect cuts immediately across the positive affects, interposing a deeply unpleasant experience. It instantly shuts down any interest, excitement, or enjoyment—the good things in life.

As long as shame is being coded in constructive cultural terms, it can be positive. It draws our attention to things impeding the positive affects so we can address them. We should be ashamed of those actions that get in the way of appropriate excitement and enjoyment. And it codes dangerous things negatively. It is a good thing, for example, if shame is tightly coded with the sexual exploitation of children. People who are sexually attracted to minors should suffer sagging shoulders, disordered thoughts, and a red face whenever they think of exploiting minors. Hence all cultures weave shame into multiple practices that are considered undesirable. We should be ashamed of various actions if we contemplate them. But herein lies the rub. Shame is frequently coded into *identities*, as well as into practices that are not necessarily especially bad. And this codes a toxic experience into peoples and practices that they must then endure. Some people have their shame affect triggered *simply because of who they are*, and this shame can then be associated with disgust and dissmell as well—a deeply corrosive combination.

---

11. Disgust and "dissmell" are the two other especially unpleasant affects, that is, the responses of nausea and revulsion from stench, although anger, fear, being startled (this being a split-second experience), and anxiety are all negative, especially if they are experienced too frequently. Only two affects are fundamentally positive: enjoyment and excitement. I introduce Tomkins's theory of affects briefly in "The Issue of Shame in Robert Jewett's Commentary on Romans."

Ancient society was just one type of extreme social hierarchy visible through much of human history that had perfected an affective stratification based on the activation of shame, and the vast majority of its inhabitants carried a daily burden of toxic emotion. This would then have been compounded by expressions of dissmell and disgust—"You stink!" and "You are nauseating!" Hence it is not surprising to see anger emerging in response to these cultural provocations, along with internalized senses of dissmell and disgust, all of these blending together into a poisonous emotional concoction. But Paul's communities offered a solution when they acted in love toward the unlovely.

Converts to his communities from paganism were baptized, which is to say, they were stripped of their old identities, immersed and cleansed through the death and resurrection of Jesus, and then gifted with new clothes and a new identity that was nothing less than a child of God. They were part of a family that greeted them at every meeting with the familial kiss (and this *might* even have been a full, open-mouthed kiss on the mouth to pass the spirit).[12] And they were able to speak and to sing in this family's meetings, provided the Spirit moved them—and none were excluded from such promptings.

We should not idealize the early Pauline communities. Hierarchies and status differentials are still detectable. Cultural and political arrangements we now find shameful— patriarchy, slavery, and tyranny—were still operative and unquestioned. However, the basis of these communities was a fictive kinship of familial intimacy because the identity of everyone was rooted in participation in Jesus—a Jesus who journeyed himself into the furthest and most shameful corners of society, enduring the cross, to draw people into fellowship and the full rights of children of God. Hence this participation was open to all and grafted everyone into a basic equality, an equality mirrored in a fundamental secondary solidarity in Adam. Moreover, the basic affective script of these communities for their members was positive. Their identities were shaped most deeply by belonging and affirmation—by the joy and peace (i.e., excitement and enjoyment) of being children of God who were loved in Christ. Hence the key entry ritual signified that their identities that had been coded with shame had been left behind, and the symbolism and underlying reality could not be stronger at this point; these identities had been *executed*. The shame of God had borne away the shame of the socially humiliated. The old stinking and shameful clothing of the past had

---

12. See Rom 16:16; 1 Cor 16:20; 2 Cor 13:12; 1 Thess 5:26; also 1 Pet 5:14. Robert Jewett's discussion is consummate; see *Romans*, 972–74.

been stripped off and cast away; the fresh new clothes of the Resurrected One had been donned in their stead. The cross and the resurrection of Jesus heal us from shame.

In my experience it takes time for the new positive identity of the baptized to work its way deeply into humiliated people's psyches. Moreover, it is critical that the community surrounding them mirrors the positive story of that new identity and not the negative script of surrounding society. But it does happen. The offer of an identity beyond shame is an enormously significant gift a Pauline community possesses—provided that the community is really committed to offering it in the way we have just noted. Do our modern communities offer shamed people a new identity, or do they subtly but firmly reinscribe the unnecessary shame differentials that structure surrounding society? Which is simply to ask,[13] do we love the humiliated as we should? After all, Jesus loves them. He loves them so much that he journeys to be with them, right alongside them, and even beyond them in their shame, to gather them back and to heal them, which was just the journey Paul also took wherever he went. (We will talk more about the practicalities of this in a later chapter when we describe his costly missionary practices.) It is this love, with its accompanying communal embrace, that heals people who have been inscribed with shame; and ultimately if we are to have peace in our communities, we need to learn how to heal shame. Shamed people seldom live in peace with one another and with those around them.

Dare we dream of modern churches that look like this—as incubators of peacemaking, as against ones of conflict propagation? And dare we dream of leaders who can work with as much dedication and courage as Paul to bring peace? I hope so. But peacemaking will not simply fall into our laps once we realize how important it is. We will need to acquire a number of key subordinate virtues if we are to enact it.

Additional Virtues for Peacemaking

To be loving entails restoring relationships that are fractured or damaged, and doing so in a way that is loving; it is to be a peacemaker who knows how to promote and to pursue peace. But peacemaking is itself informed by several

13. I suspect that a key marker here will be the leadership. Do our communities' leaders send the message that they live alongside their struggling members, as one of them? Or do they appear, somehow, above them?

further important virtues. Paul wrote a famous list of virtues in Gal 5:22–23b, referring to them, in biblical parlance, as fruit.

> But the fruit of the Spirit is:
> love,
> joy,
> peace,
> patience,
> kindness,
> goodness,
> faithfulness,
> gentleness, and
> self-control.

We can see from this list that if love expresses itself in damaged situations as peacemaking, then it will also require, within this general practice, *patience, kindness, faithfulness, gentleness,* and *self-control.* Hence peacemaking explains the majority of the virtues fruiting in the lives of the followers of Jesus (or it ought to…). The first three subordinate virtues on this list—patience, kindness, and faithfulness—can be dealt with reasonably quickly, in part because we have already spent some time talking about faithfulness. However, a more detailed articulation of the last two—gentleness and self-control—should result in some particularly illuminating insights for our discipleship.[14]

Patience, Kindness, and Faithfulness

We know already that love in certain circumstances results in behavior we would call faithful. And clearly Paul's reconciling efforts with both Jerusalem and Corinth were overtly faithful in this sense. His actions were deeply steadfast and enduring, to the point of arrest, imprisonment, and execution. Peacemaking is difficult work and needs this sort of perseverance—the perseverance of Jesus on the way to the cross. It also needs leaders who are kind and who possess supernatural degrees of patience.

---

14. "Goodness" either refers to generic goodness, so right behavior of any kind, treated by the entirety of part 2, or it refers more specifically to generosity, which has been treated here already in terms of giving and benefaction.

Quite obviously, peacemakers need to be kind, while I often insist that Jesus followers should simply be kind in general. Moreover, this can seem to be a more manageable relational practice than the constant practice of covenantal and self-sacrificial love. For those of us who quail a little at the thought of being loving all the time as Jesus was—who did, after all sacrifice himself for us on the cross—kindness seems more realistic.

Having said this, kindness is quite hard to define precisely, although we know it when we see it. At the least it denotes a gentle attempt to enter into the situations of others, even when they might seem initially to be forbidding or just plain wrong. We give people the benefit of the doubt. In fact, when we let people tell their own stories, we often go on to learn that we have misunderstood things in any case, so kindness might save us from the tyranny of some of our own assumptions. Similarly, it tends to forgo harsh and quick responses to slights and insults and problems. It is measured and considerate. It puts other people's interests before our own. So it behooves us to ask: are we kind? Do we live in kind communities? When people walk in the door and experience our meetings and our interactions, is kindness one of the first descriptions that springs to mind? There will be no peace without kindness. And there will be no peacemaking without patience.

I recently attended an intensive training for leaders in restorative circle practices led by the renowned circle-keeper Kay Pranis. She began the training as she usually does—by placing a bag containing a pile of driftwood in the middle of the group next to a small table and instructing us to proceed in silence as a circle (i.e., one by one, in sequence). We could take one or more pieces of wood out of the bag—as many as we wanted to—and arrange them on or around the table. Or we could put them back in the bag, whether one, several, or all of them. This had to continue until the entire group "passed" in a circle, indicating its acceptance of whatever arrangement of wood had eventuated.

I knew the driftwood exercise was coming and had fortified myself internally with the suitably chilled attitude, but even with this foreknowledge, it turned out to be difficult to sit in silence—with occasional sculptural moments in the middle—for the sixty-five minutes that it took our group to eventually settle on something. (We eventually tipped over the table and then created the word "LOVE" on the floor, with a mirror image of the word next to it so that both sides of the circle could benefit.) I was well aware that people around me were huffing and puffing, especially when I and a few others still insisted late in the exercise on getting up and rearranging things. Even more testing was experiencing a beautiful arrangement of small driftwood sculptures that had taken several rounds to create being swept to the floor by someone to begin again!

I knew that we were supposed to be learning something, although I didn't know exactly what it was. First impressions suggested that the exercise was silly, and it certainly drove everybody nuts. But this was just the point. As Kay explained after we had concluded, leading a circle, especially when it involves any resolutions of harm or conflict, involves "sitting with the discomfort." A circle-keeper has to keep still and silent and to accept that he or she has no control over the outcome of the process. The process will end when *everyone* in the circle is ready for it to end, *and not before*. It does not end when *we* might be ready for it to end. Hence circle-keepers can keep circles effectively, especially circles addressing challenging issues, only if they grasp and then live fully into this posture.

Kay went on to observe that our group had shown unusual restraint because no one at any point had put all the wood in the bag in a fairly strong signal that the stupid exercise should just stop. (We had all thought about doing this.) Usually someone does this. (On one occasion, a person took the bag and locked it in their truck in the carpark.) But when this happens, *someone else invariably goes and gets the bag and gets some wood out and keeps going.* In other words, no one person can ever take control over the process and say when it has to end. The entire group controls the process, and it ends when everyone is ready for it to end—and this is the only way in which communities can move forward with every person, important or unimportant, hurt or hurting, having been included and felt heard and valued. This is how conflicts are resolved and harm is addressed effectively, and really in this way (broadly speaking) and no other. Harm is addressed only when everyone who has been affected has been included and has spoken. Until this has happened, anyone leading the process, maintaining the fragile quality of the space within which the conflict is being addressed, must "sit with the discomfort."

But a way of naming this attitude—of sitting with the discomfort until everyone has reached a point of resolution, and the entire circle has settled—with a single word would be to say that the circle-keeper needs *patience*. Proper, deep conflict resolution and peacemaking requires patience at a level our modern culture can barely imagine.

In a *New York Times* op-ed, Timothy Egan cited a study undertaken by Microsoft in Canada that had discovered that the average attention span of a person in 2015—"the amount of concentrated time [spent] on a task without being distracted"—had dropped from the twelve seconds recorded in 2000 to eight. Apparently, this is a shorter attention span than that of a goldfish.[15]

15. https://www.nytimes.com/2016/01/22/opinion/the-eight-second-attention-span.html?_r=0.

Many of us experience the same phenomenon in traffic. I seethe with frustration if someone is too slow moving off on a green light and I am forced to wait for another change of lights—maybe a minute or two of my time—and I not infrequently see drivers around me reacting even more impatiently than I do. Things have changed for me since I have started treating traffic and traffic stops as small exercises in patience training. I am pleased to say that I have made some progress and can now happily endure a light change or two. But we will need to be more patient than this if we want to sit with the discomfort of conflict resolution as we make peace within fractured communities. The Truth and Reconciliation Commission that brought so much healing to post-apartheid South Africa met in multiple ways *for five years*.[16] (The TRC was by no means a perfect restorative justice process, but it has been constructive and significant, and especially when some of the alternatives are considered.)[17]

In short, as Paul said rightly, love is patient; and we can now add the coda that peacemaking is the place where patience is needed in an especially large measure. It requires training in a way that our modern culture constantly militates against. "Driftwood before cellphones" might have to be our motto moving forward, at least when it comes to certain group activities.

Similarly important is self-control.

Self-Control

Our prevailing cultural narrative of peacemaking tends to involve force. Problems are solved, we are told, by the application of an amount of pain to the perpetrators of offenses that is equal to the amount that they have perpetrated on others. This approach feels equal, equivalent, and balanced. We might even name it "just." The word we often use to describe this broader theory of con-

16. See especially Desmond Mpilo Tutu, *No Future without Forgiveness*; Peter Storey, "A Different Kind of Justice: Truth and Reconciliation in South Africa," *Christian Century* 114, no. 25 (1997): 788–93. Note that this essay was written while the TRC was in the midst of its work, which ran from 1995 to 2000. Storey was on the committee charged with selecting the TRC commissioners. He notes, "Selecting the truth commissioners was . . . a challenge. They had to be people of proven integrity and capable of impartiality, with a track record of commitment to human rights *and the inner strength to cope with the emotional strain of the job*. A balance of race, gender, region and vocational or professional background was also crucial" (emphasis added).

17. See James L. Gibson, "On Legitimacy Theory and the Effectiveness of Truth Commissions." and L. Gregory Jones, "Truth and Consequences in South Africa."

flict resolution is punishment. The underlying Latin *punire* means "to inflict a penalty on" or "to cause pain for some offense." However, although it contains important intuitions, this narrative of conflict resolution, despite its cultural dominance, is not fundamentally informed by the Pauline gospel.

God's way of dealing with the problem of a disordered and fractured world was to enter into it and to bear its pain, terminating it, and then to reconstitute a reality beyond it that is now accessible to those still struggling within the old dispensation. And on the way, everyone who was implicated in the wrongdoing of the old order—which means everyone—was forgiven. The obligation to repay the debt accumulated by their sin was simply released. The new reality now draws us into deeper relational wholeness, restoring us and teaching us about wrongdoing consequentially (something we will talk more about in the next chapter). This is God's solution to wrongdoing, including to conflict, *and force is nowhere in sight*, except as a possible means of effecting termination, although even there it is unnecessary.[18]

As appropriately tutored followers of Jesus, we must consequently resist the introduction of force into conflict and dispute resolution as something evil. It will more than likely take a bad situation and make it worse. As the old adage goes: "Two wrongs don't make a right." The infliction of an amount of pain on people equal (supposedly) to the pain they have inflicted is a deeply pagan account of problem-solving, and a thoroughly nasty one to boot. It is, in the end of the day, problem-solving understood as revenge.

We should recall that Paul himself was originally a violent man. Few would have felt as justified as he did inflicting pain on the bodies of the messianic Jews he apprehended before he was called so dramatically to the apostolate. His use of force was righteous, and presumably thoroughly supported by statements in the Scriptures. But he was of course utterly mistaken. It is highly significant that Paul did not prosecute his mission violently. He clearly renounced this approach, even as he endured it from others. His martyrdom, following in the footsteps of Jesus's and echoed by so many other leaders in the early church, places a final accent on the way in which violence is something evil that the church must turn its back on.[19]

---

18. The gratuity of the crucifixion of Jesus—of the infliction of pain on him resulting in death—speaks primarily of our deep hostility to God and of the evil of the powers who oppose him. They apply force and pain, and they kill: see 1 Cor 2:8. All Jesus had to do was die; he didn't have to be tortured to death. We and our evil cosmos did that.

19. It follows that an uncontrolled or undisciplined expression of the affect of anger can be deeply sinful.

But if force is not the way to solve a problem—recalling instead the healing offered by processes like restorative justice—we still need to give some account of force. By this I mean only to suggest that occasionally it might be right to do something coercive to someone else's body.

When my children Emile and Grace were small, although still large enough to get into trouble, I would sometimes restrain them, as any parent would do. I would stop them from—to put matters generically—jumping into a river or into a fire, or from running in front of a car. This action involved force, and it was the right thing to do; force here was good. But note carefully how it is not a fundamentally constructive act, even in these circumstances. I was not solving anything or creating anything. I was simply acting preventatively. I was stopping a further slide into evil.

I suggest, then, that we follow Paul's lead and renounce force as in any way a constructive thing—that is, renounce it as "violence"—and apply it only rarely and preventatively, informed by the virtue of *self-control*. This virtue prevents the unleashing of force as violence and revenge, even when our emotions and culture are screaming for it. It holds force within its necessary but limited preventative role. Can our communities model an exercise of force that is only ever self-controlled? And when even preventative force fails, as it sometimes must, can we turn our other cheek and, if necessary, accept the fate of a martyr, exposing the evil of violence more fully? Making this response would be like Paul—and even more important, it would be like Jesus.[20]

---

20. I fear of course that we are some distance away from this level of response. In the wake of the horror that took place in 2015 at the Emanuel African Methodist Episcopal Church in Charleston, SC, where nine African American worshipers were massacred by a young gun-toting racist, HuffPost published "Pastors and Faithful Pick Up Gun Training: 'We Need It in Church,'" on Tuesday, June 23, 2015 (http://www.huff ingtonpost.com/2015/06/23/gun-training-church_n_7647788.html). Bianca Graulau reports in this article how Pastor Geof Peabody recommends a much more aggressive policy of gun-training and gun-ownership in the wake of the Charleston tragedy. He has already trained over four hundred pastors, he says. The ministers "first learn about safety. Then, they move over to the shooting range to get hands-on practice." One of his students commented in the same article: "We need protection. People that go through classes and get licenses and stuff to carry a gun. I fell [*sic*] like we need this in our lives. We need it in church and in our businesses." But force dependent on the practiced use of a gun is unlikely to be merely preventative. It is much more likely to be fatal to the aggressor, if it isn't fatal to the gun-owner. And prevention based on the rationally perceived threat of deadly force is not the same thing as force applied in a directly preventative way. (Preventative force in relation to Charleston could presum-

One final virtue now needs to be noted here. It is a critical part of peacemaking, although it extends well beyond this particular practice into every aspect of our lives as followers of Jesus. We ought to pursue gentleness.

Gentleness

Self-controlled force, as against violence, is acting in a way that is *gentle*. Peacemaking requires constant, enduring, gentle actions, while kindness is in many respects simply gentleness. And I can think of few better ways of learning to be gentle than by working with plants or with animals. Most plants and animals can't fight back. But we learn from the way we treat them that gentleness elicits flourishing, along with obedience when that is relevant, while harsh and bullying ways elicit damage and recalcitrance.

When pondering these things, I often think of my grandfather. A great influence on my life, he was a famously encouraging, kind, and gentle person. He was a farmer and was particularly skilled with sheepdogs and horses. Sometimes other farmers would send him talented dogs that had been rendered useless through bullying and poor training, and he would patiently regain their trust, rebuild their confidence, and teach them again to do their highly skilled jobs. He would never beat them, this usually being the root of their problems. He did the same with horses.

For much of my early adulthood he rode a horse imaginatively named Red, who had been traumatized and was profoundly nervous. On one occasion, as a young horse, a canvas horse cover had detached from his hind legs and swung around to cover his head. He had gone through two wire fencelines, getting tangled in them, before he could be caught and calmed. But Red was a magnificent chestnut who would do anything my grandfather asked him to, whether it was cutting stock or dressage. I watched Red touch his arm gently in the stables from behind one day with his nose, and my grandfather turned to me and said, "Look, that's the way a horse tells you that he loves you."

But I think of my grandfather here not just because he modeled these virtues to me but also because of the way he acquired them. My grandfather *learned* to be gentle. He was a wonderful grandfather and a terrible father. Prior to being a farmer he had worked doing deliveries and then had volunteered to serve in the New Zealand division during the war. In those days he

---

ably involve restraining people from obtaining access to the tools of deadly force, in this case guns—something that multiplies their capacity to do harm to others.)

was "a man's man" who played rugby and boxed and frequently got into bar fights and brawls. Only close friends saved him eventually from his demons, which were worked out with a conspicuous lack of self-control in relation to alcohol. Then animals taught him to be kind and gentle, because that was really what he wanted to be. (His journey also shows us how a particular construction of masculinity can be very problematic for Jesus followers; his disciples sometimes need to learn how countercultural their identity should be.)

If we want to learn how to be gentle, there might be few better ways of doing this than by picking up a nervous dog from the pound. We will have the opportunity to learn to be gentle, as well as self-controlled, patient, and kind. If we can't develop these patterns of behavior with a dog, we should think twice before we take charge of other human beings, especially small ones. Dogs are much more compliant and forgiving partners, with far fewer demands, than people, as my grandfather often used to say.

But gentleness should characterize more than our direct actions on the bodies of other things and people. It should characterize a particularly important area of human behavior for peacemaking, not to mention, for relating in general.

Gentle Speech

The eleventh step of humility in the Benedictine Rule begins, "When [a monk] does speak, he should do so gently and without mockery, humbly and seriously, in a few well-chosen words."

One of the most curious things about Paul's more generic ethical instructions to his communities is how much time he spends on speech ethics. He is concerned about other sins as well—behavior like theft and drunkenness. But the only ethical preoccupation comparable in extent to his concern with speech is his anxiety about aberrant sexual activity. Paul spends a great deal of time exhorting his converts to speak in the right way, not merely truthfully, but constructively and lovingly. And this instruction was highly countercultural.

The lower echelons in hierarchical cultures tend to develop "strategies of resistance," as James Scott calls them.[21] It is usually too dangerous for poor and low-status people, especially servants and slaves, to confront an oppressive hierarchy directly; it requires considerable organization, talent, and courage to do so.

---

21. See Scott's classic study *Domination and the Arts of Resistance: Hidden Transcripts*.

But it is always possible to do things that cause a bit of trouble or that at least get back at one's superiors to some degree—things like loitering, pilfering, and sabotaging. Particular language games are key weapons in this resistance. The lower ranks use double entendre and tone to mock their superiors to their face, and then also parody them behind their backs. As Scott's seminal Ethiopian proverb puts it: "When the great lord passes, the wise peasant bows deeply and silently farts." In any hierarchical society, such as the ancient Greco-Roman empire, language is caught up tightly with this generalized pattern of resistance. It is used to express resentments, hatred, and scorn.[22] This context makes Paul's frequent admonitions about appropriate community language all the more remarkable.

He insists that his converts, the vast majority doubtless drawn from the lower social orders and hence well aware of these special language games, speak out of the interpersonal reality that they now overtly indwell, which is the divine communion. They are to speak in love, with gentleness, to build up and to correct one another, and not to mock, deride, or attack. This advice all makes perfect sense, however challenging it might prove in practice. Relationships are profoundly affected by how we speak within them. To a large degree they exist through our language practices, so how we speak is very important. But speaking rightly is very difficult. Paul's point is not so much, then, whether disciples should cuss or not. He doesn't approve of this (Eph 4:29; 5:4), but it is not his main concern. His principal priority is the constructiveness of our speech. Are the relationships within the body being nurtured and enhanced by our speaking, or are they being eroded and damaged?

A quick glance at the plethora of Christian blogs on the internet will reveal that many Christians are woefully out of touch with Paul's mediation of the divine priorities here (and I count myself among them at times). How much writing, preaching, and teaching is conveying the spirit of the world and the Flesh, rather than the Spirit of God? Is our internet presence a gentle one? Moreover, we see here very clearly that the how is as important as the what. We can be right in substance and utterly wrong in style, which is in fact to be wrong in substance. Marshall McLuhan's famous adage is worth quoting here: "The medium is the message." This dictum applies *exactly* to how the followers of Jesus should speak.

I suspect, then, that Paul would simply ask a lot of us to step up here, to repent of our linguistic partisanship and aggression, and to practice speech that is self-controlled and gentle—speech that by its very manner conveys the gentle

---

22. I am not excusing higher-status figures from difficult dynamics here too. They faced particular challenges in relation to the intense competitiveness of ancient society, especially its partisanship, which also tends to provoke unethical speech.

and loving relationality that we are involved with. Our communities should offer the world the gift of a community that speaks gently both to its members and to outsiders, a community that knows how to speak both rightly and kindly. Only communities who have learned to speak like this can make peace after conflicts have escalated emotions, and vicious and aggressive language has compounded harm with harm, whether these disputes take place in the office, at the local café, after a church meeting, over international borders, or over the kitchen table. Where violent speech deepens a dispute, gentle speech can begin to defuse it. Such speaking flows from peace and fosters peace.

In sum: Paul, contrary to how he is often portrayed, was a dedicated peacemaker. He pursued peace doggedly and courageously with other church leaders in his day, and he encouraged it when his communities fractured as a result of incidents like theft and adultery. Behind some of his specific recommendations, especially in 1 and 2 Corinthians, we can also detect a traditional restorative approach to conflict and dispute resolution that differs markedly from the retributive and punitive story that so dominates modern Western society but that enacts the restorative relationship God has with us by way of Jesus's crucifixion and resurrection. It follows from all this that Pauline communities are called to peace and to the practices of peacemaking. And we now know that leaders involved in this sort of work today will need to pursue certain key virtues. Peacemaking and restorative work require love. And it will need those who know how to love in ways that are faithful, kind, patient, gentle, and self-controlled. Fortunately, even though the example that Paul set practicing these virtues can at times seem a little overwhelming, he himself was merely responding to the one who embodied all these virtues supremely and who gifts them to us as well, by his Spirit, as we heed his call and obey. So let us heed that call and obey, learning to walk together—and to lead others—on the difficult pathways of peace. What could be a more powerful witness to the world of the truth of the gospel than the sight of Jesus's followers coming together, healing their differences, gently restoring their members who struggle with inappropriate shame, and then going out to patiently heal other deep social wounds as well?!

Theses

> The virtue of peace suggests that Jesus followers should address conflict constructively.
> Sadly, many churches are better at starting conflicts than resolving them.

- Paul is sometimes portrayed as an oppositional figure, akin to Martin Luther. His fiery letter to the Galatians is taken to be paradigmatic of a fundamentally confrontational approach.

- A closer look at the evidence suggests a different picture, however. If we reconstruct Paul's relationship with the Jerusalem leadership, he evidenced in his journeys, negotiations, and eventual capture and execution, an extraordinary patience, fidelity, and bravery, along with a great dedication to church unity.

- In this dedication we see the third critical "moment" in Jesus's life figuring forth in Paul's life—the dedicated healing of the broken cosmos by his cross and resurrection, and the restoration of its relationality—the bringing to the cosmos of peace.

- Second Corinthians 2 and 7, in combination with 1 Cor 6:1–11, suggest a local communal process that addressed some sort of harm (ch. 7) but that also reintegrated the person who had caused it (ch. 2).

- This process is recognizable as an ancient communal approach to problem-solving known today as restorative justice.

- Restorative justice centers on those who have suffered harm or been victimized. It emphasizes face-to-face storytelling in relation to harm and conflict; it includes the voices of all, and it focuses on communal restoration and healing both of those who have been harmed and of those who have caused harm.

- Its relational approach to resolving conflict stands in stark contrast to modern Western institutional procedures and to punitive justice.

- But it is very close to Paul's theological insights into a relational and covenantal God, especially, again, in the third moment in Jesus's story when he heals and repairs the relationality of the cosmos through his death and resurrection. This example suggests that processes of restorative justice enjoy strong theological warrant.

- Closely related to this restorative process, Pauline communities should restore and heal those who have been inappropriately shamed, largely by affirming the gift to them of a new affirming identity in Jesus as a child of God.

- The virtue of peace, understood especially as peacemaking, is necessarily supplemented and effected by the virtues of patience, kindness, faithfulness, gentleness, and self-control (see Gal 5:22–23).

- Peacemaking requires perseverance—very much so, which Paul demonstrated in his extraordinarily faithful relationship with Jerusalem. In doing so, Paul reenacts Jesus's faithfulness.

- ‣ Peacemaking requires kindness—the willingness to extend inclusion and voice to everyone involved in a situation, and to act gently and considerately.
- ‣ Peacemaking requires patience—the patience of a saint! Circle-keepers processing harm or conflict must learn to "sit with the discomfort." The process will not end until everyone in the circle feels heard and included. This takes time and cannot be forced or controlled.
- ‣ All conflict resolution presupposes a story of how a problem began, what it consists of exactly, and (consequently) how to fix it.
- ‣ A story rotating around retributive justice in punitive terms is culturally prevalent, if not dominant. This supposes that a problem is fixed by an application of pain to a perpetrator of harm equivalent in amount to the pain the perpetrator inflicted. At bottom, this is the assumption that problems are solved by revenge.
- ‣ Paul's deepest theological insights offer no support to this story. They offer a very different, restorative account of problems and their resolution.
- ‣ Force, in the sense of coercive actions on someone's body, can still be necessary at times in a preventative role. (Think of parenting small children, who sometimes have to be physically restrained from getting into trouble.)
- ‣ This forceful activity should be strictly disciplined by self-control.
- ‣ It should also be gentle.
- ‣ The virtue of gentleness can be learned by taking good care of plants and animals. Responsible dog ownership is a school for the virtue of gentleness!
- ‣ Speech should be gentle. (Speech is a key dimension within all human relating.)
- ‣ This is profoundly countercultural advice, since the lower orders in Paul's day no doubt used strategies of resistance that involved mockery, parody, and more. The upper classes would have been shaped by harsh partisanship as well.
- ‣ Relationships are profoundly shaped by speech patterns, so Paul rightly insists on patterns that promote, as against erode, a loving relationality, principally as they are informed by the virtue of gentleness.
- ‣ Pursuing this habit of gentle speech is the more necessary because the followers of Jesus attest to his truth and his love by how they do things, as much as by what they assert and where they say that they are going. The means is the end.

Key Scriptural References

A peace wish opens and closes every Pauline letter, in association with the language of giving and benefaction (i.e., "grace," Gk. *charis*).

Reconciliation texts are also significant, for they possess an important countercultural dimension. In surrounding Greco-Roman culture, the offender would (possibly!) reach out to the offended party and make overtures, gifts, and other reparations. The onus was on the offender to initiate and to effect reconciliation, as seen in the Bible most clearly in the approach of Jacob to his offended brother Esau. Jacob has to make quite an effort! In the process Paul describes, however, *God*, the offend*ed* party, reaches out to the offender. This demonstrates his limitless love for us, but it also instructs us about the nature of reconciliation. It is not a contractual process demanding that conditions be met before reconciliation can be undertaken, although it is common for reparations to arise from the process later, if it is successful. It can, and perhaps should, be initiated by those who have been harmed. It is grounded in God's love and hence, at bottom, is unconditional. See Rom 5:10–11; 11:15 (1 Cor 7:11 is less relevant); 2 Cor 5:18–20.

Paul's relationship with Jerusalem is recounted especially in Gal 1:11–2:15 and Rom 15:23–32.

Second Corinthians 2 and 7 describe a restorative process.

Galatians 5:22–23 articulates further secondary virtues that can elaborate on the virtue of peace, most notably patience, kindness, fidelity, gentleness, and self-control.

Key Reading

The healing of conflict, which often involves the transcendence of shame, is introduced with particular wisdom and precision by Howard Zehr (who is widely known as the grandfather of restorative justice in the United States), in *The Little Book of Restorative Justice*; and by David Moore and John M. MacDonald in *Transforming Conflict*.

Jared Diamond provides a charming account of the roots of many restorative justice practices in small-scale ancient communities in "Peace and War," from *The World until Yesterday* (79–170).

The church has much to learn from circle processes, and especially from healing circles: see especially Kay Pranis's little primer, *The Little Book of Circle Processes: A New/Old Approach to Peacemaking*; and Rupert Ross's fascinating exposition, *Returning to the Teaching*.

Further Reading

Contrary to some presentations of his work, Barth spends a considerable amount of time on the church, usually in the final sections of his treatments of the three key aspects of reconciliation, but in many other places within the *Dogmatics*. Ecclesial peacemaking is not one of his key emphases, although *God's* making of peace with us certainly is.

A powerful account of the life and death of Martin Luther King is Stephen Oates's *Let the Trumpet Sound*.

Here also I presuppose the biography argued for in my *Framing*, as well as related, more technical essays.

Chris Marshall has written some especially germane and important studies linking processes of restorative justice with biblical and theological insights; see especially his *Beyond Retribution* and *Compassionate Justice*. His mentee, Thomas (Tom) Noakes-Duncan, has now also provided a seminal analysis, bridging biblical, theological, and practical restorative terrain; see his *Communities of Restoration*. See also my "Mass Incarceration: Pauline Problems and Pauline Solutions."

A useful place to begin when trying to understand Paul's countercultural development of the narrative of reconciliation is Jewett's analysis of Rom 5:10 in its broader context (*Romans*, 364–67). He points to studies by Martin and by Fitzgerald as well, which grasp especially clearly the key emphasis I am making here—that the offend*ed* party is the one reaching out and actively reconciling, not the offend*ing* party. (Jewett's magisterial commentary on Romans is also particularly attentive to shame dynamics, as my short review essay suggests.)

Shame is addressed by Donald L. Nathanson, *Shame and Pride: Affect, Sex, and the Birth of the Self*; and ultimately by Silvan Tomkins in his seminal *Affect Imagery Consciousness*. Incidentally, concise and accurate information can be found at www.tomkins.org, with a specific link provided to the connection between neuroscience and restorative justice. A jaunty but sadly inconsistent and somewhat unreliable introduction to Tomkins's thought and related issues is Malcolm Gladwell's *Blink: The Power of Thinking without Thinking*.

Further information on circle processes can be found in Kay Pranis, Barry Stuart, and Mark Wedge, *Peacemaking Circles: From Crime to Community*.

Information about the Truth and Reconciliation Commission in South Africa can be found in Tutu's readable history *No Future without Forgiveness*. Peter Storey's essay is also particularly interesting, containing profound theological insights, even while being composed in the middle of the process. Other relevant essays include studies by Jones, by Pisani and Kim, and by Gibson.

The monks of New Skete (found in upstate New York) have written a charming account of appropriate dog training, *The Art of Raising a Puppy*.

Bibliography

Barth, Karl. *Church Dogmatics*. IV/1; IV/2; IV/3.2.

Campbell, Douglas A. "The Issue of Shame in Robert Jewett's Commentary on Romans." Pages 255–66 in *From Rome to Beijing: Symposia on Robert Jewett's Commentary on Romans*. Edited by K. K. Yeo. Lincoln, NE: Prairie Muse, 2012.

———. "Mass Incarceration: Pauline Problems and Pauline Solutions." *Int* 72 (2018): 282–92.

Diamond, Jared. *The World until Yesterday: What Can We Learn from Traditional Societies?* New York: Penguin, 2012.

Fitzgerald, John T. *Cracks in an Earthen Vessel: An Examination of Catalogues of Hardship in the Corinthian Correspondence*. SBLDS 99. Atlanta: Scholars Press, 1988.

Gibson, James L. "On Legitimacy Theory and the Effectiveness of Truth Commissions." *Law and Contemporary Problems* 72 (Spring 2009): 123–41.

Gladwell, Malcolm. *Blink: The Power of Thinking without Thinking*. New York: Little, Brown, 2005.

Jewett, Robert, with Roy D. Kotansky. *Romans: A Commentary*. Hermeneia. Minneapolis: Fortress, 2007.

Jones, L. Gregory. "Truth and Consequences in South Africa." *Christianity Today* 43, no. 4 (1991): 59–63.

Marshall, Christopher. *Beyond Retribution: A New Testament Vision for Justice, Crime, and Punishment*. Grand Rapids: Eerdmans, 2001.

———. *Compassionate Justice: An Interdisciplinary Dialogue with Two Gospel Parables on Law, Crime, and Restorative Justice*. Eugene, OR: Cascade, 2012.

Martin, Ralph P. *Reconciliation: A Study of Paul's Theology*. Atlanta: John Knox, 1981.

Monks of New Skete. *The Art of Raising a Puppy*. Rev. ed. New York: Little, Brown, 2011.

Moore, David, and John M. McDonald. *Transforming Conflict in Workplaces and Other Communities*. Sydney: Transformative Justice Australia, 2000.

Nathanson, Donald L. *Shame and Pride: Affect, Sex, and the Birth of the Self*. New York: W. W. Norton, 1992.

Noakes-Duncan, Thomas. *Communities of Restoration: Ecclesial Ethics and Restorative Justice*. London: Bloomsbury, 2017.

Oates, Stephen B. *Let the Trumpet Sound: A Life of Martin Luther King, Jr.* New York: HarperCollins, 1982.

Pisani, Jacobus A. Du, and Kwang-Su Kim. "Establishing the Truth about the Apartheid Past: Historians and the South African Truth and Reconciliation Commission." *African Studies Quarterly* 8, no. 1 (2004): 77–95. http://www .africa.ufl.edu.proxy.lib.duke.edu/asq/.

Pranis, Kay. *The Little Book of Circle Processes: A New/Old Approach to Peacemaking.* Intercourse, PA: Good Books, 2005.

Pranis, Kay, Barry Stuart, and Mark Wedge. *Peacemaking Circles: From Crime to Community.* St. Paul: Living Justice Press, 2003.

Ross, Rupert. *Returning to the Teachings: Exploring Aboriginal Justice.* Rev. ed. Toronto: Penguin, 2006.

Scott, James C. *Domination and the Arts of Resistance: Hidden Transcripts.* New Haven: Yale University Press, 1990.

Storey, Peter. "A Different Kind of Justice: Truth and Reconciliation in South Africa." *Christian Century* 114, no. 25 (1997): 788–93.

Tomkins, Silvan S. *Affect Imagery Consciousness: The Complete Edition.* 4 vols. Philadelphia: Springer, 1962–92.

Tutu, Desmond Mpilo. *No Future without Forgiveness.* New York: Doubleday, 1999.

Zehr, Howard. *The Little Book of Restorative Justice.* Intercourse, PA: Good Books, 2002.

CHAPTER 15

Loving as Enjoying

Joy

We step now into the fourth major moment in Jesus's life, one that scholars often curiously neglect—his ascension. After the great act of giving that was his incarnation, his faithful and obedient walk to the cross, and the event of the cross itself followed by the resurrection, which effected the healing and reconciliation of the cosmos, we see Jesus lifted on high by the Spirit and enthroned at the right hand of his Father. We see a great moment of celebration and acclamation. He is feted as Lord and as the long-awaited Messiah, even as he cries out "Abba!" to his Father in recognition and appreciation. The moment is filled with joy, singing, and praise, and doubtless with the celestial equivalent of dancing. But as we know, God's gracious plan is for us all to enter into divine communion, which, thanks to the resurrection, we are entering into now, albeit partially. Hence, as we experience the resurrection in our lives, principally by way of our new minds of spirit, we taste the joy and celebration of Jesus's enthronement, and this is the state for which we were made and for which we are destined. And we learn from this foretaste that to experience loving relationality in all its fullness is to experience *joy*. So presumably we should allow some of this joy to overflow into our lives right here and now. God delights when we do so.

Paul was profoundly aware of the importance of joy. In Rom 15:13 he utters an important blessing:

May the God of hope
fill you with all joy and peace in your believing,
so that you go on to overflow with hope,
through the power of the Holy Spirit.

Paul speaks here of four relational gifts from the Spirit that he prays will overflow through his Roman audience. We have already discussed three of them: believing as implicit in the virtue of faithfulness, hope as a further element within faithfulness, and peace, especially in the sense of active peacemaking. All are appropriately grounded in Jesus. But we have not yet considered joy, and I am increasingly convinced that we ought to treat this as a key virtue in addition to the others, bringing it to the forefront of our journey in discipleship. It was, after all, the state in which Jesus finally arrived, there to remain in a certain sense forever.

It is interesting to note in this relation that in Eph 5:18 Paul instructs his listeners to avoid drunkenness and, instead, to be filled with the Spirit. He goes on to say that they should all speak and sing to one another.

> Do not get drunk on wine, which leads to debauchery.
> Instead, be filled with the Spirit,
> speaking to one another with psalms, hymns, and songs from the
> Spirit.
> Sing and make music from your heart to the Lord,
> always giving thanks to God the Father for everything,
> in the name of our Lord Jesus Christ. (5:18–20)

Similar instructions to avoid drunkenness and the ancient party culture of banqueting are given to other communities: to the Thessalonians (1 Thess 5:6–8) and, in a slightly different sense, to the Corinthians (1 Cor 6:10; 10:6–22; 11:21–22; see also Gal 5:19, 21).

These are actually instructions to avoid the ancient equivalent of substance abuse. This is bad in its own right, and bad things happen when it is indulged in. I am particularly struck here, however, by the juxtaposition in the Ephesian text between the avoidance of partying and substance abuse and the legitimate intoxication with the Spirit that issues in community speech and music. This sort of exuberant celebration is evident in other Pauline communities, although most notably at Corinth, where its enthusiasm has spilled over into disruption and disrespect. But Paul merely tempers this situation in his response; he does not preclude it. Although the word is not used, Paul is speaking here of joy—of rejoicing and celebrating.

An important lesson is detectable within these brief instructions.

Our modern society is awash with substance abuse. The epidemic of deaths from heroin addiction that is now sweeping poor rural areas in the United States is currently starting to break into the national news. Over 33,000 people are now dying from overdoses a year—more than from traffic accidents or from gun deaths. And this is just one glimpse into the practices of a broader culture that consumes mind-altering substances at a truly staggering rate—while it is also a glimpse into the wisdom of attending to sin's consequences. Substances like heroin promise a lot and then tend to deliver untold damage that is not mentioned in the advertising. (The most destructive force in the Western world currently, in medical terms, remains alcohol.)

Paul declares, quite accurately, that this dependence upon substances is unwise and ultimately destructive. But he also offers an antidote, *which is an even more intoxicating experience of the Spirit*, issuing in turn in singing and praising. Paul does not merely utter a prohibition here, which is critical. He is not just saying "no" to drugs, which would almost certainly prove largely ineffective (see Rom 7:7–25!). He is offering a positive alternative, which is the rich emotional "high" that comes from praising God in the fullness of the Spirit. And again this Pauline alternative is deeply challenging.

Is our experience of communal praise so intoxicating that it can displace the substances and partying of the secular world that surround us? The competition here is pretty fierce. The pagans I am acquainted with really know how to party. But Paul's communities were meant to be able to match this exuberance and then some. Moreover, they offered a healthy high.

I suggest that we learn how to party as well as or better than the pagans. The creativity and exuberance of the Spirit is waiting for us to shed our inhibitions and to rejoice in the presence of the Lord in a way that will astonish even the most hardened regular at the Ministry of Sound or its US equivalent. Moreover, this is a *practice*. So we need to classify it as a virtue that we then pursue and learn about. Emotions are involved, as always; no human activity takes place without the activation of affects, and joy is one of them. But it is more than mere affect. It is part of a script, Tomkins would say; so it is something that we both experience and learn to do. So Jesus rejoiced, as did Paul. But we seldom associate their abandoned joy in the presence of God with our church meetings, which is a sad loss. As Paul says repeatedly through Philippians,

Rejoice in the Lord always. I will say it again: Rejoice! (4:4)[1]

But there is another aspect to joy that is worth quickly noting here. Thinking about joy encourages us to think about fun and, in the same breath, to think about play. The connection joy-enjoyment, which is a deeply positive

---

1. See also Phil 1:4, 18, 25; 2:2, 17, 18, 29; 3:1; and 4:10—in all, thirteen instances of "joy" and "rejoice."

affective spectrum, can be experienced after the cessation of a negative affect like anxiety. For sustained health, however, joy really needs to follow the other positive affect, which is interest, a spectrum that shades into excitement. Enjoyment and joy cannot exist by themselves indefinitely. They are principally a signal of relief—possibly immense—from some other pressing concern, so in order to be experienced fully and repeatedly, they need to alternate with other affective states. And the only positive affective concern is generated by the pressure of interest and excitement. After episodes of interest, joy can intervene, with its relief, its upwardly crinkled, slightly closed eyes, and its smiling face. But it must be both preceded and succeeded in turn by the slightly furrowed brow and attentive stare of excited interest. This connection—this script—that sequences interest and joy, shading at times into the more intense oscillation of excitement and rejoicing, is arguably best captured by the phenomenon of *play*, which might be more understandable if we also refer to it by its adult name, "hobbies."

We already know that play lies at the center of God's plan for the cosmos. That plan is ultimately for the divine communion to embrace humankind and to share its overflowing love so that at the center of all of reality—of time and space—is an unending experience of joy and delight, coupled with excitement in the company of one another. And this reality seems present in our most playful moments. Those who learn to play and to play well tend to be joyful; those who don't or won't tend not to be. But they are joyful because they are *enjoying* something, which means that they are actually excited about it and interested in it. Play suggests that we do something for its own sake, because it is interesting in and of itself—because it is "fun," we usually say—and this experience generates enjoyment when our period of interest pauses.

I dabble in chess because I find it fascinating in and of itself. Its tactical puzzles, its history, the brilliance of its outstanding players, its complexity, and its elegance interest me ever more deeply. I stand over my board fiddling with openings for hours with my brow furrowed with concentration, which is to say, with interest, and even with excitement as I stumble upon a particularly wicked new variation. I then usually finish my time and relax and sink into the feeling of relief and rest, and I smile. I experience joy (if, that is, I am not trying to move on from the experience of shame if I have just been soundly outmaneuvered!). Play then doubles its value if we play together, in projects of mutual interest—in hobbies, games, and other pastimes—or even as projects of interest to one another.

At the heart of God's plan for the cosmos is play, and play together; and it follows that Paul's communities need to play. And if they can't, they need to learn to do so. Without this activity, there is nothing positive to summon people to join! We are calling people to respond to the presence of the divine communion because it is, in and of itself, the most important and special thing in existence. And it should follow that it is enjoyable. It is something fun. We will find humor and laughter—a great, healthy, overwhelming party. We will be splashing around together in a pool, as I have heard some people describe it, and this is all about play and the joy that goes with it. So we need to model this, and to do so authentically. It will speak like nothing else of the reality that we claim we are being drawn into.

I suspect Paul's converts knew how to have fun, just as he did, along with Jesus himself. We will see later that we can detect a joke in Phlm 11, while I certainly detect a wealth of sly humor in Romans.[2] So, somewhat paradoxically, we should work on having fun. Those gifted with playfulness often get treated like naughty children, when they are actually the life of the party; they are gifts to teach the rest of us to lighten up a little. We need to learn from those who know how to play and how to rejoice, which should inject a hearty dose of fun into our learning.[3] But this line of thought leads us to a closely related practice.

A key aspect of celebration together also seems to be the unleashing of the creative gifts of all of the community's members. Paul speaks of an intriguing practice in his communities; everyone was supposed to bring along contributions to worship, which he defines primarily in terms of different types of songs. This is incredibly interesting. All the community members were apparently composing their own songs, which they would bring to the worship gathering and which would presumably be learned and sung. And this practice speaks of a joy and sense of celebration so palpable that it issued forth in the composition of praise songs during the day. It also suggests a radical democratization of the process, so that everyone had their contributions to the worship gathering included. (Moreover, they were not to dominate one another, speaking on top of one another.) Arguably we can even detect some of Paul's songs that he has woven into his letters, and we can see that they are deeply thoughtful and profound compositions useful not just for praising and celebrating but for teaching and exhorting.[4] Indeed, we have been using

---

2. The voice of the Teacher in Rom 1:18–32 and 13:1–7 is delightfully pompous.

3. Humor is also an important and deeply healthy response to shame; see Donald Nathanson's *Shame and Pride*.

4. Common suggestions here include Rom 1:3–4; 3:24/25–26; Eph 1:3–14; and Col 1:15–20.

what was almost certainly one such song extensively here—Phil 2:6–11. All this seems to be summarized by Paul in Col 3:16:[5]

> Let the speech that comes from Christ
> dwell in you richly,
> with all wisdom,
> as you teach and exhort one another,
> with psalms, hymns, and other spiritual songs,
> by means of this gift,
> while you sing from your hearts to God.

It seems, then, that these songs were diverse in form and function. They praised God the Father, spoke of important theological truths, gave thanks, especially for the work of Jesus, and articulated his life and its implications. Paul's thanksgivings, which begin every letter except for Galatians, should be folded into this dimension of church life as well,[6] along with his prayers. These thanksgivings celebrate and rejoice, often doing so by articulating gratitude in highly specific terms for the converts with whom he is involved—and many of whom are clearly not model converts!

It is both exciting and slightly worrying to think of our gatherings working in this way today. Presumably the quality of the praise contributions would vary, and in a certain sense, that is just the point. It doesn't matter. A certain intensity of commitment seems to underlie this practice, and perhaps rather more than we currently experience. But there is something charming about the thought that we might all be able to bring our creative talents to bear on contributions to our gatherings, and we do not need to contribute just by way of songs. As Paul notes in 1 Cor 14:26, members could bring a number of different words to worship, whether a teaching, a revelation, glossolalia, an interpretation, or a crafted act of thanksgiving, blessing, or prayer, which is not

---

5. I am grateful to Amy Whisenand for bringing this text and its communal implications to my attention.

6. See Rom 1:8–12; 1 Cor 1:4–9; Phil 1:3–11; Col 1:3–12; 1 Thess 1:2–10; 2 Thess 1:3–12; Phlm 4–7. Second Corinthians is unusual, segueing out of a blessing into a communal act of thanksgiving; see 1:3–11, but a positive opening paragraph of praise and gratitude is certainly present. Ephesians postpones its thanksgiving until after its exuberant opening blessing; see 1:15–23. And 1 Thessalonians, it should be noted, returns to thanksgiving two times in the body of the letter; see 2:13 and 3:9. Alternatively, Paul structures the first three chapters of the letter in terms of thanksgiving.

to exclude contributions in the moment. Many now would add the importance of art and dance. And I would add only that these, and any other creative activities not mentioned here, ought to spring from the joyfulness, celebration, and sheer playfulness of being lifted into the presence of God. To commune with God is a great gift and is, at bottom, sheer joy. And we should probably let this reality overflow into our lives a little more dramatically than it sometimes currently does. We should give ourselves permission to be caught up into the wild, inexpressible, and rapturous delight of communing with God the Father, God the Son, and God the Holy Spirit.[7] And this openness also means being alert to the ways in which our joy can be *stolen*.

Joy-Stealers

In a classic analysis written in 1985, Neil Postman argued that the modern media are effectively in a bargain with the devil (my words, not his).[8] They engage their consumers emotionally with stories that people far away are experiencing. This engagement has an addictive dimension that has only increased since 1985; modern media are deeply absorbing. Yet, by virtue of their technology—the importation of information from locations vast distances away—their consumers have absolutely no power or leverage in relation to the situations being reported. Information is simply received, complete with emotional orchestration, in relation to people and events and situations *on the other side of the planet*. And the result is a steady emotional diet of helplessness. Media consumers are drawn into stories and people that they have no relationship with at all. And yet they go on to judge, to resonate with, and to devote a great deal of mental time and energy to *an utterly artificial situation*. Many engaged readers (or hearers) of media might, for example, be giving a lot of attention at the time I am writing this to a nasty, long-lived conflict in Syria—to the atrocities, the factions, the outside influences, and so on. Yet few of those readers work in international peacekeeping organizations or are high up in state systems, where they might actually have a degree of involvement and leverage in that situation. So what exactly is the point of feeding us all

7. Adapted from a bon mot that, I am told, originally applied to drinking at somebody else's expense. G. K. Chesterton's wonderful aphorism has already been noted in ch. 4: "The true object of all human life is play."

8. Neil Postman, *Amusing Ourselves to Death: Public Discourse in the Age of Show Business*.

this information?[9] Slightly closer to home: at the time of writing, much of the US electorate is probably weighing its options in relation to an important midterm election. Citizens like me are deciding, first, whether to vote and, second, whom to vote for. Speaking with complete rationality, it is clear that I will need about ten minutes to vote at the booth erected conveniently on my campus, and I will need about ten seconds to decide which ticket to vote—although that is because of all the prior research I have done, having spent hours every week for the last two years poring over reports, satires, and polls and discussing the situation vigorously with anyone who will listen to me. In fact, it would have been more efficient for me to have researched the performance of the current administration just prior to voting, and I estimate that this might have taken two hours. All the rest of my engaged activity—with all its harrowing emotional registers—has really been a complete waste of time ginned up by the modern media, just as Postman observes. And has it ever made me miserable!

If I am paradigmatic of many, and if our frequently pointless involvement in media is granted, we need note now only that this involvement *steals our joy* (even as it models partisan patterns of behavior for us that are profoundly unlike Jesus). Most of the stories that the media serve up for us are stories of pain. Few things engage media consumers like narratives of people who are struggling with tragic circumstances—an argument in terms of *pathos*, Aristotle would slyly note. And alongside the viewing of horrible tragedy is a daily presentation of awful behavior by leaders that really serves only to make us angry. We willingly consume a daily diet of grief and anger—a toxic emotional state, as Tomkins would remind us. And while we stew, we lose our joy. The weight of the world is too heavy for levity. Too many people are suffering, and too many leaders are corrupt and bullying—failing to heed our wise counsel that we offer from our breakfast tables. Too much is going wrong. What a catastrophe—for our lives of discipleship!

We badly need to identify the traps we have fallen into—the bait we have taken—that lure us essentially pointlessly into mental spaces where joy is choked out and stifled, traps such as an overconsumption of modern media. And we need to identify church teaching, and even church leaders, who major on pain. Of course, pain should not ever be overlooked, but Jesus did heal lepers who were standing in front of him. He could talk to them (which is

9. Someone might respond that prayer and charitable giving could flow in response. I agree completely. But how much of our news consumption results in prayer and/or in giving? Provided that it does, read away!

perhaps a useful test for the measure of our involvement: can we talk to the problem we are thinking about trying to solve? If we can't, then what are we doing?!). Pain is not God's first word to us or our destiny. Joy is. And a world of pain needs, above all, to be reminded that joy still exists and that joy will eventually triumph. We must identify joy-stealing, along with its apostles, and eschew them!

And with this last concern named, my basic enumeration of the key virtues in Paul's communities is complete—the four frequently quite gritty ways in which love is expressed in specific circumstances as we follow in the footsteps of Jesus as Paul both described and experienced him. But before moving on to the next major phase in our discussion, we ought to pause to consider the deceptive robustness of this Pauline account of church ethics. That is, as I endlessly extol the goodness and the love of the God who lies at the heart of Paul's thought, some of my students invariably voice concerns, apparently fearing an ethical collapse—and Paul apparently faced this question repeatedly in his own lifetime as well (which I take to be a good sign). "Why should we not sin?" his interlocutor asks understandably, if a little truculently, in Rom 6:1. An anxiety that all this is dangerously libertine is surfacing here—and libertinism is not a good thing. My students want something stronger and harder to enforce ethical behavior when my sentimental appeals to love prove too weak to make people act properly. Ethics needs an edge, we might say, if it is to work. But when they make this challenge, my protesting students are risking falling into the trap of what we will call *extrinsic ethics*. This is so pervasive and important that we must spend a bit of time addressing it, along with the right, *intrinsic* approach to our behavior.

Extrinsic and Intrinsic Ethics

Sometimes we care about ethics so much that we oversupply reasons for good versus bad behavior and thereby end up—rather ironically—unleashing further unethical behavior. As we pile on the pressure, we provide reasons for acting in a good fashion that are *external* to its goodness (goodness being rooted in the good God). Similarly, we provide reasons for avoiding bad behavior that are *external* to the behavior's actual evil. And these considerations *are themselves evil*; they *undermine* a good approach to good behavior! This might sound a little abstract, so let me clarify that I am really just talking about appeals to future rewards and punishments as primary motivators for good behavior.

We often speak of acting in the right way and ultimately getting a reward for doing so. In particular, we hope one day to go to heaven. And we should avoid bad behavior because we might well be sentenced to death on the day of judgment. "Do the smart thing, then, and avoid hell and get to heaven. Act rightly!" But this is all a nasty trap. We have been lured here onto treacherous ethical ground by embracing *external*, or *extrinsic*, rewards for doing the right thing.

Think carefully about what we are saying when we urge someone to be good so that he or she can get to heaven. *Why* exactly is this person going to be good? If it is because he or she hopes to get some future reward, then it is a selfish decision that now has nothing to do with the goodness of the behavior in question or the God doing the asking. It is purely self-interested. (It is also overly rationalistic, but we won't worry about this problem for the moment.) If I behave well in the expectation of a reward, then my behavior has nothing to do with the goodness of the action in question or the person asking me to act well. Similarly, if I behave well only to avoid a negative outcome, I am not behaving well because that activity is good and the avoided activity is evil, or because I care about it particularly. I am just trying to save my own skin.

Imagine I am heading off to a conference in Amsterdam, famous for its fleshpots (which in fact, as I write this, I am; a New Testament conference is about to be held there). I am a happily married man, and a faithful one. But why should I remain faithful in Amsterdam, while my wife waits patiently and innocently for me back in North Carolina? For extrinsic reasons or for intrinsic reasons?[10]

Thinking extrinsically, I might reason that I must not indulge myself in the fabled fleshpots because I could lose the reward eventually of heaven and might get sent to hell. Moreover, I might suffer some practical, this-worldly losses as well. My wife might find out and would probably divorce me. I would have to pay her a great deal of alimony. And I would be lonely once I got back to North Carolina. I might reason, however, that there is not much likelihood of her finding out and that I could take the risk—many presumably do. I would just have to lie about it all when I got back to the United States. However, I might then think the risk is too great. How would I disguise the costs on my credit card or my large withdrawals of cash? So I refrain from visiting a brothel and come home ethically triumphant.

My wife meets me at the plane and says, "Did you indulge yourself, dear?" And I reply, "No, I thought the risk of you finding out if I did so was too great,

10. Alan J. Torrance is the master at deploying this (fictional!) illustration.

and the potential financial inconvenience if I was discovered would be too high." I might then add, if I was being completely honest, "Those risks apart, of course, I would have"—at which point, any right-thinking wife would divorce me in any case! Clearly, I haven't really done the right thing here, even though I behaved technically in the right manner. My extrinsic motivations undercut my action's goodness. But how might I approach this situation intrinsically?

As I sit on the plane and contemplate the fleshpots of Amsterdam, I think to myself, "If I indulge myself with one of these women, I betray my wife, whom I love dearly. I inflict awful hurt on her and damage my covenant with her deeply and possibly fatally—and much of this irrespective of whether she ever finds out. I love her and want to be faithful to her, and so will skirt these fleshpots like the plague, since that's what they are." And it is the same with God.

We do not behave in the right way because we covet or fear the final consequences. To behave in this way is a betrayal of our relationship with God. Reasoning in this fashion, *we don't care about God*, and we don't care about the good either. We are behaving fundamentally selfishly—and so if we behave correctly for this reason, we still in fact sin! We should behave in the right way, rather, because we love God and want to do what pleases him. And he has shown us what the good thing to do is, and so we want to do the good thing because it is good. Church ethics is *intrinsic* because it flows from personal relationships and is internal to them. And we must hang on to this kind of ethics, the protests of earnest extrinsic ethicists notwithstanding.

Once we have grasped this point—essentially, that we obey God because we love God and for no other reason—we can nevertheless supply a strong secondary consideration for good behavior that arises from within this appropriate relational matrix.

Evil as Negation

We have spent a lot of time up to this moment exploring the learning that the followers of Jesus undertake, and in largely positive terms. We are supposed to grow in certain key virtues. In all of this we are pressing more deeply into the good. As we are folded more and more deeply into the divine reality and as that reality pervades our thinking—as we are infused with goodness from Jesus and the Spirit mediated through our leaders and mentors, and simply through those good messianic Jews and/or Christians around us—we grasp more and more clearly what goodness is. It is relational and personal, loving and covenantal, and virtuous and life-giving. And in the light of this growing appreciation of our good God, we see more clearly what evil is as well, and we need to grasp this phenomenon too, insofar as it can be grasped.

Evil, it turns out, is basically *negation*. As Augustine saw with great lucidity (although he was not the only one), evil is fundamentally parasitic. It does not really exist in its own right. It exists only by destroying that which already exists, all of which is created by God and is good. Evil attacks good things, bending and distorting and eroding them. We see an example of the actions of evil in Paul's thinking as he recounts how the tenth commandment—"Do not covet!"—good in and of itself, provides an opportunity for sin to seduce and to enslave someone attempting to obey it (Rom 7:7–25). Evil twists something here that is good into something that damages. But Paul takes pains to point out that without the good, it cannot function at all. However, we can also infer the presence of this lesson in Paul's repentance of his violent persecution of the church prior to his calling. That deeply vicious activity was undoubtedly underpinned by good scriptural texts that the forces of evil preyed on and manipulated. Things that were good here again—devotion to God, preparedness to die for him, and a great love of the land, the temple, and the Scriptures— were twisted and distorted into an evil activity. Moreover, it just seems to be an obvious inference that if reality is fundamentally personal, relational, and covenantal, evil is at bottom an ongoing attack on persons, relationships, and covenants. It breaks down people, frays relationships, and undermines covenants. So Paul, as Saul, was deceived into attacking the early church. But there is something ethically useful going on in this somewhat depressing realization.

We can see now, in the light of all this, that the reality we inhabit is constructed "consequentially," using this last word in a very particular sense.[11] When we sin, we turn away from goodness and relationality and life. We turn to damage and distortion and negation. But we can now grasp that these apparently distinct phenomena are actually the same thing. To sin *is* to damage and distort and negate in some way, parasitically breaking some part of God's good reality. When we sin, we are inflicting damage. We are destroying something and someone. We are twisting and scorching our relationships, which is to twist and scorch what we are as well. When we sin, we are effectively sticking our leg into the grate in front of us, where a log fire is happily burning and crackling. We are destroying our leg and damaging our bodies by doing this. Just so, sin is *relational damage*. It is, in and of itself, distortion and destruction, and hence it is ultimately painful. This is what it "is," which I place in

---

11. That is, *not* in terms of the ethical school and philosophical system dubbed consequentialism.

quotes because it isn't really anything in a positive sense. It is the destruction of something else, and so the absence of goodness.[12]

The important point for us to grasp here in all this conceptual slipperiness is that we can learn from evil and make further progress in virtue, albeit painfully, because of the painful consequences of evil.

We should behave in a good way fundamentally because we want to please our good God. Our motivations are positive and flow from our relationships, which are loving and responsive. And we learn as we grow in these relationships what things are good, and that we should do good things because they are good. But we can now add the further motive that not to behave in a good way, destroying the fabric of our creation at some point and our healthy relationality, will be fundamentally stupid and self-destructive, not to mention, painful. It will be to walk willingly into self-inflicted pain! We will be sticking our feet into a fire, and that's just not smart.[13] Moreover, because we are constituted as persons intersubjectively, by our relationships, to damage those relationships is automatically to damage others, even as we damage ourselves. So self-interest and mutual loving interest now coincide. We learn, in short, that sin is *intrinsically* sinful. It is awful *in its own right*. We should not sin, then, not just because we want to walk obediently in relation to God, *but because every time we do sin we are damaging or hurting people, including ourselves.* Sin is damage, and damage hurts. This is an important additional reason why sin should be avoided so urgently.

We can now begin to push past the deceptions and seductions of sin—its false forecasts about the happiness that awaits us if we take its deceptively easy steps. Sin promises much that it generally fails to deliver, but it delivers things we would avoid if we saw them coming. Satan, we might say, is the prince of false advertising. Sin traffics in lies. However, as we grasp the consequences

12. Later, when discussing creation, we will connect this account with a cosmic account of evil, drawing on the narrative of chaos that is found in the Jewish Scriptures; see ch. 24, "Rethinking Creation."

13. I would contend that self-interest is not operating here in quite the same way that I argued it is, unacceptably, within an extrinsic ethics. When we damage ourselves, we damage our relational networks and thereby damage others around us, and cognizance of this, and a wish to avoid it, is not deleteriously or unacceptably self-interested. It is not self*ish*. Moreover, we can rely on a certain account of creation here. God has constructed things so that joy and happiness and rightness *correlate*. So persistent emotional dysregulation is a signal that something is wrong. The self and its concerns are not placed at the center of ethics, as they are in any fundamentally extrinsic approach. But they are in play, in the right place, as they need to be.

of sin increasingly clearly, we gain a better grip on what sin really is—on its truth—and learn not to be ensnared by its false promises. We turn from the ways that the Bible links to being a fool and instead grow in *wisdom*. And in doing so, we also inhabit more deeply a tradition. Followers of Jesus who have lived before us—and lived for longer than us[14]—have gathered a great deal of information about the consequences of sinful patterns of behavior that we would be fools to ignore. This secondary, complementary education of converts in terms of consequences is an important part of our pedagogy. None of this learning comes naturally!

And with these important final insights into a Pauline ethic in place, we need to turn at the end to consider one last practical question, which arises now in relation to how we most effectively learn all this.

The Intensity of Community

We grasped earlier on that our leaders in particular are supposed to model the key virtues that shape the community. It is important to add immediately that leaders are not the origin of these practices; they originate in God. However, leaders mediate the virtues to the community in an embodied way, reflecting, with the Spirit's all-important help, the incarnation of the Son and the subsequent life of Jesus. But the comprehensiveness of these practices, as well as their infusion into daily life, prompts us to consider now whether Paul's communities might not have been rather more tightly knit together than our modern church communities are with their characteristic Sunday rhythms, thereby summoning us to a deeper intensity of life together. The Thessalonians, for example, ate together every day.[15]

14. Daniel Gilbert points out that the human mind is poorly constructed to project into the future with much accuracy, extrapolating from the present, including especially from its emotional tenor. These aspects of our thought make our predications about our future lives almost certainly wrong. (Gilbert is especially concerned with predications about what will make us happy in the the future.) A far surer guide to the future situations in our lives is *to consult with those who are older than us.* See his *Stumbling on Happiness.*

15. It is more difficult to determine whether the entire Corinthian church did as well, but I am not convinced that it didn't; certainly I cannot detect probative evidence suggesting only a weekly gathering. See Rom 16:23; 1 Cor 11:18–34.

As we know, our communities are supposed to be communities of learning. Our members are supposed to grow in virtue, largely by copying one another. So we need to ask, Are our communities "intense" enough to achieve the movement forward in virtue, along with any necessary corresponding abandonment of sin, that they need to? If not, then they probably need to become more intense in the sense of being tighter and more closely knit together. (The sociologists call this [re]socialization, and they call intense organizations that ask a lot of their members "greedy" organizations.) The bigger the problems, the higher the intensity needs to be so that the learning of new relational patterns can take place, face-to-face.

Think for a moment of some of the key communal practices that we have just enumerated. Jesus followers are supposed to exercise gentleness and self-control in relation to bodily force. They are supposed to exercise the same in speaking. They are to act with scrupulous fidelity in sexual activity, avoiding promiscuity or any hint of adultery (an area of ethics we will discuss in more detail later). But any progress forward in these practices, especially for some, cannot realistically take place without constant involvement within a community, and without a dedicated, present leadership. The possibility of imitation will need to be constant. Without this, the virtues simply will not be learned. They might be preached, but they won't be practiced. They are learned, after all, *by being copied*. We might hear about their importance, then, for a limited period of time for part of one day a week, and be shown where to read about them in the Bible, but they really need to extend, in a personal way, through the entire seven-day cycle that people inhabit. And large problems require very tight, intense community if they are to be displaced by the right relational practices.

I know someone well, a woman now in her thirties, who has had a long struggle with addiction. She has been particularly fond of "ice," that is, methamphetamine, which is widely available, since it can be made with easily accessible chemicals. Her addiction has been so severe that it has threatened her life on several occasions. No lecturing, repentance, anxiety, illegality, or bankruptcy enabled her to break free. However, at rock bottom—as is often the case—she entered a Fundamentalist rehab organization that enforced what amounted to a Benedictine Rule on its members, coupled with a certain amount of group therapy. The members lived in a compound. The discipline was firm and consistent. Clothing was modest, basic, and closely monitored. Makeup was forbidden. Viewing of TV was tightly controlled, as was internet access. Major infractions resulted in expulsion. Minor infractions resulted in long cleaning details, and everyone had to learn to clean everything anyway (so, as I said, Benedictine).

As a result of all these practices, the participants learned to clean, to observe a regular timetable, and to be honest. (They learned many other things as well.) Two years later she graduated from the program, clean, enthused, and dedicated. In fact, she now works in it as a leader. Her life has been transformed.[16]

This is a story of Christian transformation, but it is also a story of Christian resocialization within an intense, "greedy" communality. Its intensity mirrored the extent to which its members needed to be reshaped constantly and vigilantly by one another, and particularly by leaders. And I suspect that the faithful adoption of many of Paul's key practices in the midst of what is really our modern pagan society might well require the same.

Paul expects his converts to abandon substance abuse. He expects them to learn to speak in a certain way. He expects them to abandon violence and to embrace peacemaking. He expects strict sexual self-control and fidelity. But how can converts learn to consistently act in these ways without being significantly reprogrammed by a tight community of virtue? These practices are dramatically countercultural, and perhaps increasingly so. But do our churches offer their struggling members this sort of pedagogy, and this sort of haven, away from the things that tempt and enslave them?

However, I am not suggesting that the way forward for all modern Pauline communities is effectively monastic, although interesting new examples of monasticism are currently flourishing, and there is much to learn from them.[17] Paul advocated a dynamic and flexible ethic (which will be even more apparent in part 4). But I *am* suggesting that our communities should possess this dense communal association at times and in certain places *to the degree that it needs to for its members to be schooled effectively in the ways of Jesus.* In short, Jesus's followers live in community, and that community needs to be tight and intense enough to reshape them—if necessary, dramatically. We need to be close enough together to learn from one another the practices of giving, being faithful, peacemaking, and delighting. But it is also critical to map these communities correctly in mental terms. This is a practice, when it is needed, and not a law.

16. http://www.abc.net.au/news/2015-06-16/former-ice-addict-dedicates-life-to -helping-others-beat-drugs/6548594. This is not to suggest that life for this woman is now perfect and without ongoing challenges.

17. The movement is known as new monasticism.

The Rhythm of Community

To pick up an earlier thread of discussion here from part 1: when my students diagram the community that is the church in relation to the world on the seminar room's whiteboard, they tend to reproduce the Western spatial categories that they also use to diagram a person. The community is a circle within a larger circle that is the world, and the boundary between the two spaces is strong. Now there is some value approaching things in this way. Moreover, we can be further encouraged to think in this fashion by the realization that our communities are supposed to resocialize their members, at times quite intensely, as we have just learned. It is easy to think in these terms of modern Christians or messianic Jews drawing together into an in-group and drawing apart from the distorting practices that surround them, from which they are protected by some sort of wall or boundary. But this conceptualization also risks major distortions. In the first instance, it simply isn't true.

People are fundamentally relational, and so groups are really *networks*. See, for example, the map of human relationships at Framingham, Massachusetts, based on the data of a famous longitudinal study that we have already referred to.[18]

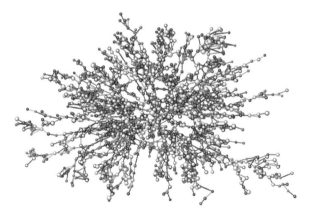

Church community is simply not a bounded space like a circle. It is a spider's web of relationships spreading out in all directions—a complex molecule of relations, polarizations, and orbits. People attending a Sunday service will often have many key relationships with people who don't, so there is no clearly demarcated border or boundary between attenders and nonattenders.

18. http://www.ssc.wisc.edu/cde/images/framingham_christakis.jpg.

We could insert a boundary in these terms, but we would thereby be artificially overlooking a hundred and one important connections. And as we rethink community in terms of a network, we need to appreciate that the spiderweb of relationships that is human community shifts over time. People flow in and out of their key relationships during the course of days, weeks, and years. For all sorts of reasons, the intensity of relationships waxes and wanes. So mapping a community in terms of its networks of relationships looks more like a fractal playing across a computer screen. It moves, growing and contracting in different directions. (A more complete model of the Framingham community over time contains several rather different maps.) And we learn something important from all this. The network that is the church community really has a temporal *rhythm*, and we can detect certain regular and very basic pulses or beats in its movement that help us to articulate a constructive solution to the need for intensity or proximity and any attendant communal resocialization.[19]

Sometimes the fractal network concentrates on itself and gathers together. In our day these are frequently meetings, and after these events, our fractal spreads out again into its primary locations and networks—homes and places of work and play. But we have just been thinking, does the pulse that is our gathering need to be more frequent, and perhaps daily as against weekly? Certainly the indrawing pulse of the network was quicker in Paul's day. But we have also seen that a simple test lies to hand for testing our network's health. Is the heartbeat of closer communality needed for Christians to conform more closely to virtue, and especially to the virtuous relationality being modeled by their leaders? Our network should pulse with the beat it needs for it to grow and to advance in virtue. The surrounding, less virtuous relationships of pagans—and of any partly pagan Christians—are constantly influencing the Christian and messianic nodes and hubs and clusters, and so the key question is always, *who is influencing whom?* If Christians, along with their messianic counterparts, are fading into the ways of the world, then they need to gather with one another more intensely and to copy one another more faithfully. The

19. I am not using the metaphor of a beat or rhythm here in the way it is sometimes used to connect worship services with action and service "out in the world." I am not denying the validity of that usage (although I am implicitly mitigating it), but I am applying the metaphor to something rather different here, namely, the question of resocialization in the virtues. On the alternative usage, see, among others, Miroslav Volf, "Worship as Adoration and Action: Reflections on a Christian Way of Being-in-the-World," in *Worship at the Next Level: Insight from Contemporary Voices*, ed. Tim A. Dearborn and Scott Coil (Grand Rapids: Baker Books, 2004), 30–41.

rhythm of gathering needs to quicken. But another critical dimension to the pulse of this network is detectable at this moment.

There is always an ongoing dynamic interaction with parts of the network that are not yet folded into the church's rhythm of gathering and clustering. The church network pulses outward and spreads, even as it gathers rhythmically inward. It is as if our fractal is always seeking to draw the rest of the network with which it is connected into its rhythm beat by beat, pulse by pulse. Moreover, this outward movement and connection is clearly an integral aspect of the network that is authentic community. A network of Jesus followers is an emphatically open network, so this critical dimension to our relating and community that was so central to Paul's life now needs to be addressed. Properly pursued, it can bring much joy; improperly pursued, it can bring much pain and damage.

Theses

> - A fourth critical moment in Jesus's life that we now share is joy—the joy, delight, play, and sheer fun, of sharing in the divine communion and, in particular, in his enthronement and acclamation.
> - Paul counsels his converts to avoid substance abuse, which in the ancient world meant alcohol and drunkenness.
> - He does so in part, however, by affirming the greater and far healthier "high" that is joy in the Spirit, involving singing and dancing.
> - Substance abuse should not, then, simply be avoided but should be displaced, which constitutes a challenge to much current church practice.
> - The virtue of joy also connects with the practice of play, which is at the center of God's plan for the cosmos.
> - Divine and human communion presupposes the enjoyment of one another, necessarily at times at least in playful terms that involve humor and fun.
> - Communal life and learning together should be joyful as well—both exuberant and exciting, playful and fun, and filled with laughter.
> - The enjoyment of the divine communion should elicit creative contributions (such as new songs) from everyone to worship gatherings.
> - Paul himself exemplified this creativity with his composition of songs, some of which arguably appear in his letters. They are profound compositions with important didactic implications as well. See especially Phil 2:6–11 and Col 3:16.

‣ We can also learn from Paul's composition of thanksgiving paragraphs, of blessings, and of prayers. Joy, thanksgiving, and blessing are closely related.

‣ In complement to pursuing the practices of joy—of delight, play, and fun—we ought to identify and to avoid "joy-stealers."

‣ A depressingly relevant example of joy-stealing is the modern media—a commodity that, after consumption, elicits engaged negative emotion with no practical engagement. A better recipe for stealing joy is hard to imagine.

‣ Followers of Jesus ought to think carefully about the mode of their media consumption, and the amount. Media fasts might even be useful (which, admittedly, and despite the best of intentions, I have never managed to sustain myself).

‣ We should avoid a deceptively destructive extrinsic approach to ethics, according to which good behavior is encouraged by way of external rewards and punishments.

‣ The appropriate motivation for all our progress in virtue and relationality is intrinsic, and it is loving. We want to obey God because we love God.

‣ An extrinsic approach to ethics is actually self-centered and fails to encourage a recognition of the evil of sin in and of itself.

‣ It is also ineffective because it works only if the threat of exposure is real. And it fails to encourage an appropriately relational approach to ethical behavior that issues in constraints, irrespective of surveillance.

‣ As we press into the good more deeply, through communal learning and formation, we also learn about evil.

‣ Following Augustine and those who think like him (i.e., Barth), evil is negation. It exists only parasitically, destroying God's good creation, and hence does not really "exist" at all.

‣ This characterization of evil leads to a recognition of the phenomenon of consequences. Sin has consequences that are intrinsically destructive and painful. (This is not philosophical consequentialism.)

‣ We are motivated to behave well, secondarily, to avoid the painful consequences of sin and to advocate the same. (We behave well primarily to please the God whom we love and who loves us.)

‣ We also learn that sin is intrinsically evil; it is best avoided because of what it is and does to our loving relationality.

‣ This understanding helps us to penetrate past the deceptive side to sin—its false advertising—to what it really is and does, and thereby to avoid it and to counsel others to do the same.

▸ We can call this growth in our understanding of sin and evil wisdom, which grows principally as we grasp the intrinsically damaging nature of evil and consequences of sin.

▸ We need now to return and to consider the best structure for the formation of appropriate relationality.

▸ Virtues, as defined by Jesus and mediated by his followers, especially the leaders of his communities, extend through every part of life.

▸ Learning is supposed to take place imitatively and face-to-face.

▸ Consequently, community may need to be quite "intense." Leaders should be present enough to shape its members in virtue in their daily lives.

▸ Moreover, people leaving deeply engrained practices of sin require intense community—resocialization—to change.

▸ The test for the appropriate intensity in a community is whether or not it is in fact promoting growth in virtue. The need for intensity will therefore vary from group to group.

▸ There is a temptation now to think spatially about community as an in-group walled off from a different, distorting population.

▸ But people are relational, and communities are networks, so thinking of walls between them is a false conceptuality.

▸ Relationships also change over time, so networks are constantly shifting around, like a fractal.

▸ Church community consequently has a rhythm of gathering and spreading, and the question of intensity can now be posed more dynamically and constructively.

▸ Christians and messianic Jews should cluster intensely together to the degree and for the time that they need to in order to grow in virtue—the rhythm of gathering.

▸ They should then spread out, opening into those relationships that are less or non-Christian in mission—the subject of part 3.

Key Scriptural References

Romans 15:13 notes the importance of joy among the key virtues.

Joy is implicit in the celebration of Jesus during his ascension, enthronement, and heavenly acclamation, outlined in Phil 2:9–11 (and joy is threaded through the rest of the letter). See also his implicit cry to his Father in Rom 8:15 and Gal 4:6, which is a cry of acknowledgment, inheritance, and enthronement.

Ephesians 5:18 briefly touches on the competition between pagan substance abuse and Christian joy.

Colossians 3:16 and 1 Cor 14:26 point to participatory worship compositions and practices.

Key Reading

Barth provides a matchless account of evil as "not-ness," or negation—rendering here the untranslatable German phrase *das Nichtige*—in III/3, §50. An understanding of evil in terms of negation is also summarized with particular clarity by Stanley Hauerwas in his essay "Seeing Darkness, Hearing Silence." It departs from Augustine, and we will return, with a caveat, to this analysis in what follows.

In order to grasp some of the key arguments here, especially between intrinsic versus extrinsic ethics, it is important to revisit James Torrance's seminal essays "Covenant or Contract" and "The Contribution of John McLeod Campbell."

Further Reading

Barth's great sense of humor emerges repeatedly throughout *CD*. Similarly, Hauerwas's work is often an excellent example of humor in action within church pedagogy.

Nathanson's account of how humor contributes directly to the defusing of shame is fascinating. The importance of play was originally noted in chapter 4, quoting G. K. Chesterton and referencing studies by Cone, *The Spirituals and the Blues*, 32–33; and Harvey, *A Brief Theology of Sport*.

I have undergone a long journey in relation to the hypothesis that Paul's texts contain small, dense hymns or their equivalent. My doctoral work was skeptical of this theory in relation to Rom 3:24/25–26. I continue to be skeptical that Paul is quoting preformed early church traditions (except when he tells us he is, as in 1 Cor 15:1–3 and elsewhere), this view being a remnant of the comparative religions school, which sought to reconstruct the theology of pre-Pauline Hellenistic Christianity from these fragments. But the theory that Paul is quoting his *own* preformed units, integrating *songs* into his letters, now strikes me as an excellent explanation of the dense christological sentences he not infrequently drops into. The important insight that these sections have narrative structures, advocated by figures like Hays and Fowl, can be maintained, since we would expect songs by Paul about God acting in Jesus to have a narrative structure.

Neil Postman's short analysis of the impact of modern media on our lives, *Amusing Ourselves to Death*, is, I would suggest, a prophetic statement. It is especially helpful at this moment as it illuminates the way that modern media, which are a commodity, can steal our joy, leaving us riled up and yet helpless. I recommend attending to its argument and implications carefully.

The approach of new monasticism can be usefully represented by Shane Claiborne and Jonathan Wilson-Hartgrove. Having said this—and as new monastics know—there is much to be learned from traditional monasticism. Accordingly, Wilson-Hartgrove has published a version of Benedict's Rule.

Information about the Framingham data can be found, specifically on the medical aspect of the study, at https://www.framinghamheartstudy.org/; and more generally, at https://en.wikipedia.org/wiki/Framingham_Heart_Study.

Bibliography

Barth, Karl. *Church Dogmatics*. III/2.

Claiborne, Shane. *The Irresistible Revolution: Living as an Ordinary Radical*. Grand Rapids: Zondervan, 2006.

Cone, James. *The Spirituals and the Blues: An Interpretation*. New York: Seabury Press, 1972.

Fowl, Stephen E. *The Story of Christ in the Ethics of Paul: An Analysis of the Function of the Hymnic Material in the Pauline Corpus*. Sheffield: JSOT Press, 1990.

Harvey, Lincoln. *A Brief Theology of Sport*. Eugene, OR: Cascade, 2014.

Hauerwas, Stanley. "Seeing Darkness, Hearing Silence: Augustine's Account of Evil." Pages 8–32 in *Working with Words*. Eugene, OR: Cascade, 2011.

Hays, Richard B. *The Faith of Jesus Christ: The Narrative Substructure of Galatians 3:1–4:11*. 2nd ed. Grand Rapids: Eerdmans, 2002.

Nathanson, Donald L. *Shame and Pride: Affect, Sex, and the Birth of the Self*. New York: W. W. Norton, 1992.

Postman, Neil. *Amusing Ourselves to Death: Public Discourse in the Age of Show Business*. New York: Penguin Group, 2005.

Torrance, James B. "The Contribution of McLeod Campbell to Scottish Theology." *SJT* 26 (1973): 295–311.

————. "Covenant or Contract: A Study of the Theological Background of Worship in Seventeenth-Century Scotland." *SJT* 23 (1970): 51–76.

Wilson-Hartgrove, Jonathan. *New Monasticism: What It Has to Say to Today's Church.* Grand Rapids: Brazos Press, 2008.

————. *The Rule of Saint Benedict: A Contemporary Paraphrase.* Brewster, MA: Paraclete Press, 2012.

PART 3

Mission

CHAPTER 16

An Apostolic Foundation

The Mission of God

The origin of the church network's open, inclusive dynamic lies in the plan that characterizes the arc of the universe, which is to say, it belongs in the very nature of God. We learned some time ago, in chapter 3, that the God of love created us for communion and is drawing us back as we have gone astray. Fulfilling this plan, consequently, has two broad dynamics: we must learn to live in communion with God and with one another in the sorts of loving relationships that characterize the triune God, and those of us whose faces are turned away must be reached and drawn back into this communion—the tasks of shaping and establishing community, respectively.

We have spent some time already articulating the first of these dynamics. We know what a community in communion with God is supposed to look like as Paul envisages, crafts, and mediates it. It ought to evidence Jesus's relational qualities in increasing measure—his loving activities of giving, being faithful, peacemaking, and delighting—especially when it is well led. But our account of this community is by no means complete because it is, like the God it knows and worships, extrinsic in its very being, and we now need to explore this critical dynamic in more detail. A Pauline community reaches out to those who lie outside of it just as God does, because loving involves reaching out and journeying, and especially to those who are different from it and indifferent to it. Love is not just giving, faithful, restorative, and joyful. It is missional. It seeks and saves the lost.[1]

---

1. This motivation for mission seems deeply obvious, and yet the motivations for mission tend to be variations on the stories either that God, by way of Christians, is here to help you in your deep impoverishment or that God will eventually execute you if you do not turn to him in faith.

As a key aspect of God's loving relationality, we would expect all Jesus's followers to mediate this reaching, missional dynamic to some degree. But it is clear from Paul that the principal responsibility for this outreach falls again at the feet of the community's leaders. Moreover, the key leader is, as always, the apostle. Indeed, it is here that we encounter some of the apostle's most distinctive features. Both Paul and later church tradition viewed apostles as the basis of the church, although their understandings of apostolicity arguably differ a little. We begin with Paul's viewpoint.

Call and Identity

Most of what we need to know about Paul's view of an apostle can be found in Gal 1:15–16.

> But when God,
> who set me apart from my mother's womb
> and called me by his grace,
> was pleased to reveal his Son through me
> so that I might proclaim him among the pagans,
> my immediate response was not to consult any human being.

Every element in this short story is important, but we begin with Paul's sense of call.

Paul says here that he was personally called by God, although there is rather more than just a call going on. God did not simply shout out Paul's name to get his attention and then proceed to have a series of convivial chats. Furthermore, this call wasn't just a revelation both of and by the Lord Jesus, although it included these things, and they are important (so ch. 1). Paul was called to do something on this basis, so his call was really a commission, and Paul's call consequently had quite specific content. Furthermore, he was called to at least two activities: to go to a particular constituency, the pagan nations, and to preach and to proclaim a certain important, and fundamentally positive, message concerning Jesus to those people, which Paul calls the gospel, or good news, about him.

There can be little question that Paul's entire subsequent life and very identity were oriented by this divine commission that took place near Damascus. It was this task that defined who he was and what he was to do, who he was being largely defined by what it was he was to do. He was "sent," or we might say "apostled," to proclaim the good news (Gk. *apostolos,* a noun, is a cognate of the verb *apostellein,* "to send"), hence he was, above all, an apostle.[2] Moreover, this definition came from God. At bottom, God had a job for him to do, which, from the moment of its disclosure, defined him. I belabor this point because it speaks to such a deep hunger—and perhaps to an equally deep confusion—in so many of the lives that surround me.

Everybody these days seems to want to know who they really are, and this project seems to be something, moreover, that they work out for themselves by searching deep within. Apparently, this act of prior definition has to take place, in full autonomous terms, before any further external action can actually take place, with the result that many people spend all their activity spiraling around thinking about who they are deep down inside, with predictably confused results.[3] The indigenous people of New Zealand, the Maori, call their navel a *pito.* I once heard Manuka Henare, a wise Maori leader, saying, "When Maori sit around endlessly examining their *pito,* all they end up with is the conclusion that they have a *pito.*"

Paul's call liberates us from any such narcissistic quagmire. It reminds us that our identities derive from the work that God has ordained for us to do, not from our own internal inquiries. Our identities unfold in action, in activity that has been divinely appointed and organized to serve the plan that lies at the heart of the cosmos, so one could hardly wish for more meaningful work. And we no longer need to ask, like good liberal individualists, Who am I? or What am I going to choose to do with the rest of my life? There are no cogent answers to these questions on the basis of our own resources. We do not find them for ourselves, and we do not find them deep down within ourselves. We need to ask, What is God calling me to do out there? And if we ask, God will answer, if he has not done so already, although Paul provides us with further guidance at just this moment.

---

2. He uses the word *apostolos* 29x, usually about himself; the cognate verb, 3x. But it is apparent, especially in the opening verses of Galatians, that apostleship for Paul is entwined tightly with *euangelion* ("proclamation" or "declaration," usually translated "gospel" or "good news"), which he uses 56x; the cognate verb *euangelizō* ("proclaim" or "declare"), 21x.

3. This focus on one's inner understanding is a particular trap in modern philosophical liberalism, but it is evident also in the roots of the Western intellectual tradition, which depend on introversion. Socrates's philosophical dictum, drawn from the oracle at Delphi, was apparently *gnōthi seauton* ("know yourself!"). Further development of the narcissism of modernity can be found in Alan J. Torrance, "The Self-Relation, Narcissism, and the Gospel of Grace."

Paul says in Gal 1:15–16 that he was called by God to go to the pagan nations, that is, to a particular constituency (and to one he had serious problems with). So we too will ordinarily be commissioned by God to go to certain specific groups or people.[4] God is primarily interested in people and relationships, and he is very particular. It follows that his calls are as well. Are there specific people, then, whom God is actually calling us to engage with, whether in ongoing service, evangelism, or guidance (i.e., as a teacher, evangelist, or prophet)? Is our divine task right in front of our noses? Are we looking in the wrong place for meaning and direction, or thinking about it in the wrong terms? If so, Paul's specificity can help us once again. Our identities are likely to be bound up closely with particular people.

However, Paul's call may also differ from ours a little in that he was sent on Jesus's behalf, effectively as his chosen delegate, to announce him to a foreign group of people. So he was rather like an ambassador or diplomat tasked with representing a monarch to an alien empire, and this is the basic sense that we should give to his own favored title of apostle. In this sense, an apostle is a missionary. Without this apostolic call to foreign fields (and we will detail the critical components within this skill set in more detail shortly), we should probably stay where we are. But setting this important distinction aside, we share with the apostle the task of proclaiming Jesus to the particular people with whom we are in relationship. And a further challenge is lurking here.

The Unlovely

The people we are called to engage with, whether right alongside us where we are or in some distant land or place, might be unattractive to us. We might even fear, despise, or hate them. But God loves them and has a wonderful plan for their lives, and we may well be a part of that plan.

The initial call by God to Paul to reach out to the pagan nations was a shocking one that caused him a great deal of trouble. Ancient society was far more polarized ethnically than modern liberal society. What progressives today call "racism" was largely endemic in the ancient world. There had been no long social progress by constitutional societies to various forms of equality (however imperfect), abetted by bills of rights and liberation

---

4. Although we are not all called to be apostles, Eph 4:11 describing at least three other major leadership roles, we are, I would suggest, all called to engage with particular people and/or constituencies in the way that Paul's apostolic call in Gal 1:15–16 attests.

movements.[5] Information was poor, and postures were, we might say, more traditional. Outsiders were generally viewed with a mixture of fear, hostility, and contempt. Xenophobia was the norm.

Somewhat sadly, various Jews were not much different. There were Jewish figures who exhibited greatness of heart, and many Jews were located in culturally intermingled locations who mingled themselves and found the horrifying pagan other rather less exceptionable than they previously thought. Some Jews in the Diaspora, living in pagan cities, may well have tended toward this posture. But other Jews, and especially those located in Judea, were "patriots" and viewed pagans as highly problematic. Their literature could paint the pagans in lurid colors, as addicted to disgusting religious celebrations that worshiped dead images, indulging in the ancient equivalent of substance abuse, not to mention, outrageous sexual excesses, and even rejoicing in child sacrifice. And note that the pagans here are not just fearsome. They are contemptible, a very strong emotional posture evoking the reflexes of stench and nausea (technically, dissmell and disgust).[6]

We can be fairly confident that Paul shared this viewpoint and policed his people's boundaries vigilantly. This, after all, is basically what he tells us in Gal 1:13–14.[7]

> For you have heard of my previous way of life in Judaism,
> how intensely I persecuted God's assembly and tried to destroy it.
> I was advancing in Judaism beyond many of my own age among my
>   people
> and was extremely zealous for the traditions of my fathers.

So God's call to Paul to go *to* the pagan nations was a shocking one. He was called to go to a group that he despised. Small wonder, then, that his call

5. This progress is also arguably underpinned to a large degree by a great expansion in productivity, ensuing creation of a middle class, development of education, welfare, and the rule of law, and the resulting potential liberation of many women from traditional gender roles.

6. The portrayal of pagans in the Wisdom of Solomon is especially aggressive and negative.

7. Technically, this is an argument a fortiori; if Paul was prepared to hunt down messianic Jews, which is to say, his own people, for their aberrations, exacting violence on them for insufficient vigilance or a contaminated piety, then he almost certainly would have regarded the pagans as beneath contempt and worthy only of God's destructive wrath.

had to be so irruptive and dramatic. God clearly did not hate and despise the pagans. God loved them. But Paul was not in a position to grasp this until his call. And many of his fellow Jews continued to be outraged by his proclamation of this agenda—the story of much of the book of Acts.

> Then he [Ananias] said: "The God of our ancestors has chosen you to know his will and to see the Righteous One and to hear words from his mouth. You will be his witness to all people of what you have seen and heard. And now what are you waiting for? Get up, be baptized and wash your sins away, calling on his name."
>
> "When I returned to Jerusalem and was praying at the temple, I fell into a trance and saw the Lord speaking to me. 'Quick!' he said. 'Leave Jerusalem immediately, because the people here will not accept your testimony about me.'
>
> "'Lord,' I replied, 'these people know that I went from one synagogue to another to imprison and beat those who believe in you. And when the blood of your martyr Stephen was shed, I stood there giving my approval and guarding the clothes of those who were killing him.'
>
> "Then the Lord said to me, 'Go; I will send you far away to the Gentiles.'"
>
> The crowd listened to Paul until he said this. Then they raised their voices and shouted, "Rid the earth of him! He's not fit to live!"
>
> As they were shouting and throwing off their cloaks and flinging dust into the air, the commander ordered that Paul be taken into the barracks. (Acts 22:14–24)

We could paraphrase the thinking of the enraged Jewish crowd here as follows: "The disgusting pagans included in the age to come—the age of blessedness—with us, God's people, who have endured humiliation and scorn from them?! No way! Perish the thought! And anathema on any person who suggests this! Surely such a person is a traitor to his own people!"[8]

---

8. This, incidentally, is one of the most important insights within the so-called new perspective on Paul, although the position must be handled carefully. There were boundary issues and racist dynamics at work in Paul's context, some of which have just been noted. The classic introduction to the new perspective is J. D. G. Dunn's "The New Perspective on Paul," a lecture given in 1982 and first published in 1983. His later essay "The Justice of God" is also instructive. I describe the new perspective and criticize some of its shortcomings (which I regard ultimately as dangerous when they are not

A critical truth is present here for mission. God loves the unlovely. He is this sort of God. So missionary calls are often unexpected, if not shocking. The Spirit will frequently commission apostles to go to groups of people who have been previously unnoticed or who have been previously despised and—in a much-used word—marginalized. Furthermore, while the church can be very good at recognizing yesterday's marginalized group that lacked engagement, this agenda must not obscure the possible call by the Spirit to reach *today's* marginalized group, which might be living in a very different place. And such groups are not necessarily merely marginalized. They are not the people we feel sorry for. They can be hated, feared, and despised, which are rather different things.

My own view is that the Spirit is calling the Christian network where I live to engage more closely with the mentally and physically challenged and with the imprisoned, in addition to more standard and recognizable engagements across gendered, racialized, and state-regulated boundaries. But I suspect the Spirit is also calling apostles who are convinced Democrats to reach out to Republicans, and Republican Christians to do the same to Democrats, an action that reaches across a (perceived) gradient that is not one of need or marginalization but one of hatred and scorn (and this is not just a missionary calling but a summons to basic church unity). God may well be calling his apostles to a group that *they* have not noticed yet—to a group on their margins, in the sense of being on the margins of their approval or attention. When it comes to God's desire to include, we must expect the unexpected.

Paul now provides us with a further critical insight into the phenomenon of calling—one that flows directly out of the discomfort that we have just noted is a potential factor in any calling we might receive.

Journeying

After his call, having spent his previous period in unwitting but vitriolic opposition to God, Paul seems to have made haste to do as he was told. An astonishing amount of missionary work duly took place over the next twenty years or so, largely in the coastlands of the northeastern quadrant of the Mediterranean, so working "in a circle," as he put it "from Jerusalem around to Croatia" (Rom 15:19). This area included much of modern Turkey, the coun-

---

detected and resisted) in *Deliverance* ("Wide and Narrow Paths," ch. 12, 440–59). We will return to consider the New Perspective briefly again in part 4.

tries around the Aegean Sea, and the coast of the eastern side of the Adriatic, although Paul's first years of work seem to have been inland and eastward from Jerusalem, working up and down what is now the country of Jordan and parts of southern Syria.

We see from all this that Paul was obedient to his divine charge. Moreover, it is blindingly apparent that *he went to where his constituency was located, and not the other way around.* The mountain did *not* come to Muhammad. This obedience involved concrete, bodily relocation and built mobility into the basis of Paul's work. And this observation flows directly, once we notice it, from an underlying posture. "Since I care about you, *I* will move and come to you. *You* do not have to come to me." So Paul says explicitly in Galatians, in passing: "I plead with you, brothers and sisters, become like me, for I became like you" (4:12).

But this journeying is no more than a dim reflection of the initial posture and subsequent movement of God toward us in Jesus Christ. The Father and the Spirit send the Son, and the Son, in obedience, journeys into our location in an inconceivably costly act of relocation (Phil 2:6–8). Hence it follows from the nature of God apparent in his self-giving that his followers should also, strictly speaking, be prepared to move in order to engage with those whom they have been called to, while this very movement on the part of Paul (and others) attests to this particular God. We must be prepared to go to those to whom we have been called. Love reaches out to the unlovely. It journeys to them. And so we all, although apostles in particular, are called to enter into potentially uncomfortable spaces that we are unaccustomed to if that is where the people we are being called to engage with are located. It is what Jesus did for us. It is what Paul did. It is what every missionary does. And it is what all Jesus's followers should be prepared to do, excepting the important caveat about formation that we have already noted. (We must sometimes withdraw if we are being relationally deformed by this journey and engagement.)

Moreover, given our ease of travel today, we might overlook the fact that in the ancient world this journeying was an immensely costly and frequently dangerous act. In order to cover the ground that Paul evangelized—a vast area—he must have walked or sailed in all kinds of seasons and weather for many thousands of miles. And this accomplishment fills me with *deep* appreciation this week of all weeks as, at the time of writing, I have just returned from a short stint on the Camino de Santiago, where I managed a paltry total of about sixty miles. The sheer physical challenge of walking, day after day—and in Paul's case with no shapely modern boots, walking poles, and lightweight all-weather gear—on stony ground, then sleeping in some hard, noisy bed, and resuming walking the next day has to be experienced to be understood. The damage to feet and muscles and joints, also to the gastrointestinal tract, done by foreign roads and food and water—the blisters, cramps, sunburn, cold, diarrhea, hunger, and dehydration—would have been constant. Traveling is costly; it leaves one vulnerable. And yet loving as journeying means that one must be prepared to pay these prices. Indeed, only a journeying built on love will consistently pay these prices.

Paul is well aware of the toll this takes on his appearance as he shows up in an ancient city like Corinth and then declares that he is the messenger of God. He sure doesn't look like one! But we are fortunate that the worldly Corinthians challenged him in this relation because the result was a deep theology of apostolic leadership in terms of vulnerability and costliness. We will probe this theology carefully when we investigate the appropriate manner of engagement with those who are not like us. For now we merely need to set the marker in place that to love entails journeying, and journeying entails vulnerability, costs, and frequently, the cost of suffering. To journey, especially in ancient times, is to enter into a fundamentally martyrological story.

In sum, then, we learn from Paul that an apostle receives a divine summons from God to a particular job—a job involving specific people. These people are often quite different from us, possibly unnoticed and even unlovely. Apostles, however, dimly mirrored by local evangelists and ordinary local community members, are called to engage with a specific people in their own spaces, hence by traveling to those spaces, absorbing and enduring any costs involved. And all of this flows from the loving heart of God, who reaches out through us to draw all of humanity back into the communion with God for which they have been destined from before the foundation of the cosmos.

The Apostolic Basis of the Church

Later tradition placed a great deal of emphasis on the apostles as the basis of the church, although it generally meant by this the writings of the twelve apostles and of some of their key followers collected in the New Testament (and strenuous efforts were made at times in support of these authorships), along with the succession of church leaders—which, within a hundred years or so, included bishops—that stretched back in a supposedly unbroken line of transmission to the original apostolic leaders authorized by Jesus himself.

The church, it is said, is built on these texts and this line of transmission—the position of Irenaeus and of many great church leaders subsequently. I have no wish to deny many of the insights in this position, some of which we will revisit when we discuss the Pastor's development of Paul's work for a later generation (i.e., the program found in 1 and 2 Timothy and Titus). However, Paul does tell us a slightly different story.

Paul places apostles at the basis of the church, not so much because he thinks that they are the only leaders that matter, because he doesn't. It is just that new networks of Jesus followers, Jewish and Christian, spring up necessarily because of the work of apostles, which is to say, because of missionaries, who convert people and so found these networks in the first place. And those missionaries then exercise "founder's rights" over the community in the way that (responsible) parents exercise primary care over the children that they have made. Paul gives birth to his communities, and thus he loves them unconditionally and extravagantly, and he expects them to love him in return. Within these limits, he seems to welcome input from other prophets, teachers, and evangelists—provided it is appropriate. (If it is not, he fights back hard, as any parent would.)

Hence Paul confirms that the church has an apostolic basis, but that basis is a leadership group comprising missionaries who have been chosen and sent by God to those who do not yet know him. As a result of this dynamic, at the foundation of the entire church—at its very basis—we find a group that is constantly in motion, reaching outside of itself to those who are not yet fully part of the community. The church at its heart, through its all-important leaders, *faces outward*, determinedly and inclusively. The church is inextricably related to those who are not officially a part of it.

It is a fascinating thought experiment to imagine local congregations, and even entire traditions, who are arranged under the leadership of proven missionaries. What would the resulting priorities be for training and funding and organizational design? Rather different from what they are at present, I'll wager. But this is how Paul set up his church tradition. Its leadership was fundamentally extrinsic.

If we have grasped how critical missional dynamics are to the church, and especially to its foundational leaders, arising as they do from the heart of God, we need now to grasp the equally critical nature of those dynamics, which must also arise from God. It is not enough to be missional. We must be missional *in the right way*. This challenge can be brought into sharp relief if we return to some episodes in history when the church clearly lost its way—for example, at Cajamarca.

Cajamarca

On November, 16, 1532, in Cajamarca, Peru, 168 Spanish infantry and cavalry, supported by a few small cannon, ambushed and routed a massive army of Incas, killing thousands. The day that Pizarro, the leading conquistador, arranged his ambush, Friar Vicente de Valverde first met the Inca emperor, Atahuallpa, ostensibly to parley, although the plaza designated for the meeting had been ringed with armed Spanish troops in hiding. Atahuallpa was accompanied by his usual six thousand retainers, most if not all unarmed. The meeting began with the priest showing the emperor a Bible and expounding the doctrines of the true faith (ostensibly in translation). The friar demanded Atahuallpa's immediate submission as a vassal to King Charles of Spain, who was God's appointed earthly regent. Unsurprisingly, the Inca emperor refused, casting the Bible that had been handed to him onto the ground, at which moment the friar signaled the attack to begin. Pizzaro's brothers were there and recorded the friar's words: "Come out! Come out, Christians! Come at these enemy dogs who reject the things of God. That tyrant has thrown the book of holy law to the ground! Did you not see what happened? Why remain polite and servile toward this over-proud dog when the plains are full of Indians? March out against him, for I absolve you!"[9]

The surprised Inca retinue was routed, up to two thousand of them were massacred immediately by the Christian soldiers, and Emperor Atahuallpa was captured. The brothers went on to write, "If night had not come on, few out of the more than 40,000 Indian troops would have been left alive" (73).

Atahuallpa was later ransomed for a room filled with gold and two with silver. He was not released, however, but was charged with polygamy, incestuous marriage, and idolatry. He was told that he should convert to avoid death, but having done so and been baptized as Francisco, still he was garroted on August 29, 1533 (although not all the Spanish leaders were apparently in favor of this verdict).

It is sobering to think that a few score Christian conquistadores felt justified ambushing and then slaughtering so many Incas, many of them unarmed, going on to demand unspeakable sums of money for the captured Inca emperor's release, then betraying that bargain and killing him anyway, bearing in mind that all of this was done explicitly in the name of the Christian gospel.

---

9. Jared Diamond, *Guns, Germs, and Steel: The Fates of Human Societies*, 72. Diamond provides a nice account of the entire confrontation on pages 67–74, analyzing its military and technological side through page 81.

Something had clearly gone horribly wrong. In this most significant moment of "first contact" with non-Christians—here an entire continent of Indians indigenous to South America, and hence the advent of one of the most extensive missions in church history—the church had clearly lost its way.

The calling of people into community with God is a fraught business. We need to identify some of the traps that lie here if we are not to damage those who do not self-identify with our community as we try to include and to embrace them. We must, in particular, set our faces against any colonial account of mission—the mentality clearly on display at Cajamarca—and Paul will help us as we do so. He was not a colonizer, evangelizing pagans from a place of great wealth and power. So as we attend to his missionary practice, we will be able to recover a thoroughgoing noncolonial missionary approach. And what we will find, I suggest, will be four intertwined missionary modes—distinguishable within appropriate missional relating, but not separable. Each of these must be present if missionary work to outsiders is to possess integrity.

The first will provoke the most discussion in what follows, running through most of the two subsequent chapters. Missionary activity must be undertaken with the right framing, or *definition*, of perceived outsiders in place, a discussion that leads to a consideration of universalism. We must think in the right way about the relationship between us and the benighted non-Christians who surround us; otherwise things will go wrong from the beginning. (The friar's unfortunate definition of the non-Christian is plainly apparent in the foregoing account.) But we must also be correctly positioned in terms of our *motive*, our *method*, and our *manner*. A particular motive is crucial, for the wrong motives for approaching outsiders contaminate our relationships with them irretrievably (and one does harbor doubts about Pizarro's). Our method of approach must also instantiate what we say we are doing, as well as the sort of God we say that we are involved with (and clearly the confrontation at Cajamarca lacked Christian charity; it was prosecuted with suspicion, steel weapons, gunpowder, and utter ruthlessness). And we must approach people concretely, with the right manner—alongside them, not from above or beyond them, for the same reasons (i.e., not wearing armor and touting superior weaponry). In short, in what follows we will develop a Pauline approach to mission characterized by the following four missional modes: an appropriate definition (of the other), motive (for engaging with them), method (of engagement), and manner (of engagement). And we will do so because we will see, at bottom, that to love someone unlike us, to the point of conversion, entails all these modes and is incomplete when any one of them is missing.

Theses

- The underlying reason for the outward missional dynamism in the church is the outward movement of the God of love. We were created for communion, and we must be drawn back, ceaselessly, when we have turned away from it, as we have.
- This mission takes place especially through apostles, although evangelists, and at some level, all of Jesus's followers, whether messianic Jews or Christians, mediate God's mission.
- The programmatic text Gal 1:15–16 identifies several critical elements within apostolicity, which also speak to the missional call incumbent upon all.
- At the outset, this text identifies a call (presupposing a particular revelation of the Lord Jesus) to a task, hence it is also a commission.
- For Paul this was the task of going to the pagan nations to proclaim the Lord Jesus.
- This divine commission defined Paul's identity as an apostle, just as our divine commissions define us.
- Our identities should not, then, be sought by ourselves, and they cannot be chosen or pursued by way of some "deep" introverted journey.
- A divine calling is to particular, specific people.
- Apostles are called cross-culturally, analogous in this respect to ambassadors.
- We may be called, like Paul, to those we do not love, and may even despise or hate.
- These constituencies may be unexpected.
- To love these constituencies and be called to engage with them entails journeying to them, to where they are.
- Journeys, especially in the ancient world, entailed vulnerabilities and costs.
- A Pauline account of the apostolic basis of the church grounds any Pauline community on its missionary founders.
- Missionaries bring communities into being and "birth" them, thereby becoming their parents, enjoying certain rights as a result.
- Communities based on apostles are necessarily outward-facing and extrinsic.
- Given the criticality of mission to the church, its appropriate dynamics also need to be articulated carefully; much can go wrong.
- The massacre of Atahuallpa's retinue at Cajamarca is merely one notable

incident among many of Christians approaching non-Christians in an inappropriate way—here largely by way of a self-righteous massacre.

➤ Four distinguishable but inseparable *modes* can be identified within an appropriately loving missional engagement with those outside the church: (1) a right *definition* of outsiders (which links up with a discussion of universalism); (2) a right *motive* for engaging with them; (3) a right *method* of engagement; and (4) a right *manner* of engagement. These are explored in detail in three subsequent chapters.

Key Scriptural References

Romans 8:29 is perhaps the key Pauline verse articulating briefly the plan that lies at the heart of the cosmos, which thereby grounds the mission of the church.

Galatians 1:15–16 is a short but programmatic account of Paul's call. (His call is also referenced in 1 Cor 9:1; 15:3–11 and, more metaphorically, in 2 Cor 4:6.) Galatians 1:13–14 sets up the unexpectedness of his call.

Paul's apostleship, intertwined with his proclamation of the gospel, is apparent especially in Gal 1:1–12.

Paul's gestation of communities and consequent authority is apparent in Gal 4:19 and in 1 Cor 4:14–15 and Phlm 10.

The basal role of apostles in his communities is noted more programmatically in 1 Cor 12:28; Eph 3:5; and 4:11.

Key Reading

We have discussed God's election and plan for the cosmos in chapter 3, leaning on Barth's programmatic analysis in *CD* II/2; this material remains programmatic here.

Further Reading

The grounding of mission in the missional character of God is nicely expounded by John Flett.

I prefer the translation "pagans" instead of "gentiles" or "nations" for Paul's frequently used phrase *ta ethnē*, Robin Lane Fox's contentions notwithstanding. It conveys some of the pejorative connotations of that designation for many Jews, including for messianic Jews.

The diversity of Judaism in Paul's day, along with the xenophobia that can be detected in some variations, is charted by John Barclay and Shaye Cohen. Barclay notes the venom in relation to pagans expressed by the Wisdom of Solomon.

Alan Torrance analyzes the characteristic collapse of Western thinkers into an introverted spiral, and its radical contrast to the open, extrinsic, nature of the gospel, in "The Self-Relation, Narcissism, and the Gospel of Grace." It is not an easy read, but it is worth working through.

Hauerwas's work frequently evidences a similar concern and critique. That we think we can decide what and who we are, especially in any independence from a tradition and its overarching narratives, is a singular conceit, also a fallacy, of liberalism; see especially Hauerwas's *After Chrisendom* and *Unleashing the Scripture*.

Although I have introduced the challenge of colonialism here by way of Jared Diamond and a brief account of Cajamarca, it is explicated helpfully— and exquisitely painfully—by Willie Jennings in his widely recognized study *The Christian Imagination*. Stanley's sober study is also programmatic. We will revisit various aspects within a broadly colonial dynamic several times in the chapters that follow.

Bibliography

Barclay, John G. *Jews in the Mediterranean Diaspora from Alexander to Trajan (323 BCE–117 CE)*. Edinburgh: T&T Clark, 1996.

Barth, Karl. *Church Dogmatics*. II/2.

Cohen, Shaye J. D. *The Beginnings of Jewishness: Boundaries, Varieties, Uncertainties*. Los Angeles and Berkeley: University of California Press, 1999.

Diamond, Jared. *Guns, Germs, and Steel: The Fates of Human Societies*. New York: W. W. Norton, 1999.

Dunn, James D. G. "The Justice of God: A Renewed Perspective on Justification by Faith." *JTS* 43 (1992): 1–22.

———. "The New Perspective on Paul." Pages 183–206 in *Jesus, Paul. and the Law*. London: SPCK, 1990.

Flett, John. *The Witness of God: The Trinity, Missio Dei, Karl Barth, and the Nature of Christian Community*. Grand Rapids: Eerdmans, 2010.

Fox, Robin Lane. *Pagans and Christians*. New York: Random House, 1987.

Hauerwas, Stanley. *After Christendom: How the Church Is to Behave If Freedom, Justice, and a Christian Nation Are Bad Ideas.* Nashville: Abingdon, 1991.

———. *Unleashing the Scripture: Freeing the Bible from Captivity to America.* Nashville: Abingdon, 1993.

Jennings, Willie J. *The Christian Imagination: Theology and the Origins of Race.* New Haven: Yale University Press, 2010.

Stanley, Brian. *The Bible and the Flag: Protestant Missions and British Imperialism in the Nineteenth and Twentieth Centuries.* Trowbridge, Eng.: Apollos, 1990.

Torrance, Alan J. "The Self-Relation, Narcissism. and the Gospel of Grace." *SJT* 40 (1987): 481–510.

CHAPTER 17

Defining the Other

Othering

While the jargon involved in discussions of "the other" or "alterity" can verge on the amusing (when it is not impenetrable), an important underlying issue is at stake. It matters a great deal how we define those who are not like us, whom we can usefully refer to as the other. History shows us that deeply sinister practices can operate within this process, so we had best identify and avoid them. Moreover, both Christians in general and missionaries in particular have at times been implicated in these practices—think only of Cajamarca, with which the previous chapter closed, and the way that the massacre was both justified and triggered by Friar Vicente de Valverde. The modern interpreter of the seminal missionary Paul needs to be doubly attuned to the dangers lurking here.

We all "frame" people essentially by telling a particular story about them. Christians do this framing of outsiders all the time; a definition of the non-Christian is built into Christian identity. So we all have a characteristic story we tell about non-Christians—about what they are really like, deep down, how they are not like us, and what they should do about it.[1]

The importance of our frame cannot be underestimated. Our particular frame affects our basic posture toward outsiders as and when we approach them. Indeed, if we frame them in a certain way, we may not want to approach them at all. Our construction will permeate our language and our practices and eventually even our very body language, with the result that outsiders will

---

1. Presumably messianic Jews can often do the same, although their special location, as a minority both in solidarity with and in distinction from nonmessianic Judaism, may well generate other more complex and constructive definitions of the other from the outset.

detect subliminally, in the blink of an eye, what we really think about them as we try to approach them, and the success or failure of our missionary efforts may turn on this assessment.

What is our body language transmitting to people we view as outsiders as we walk among them and speak with them? Do they detect a fundamental posture of judgment, in which case we are positioning ourselves as morally superior to them? Are we in effect speaking down to them from a height somewhere above them? And are we asking them—perhaps before we open our mouths—to change and to be more like us as a condition of our continued relationship? Are we saying, "You and I are fundamentally different, and I'm basically a little superior to you, so you need to become like me"? Or are we sending a more constructive and affirming message about their personhood and value, irrespective of their visible differences from us?

I have spoken with men doing serious time in a federal prison, and they tell me that they can tell in a moment what their volunteer visitors are really thinking about them as these people walk through the door. Sadly, they report that the majority of these visitors have placed the men in a fundamentally different category from themselves—a category of wrongdoing and inferiority. The visitors are doing a good deed and coming to help them—provided, of course, that the people doing time wisely accept this help. Rather unsurprisingly, the men on the inside don't trust these volunteers. They close themselves off from the relationship, adopting a well-practiced facade. And sure enough, many of these visitors don't prove particularly committed to their constituency and tend not to show up faithfully, especially if "results" are not quickly forthcoming, further embittering their audience. Every prison visit risks being a little colonial venture rather than an authentic and successful mission if the framing issues are not recognized and dealt with—but so does *every* contact with non-Christians. So how do we deal with the challenges that lie here?

It all depends in the first instance on how we frame the outsider in relation to our broader understanding of God's relationship with humanity and of the role that Christ plays within this relationship. Not surprisingly, I think that Paul basically got things right here, although his skill in framing the outsider is often overlooked by those less sensitive than he was to the underlying practices. (I suspect that one has to be approaching outsiders regularly to intuit what is going on here for much of the time, and presumably most Pauline scholars aren't.)

We have three options available when we start to think about those who lie outside the key group we identify with, and who we think are not like us in various supposedly important respects. We can frame these outsiders negatively as we proceed to think in foundational terms, forward; as we will see momentarily, this is the most dangerous procedure. Or we can proceed retrospectively, and so free ourselves from the foundationalist trap, but still frame outsiders fundamentally negatively. This is not as dangerous as the first option, but it is still potentially destructive. Or we can frame outsiders retrospectively *and* fundamentally positively. This is clearly rather more constructive. However, it leaves certain key questions dangling that we must still be able to answer, among other things, why people should become Christians, and what now distinguishes Christians from non-Christians. (These two questions amount to the same thing.)

It will be clearest to begin a slightly more detailed discussion of these approaches by asking, first, what the foundationalist framing of the other is, and grasping why it is so dangerous.

Foundationalist Othering

As we saw already at the inception of this book, in part 1, a foundationalist makes truth claims about God and God's ways by appealing to some ultimate truth other than Jesus Christ—and often with the best of intentions. (The road to hell, Dante reminds us, is paved with them.) But foundationalism will prove particularly tempting right now, when thinking about outsiders and how to convert them. A well-intentioned evangelist, unaware of the pitfalls of foundationalism, might suppose that the best way to make people Christians is to convince them on rational grounds that their current location as non-Christians is awful, futile, and doomed—to appeal to them where they are currently located, in terms that they accept and understand right there. On grounds of sheer rationality, combined with self-interest, such outsiders should choose to accept Jesus and thereby become Christians. But by making this understandable decision, our well-intentioned evangelist has activated a forward-moving story, from plight to solution. We are telling the story of Jesus like a quest, setting up a problem self-evidently to which Jesus will be the ultimate solution, and we have thereby overridden critical disclosures from Jesus *about* our problem. His contributions will be fixed in advance of his arrival by our account of the problem that he will definitively address.

The widely used tract "The Four Spiritual Laws," originally developed by Bill Bright for Campus Crusade (and, I add again, with the best of intentions), is a nice example of this equally widespread evangelistic practice. The first law is quite acceptable: "God loves you and has a wonderful plan for your life." (If only things had been left here!) But the second law inaugurates a foundation-alist and rationalistic progression: "All of us have said or thought things that are wrong. This is called sin, and our sins have separated us from God." Citing Rom 3:23 and 6:23b, it adds that "our sins separate us from God forever," and "the wages of sin is death." The key point to recognize here is that the situation as it has just been presented is objectively true, and we know it, so it is neces-sarily self-evident. Consequently, we have achieved these judgments through some truth process that functions independently of the revelation of God in Jesus, which hasn't come yet. We have not become Christians, but we still seem to know certain things. Moreover, as the basis of our conversion, *these truth claims will have to stay*. They must frame and control Jesus's later arrival, as the foundation for our acceptance of him.

The third law outlines the first component within a two-part solution: "God sent his only Son Jesus Christ to die for our sins." This action pays the penalty for our sins, indicating clearly that our initial problem was framed retributively. (Somewhat paradoxically, Rom 5:8 is cited here.) The fourth law then makes the all-important pitch for our acceptance of this offer by exer-cising the second component in the solution: "If you want to accept Christ as your Savior and turn from your sins, you can ask him to be your Savior and Lord by praying a prayer like this . . ."—the decision, in other words, of faith. The conditional relation of faith to what precedes is clearly apparent in the foregrounded "If," thereby sharply limiting the sense in which God loves the tract's reader. God is separated from non-Christians and will execute them unless they undertake an act of repentance, and only then will he love them. So this "love" is conditional. Moreover, it is now apparent that the love of law 1 is strictly limited in its scope. It plays no generative role in the schema. The driving force for the narrative is God's retributive justice.

We already know that the endorsement of theological foundationalism by way of this simple evangelistic schema is very unwise, not to mention, disobedient; the central, sovereign truth that is God revealed in Jesus has been subtly but permanently undermined by its forward-oriented argument. But we are particularly interested here, as we explore mission, in the implicit account of the other. What is the non-Christian like? And how important is this definition to the rest of the schema?

The non-Christian is framed punitively by this schema. Non-Christians are in effect cosmic felons destined for execution. Moreover, if they remain in this state, they are stupid, as well as immoral; they are resisting the rational, obvious, and right thing to do, which is to convert and to become like the evangelist promoting this pamphlet. So they clearly deserve their fate.

It is hard, then, to imagine a more negative account of the Christian outsider. It is self-evident that they are deservedly under a deathly judgment, and if they resist this suggestion, they are doubly deserving of it.

But where is this harsh account of the outsider located theologically? How important is it to the overall program?

It is located in the very warp and woof of this account of the gospel, in its first key law. (It inaugurates the rational progression to conversion, although it appears in position 2, so, significantly, the variation on this model known as the Roman Road begins right here, citing Rom 3:23.) Hence this negative definition of the outsider is built into the foundation of the gospel. It is nonnegotiable.

Clearly, then, we are dealing here with a profoundly sinister notion of alterity. Christian identity in this model depends on the negation of the non-Christian in punitive terms. And this negation will have to be maintained at all costs, or the entire account of Christian identity being supplied will collapse. Equally clearly then, we desperately need to find some alternative account of the other, which will be rooted in some alternative account of the Christian gospel. But how do retrospective accounts of the non-Christian fare?

As we turn to consider them, we will begin with a description of an entirely positive scenario developed on a retrospective basis before considering whether Paul limited it, and, if so, whether he should have. We will adopt this approach because it turns out that any limitations here—that is, moments when the other must be coded negatively—are modifications of a fundamentally positive viewpoint—the view of humanity from the vantage point of Christ!

Christological Othering

In a surprisingly large number of texts Paul gives an account of creation and of the entirety of humanity in fundamentally christological terms. The most extensive is Col 1:16–17:

Everything was created through him—
in the heavens and on the earth, the visible and the invisible,
whether thrones, rulers, powers, or authorities,
everything was created through him and for him—
and he is before everything,
and everything through him holds together.

As we saw already in chapter 1, the same point is made more compactly by 1 Cor 8:6, using the same instrumental phrase as the longer passage in Colossians:

for us . . .
[there is] one Lord, Jesus Christ,
through whom everything [exists],
and we [exist] *by means of him.*

Everything that has been created is created in some relation to Jesus, its creator.[2] (He is not the only creator, but he is the creator.) Paul is no Marcionite.

Jesus's reach through all of humanity is apparent again when Paul uses his favored couplet of stories to talk about salvation. The story of Jesus is the story of salvation, which, as we have already seen, Paul narrates combining fragments of earlier Jewish stories. When he wants to talk about the contrasting, problematic situation from which we have been saved, he uses the story of Adam.[3] And this choice tells us immediately that Jesus's saving reach, like his creating reach, is universal. What Jesus did affected all of humankind, in counterpoint to the universal effect of Adam's sin. So Paul can write compactly in 2 Cor 5:14, "One died on behalf of all, therefore *all* died." And what else would we expect? When God comes to visit his creatures in person, is his impact limited?! Is there some fundamental separation within God between creating and saving actions, with the latter being drastically curtailed in effect? Presumably not (on both counts). Jesus's impact is vastly superior to Adam's reach and impact, as Paul is well aware. This is quite clear in Rom 5.

Paul wants to begin a detailed discussion at this point in Romans that will continue through chapter 8 of various aspects of salvation, so he introduces the story of Adam, which he uses in counterpoint to his story of Jesus—the story of the problem to which Jesus is the solution. But before setting these stories in parallel and beginning his compare-and-contrast exercise (see 5:18–21), he introduces a series of caveats that are clearly intended to remove any shadow of doubt that this parallel is in any sense remotely equal or symmetrical. It is a vastly disproportionate juxtaposition. Jesus is immeasurably superior to Adam. We need to appreciate before thinking about this parallel, then, that it is not a full parallel:

2. See also Rom 8:29; Eph 2:15.
3. See especially Rom 5:12–21; 7:7–25; 1 Cor 15:22, 45–49; 2 Cor 5:14.

But not as the transgression,
so also is the gift. . . .
For the verdict came from one transgression
and led to a sentence of death [for the many],
but the gift followed many transgressions
and led to release. (5:15–16)

That is, if one transgression, by Adam, can have the effectively nuclear impact of death for all of humankind, how much more powerful must the one act of Jesus be, which follows an entire humanity of transgressors, each one of which has committed a potentially nuclear sin, and yet solves everything. Alternatively, reading the key phrases here in a less Augustinian fashion, if one transgression leads to the death of the transgressor, and all of humankind then transgresses and inaugurates death for themselves, how much more powerful must the single act of Jesus be that overcomes all these transgressions and their deathly consequences?

I labor this point a little because Paul's interpreters can lose sight of it so easily, and yet it is so important. Jesus is bigger and better than Adam, so Jesus's work encompasses Adam, which is to say that he encompasses and defines humanity. We are all who and what we are in relation to Jesus and as defined by him. And this includes "outsiders." Indeed, there are now no real outsiders. We are all inside Jesus, even those who do not know it. The truth of each person is the truth that he or she is informed by Jesus deeply and significantly. This relation is what makes people good and right and true, insofar as they are these things. Jesus is at work in them because Jesus comprehends and is at work in the world as its creator, as well as its redeemer. But someone will say to me, "What about sin and evil?" There still seems to be a lot of that around.

We should recall our musical analogy here again. We are all in Jesus, which is our determinative reality. But as we already know well, we are also all in Adam. The discordant music of the Flesh is playing simultaneously in us alongside the music of heaven. We live in these two dimensions at the same time. But we must affirm that our determinative reality is God, which is to say, Jesus. If we deny this relation, then we lapse into a functional Marcionism, as T. F. Torrance once observed so insightfully.[4] Any denial of the full determination of us all by Jesus commits us to the existence of some part of creation—and this instance a very important part, namely, all those people who are not in the church—in a state of separation from Jesus, which is really

4. T. F. Torrance, *Space, Time, and Resurrection*, 64.

just theological nonsense. Where God the creator is present, whom we often think of as the father, God the savior, Jesus, is present as well; *it is the same God*. Marcion separated creation from salvation, and he separated two Gods here as well—as he had to—and the church rightly repudiated these mistaken assertions. So we must continue to repudiate this separation, following Paul's lead in the texts we have just noted. We must not fail to affirm that God's actions on us in Jesus are superior to the evil erosion of our goodness that the Adamic story speaks of. Who is more powerful, more important, more determinative: God or the devil?

These strong universal affirmations are ultimately a very good thing. We can now supply a delightfully affirming account of the outsider, an appropriately humble account of the insider, and a suitably nuanced account of the church.

As we saw a moment ago, we can—and must!—now define the non-Christian positively, in relation to Jesus. *There is no inside and outside here anymore*. There are no more "outsiders." (Rejecters, maybe, but outsiders, no.) Furthermore, if Christ is present with and at work in non-Christians, then we are free to recognize and to affirm this. And Jesus is at work in non-Christians, often to our shame.

I was involved for a time in a local organization focused on the mentally and physically challenged. One of the most challenged of the many enthusiastic members of this group—I will call him Sam—was effectively a quadriplegic, living in a motorized wheelchair. He had no sight and almost no hearing. Thought for years to be significantly impaired mentally, a computer-assisted eyeball-activated communication system revealed an astonishing thing: Sam was deeply and fully cognizant. We learned this when he almost immediately wrote a rhyming poem about his attendance at the group.

But Sam has been largely abandoned by his family. He is now cared for full-time by his social worker, whom I will call Brenda, and his needs are very extensive and exhausting. What makes Brenda's involvement so astonishing, however, is that after Sam's abandonment by his family, she basically adopted him. Brenda is not a Christian. But her love, service, and fidelity put most Christians to shame. Moreover, we must recognize that Jesus is powerfully at work in this relationship. He is present here. And Paul's framing of the non-Christian can account for this presence. But our posture toward the non-Christian might now need to alter a little.

Jesus is present there. So we ought to treat everyone *as* Jesus. When we serve anyone, we serve Jesus. When we meet anyone, we meet Jesus. However, even as we recognize Jesus in others, we must also recognize the Adamic di-

mension that is present in all of us as well. So while we might be open to the
work of Jesus in non-Christians, we should not be surprised to see the powers
of evil at work there as well. Of course we should be equally unsurprised to see
the powers at work in us. We are all in Adam. So we actually possess a double
solidarity with the non-Christian: the solidarity of a fundamental if subtle
determination by Jesus, *and* a shared collaboration and solidarity with the
forces of evil and sin. We are in solidarity both in Jesus and in Adam. Hence
our fundamental relationship with the non-Christian is one of solidarity, and
not of otherness at all.

Paul's Initial Proclamation

We need to let these insights restructure how we think about Paul's presentation of the gospel. We will have a lot more to say about this topic shortly, but
let us imagine for the moment that we are fortunate enough to be stitching a
canvas awning alongside Paul in the workshop he is sharing in Thessalonica.
He is, as usual, talking away. Busy artisans are seated all around him trying to
catch what he is saying. (Those who are bored and irritated have already left.)
And he is talking about them, at least for some of the time. Certainly he is
issuing some challenges. But how is he portraying them? What is he actually
saying?

Unfortunately, scholars have been led astray in this regard for a long time
through a mistaken emphasis on the opening chapters of Paul's letter to the
followers of Jesus at Rome, and in turn by a mistaken construal of this material. As that material legitimately suggests, there is a stern side to what Paul is
saying. Disobedience kills. But this is not his *first* word. From what we have
seen above, his first word must be a "yes" on behalf of God to those seated
around him. It is only after this "yes" has been spoken that Paul, on behalf of
God, utters a "no." But how does Paul actually put all this?

Paul mentions in a few places (although one could wish for a few more)
what he said when he first arrived and managed to found a community, and
we have already drawn some insights from these texts. In his letter to the Galatians he says rather cryptically that "Jesus Christ crucified" was portrayed
graphically before their eyes (3:1–5). He then states that the Holy Spirit arrived
at this time as well, effecting wonders among them. In 1 Thessalonians Paul
talks about the Spirit working through his words to effect real conviction. His
report to the Thessalonians was "about God" (2:13), and presumably about
"the living and true God" of 1:9. A little more detail is supplied by 1 Cor 2:1–5.

Paul repeats here that his message focused on the crucified Christ. He tells us in fact that he resolved to know *nothing* except this story, although the presence of the Spirit is again significant. This approach produced conviction, despite the tremors, the vulnerability, and the lack of eloquence of Paul the speaker. A bit more content can then be found just in advance of these statements.

In all this, Paul is revealing a heavenly secret, he says, which ancient Greeks called a mystery. This heavenly secret has been present since the foundation of the world and is bound up with God's Wisdom, but it has now been revealed to Paul, who reveals it in turn to those who will listen to this bedraggled messenger. It is, in some sense and despite appearances, a message of power. Jesus, the crucified one, *is* the Wisdom of God, and those "in him" receive "deliverance and cleansing and release" (1 Cor 1:30). Moreover, this God is interested in *everyone*.

Those possessing status, learning, and pedigree, as well as those possessing significant reservoirs of prior religious knowledge, tend to deride this message. But God has sent his Son to experience the shameful death of crucifixion—the death of a low-class felon. And in doing this, Paul says, God has shown that he is deeply committed to those the world regards as unimportant. He reaches down into the very depths of our existence and into the most distant and shameful corners of our society to touch and to gather back the people living there. So Paul's Corinthian converts are primarily an unimportant group, ill-born, despised, and possessing little or nothing. *This* stooping, affirming, including event is the message of the crucified Lord. And it links hands directly with parts of Paul's message that are already well established for us.

A God and Father who sends his only beloved Son to die shamefully for a sinful and hostile humanity is a God who will endure any distance and shame to reach people. God speaks a "yes" here to everyone, irrespective of their social location and status. Everyone matters. There are no outsiders here to the purposes of God.

Moreover, all those responding to this absurdly humiliated God can receive release and cleansing. In Jesus they are transformed. By entering the person who took this shameful path, release is possible, which can only mean release through death and resulting resurrection. So the baptismal statement of 1 Cor 6:11 neatly resumes the triad of events articulated in 1:30 of cleansing, purification, and release.

It can hardly be overemphasized that this is Paul's first word in his preaching. There is no preamble because *there can be no preamble to the revelation of a divine secret*. This can only be *declared* by an appointed ambassador like

Paul.[5] The declaration focuses on a divine Father who sends his only Son to die a shameful death for you, whoever you are. Your baptism declares how you have entered his death and thereby entered his new life. And if all this seems a little hard to credit, the signs and wonders of the Spirit affirm that this new life is present, albeit in some oddly invisible way. The strangely vulnerable figure before us is speaking the truth about God, a God who loves you enough to send his Son to gather you back and his Spirit to heal you.

So we can see now that Paul's preaching—at least insofar as he tells us what it is—is fundamentally inclusive. It does not "other" its target constituency but proclaims its inclusion, irrespective of social status, within the divine purpose for the universe. There will be exclusions in due course, to be sure, but the basis of everything is positive.[6]

But we now have an important question to answer. Have we now erased any meaningful distinction between the world and the church?

Emphatically not. But what exactly does the distinction between the followers of Jesus and those who are overtly resisting that designation now consist of? Our very rationale for declaring the gospel must lie in this distinction. This distinction is why we are asking people to become Jesus's followers.

In order to answer this question, we will have to talk again about the basic shape of Paul's ethics, especially the phenomenon of consequences.

Ethics

It is important at this moment to recall our basic ethical situation. We are made for relationship with God in Jesus and, through him, with one another, and we are called to correspond to the dynamics of this relationship—to its virtues, its commands and requests, and its covenantal commitments.[7] In free obedience within this relationship lie our joy and peace and our true freedom. Conversely, if we bend away from this situation, following the allure of evil, we plunge into self-destructive and painful ways. We stick our feet boldly into the

---

5. A point made tirelessly by J. Louis (Lou) Martyn, especially in relation to the word "gospel" itself; see his *Galatians*, especially comments 7 (127–36) and 9 and 10 (146–51).

6. We take up the interpretation of Paul's overt exclusion texts in ch. 18.

7. We have already talked a lot about virtues in part 2; in part 4 we will describe in more detail the dimension to Paul's account of ethics best captured by the notion of a command or request, something Barth treats in *CD* III/4.

fire and arrogantly insist that we are doing the right thing, irrespective of the pain. (Perhaps we are thereby exercising "our right to choose.") In short, joy and peace flow from living in obedient and loving relationship with God, and pain and death flow as consequences from any disobedience.

So the church is—at least in theory—living overtly and vigorously within its relationship with God. It is self-consciously walking in obedience and thereby in joy and peace, and it is teaching its members to resist the allure of evil, aware that any lapses lead to pain and destruction. This is not to claim that the church's correspondence with the ways of God is perfect or that the world's lack of correspondence is total. But it is to affirm that a wholehearted commitment to God is the pathway to life, and any rejection of this commitment is to stray onto the pathway to death. And herein lies the basic distinction between the church and the world.

The church is—to some degree—obeying and so living; the world is—to a large degree presumably—disobeying and so dying; it is inflicting ongoing damage on itself. The church is pulling its feet out of the fire. The world is—through gritted teeth—stubbornly holding them in it.

My students sometimes protest a bit when I suggest all this. They seem to want something rather stronger here to distinguish the church from the world. But the distinction I make here is pretty strong, once one thinks about it. There is precious little enjoyment present in a life that denies God. The author of life, peace, and joy is being ignored and resisted in a way that will also have damaging consequences.

Imagine a situation in which a young heterosexual woman is living in a house. She has a good job. Life is prosperous and anxiety-free. But she is lonely and wants to find the perfect man to marry so that she can enjoy the riches of that relationship. Somewhat strangely, however, she is in fact married, to a lovely man, who sleeps next to her at night in her bed, gets up and makes a glorious breakfast in the morning, with French toast and fruit garnishes and a steaming cup of coffee, and talks to her happily when she gets home in the evening from work. (It is a somewhat old-fashioned relationship.) But she does not believe he is there and steadfastly refuses to acknowledge his presence. As far as she is concerned, she sleeps alone, she has to make her own breakfast—a hurried mix of bland instant porridge—and her days pass silently. As the years pass, she spirals into narcissistic despair and bitterness. She turns to alcohol, becomes angry, bitter, and ill, and she dies cynical and desperately alone. And all the while, this lovely man calls out to her, lives with her, puts delicious food and drink on the table in front of her, and offers to spend time with her. At any moment, she can respond to his presence, and then what she yearns for will unfold for her in all its fullness. As a friend of mine puts this, "She just needs to wake up and smell the coffee." But she refuses to.

The church is responding to the presence in the room. Life is unfolding as it is meant to. We are smelling—and drinking—the coffee. We are living and loving. Non-Christians are resisting this relationship, however, and condemning themselves in the process to unreflectively lonely and twisted lives.

This seems like quite a sobering distinction. And yet it is not a fundamental *ontological* distinction in the basic relationships and constitutions of the people involved. It is not a difference in the way that they are actually made. Jesus is fully present to everyone. It is just that one party is responding obediently to the call of God, and the other is unnaturally resisting and twisting away from it.[8] One party is responding to God, growing in virtue and consequently growing in things like peace and joy; the other is rejecting God and experiencing the consequences of this—a spiral into sinful habits that inflict ongoing relational damage and all the consequent pain. It is the difference between obedience and sin.

In the light of this parable, we can nuance our earlier account of the church's relationship to non-Christians in some further respects. In particular, it will be helpful to return here for a moment to our earlier account of sinners in terms of substance abuse.

We are all substance abusers. In this respect, we are in complete solidarity. But the church is in rehab and is cooperating as fully as it can with the program (again, at least in theory). The non-Christian in general, however, is the substance abuser who is still in denial, and such figures are living fundamentally self-destructive lives.

Consequently, it is imperative that the church continues to attest gently, clearly, and faithfully to the importance of the rehab program, along with the programmer. "This is the way to recovery. I am in it, so I know. It's not apparent from where you are, but trust me. Come and join me, and you will see." The church is called, that is, to witness to the salvation that is obedience to God. It is not called to actually save the world. (What a relief.) God is saving the world

8. Hauerwas characterizes this distinction slightly unhelpfully as a difference of agency *as against* one of ontology in "Seeing Darkness, Hearing Silence." But agency *is* ontology, so this distinction is false. Moreover, the key difference is not agency per se but the *exercise* of agency, with Jesus's followers trying to obey and those rejecting and resisting him sinning—something Hauerwas is basically well aware of. Having said this, there is a sense in which we must grant that those exercising their agency to follow Jesus more closely will presumably change for the better, and that this is arguably to be different ontologically—at least in this way and to this degree.

and has saved the world. The church is called to witness constantly to this present fact. Moreover, it does not do so from any location of superiority. As one substance abuser speaking to another, it says, "This works for us all." And its advice is consequently informed fundamentally by mercy and compassion.

A slightly more biblical way of putting all this would be to suggest that, as a result, the church functions, in its greater correspondence to God, in a representative and hence priestly relationship to the people around it.[9] Like priests robed and serving in the temple of God, walking in its daily and seasonal rhythms and attending to their God's sacred texts and commands, a priestly church walks and serves among the people, characterized by a visible holiness—which is to say, by something both right and different from the world. It represents God and the ways of God to the world as it faithfully serves him. And it calls the world to recognize the presence of God with us all in the world. Consequently, the world can look and see what correspondence to God looks like as the priests model and teach the same. And the priests themselves ask the rest of humanity to come and to join them. (This is a priesthood of all believers and, beyond that, of all humanity.)[10]

I am going to abandon now—just for a moment—my usual antipathy to spatial analogies, because they are helpful here in their depictions of inclusion and exclusion. We often think of the relationship between the church and the world, which is to say, with the outsider, as in the following diagram:

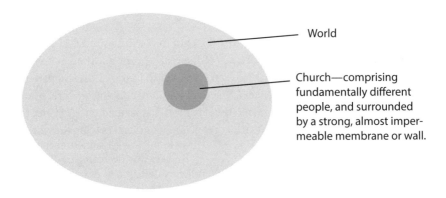

World

Church—comprising fundamentally different people, and surrounded by a strong, almost impermeable membrane or wall.

9. Paul doesn't use directly priestly language very much. A cultic theme that implies priests can be detected in Romans. The imagery is more overt in 1 Peter, Hebrews, and Revelation.

10. James B. Torrance, "The Vicarious Humanity of Christ" (Calvin lies behind much of this article).

But a lot of problems are now evident in this depiction.

It is functionally Marcionite because it separates God's work as creator off sharply from God's work as redeemer. Moreover, it calls the success of God's work as a redeemer drastically into question. Look at how limited this rescue attempt is in relation to the great expanse of creation. How ineffective God's solution seems to have been—and God was personally present to effect it!

In addition, this approach—this frame—encourages us to think about the church as a bounded entity. It is separated from the outside world by some sort of wall, which we must now spend a lot of time defining. And its relationship with non-Christians is now significantly differentiated. There is a *qualitative* difference between those on the inside and those on the outside. Non-Christians are being "othered" as something different and inferior (and the Jews are often the quintessential other). And missionary work is now a foray by morally superior people out into hostile and debased territory. It is a dangerous sortie. Furthermore, if the missionaries are using a foundationalist account of the situation, narrating the journey of the non-Christian from the outside in, so to speak (i.e., beginning with the broad situation of the outsider, under judgment, then trying to supply them with good reasons for becoming a Christian), the negation of the outsider will be written permanently into the constitution of the Christian church, along with a foundationalist approach to theology as a whole.

Fortunately, Paul did not think like this (although, as we will see momentarily, in the next chapter, he could think like this on occasion). When he was thinking directly out of God's action in Christ, he thought more like the following:

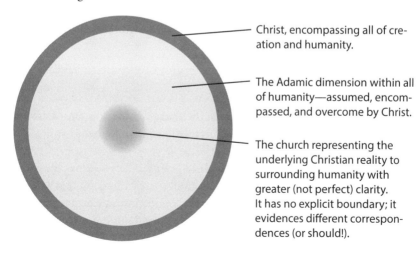

Christ, encompassing all of creation and humanity.

The Adamic dimension within all of humanity—assumed, encompassed, and overcome by Christ.

The church representing the underlying Christian reality to surrounding humanity with greater (not perfect) clarity. It has no explicit boundary; it evidences different correspondences (or should!).

As we have just seen, Paul was no Marcionite. His vision of reality is Christocentric. And the church is consequently not set off qualitatively from the rest of humanity. It is in solidarity with humanity, both in Jesus and in Adam. However, it is set off by its obedience. When messianic Jews and Christians live in obedience to Jesus—when they follow him—they fulfill a priestly role, attesting to the world around them what the ways of God are really like. So there is no need to spend time articulating and specifying—and perhaps even erecting—a barrier between the church and non-Christians. There is a comprehensive difference operating here all the time as those in the church obey God, bearing in mind that non-Christians obey too for some of the time, even as many in the church do not. Nevertheless, the church is that specific part of the broader circle of humanity that enjoys the presence of God and walks self-consciously on the pathways of life. It is the primary place where the peace and joy flowing from that relationship can be found.

I trust, then, that it is clear that it is entirely possible to frame non-Christians in fundamentally positive terms, not to mention in full solidarity with the church, in relation both to Adam and to Christ, and yet to supply an entirely convincing account of the difference between the two groups in terms of a difference of ethics or obedience and its attendant consequences.

But fairly obvious questions now arise. We will need to ask whether the retrospective and positive account of the other that we have been developing here has limits, and also reflect on what to do with the texts in Paul that seem to suggest that it does—the subjects of the next chapter. In particular, we need to ask, What is going to happen in the future? Does God judge everyone then punitively, excluding some? If he does so, then perhaps the account being developed here needs to be either substantially modified or even abandoned. So the stakes for this next chapter of discussion are high.

Theses

- ‣ Much depends now on how those in the church define non-Christians, or the other, as they arrive to enter into relationship with them.
- ‣ The story we tell about the other affects our very body language.
- ‣ The popular evangelistic tract *The Four Spiritual Laws* defines the other punitively and foundationally. But it cannot change this definition without self-destructing—without destroying the foundation on which its account of the gospel is built. But clearly this kind of definition is undesirable. It builds negation of non-Christians into the basis of the Christian gospel.

- Another way of defining the other is positively and retrospectively, as Paul does when he places the stories of Christ and Adam side by side in passages like Rom 5:12–21.
- We learn here that Christ is superior to Adam—indeed immeasurably so—so we must in some sense include all of humanity in Christ, as well as in Adam. The reality of Christ must be more determinative and important than that of Adam, even if it is less visible. He is our creator and lord. (To fail to affirm this inclusion is to lapse into "functional Marcionism.")
- Paul's preaching is therefore fundamentally positive. It begins with a "yes" of inclusion in Christ, before proceeding to a "no" that addresses the sinful reality of Adam.
- This "yes" is proclaimed to everyone, irrespective of one's social location. No corner of society is too shameful or unimportant for God to reach with this positive word. Indeed, God seems to like these places especially.
- But given this double solidarity of all of humanity in Christ and in Adam, in what does the distinction between the church and non-Christians consist? Why should non-Christian become followers of Jesus?
- The difference is not one of existence or being at a fundamental level—of how everyone is made and determined—but of *agency and its exercise*. Jesus's followers are responding to God differently—or they should be. They (ought to) correspond to the life-giving ways of Christ more closely than non-Christians, and this can amount to a very big difference.
- There is a sense in which all of humanity is caught up in substance abuse. (Our sin functions very much like substance abuse.) But the follower of Jesus is responding to rehab; the non-Christian is not.
- It is important to recall the consequences of sinful activity at this moment. Sin distorts and destroys. So to sin is to live in pain and to inflict pain on others.
- Understood in this way, the church functions in a priestly, representative way. It represents more clearly, although still imperfectly, the healing ways of God to surrounding humanity.
- There is no hard boundary between the church and non-Christians. Members of the church represent what everyone, in a very real sense, is.

Key Scriptural References

Jesus's universal implications as creator are implicit in the basic claim that "he is Lord"—see 1 Cor 8:6—and explicitly affirmed in Col 1:15–17. They are also affirmed more briefly in texts like 2 Cor 5:14.

Jesus's qualitative superiority to the universal reach of Adam is affirmed explicitly in Rom 5:15–17. His determinative significance for humankind over against Adam is affirmed in 1 Cor 15:22, 45–49 as well, and more subtly in texts like Col 3:11.

Paul provides details about his preaching in 1 Thess 2:13; Gal 3:1–5; and 1 Cor 1:17b–2:16.

Key Reading

The theological presuppositions for an appropriate account of the other are articulated by Barth in various places. They are especially clear in his short treatment *Christ and Adam*.

This position is also very nicely described by Jeff McSwain on 74–89 of his insightful short book *Movements of Grace*.

Further Reading

The classic account in Pauline interpretation of othering leading to erasure is provided by one of Daniel Boyarin's early works, *A Radical Jew* (see esp. 1–85, 180–200). (Incidentally, Boyarin uses here a subversive method often identified as postmodern, but in fact one deeply at home within modernity and developed—in the modern period—originally with the most power and sophistication by Nietzsche. MacIntyre's account of this discourse, couched in terms of "genealogy," is superb. It should be required reading for all Christian engagements with "the genealogists.")

Barth lays the theological foundations for an appropriate account of the other, both anthropologically (where Christology is determinative) and ethically (where a command ethic allows the flourishing of legitimate and highly context-sensitive variations).

James Torrance also supplies a definitive account of the priestly and representative role of Jesus Christ, and hence of the church, in his essay "The Vicarious Humanity of Christ."

It is also important to recall an appropriate theological understanding of evil in terms of negation, as summarized with particular clarity by Stanley Hauerwas (although also suitably qualified) in "Seeing Darkness, Hearing Silence."

The sort of universal inclusion in Christ I am advocating here necessitates a particular account of the sacraments of baptism and Eucharist. At this moment, however, an intriguing connection is apparent with John Wesley's emphasis on the sacraments as "converting." They could bring home to those already converted a sense of the love of God—something Wesley said happened to his mother later in life. Wesley's concerns are not precisely coterminous with mine, but there is significant overlap. The sacraments *declare the truth about every human being as they are defined in Christ,* and they urge an emotional and personal response within and to that objective truth. Wesley's views are articulated by Randy Maddox in his *Responsible Grace*, 219–21 (and my thanks to him for these references and insights).

The rationale for mission that I am articulating here is close to the position of Peter Cotterell; see his *Mission and Meaninglessness: The Good News in a World of Suffering and Disorder.*

Bibliography

Barth, Karl. *Christ and Adam. Man and Humanity in Romans 5.* Translated by T. Smail. New York: Collier, 1962.

———. *Church Dogmatics.* II/2; III/4; IV/3.

Boyarin, Daniel. *A Radical Jew: Paul and the Politics of Identity.* Berkeley: University of California Press, 1994.

Cotterell, Peter. *Mission and Meaninglessness: The Good News in a World of Suffering and Disorder.* London: SPCK, 1990.

Hauerwas, Stanley. "Seeing Darkness, Hearing Silence: Augustine's Account of Evil." Pages 8–32 in *Working with Words.* Eugene, OR: Cascade, 2011.

MacIntyre, Alasdair. "Genealogies and Subversions." Pages 284–305 in *Nietzsche, Genealogy, Morality: Essays on Nietzsche's Genealogy of Morals.* Edited by Richard Schacht. Berkeley: University of California Press, 1994.

Maddox, Randy L. *Responsible Grace: John Wesley's Practical Theology.* Nashville: Abingdon, 1994.

Martyn, J. Louis. *Galatians: A New Translation, with Introduction and Commentary.* AB 33A. New Haven: Yale University Press, 1997.

McSwain, Jeff. *Movements of Grace: The Dynamic Christo-realism of Barth, Bonhoeffer, and the Torrances.* Eugene, OR: Wipf & Stock, 2010.

Torrance, James B. "The Vicarious Humanity of Christ." Pages 127–47 in *The Incarnation: Ecumenical Studies in the Nicene-Constantinopolitan Creed, A.D. 381.* Edited by T. F. Torrance. Edinburgh: Handsel Press, 1981.

CHAPTER 18

The Triumph of Love

Paul's Notion of Resurrection

Recently a clever graduate student opened my eyes to an aspect of the data in Paul that I had not really noticed before but that, once I had had it pointed out to me, made a very big difference to the consideration of our current questions concerning the future and its judgments.[1] In order to grasp it, however, we must turn in our analysis to Paul's context and quickly reconstruct the thinking of his contemporaries about resurrection.[2]

Many Jews in Paul's day were convinced, as he was, that one day God would usher in a great future age that would transform the earth—the age to come. Basically heaven would be reunited with the earth at this time, God would dwell with humanity, and the primeval glory lost in Eden would be restored, or something similar to this scenario. All the problems of humanity, and of Israel in particular, would be resolved by this making of all things new. But although many Jews agreed that this was the case, they disagreed on the precise mechanics, which is understandable because it hadn't happened yet. In particular, some disagreed on just what role a bodily resurrection would play. Setting aside the variations that don't concern us here, there were two broad camps.[3]

---

1. Thomas D. McGlothlin, *Resurrection as Salvation: Development and Conflict in Pre-Nicene Paulinism*, 17–47.

2. An earlier, abbreviated version of the argument in this chapter appears in *Journey* as "God Wins," ch. 13, 162–70. The argument has been significantly reordered and expanded here.

3. I am setting aside here the Sadducees and those like them, who apparently did not believe in a resurrection at all. Conversely, many Jews were influenced by the Greek notion of the immortality of the soul. They didn't need a bodily resurrection. This

Some Jews thought that everyone would be resurrected to face a final judgment. See, for example, Dan 12:2–3:

> Multitudes who sleep in the dust of the earth will awake:
> some to everlasting life,
> others to shame and everlasting contempt.
> Those who are wise will shine like the brightness of the heavens,
> and those who lead many to righteousness,
> like the stars for ever and ever.[4]

The resurrected, that is, would receive a body, having been raised from the dust of death, which would allow God to evaluate them for their deeds. This final, essentially retributive judgment would then divide people into the innocent and the guilty—the proverbial sheep and goats—and the two constituencies would be sent off to their assigned locations: the sheep, to the glories of the reconstituted earth; the goats, to burning annihilation or even to torment. So bodily resurrection functions here essentially as a precursor to a divine act of retributive judgment; it is the necessary presupposition for this event.

However, some Jews thought differently. They understood bodily resurrection as a fundamentally good thing that obtained access into the glories of the age to come.[5] There was a sense, then, in which any judgment had already

---

position could also display variations: the soul could ascend to heaven immediately after death, or it could wait until the last day for this ascension. There were also hybrid positions that intertwined the two main options, or the two main views of bodily resurrection. So some Pharisees apparently thought that only the righteous would experience a full-fledged bodily resurrection, but that the souls or spirits of the wicked would be judged. (There is a hint of this position in Rom 2:9.) And the book of Revelation resurrects only the righteous bodily for a thousand years, then resurrects everyone bodily to face judgment, thereby fashioning an ingenious synthesis of the two main positions.

Fortunately, we have already moved beyond any endorsement of the immortality of the soul earlier on, in ch. 7, resolving the key tensions there by shifting to a more accurate view of time as a field or continuum rather than as a constant. This dualistic view of the person should be rejected in any case on solid theological grounds. The incarnation and the resurrection establish unequivocally that people are embodied. So we will continue to set it to one side here as well as we move forward.

4. See also 4 Ezra 7.31–33, 36–38; 2 Bar. 50:2–4; 51:1–3; Josephus, *Jewish Antiquities* 18.14.

5. See, e.g., 2 Macc 7:9, 11, 14, 23; 14:46; and Josephus, *Jewish War* 2.163. Note that Josephus suggests here that the souls of all can be affected by reward or punishment. But only the righteous receive bodies on the last day ("The souls of good men only are

taken place. The resurrection was part of the reward for a virtuous life or some variation on this rationale. If people had been resurrected, then they had *already* been judged worthy of entrance into the coming age, something the resurrection of the body effected directly. One simply wanted, then, to be one of the resurrected—to be one of the few who would recline to eat at the great feast in the kingdom of God (Isa 25:6–8). This was the big hope. Everyone else would remain in the dust of death, effectively annihilated by death.

There is an important difference between (1) wanting to be resurrected and *then* be judged worthy of life in the age to come and (2) wanting simply to be one of the resurrected who thereby *is* part of the life of the age to come. The resurrection is doing different things in these two stories. And although Paul is often read in terms of the former scenario, where all are resurrected bodily, judged retributively, and then the virtuous are rewarded with eternal life, a careful consideration of his letters suggests that he was an advocate of the latter scenario, where only the righteous are resurrected. And this understanding will change some things.

Paul seems to have believed that the resurrection is a gift to the loyal followers of Jesus, with only a limited number of folk receiving it. This scenario, essentially of an entirely positive but limited bodily resurrection, can explain why, on the one hand, he excludes recalcitrant sinners from any part in the future blessed kingdom at all.[6]

> Do you not know that wrongdoers will not inherit the kingdom of God?
> Do not be deceived:
> Neither the sexually immoral nor idolaters
> nor adulterers nor the effeminate nor men who bed men
> nor thieves nor the greedy
> nor drunkards nor revilers nor thugs
> will inherit the kingdom of God. (1 Cor 6:9–10)

But on the other hand, his account of the future kingdom's consummation is explicitly saving and universal.[7] "Everyone" in the new cosmos will be

---

removed into other bodies"). So, as McGlothlin points out, this view entails that bodies themselves are positive and not a prerequisite for judgment (*Resurrection as Salvation*, 17–47). See also 1QHᵃ cols. 11 and 19.

6. Paul speaks of this exclusion in 1 Cor 6:9–11; Eph 2:3; 1 Thess 1:10; 5:3, 9; and 2 Thess 1:6–10.

7. Paul speaks of this universal eschatological acclamation supremely in Phil 2:9–11; but see also 1 Cor 15:22, 27–28; Eph 1:23; Rom 5:18–19; and 14:10–12.

bending the knee to Christ and confessing him on that glorious day, he says clearly and repeatedly.

> At the name of Jesus
> every knee in heaven and on earth and under the earth should bow
> and every tongue confess
> that Jesus Christ is Lord
> to the glory of God the Father. (Phil 2:10–11).

That is, everyone who is resurrected is confessing the lordship of Christ and therefore is presumably both righteous (in him) and saved.[8] The only way to make sense of these two positions consistently—exclusion of some people right beside the universal confession of Jesus's lordship by the resurrected—is through a limited resurrection of the righteous only, but this expectation does explain things neatly.[9] Only some people are resurrected and saved, and all the resurrected are consequently obedient followers of God. They all bend the knee to him and confess him as Lord. The disobedient simply do not get resurrected, which is why pagan converts in Corinth were being baptized vicariously on behalf of dead family members (1 Cor 15:29). They wanted them to be resurrected as well. So sinners are indeed excluded from the future kingdom. And this all has the added convenience that it is a more consistently christological account of resurrection.

When Jesus was resurrected, he in effect coded bodily resurrection with an indelibly positive function. That event and process were taken up into him. Moreover, he did not get resurrected and then face judgment. Jesus's resurrection is, for Paul, a saving event in its own right. It is the reconstitution of humanity beyond the contamination of Sin and the grip of Death. The resurrection is, then, by its very nature, saving, although it is also rather more than

8. Paul also consistently describes this scenario using the word "all"; see Rom 5:18; 11:32; 1 Cor 15:22; 2 Cor 5:19; Eph 1:10; Col 1:20. It could be countered that he also speaks of a judgment scenario by Christians of other agents after death in 1 Cor 6:2–3. However, this seems to refer to nonhuman entities or the powers. Paul views these as being defeated after the *parousia*; see 1 Cor 15:24–26.

9. A variation here could be a resurrection of just the righteous bodily, with a judgment of the *souls* of the wicked. The only evidence for this position in Paul would be Rom 2:6–10, which I take to be representing an interlocutor's position, and Acts 24:15 (and perhaps also v. 25), although this would represent the position of the author of Acts before it represented Paul's. Lacking confidence in this potentially countervailing data, I am sticking with the simpler scenario I am outlining here.

this. It is liberating, life-giving, and glorious. In view of this, it is extremely difficult to make sense of a future scenario within which some are resurrected bodily, only to be judged unworthy and sentenced to death and possibly also to hell. Gifted momentarily with bodies free of sin, contamination, and death, and temporarily glorious, thanks to the work of Jesus—raised in him, bearing his image—these people are nevertheless herded after their sentencing onto the heavenly equivalent of cattle cars and sent away to be exterminated. If the resurrection is to function as a salvific act in and of itself—and Paul's ethic depends on it—then this scenario doesn't make much sense.[10] So I think we should endorse the presence of the alternative scenario in Paul within which only the righteous are resurrected. Those who presently have a resurrected mind, and no one else, are guaranteed a resurrection body.[11]

Doubtless someone will now cite several of Paul's texts which seem to describe a process of future judgment, however, and this seems to point in turn toward the first narrative of resurrection discussed above, within which all are resurrected bodily to face sentencing. Certainly these passages are often read this way.

Judgment

I admit that Paul does frequently talk about a process of judgment in the future that will presumably take place after death or at the end of time,[12] whichever comes first.[13] However, the entailments here are false. These objectors have not had their understanding of judgment sufficiently transformed by the great process of judgment that stands at the heart of the cosmos—and that stands at the heart of all healthy parenting as well. The judgment that Paul has in view in all these texts is, I would suggest, an *evaluative* and not a *punitive* judgment.[14]

10. McGlothlin charts the way many of the church fathers have nevertheless valiantly tried to square this circle.

11. So especially Rom 8:9–11.

12. Paul's most important judgment texts are Rom 2:16, 28–29 (although see more on this just below); 14:10–12; 1 Cor 3:13–17; 4:3–5; 2 Cor 5:6–10; Eph 6:8; 1 Thess 2:4; and 2 Thess 1:5–10.

13. We made an important adjustment here in part 1 on the grounds of *Sachkritik*, introducing a post-Einsteinian view of time and adjusting our understanding of God's eschatological action on the cosmos accordingly.

14. The possible exception is Rom 1:18–3:20, supported indirectly by 13:1–7. I have made an extensive case elsewhere, however, that neither of these texts actually reflects

Once our eyes have been opened and our ears attuned to this alternative type of judgment to the strictly retributive, we can see that this is what Paul has in mind in his judgment texts that discuss a future evaluation, and consequently only of the saved before God's throne. We learn from these texts, that is, that the righteous who are resurrected will still face some sort of scrutiny. They will be held accountable. (*We* will be held accountable.) But mercifully, salvation itself does not depend on this divine evaluation.

I sometimes explain this to my worried students in terms of the difference between a job interview and a job evaluation. A job interview amounts to a sentencing. We are in or we are out. It is thus analogous to a retributive tribunal. But although these dramatic processes stud our imaginations, probably because they infest our universe of entertainment, we rarely face them in real life. Much more common is the job evaluation. In this sort of judgment our actual position is not technically on the line. But we are being scrutinized, which is to say, held accountable for what we have done so that we can address any issues, improve, and move on. And this is how most parents operate, not to mention teachers, including even the occasional professor.

Parents seldom if ever judge their children retributively. I have not come across a parent yet who says, after a particularly egregious sin, "You are no longer my son!" (i.e., who says this and really means it). But parents judge their children *all the time.* I am a parent, and a child, so I know this statement to be true. We are constantly being evaluated in relation to our behavior by our parents, and we constantly evaluate our children in the second type of evaluative judgment process just described. And clearly this is still excruciatingly accountable.

Few things are tougher than facing scrutiny from someone we respect and love after we have done something wrong. Real shame is likely, which is one of the most unpleasant scenarios a human being can contemplate. (I hesitate even to recall my own memories of such events because of the burning sense of shame that is still with me. One of the more innocuous but still painful episodes involved me spending rather too much time at a friend's house showing off the family's new car.) But this process is framed unconditionally, by the parent's love, and not conditionally, as the retributive judgment scenario is. We are not facing ultimate exclusion or inclusion. Right evaluative judging is

Paul's own thinking about things directly. See my *Deliverance of God*, presaged by *The Quest for Paul's Gospel* and summarized by Tilling, *Beyond Old and New Perspectives in Paul.* Moreover, even Rom 1–3 is only a possible exception, as the careful use of *psychē* in 2:9 might suggest.

a fundamentally pedagogical process through which we are being helped to learn from our mistakes. Hence it is worth recalling how good parenting will also factor in attention to consequences.

As we have already seen, bad decisions on our part and any resulting foolish behavior lead to concrete results that are themselves painful and damaging, a fact deriving from the nature of sin and evil as privation or negation, with its inevitable attendant harmful impact. A good pedagogy will lead a person to grasp such sinister dynamics and to turn wisely away from sinful behavior in the future. Parenting helps children to grow in wisdom, drawing the connection between a bad decision and its resulting set of painful consequences that is obvious to us but far from obvious to our children in their youth and stupidity. "I shouldn't do this anymore. It is hurting others and hurting me—I see that now." This critical learning all takes place during evaluative judging. And note how this sort of parenting also stays within a healthy, intrinsic approach to ethics that we have spoken of earlier as well. People in this type of relationship can learn that certain acts should be avoided because they are in and of themselves evil, which is as it should be, and not because we are supplying additional threats, thereby diverting attention from the evil of the acts themselves.

Retributive judging and parenting, meanwhile, remain extrinsic and thereby run the risk that the appropriate connections will never be drawn and the appropriate behavior never adopted for the right reasons. Forgoing the innate unfolding of consequences, retribution adds pain in the form of punishment to negative acts, thereby obscuring the connection between the acts and their own intrinsic evil consequences, and focusing the attention of the people being punished on the punishers and the pain of the punishment. Moreover, people are being framed here in explicitly self-interested terms. As a result of these deficiencies, people being punished in retributive and extrinsic terms might never learn the appropriate lessons about evil behavior. They might never grasp that certain acts and habits inflict pain on them and others. They might simply learn that if they can avoid the punisher, they can do what they like. Are there any good reasons not to? Moreover, they might learn that the punisher is a tyrant. They might learn that the basis of all ethics is self-interest. They might even learn all of the above. And the result would be deeply unethical people and a considerable failure in parenting.

Once we grasp the ubiquity of evaluative as against retributive judging, particularly in healthy parenting and in analogous managerial and pedagogical situations, its stringent accountability, *and* the inherent unhealthiness of retributive accountability, it is easy to see that this is what Paul is talking about when he speaks of his charges appearing before the judgment seat of Jesus, the one whom they ultimately respect and love. The prospect of this scenario should motivate his followers powerfully. They want this job evaluation to go especially well. It is the big one. They want Jesus to be pleased, not disappointed. And they will doubtless concur with God at this moment that everything caught up in their Flesh needs to be eliminated, even if this includes some of their cherished practices and achievements—practices and achievements that turn out, under scrutiny, to be constructed of chaff. Nothing impure or evil must enter the age to come. This judgment will scrutinize and cleanse.

"All of us must be presented before the throne of God," says Paul in Rom 14:10. "Every knee will bow and every tongue confess to God," but he then adds that at this moment "each of us will give an account concerning ourselves" (14:11–12). It seems clear, then, that everyone who is resurrected is both confessing the Lord appropriately and supplying an account of their behavior. And this makes sense only if those resurrected are community members who then face their Lord and master. They and they alone are resurrected and then judged in an appropriate moment of accountability.

But if we are still a little unsure about all of this, 1 Corinthians supplies even more clarity. In 1 Cor 3:10–12, using an extended construction metaphor, Paul pointedly warns other builders of the Corinthian community (i.e., Paul's rival there, Apollos, along with his colleagues) to be careful how they build. The quality of their work will become clear on "that Day" because fire will test it. Good work that remains will entail some sort of recompense—presumably praise and delight from the Lord. Bad work will not survive, however, being incinerated, although the person who did this shoddy construction will still be saved. It is just that they will suffer loss, having passed through this purifying fire.

> By the grace God has given me,
> I laid a foundation as a wise builder,
> and someone else is building on it.
> But each one should build with care.
> For no one can lay any foundation other than the one already laid,
> which is Jesus Christ.
> If anyone builds on this foundation using gold, silver, costly stones,
> wood, hay or straw,
> their work will be shown for what it is,
> because the Day will bring it to light.
> It will be revealed with fire,

and the fire will test the quality of each person's work.
If what has been built survives,
the builder will receive a reward.
If it is burned up,
the builder will suffer loss
but yet will be saved—
even though only as one escaping through the flames. (3:10–15)

This is a nicely Jewish account of an eschatological, or final, job evaluation. Paul is clearly confident that he is doing stellar work. He is expecting recompense from his Lord, whom he serves so zealously. His work of community building will survive the burning fire of the final day. However, he is not so sure about other teachers. They will not be excluded, but they will be chastened, and their rough and consequently inflammable work will be burned away.

Nevertheless, some people will be excluded altogether, Paul says in 3:17—those who "destroy God's temple." It seems that they will not even be evaluated. They will simply be incinerated, this being the second main aspect of the final judgment that we need now to think about.

We have just seen that all Jesus's followers will be resurrected bodily and judged in the sense of being parentally evaluated. Everyone who is so resurrected and judged will be a community member, hence a messianic Jew or a Christian, and no one else will enjoy this second life. Paul is confident, that is, that God will destroy all remaining evil and evildoers on the last day, leaving dead evildoers unresurrected, and this position is especially apparent in his earliest letters, which were written to the Thessalonians.

The Thessalonians were suffering greatly from their fellow countrypeople, but Paul was confident that the Day would turn the tables. Those who had pivoted away from disgusting idols to serve the living God who cannot be imaged would be saved; they would be resurrected and evaluated, responding with confession, obeisance, and praise. But those who had resisted this call would be destroyed when Jesus returned, this act of destruction attesting to God's righteous disapproval of idolatry and other evils, which would also effect a payback for those who had previously been persecuting the Thessalonians. They will be wiped out.

Intriguingly, when Paul exhorts the Thessalonians later in his first letter to them not to grieve too much over those who died, he comforts them with further details about this future scenario and its resurrection. When the Lord arrives to great fanfare, the dead in Jesus will rise and meet him, after which those left alive will be caught up in the clouds to be with him forever (4:13–18), when the great eternal party in the sky begins—although presumably this includes a searching assessment at some point. So the Thessalonians need not worry about their Christian dead. They can have the precious thing that so many ancients—and not a few moderns—lack: hope in the face of death. They will all meet again, the creeds phrasing this gathering as "the communion of saints." But note that no universal resurrection and ensuing punitive judgment are mentioned here, and it is difficult to see where these could be inserted into the story without disrupting it.[15] Community members left alive are transformed "in the blink of an eye" and caught up to be with Jesus, as 1 Corinthians explains (15:51-53). Conversely, 1 Thessalonians states that any remaining idolaters will simply be caught unawares by this sudden appearance by the Lord and destroyed as labor pains suddenly overwhelm a pregnant woman (5:3).

It seems, then, that bodily resurrection in Paul, however we understand it, pertains only to the elect. The impure are destroyed by the fiery cataclysm of the Day (see also 1 Cor 6:9-11; Gal 6:7-9), which seems consistent with Paul's famous words in Rom 8:18-23, which we can now perhaps understand a little better than we used to.

---

15. That is, if Paul thinks resurrection is universal, he has now committed to two different narratives of resurrection that do not align with one another. On the one hand, community members are all saved, and those left alive are fortunate enough to avoid death altogether. They are transformed, which is to say, resurrected, on the spot. However, idolators and the like are all annihilated. So if resurrection is in fact universal, this group, on the other hand, will need to be resurrected after God has killed them, which is both unnecessary and asymmetrical. Moreover, they will either be resurrected in a transformed state, victorious over sin and death (1 Cor 15:54-57), only to be judged deficient and executed again because of past failures, or they must be resurrected in their original embodied state, which is both odd and unattested.

The only way beyond this conundrum is through the introduction of the hybrid position noted at the beginning of the chapter that was endorsed by some Jews in Paul's day. The righteous are resurrected bodily, proceeding after their evaluation to enjoy the communion of saints, and the unrighteous are not resurrected bodily but have their souls judged retributively, as possibly suggested by Rom 2:9. But there are many good exegetical reasons for querying the relevance of Rom 2:9, and many powerful theological objections to any sustained deployment by Paul of the notion of an immortal soul (see esp. ch. 7). To these objections, we can now add the observation that no souls of idolaters and sinners seem to survive the fiery annihilation of the Last Day in 1 Thess 5. This group is destroyed. So God would have to resurrect just the souls of the unrighteous dead so that they can face a punitive judgment, making this narrative even stranger than the scenario it is trying to improve upon.

> I consider that our present sufferings are not worth comparing
> with the glory that will be revealed in us.
> For the creation waits in eager expectation
> for the children of God to be revealed.
> For the creation was subjected to frustration,
> not by its own choice,
> but by the will of the one who subjected it,
> in hope that the creation itself will be liberated from its bondage to
>   decay
> and brought into the freedom and glory of the children of God.

Here Paul suggests that creation is eagerly awaiting the revelation of the children of God beyond mortality, in all their incorruptible glory, at the second coming. Creation is waiting, that is, *to see who makes it in.* This group includes both Paul and those he is writing to, who have the firstfruits of the Spirit, but its outer boundaries are unknown. At the wonderful moment he is anticipating here, however, all previous suffering will seem worth it, and the children of God will be explicitly identified in blazing glory and will enter into a wonderful new world, hand in hand with the creation itself, which will then be set free from all its struggles with corruption. A judgment awaits, which might have its embarrassing side, but it is a long-awaited moment of accountability. Most important for our present concern, to be resurrected here is simply to be glorified (so Phil 3:21; Col 3:4). Only some blessed people will experience this, says Paul, which is why (at least in part) creation is "craning its neck forward" (Gk. *apokaradokia*), and "eagerly awaiting" this moment.[16]

Covenant or Contract?

There can be little doubt, then, that Paul saw the future playing out very differently in relation to two contrasting groups of people. The chosen will be saved. They are marked now by the Holy Spirit and are supposed to live spotless lives. On the last day if they have died, they will be fully resurrected and glorified, along with the suffering cosmos, or if they are still alive, they will be transformed in the blink of an eye. They will all then be presented blameless before God, where they will give an account of their work—a moment that

16. This is also because the creation is suffering and groaning within a general corruptibility that it did not bring upon itself but must bravely endure.

could be exquisitely embarrassing but that will not result in ultimate exclusion. Shockingly, Paul made the offer of salvation indiscriminately to pagans, and in a double shock, his definition of righteous living did not include many standard Jewish activities (something we will discuss shortly in more detail in part 4). So there will be some surprises in this happy throng and their divine evaluation. But Paul clearly held that the rest of humanity, lost in idolatry and general wickedness, will be destroyed in a fiery cataclysm. Sin, death, evil, the powers, Satan, corruption, and the entire world of the Flesh will be annihilated. Paul expected this extinction to reach a vast number of idolatrous pagans, including those who had been mean to his small Christian communities.[17]

So the stakes were fairly high for becoming a Christian or a messianic Jew loyal to Jesus. Only this relationship could guarantee eternal life. *And this seems to suggest in turn that there might be something like a contract lurking in Paul's theology after all.* Certainly, Paul attributes the responsibility for ending up unsaved largely to a refusal to accept the offer of the gospel. Satan plays his part.[18] But Paul's longest discussion of rejection and its causes is in Rom 10, where he discusses the rejection of Jesus by a large number of Jews. And he places the blame for this rejection squarely at the feet of those who have repudiated Jesus. God has come right down to his people, reaching out to touch their hearts and minds, both in person and through chosen messengers, and they have pushed all these overtures stubbornly away. It is their fault.

Does this mean that deep down Paul thinks about salvation conditionally, that salvation is structured like a contract, and that people have to do certain things in order to be saved, failing which they are struck down on the last day? If you get damned for not doing something, then doesn't it follow that you will get saved by doing something, at which moment we have a contract?

Not necessarily, although there are some real challenges here that we need to face.

In the first instance we need to grasp that it is entirely possible for people to push an arrangement away, however destructive and irrational that rejection might be, but this refusal does not mean that the overarching arrangement is a contract, as any parent of troubled teenagers knows. They could be pushing a covenantal arrangement away and refusing to live out of that basic reality. If people reject these arrangements and turn away, then they lose the benefits of living in these arrangements. This does not mean, however, that a contract is in place. It's just the universal reality of consequences.

17. See 1 Thess 1:10; 2:14–16; 2 Thess 1:3–12.
18. See 2 Cor 4:4.

Jessie was born to a stable and happy family. Her parents are kind, faithful, and consistent. But for whatever reason she was angry and decided as a teenager to explore drugs. She pushed her parents away and spiraled into serious substance abuse, eventually becoming deeply depressed and ultimately vagrant. At any moment she could enter a rehab clinic and engage in recovery with a fully supportive family. But she refuses. One day an acquaintance asks her, "Where are your parents?" She replies, "They are dead. I have no parents. I am all alone. Nobody loves me."

This is a lie. She has parents who are still her parents and who love and support her unconditionally. They have not withdrawn from her and are ready at a moment's notice to stand by her during any attempted recovery. (Addiction specialists tell me that such parents will need to be ready to do this for the seven attempts that most addicts will make to reach full recovery.) Jessie is located in a covenantal relationship. But she is rejecting that relationship and refusing to live out of its reality. Her rejection of this reality and its ongoing gracious invitation does not mean that she can do anything to reestablish the relationship itself and thereby turn this covenant into a contract. The covenant is still in place. It is there. It is always there. She is just rejecting and abusing it. She should *respond* to this covenant as is appropriate; in doing so, she would stop damaging herself, as well as the other people who love her and are engaged with her. It is this dimension in the situation that she is messing with, and she is experiencing the consequences.

Hence the fact that large numbers of people contemporary to Paul were rejecting Jesus and courting the consequences does not mean that they were in a contract with God. They were in a covenant. That's what made the rejection so acutely painful and incomprehensible. Covenants can be violated and damaged. They are restored when they are recognized and people turn from their foolish ways—when, in other words, they repent. And as the Karl Barth of *Church Dogmatics* III/2 says, God is then under no obligation to save such people in the future in spite of themselves. He is free to endorse their rejection, to leave them in their vain imaginings, and to continue into eternity with the grateful saved alone. Those who are saved in the meantime ought to *pray* and to *hope* for the salvation of all; this is the loving thing to do. We are to love our enemies, or at least to try to. And loving them presumably includes both hoping the best for them—that they will be saved—and praying accordingly. But we are not in a position either to tell God what to do or to affirm confidently that universal salvation will in fact happen. That is up to God. And this eschatological agnosticism does not entail that God is contractual. It is just that the covenantal God will not override the stupidity of sinful people, and it may even arguably be the covenantal thing not to do so.[19] So Paul's harsh exclusionary texts in relation to the future do not undermine his central claims about God's love, depressing though this ultimate prospect might seem.

But can we let things rest here?

Some further questions arise at this point that we ought at least to consider. First: is this view of the future, rooted in Paul's texts, not problematic for God? There is a question of the divine integrity that now arises, and we need to consider it carefully. Closely allied is another question: will our visions of an exclusionary future and of how God ultimately acts now overwhelm our understanding of God in the present, which is rooted in how he *has* acted, in Jesus? This would be a particularly subtle form of foundationalism—a futurist foundationalism, we might say. And we need to be alert to it because even though our visions of the future are important and powerful, they are really just our imaginative projections into the future of what *we* think is going to happen. Given that they haven't happened yet, it would be unwise to let these flimsy constructs override our present understanding of God, rooted in what he has actually done.[20]

Plausible answers to these questions prompt me to undertake a tentative Pauline reconstruction of the future that is subject to rigorous christological control.

Who Wins?

In view of what Jesus has disclosed about God's deepest nature, it is hard to comprehend how God can be both a loving, covenantal God *and* an omnipotent God (although omnipotent in his own way) if everyone is not eventually saved. If God's great plan fails—his plan to create us and to play with us eternally—then one possibility is that God does not really love us. But we should immediately dismiss this idea as ludicrous; this conclusion is clearly contrary to what God has revealed about himself, at great cost, through Jesus. God loved

---

19. It is unloving to coerce people into a response, even when that response is healthy and appropriate. Any account of a universalism that assumes this sort of future divine action therefore ought to be rejected.

20. The flimsy nature of the future—essentially being an emotional and conceptual projection of our present—is nicely detailed by Daniel Gilbert in *Stumbling on Happiness* in his chapters "In the Blind Spot of the Mind's Eye" (83–105) and "The Future is Now" (123–43).

us enough, on the one hand, to deliver up a beloved, only child *to death* on our behalf *while we were still hostile to him* (the sacrifice of the Father and the Spirit) and, on the other hand, to accept this need to die for us while we were still hostile. God loves us (the sacrifice of the Son). There is nothing truer in the universe than this assertion. But the only other possibility, if God were to fail to save everyone, seems to be that God is not capable of carrying out his benevolent plan. Some of the people whom God created for eternal fellowship to love would be twisted, damaged, and eventually lost forever. This conclusion would suggest that a great opposing power had wrenched them from his grasp and defeated his ultimate purposes. And if this is the case, then the universe is really Manichaean, with two great and largely equal powers contesting it, one good and the other evil. In this scenario, evil would triumph, at least to some degree, which seems intolerable.

It is a nasty conundrum. What are we going to do?

Sachkritik might help us to find a way forward that is Pauline even if it is not Paul's.

We saw earlier that Paul gives an account of the problem facing everyone in terms of Adam, in counterpoint to an account of the solution in Jesus. In doing so, he claims that Jesus's solution is humanity-wide. It corresponds to Adam, the original image of all humanity, so this solution must be equally universal. Paul goes out of his way to affirm this in 1 Cor 15:22 (see also vv. 45–49):

> In Adam all of us die.
> In the same way, in Christ all of us will be made alive again.

But in Rom 5 we have already seen that Paul goes further than this. He writes that Adam is only a "type" of the one who comes later. He is an inferior negative copy of an original in the sense that a carefully carved and molded stamp can be used to press imprints into small discs of metal to make coins (Rom 5:14). Ancient coins were never as clear and sharp as the original stamp—and they face in the opposite direction. Jesus is primary then; he is the stamp. Adam is secondary; he is the inferior negative imprint.

Paul goes on to argue in this paragraph that Jesus's solution to Adam's problem is so superior that it is almost incomparable to the latter. It is vastly greater both qualitatively and quantitatively. Only when this incommensurability has been grasped from verses 15–17 can we proceed to a parallel comparison between Jesus and Adam in verses 18–21, although this is only what we would expect from a personal intervention by God into a problematic situation.

But the gift is *not* like the transgression.
For if through the transgression of the one, the many died,
how much more did God's benefaction—
the gift given through the benefaction of the one person, Jesus
    Christ—
overflow to the many!
And the gift is not like the results of the one person's sin.
For, on the one hand,
the judgment followed the transgression of the one person leading to
    condemnation;
but, on the other hand,
the gift followed many transgressions and led to release.
For if, by the trespass of the one person,
death ruled through that one person,
then how much more will those who receive God's overflowing
    benefaction,
which is to say, the gift of deliverance,
rule in life through the one person, Jesus Christ! (Rom 5:15–17)

It stands to reason that God acting in Jesus must be vastly superior to the created but corrupt situation that he is engaging with. After all, he runs creation. When it comes to God getting involved with creation as a person as against a person he created dictating the future of humanity, God's person is going to be bigger, better, and more important. The formula is: Jesus > Adam.

This all suggests to me that God's plan being effected in Jesus is going to work *better* than anything that might happen to us in Adam, and God's plan for us in Jesus is saving. Moreover, to leave any loose ends unresolved would imply that God's solution was, to this degree, ineffective. We would be faced with the awkward conclusion that God's plan in Jesus, having been disrupted by evil, is never completely executed, despite God's personal involvement, and evil would be victorious to this degree. The extinction of the personal would have succeeded. God's plan for fellowship, reestablished in the face of evil by a personal intervention and salvation, would have failed in relation to these particular people. The rescue mission didn't work here. (Imagine a hostage rescue attempt in which the commandos saved two out of two hundred captives. Would we view this as a success?) This would be the conclusion if any people who were created good are eternally lost, ultimately to the nothingness of death.

If we placed this problem to Paul in this exact form, we could wonder how he would react. "Paul, did God's plan to rescue the world through his own

Son come up short? Did it fail to some degree? Was it perhaps as much as 40 percent ineffective? Or more? Was it—if we are deeply committed Calvinists—perhaps 95 percent ineffective? Putting things slightly more technically, are God's created acts ultimately more powerful than, and because of this failure, also disconnected from, his redeeming acts?"[21]

I imagine his answer would be, "Hell no!" If God is going to win and his plan be brought back on track, we must expect everyone to be drawn back into fellowship with him through the work of Jesus. Jesus's mission was perfect and complete. No one gets left behind. So the theological inferences here are quite straightforward, and they infer forward from Paul's most basic insights into God. If God is really the Lord, then his plan will work, and his plan in Jesus is for everyone who is created to be drawn into communion with him, to play, delight, love, and worship forever. His redemption will correspond—even as it vastly exceeds—his creation. So this plan will work. We might not know how exactly, but we do know *that* it will succeed.

However, we have another quite strong card to play in this particular hand. There is some fairly clear evidence that Paul viewed God as being capable of overcoming human resistance when he really wants to.

Unbelieving Israel

In Rom 11 Paul spends some time arguing that unbelieving Israel will eventually be saved. The conundrum that many Jews rejected Jesus as both Messiah and Lord was a painful problem for Paul (9:1-3, 31), and he basically throws the kitchen sink at it. Over the course of this long chapter he makes numerous arguments, large and small. But most of them are designed to take his listeners to the conclusion that "all Israel will be saved" (11:26a), even though they are presently largely hostile to God acting in person in Jesus.[22]

---

21. Our discussion links hands here again with the problem of functional Marcionism.

22. The precise meaning of Rom 11:26 is widely debated. But the immediate context suggests that Paul is not merely using the word "Israel" symbolically to refer to the church here. Israel is a group that *will* be saved, suggesting that currently it is not, which can really only be "ethnic" Israel, meaning Jews living in the present cosmos.

There are no difficulties with the suggestion that Paul can think of *future* Israel in the age to come as including resurrected Jews and Christians. The opening stages of this broad sweep of argument in chs. 9–11, in 9:6–26, suggest that converts from paganism could be included in Israel. Paul quotes Hos 2:23 and 1:10 there, which speak of "those

Paul points out, first, using the motif of the remnant, that God never lets go of Israel (11:1–7; see also 9:27–29). The existence of a remnant indicates God's commitment to the wider group from which the remnant comes. It is preserved precisely in order to preserve the future of the broader group, which will sprout from this stump, despite its experience of being cut off in judgment. Hence the existence of a remnant indicates that God has not let go, and will not let go of Israel but will bring a future flourishing to this presently truncated people. Paul argues, second, and somewhat cryptically, that if the firstfruits of an offering are holy, then the entire mass is, and that if the root of a certain tree is holy, the branches are as well (11:16). (Paul's claims here are best explained by some technical rabbinic arguments.)[23] He adds, third, that God is able to graft broken branches from a cultivated olive tree back into their own tree, since there is something natural about this reinsertion (11:24b). It is, after all, their own tree, so this is easier than grafting unnatural pagan branches into the trunk.

As we read on, however, we discover that these three organic images in Rom 11 are grounded by a fourth argument that reaches all the way back to Rom 9. Israel will be saved in its entirety because the later descendants of the patriarchs are beloved on account of the patriarchs. God's original gift of life to the ancestors of Israel—to Abraham and Sarah, Isaac and Rebekah, and to Jacob and Leah and Rachel—is *irrevocable* (11:28b–29; 9:5–13).

> As far as election is concerned,
> they [the Jews] are beloved because of the patriarchs [and matriarchs],
> for God's gifts and his call are irrevocable. (11:28–29)

---

who are not my people being called my people." "Israel" is the Hebrew for "God's people," and this view is supported by Eph 2:19. But in future Israel we all bear the image of the resurrected Son, who was a Jew, but is now a significantly transformed one.

On balance, I tend to see "Israel" in Rom 11:26 as more restricted in reference. But a more inclusive reading, with messianic Jews and Christians in view, does not undermine my current claim in any case. An *exclusive* reading, with a reference *only* to future saved believers who are being coded strictly symbolically as Jews—in effect to a "spiritual" Israel—would affect my argument, but this reading seems highly unlikely. This case can be made only by overruling the clear local contextual information in the name of other Pauline axioms that are themselves ultimately contestable—a doubly dubious procedure. Ross Wagner provides a deeply nuanced account: *Heralds of the Good News*, 276-98; as does Susan G. Eastman, "Israel and the Mercy of God: A Rereading of Galatians 6.16 and Romans 9–11."

23. See Benjamin D. Gordon, "On the Sanctity of Mixtures and Branches: Two Halakic Sayings in Romans 11:16–24."

This, then, is the holy offering of firstfruits that sanctifies a polluted offering, the root of a tree planted on holy ground that sanctifies the branches that spread into unclean space, and the cultivated and fruitful olive tree into which broken branches can be regrafted. The irrevocable election of Israel's founding families also undergirds the preservation of a remnant, which continues the existence of Israel after it has strayed into disobedience and suffered the deathly consequences of that foolishness, thereby guaranteeing its later flowering into full fruitfulness. And this all makes perfect sense.

Paul's God is a covenantal God. This God calls people into existence, loves them, enjoys them, gives to them (see 9:3–4), and never lets them go. He gifted life to the patriarchs and matriarchs and called Israel into existence. He *elected* them. So he preserved them through their rebellions and hostilities. And he will draw them back to him in their fullness because he is this sort of God. His love never gives up, never lets go.

We don't know exactly how this will happen or when. Scripture tells Paul that "the rescuer," who is probably Jesus, will turn ungodliness and transgressions away from the descendants of Jacob. (So this really has to be Jesus.)

> As it is written: "The deliverer will come from Zion;
> he will turn godlessness away from Jacob.
> And this is my covenant with them—
> when I take away their sins." (Rom 11:26b–27)

But we don't know any more than this. Paul's statements here are not very detailed, and he is basically just quoting scriptural texts. This quotation could refer to a future personal visit by Jesus, or it could refer to an obedient response to his original presence and work, or it could refer to something else again. However, we do know *that* it will happen. Paul is quite clear about this future:

> All Israel will be saved. (Rom 11:26a)

And we are now in a position to draw the key inference for our present discussion.

Paul is facing the fact of widespread Jewish rejection of Jesus (9:1–3; 10:1–3; 11:28a). Few Jews have, like him, become messianic Jews and then even missionaries to the pagans, and perhaps very few. The vast majority of Jews seem to be unbelievers. But Paul is confident that all Israel will eventually be saved. Why? Essentially because of the nature of the God who summoned Israel into existence in the first place. God called Israel into being and loved Israel by way of its famous ancestors. He gifted Israel with existence and life at that time and will now never let go. He is this sort of God, a God who lovingly elects and then maintains this commitment in spite of any hostility and foolishness in the objects of his love. His love will eventually triumph over Jewish unbelief. In short, in the contest between divine benevolence and human recalcitrance fought out in the space that is Israel, God will win. All Israel will be saved.

But there seem to be no good reasons for withholding exactly this narrative from humanity in general. (Paul himself did withhold it, but we are extending his thinking here consistently.)

God created humanity, lovingly electing them into existence and fellowship, preserving them through their self-destructive hostility and foolishness, and refusing to let any of them go, as seen especially in the great missionary outreach to the pagan nations. God loves humanity as much as he loves Israel, Israel standing as a remnant and hence as a saving sign in relation to the rest of humanity, just as the believing Jewish remnant stands as a sign to the rest of Israel. God's Son came to save the human race, undoing the destruction of Adam, not just the destruction of Jews. Hence it seems that exactly the same rationale should apply. God will not let humanity go. In the contest between divine benevolence and human recalcitrance fought out in the space that is the human race, God will win. All humanity will be saved. And God really is a covenantal God, committed to us all permanently and irrevocably.

We still need to know how to handle the Scriptures that push against this view, and many do. But we should recall at this moment that Christians should read the Scriptures in the light of Jesus and at his command (something that we discuss more shortly; see esp. ch. 22). They cannot be used to go against him or to correct him. If he wants to save everyone or seems poised to, we must learn to read the Scriptures accordingly—and there are lots of ways of handling Paul's judgment texts, along with the other judgment texts in the Bible, so that they speak of this overarching story.[24] And it might also be helpful

24. We all handle (i.e., reinterpret) some texts in the Bible in light of other texts. Whatever position we adopt here, we will have to reinterpret certain other biblical texts. There are explicit commitments to universalism in the Bible. See especially 1 Tim 2:1–4, especially v. 4: "I urge, then, first of all, that petitions, prayers, intercession and thanksgiving be made for all people—for kings and all those in authority, that we may live peaceful and quiet lives in all godliness and holiness. This is good, and pleases God our Savior, who wants all people to be saved and to come to a knowledge of the truth." Indeed, everything that has just been said about universalism is from the Bible.

My hunch is that exclusion texts that cannot be handled restoratively, in terms of a judgment process that evaluates rather than punishes, should be redeployed to warn

to recall at this moment too that a healthy approach to ethics is covenantal and not contractual;[25] people who resist joining God's people are only hurting themselves and damaging those they love. But this still leaves us with what Paul actually said.

Paul himself was not an explicit universalist. However, I believe we are entitled to suggest that he is one implicitly. If we do not infer this, we unleash the horrible internal contradictions that we tabulated earlier on. Jesus is qualitatively and quantitatively superior to all of humanity as represented by the story of Adam, not inferior. His story, which is God's story, must dominate the story of Adam, and not the other way around. Moreover, Paul is explicitly universalist in relation to unbelieving Israel. In view of the tensions in his writing, then, it does seem necessary to push through his deepest insights, which are grounded in the God revealed by Jesus, and let Paul reinterpret Paul. God really is love all the way across and all the way down. The covenant is unbreakable, and it ultimately enwraps us all in the gracious purpose of God that was established with us through his Son before the foundation of the world.

I am not going to insist on this position. This view must be suggested and then left largely at that. My insights are always distorted and limited; the events in question have not happened yet, and I am not in charge of them when they do—and they are massive, namely, a full transformation of all of history through time and space. What I can say with confidence is that there is every ground for hope and that we can trust the one who is in charge of this process to do a good job on that day. More than this does not need to be insisted on. Having said this, however, I do worry that I am being just a little bit cowardly.

As soon as the dreaded word "universalist" is used, a lot of people just get off the train. But I hope it is obvious by now that this is unnecessary. Furthermore, it might even be necessary to stay on the train to preserve God's integrity, along with the integrity of Paul's gospel. As far as I can tell, Jesus is

---

us of the terrible consequences of sin, a phenomenon we constantly trivialize. It is just that the punishment for sin will be internal to the sin and not external. Sin *is* destructive in and of itself. We need to face this fact squarely and not postpone or relocate it. Hence a reinterpretation of some of the Bible's future punishment texts might help us to be more honest about the sins we are presently involved with.

25. A covenantal approach relies for its ethical pressure on an existing relationship of love. Good behavior flows from such an approach. Only contractual ethics likes to induce good behavior by promising rewards and threatening punishments. So we are not weakening our ethics by rejecting the possibility of a horrific future state for those who sin. We are strengthening our ethics as we resist this scenario.

still on the train. Universalism (in the sense I am using it here) is really just a defense of God's integrity. We shouldn't want God's plan to fail, and we shouldn't impugn what God is like. God's work is compassionate and perfect. He created everyone to love and to live with him. Moreover, God is God. So God gets what he wants, eventually. Hence we have ended up here sounding more like the Barth of *CD* IV/3, who extols the triumph of God, than the cautiously optimistic Barth of *CD* III/2. It follows that we should also resist reducing Jesus in size, making him smaller and less significant than Adam and his work. This would be to get things the wrong way around. The plan in Jesus is far bigger, better, and more glorious than anything that happens foolishly because of Adam and Eve. God's plan is going to work and to work perfectly. So perhaps we need to put things slightly more strongly.

Let me say that I know as yet of no good theological arguments that lead me to expect another outcome regarding the scope of the future resurrection besides universalism. No other scenario seems to be grounded in Jesus so strongly. I expect everyone to be raised in glory, although some rather more shamefacedly than others.[26] The caveats just noted still apply: I have limited theological insight; the events have not taken place and are enormously complex; and I am not the one who makes them take place. I am not in a position either to know everything about this or to insist on this scenario.[27] But I am quietly confident.[28]

God is love.

Love never lets go.

Therefore God never lets go.

Theses

> ⏵ We need first to address an often-unnoticed issue—whether future bodily resurrection in Paul is limited to the righteous or whether it is universal, thereby enabling all to face a retributive judgment. The evidence, con-

---

26. Recall that there will be a stringent accountability.

27. In particular, I don't know *how* exactly this is going to happen, although I toy with the idea of a vast process of restorative justice unfolding at the "beginning" of eternity—a bracing prospect!

28. It is not necessary to endorse this view of God's final saving action, however, to frame or to define the non-Christian appropriately, and ultimately christologically. An agnostic stance toward universalism will suffice in this relation—and for the rest of the argumentation in this book.

trary to how it is often presented, suggests that Paul believed only in a limited resurrection of the righteous. This explains how everyone who is resurrected in his texts confesses Jesus's lordship, thereby evidencing being saved, and yet egregious sinners are in Paul's view excluded from this future kingdom.

> But is this view compatible with the scenarios in Paul of future judgment?
> Careful reading suggests that these are not retributive as much as evaluative—not a job interview but a job evaluation (or a parental evaluation!).
> A question now arises concerning future judgment in Paul. Does either the failure of God to save everyone or his active destruction of some suggest that God's relationship with humanity is ultimately conditional and effectively contractual, as against loving, elective, and irrevocable? If people by not doing something are not saved, then are people by doing something saved, suggesting that God relates to us contractually after all?
> In fact, people can reject a human covenantal relationship, cut themselves off from it, and live painful and damaged lives as a result. But this response does not entail that a constant covenantal invitation to relationship is not present. Many parents of troubled teenagers know this awful dynamic well.
> It is possible, then, to be a hopeful, prayerful, but agnostic universalist, like Barth in *CD* III/2.
> But a further question arises at this moment in relation to God.
> If God does not resurrect all his human creations, then this would be a puzzling failure.
> God loves all and wants all people to be gathered into communion.
> Moreover, God in his omnipotence should win; his plan should work and his purposes be ultimately achieved. This inevitable triumph implies a stronger form of universalism (see Barth in *CD* IV/3).
> Paul did not present this view, but he may imply it.
> In fact, there is direct evidence in Paul of a divine ultimate overcoming of human recalcitrance taking place somehow in relation to unbelieving Israel (see the argument of Rom 9–11). (The mechanics of this overcoming are not specified, but the ultimate fact of overcoming is affirmed.)
> This evidence suggests that we could read Paul's explicit expectations concerning the scope of future salvation—which are limited—in terms of his implicit and more important theological principles—which are universal—in an instance of *Sachkritik*. He is then an *implicit* universalist, although not an explicit one.

Key Scriptural References

Wrongdoers are clearly condemned by Paul in 1 Cor 6:9–11, as in several other texts. They do not inherit the kingdom of God.

The resurrected all seem universally to acclaim Jesus as Lord in Phil 2:9–11, as in several other texts.

We can explain this conundrum by grasping that only the righteous are resurrected in Paul.

Paul's evaluative, as against retributive, understanding of judgment is most clearly seen in Rom 14:10–12 and 1 Cor 3:13–17.

First Thessalonians 4:13–18 and 5:2–3 articulate a sequence in which the righteous are resurrected or caught up to meet Jesus "in the clouds" and "in the air" when he returns (which scholars know as his *parousia*, or "[royal arriving] presence"), and the unrighteous are destroyed "in the blink of an eye." This seems to confirm the scenario of a bodily resurrection of the righteous only.

Romans 5:12–21 suggests the superiority of the last Adam, Jesus, to the first Adam—and understandably so. The last Adam is the Lord.

Romans 9–11 argues, among other things, that, despite its present unbelief (ch. 10), "all Israel will be saved" (11:26), providing warrant for God's triumph over human resistance. (This use of "Israel" certainly includes unbelieving ethnic Israel at the least, and must not be reduced to a merely "spiritual" Israel.)

Key Reading

Hart's essay is a powerful, learned, although occasionally difficult articulation of the case finally being argued here. (See also his lecture on much the same material at https://www.youtube.com/watch?v=3dOsKzh7Kyw.)

De Boer is a learned Pauline scholar who has explored the universalist dimension within Paul's thinking both accurately and astutely.

Further Reading

McGlothlin canvasses the data in the New Testament and the church fathers incisively. Wright and Perrin provide a useful overview of the data but are insensitive to the issues that McGlothlin identifies and so should be used in with caution. (They run into infralapsarian problems too, which are illuminated by ch. 24.)

Barth has often been accused of universalism, but he steadfastly denied it (see the final paragraph of *CD* III/2), and we owe it to his intelligence and subtlety to at least examine his claims in this relation. One of his key points was a denial of any overriding of human freedom by God, although he defines that topic very carefully. This stance certainly excludes crude forms of universalism (and I myself endorse this exclusion). Another key point was his recognition of God's freedom, which certainly seems fair as well. God acts freely, and so we cannot really circumscribe God's activity in advance. Barth did point toward the legitimacy of hope, and even of prayer, for universal salvation. However, he stopped short of predicting it. (Part of Barth's repudiation is explicable in terms of his rejection of a form of universalism understood in a "hard" Origenist fashion, as seen also in Maximus the Confessor, which overrules divine agency. These theologians claim that salvation of all *must* follow on the successful theosis of all—a Pelagianizing account of universalism that Barth was quite right to reject.)[29]

Having said this. I am not sure that his development of the notion of the ultimate victory of God at length in *CD* IV/3 did not lead him to a theological location where the denial of universalism would in fact lead to the denial of key christological warrants, even after taking human freedom fully into account. And his christological account of election can also be invoked here in relation to God's freedom (II/2). God's freedom is not freedom per se but his free love toward us, which is definitively enacted in the Son prior to the foundation of the world. So perhaps some *Sachkritik* in relation to Barth himself is in order at this moment.

MacDonald, along with Parry and Partridge, introduces the contemporary debate usefully. Travis provides some important new angles on the Bible's judgment material, although his treatment needs further development. The imaginative and narrative resources in Lakoff, developed in terms of "nurturant" parenting, are extremely helpful in this relation, as we try to think about different types of judgment. A nice popular account of the view I am developing here is Rob Bell's much-maligned *Love Wins*. Its scholarship is by no means flawless but it still is a pretty good book; certainly its heart is in the right place, and it makes a number of the key moves clearly and engagingly. C. S. Lewis is also a useful popular point of access to this position; see his *Great Divorce*.

Come Sunday (dir. Joshua Marston, 2018), starring Chiwetel Ejiofor, traces the (in)famous journey of Pastor Carlton Pearson, a protégé of Oral Roberts, from a conservative to a universalist gospel. Theological, biblical, pastoral,

29. My thanks to Ethan Taylor for this set of insights.

and ecclesiological/institutional pressures are all in play in his journey in a rather fascinating way.

A footnote observed that another interpretative angle on Paul's texts about the future can be developed from the relatively recent progress of neuroscience concerning the mental construction of the future. Future scenarios are largely projections into the unknown of present states, both structural and emotional. So accounts of the future really tell us more about an author's experience of the present. This projection is introduced by Gilbert (esp. 83–105, 123–29, 140–42).

Bibliography

Barth, Karl. *Church Dogmatics*. II/2; III/3; IV/2; IV/3.

Bell, Rob. *Love Wins*. New York: HarperOne, 2011.

Boer, Martinus de. "Paul and Apocalyptic Eschatology." Pages 345–83 in Vol. 1 of *The Encyclopedia of Apocalypticism*. Edited by John J. Collins. New York: Continuum, 1998.

Gilbert, Daniel. *Stumbling on Happiness*. New York: Vintage (Random House), 2005.

Gordon, Benjamin D. "On the Sanctity of Mixtures and Branches: Two Halakic Sayings in Romans 11:16–24." *JBL* 135 (2016): 355–68.

Hart, David Bentley. "God, Creation, and Evil: The Moral Meaning of *creatio ex nihilo*." *Radical Orthodoxy: Theology, Philosophy, Politics* 3, no. 1 (2015): 1–17.

Hauerwas, Stanley. "Seeing Darkness, Hearing Silence: Augustine's Account of Evil." Pages 8–32 in *Working with Words*. Eugene, OR: Cascade, 2011.

Lakoff, George. *Moral Politics: How Liberals and Conservatives Think*. Rev. ed. Chicago: University of Chicago, 2002 (1996).

Lewis, C. S. *The Great Divorce*. New York: HarperCollins, 2001 (1946).

MacDonald, Gregory. *"All Shall Be Well": Explorations in Universalism and Christian Theology from Origen to Moltmann*. Cambridge: James Clarke, 2011.

McGlothlin, Thomas D. *Resurrection as Salvation: Development and Conflict in Pre-Nicene Paulinism*. Cambridge: Cambridge University Press, 2018.

Parry, Robin A., and Christopher H. Partridge, *Universal Salvation? The Current Debate*. Grand Rapids: Eerdmans, 2003.

Torrance, James B. "The Contribution of McLeod Campbell to Scottish Theology." *SJT* 26 (1973): 295–311.

———. "Covenant or Contract? A Study of the Theological Background of Worship in Seventeenth-Century Scotland." *SJT* 23 (1970): 51–76.

Travis, Stephen H. *Christ and the Judgment of God: The Limits of Divine Retribution in New Testament Thought.* Peabody, MA: Hendrickson, 2009.

Wagner, J. Ross. *Heralds of the Good News: Isaiah and Paul in Concert in the Letter to the Romans.* Leiden: Brill, 2003.

Wright, N. T., with N. Perrin. *The Resurrection of the Son of God.* Minneapolis: Fortress, 2003.

CHAPTER 19

Mission as Friendship

A Brief Theology of Mission

We might adopt the right frame and consequent posture toward non-Christians, defining them christologically and so in solidarity with our own better, as well as with our worse, selves. We might dedicate ourselves to the truth that God loves them and has a wonderful plan for their lives, and that we have a key part to play in letting them know about it. But when we try to make actual contact with non-Christians, there are still traps lurking that we must identify and navigate around. We might still violate their integrity in a number of ways, as serried critiques of colonialism and any attendant missional distortions have tirelessly pointed out.[1] So what is the right way to do mission?

---

1. We have already noted the challenge of colonialism in part 3. This topic returns here, although it is only fair to note that colonialism as a historical process was complex, with many dimensions, some good and some bad. It is important within any critique not to flatten out the particularities of Christian mission into an unethical caricature, which is also ironic because a frequent complaint by the critics is a failure by colonizers to attend to the voices of the colonized, that is, to detailed realities on the ground. There is also a frequent overlooking of the vast benefits, especially medical, accruing to the colonized, and of the attendant sacrifices by missionaries. Advances in medicine and sanitation greatly improved the lives of millions of people. But there is truth in the critiques as well. Colonialism could be profoundly problematic, and when it was intertwined with missionary work, mission was often compromised deeply in turn, in a number of different ways. Earlier, in part 3, I was more concerned about how to navigate the relationship between the Christian and the non-Christian so that it is not forced, coerced, or manipulated by inappropriate types and uses of power. Here and following I address the problem of inappropriate local cultural *erasure*.

As always, we should begin from first principles. We have already learned that the God revealed through Jesus is a personal God and that persons themselves are intrinsically relational beings. Indeed, we are relational to the point that we are constituted and live as persons in and through one another, intersubjectively. And we learned this truth from a God who became a human being. Consequently, it is absolutely no surprise (in retrospect!) that the truth continues to be revealed by people to one another. God is mediated through people, although this mediation is superintended, mercifully, by God, and especially by the nurturing divine Spirit. But this direct, concrete, relational outreach now needs to be parsed carefully; it contains several very particular modes. When one of these is absent, the authenticity of the entire missional relationship is thrown off and compromised, and before any personal contact begins, the problems can begin with our *motive* for engaging in the first place.

Motive

Having the right motive is critically important to a correct approach to mission. If, for example, any outreach to non-Christians arises principally from a sense of perceived need within them, then there is actually something inauthentic about any conversion, or even just any relationship that proceeds on this apparently charitable basis. We have thereby designated the non-Christian as "needy," thereby arrogating to ourselves a superior, less needy, position. Our relationship must then proceed on a fundamentally paternalistic basis. Moreover, because we have defined these needs externally to the person, prior to getting to know her (a woman, let us assume), we have imposed our concerns onto the situation before we have heard the concerns of the person herself; we are speaking for her and over the top of her in this most delicate of situations, defining her struggles and deficiencies for her. So although this sort of relationship proceeds with the best of intentions, it conceals a sinister, superior, fundamentally colonial dynamic that we ought to avoid if we can. We need to value the person for her own sake and not because we feel her pain and want to fix it. She is not fundamentally a problem; she is, at bottom, a person. (Note: I am not denying that a definition of a problem might ultimately be involved or that there might be pain present, but it cannot be our first word to someone.)

Similarly, I might want to reach out to people because I want to convert them, and I have been told from my first conscious years in Sunday School that this is what all my relationships with non-Christians are about. Their becoming Christians is the primary goal of my activity. But this is again external to who they really are and want to be themselves at present, however misguided their goals might be, and so I am again disrespecting their personhood. If we approach people merely as potential converts and lose interest in them if they don't become actual converts, then we are not valuing them as people. We are valuing them as statistics and as markers of our own piety—in terms of our own goals—and the integrity of our missional relationship has been undermined once more, along with the integrity of our witness to the gospel of a loving, Trinitarian God who loves and respects us as people, right where we are. This motive also badly needs to be avoided. But how do we do this?

We avoid instrumentalizing potential converts—which is what we are doing here—and we stay in touch with the very heart of our gospel and our God if we approach people in the first instance for the right motive, and this must be the goal simply of being in relationship with them and getting to know them as people. Basically *we must want to make friends with them*. Authentic mission is "friendship evangelism" (as it is usually known), with the emphasis on the friendship.[2] Fortunately, our christological account of the other will supply us with a deeply convincing warrant for this approach.

We have already learned that Jesus is at work in everyone. He loves them, created them, and is relating to them, and we cannot deny this activity without denying his lordship. So everyone, whether they are overtly confessing Jesus as Lord or not, witnesses on *some* level to the divine presence and has value as a mediation of God's unconditional love. And so we can approach them on this basis. Everyone has value. (They are probably not pure value, so to speak, but they have some value, just as we do.) So we should approach people to make friends with them because we value them in the first instance for who they are and what they bring to a relationship with us, knowing that they can tell us something about God and are consequently worth knowing in their own right. Each person, in short, is worth making friends with. The basis of any engagement should be this positive recognition of the value of the other. And there is a simple test to see if we are really doing so.

A former teacher of mine who had lived for many years in Israel as a Christian was once asked this question by a Jewish friend: "Will you love me even if I never become convinced about Jesus?" The answer was, "Of course." And this is certainly the correct answer. But while it slides glibly off the tongue,

---

2. This is a moment where familial values need to be displaced by the primary category of friendship, although understanding friendship in the appropriately familial terms as those have already been defined, covenantally.

it is a costly act in practice. Yet it is the only posture that generates and maintains integrity in any relationship with a non-Christian.

Do we desire a given relationship if at bottom that person never commits
overtly to Jesus? Are we desirous of a friendship—a full, honest, committed
friendship—because we value and enjoy the non-Christian person in question? Will we hang out indefinitely with someone who is very different from us
in many key respects, not because we are hoping that the person will eventually
convert, but because we value that one just as he or she is? (We do hope for a
conversion, but that must be an ancillary motive.) We must be able to answer
"yes" to these questions if our missionary work is ultimately to have any integrity, and we must learn to relate to non-Christians primarily on this basis.

It is hard to tell whether Paul himself was this motivationally pure. He does
not seem to have been an introvert, and he doesn't tell us much about his inner
life.[3] He certainly evidences strong desires for non-Christians to convert, but
this is not necessarily bad in and of itself. It just cannot be primary. I think we
can say that he was a good friend-maker (and apparently a good enemy-maker
too, although there were different reasons for this).[4] A circle of loyal and affec-
tionate supporters is generally discernable buzzing around him. And perhaps
we can point to the conversion of Onesimus ("Handy Andy") and detect a real
depth of affection and commitment in at least this particular relationship.[5]

Onesimus was an unhappy slave who had sought an intervention from Paul
into his troubled relationship with his master, Philemon. Paul possessed a degree
of spiritual authority in relation to Philemon as the apostle who had converted
Epaphras, the original Colossian missionary, and so Onesimus saw value in approaching him for help. But the cultural distance between Paul and Onesimus
was extreme. Paul didn't look like much, but he was an older, educated, freeborn,
and spiritually authoritative figure, with an impeccable Jewish ancestry. Onesimus was a young, white, "Russian" slave of ill repute. (A Scythian was a slave from
what are now the Russian steppes, to the north of the Black Sea, which is probably
why Paul mentions this unusual group in Col 3:11.) So Paul and Onesimus were

3. Romans 7:7–25 should not be misread as an introspective or psychological
analysis, although it has distant implications here. It is, as we saw earlier in ch. 6, a
programmatic account of the nature of fleshly humanity that is heavily informed by
Jewish narrative and Christian theological concerns.

4. See more on this shortly. Much that Paul wrote was shaped in response to a
group working through his congregations, subverting his gospel, whom he calls at one
point his "enemies" (Phil 3:18).

5. Paul puns on this name in Phlm 11, an interesting fact we will discuss more in
ch. 20.

separated by gulfs of status, class, and ethnicity. Yet Paul evidences a deep affection for Onesimus in the pleading letter he writes to Philemon. "I am sending him back to you—who is my very heart" (12). And by turns he exhorts, cajoles, and even subtly threatens to try to ensure Onesimus's safe reception back at Colossae. This is clearly a friendship, then, and a rather strange one.[6] But a conversion was involved as well. Paul "begot" Onesimus while he was in prison (10).

We cannot say for certain on the basis of these data that Paul was initially committed to Onesimus as a person to be befriended and enjoyed, and only secondarily in terms of conversion. But we can say that he crossed a massive gulf of social distance and that he seems to genuinely have loved the unhappy young slave (who might also have been somewhat light-fingered),[7] and this relational impetus could certainly flow from a motive of genuine friendship. Furthermore, we can ask whether Paul would *not* have written his charming letter to Philemon if Onesimus had not converted. This seems very unlikely. We can legitimately infer, then, that the master of friendship evangelism, as this method is often known today, was a master because, in the first instance, he was a master of friendship, thereby setting us an important example.[8]

If we want to convert people, then, our motive for engaging with them concretely, as we have to, must paradoxically be the goal of making friends with them even if they never convert. This is where all healthy mission begins. We want the best for our new friends, which would involve their conversion, but this is not our primary motive for reaching out to them in the first place. They are people, and we approach them as such, sending the message that they have value right where they are and as they are, and that we value them in the first instance as our potential friends. Conversion would be a bonus.

Fortunately, friendship evangelism is incredibly effective—although why would this surprise us? We were made for friendship. And Paul did make friends—a lot of them.

Method

My eyes were opened to the method operative within Paul's mission through the research of sociologist Rodney Stark and his colleagues into the beginnings of new religious movements in the United States. In a salutary sentence Stark

6. We will talk more about this critical dimension of Christian mission momentarily.

7. See Col 3:22–25.

8. That is, Paul would have been a friend of Onesimus's even if he had not converted, suggesting the underlying primacy of the relationship of friendship.

says, "In the early 1960s John Lofland and I were the first social scientists to actually go out and watch people convert to a new religious movement."[9] In San Francisco they followed around Young Oon Kim, a woman missionary from Korea who was trying to convert people to the Unification Church, better known as the Moonies. Later on they studied conversions to the Church of Jesus Christ of Latter-day Saints (LDS), that is, to the Mormons. They found that, contrary to all the theorizing, conversions took place informally through preexisting relationships of friendship and family.

All the formal attempts at conversion by Ms. Kim—using public meetings, pamphlets, press releases, and so on—yielded no converts at all. But her community did come into being and grow, and it was through the young housewife she first lodged with. A group of three neighboring housewives and friends converted at this time, followed by their husbands, and then some relatives who visited from Oregon. And the study of conversions to the LDS community yielded the same results. Indeed, the LDS statistics are particularly compelling.

The LDS community gives an enormous amount of time and talent to formal evangelism. Its leaders devote two years to this practice full-time. Who has not met LDS missionaries many times knocking on the front door? But the actual conversions from these efforts are next to negligible: about one in a thousand. The impressive growth rate of the community—about 4 percent yearly—is achieved almost entirely through the conversions of relatives and close friends: an astonishing 50 percent of them are converted after a period of around three years of general informal contact. Conversions take place through informal networks.[10]

This sociological lens helped me to see the same phenomenon playing out on the pages of Paul's letters.

A large circle of supporters and coworkers is evident in Paul's writings— (without any claim to completion) see Aquila, Aristarchus, Barnabas, Chloe, Demas, Epaenetus, Epaphras, Epaphroditus, Erastus, Evodia, Gaius (from Corinth), Gaius (from Derbe), Jason, Jesus/Justus, Lucius, Luke, Mark, Onesimus, Phoebe, Prisca, Secundus, Silvanus/Silas, Sosipater/Sopater, Sosthenes, Stephanas, Syntyche, Timothy, Titus, Trophimus, and Tychicus.[11] This is a long list of traveling companions, helpers, and hosts and hostesses, and to

---

9. Rodney Stark, *The Rise of Christianity*, 15.

10. Many of these conversions are unfortunately not characterized primarily by the motive of friendship; they are, precisely, characterized by a desire to convert.

11. I would not include Apollos or Crispus on a list of Paul's friends. I would include Sosthenes. Crispus was, I would suggest, converted by Paul but "defected" to Apollos; Sosthenes did the reverse.

fulfill these roles in an ancient Pauline church network meant that these men and women were basically Paul's friends. So Paul clearly had a lot of friends, which is also to say that friendship evangelism worked for him, and this in large measure because *friends convert friends*. Once one has made a friend, all the preexisting friends, along with the close family members, of that person become exposed to the new movement, and so it almost inevitably spreads through those networks. Furthermore, we have already seen how highly intersubjective and networked people are. The good news echoes and resonates through our new friend's network; his or her newfound happiness spreads like a beneficial virus. Moreover, if the process keeps going, as Stark asserts (although arguably a little too optimistically), it increases exponentially. Friends convert friends, who have further friends to convert, and so on. If things move on in anything resembling a constant, then at a surprisingly early moment, the movement reaches a tipping point and, in numerical terms, virtually explodes.

But there is a further critical insight lurking within these data. These are not merely friendships. They are highly diverse friendships with very different people. Note how many of the people on our earlier list of thirty friends are pagans, not Jews—nineteen.[12] And note how many are women, not men—five (which is a high number for a male network in the ancient world).[13] These are *strange* friendships in just the way that Paul's close relationship with Onesimus was. What explains this? The key lies in the *manner* in which Paul made his friends, the third key mode in appropriate mission work.

Manner

One of my favorite Pauline verses—although I do have a lot—is 1 Thess 2:9:

> Remember, brothers, our toil and labor;
> while we worked night and day so that we would not burden any of you,
> we proclaimed the good news about God to you.

12. Aquila, Aristarchus, Barnabas, Jason, Jesus/Justus, Lucius, Mark, Prisca, Silas/Silvanus, Sopater/Sosipater, and Timothy, are explicitly identified at some point as Jews—eleven of the thirty people named.

13. Five is probably a high percentage for an ancient, androcentric culture, and especially when all of these women seem to have positions of authority (perhaps excepting Chloe).

It is evident from this statement that when Paul arrived in Thessalonica he worked alongside the handworkers whom he eventually befriended and con-verted. A further critical insight into mission in terms of friendship is present here, concerning its manner.

Paul was clearly prepared to travel to those he was called to. He was ready to go, just as God commanded him to; his very title "apostle" suggests he was, as one who was sent ("apostled"). But implicit in this preparedness is not just a geographic charity—the preparedness to go to where someone is to befriend them. We also see in Paul's life what we might call a sociological charity as well, although this is directly continuous with geographic charity. Paul did not just travel through different places engaging with people indiscriminately from a great social height. Insofar as he could—and he went a very long way in this regard—*he adopted the practices of the people he was befriending*, so he lived and worked *alongside* them. He assumed their identities, thereby extending the incarnational dimension already apparent in his missionary activity from a mere preparedness to go and travel to a far country to an adoption of the practices of those who lived there (although with an important caveat con-cerning sin that we will develop in due course). And this shows us particularly how to avoid colonizing our potential converts through the inappropriate use of power, here in the form, strictly speaking, of any deployment of superior social capital. Like the God acting through Jesus, Paul becomes just like those he is approaching and befriending, which is the approach of one who seeks a relationship based not on power but on love.

Paul speaks explicitly of this aspect of his missional relating in a couple of important texts, where we also see how adapting to those one is befriend-ing in different situations entails diversification (an important Christian phe-nomenon that will occupy us a great deal in the chapters that follow). Paul's programmatic statement of this missionary mode is in 1 Cor 9. He writes there of becoming a Jew to Jews, under Torah to those under Torah (although he is not, he asserts, actually under Torah), of (nevertheless) lacking Torah among those who lack it (although he does not lack the Torah of Christ of course), and of being weak among the weak.[14] In this way he has become everything to all, with the result that he might save some (9:22).

14. The "weak" is a reference to converted worshipers-of-God, or Godfearers, who converted to Christianity from a location quite close to Judaism but not fully integrated with it. Any men in this group, for example, were probably not circumcised. These converts consequently continued to practice various Jewish customs, even though, as converted pagans, in Paul's view they did not have to. Their consciences in this respect were "weak."

The book of Acts also records numerous instances when Paul adopted Jewish practices as he headed into Jewish contexts,[15] while his own attested endurance of no less than five synagogue lashings (2 Cor 11:24) suggests a determined presence in various Jewish communities as well. That is, he endured this extreme discipline, which was appropriate only for Jews, rather than simply withdrawing from Jewish contexts (and this should also ease the misgivings of some scholars that Acts is exaggerating Paul's commitment to Jewish contexts in Jewish terms). Paul clearly meant what he said in 1 Cor 9:20. But his work as an artisan among artisans in Thessalonica confirms this practice as well among low status, out-and-out pagans, which is what he says in 1 Cor 9:21. He worked night and day alongside them, eating and drinking with them, living just like a pagan handworker. And just the same point is expressed more succinctly in Gal 4:12, when Paul challenges his formerly pagan Galatian converts "to become like me, for I became like you."

All these data suggest that we are on firm ground when we infer that Paul adapted himself to his different constituencies significantly, becoming like them and living alongside them. Not only did he travel to them, but he contextualized himself among them; the movement involved in reaching them extended through to a deep involvement in their situations.

Missionaries sometimes refer to this manner of getting alongside friends and potential converts in terms of "immersion" in the local culture, or "contextualizing." And a key marker of immersion will usually be learning the local language. As the locale of a given mission's language is mastered, so too its culture should be mastered. It must be indwelt as fully as it can be. This indwelling and language learning, both in literal and in broader cultural terms, is the baseline for the further process of Christian community formation, and there is another simple test for this. Do you know your people well enough to laugh at their jokes and to make them laugh? If not, stay a bit longer and learn a bit more.

An interesting aspect of this practice of immersion is that it is a posture of listening more than it is of talking. We often tend to think of missionaries arriving and proclaiming the gospel to a city or town from some street corner. They stand there and announce what God is doing like a person standing on a box declaiming at the corner of Hyde Park in London. This is true in certain respects, but we need to think again about when exactly this announcement takes place and in what mode. We really need to win the right to speak. And that begins with listening.

---

15. See Acts 13:14–43; 16:3; 18:18, 22; 20:6; 21:24, 26, detailing, among other things, a circumcision and two Nazirite vows.

We only hear Paul speaking, because we have only his letters. But I believe one can detect a listener in them.

They are astonishingly diverse. Romans and Galatians are very different from the two letters we have preserved from his correspondence with the Corinthians—and Galatians has a long biographical section where Romans has none. The Thessalonian letters are different again, as are the more liturgical Ephesians and abbreviated Colossians. And who would have expected a letter like the plea to Philemon from the author of the rest of this correspondence to Christian communities?

Some scholars offer a somewhat cynical explanation for this—that Paul was a jumbled thinker who could not maintain much conceptual consistency from one letter to another. Or still worse, he was a cynical speaker, who told his listeners whatever their itching ears wanted to hear. But a more constructive explanation of this diversity is the process of immersion we are describing here. If Paul was operating in these terms, then he would have responded deliberately and carefully to the specific circumstances of each of his communities, and these were very different. So his letters were different. In this marked divergence among his letters, then, we can detect an underlying posture of listening and specific responding. He indwelt the problems and struggles of his communities, and so we see this contextual sensitivity in the diversity of his letters addressing those when he could not—or judged he should not—be personally present with them.[16]

Strange Friendships

The result of Paul's willingness to travel into different geographic and social spaces and then to live alongside their occupants is not merely an impressive record in the Pauline data of successful friendships and conversions. Paul's friendships took place across challenging social gradients, in spaces that were very different from his origins after he had adapted himself to the customs and mores around him. So they were frequently strange friendships. One of my favorite examples is the conversion of Lydia, recounted in Acts 16:13–15.

16. Paul usually sent letters only when he could not travel to defuse a crisis in one of his communities, but in the case of Corinth he found that letters were more effective there than his presence, especially when they were conveyed by Titus.

On the Sabbath
we went outside the city gate to the river,
where we expected to find a place of prayer.
We sat down and began to speak to the women who had gathered
   there.
One of those listening was a woman from the city of Thyatira named
   Lydia,
a dealer in purple cloth.
She was a worshiper of God.
The Lord opened her heart to respond to Paul's message.
When she and the members of her household were baptized,
she invited us to her home.
"If you consider me a believer in the Lord," she said,
"come and stay at my house."
And she persuaded us.

Lydia was a female business owner in Philippi, involved, Acts tells us here, with the purple dye business, although she originally came from Thyatira. There is a great deal of interesting information buried in these cryptic details.

Lydia was probably involved in Philippi with the ersatz toga business. But to understand the full significance of this job, we will need to plunge more deeply into the industries and snobberies of the ancient Roman Empire.

Roman citizens had a carefully coded public profile. They wore a distinctive white, very expensive Roman garment, the toga, which was often marked with purple to denote their different statuses. Children, magistrates, and senators wore togas marked with purple bands of various widths, the toga praetexta, while emperors, curule magistrates at important public occasions, and consuls wore the completely purple and comprehensively embroidered toga picta (so an emperor was "born to the purple"). The city of Philippi was "a little Rome," and so it aped the garments and codes of its mother city. (And many people simply liked purple cloth.) But it faced a problem. Purple dye was enormously expensive.

The genuine article, Tyrian purple or porphyry, was obtained by crushing the purpura rock snails found in the eastern Mediterranean, in particular abundance near Tyre, hence the name. But it took perhaps twelve thousand snails to produce 1.4 grams of dye sufficient to stain the hem of one robe. So Tyrian purple cost a small fortune—it would have been cheaper to sprinkle a toga with gold dust—and we can see immediately that even striped Roman togas signified enormous wealth. They were key ancient items of conspicuous consumption, and hence the reason for the Romans wearing them. So what were the rather poorer, provincial Philippians to do?

They did what many Roman imitators did and obtained a cheaper substitute, which was derived from a plant known as madder, from which was extracted Erythrodanon, or "dyer's red." It was found in many ancient locations, including the regions of Phrygia and Lydia (in today's western Turkey). The product was nowhere near as good as Tyrian purple, but neither was it anywhere near as expensive. And it seems that Lydia was involved in this business—the ancient guild of the purple-dyers, or purpurarii.

However, her name also suggests that she had probably been a slave.[17] Slaves were frequently named by their owners after their places of origin, since their original barbarian names would have been both unpronounceable and inappropriate. So we can deduce that she came from the ancient territory of Lydia. But her behavior in the story in Acts suggests that she was now a freed slave who ran her own business. She still most likely worked hard with her hands in this despised manual labor. And Acts also states that she was a Jewish sympathizer, or "reverer of God."

Paul meets Lydia at a Jewish meeting point because of her Jewish sympathies. But she is technically a pagan. And despite her relative independence, she is a fairly low-status person—a foreigner, a freed slave who continues to work with her hands, and a woman. Yet he converts her and then accepts her hospitality. This, then, is a strange friendship. The place is not entirely unexpected, but a river bank in Philippi is a long way from Jerusalem. And a friendship between a high-status Jewish man and a low-status, formerly enslaved woman is clearly a strange one. Yet this encounter and its subsequent friendship led to a Christian community in Philippi that would live on for a very long time.[18] Polycarp wrote a letter to it around 150 CE.

17. Lydia is not always a slave name, but it is combined here with her origins from Thyatira in Lydia, and with her status as a handworker in an industry known to be a speciality of the region of Lydia. In combination, this evidence for her humble background seems decisive.

18. Note also that twenty years later, in Philippians, he begs two important women in the local community at Philippi, Euodia and Syntyche, to get on with one another—and he begs; he does not command. It seems possible if not likely that one of these is Lydia, the original patroness of the church, here using her preferred, not her slave, name. This would neatly explain why two women occupy such a powerful position within the community. Lydia, being a woman, probably had important friendships with other women and carried those into the church, here in another instance of friendship evangelism. However, being a relationship between frail creatures of flesh,

But the conversion of Lydia is significant for one further reason. We see, as we trace out her subsequent influence on Paul, that evangelism, done for the right reasons of friendship and with the right immersive manner alongside, catalyzes an extraordinarily effective additional dimension within Paul's missionary method. These practices result not just in strange, unexpected, and surprising friendships that open up further conversions by way of existing friendships and family connections in that person's network. They result in network *multiplication*.

Network Multiplication

Shortly after befriending Lydia and establishing a small church in Philippi, Paul traveled down the magnificent Roman highway that is still partly visible today in northern Greece, the Ignatian Way, to Thessalonica, the capital of the province of Macedonia and the Aegean Sea's key northern port. And he succeeded in starting a community there as well. It had a rocky start, however. There seems to have been strong local opposition, apparently from both Jewish and pagan figures, and Paul and his fellow missionaries were forced out of the city prematurely, leaving the young Thessalonian church exposed to its local antagonists.[19] However, the Thessalonians' misfortune is our good fortune. Because of this pressure, we now possess two letters from Paul to Thessalonica, written to sustain that community in those difficult days. Indeed, these letters are doubly fascinating because they are so early. They were written around 40 CE, thus a good ten years before his other letters. And they tell us, as we have already seen, that Paul converted the Thessalonians by working alongside them, "night and day," in manual labor (so 1 Thess 2:9).

Now one does not simply arrive in an ancient city and practice a trade. There are local organizations that protect the precarious lives of particular

this friendship had, like so many, deteriorated, thereby disrupting the rest of the little community. Paul strives repeatedly to make peace within this relationship in his letter. The famous song, Phil 2:6–11, is oriented largely toward this goal, as v. 5 suggests. Moreover, the cause of the deterioration seems to be status competition, which was a particular problem in highly competitive, status-sensitive Hellenistic society, as some of the difficulties at Corinth also attest.

19. A brief overview of Paul's relationship with the Thessalonians can be found in my *Journey*, ch. 3–5, 41–74; a more detailed analysis of his travels and their date is provided in *Framing*, ch. 4, 190–253.

artisans, and there need to be opportunities to work—shops, contracts, materials, and so on. Hence one shows up in an ancient city unannounced only if one has either a lot of money or a death wish (or is just passing through). Life in the ancient world was proverbially nasty, brutish, and short. There was no social welfare and little sympathy for outsiders. Without an introduction, then, starvation and exposure were probable outcomes, especially for poor people. So it is highly likely that Paul had an introduction to certain artisans in Thessalonica asking them to welcome him and to provide him with work. It was this work opportunity that opened up in turn into relationships that formed the community.[20] Moreover, this opportunity almost certainly came from Lydia's contacts as an artisan with the handworking communities in this city neighboring hers (and presumably from any other business-people in the Philippian congregation). And it is now clear that some rather significant things seem to have happened on the most basic social and relational levels to further accelerate Paul's missionary work.

Paul is connecting with potential converts through networks of friendship, accessing new networks by way of strange friendships. But we already know this. However, something new is apparent here. Paul is also jumping *between* overlapping networks to obtain maximal advantage by exposure to new opportunities, something he can do only because he is prepared to travel into new situations and to make new friends in different locales with different lifestyles. I call this network multiplication or, more colloquially, missionary snakes and ladders. We see here initially, in Lydia, a Jewish network that turned out to overlap with an artisan network. Paul met Lydia at a Jewish meeting place, then befriended her connections with other artisans. (A network of military veterans is also possibly detectable at Philippi, although veterans were often artisans as well; see Phil 2:25.) And it was this new, artisanal network of business contacts that allowed him to travel safely to Thessalonica and to be accepted by handworkers there, among whom he worked, and many of whom he subsequently befriended and converted. Artisan networks then also helped him as he moved south, especially to Corinth, where both his Jewish connections and his handworker connections were in play. Indeed, we can now see how Paul constantly worked several overlapping networks during his

20. There is evidence of a Jewish connection at Thessalonica as well, namely, Jason, Aristarchus, and possibly also Secundus (who was a slave), but it does not seem to have been a significant element in the ongoing life of the church in the way that it was at Corinth, and probably also at Berea. Jason, Aristarchus, and Secundus seem to have traveled with Paul, which may go some way toward explaining their inclusion.

missionary career, hopping between them whenever he could—the missionary equivalent of landing on a ladder and shooting up several squares in the board game just mentioned.

Paul exploits family or *kinship* networks whenever he can, including his own and those of his fellow workers (and these are always important). So not long after his call he traveled to Syria and Cilicia, the latter region being where his home town of Tarsus was. Then later he traveled with Barnabas to that missionary's home town on Cyprus. He also clearly worked Jewish networks, which was an *ethnic* network, trying to get a footing in local synagogues, although usually without success. But he also worked any *aristocratic patronage* networks he could gain access to. This is the most likely explanation for his journey to Pisidian Antioch after the conversion of Sergius Paulus on the island of Cyprus, an episode we will discuss more momentarily. The Sergii Paulii were a prominent family in this somewhat obscure Roman colony in the distant uplands of what is now central Turkey. This type of elite, international patronage network (or, at least, regional network) should be distinguished, however, from the way Paul benefited from local city, or *municipal* patronage networks, where prominent businesswomen seemed to have helped him especially. Phoebe, the deacon and host of the community that met in Corinth's port city of Cenchreae (Rom 16:1–2), took Paul's magisterial letter to Rome, to the Jesus followers there, suitably escorted. (Her interpretative explanations would have been the first commentary on Romans!) She had nowhere near the reach and influence of a family of aristocrats like the Sergii, but she had local power and some international contacts. Moreover, Paul seems to have worked his periods of *imprisonment* hard as well. Prisons are excellent places to network. So as many as seven overlapping networks are detectable in Paul's missionary work—kinship, artisan, ethnic, veteran, both elite and municipal patronage, and carceral. His skill in jumping from one to the other and back again is probably what led in large measure to his success in establishing communities in various cities around the Mediterranean coastlands.

We now have a nice account in place of a Pauline missionary method, one modeled by the great missionary himself, and I would suggest that it will still prove powerfully effective, provided it is undertaken accurately. This basic approach to mission will already be known by many as friendship evangelism, but it is a highly particular type of friendship evangelism. It begins by defining non-Christians christologically, valuing them in and of themselves, wanting to befriend them for their own sake. It consequently establishes relationships with non-Christians that are not primarily evangelistic (or patronizing) but rooted in friendship. This is the motive for concrete engagement with other people, face-to-face. But this is also the method—making friends—that can result, happily, in the friends of those friends converting, and their friends and family, and so on. These friendships are attempted and pursued, moreover, immersively, by getting alongside those being befriended, no matter how different—or especially, how low—the social spaces are that they occupy. The manner in which we pursue friendship is, in short, incarnational. And the result will probably be strange friendships, and many of them, resulting in turn in the possibility of network multiplication. In short, we have given a Pauline account of mission here in terms of its initial definition of the non-Christian other; and then of the motive, method, and manner of relating to him or her. These are the four key Pauline missional modes—definition, motive, method, and manner—which, properly followed, should result in strange friendships and network multiplication. But our account is not yet complete.

We need now to consider quickly how costly this type of mission is, and not merely in terms of the sheer physical and cultural costs of relocation. Missionaries acting in the Pauline mode we have just detailed, getting alongside people, will court vulnerability, resulting in a deeply counterintuitive account of leadership. Moreover, the exploration of this distinctive leadership mode will open out into an absolutely critical aspect of mission that we have not yet sufficiently described, namely, the leading of the Holy Spirit.

Vulnerability

Implicit in Paul's mode of arrival as a missionary, befriending and getting alongside the unlovely, is a feature of authentic leadership that we would do well to attend to. It is so counterintuitive—which is really to say "counter-fleshly"—that we seem frequently to lose sight of it, fixating on incorrect markers of leadership and thereby following inauthentic voices and losing our way.

We saw earlier on that Paul's missionary activity originated in a personal call from Jesus himself. Few church leaders can point to events as dramatic and overt as Paul's, but the point nevertheless remains valid that community leadership must be initiated by the call of God and not by the person in question. It is not self-initiated. But we can add quite a bit of information to this point now that might enable us to evaluate when someone is divinely appointed and energized as against being merely self-ratified.

As we saw, Paul's practices of arrival entailed traveling far away from his own people and his home. He clearly had a readiness to go, as well as a readiness to follow new networks into strange and marginal social spaces.

Moreover, in doing so, he tried to adopt the practices and lifestyles of his new contacts. He lived alongside them. And the basic result of this lifestyle, especially in an ancient context, was *vulnerability* on a number of levels, for which Paul's word was "weakness" (Gk. *astheneia*, which he uses 11x).

Foreigners lacked the resources of their own local networks—their families, villages, tribes, communities, and patrons. And they could lack very basic necessities like food, shelter, and work. Moreover, they were subject to the suspicions customarily directed toward foreigners by the highly xenophobic communities that composed the ancient Roman Empire (2 Cor 11:24–25!). So Paul was apparently subjected to punitive action by suspicious local authorities in almost every area he entered. Furthermore, his policy of living alongside his new contacts entailed a deliberate abandonment of cultural status markers. If one becomes like low-status artisans, one looks like an artisan and enjoys none of the advantages possessed by elite figures—eloquence, learning, patronage, wealth, and so on. This deliberate contextualization consequently doubled his vulnerability, creating a further exposure to misunderstanding and rejection. "Is this what a messenger from the Lord of the universe looks like?" people must have asked.

But in this very vulnerability Paul is enacting key aspects of his theology. If he perseveres in his ministry, sustaining its costs, enduring its sacrifices, and pressing on faithfully in spite of misunderstanding and outright opposition, he attests to the presence of a number of key virtues that are attested in the life of Jesus himself. His self-sacrifice, nonviolent endurance, and fidelity speak powerfully of the grace, the obedience, and the faithfulness of Jesus. Hence, although Paul might not look like much to the unenlightened outsider, the careful observer could see the life of Jesus figuring forth in his behavior in a deeply authentic way, because Jesus's life didn't look like much to the outsider either.

Moreover, the costliness of this lifestyle automatically guarded it against phony reproduction; no insincere leader would willingly endure the pressures of this type of ministry; it simply cost too much. Two "payments" in particular are worth emphasizing. First, Paul was a celibate. He traveled without a wife, which probably means he had none, although he maintains that he had a right to be married (1 Cor 9:5). (And this decision seems wise, given the rigors of his work. Paul's tough, itinerant lifestyle was no place for child rearing.) Second, he preached the gospel free of charge. He would, it seems, accept money from communities that had already been founded in other places, but he would not accept money from the people he was immediately living among, which further enhanced the authenticity of his proclamation (1 Cor 9:12, 15–18; 2 Cor

12:13). He was no charlatan, unlike many in the ancient world, although he could not entirely escape suspicion (1 Thess 2:1–12).

These, then, are the marks of an authentic apostle—a person tasked by God with taking the gospel to a foreign location, whether that is geographic, social, or both, and planting a community there. And such workers are radically countercultural in their abdication of all the key cultural status markers— if, that is, they were possessed in the first place. These are set aside, including spouses and wages. The positive marks of authenticity are seen especially clearly, however, as these leaders endure the pressures elicited by their vulnerability. In their faithful and committed endurance of misunderstanding, rejection, and suspicion, of the basic physical challenges of life in a poor and hostile situation, and even of interrogation, their instantiation of the life of Jesus is evident to those with the eyes to see. And this endurance doubtless extended to the struggles necessary to preserve the unity of the church and in the patient explanation of the legitimacy of the shockingly novel developments currently taking place—dynamics we talk more about shortly. Their authenticity is apparent, in other words, as they suffer, provided they respond to this suffering in an appropriate way. Vulnerability and suffering segue into one another rapidly and inextricably. Indeed, I am tempted to say at this point, if anyone out there still wants to be an apostle, think again.

Authentication by the Spirit

A problem of authentication, however, remains visible in the apostolic praxis that we have just sketched out. How is anyone to recognize in such a vulnerable, rejected, and struggling figure the ambassador of the creator of heaven and earth, and of his resurrected Son? And how is anyone to see that a story culminating in crucifixion represents in fact the power of God to re-create humanity through resurrection? It seems that neither God nor Paul depended entirely on the introduction of an appropriate christological hermeneutic by his new friends, which would have been asking too much. So at this moment, Paul does something highly significant that is so embarrassing to modern ears—especially to those trained to listen by modern universities—that we interpret it rapidly out of sight. He appeals to "signs and wonders," to the "deposit," or "down payment," of the Holy Spirit, who guarantees the future fullness of the reality that is now breaking in upon his listeners. This is in fact the final key component in Paul's missionary approach that we need to recognize and arguably also to recover.

The work of the Spirit is by no means limited to signs and wonders, as we see in relation to many other aspects of Paul's thinking. But signs and wonders do attest to the presence of the Holy Spirit in conjunction with Paul's preaching, and we are probably meant to think here of some people speaking miraculously in diverse languages ("glossolalia"), of others prophesying the secrets of people's hearts that could not be known except by divine illumination, and of the interpretation of the former generating more of the latter. But we should also probably think of the discernment and deliverance of demonic forces from people, of events of healing, and of acts of compassion and mercy that are so overt they must be charged by another spiritual world—acts of extraordinary service and generosity (see 1 Cor 13:1–3; 14:22–25). All this activity is attributed by Paul to the Holy Spirit and attests directly to the truth of his proclamation. And it is on *this* evidence rather than on eloquent demonstration and persuasion that the Corinthians' belief rests (1 Cor 2:1–5), not to mention, that of the Galatians (Gal. 3:1–5). These nakedly divine events attest to the truth of the reality to which Paul is pointing—the reality of God and of resurrected life through Jesus Christ in the power of the Spirit.

Paul's assertions here are of course deeply embarrassing to most modern readers. A colleague once remarked to me that when Paul appeals to the overt presence of the Spirit working wonders in Galatia in support of his gospel proclamation, arguing that undertaking works informed by the Torah does not enjoy this sort of authentication, he is supplying a test that most modern Christian churches today would not merely fail but would probably find unintelligible. But I would suggest that we cannot avoid this challenge. If it is unintelligible, we ought to take drastic steps to recover its intelligibility.

Part of this pneumatological poverty seems to derive from a long post-Reformation antipathy to "enthusiasm,"[21] which has devolved in more orthodox circles into an equally narrow-eyed suspicion of modern narcissistic piety. It seems that a ready endorsement of the work of the Spirit leads all too easily to divisive and oddly radical behavior, as well as, in the modern period, to an endorsement of individual experience and emotion. The Holy Spirit is often collapsed into the human spirit, at which point the ruin of the gospel is complete.

I certainly share these misgivings. But it seems to me that the baby has gone out with the bathwater—and it is quite a baby! The correct response to abuse is not disuse but right use. And the right use of the Spirit is her inter-

---

21. A brief overview can be found at https://www.encyclopedia.com/history/modern-europe/ancient-history-middle-ages-and-feudalism/enthusiasm.

pretation in a constant and unbroken connection with the Father and the Son. The Spirit is the Spirit of God the Father and the Spirit of Christ. If the triune identity of God, comprising distinct but inseparable persons, is kept constantly and fully in view, then it seems to me that the excesses both of enthusiasm and of individualistic experientialism can be avoided. The Spirit does not point us to tyranny and debauchery, or even simply to human emotions (although these last will hopefully be suitably involved); the Spirit points us constantly and consistently back to Christ, and thereby to the Father. If the underlying problem here is a lapse into tritheism—the heresy of the third article—then the correct response is a mature Trinitarianism, and not a functional binitarianism or, even worse, a crude version of monotheism that operates as though God has not really entered into and assumed our condition at all. In short, Paul's unavoidable emphasis on the overt and dynamic presence of the Holy Spirit alongside his preaching is a challenge to many of us to open ourselves up anew to the fullness of the work of God within our lives and ministries. And this challenge leads us to recognize a last important dynamic within Paul's missionary activity that we have already described in passing but can now deepen quite significantly.

New Networks

It is apparent in Paul's missions that the Holy Spirit is often instrumental both in accessing new networks and then in breaking them open through spectacular wonders that cause instant conversions. So Paul's patient work creating strange friendships and then working through them to overlapping networks needs to be supplemented with the possibility that the Spirit has specifically directed him in a particular unexpected direction—has "opened that door"— and has sometimes caused a very sudden conversion that opens up an entirely new set of connections. A paradigmatic instance of this is the conversion of Sergius Paulus, the governor of Cyprus, recounted in Acts 13:6–12.

As was customary, Paul was accompanied by another missionary at this time, namely, Barnabas. The two missionaries were on Cyprus utilizing Jewish and kinship networks (Barnabas was from Cyprus). They were summoned in front of the governor in the town of Paphos, where what was in effect a magical competition ensued. The governor's Jewish magus Elymas, otherwise known as Bar-Jesus, was apparently cursing Paul with blindness. He might have been playing cleverly here on an eye condition that Paul already had (see Gal 4:14–15). A bedraggled Jew with weeping, infected eyes would hardly have cut an impressive figure for the immensely wealthy and privileged governor, who was a former praetor at the least (i.e., a very important dignitary from Rome's ruling aristocracy). Paul's malady, moreover, would have been proof of the superior access of Elymas to the spirits populating the unseen spiritual realm, and of the superiority of the forces he could call upon and manipulate. However, Paul responded in kind and really went one better, striking Elymas blind with a curse—an instance of the "evil eye." Acts then notes drily that the governor, "being an intelligent man," converted on the spot, doubtless hoping to avoid a similar fate. The consequences of this wonder and subsequent conversion were significant.

The governor, a member of the prestigious Roman Sergii Paulli family,[22] seems to have sent Paul from Cyprus directly to his brother's country seat in the town of Pisidian Antioch, in the uplands of modern Turkey—in his day, the Roman province of Galatia. The family owned vast herds of sheep, so they were the ancient equivalent of oil billionaires. (Wool was an important luxury item, being waterproof and warm, and was also very expensive.) And this connection was the starting point for the establishment of a cluster of Christian communities in Galatia generated by out-and-out pagan connections—specifically, a Roman, upper-class network. So Paul must have functioned at this time as a client, exploiting his wealthy patron's vast network of connections with other friends and clients, perhaps eventually reaching as far as the city of Philippi, where he crossed over, as we have already seen, into a network of artisans by way of Lydia (although this last connection with Philippi can be little more than a suspicion).

We see here, then, how a dramatic wonder by the Spirit converted someone immediately, in this case, the most wealthy, high-status person Paul probably ever converted, and thereby opened up a completely new pagan network related to this figure's upper-class Roman family. The new network then connected Paul with (1) other family members, many of them apparently living in Galatia, (2) their friends and, most numerous of all, (3) their clients. It was a rich vein of potential converts for Paul to mine, which he clearly proceeded to do for perhaps two years (37–38 CE). And so we see here a vital further dimension within the Spirit's work.

The Holy Spirit breaks open new networks for Christ's appointed missionaries, at times dramatically and unexpectedly. On these fronts we see overt evidence of the Spirit's work—the all-important signs and wonders—as key new figures are dramatically converted. And it is the same today.

---

22. The Latin inscriptions attesting to the presence and influence of this family in Pisidian Antioch spell their family name this way.

I would suggest that the Spirit is still at work breaking open unexpected new networks and calling and attesting the truth to key figures within those. It is incumbent upon us, then, to try to be sensitive to the leading of the Spirit. Which constituencies are we being prompted to engage with? Sadly, yesterday's constituencies can sometimes blind us to those the Spirit wants to lead us to today. I am convinced that we are in the presence of a marked turn toward new groups of people on the margins of our social structures but in the center of God's purposes. I think immediately of the mentally and physically challenged, as well as of the vast population that is currently incarcerated, especially in the United States, which is disproportionately poor, colored, and mentally troubled.[23] The Spirit is clearly at work among these constituencies (which is emphatically not to overlook promptings in other directions). Hence it is quite right to recognize here God's "preferential option for the poor."[24]

This is also the point where we can finally address the questions of the sincere doubting student, whom we first met in chapter 2. (He or she is to be distinguished from the aggressive atheist, who demands further epistemological warrant for our truth claims, which were made in sole dependence on the God who is the truth.) Some people simply doubt that God exists. They want to believe but can't. They just don't believe, and as we saw earlier, people cannot simply choose, by an act of will, to believe things are true that they don't believe. How are we to respond to these troubled souls?

Paul would probably have said to our modern doubter that the Spirit will attest to the truth of what he is saying, as well as to the surety of the things Christians believe, through signs and wonders. But there is a sense that we

23. See here now http://www.umc.org/news-and-media/retired-bishop-serves-memory-care-unit-as-chaplain.

24. A much-debated phrase; see https://en.wikipedia.org/wiki/Option_for_the_poor. Using it in primary dependence on Gustavo Gutiérrez and liberation theology, where the emphasis "preferential" is usually found, it is important to appreciate that it is not exclusive of God's love and outreach to all. Within this framework, however, Gutiérrez and others recognize a special preference for the marginalized, and I am happy to endorse this emphasis, especially having seen God's overt involvement with the incarcerated. (The designation "marginalized" must also be used advisedly.) However, my endorsement of this phrase is not framed simply in terms of social policy and justice, as it is by much Catholic social teaching. I agree with that emphasis but want to employ the phrase more programmatically to denote God's sheer preferential inclusion of the poor within the community, initially through the work of the Spirit in mission. Appropriate resourcing should follow on this as a matter of course, as we have seen in relation to the virtue of giving in part 2, ch. 12, and will see in part 4, ch. 21.

need to be where those signs and wonders are taking place if we want to experience those attestations—so we need to be where the wave of the Spirit is breaking through into new, unreached, and marginalized constituencies. God is at work all around us. But it is quiet, localized work caught up with the proclamation of the Son by the Spirit and by God's specially commissioned leaders to the people whom God is particularly interested in. This is where the Spirit tends to be overtly at work. Perhaps if we doubt the presence of God, then we simply need to move to the strange, obscure corners of the world where God is actually doing things. Perhaps we just need to catch up to the Spirit.

As we close out this Pauline account of mission, it is largely superfluous to point out that something shocking has been unfolding. All Paul's befriending and converting is not merely an appropriately sensitive process, treating the other at bottom with dignity as a person whom Christ loves and sometimes even speaks to us through. It is a radically inclusive process, in Paul's case involving outreach to the despised and hated pagans. His friendships are strange friendships, resulting in a radical and unavoidable *diversity* in his communities. Christians, after all, are not messianic Jews, and Christians themselves differ a great deal from one another. Lydia dyes cloth and sings and dances with former slaves and other stinking undesirables in Philippi, while Sergius Paulus reclines in his dining room with members of Rome's political and cultural elite. And diversity of this magnitude causes trouble. It caused tremendous conflict in Paul's day, and in different forms, it still does in ours. So we must try now to give an appropriate account of this signature feature of Paul's missionary work and of a Pauline church network, which is the subject of part 4. If we can do so, we will show that we have really grasped what Paul was all about, and we will also provide the modern church with some much-needed guidance as it seeks to avoid massive—and many ultimately unnecessary—internal fractures over much the same sorts of questions.

Theses

- Just as God first came to us as a human being, meeting us concretely, in person, face-to-face, so too the message about God spreads through people, concretely, face-to-face, although superintended especially by the Holy Spirit. A relational God calls people to relationship through relationship.
- The *motive* involved in these encounters is critical. It is important for any

missionary not to want to convert people because they are needy or for the sake of their conversion. This approach turns people into instruments of other more selfish goals on the part of the missionary, unavoidably patronizing them, by defining their needs for them or using them for self-centered increases in status if one succeeds in making converts.

> Potential converts must, somewhat paradoxically, be approached first for their own sakes and valued simply as people to be enjoyed, whether they intend to convert or not. They must be approached in the hope of genuine friendship.

> A christological *definition* of the other—the corresponding conviction that Christ is involved in the other—helps us here again, as it underpins the belief that everyone has value, including non-Christians, in part because Christ is, in some way, involved with and present to all. So this sort of open-ended offer of friendship for its own sake can be made appropriately.

> The test of the genuineness of a friendship is that it will be maintained, even if the new friend does not convert.

> Onesimus is the most detailed instance we have in Paul of a friendship and may well attest to Paul's motives of friendship. Paul would almost certainly have loved him, befriended him, and advocated for him, even if Onesimus had not converted.

> Friendship evangelism is a highly effective missionary *method*, as research on new religious movements has shown. The conversion of a friend opens up his or her preexisting networks of friendship and family to further conversion, potentially generating an exponential growth as further conversions open up those networks in turn.

> Paul's letters evidence the conversion of many friends and of many surprising or strange friendships, with people very unlike him.

> This response can be explained in part by the *manner* in which Jesus's followers make friends, as exemplified by Paul and warranted by first principles.

> Paul adopted as many of the local customs and practices of the network he was engaging with as he could, living *alongside* those he was meeting and embodying Christ's incarnation.

> This immersion into local culture, when it plays out today, usually involves learning the local language well enough to master its sense of humor.

> It also involves listening more than talking.

> The result of Paul's preparedness to travel into odd new locations and to make friends with very different people was the phenomenon of *strange friendships*.

‣ A nice (further) example of this is his conversion of Lydia (see Acts 16:13–15), who was probably a freed female slave from Lydia (i.e., western Turkey) working in the purple dye industry. Onesimus is another example that has already been noted.

‣ The conversion of Lydia, combined with Paul's subsequent mission to Thessalonica, reveals an important result generated by Paul's approach to mission.

‣ An openness to strange friendships and a preparedness to enter into new social spaces and locations lead to network *multiplication*.

‣ Networks overlap with one another, especially through key people, and Paul could thereby move between different networks, trying to befriend as many people as he could.

‣ His exploitation of seven networks is detectable: familial, Jewish, artisanal, veteran, patronage at the international and civic levels, and carceral.

‣ However, this type of missionary activity is costly, if not dangerous, and hence is best pursued by celibate missionaries like Paul.

‣ Paul's approach consequently results in vulnerability, both a result of travel and related practical vulnerabilities and a result of his deliberately getting alongside those of perceived low status.

‣ The gospel is also best offered free of charge, as Paul offered it, thereby ironically increasing vulnerability in the ancient world in certain respects.

‣ Authentic and mature church leadership involves this vulnerability, which is counterintuitive.

‣ The virtues of giving, fidelity, and endurance are nevertheless several of the key virtues of Jesus himself.

‣ The works of the Holy Spirit also attest to the truth of the proclamation of a resurrected Lord and a resurrected future for all; miracles authenticate the proclamation of otherwise unimpressive messengers.

‣ When invoking the Holy Spirit, it is critical to avoid functional tritheism. The Holy Spirit is the Spirit of the Son and of the Father, and her work must always be discerned in direct connection with the other two persons in the Trinity.

‣ The Spirit can be seen opening up new networks dramatically, like Sergius Paulus's family and his patronage network.

‣ A preferential option for the poor is discernable in the Spirit's missional leading.

‣ If we seek to respond to genuine doubt today, we ought to try to recover a sense of the Spirit's presence. Hence, it might be necessary to move to those marginal places where the Spirit is currently at work.

> ➤ Missionary work conducted in these terms automatically leads to diversity, which can cause conflict. The navigation of appropriate as against inappropriate diversity is a critical issue and the subject of the book's final part, part 4, and is as important for the church today as it was for Paul.

Key Scriptural References

Paul's close relationships with his converts are revealed especially by his letter of Philemon, which speaks of his intimate relationship with the unhappy slave Onesimus; see especially verses 10 and 12. (See also Col 3:11.)

Evidence of the key practice of arriving in a network by adapting to it, if not immersing into it, is supplied by 1 Thess 2:9; more programmatically, by 1 Cor 9:19–22 and by Gal 4:12. Acts also supplies frequent evidence of Paul acting like a Jew in Jewish spaces; see especially 16:3; 18:18; and 21:23–26 (and probably also 20:6; see 16:15). This evidence is corroborated especially by 2 Cor 11:24.

My favorite example of a strange friendship, in addition to Onesimus, is Paul's relationship with Lydia, as recounted in Acts 16:13–15.

Paul's vulnerability is articulated in relation to weakness extensively in 2 Cor 2:14–6:10; 10:7–12:10; this line of defense is anticipated in 1 Cor 4:7–18.

The importance of signs and wonders attesting to the truth of the gospel proclamation is noted in several places by Paul; see especially Rom 15:18–19; 1 Cor 2:1–5; and Gal 3:4.

The story of the conversion of Sergius Paulus can be found in Acts 13:6–12.

Key Reading

The correct motivation for outreach is articulated simply, powerfully, and superbly by *Living without Enemies*, coauthored by Sam Wells and Marcia Owen.

A charming theological account of friendship (and such accounts are quite hard to find!) is supplied by Hauerwas and Pinches in their *Christians among the Virtues*, in which see "Companions on the Way: The Necessity of Friendship," 31–51; and "Friendship and Fragility," 70–88. A classic account of the subject is provided by Aelred of Rievaulx.

The importance of networks is articulated helpfully by Rodney Stark. He has written a great deal, but I lean here especially on his first key work, *The Rise of Christianity*.

The importance of pneumatological and charismatic activity, especially in marginalized spaces, is captured by Ekblad's *New Christian Manifesto*.

Further Reading

The grounding of mission in the heart of God, as well as the relationality of the Trinity, has already been covered at length in previous chapters; see the relevant reading there (i.e., Zizioulas, Flett, the relevant parts of Barth's *CD*, and others).

An insightful, powerful, and profoundly helpful account of getting alongside those we are befriending is Michael Duncan's *Alongsiders: Sitting with Those Who Sit Alone*.

I collect stories of strange friendships. A powerful account local to my present context of Durham, NC (USA), is Osha Davidson's *The Best of Enemies*. A wonderful and utterly seminal friendship at the heart of mission in New Zealand unfolded between Samuel Marsden and the Maori chief Ruatara. It is described briefly in broader accounts by Allan Davidson and by A. H. Reed. Intriguingly, Barth clearly evidences a special friendship at the end of his life with Carl Zuckmayer, a young Catholic. (It was not of course his only special friendship, as Busch's devoted biography attests.) Films dramatizing true stories of remarkable friendships make this point powerfully as well. I am especially fond of *Les Intouchables* (dir. Olivier Nakache and Éric Toledano, 2012).

Friendship in Paul is not generally discussed in quite the terms that I have used here, but relevant aspects of his life are described in helpful ways. See, for example, the classic—although distinctly androcentric—short study by F. F. Bruce, *The Pauline Circle*.

John Barclay introduces the key issues in relation to Philemon with customary insight; see also my *Framing*, ch. 5, "Locating Philemon, Colossians, and 'Ephesians,'" 254–338. Richard Ascough introduces the issues in relation to Lydia (although we disagree over some of the details).

A book I often mention in the same breath as *Living without Enemies* is *Friendship at the Margins*, by Chris Heuertz and Christine Pohl. It addresses the issue of motivation within mission especially directly. The title was not, incidentally, the choice of the authors. One of the book's main points, which I endorse, is that the margins are only so-called. The groups and networks often designated as marginal are *central* to God's concerns and activities. Moreover, there is frequently something artificial, constructed, and even just incorrect about cultural, political, and social designations of certain groups as marginal.

Having said this, the category remains important. We do need to speak at times of relative deprivations. One important solution is to insist on a significant degree of emic, rather than just etic, definition.

Note Mark Granovetter's seminal work on relationships within networks characterized by weak, as against by strong, ties; it encourages us to detect when weak and strong ties are operative. As he theorizes, missionary apostles access new networks from outside, "bridging in," by way of what he would call a weak tie—a very weak tie sometimes. But they then establish communities established by strong ties. After they depart, the evangelists left behind, who have been entrusted with the local community's ongoing growth, are probably characterized by a mix of strong and weak ties. The weak ties are, counterintuitively, the most useful relationships for innovating, diffusing, and converting.

One of the critical side effects of strange friendships is their capacity to overcome prejudices of various sorts. This has been theorized for some time by (social) contact theory, intergroup contact theory, and the contact hypothesis (see https://en.wikipedia.org/wiki/Contact_hypothesis), an approach pioneered by Gordon W. Allport in 1954. Christena Cleveland provides a more tightly focused application of contact theory to current church challenges.

The seminal account of the interaction between circumstantial diversity, which J.-C. Beker calls contingency, and Paul's underlying theological core, which he calls coherence, is provided in his classic account *Paul the Apostle*.

A useful study of the Spirit in relation to Paul's missionary work is Mehrdad Fatehi, *The Spirit's Relation to the Risen Lord in Paul*. A broader treatment of the Spirit's critical role in modern incarnational—gritty!—evangelism is Bob Ekblad's *A New Christian Manifesto*.

Bibliography

Aelred of Rievaulx. *Spiritual Friendship*. Edited by Marsha L. Dutton. Translated by Lawrence C. Braceland. Collegeville, MN: Cistercian Publications/Liturgical Press, 2010.

Allport, Gordon W. *The Nature of Prejudice*. Palo Alto, CA: Addison Wesley, 1954.

Anglican Church in Aotearoa, New Zealand, and Polynesia. *New Zealand Anglican Prayer Book / He Karakia Mihinare o Aotearoa*. New ed. Christchurch, N.Z.: Genesis Publications, 2005.

Ascough, Richard S. *Lydia: Paul's Cosmopolitan Hostess*. Collegeville, MN: Liturgical Press, 2009.

Barclay, J. M. G. *Colossians and Philemon*. New Testament Guides. Sheffield: Sheffield Academic Press, 1997.

———. "Paul, Philemon, and the Dilemma of Christian Slave-Ownership." *NTS* 37 (1991): 161–86.

Barth, Karl, and Carl Zuckmayer. *A Late Friendship: The Letters of Karl Barth and Carl Zuckmayer*. Translated by Geoffrey W. Bromiley. Grand Rapids: Eerdmans, 1982.

Beker, J.-C. *Paul the Apostle: The Triumph of God in Life and Thought*. Philadelphia: Fortress, 1984 (1980).

Bruce, F. F. *The Pauline Circle*. Exeter: Paternoster Press, 1977.

Busch, Eberhard. *Karl Barth: His Life from Letters and Autobiographical Texts*. Translated by J. Bowden. 2nd rev. ed. London: SCM, 1976.

Campbell, Douglas. "Strange Friendships." *Divinity* 14, no. 1 (Fall 2014): 4–9.

———. "Unravelling Colossians 3.11b." *NTS* 42 (1996): 120–32.

Cleveland, Christena. *Disunity in Christ: Uncovering the Hidden Forces That Keep Us Apart*. Downers Grove, IL: InterVarsity, 2012.

Davidson, Allan. *Christianity in Aotearoa: A History of Church and Society in New Zealand*. 3rd ed. Wellington, N.Z.: Education for Ministry, 2004.

Davidson, Osha Gray. *The Best of Enemies: Race and Redemption in the New South*. Chapel Hill: University of North Carolina Press, 1996.

Duncan, Mick. *Alongsiders: Sitting with Those Who Sit Alone*. Dandendong, Victoria: Urban Neighbors of Hope, 2013.

Ekblad, Eugene Robert. *A New Christian Manifesto: Pledging Allegiance to the Kingdom of God*. Louisville: Westminster John Knox, 2008.

Fatehi, Mehrdad. *The Spirit's Relation to the Risen Lord in Paul: An Examination of Its Christological Implications*. Tübingen: Mohr Siebeck, 2000.

Granovetter, Mark S. "The Strength of Weak Ties." *American Journal of Sociology* 78 (1973): 1360–80.

Gutiérrez, Gustavo. *A Theology of Liberation*. 15th ann. ed. Maryknoll, NY: Orbis, 1988.

Hauerwas, Stanley, with Charles Pinches. *Christians among the Virtues: Theological Conversations with Ancient and Modern Ethics*. Notre Dame, IN: University of Notre Dame Press, 1997. (See especially "Companions on the Way: The Necessity of Friendship," 31–51; and "Friendship and Fragility," 70–88.)

Heuertz, Chris, and Christine Pohl. *Friendship at the Margins: Discovering Mutuality in Service and Mission*. Downers Grove, IL: InterVarsity, 2010.

Marsden, Samuel. *The Letters and Journals of Samuel Marsden, 1765–1838*. Edited by John Rawson Elder. Dunedin, N.Z.: University of Otago, 1932.

Reed, A. H. *Marsden of Maoriland, Pioneer and Peacemaker*. Dunedin, N.Z.: A. H. & A. W. Reed, 1938.

Stark, Rodney. *The Rise of Christianity: A Sociologist Reconsiders History*. Princeton: Princeton University Press, 1996.

Wells, Samuel, and Marcia A. Owen. *Living without Enemies: Being Present in the Midst of Violence*. Downers Grove, IL: InterVarsity, 2011.

Wilson-Hartgrove, Jonathan. *Reconstructing the Gospel: Finding Freedom from Slaveholder Religion*. Downers Grove, IL: InterVarsity Press, 2018.

PART 4

Navigation

CHAPTER 20

Missional Diversity

Trouble

Missionaries frequently seem to get into trouble with their headquarters back home. A classic example from church history is the great Matteo Ricci, who in the late sixteenth century experienced recall and discipline from the Vatican for making too many concessions to Chinese culture. In particular, with extraordinary foresight, he had urged acceptance of Chinese ancestor veneration, a custom that has proved to be an ongoing problem for Christian missionaries.

Those insufficiently attuned to Chinese culture tend to assume that the veneration of ancestors, which involves rituals before small statues, is unvarnished idolatry and therefore to be judged and erased in just the manner that Paul denounces idolatry in a text like 1 Thess 1:9–10:

> You turned to God from idols
> to serve the living and true God,
> and to wait for his Son from heaven,
> whom he raised from the dead—
> Jesus,
> who rescues us from the coming wrath.

But those more immersed in Chinese culture know that this practice is not worship as much as the respectful recall of progenitors, which is technically another thing, and even something the Bible spends some time doing and commending. So this difference from European culture can be affirmed without compromising the gospel. Bowing before ancestral statues was not an act of worship either, but an act, in Asian terms, of veneration and respect. So this too could be accommodated, provided that it was correctly understood. Sadly for the success of the Chinese mission, however, the distant bureaucracies underpinning these missions, insensitive to the local Chinese context and ignorant of the particular Chinese meaning informing these practices, tended to win the day, severely setting back the formation and establishment of Chinese Christian communities in every instance, as missionaries were instructed to demand the renunciation of ancestor veneration by their converts or face discipline—Ricci's fate.

Similarly, the zealous Baptist missionary Timothy Richards was engaged in the evangelism of China from 1869 for almost fifty years. After decades of struggle, he became fairly successful as, we onlookers would say with hindsight, he began to contextualize his message more effectively. He switched from the standard evangelistic techniques of his time—daily preaching in street chapels and the handing out of scriptural tracts—to more Sino-sensitive techniques, including the use of wall posters with gnomic sayings (which were a standard feature of Chinese culture), famine relief (sadly, a new notion), and the promotion of general literacy, with a particular concern for sympathetic engagement with local religious texts and traditions like Buddhism. But these "radical" suggestions got him into trouble with some of his fellow missionaries, and with his funding bodies back home. Like Ricci many centuries earlier, Richards experienced criticism, hostility, and a withdrawal of support.[1]

Armed with these and similar insights from church history, of which there are many, we can see just the same dynamics playing out within the early church in relation to Paul's mission to the pagans. There was something uncomfortably different about his movement too, and it got him into trouble with the other leaders in the church. They seem to have found his divergence from the usual ways of pious living offensive and unacceptable. But in order to see this tension, we must grasp what it meant that Paul established communities of "Christians." Modern Christians are so familiar with this name that they tend to overlook its significance when it was first used.

The Christians

The book of Acts says that the name "Christians" was coined in Syrian Antioch (11:26), and it was most probably thought up by the Roman authorities.[2] The

1. See here in particular Andrew Walls's fascinating essay "The Multiple Conversions of Timothy Richards." My thanks to John Stenhouse for this reference. The Chinese Rites Controversy is also well documented by George Minamiki.

2. I am unconvinced by contentions that Acts is being anachronistic, given that

name is Latin, whereas the languages of the early mission were Aramaic and Greek. It suggests that Paul converted former pagans who joined a group who were known as "members of Christ's household," the *Christiani*, which was a Roman joke. With due apology to my American readers, we might helpfully recall at this moment that the name "Yankees" is quite possibly an insulting moniker derived by English troops from the word "yankers." So too "Christians" sounded to the Romans like "Chrēstians," and Chrēstus was a common slave name meaning "useful." Paul puns on this name himself in his letter to Philemon in verse 11, when talking about Onesimus, which is the Latin equivalent for the Greek "useful." "Formerly he [Onesimus or 'Useful'] was useless [*achrēston*] to you, but now he has become useful [*euchrēston*] both to you and to me." This phonetic similarity meant that the "Christians" were members of a slave's household and not members of some important, wellborn house like the Juliani or Claudii—an absurd notion that the Romans clearly found deeply amusing. For them this was a little like a group today celebrating its descent from ancient cockroaches. And doubtless because of its ridicule and outsider status (it was an "etic" designation), most members of the movement avoided using it, so it occurs only three times in the NT. But there are no good reasons for doubting that this is how the name arose, not to mention when, as Acts tells us. Beyond its sly ridicule, however, the invention of this new name is telling.

The Romans had apparently investigated this new religious movement, as they were wont to do. They were suspicious of groups meeting together, fearing blasphemy, sorcery, or sedition. Clearly, however, after a suitable inquiry, they had found Paul's converts in Antioch merely laughable—the followers of a figure who had been shamefully executed as a slave. They had therefore named them, in a typically derogatory fashion, because they were something new, *meaning that this group no longer looked sufficiently Jewish to be identified in those terms*. So the Romans had coined the mocking new name—"members of the household of the executed slave Useful"—which eventually stuck.

Ancient peoples like the Romans knew various basic things about Jews that enabled them to be identified—that they met together on the Sabbath, then rested, and that they ate a particular diet, avoiding food like pork and shellfish. The men practiced the grotesque custom of circumcision. They married one another and often refused to engage in various social activities with outsiders like communal banqueting and religious festivals, so they were abused for being exclusive misanthropes. And they all had some sort of at-

---

the historical situation being described is so accurate. See my study "Beyond the Torah at Antioch."

tachment to their homeland of Judea, which surrounded the sacred city of Jerusalem.

But Paul's converts did not follow the Jewish calendar rigorously and certainly did not worry about Jewish dietary scruples. Moreover, their men, insofar as it was apparent—and it might well have been in the public toilets, gymnasiums, or bathhouses—were not circumcised. They seemed to socialize more freely with their neighbors. They married non-Jews. And they had little or no connection with Judea. So the Romans did not recognize these converts as Jews. And these differences were all sufficiently novel to warrant investigation and a new name, as a result of which the Romans supplied their derisive pun.

Because of this origin, however, the name "Christian" applied—when it was first coined—*only* to converts to the Jesus movement from paganism who did not go on to convert fully to Judaism. They were the non-Jewish members of the Jesus movement. So in these terms I am a Christian. But those Jews devoted to Jesus were not Christians. They were messianic Jews, in the sense that they specifically held Jesus of Nazareth to be the Messiah.[3] In order to respect this important distinction, then, I will continue to refer in what follows as I have throughout this book, on the one hand, to Christians, meaning by this term pagan converts, and on the other, to messianic Jews, understanding the further qualification of messianic loyalty specifically to Jesus as being present. The early church was composed of *both* these constituencies: Christians and messianic Jews. So when I talk of the community as a whole or of the early church, the same distinction is being presupposed. We are discussing a fundamentally *diverse* community. In fact, after Paul got going, it was shockingly so.

Diversity

To cover the main points here briefly: Paul's communities of pagan converts were obviously still ethical. We know from his letters that he had very high expectations of their behavior, which we have spent much of part two articulating. Paul expected his converts to behave virtuously, and stringently so. But it was by no means a standard Jewish ethical system any more, although it was so in part.

3. The signifier "Christian" clearly shifted in a more encompassing (and positive) direction in due course (as evidenced perhaps by Acts 26:28–29), but I am interested here in its original use, during the Pauline mission.

Quite a bit was still held in common with Judaism. Paul enforced a prohibition against direct idolatry, although he seemed to be a little more relaxed around the edges of this than some of his Jewish contemporaries. Magical activities had to go as well. And he advocated strict Jewish rules in relation to sexual activity and marriage, as well as ethical behavior in general. So things like theft and drunkenness were firmly prohibited. He enjoined regular meetings together for singing, prayer, and teaching. These gatherings occurred at least weekly, but often daily. He had expectations of how money would be shared, analogous to the concern of many contemporary Jews with almsgiving. Standard Jewish commitments to other virtues were also present throughout— to kindness, faithfulness, and so on. Of course, Paul grounded these practices tightly in Jesus, but Jesus was a Jew, and most of these virtues would have been quite familiar to Jews already.[4]

There were admittedly some strange messianic additions that stretched the contours of acceptable Judaism. The worship services were oddly exuberant. People claimed to have received healings and visions, along with liberations from the dark powers. They sang and danced, and even the women were involved. And although they claimed to worship the Jewish single God as Lord, who was not imaged, the Christians also worshiped a person, Jesus. He had been raised from the dead, they claimed, had ascended to heaven, and now sat at God the Father's right hand. One day he would return in glory to judge the cosmos and to gather his people into the new age. And the Christians claimed that this future inclusion was guaranteed by the presence of God's Spirit in their communal meetings in a fashion that most Jews connected only with special episodes recounted in the Scriptures or with the heart of the Jerusalem temple—although some Jews, like the Essenes, were deeply involved with the Spirit as well.

But although this is all somewhat marginal, it is still Jewish in some sense, at least arguably—the worship of Jesus was presumably especially contentious. (The worship of God was not.) However, many important Jewish practices were absent from Paul's communities of converts altogether.

As we noted earlier, Jewish calendrical and dietary practices were not being followed. Paul's converts did not rest on every seventh day, so the dis-

---

4. Indeed, because of these practices various pagans thought that the early Christians, like the Jews, were a variation on ancient philosophers; they gathered, but without worshiping statues of gods or gathering in the large local temples. Instead, they gathered in houses, studied texts, and practiced a distinctive communal ethic.

tinctive weekly rhythm of the Jews was not always in evidence. Presumably they could also take the day off if it was an important pagan god's festival, since pagan gods were nothing (1 Cor 8:4). And they certainly weren't as fussy about eating as normal Jews were. They ate meat from the secondhand meat market, which had been previously sacrificed to pagan gods. They ate *any* meat in fact, including pork, and it didn't need to have been properly strained of blood. They drank any wine. And they continued, as a result, to socialize much more easily with their pagan neighbors than most Jews did. The Jerusalem temple was not visited or provided with money. Codes of dress, insofar as they existed, were probably diverse. (They were still modest; see 1 Cor 11:2–16.) The men were not circumcised. One assumes that learning Hebrew was not venerated. In fact, it does not even seem that scriptural acquisition and learning were mandatory; certainly the instructions of Moses were not being followed very literally. Moreover, some of the community members came from "mixed marriages." If someone in a pagan household converted, he or she sometimes stayed married to his or her partner, although sometimes they divorced, and some converts did not marry at all.

There are some significant omissions here, and not a few scandalous additions. Various Jews in Paul's day would have regarded the failure by Jews to undertake even one of these practices as apostasy and meriting an immediate stoning.[5] And some of the additional practices and claims are equally shocking. The inclusion of pagan converts in the age to come, and in these odd ethical terms, would have been especially inflammatory. Hence it is not surprising to learn that the mother church back in Jerusalem, which was basically Jewish, albeit messianic, eventually tried to rein these new communities in, in a manner parallel to the fate suffered by the Chinese missionaries contextualizing within their vastly sophisticated, non-Western contexts like China in ways that upset their funding bodies back home. The leaders distantly managing the early church seem to have become suspicious of these odd new groups of converts from paganism with their lax practices who were so different that they were not known as Jews at all but as "Christians," and tried to bring them to heel. "Converts to Jesus who are not Jews? How could this be?! What *is* a Christian? Surely being a messianic Jew is sufficient trouble for the day?!"

---

5. See, among many other texts, 1 Macc 2:24–26, 44–48, which describes the killing of Jews who sacrificed to pagan gods, the tearing down of pagan altars, and the forcible circumcision of male infants.

The Mother Church

At some point around the fall of 49 CE, emissaries from James, the brother of Jesus, who was based in Jerusalem, arrived in Syrian Antioch, where an important community of Pauline converts, which is to say, Christians, gathered alongside the messianic Jews, some of whom had converted them. The delegates prohibited eating together between Christians and messianic Jews unless the former converted fully to Jewish ways (Gal 2:11–14), and a hard underlying exclusion is probably implicit in this command. Groups of Jesus followers excluded from the table were excluded from participation in the very body and blood of their Savior as that was commemorated and shared in by the Eucharist. So this demand probably carried the implication that those who did not convert fully to Jewish ways were not in fact saved at all. Unsurprisingly, these events caused a confrontation at Antioch between Paul and Peter, and also implicitly with Barnabas (who apparently was siding with James at this moment), so much so that the key figures involved decided to go to Jerusalem to consult with all the early church's main leaders. In any case, James, Jesus's brother, and the apparent instigator of the Jewish crackdown, was in Jerusalem (2:1–10).

Now we really have to try to appreciate what the leaders of the messianic Jews in Jerusalem were probably feeling at this point. One person's contextualization is another person's apostasy, as we have already seen briefly in the ongoing saga of Christian missionary work in China.

Imagine that an astonishingly successful mission suddenly explodes in Utah. Young ministers, graduates of Duke Divinity School and so highly trained in the importance of noncolonial sensibilities, have been sent there by the bishop of the eastern conference of North Carolina to do mission work, and people have begun to flood into the Methodist churches in and around Salt Lake City. The mission's success verges on being a revival. The bishop is initially very pleased. But then disturbing reports begin to reach her.

Apparently, these flocks of new converts all happily confess that Jesus is Lord and endorse the triune God of grace. But churchgoing with special linen undergarments is viewed as acceptable, if not as standard. Sayings from the book of Mormon are being quoted liberally in the church alongside quotations from the Bible. And most disturbing of all, there are rumors that polygamy has been ruled acceptable, and many male converts with multiple wives are coming tearfully out of the closet and living and worshiping openly with their impressively large families.

The bishop contemplates simply excommunicating the young missionaries and their new congregations immediately. But she generously sends a letter instead ordering all those involved to return to traditional Christian practices pending further consideration.

To her surprise, the missionaries involved confront her representatives very directly about these instructions and a heated public argument ensues. The orders, moreover, are rejected by these Utah missionaries in no uncertain terms, with copious quotations from Scripture and tradition in ostensible support of their radical departures. Fortunately, all the parties concerned subsequently agree to journey back to North Carolina to meet together to try to decide what should be done (before, that is, they go to general conference). They will seek the will of God together concerning this entire controversy.

In just this sense but more so, Paul's Christian communities were a shockingly radical departure from standard Jewish practices. Many of the things that Jews hold most dear were not being taught and practiced. Small wonder that a delegation from Jerusalem sought to take matters in hand.

However, it is clear from Paul's perspective that this intervention was equally unacceptable. The Jerusalem church, fully immersed in Jewish practices, was attempting to impose its own culture comprehensively on his pagan converts without the necessary sensitivity to the local pagan practices that he had discerned, from the midst of his mission, were legitimate.

It is worth recalling at this moment that, despite his opposition, Paul bent over backward to maintain his relationship with the conservative Jewish leadership of the early church in Jerusalem. His commitment to ecumenicity was, as we saw earlier in chapter 14, when discussing peacemaking, extraordinarily steadfast. But at the same time he trenchantly resisted the comprehensive imposition of Jewish practices on his converts. His converts were not to fully adopt the Torah. I don't think that Paul was asking the messianic Jews in Judea to abandon their Jewish practices, but he certainly opposed their full introduction to his communities of converted pagans. So, as we have just seen, Paul confronted Peter at Antioch and defended his converts' radical ethic. He then journeyed to Jerusalem to meet with all the key figures. And the amazing thing is that he seems to have succeeded in gaining acceptance there for his new way of doing things—a considerable achievement, on the part both of Paul and of the messianic Jews who eventually affirmed him.

In the midst of these negotiations, Paul also pledged to raise a large sum of money from his pagan converts for the impoverished members of the church in Jerusalem (Gal 2:10), which inaugurated the great collection that we have already talked about under the rubric of giving. Raising this collection took Paul as long as two and a half years, from early 50 through mid-52, and pulled him away from his principal work of mission in areas "where Christ had not yet been named" (Rom 15:20). Nevertheless, he returned to Jerusalem personally in due course with the money, knowing that he faced death there. (As things turned out, he narrowly escaped with his life, but a long incarceration ensued that ended his missionary work and led eventually to his execution.)

In short, Paul was prepared to lay down his life for church unity, a point that is not always fully appreciated. But neither at any moment is a major abandonment of his radical new approach to mission apparent either. He was prepared, that is, to lay down his life for his new converts as well—for the Christians.[6]

The practical diplomatic and reconciling skills evident in Paul's relationship with Jerusalem were clearly vital for holding the members of a diversifying church together. But he also had to legitimize and to authenticate his new, divergent constituencies. He had to provide convincing arguments to the other, more conservative leaders, that this was a valid work of God and not the creation of a self-serving missionary empire or an evangelistic ego trip. And in one of the most important theological moments in the history of the church, he did so. Before introducing this, however, we need to pause to note the way the phenomenon of diversification within the early church—of ethical and ecclesial divergences as its different communities were founded and took shape—corresponds exactly to the initial phenomenon of missionary immersion and contextualization. To contextualize *is* to diversify and to diversify *is* to have contextualized. So the same rationale should uphold—or fail to uphold—both these critical missional practices.

---

6. We can see at this moment that the diversity within the early church was extreme—so much so that it threatened to rupture into Christian and messianic Jewish constituencies, the latter denying the former legitimacy. (This is the enduring insight in the work of F. C. Baur, a figure from whom scholars of Paul still have much to learn.) And Paul had contributed to this problem. His radical mission was probably the most divergent constituency within the spectrum of groups and related practices that made up the early church. He labored mightily to hold the church together, and seems to have succeeded in working out a modus vivendi with the key leaders of the troubled messianic Jews. And the cost to him personally was very significant. But his practices also contributed directly to this diversity, generating the tensions that he had to manage, although he seems to have been able to do so, at least for a time.

Missional Immersion

We have talked a great deal in part 3 about how missionaries ought to arrive among non-Christians so that mission does not descend into a manipulation or a power game but begins in a way that respects the personhood of everyone involved. Missionaries must frame non-Christians as people with whom Jesus is already involved. Moreover, to this end, they must incarnate as best they can into their contexts, walking alongside the people there, eschewing the use of power and resources to effect relationships and conversions, which would be manipulative. They must become like those they want to convert. "Brothers and sisters, become like me, for I became like you," Paul says insightfully in Gal 4:12. And he makes the same point more programmatically—and rather famously—in 1 Cor 9:19–22 (which is a chiasm).

> Though I am free and belong to no one,
> I have made myself a slave to everyone,
> to win as many as possible.
>
>> To the Jews I became like a Jew,
>> to win the Jews.
>>
>>> To those under the Torah I became like one under the Torah
>>> (though I myself am not under the Torah),
>>> so as to win those under the Torah.
>>>
>>> To those not having the Torah I became like one not having
>>> the Torah
>>> (though I am not free from God's Torah
>>> but am under the Torah that is Christ),
>>> so as to win those not having the Torah.
>>
>> To the weak I became weak,
>> to win the weak.
>
> I have become all things
> to all people
> so that by all possible means I might save some.

But we have left a critical issue here largely unaddressed until now. How can a missionary do all this without sinning? How can he or she leave a godly country and culture—in Paul's case, Judaism—and simply adopt various practices within the godless pagans without harm or sanction? Is this not obviously and overtly sinful? Isn't Judaism good because it has been given to the Jews by God?, and so isn't everything else that is different, by definition, bad? In view of such considerations, isn't it entirely understandable that other Jews in the early church were puzzled, offended, and even outraged by the new practices, their puzzlement being echoed through the ages by Christians located in godly cultures of their own who are viewing suspicious diversifications unfolding on the fringes of their purview? Yet clearly this adoption of a different and problematic culture is what an incarnational mission demands, and what Paul and those like him constantly did and do.

When we step back and look at it carefully, we can see that this phenomenon is effectively the same as the phenomenon of diversification as any new Christian community forms. In both instances, new forms are being adopted, and old forms are being left behind. In fact, this process of worrying divergence actually begins with the missionary-apostles contextualizing into their given context, continuing as their new praxis is accepted as a valid form of piety and a new type of Christian expression begins to take shape among their converts. The legitimate indwelling of the local culture by the community's founders is the inauguration of the diversity; as the missionaries gather followers who imitate them in turn, the new Christian form results.

We have already signed off on the validity of the practice of immersion at a broad level; indeed, we are committed to the presence of Jesus in some concrete way in the non-Christian other. Jesus must be present to all of humanity in a way that is superior to the presence of our contaminated Adamic reality or we trigger functional Marcionism. So it is safe for us to walk alongside our new potential friends and converts, adopting their customs, because we can trust that Jesus is there already, acting within their culture and practices, at least to some extent. Where they are and how they behave are in some measure necessarily good.

But in certain respects the introduction of this insight merely inscribes the problem we have raised here yet more deeply. How do we *explain* that this is in fact true, especially given the fact that Jesus seems to have taken special pains to call out a people for himself, revealing his ways to them in a distinctive way? How is Jesus at work now in a real, pure way in Jewish and Christian, not to mention in non-Jewish and non-Christian situations? How can he be at work now in everyone as their creator and Lord?, which is also to ask, How did Paul avoid sinning as he sank into local pagan customs? And it is to ask as well, How can the original Christian divergence from Judaism possibly be legitimate?!

Clearly the stakes are high then as we turn to consider Paul's answer to these intercalated questions.

The Critical Insight

I suggest that a distinction between *structures* and *relationality* is the key to Paul's justification of Christian diversification from messianic Judaism, and hence of his incarnational, contextualized missionary approach, and ultimately of the acknowledgement of Jesus's concrete presence in all of humanity. This all-important distinction emerges directly out of Paul's gospel, which we have already described in parts 1 and 2.

As we know, Paul has a theory about how God, working through Jesus, has made us into people who can behave in the right way, and we needed help to do so. Humanity, without this help, is made of Flesh, which denotes a state that is dominated by evil powers, enmeshed in sinful desires, and destined for death. "Oh wretched person that I am!" the human being made of Flesh cries out in Rom 7:24a. But members of the community, Paul holds, live now in a new way because they live, at least to a significant degree, in a new age.[7] The Flesh has been executed, terminated on the cross, and people have been raised in Jesus into a glorious state beyond its contamination and mortality. "Thanks be to God—through Jesus Christ [I have been rescued] . . . ," Paul says in Rom 7:25 immediately after his fleshly cry in Rom 7:24. The divine Spirit works through the Son at the behest of the Father to effect this shift, reconstituting us—resurrecting us—as spiritual people (1 Cor 15:44, 53–54), with resurrected minds that are participating in the long-awaited age to come.[8]

---

7. Although we extended this life through the rest of humanity, to avoid functional Marcionism.

8. Paul, with his traditional view of time, thought that this resurrection would happen in two stages. We have a resurrected mind now, and we will receive a glorious new resurrected body when Jesus returns, waiting with Jesus for that moment if we happen to die first in an intermediate, soulish state. The tensions implicit here are smoothed out if we adopt a more accurate view of time as a field. With the help of Einstein, we now know that when we die, we enter directly into God's perfect time, so there is no period of waiting in a strangely disembodied state. But whatever the temporal mechanics, this glorious new constitution dramatically transcends our former fleshly condition, solving any problems of capacity. Our new resurrected minds think and act in the right ways, and we have this capacity to act well right now, recalling also that to think rightly is already to this degree to act correctly.

In view of this eschatological transformation, it is unsurprising that the entry ritual for Paul's converts into the community is not an embodied marker like circumcision, which was given just after birth to recognize physical ancestry, but the highly transferable ritual of immersion. People are not simply born into the new community, biologically, in the same way that they might be born Jewish—or English, or Korean, or Nigerian. The "birth" effected through the gospel takes place miraculously, through the Spirit, like Isaac's conception (Gal 4:28–29), and this new birth is recognized in the ritual of immersion, which enacts the deaths of converts and their resurrection into a new reality.

Paul now thinks, and also constantly instructs his converts, on this basis, which is to say, in terms of what we can call a "resurrection ethic." Our capacity to act in a good way comes from the fact—the fact!—that we have been reconstituted mentally within the new age, that is, the age to come, from the future (Col 3:1). But what is the new age exactly? What are the contours of this resurrection?

Paul is convinced that we are being drawn into the communion of the Trinity, around which the new age revolves. This was God's plan for us from before the foundation of the world, so it is the reality into which we are being pulled after we have foolishly turned away from it, following the siren call of evil (Rom 8:29). *The determinative reality in our lives*—in *all* our thinking and related acting—*is the triune God*, which is to say, the divine communion; this is our origin, our destiny, and our most important present reality.

We have learned well by now, furthermore, that this reality is interpersonal. God's nature is intrinsically and supremely relational. A resurrection ethic is consequently a comprehensively *relational* ethic. So it follows that a relational reality is now pressing down upon us, imprinting us as a mold shapes a slab of dough that has been rolled out on the kitchen counter. And we also know well by now what these relationships are supposed to look like, the subject especially of part two. We are to live like Jesus, in full, loving relationships with God and with others, with that love expressing itself (Gal 5:6) in different situations as giving, obeying and being faithful, peacemaking, and rejoicing—or, as Paul himself puts it on one occasion, in loving relationships characterized by joy, peace, patience, kindness, goodness, faithfulness, gentleness, and self-control (Gal 5:22–23). A resurrection ethic is a relational ethic of love, in all its flourishing specific instantiations. This is the primary reality for which we were destined and that we now live out of.

It is important to reiterate at this moment that this activity is still embodied. Paul never endorses a destructive dualism between body and spirit or soul, as later Gnostics did. Paul is frequently so excited about the way that the new resurrected reality solves the problems of the old cosmos, and about its over-whelming superiority, that his language can get him into trouble, especially when he is deploying short summary statements. See, for example, his claim:

> If someone is in Christ, he is a new creation.
> The old has departed. Behold, he has become quite new. (2 Cor 5:17)

This isn't quite true of us, although it is true of Jesus himself. One of Paul's most famous claims about this new resurrected state, Gal 3:26–28, evidences the same sweeping claims.

> All of you who are in Christ Jesus are, by means of that fidelity,[9] sons
>   of God.
> For you have been immersed into Christ;
> you have been clothed with Christ.
> There is no "Jew" or "pagan," no "slave" or "free," no "male and female."
> All of you who are in Christ Jesus are one and the same.

Again, however, it is only fair to note that Paul does continue to live on, to some degree, as a Jew, a freeman, and a male. We grasp his point that these dimensions are all emphatically secondary to the impress of the new reality in Christ, which is one of divine "sonship." But we are still stuck with our particular bodies of flesh. And Col 3:9–11 is similar:

> You have taken off your old self with its practices
> and have put on the new self,
> which is being renewed in knowledge in the image of its Creator.
> Here there is no Gentile or Jew, circumcised or uncircumcised,
> barbarian, Scythian, slave or free,
> but Christ is all, and is in all.

A little sadly, Philemon is still a barbarian master—probably a Phrygian if his wife's name is any guide (Phlm 2)—and Onesimus is still a Scythian slave. These embodied identities are structuring the way in which they relate to one another. Hence it would be a grave mistake to suppose that the old age has

---

9. This phrase is a reference back to a key motif in the previous argumentative stage. It refers primarily to Jesus's "fidelity" and not to ours. His coming has made our sonship possible.

been completely abolished. Even if the present body of Flesh is inadequate, Paul is still convinced that all human existence and action is embodied. The limitations of the body of Flesh will be dealt with by God's generous provision of a new, spiritual body in due course. (Paul talks about this provision at length in 1 Cor 15.) But Paul never envisages human life apart from an embodied existence, and he was quite right to emphasize this point. Jesus was always embodied from his incarnation onward, and as we wait for our perfected spiritual bodies, we still act in a concrete world. It is just that this is no longer primary or determinative.

Paul's main claim is that these embodied forms are nevertheless distinctly secondary to the main reality, which is the baptismal identity of both Philemon and Handy in Jesus—or at least they should be. It is impossible to avoid the punch in these statements that is coming through from the new age, which we already enjoy. This is what matters, and it matters now as signaled by the fact that Paul is using the present tense. The divine relationality of love acts through our imperfect and embodied lives. It is this relationality that is now all-important, coming as it does from beyond, which is to say, from God, although bodies and their locations remain in play as the vehicles through which this relationality takes place.

It is here, then, that we see our vital distinction emerge into view—between the embodied forms and structures in the old age that we still indwell, and the relationality of the new age that works through them. Note, this is not a distinction between form and content, which would be spurious. These are two dimensions within the same activities so they are never separable, although they are distinguishable, from one another, this being a further moment when Chalcedonian categories can help us.

On the one hand, then, God is deeply involved in all the details of our existence. Every hair on our head matters, as the incarnation shows. Furthermore, this affirmation stands to reason. If our acting and present existence is embodied, then all our relating takes place through embodiment. Nevertheless, on the other hand, the specific structures and forms that our embodied actions are working through are less important than the quality of the relationality involved, which is pressing down upon them, and this is the critical dimension within the navigation of any situation. The forms and structures of everyday life are not unimportant. That would be to collapse into Gnosticism. They are not trivial, to be erased or abandoned. But they have been transcended in some sense as well, *which opens up the possibilities of missional contextualization and of consequent ethical and ecclesial variation.* Embodied structures belong to a cosmos that has been executed and reconstituted in Jesus, so their value comes only from the way that they are intertwined with and make possible the relationality of the new age. That relationality is what really matters because this is both what we were made for and where we are going, and the forms and structures themselves matter only to the degree that they freight this relationality. In essence, then, structures have been relativized, hence not abolished or erased, or reified and universalized, to move to the opposite pole of importance, but located between these two false extremes—a distinction that is so important, it is worth spending a little more time on it.

Indifferent Structures

All relationships operate within forms or structures that contain multiple dimensions providing options for individuated behavior. Without such structures freedom is not even possible (see ch. 9!). We all live and act through various structures and forms all of the time. But as we saw earlier, Paul is not always that interested in these relics from the old cosmos. They are vehicles for living and little more. But every specific action that takes place through them can be assessed in terms of its charity and its relational tenor, which is the key ethical determination. This dimension within the situation is coming from eternity. So we always need to ask, Is an act or activity loving? If appropriate, is it covenantal? In the right circumstances, is it gentle, and/or kind, self-controlled, patient, and so on? Putting these questions in terms of their common denominators, we need to ask *how* things are working as against *what* those things are.

So, for example, if, in an act of kindness, I offer to get my coworker a free beverage, it does not matter whether he or she asks for a cup of coffee, of cocoa, or of tea. The act can't take place without a concrete drink, but the *what* of the drink does not matter as much as the *how* of the offer and its delivery.[10] Just so, Paul is not very concerned when someone is eating meat that has been previously sacrificed to an idol and not drained of its blood.[11] But he knows

10. Joseph Chancellor, Seth Margolis, Katherine Jacobs Bao, and Sonja Lyubomirsky, "Everyday Prosociality in the Workplace: The Reinforcing Benefits of Giving, Getting, and Glimpsing," *Emotion*, June 5 (2017): 1–11; http://dx.doi.org/10.1037/emo0 00032.

11. His principal navigation of this situation can be found in 1 Cor 8–10, but a more generic treatment also appears in Rom 14. A subtle analysis of Paul's navigation of these questions is supplied by David Horrell, *The Social Ethos of the Corinthian*

that this what will scandalize anyone with Jewish commitments, so he counsels his converts not to cause offense—the how of the situation. If someone will be upset or perhaps even theologically thrown by seeing community members feasting on such meat, they should determine never to eat meat again!

> If your sibling is grieved because of food
> then you are no longer walking in love. . . .
> For the kingdom of God is not a matter of food and drink
> but of goodness and peace and joy in the Holy Spirit. (Rom 14:15–17)

It is clear, then, that Paul was not that worried about the what any more (at least in relation to this question).[12] He was quite confident that any relationship with God was not materially affected by food per se. The form or structure of the actual food and its consumption did not matter. These had been transcended. But he was very concerned about how eating practices would affect these communities relationally, and so he offered strong and potentially quite costly advice about behavior designed to enhance their fundamental concord. If my eating meat sold in the temple market causes offense, I will never eat it again, he says (at least, in front of you). Similarly, I won't let pork—or any dubious meat—touch my lips if it is going to upset you. If we think about this for a moment, we can see that it is quite challenging advice. How many of us are prepared to become vegetarians because of the scruples of our friends and neighbors? But it is thoroughly relational. Paul is thinking about the how, not the what.

Paul can take this line only because of the way that the new age relativizes structures within the old fleshly cosmos, but he is quite clear about this transcendence. His resurrected converts live from a state beyond ingestion and the stomach, with the result that food is just not that important in and of itself (see Rom 14:1–15:6; 1 Cor 6:12–13; 8; 10:23–33; Gal 2:11–14). "Food does not bring us closer to, or take us away from, God" (1 Cor 8:8; see also Rom

---

Correspondence: Interests and Ideology from 1 Corinthians to 1 Clement (Edinburgh: T&T Clark, 1996); and John Barclay's treatment of Rom 14 is also typically probing: "Do We Undermine the Law? A Study of Romans 14:1–15:6," in *Paul and the Mosaic Law*, ed. James D. G. Dunn (Tübingen: Mohr Siebeck, 1996), 287–308. (Having said this, I am not sure that either study grasps the underlying relational ethic that I am identifying here.)

12. Where Paul is concerned about structures will be described and evaluated carefully in due course. His principal structural impositions are pedagogical and in relation to sexual activity.

14:17). Indeed, "God will destroy them both" (1 Cor 6:13). The new world of relationality dramatically transcends the old cosmos and its structures.

Intriguingly, he applies the same reasoning to the division of time, which for Paul was under the supervision of the present heavenly bodies (as even for us today, to a large extent, it still is). The new community is structured by a different time altogether, the perfect time in the new age, along with its eager anticipation here of this glorious event, and so it can observe whatever local constructions of time it needs to "in the meantime" as the relational needs of its contexts suggest. Consequently, Jews can actually continue to follow their treasured Jewish calendar, with Sabbaths, new moon intervals, and feasts. But pagans can follow their own calendars too, which divided up time differently (Rom 14:5). Moreover, these calendars do not need to be transferred. And Paul even scolds the Galatians, who were former pagans, for thinking that they should switch to Jewish time: "You are observing days and months and seasons and years" (Gal 4:10–11). He fears that if they do switch, then they are denying the validity of the entire underlying reality of life in the resurrected Christ beyond such structures, and he is right. Intriguingly, the Colossians were making a similar mistake. They too should stay with Colossian practices of eating, drinking, associating, and calculating time (Col 2:16, 20). To adopt Jewish customs was to embrace "a shadow of the things that are to come, namely, the body of Christ" (2:17), and to be subject to essentially weak and useless realities, namely, the temporary structures of the present passing age.

In sum, we must learn, like Paul, to ask constantly what relationality is operative in any given missional context, whether during our initial immersive mission, or during ongoing community formation. We must *evaluate* the local pagan structures and forms in the light of this primary distinction. Some forms can be judged safe—and some not so much; it is the tenor of the relationality in play that is our key concern. A simpler way of putting this is to say that the how matters more than the what, while the what matters only to the degree that it is affecting the how.

This distinction, generated, the scholars would say, by realized eschatology, articulates the way that the loving relationality of the Trinity places pressure on the entirety of our situation with all its structures, pressuring them into conformity with itself but, paradoxically, allowing diverse communal expressions as diverse peoples and communities are encountered. It is this distinction, then, as well as the implications that result from it, that explain the shocking diversification in much missionary work that we began this chapter with, and much else besides (e.g., missional immersion), although this is a complex tale that will require further unraveling. When this distinction is pressed, contextualization is not the only thing that happens. In fact, a spectrum of *four* options for any engagement with the elements within pagan culture has now been created. Adumbrating this full suite of options will be the subject of the next chapter.

Theses

- Missionaries often seem to get into trouble back home with the "head office" as they contextualize their converts' ethic, something especially apparent in the history of missions in China.
- That the Romans named converts to Paul's gospel in Syrian Antioch "Christians" (Lat. *Christiani*) indicates that a strand had formed within the early church that was not recognizably Jewish, and this diversification is a familiar missionary dynamic, as was just noted.
- From this point onward, the early church comprised both Christians and messianic Jews (the latter being messianic in the specific sense of affirming Jesus of Nazareth as the Christ).
- The ethic of the new Christians was partly Jewish, but in part not so, and here to a shocking degree, abandoning the Jewish calendar, diet, and circumcision of males. Paul endorsed this ethic. There were also shocking additions to much Judaism at the time, for example, the inclusion of converts from pagans qua pagan converts in the age to come.
- These radical departures elicited an attempted suppression from the "head office" in Jerusalem, which was rejected on site in Antioch and was followed by an important conference back in Jerusalem of all the key leaders, from all of which a modus vivendi seems to have resulted. The early church accepted the legitimacy of both Jewish and Christian converts.
- Paul worked very hard to maintain church unity, even as he resisted the imposition of comprehensive Judaism on his converts, the practice that had created the difficulty in the first place. He made trips to Jerusalem, raised money for their work, and eventually risked death to deliver this gift to the leaders there personally.
- But he also formulated a theological and scriptural rationale for the situation—the "gospel" of salvation and its accompanying ethic that we have already described in parts 1 and 2.
- We have identified a basic distinction operating in Paul between structure and relationality—between the structures and forms within which people are embodied in the present age and through which they act, and the lov-

ing relationality of the Trinity, which is pressing through those structures as well. When a missionary-apostle engages with a particular context, in Paul's case a pagan context, this distinction is the key.

> It also allows a missionary-apostle like Paul to immerse into a new and pagan context legitimately, without sinning, *and* to accept and include many local pagan forms and structures within a new expression of the church.

> The key ethical question to ask now is, How is the relationality of the situation working?

> It is worth quickly reprising the theological grounds of this key concern.

> We begin by recalling God's gift of ethical capacity to us by executing our sinful Flesh and raising us within Jesus through the Spirit. Our minds are resurrected now, and we await our glorious new bodies. We have stepped into the age to come, as instantiated by baptism.

> The new age we experience is a divine communion and hence structured fundamentally interpersonally and relationally, in relationships of love.

> Activity is still embodied, and consequently inseparable from forms and structures. Paul emphasizes strongly the superiority of the New Age. But he is no Gnostic. Forms and structures are not irrelevant but they are secondary. They are the means through which relationality in the present is enacted. Hence structures and forms in the old cosmos are not erased, but they are relativized by this new situation.

> Ethically, the focus is on the quality of relationships operative in any given situation, and as a result on the "how" of any situation rather than on the "what."

> In fact, however, a spectrum of four options for evaluation and engagement with any given context has now been generated, and they are not all affirming.

Key Scriptural References

Jesus followers are called Christians in the Apostolic Writings (NT) only in Acts 11:26, 26:28, and 1 Pet 4:16. But there are good reasons for both holding Acts to be accurate at this moment, and explaining why the AW seldom use this nomenclature.

The key summaries of Paul's eschatologically transcendent ethic were listed in chapter 5 and should be well-known by now: see 1 Cor 12:13; 2 Cor 5:17, Gal 3:26–28; 6:15; and Col 3:9–11.

The texts denoting Paul's adaptability to local contexts have been listed before: see especially 1 Cor 9:19–23; Gal 4:12, and 1 Thess 2:9. But now they receive a more robust explanation.

Key Reading

Walls's account of Timothy Richards's missionary career in China should be standard reading for anyone thinking about mission in any capacity—and Pauline interpreters should always be thinking about mission.

"Everyday Prosociality in the Workplace: The Reinforcing Benefits of Giving, Getting, and Glimpsing," an essay by Joseph Chancellor, Seth Margolis, Katherine Jacobs Bao, and Sonja Lyubomirsky, is a delightful analysis that beautifully conveys the key distinction between structure and relationality, although this has to be mined from the paper's prosaic statistical evaluation of the impact of kindness in a modern institutional setting.

Further Reading

Useful observations about the church's later missionary work and their dynamics, especially in China, are supplied by Minamiki and by Walls.

The biography assumed in this chapter is argued for in detail by my *Framing Paul*, especially in chapters 2 and 3, and by my two articles "Galatians 5:11" and "Beyond the Torah at Antioch." Gordon describes how the Romans reacted to "new religious movements."

A famous treatment of bodiliness in the Christian tradition is Peter Brown's *The Body and Society*. It is an extremely useful map allowing the specific location of Paul's position.

Bibliography

Baur, F. C. *Paul the Apostle of Jesus Christ. His Life and Works, His Epistles and Teachings*. 2 vols. London: Williams & Norgate, 1873.

Brown, Peter. *The Body and Society: Men, Women, and Sexual Renunciation in Early Christianity*. 2nd ed. New York: Columbia University, 2008.

Campbell, Douglas A. "Beyond the Torah at Antioch: The Probable Locus for Paul's Radical Transition." *JSPL* 4, no. 2 (2014): 187–214.

———. *Framing Paul: An Epistolary Biography*. Grand Rapids: Eerdmans, 2014.

———. "Galatians 5:11: Evidence of an Early Law-Observant Mission by Paul?" *NTS* 57 (2011): 325–47.

———. "The Trinity in Paul: From Confession to Ethics." Pages 193–217 in *Essays on the Trinity*. Edited by Lincoln Harvey. Eugene, OR: Wipf & Stock, 2018.

Chancellor, Joseph, Seth Margolis, Katherine Jacobs Bao, and Sonja Lyubomirsky. "Everyday Prosociality in the Workplace: The Reinforcing Benefits of Giving, Getting, and Glimpsing." *Emotion* 18 (2017): 507–17.

Gordon, Richard. "*Superstitio*, Superstition, and Religious Repression in the Late Roman Republic and Principate (100 BCE–300 CE)." *Past and Present* 199, supp. 3 (2008): 72–94.

Minamiki, George. *The Chinese Rites Controversy from Its Beginning to Modern Times*. Chicago: Loyola University Press, 1985.

Walls, Andrew. "The Multiple Conversions of Timothy Richards: A Paradigm of Missionary Experience." Pages 271–94 in *The Gospel in the World: International Baptist Studies*. Edited by David Bebbington. Carlisle: Paternoster, 2002.

CHAPTER 21

Evaluating Paganism

The distinction between structures and relationality allows a flexible immersion by missionary-apostles into local contexts, and the consequent generation of new Christian forms, and this speaks in turn to a perennial problem within much Christian mission. So often Christian missionaries have overridden local cultures and practices too aggressively, judging and erasing them in favor of communities constructed in their own image. A Christianity that sensitively employs the structure-relationality distinction, however, can avoid the inappropriate erasure of local cultures as it engages with them (although resistance from Christian traditionalists, offended by the resulting differences, will then almost inevitably have to be faced).

But it turns out that the adoption of new local practices is only half the story. Missionary-apostles must still avoid sinning and go on to address and resist sinful structures operating in any local context as well. So the pressing of the structure-relationality distinction is not a simple matter of contextual affirmation *carte blanche*. It actually generates various possible responses to different aspects within any local context, specifically, four: (1) affirmation; (2) admonition; (3) reformation; and (4) condemnation.

Basic Modes of Evaluation

As we just noted, the relational question is the key. Missionary-apostles should constantly be asking, How are people in this particular context acting toward one another? What is the tenor and quality of their behavior? In particular, is it loving? This is to ask about "how" things are happening as against "what" is in play. When this primary concern is combined with the various structural vehicles through which all the relating is taking place, four types of judgment emerge into view, recalling that relationality always unfolds through some sort of structure.

1. First and most positively, a structure might be judged neutral, and its relationality entirely healthy and loving, leading to judgments of *affirmation*. How things are working, both in terms of structure and relationality, is just fine. "Good job," says Paul in such instances.
2. Although a structure might be judged neutral, the relationality currently operating through it might be judged inadequate and unloving, at which moment the apostle will *admonish* his converts to practice the loving relationality made available to them through Jesus within the structure as it presently stands. The structure doesn't need to change; the relationality does.

These two evaluative modes can lead to strong contextual affirmations of local structures and forms, and hence to ecclesial diversification (which are two sides of the same coin). New forms of Christianity flourish. So these two modes lead to the shocking diversification in the nature of the church that was described in the previous chapter. They also do much to move mission past any deleterious colonialism, especially cultural erasures. But navigation is by no means finished with this happy endorsement of local structures.

3. It might become apparent that a certain structure is impeding or hampering a loving relationality, so it needs to be modified or *reformed* so that it can be a better vehicle for the ways of Jesus to unfold. Some structural change is consequently necessary, along with relational change. (Note, the structural impediment is revealed by its inability to convey a loving relationality adequately.)
4. A structure might be so distorting and damaging that Christians should stop participating in it at all, eliciting a judgment of *condemnation*. Some structures just have to go. No loving relationality is possible within them. The loving "how" is being blocked completely.

As was the case for the four missional modes, when one or more of these four key evaluative modes is dropped, distortions result. The ongoing formation of converts into Christian communities will lapse into the worst form of colonialism or into some complementary libertine aberration. When the four modes are all enacted, however, an appropriate diversification results. Each evaluative mode, in other words, is a sine qua non for diverse but healthy community formation. It is clear that in both the first two modes Paul is happy to let pagan structures stay intact, and it is this phenomenon that creates Christian communities that are different from the parent culture of their missionaries. An account of sin kicks in with mode 2, we might say, but the challenge to reform local structures, leading to overt deviations from the local culture of the converts in question, only kicks in significantly with mode 3. In modes 3 and 4 the new communities of Christians deviate from their own local cultures, generating challenges on that front. So in any authentic missional situation Christians will probably end up taking heat from both sides—the story of much of the book of Acts.

Evaluative Mode	Local pagan culture	Structure	Relationality	Repentance
1. Affirmation	Endorsement (ecclesial diversification)	Good	Good	Unnecessary
2. Admonition	Endorsement (ecclesial diversification)	Good	Problematic	Sin challenged
3. Reformation	Deviation (local divergence)	Problematic (so reform)	Problematic	Sin challenged
4. Condemnation	Deviation (local divergence)	Unacceptable (so abandon)	Blocked	Sin challenged

Analogies for this fourfold process of evaluation are difficult to find, but a musical parable might again help us.

Music Again

Let us imagine that I am a conductor arriving at a concert hall one night for a new assignment—to teach and then lead the musicians gathered there in a performance of *The Firebird*. The orchestra is waiting for me, music on the stands, instruments tuned and upright. I raise my baton to signal the beginning of the piece to see where they are placed and how much I need to teach them, and as I begin conducting, an extraordinary, flawless performance of *The Firebird* follows. I can do little more than mark the time, and even that often seems unnecessary. The music is inspiring, and its performance equally so. Tears come to my eyes. After the piece finishes, I can only say, somewhat damply, "Phenomenal job; I can teach you nothing. Just keep doing whatever it is you're doing." I comprehensively, sincerely, and happily affirm my charges.[1]

I return to the concert hall the next week to the same assignment with another group of musicians. I raise my baton to signal the start of the music and, to my surprise, a rather awful performance of *The Firebird* unfolds. The players in the orchestra are not listening to one another. They don't know the music well, and they struggle to render it. They are insensitive to all the emotion of the piece. It is just horrible. It is clear, then, that we have a lot of work to do simply to play the piece well. The musicians must practice, and they also must play together and do so repeatedly and carefully, although I remain hopeful that, at the end of this process, a beautiful performance of *The Firebird* will be possible. I finish with a speech challenging the musicians—who are evidently quite competent—simply to play the music better with one another. They can do it. The basic task is a simple one. Everything is in place. They must listen more carefully, feel the pulse of the music more deeply, and care about what they are doing. I admonish them just to play better.

Sometime later I return to the hall to conduct another ensemble. I walk in and raise my baton. Complete musical carnage ensues. Many of the musicians have the wrong music. Many have not practiced, and for some, any amount of practice will not lift them to the level required to render *The Firebird* well. Some even have the wrong instruments for the piece. Other key pieces are missing. Someone is pounding a bass guitar; others are strumming ukuleles. Before we even begin to practice, then, we must reorganize things thoroughly. Certain instruments must go. Others must be brought in. Where are the all-important trumpets?! Some musicians must be demoted from the group. The right music must be found for everyone. Only when all this is done will the orchestra even be in a place to begin learning to play *The Firebird* well, and this could take some time. There is no actual orchestra possessing the requisite musical competence present. So the entire situation—its very organization— must be significantly reformed and modified before we can move forward.

I return later in some trepidation to the same concert hall for my final teaching assignment. I walk in and raise my baton. This time, it is not simply a matter of musical carnage. It is physical carnage, plain and simple. Apparently a team of rugby players is present who proceed to practice tackling, scrummaging, and kickoffs. And other players are present as well. Someone

---

1. https://www.youtube.com/watch?v=RZkIAVGlfWk&list=RDkd1xYKGnOEw &index=2.

is practicing squash; someone is bowling a cricket ball. It is a complete chaos. There is not a note in sight. I manage to gain control of the situation and begin to eject everyone from the hall. There will, of course, be no performance of *The Firebird* tonight, or ever, unless some of the players present convert to musical careers and begin the long, arduous task of learning to play their instruments to the requisite standard, which some of them assure me they want to do. In fact, I find out on inquiry that some of the musicians from the other weeks are present. But they have no instruments or music with them, and I watch in horror as they begin to damage their fingers and hands during tackling practice. I exclaim to them that they cannot play rugby to a high standard and music to an equally high standard. It is one or the other. And as I see one particularly gifted pianist nursing a broken finger, I burst out in condemnation, "This must stop!"

If this is all beginning to clarify, it is time to press into Paul's texts to discern where he is utilizing these four evaluative modes. Clearly he does not state things in these schematic terms, but I suggest that the basic modes are all apparent.

Evaluative Mode 1: Affirmation

As we noted earlier on, there may be structures already operating among an apostle's new friends with the appropriate loving relationality at work as well, to which he or she need only say, "Good job; keep at it." And we would even expect some structures to be of this nature. We must be able to affirm some appropriate Trinitarian relationality in any new location. Jesus is at work there already, probably not very overtly or clearly, but concretely and recognizably, and he always is. So, for example, people are generally born into families, however dysfunctional, and make friends, however sporadically. And most families and friendships will contain moments of loving relationality, while some will operate constantly in these terms. Hence the basic structure of many of these families and friendships does not need to change. And it follows that God is already at work to some degree in any given context, which should simply be recognized and affirmed. Insofar as relationality in the new pagan context is already loving, and loving in ways that specifically instantiate love as giving, being faithful, making peace, and delighting, the structures freighting that love can be fully affirmed.

There is a hint of this in Paul at times. He reminds his Galatian converts of their loving reception of him when he was ill—of how they were a "blessing" to him. They were not yet his converts at the time or even his friends. But they loved him well (Gal 4:13–15 NIV modified).

> As you know,
> it was because of an illness that I first preached the gospel to you,
> and even though my illness was a trial to you,
> you did not treat me with contempt or scorn.
> Instead, you welcomed me
> as if I were an angel of God,
> as if I were Christ Jesus himself.
> . . . I can testify that, if you could have done so,
> you would have torn out your eyes
> and given them to me.

Putting things a little more technically, we can say that a pagan structure of welcome—clean clothes, warmth, shelter, food, care, local medications perhaps, certainly a bed, drink, and security—was indwelt here by a loving relationality and was entwined into a blessing. So nothing here needed to change. It needed only to be affirmed. The structure of hospitality was fine, and the relationality operating within it was fine.

In a similar way, the Thessalonians already know how to love one another. They do not need to be taught this, so this too needs merely to be affirmed (1 Thess 4:9–10, NIV modified):

> Now about your love for one another
> we do not need to write to you,
> for you yourselves have been taught by God to love each other.
> And in fact, you do love all of God's family throughout Macedonia.
> And so we urge you, brothers and sisters, to do so more and more.

A specific structure is not in view here, so we must supply a panoply of unstated forms that are all clearly working within this community as well as they needed to, channeling the love of God. Paul is pleased (for once!) and affirms this.[2] Nothing needs to change. "Good job; keep at it," is all that needs to be said.

2. It could be argued that the Thessalonians' love for one another was a postconversion phenomenon, so we may have just the one example of affirmation here from Paul. Nothing significant changes either way.

But as we well know, Paul does not major on this sort of advice. Generally things do need to be corrected, leading us to a consideration of the next navigational mode. In many respects, mode 2 is Paul's signature mode.

Evaluative Mode 2: Admonition

As we saw in the last chapter, Paul is just not that worried about a lot of structures operating among the pagan peoples that he is evangelizing and teaching. Structures don't matter unless they get in the way of relating. Hence Paul seems to have judged many pagan structures as falling into a category of fundamental indifference—a bold move but one that makes sense once its underlying eschatological rationale is grasped. So he was not overly fussed about pagan structures of language (i.e., the languages they spoke). Nor was he particularly concerned with basic patterns of eating, drinking, dress, work, and the demarcation of time, or with various dynamics within family and friendship structures, or with socializing, to offer a quick list. Pagan patterns for doing these things generally didn't bother him, and so he could adopt them happily when he was evangelizing. But he was very concerned that these patterns or structures convey the appropriate relationality. His admonitions in this respect were constant because pagans were not, in his view, usually acting through these forms with the appropriate love. The forms themselves did not need to be substantially changed, then, or even to be revised; their occupants merely needed to let Jesus's loving virtues flow through them more consistently and obviously.

For example, Paul placed a lot of pressure on the relational tenor of his converts' language. We will discuss language further in a subsequent chapter when we dive more deeply into the work of the Spirit in ethics, along with the Spirit's use of the Scriptures within that guidance, so for now it must suffice to say that language in the church was both vitally important and, ideally, comprehensively loving. So it frequently needed to be more self-controlled, gentle, and considerate than it apparently was. Paul's pagan converts were supposed to stop vilifying, criticizing, boasting, cursing, slandering, and comparing. Rather, they were supposed to speak constructively, humbly, respectfully, kindly, peacefully—in a word, lovingly. So the actual structure of language did not disappear. People did not stop talking. However, the relationality that their language was conveying needed to be changed, and sometimes quite dramatically.

Similarly, the fact of eating, and what was eaten, did not matter; how it was eaten did. Christians could eat jellied eels, jugged hare, or hot sausages with mustard. None of this mattered. Was the eating taking place appropriately, though? Were participants in Christian meals either sharing from their largesse or contributing as they could without freeloading? Neither of these countervailing actions, occurring in Corinth and Thessalonica respectively, was loving. The eating didn't need to stop, and what was actually eaten didn't need to change. But it did need to take place with more kindness and respect. The relating taking place through and around the eating was paramount, and as things stood in Corinth and Thessalonica, it was unacceptable.

Clothing didn't need to change either. Paul notes in one celebrated instance that female clothing should be worn respectfully and not discarded in a frenzied abandon during worship (1 Cor 11:2–16). Within the norms of ancient marriage, this was the loving thing to do. (The norms themselves will be addressed at length in a later chapter.) So Paul did not tell people what exact types of clothes to wear—what color, material, or pattern. Paul's communities were not the ancient equivalent of Hasidic Jews, seventeenth-century eastern European clothing intact, complete with fur hats. In like manner, the local calendar could be followed, and so on.

We can probably see now quite clearly, looking back, that it is the enactment of these two navigational modes, affirmation and admonition, that underlies the formation of a local Christian community that is markedly different from the parent culture of its missionaries. Any local pagan structures or forms that can convey a loving relationality appropriately can be left intact after conversion and as the new church takes shape, and this encompasses quite a lot. Many of the key markers of ethnic identity are left essentially undisturbed by this approach to community formation, excepting the stringent demand to be more loving within them. Eating, associating, marking time, dressing, marking the body, and even speaking can all be left much the same, and as a result of this, any new Christian community is going to look rather different from its parent body. But at this moment we need to go on to appreciate that not only is this charming diversification possible; we *must* embrace contextualization, with all its creativity and risks and resulting offensive diversifications, as fully as we can. This all seems to be part of God's great plan.

Diversification

Human life is diverse. We moderns tend to use the word "culture" to describe this phenomenon, at times a little unhelpfully. But when we talk about different cultures today, we understand, broadly speaking, that people have all sorts of different ways of doing things. We speak different languages, dress in different clothes, eat different food, at different times, with different eating tools. We entertain ourselves with different stories, and we laugh at different jokes. We scream and yell at different referees making bad calls, using diverse curses, in different games. We enjoy different weather, which we deal with in part by living in different houses decorated in different ways and positioned within different gardens. And so on. Human life is complex and intertwined, but its vast networks spread inexorably into diversity across space and time. The forms and structures that make our embodied life possible differ dramatically. So what happens when a missionary like Paul encounters a new form of life—a new culture—as he did, with his friend Barnabas, at Antioch in late 36 CE, and then many times subsequently?

Once the missionaries have thought things through and grasped the eschatological basis of the new situation, with its all-important relationality, then they can conclude that God's people, as they gather new converts, will inevitably expand and diversify into new forms, and that this is fine. We see the Holy Spirit strongly signaling her approval at Antioch and subsequently.[3] It was OK to be Greek, we might say, as long as that culture was suitably reformed. In fact, a creative God clearly *delights* in this diversification as new cultures and new ways of doing things are encountered. The church is *supposed* to diversify.

But many Jesus followers still recoil from this diversification. It is so tempting to play it safe during missionary work. This attitude means pressing for a maximal adoption of *the missionaries'* structures, and even for a whole-sale transfer of the missionary team's culture into the culture of the converts. This transfer avoids any difficult questions of discernment. "What we do is already ratified, so if you do it as well, it must be alright." Moreover, any friction with the mother church back home is attenuated because it doesn't arise. The culture of the mother churches is being safely exported into the communities in question. It is also easier on the missionary end. The missionaries don't have to learn the culture of their converts inside and out. It is the other way around. They arrive and say "become like me," in a telling reduction of Paul's original twofold process, stated in Gal 4:12, to one movement in their own direction. Here all the relationality and structures of the missionary are adopted by converts.

---

3. Such approval is also a phenomenon evident throughout both Paul's writings and the book of Acts. We will discuss this point more in a following chapter.

But this approach is also thoroughly colonial, and it betrays Paul's original missionary work, which was intrinsically diverse. It also betrays the truths that this diversity was based upon, that is to say, *the reality of the person and the acts by which we have been lifted into the age to come,* so the betrayals here run deep.

It is not loving to approach people and to repudiate the structures they indwell wholesale. The culture of the converts is thereby erased, and church history teaches us repeatedly that this is a disaster of equal magnitude to those generated by plunging too fully into the cultural location of any converts. When we do so we are a very long way from the God who loved us so much—who respected us so much—that he abandoned his divine location and assumed the limited and corrupt form of a human. It simply follows from God's initial immersion into our situation—the contextualization that dwarfs all others!—that Christianity should flower as a new form out of Judaism, and flower internally itself into multiple new expressions. "Flee colonialism!" Paul would doubtless say to us today were he with us, observing all our missional scruples.

In short, a navigation into difference is a fundamental feature of Pauline mission. It is important that sins are named and repented of—things such as idolatry, which we will discuss momentarily—but it is equally important that legitimate differences from any parent body are affirmed and encouraged. To fail in the former discernment is to unleash a libertine free-for-all in the name of the gospel and to leave sinful pagan practices, with all their harm and pain, intact. To fail in the latter discernment, however, is often *to impose* harm and pain on converts as their local culture is unnecessarily quashed. Equally important, it is to resist the desire of the Holy Spirit, who wishes to affirm the legitimate differences that exist within human history and within humankind, gathering them into, and sanctifying them within, the church.

But we need to recall now that the missionaries whom Jesus commissioned and sent did not just affirm and admonish their pagan neighbors in relation to the quality of their relating. As we well know, on occasion they challenged them and even condemned them. Other navigational modes were clearly at work, then, which we need to describe in order to deepen our account of missional navigation into a context.

Evaluative Mode 3: Reformation

Paul's constant challenges to his pagan converts to practice the right relationality within their local structures and forms clearly shade over at times into challenges to reform those structures.[4] It is all very well to suppose that many pagan forms can simply freight the loving relating of Jesus as the pagans acting through them are exhorted and empowered to do this. Are you friends with someone? Be more faithful! Are you estranged? Be more reconciling! But at times, in order to convey a loving relationality—which is to say, in different circumstances, an extravagant generosity, a steadfast faithfulness, a tireless reconciling, or an exuberant celebrating—forms might need to change. A loving relationality grounded in Jesus will affect them, while presumably this change can take place along a gradient from the subtle to the significant. And in fact, we have already traced this process through earlier on in the book several times in relation to various pagan discourses that Paul has picked up and reshaped under pressure from Trinitarian realities.

We have noted, for example, how followers of Jesus indwell the ubiquitous pagan structure of benefaction, which included the presence of expectations on the part of the giver in relation to the recipient. Those have certainly not been relaxed, although their relational content might now be rather different. But Paul has placed christological pressure on this structure, reshaping it in further countercultural directions. Jesus's followers are called to give self-sacrificially, lavishly, incongruously, *and* unconditionally, at which point we suspect that the actual structure of pagan giving—*euergetism*—has been subtly but significantly changed. In particular, once we have stepped from essentially contractual arrangements into covenantal relations, we are involved with a fundamentally different social practice. But it is now also far more costly and egalitarian, more accepting and inclusive, and more long-suffering, presumably as well as being a little less self-promoting.

Similarly, the approach of Jesus's followers to reconciliation, grounded in the reconciliation of the cosmos effected by the Father and the Spirit through the death of their Son, is so different from pagan practices, which were again contractual, that we should really speak of a different *structure* of reconciliation. The victim and the offended are now supposed to reach out to their enemies, unconditionally, and where it is possible, tirelessly and even lovingly. This is a very different approach from pagan reconciliation, where that took place and insofar as it can be reconstructed, within which offenders had to take the first steps—and probably many of the subsequent steps as well—and effectively earn their way back into favor. Although the overarching relational goal is the same, namely, a mended relationship, the structure by which that is pursued seems different.

4. That is, this is not a threshold as much as a continuum.

Moreover, the celebrations that the followers of Jesus undertake were so different from the partying practices of ancient pagans—and from not a few modern ones as well—that we really need to speak again of another form altogether. Ancient pagan celebrations centered around processions and the worship of false gods and were assisted by feasting and by the consumption of mind-altering substances to excess—in ancient times principally by quaffing a horrifically rough wine. The official celebrations were also presided over by a professional priestly elite. These practices were displaced firmly in Paul's communities by celebrations in the presence of the living God, who cannot be imaged, and by intoxication through the Holy Spirit, generally in a host's house or apartment. There was also a delightful democratization of worship offerings in the local gatherings. Hence the practices generating these celebrations were different to the point that the very structure of the celebratory event seems different as well.

And similar comments are probably appropriate concerning authentic community leadership. Its actual practices are quite different from many of the practices informing pagan leaders. The pagan love affair with ancestry, wealth, achievement, education, professional speech, and popular acclamation is all displaced by benefaction by the Spirit and a Jesus-like character, the latter including virtues that militate directly against many of the key pagan criteria for leadership that have just been listed. Leadership itself is not being set aside. Church leaders are still authoritative, and they still possess their own sort of status. But the markers and practices whereby they achieve that status are very different from pagan markers, leading to a frequent inability by insufficiently Christianized pagans at Corinth to recognize an authentic church leader walking in the footsteps of Jesus, as against a pretentious showman. An authentic leader builds bridges humbly, patiently, and gently, between warring factions, and exhibits self-sacrificial generosity, faithfulness, and exuberant joy. This is *not* what a great pagan leader looked like!

We will later discuss at length what are perceived in our day as Paul's most contentious structural reforms to his pagan environment, namely, his advice about the appropriate form for marriage and hence for sexual activity. And we will shortly address an area that modern readers invariably think he should have drastically reformed but didn't, namely, slavery. Here we now think he did both too much and too little. For now, however, we need to address the type of apostolic advice that must be issued when structures pass beyond the point of reasonable reform, at which moment we reach a fourth navigational mode—*condemnation*.

Evaluative Mode 4: Condemnation

Paul insisted on the immediate cessation of idolatry, which had direct implications for pagan forms and structures, along with any associated relationality. And as we just noted, he insisted on the introduction of a Jewish sexual ethic—within a heterosexual monogamy and not elsewhere—which had an immediate condemnatory effect concerning certain standard pagan forms of sexual activity. He also condemned magical practices out of hand. Moreover, these pagan structures could not be reformed or modified. Any relationality they channeled was so distorted and inappropriate that these structures just had to go.

Loyalty to the one true God means that God alone is to be worshiped, and the worship of anything else must cease. To worship another thing as a god would consequently be a betrayal—an act of consummate disloyalty—and there is no way around this judgment. Moreover, the God revealed in Jesus Christ is to be loved, worshiped, acclaimed, and obeyed, as he revealed himself, and not through some speculative image. So idolatry must be abandoned as well. And these judgments entailed a withdrawal from one of the central organizing features of the ancient city. Its key spaces were no longer to be visited—its temple precincts—and its key practices no longer to be participated in, whether those were prayers before small images in the home or bumptious processions to the local temple, followed by gorging on meat and wine and some indulging in pagan revelry. All participation in these key pagan structures was to cease, and so pagan converts in *these* respects no longer looked like pagans. Paul did allow his converts to banquet with pagans on meat that had been sacrificed to idols and bought subsequently at the secondhand meat market, with certain caveats, so his response to the vast ancient discourse of idolatry was nuanced. He was more flexible and accepting than many of his Jewish contemporaries here, thanks to his relational approach. But his instructions concerning idolatry certainly included elements of outright proscription.[5]

The use of prostitutes was also condemned quickly and decisively by Paul (along with various other violations of heterosexual monogamy).[6] But forms

---

5. Paul's condemnation of idolatry is especially apparent in 1 Cor 10 and more briefly in 1 Cor 5:11; Gal 4:8; Eph 2:11–12; 4:17–19; 5:5–14; Col 3:5–7; and 1 Thess 1:9–10. The way I read him, he would *concur* with the condemnation of idolatry in Rom 1:18–32, although he would not concur with its broader (i.e., its self-evident, foundationalist, and rationalist) terms. For his view of human nature, see especially Rom 5:12–8:14.

6. Paul's condemnation of sexual immorality is evident in 1 Cor 5:1–13; 6:9–20;

and structures will be affected by this judgment as well—the ancient city's vibrant sex industry! Participation by pagan converts in the sex industry was to cease immediately and utterly. So was sex with anyone outside of wedlock—anyone!—so sex with minors and with those of low status was to cease as well, affecting the structure of pagan benefaction and banquets (since hosts could offer slaves to their guests, which could include children; and high-status agents could effectively rape any low-status person they desired).

Similarly, all magical practices were to cease. Cursing and any corresponding protective rituals and products were to be abandoned.[7] So the vast magic industry, with all its spells, papyri, and amulets, along with its supporting cast of street vendors and practitioners, was to be divested, at which moment another notable feature of pagan culture bit the dust.

These are not inconsiderable condemnations. Paul expects participation by his pagan converts in idolatry and its associated rituals and schemas, participation (largely by males) in the sex industry, and any use of magical practices to stop. These structures are to be erased from the Christian community and not relationally revisited or even structurally modified. They are to be eliminated—on relational grounds, of course. They cannot convey the loving relationality of the triune God in any shape or form, and so they must go. They all dictate such damaging practices in an ongoing way to all the relationships involved that the loving thing to do is just to stop. And this is all clearly *not* a contextualization within ancient pagan culture but a challenge to some of its most fundamental features. Christian communities being formed in this way no longer look like their pagan environments, then; in these respects, they are a significant departure from them. And the process of diversity is working here in the other direction. *Pagans* would be offended as converts from their midst abandoned these typical practices.

Qualifications

I hope that it is plain by this point that when we are working with a distinction between relationality and structure, four basic evaluations of local culture are likely, depending on the details of the situation we encounter. But hopefully it is equally apparent that the four modes that I have just described are not neat,

---

Eph 5:3–7; Col 3:5–7; and 1 Thess 4:1–8, again, concurring with the viewpoint in Rom 1:24–27. The use of prostitutes is condemned in 1 Cor 6:12–20.

7. See Gal 5:20. See also Acts 19:11–20.

self-contained boxes into which all actions by missionary apostles can be fitted as they shape new Christian communities out of their pagan contexts; neither are they rules to be applied mechanically.[8] The assessment of the interplay between relationality and structure in any given moment—in the particular, unrepeatable situation that missionary teams are engaging with—will require *judgments* (which are also attempts to discern and to obey an impinging divine reality, I hasten to add, which is something we address in more detail shortly, in a subsequent chapter). Moreover, it is always the same basic judgment. What sort of relationality is in play?, and how do we make that work better?[9] With these critical evaluative modes in place, however, we need to turn now to consider the other major modes of missional engagement, because the story of sensitive and appropriate community formation by missionary-apostles within pagan cultures is far from over. The first and most complex suite of judgments is behind us, but other key elements within community formation still need to be recognized and described.

Theses

> The pressing of a structure-relationality distinction will generate two evaluative modes at first, as the legitimacy of the local culture is assessed: (1) affirmation, when both a local structure and its relationality are operating lovingly and well, and (2) admonition, when a structure seems basically alright but the relationality operating through it is not loving. Here the missionary-apostle admonishes his or her converts to act more lovingly.

8. As I said earlier, these four distinguishable judgments are actually different locations on a continuum. Some things can stay as they are; some practices need to be a little more relationally sensitive, and some relational changes will impact the structures in play as well, and that impact will slide up a scale from minimal to maximal. Then eventually we reach a moment when no structural change is possible, and the structure itself must go—the other end of the continuum. So, complete affirmation lies at one end of the continuum of change, which continues through various modifications that slide over from relational change to structural change, ending in structural termination. Missionary-apostles will need to make judgments in their specific settings, and these will fall at different points on the continuum.

9. So it is a particular sort of *prudential* judgment familiar to virtue ethicists. For this reason also I have avoided using the signifier "judgment" to denote the category of condemnation. Judgment, properly understood, is a prudential act, not a punitive act, and should be made in terms of the considerations that have just been described.

- The operation of evaluative modes 1 and 2 leads to a legitimate contextualization within the local culture of any converts. They do not need to change, other than relationally, in relation to these structures.
- But this contextualization, which accepts local structures, is, at the same moment, a divergence from the parent culture of the missionary-apostles and a diversification in the forms within the mother church.
- This discrepancy often elicits concern and even resistance and hostility from leaders within the parent culture.
- But this inappropriate response needs to be resisted.
- It is clearly God's plan to include appropriate differences within the church.
- This acceptance of legitimate differences—and active seeking after the same during missionary work—is also the key ethical bulwark against colonialism. To the degree that the local pagan structures are not abandoned—and they are extensive—missionary work does not erase the local culture.
- The pressing of a structure-relationality distinction will ultimately generate two more distinguishable outcomes during any missional navigation into a new context and consequent community formation, however:
- (3) reformation, when a structure needs to be modified, which is to say, reformed, so that it can convey a loving relationality more effectively; and
- (4) condemnation, when a structure simply cannot convey a loving relationality in any form and must be eliminated.
- Modes 2, 3, and 4 all address sin in a local context, asking for repentance, although in different respects.
- In modes 3 and 4, namely, reformation and condemnation, the new Christian community will diverge from its local pagan context, perhaps in quite significant ways, modifying or erasing structures, and thereby elicit concern, and even resistance and hostility.
- The four navigational modes are not in fact discrete categories of action but take place on a continuum or spectrum from complete affirmation of both relationality and structures, through modifications of relationality and then structures, to complete rejection of structures.
- In between these two end-points, different prudential judgments will be necessary by leaders in relation to the unrepeatable details of their situations, modifying relationality and, if necessary, structures, to greater or lesser degrees.

Key Scriptural References

Paul's gestures toward affirmation can be seen in Gal 4:13–15 and possibly also in 1 Thess 4:9–10.

The flexibility a structure-relationality distinction affords Paul is especially evident when he discusses whether or not kosher meat should be eaten, along with the related question whether food sacrificed to idols can be consumed. I would categorize his responses here in terms of mode 2, admonition: see especially Rom 14:15, 17 but also Rom 14:1–15:6; 1 Cor 6:12–13; ch. 8, especially 8:8; 10:23–33; Gal 2:11–14. The unnecessariness of adopting Jewish food rules and the Jewish calendar is explicit in Gal 4:10–11 and Col 2:16, 20 as well.

Paul also spends a great deal of time placing pressure on his converts' use of language. Language use per se should not stop, but it should certainly change! Hauerwas's admonitions about language remain apposite.

Reform has actually already been addressed through much of part 2: see there in particular the texts describing, and following discussions of, benefaction and giving, reconciliation, celebrations, and leadership.

Pauline condemnation of idolatry is evident in 1 Cor 10; and more briefly in 1 Cor 5:11; Gal 4:8; Eph 2;11–12; 4:17–19; 5:5–14; Col 3:5–7; and 1 Thess 1:9–10. I would include 2 Cor 6:14–7:1 in these data, following the arguments of Fee for its inclusion in 2 Corinthians where it stands.

Paul's condemnation of sexual immorality is evident in 1 Cor 5:1–13; 6:9–20; Eph 5:3–7; Col 3:5–7; and 1 Thess 4:1–8, and concurring with the view of gender construction articulated in Rom 1:24–27. The use of prostitutes is condemned in 1 Cor 6:12–20.

The condemnation of magic, and its aftermath, are evident in Gal 5:20 and Acts 19:11–20.

Note, the reforms and condemnations associated with appropriate sexual activity and related questions of gender construction are treated in detail in later chapters. This includes the issue of female clothing during worship, which Paul addresses in 1 Cor 11:2–16.

Key Reading

A compact account summarizing the argument of the two previous chapters— and much else that I am arguing in this book about the intersection between Paul's understanding of God (and his understanding of how he came to know about God, revelationally and christocentrically), his radically inclusive mission, and his corresponding flexible, relational ethic is my essay "The Trinity in Paul."

Further Reading

Our earlier discussions of colonialism, dependent principally on the work of Diamond, Jennings, and Stanley, can be recalled helpfully here. See the bibliography in chapter 16. Boyarin's account of the problem of erasure in relation to Paul, argued specifically in relation to Gal 3:28 in *A Radical Jew*, remains seminal.

A typically subtle analysis of Paul's navigation of the questions surrounding idolatry and diet, attuned to sociological dynamics, is supplied by David Horrell, *The Social Ethos of the Corinthian Correspondence: Interests and Ideology from 1 Corinthians to 1 Clement* (and he attempts a broader account of Paul's strangely upright yet flexible ethic in the insightful *Solidarity and Difference*). And John Barclay's treatment of Rom 14 is typically probing: "Do We Undermine the Law? A Study of Romans 14:1–15:6." Having said this, I am not sure that either scholar systematically identifies and employs the underlying relational ethic that I am emphasizing here.

Barth's nuanced account of divine judgment can be found especially in IV/1.

A useful—and deeply learned—conversation partner at this moment is Oliver O'Donovan's multivolume work *Ethics as Theology*. He works at times with a structure-relationality distinction, although not quite as I suggest Paul does here.

Bibliography

Barclay, John. "Do We Undermine the Law? A Study of Romans 14:1–15:6." Pages 287–308 in *Paul and the Mosaic Law*. Edited by James D. G. Dunn. Tübingen: Mohr Siebeck, 1996.

Barth, Karl. *Church Dogmatics*. IV/1.

Boyarin, Daniel. *A Radical Jew: Paul and the Politics of Identity*. Berkeley: University of California Press, 1994.

Campbell, Douglas. "The Trinity in Paul: From Confession to Ethics." Pages 193–217 in *Essays on the Trinity*. Edited by Lincoln Harvey. Eugene, OR: Wipf & Stock, 2018.

Fee, Gordon. "II Corinthians vi.14–vii.1 and Food Offered to Idols." *NTS* 23 (1977): 140–61.

Hauerwas, Stanley. "Speaking Christian." Pages 84–93 in *Working with Words: On Learning to Speak Christian*. Eugene, OR: Wipf & Stock, 2011.

Hauerwas, Stanley, with Jean Vanier. *Living Gently in a Violent World: The Prophetic Witness of Weakness*. Downers Grove, IL: InterVarsity, 2008.

Horrell, David G. *The Social Ethos of the Corinthian Correspondence: Interests and Ideology from 1 Corinthians to 1 Clement*. Edinburgh: T&T Clark, 1996.

———. *Solidarity and Difference: A Contemporary Reading of Paul's Ethics*. London: T&T Clark, 2005.

O'Donovan, Oliver. *Ethics as Theology*. Vol. 1: *Finding and Seeking;* vol. 2: *Self, World, and Time*; vol. 3: *Entering into Rest*. Grand Rapids: Eerdmans, 2013–17.

CHAPTER 22

Transforming Paganism

Perhaps we have immersed ourselves into a local pagan context, attentive to the four modes of missional engagement, thereby absorbing many of its practices. And as we have done so, we have carefully evaluated its diverse forms, structures, and practices, attentive to the four modes of missional evaluation. We have reached a series of conclusions about what can stay and what should go. A new form of Christianity is emerging. However, we need now to add a few further missionary practices to our apostolic toolbox as we actually begin to *transform* our local pagan converts into a community. We will need, in particular, (1) to proceed to press for change in the right way, negotiating it carefully and respectfully; (2) to provide the right sort of pedagogical structure for our new community, and especially for its emerging leaders; (3) to resource it concretely in the right way if we have the means to do so; and (4) to let this community interrogate us and our locations, in a reflexive mode. Once we have noted all these essentially transformational modes—and they are not difficult in theory, although they are difficult in practice—most of what we need to know about forming Pauline communities will be in place. We will be able to engage a new context, evaluate it, and transform it, in a deeply Pauline fashion.

Transformational Mode 1: Negotiation

In fact we already know from earlier chapters that any judgments about what needs to change in a situation, whether by way of admonition, reformation, or cessation (since affirmation will change nothing), must always be closely intertwined with judgments concerning *how* this needs to happen. The means *is* the end. So any change must itself be managed with the appropriate relationality.

And this requirement clearly places what many modern progressives would consider to be dramatic constraints on the process of change.

If structures need to be reformed, don't we just condemn them, stringently and clearly, and let everyone get on with it, scolding and berating them as they lag?! Not really, because this approach to change would not itself be relationally appropriate. Indeed, to fail to recognize the importance of the means of any change is to embrace a seductive and very serious sin. If the relationality of people is not respected as we ask them to change, whether relationally or structurally, then we are employing some degree of coercion and thereby sinning ourselves. Perhaps it is merely rhetorical, but even highly pressurized rhetoric in relation to the rhetor's goals can be profoundly disrespectful to the dignity of the auditors, while lurking behind rhetorical coercion is institutional, legal, and ultimately physical coercion. And coercion is antirelational. It fails to treat people as people, in essentially loving terms. God has gone to extraordinary lengths to relate to us in noncoercive terms, incarnating alongside us, and we must learn to do the same. Hence doing the same, and observing a relational caveat in relation to our judgment that various people must change, in spite of how much it might offend our passionate liberal instincts, is not a constraint or a barrier or an imposition. It is to enter more deeply into our highest calling, and into the very heart of the matter. The means *is* the end, and the end is loving relationality, so the means too must be a loving relationality, and every other approach to change must be admonished, perhaps reformed, or even condemned!

A similar qualification applies to condemnation. When a judgment of condemnation is passed on a particularly diseased structure, the only way to erase that structure with relational integrity *is to cease to participate in it*, although we can see immediately that the notion of witness is expanded here rather dynamically. We do not coercively erase the structure ourselves, since people will doubtless be involved. This is to lapse at the end into a dominating mode.

In fact, we witness as much by the things that we do not do as by the things that we publically affirm and refuse to recant. We insist on the truth, but we also insist on not participating in structures that are generating comprehensively evil outcomes. The followers of Jesus are always entitled to withdraw their activity, and this is never coercive. One of their principal weapons in any matter requiring condemnation is consequently what we might call "the ethical strike." An evil structure should be named—truthfully and fairly, but named—and participation in it should cease. Christians are simply not to participate in idolatry, prostitution, and magical curses. (Jews already know not to do these things.) They are to withdraw from all such activities and structures. Exactly when and how to do this is of course a judgment for each community and its leaders. But in whatever way this particular navigation takes place, Christians are not to attack evil structures coercively (that is, unless protective dynamics are in play), because that would be to betray the truths upon which their disapproval rests. They should not burn down temples and brothels, and, once they have gained political power, deploy the security forces to execute magicians. The means is the end, and this is something that we must, again, learn to delight in, as against to be frustrated by. This realization sets us free.

Let us suppose then, arguably a little optimistically, that our missionary-apostles have evaluated their pagan locations with a suitable sensitivity both to local structures and to the relational demands of the loving triune God, and have gone on to negotiate changes with a suitable sensitivity to the way in which the structural shifts and demands that they have asked for have been effected—transformational mode 1. Communities of formerly pagan Christians have now been formed—people who are neither Jews nor Greeks, as Paul would say, but siblings in Christ—and a network of these diverse and decidedly odd participants is spreading. We now need to add another major element into the formational mix, although we already know it well.

Transformational Mode 2: Teaching

These converts still need to be taught. They must be gifted with a Christian structure oriented around learning, because clearly we are asking a lot of the leaders who will eventually undertake their own versions of these navigations. This is a point—and arguably the only point—where Christian leaders introduce a particular form to their converts and ask them to adopt it.

Navigating community formation as a church is not easy. It causes offense, usually on all fronts, if they are relevant, Jewish, more latterly, Christian, and pagan. And it is challenging simply in its own terms. There are no clear rules or laws to follow (thankfully in my view, but this does make things less secure for some). Prudential judgments have to be made constantly about what needs to change and how, as against what can be left, at least for the moment, or simply affirmed as God already at work.[1] At the basis of these judgments

1. We see here perhaps most clearly how a Pauline virtue ethic does belong to the broader family of virtue ethics. One of its key dimensions is the continued making of

is the realization that a loving relationality is at work that is distinguishable from the structures and forms it is working through, so the contours of that relationality must be deeply familiar. But undergirding this critical but subtle distinction and its application is the recognition of arrival of the truth about Jesus through revelation, followed by the identification of and resistance to deceptive gambits inviting its abandonment. The story of Jesus must be told, mediated, and participated in. The real importance of his incarnation, death, resurrection, and ascension, must be grasped. The various dynamics of love must be learned. The glories of the triune God must be felt on a very deep level, especially where they are revealed in odd spaces and relationships by the Spirit. And leaders must possess robust consciences that can generously enter into very different practices out of love for their frequently unlovely new friends. For converts to be formed then, ultimately into leaders many of whom will go themselves in apostolic missions to found further communities, a powerful pedagogical process needs to unfold that grounds and teaches people in the right way, and there can be little avoiding the fact that this will be imported. A certain structure from the missionary's parent culture will need to arrive and to significantly reshape the recipients' location. Things like distinctively messianic and Christian meetings will start, with their specific rituals that enact the key events at the heart of the new movement. Jewish and Christian texts will be studied. Messianic and Christian leaders will be raised up, and teach and lead in turn.

The breadth and depth of this pedagogy should not be underestimated. Many would speak at this point of a reshaping of Paul's converts in terms of an entire tradition or discourse. If this is overstating matters a little, it nevertheless does need to be acknowledged that this process takes place in addition to the navigation of the structure-relationality distinction on site. In essence, this distinction itself, along with everything that establishes it, needs to be in place for any context-sensitive navigation in its terms to take place, and it is quite a distinction. It is the tip of an entire iceberg of formation. But by introducing this pedagogy, do we not destroy our noncolonial account of Christian formation that we have been constructing so carefully up to this point? Has an inappropriate structure intruded finally into our account of mission?

I don't believe so.

---

judgments by apostolic leaders, and then by teachers, prophets, and evangelists—judgment in sense of practical reason, as Aristotle called it. This is the exercise of prudential judgment, case by case, moment by moment, and Aristotle was also quite right to note that it takes a certain sort of intense pedagogy to produce minds that can do this.

There is a sense in which, for a Pauline Christianity to flourish, all the things I have been talking about for some time in this book need to be absorbed, which will be a transformational process. There is no denying this, and we shouldn't want to—it was the subject of the entirety of part 2. But I am not sure that this change amounts to all *that* much. Only those structures should be introduced that are necessary to serve this fundamentally relational set of dynamics and its formation (and we learned in part 2 that these structures need to be as intensive and intrusive as they need to be to effect changes in virtue in community members, and no more). In essence, missionary apostles need to arrive and to be copied, and their narratives and their methods must be imbibed—*especially what they say*. That is, the vast majority of this pedagogy is actually linguistic. Ninety-five percent of being Christian, Hauerwas reminds us, is learning to talk right. So we are contemplating the introduction here of a certain language game, as Wittgenstein might put it. And further minimizing the disruption of this introduction, any copying and teaching will have been definitively *translated*.[2]

Leaders on arrival have immersed; teaching forms have therefore been contextualized; and the very content of Christian teaching will have consequently been translated. So we are talking about a minimal and highly contextualized insertion of certain types of relationships and their acquisition revolving around language. Indeed, translation is clearly critical both metaphorically and literally.

Translation

Early Christianity was, it should be recalled, a translation movement. It primarily used the Greek translation of the Jewish Scriptures, the Septuagint (which was a family of translations rather than a single authorized version). And it wrote its own key documents in Greek, the pagan *lingua franca* of its day, and not in Aramaic or Hebrew, the languages of its original Scriptures. Paul wrote Greek letters to his converts. (It is hard to say, but I wonder whether his preferred language was not Aramaic, in which case his commitment to Greek—and I suspect also to Latin on occasion—is the more impressive.).[3]

2. Lamin Sanneh's important term and insight.
3. Second Corinthians 11:22 suggests at the least that Paul spoke Aramaic—see also Acts 22:2, 3; Phil 3:5 might suggest that he was an Aramaic speaker raised by the same, and Acts 26:14 suggests that Jesus spoke to Paul in Aramaic. Paul generally prefers the

And this translation practice is clearly an instantiation of the immersion that needs to take place during mission, here fused with an appropriate pedagogy. Appropriate teaching in a missional situation should always be translated teaching.

If we observe a liturgy then—and I think this is a good practice even if it is not discernable in Paul—we should create, with our new friends, a new, appropriately contextualized liturgy for them and with them. And as this emerges, it will be a sign that a translated pedagogy is unfolding as it should.

My home country has arguably provided an especially good example of this—the Anglican liturgy of Aotearoa/New Zealand. (The indigenous name for New Zealand, Aotearoa, means "land of the long white cloud.") I notice with amusement that one of my very liturgically committed students did not particularly like it, and at first I was a little taken aback by this judgment. But on reflection now the difficulty was obvious. How could an American student resonate with this liturgy's immersion in the practices, flora, and fauna of New Zealand? While much of it arises directly out of the Book of Common Prayer, parts have been thoroughly contextualized and hence must appear foreign and even unintelligible to those not living in Aotearoa and/or deeply familiar with this location. (In fact, I don't actually use this liturgy very much partly because it makes me homesick.)

The church year includes important dates for Christianity and New Zealand, including the commemoration on 17 May of Wiremu Te Tauri, the important Maori friend of Samuel Marsden, our first significant missionary. Without this friendship, Marsden's missionary breakthrough in Aotearoa would have been impossible. And consider the following part of the liturgy.

> Katahi, e te Ariki, ka tukua tau pononga kia haere i runga i te
> rangimarie.

This is in fact Simeon's prayer, found in Luke—which the liturgy references as Ruka 2:29–32—but it is of course unintelligible to anyone who cannot speak a little Maori, the language of the indigenous people in New Zealand, which was translated into written form by some of the first European missionaries. However, perhaps the following prayer is only marginally more accessible because of its invocation of the flora and fauna of Aotearoa. On Monday mornings those following this liturgy would pray:

Aramaic name for Peter—Kephas (see esp. 1 Cor 1:12; 3:22; Gal 2:9, 11, 14). This might all suggest an underlying preference for Aramaic, combined with fluency in Greek.

O give thanks to our God who is good:
whose love endures forever. . . .
You kauri and pine, rata and kowhai, mosses and ferns:
give to our God your thanks and praise.
Dolphins and kahawai; sealion and crab:
coral, anemone, pipi and shrimp:
give to our God your thanks and praise.
Rabbits and cattle, moths and dogs,
kiwi and sparrow and tui and hawk:
give to our God your thanks and praise.

These are not fanciful or distant motifs; these are the creatures that thickly populate the New Zealand context and that ought to be exhorted to join in with creation's chorus of praise to God. The distinctive trees and fish and birds of Aotearoa have their part to play glorifying God. Moreover, the emphasis within this liturgy on these flora and fauna is a result of the superior sensitivity of the Maori people to the environment (a moment when a reflexive aspect to appropriate community formation also comes into view). I would not expect messianic Jews or Christians living outside New Zealand to pray these prayers. But I would expect foreign Christians who come to Aotearoa to teach their converts to pray in this way, which means that they must first have learned to think and pray like New Zealanders themselves, partly by living in Aotearoa's distinctive environment.

It is also important to affirm further, however, that an appropriately translated pedagogy does not stop at the appropriate transfer of information. This is important. But the teaching relationship needs to be understood more broadly than any account that would limit pedagogy to mere information. Appropriate teaching transmits an entire relationality that is rooted in God and mediated especially by Jesus. So, as Paul put it,

[We were] delighted to give you
not just the declaration about God but our own souls,
you had become so beloved to us" (1 Thess 2:8).

And it follows from this that missionaries must raise up indigenous leadership. This is clearly vital. It is the ultimate point of any introduced pedagogy. Moreover, they must also—when they can, and it wasn't always the case that the bedraggled Paul could—*resource* their communities.

Transformational Mode 3: Resourcing

Pedagogy by the followers of Jesus includes the important practice of grace, which is to say, of outrageous generosity, benevolence, and benefaction, concretized in the Father's gift of the Son to humanity, something we already discussed in ch. 12. So the pedagogical resourcing of converts is broader than the gift of right language by way of Scripture, teachings, and liturgy, important though they are. But as soon as we emphasize this practice, we can see a trap that we need to identify clearly and to skirt.

We have avoided defining the other initially as fundamentally needy, which would take us perilously close to a paternalistic relationship with any new converts who would then be defined fundamentally and perhaps permanently as victims. Arriving alongside people will avoid many of the implicit assumptions operating on both sides of this relationship that can frame it in paternal terms, assumptions unleashed when missionaries arrive with power and resources. But this is not to exclude the fact that our new friends do often have needs and it would be inappropriate to ignore those if we can help. As friends we can and should help. However, I strongly suggest locating any response to needs in this rigorously framed position, where we are listening rather than talking.

As we get to know our new friends they will tell us what their needs are. And there is a world of difference between this approach and our arrival as people with resources and know-how who immediately send the message that we know what our friends' needs are, and this possibly in spite of what they think themselves. We should respond to the needs that emerge from our new relationships, and as those relationships express those needs. And this means concretely, as we will see in more detail shortly. It means money or the equivalent. It will not be particularly appropriate or helpful to say to our new friends, "God bless you; keep warm and well fed" as they stand shivering and starving at the door. We invite friends in need inside when they ask us to, and share our resources with them as we can. After all, wouldn't we want them to do that for us? This flow of generosity and gifts should also then attest to the fundamental gifting flowing from the heart of a loving and generous God (2 Cor 9:11–15). However, this resourcing emerges from a conversation.

I vividly remember worrying about the navigation of this particular dimension within a relationship and talking about it during a recent visit to Aotearoa with a great social activist and advocate for the incarcerated, Kim

Workman. "Kim," I said. "I'm really struggling with the problems involved with being ready to help folk, and recognizing their needs, and yet trying to avoid the trap of colonizing them in a soft, paternalistic sort of way." I was concerned at the time especially with the problem of mass incarceration facing the New Zealand Maori population, which is imprisoned at the same staggering rate as the US incarcerates African Americans. And I was wondering in particular about what local conditions might contribute to this situation, and what costly actions should be taken to address them. He replied, as usual with a twinkle in his eye: "Why don't you ask them what they need?" I laughed, partly from embarrassment and partly from relief. It was so obviously right, and also simply just so obvious. Accounts of need must be addressed, and addressed concretely, but they must emerge from the friendship and not frame it. A friendship framed *by* need will not in fact be a friendship—and will often struggle to become one. But friends can have needs, and if we can meet them, in partnership with them, we should.

It might also be worth noting here in passing that we should not stop resourcing our friends in the ways that they ask us to—and that are consistent with love—if they do not convert to our communities. We hope and pray that they will; this is in their own interests. We would have them turn from the self-destructive ways of sin toward the loves and joys of an overt relationship with God. But even if they do not—and many might not—we will still act on their behalf, and act in a way that respects their own understanding of what they require. This opens up the activity of our community on behalf of other people who are not necessarily converts, which is spoken of at times by using the phrase "the common good." Jesus's followers ought to act on behalf of the good of everyone, whether they are messianic Jews or merely Jews, and whether they are Christian or pagan. Cooperative and collaborative action in this way is right and good (something that can happen a lot in modern societies, with their high degrees of complexity and communication). Such action might even be a useful test, on a grand scale, of the authenticity of the missionary practice of befriending, that is, the key practice of approaching non-Christians initially in the hope of friendship, and this irrespective of whether they eventually convert or not, believing that Jesus is already present. Sustained action with non-Christians on behalf of all is, in many respects, simply the outworking of this personal and respectful approach on a higher organizational level.

We come now to a final and particularly interesting transformational mode—*reflexivity*.

Transformational Mode 4: Reflexivity

As we will see in more detail when we discuss Paul's struggles with certain "enemies" later on, that is, his conflict with some zealous messianic Jews who felt that he had thrown out far too much important Jewish material, there is a humbling dimension to community formation for the parent community. Customs and practices—i.e., forms and structures—that are held very dear by their missionary-apostles turn out to be merely important, and not universally binding. They should be practiced by those who belong to the parent community, but they are not necessarily so superior that they should be practiced by the entirety of humankind. It is, as always, merely the relationality that matters. So as missionary-apostles navigate into new contexts, many of the practices from their parent culture can, in effect, be left behind. And here a light is shone back on *us*, exposing where we attribute too much importance to our own ways, and ultimately to ourselves.

But that light comes from our new converts, and we need to be open to its illuminations. We can resist this reflexive and fundamentally humbling process, because it is, after all, coming from mere neophytes. But we shouldn't. Paul did allow this light to shine, and then took up cudgels on behalf of his new converts when key members of the parent culture overstepped and refused to recognize limitations on their own treasured forms. Jewish food, calendar, bodily markings, and so on, did not need to be adopted by Christians. Their own food, calendar, bodily markings (et cetera), could stay in place, Paul realized, and this despite his own attachment to such practices. In like manner, it is painful but salutary to experience this sort of feedback from our new converts and their new type of community on our Christian forms and structures.

The key to these insights is a recognition when we are asking our new converts to adopt something new that it might not in fact be as strongly warranted as we think—a fact they presumably will point out to us. A specific practice we are teaching might not be attested by Trinitarian realities and the appropriate relationality but rest on some other set of claims grounded somewhere else, perhaps in "creation," or "the natural order," or some such. When such demands on our part are exposed by our students, we are brought face to face with our possible collaborations with foundationalism, and so it is wise to heed these challenges, or at least to entertain them. "Anything that is not 'by way of fidelity' is sin," Paul states in Rom 14:23, meaning that any ethical demand that does not proceed out of the resurrected mind of Christ, which we indwell, is wrong.

Although it is somewhat oblique, I am often struck by how Christian communities comprising those who are physically and mentally challenged shine a bright light on some of our own conceits. There is always something strangely challenging about the exuberance, abandonment, and simplicity of this precious constituency's ways, especially its worship. Far from imposing our worship forms on this group—which tends to happen when we let them attend our carefully orchestrated services—we need to let their worship challenge ours. And when we do, ours can be exposed as uptight, overcontrolled, and lacking in commitment. We are in the presence of the living God! Yet we don't act like it—although the physically and mentally challenged often do (2 Sam 6:12–23). They worship with true abandon and joy.

We can also learn a lot from this group's basic approach to life. Things that really matter come into view; things that really don't matter are rather ruthlessly exposed. We tend to be so caught up in cultural trivia, anxious about the unnecessary. What *does* really matter in life? The physically and mentally challenged will tell us, generally without using words. So we often experience *a judgment* as we reach out to and live and worship among these particular friends, as in a useful and salutary one (2 Cor 7:9–10), as that encounter functions reflexively.

On a more theological level, the mentally challenged who are devoted to Jesus may expose any overdependence in our own soteriology on our own actions and responses to God. If we make our relationship with God conditional on certain sorts of responses—perhaps a whole-hearted recitation, affirmation, and prayerful response to The Roman Road (not every element in which is a bad thing)—then our alternatively abled friends will illuminate our foolishness. They are clearly loved by God, and in love with God, and yet cannot undertake these cognitive acts. Are we really suggesting that God is not among them, and has abandoned them, because of their "deficiencies"? Are we really saying they are not saved?[4] It is of course our own arrogant theological program that is exposed by all this as deficient. Instead of affirming our own capacity, the physically and mentally challenged could recall us to our radical dependence on others that we spend so much time disguising.[5]

4. Sadly, this is not a hypothetical example; I have witnessed this conversation.
5. An insight beautifully articulated by Alan Lewis, "God as Cripple."

We will return to the benefits of a full commitment to reflexivity in more detail later on when we consider the indirect help Paul received from his enemies, who were inveterate Jewish foundationalists (and I hasten to add that they were Jews of a certain specific type, as well as messianic). We learn much from their misguided attack on Paul's gospel. For now, however, we can move on from our brief description of the four transformational modes, to the next cluster of closely related questions that community formation in a Pauline fashion poses.

Diversity and What to Call It

We will note shortly that a great deal can go wrong with this subtle and challenging process of community formation. But let us assume for the moment, with sunny optimism, that this is all possible. A Pauline church is a wonderful thing. However, in its very uniqueness, it presented Paul with some further intriguing challenges of an essentially positive nature. What was he to call it? And what images could he use to communicate its nature most effectively? (these two questions being closely related).

This community was quite unlike anything he had encountered before. It was something new under the sun—a network of Christians spreading in increasingly diverse clusters through space and time, although anchored at their origin in messianic Jewish groups in Judea. Ethnicity is respected within this network but it is emphatically not paramount or determinative. So he could not call it a tribe or nation. The church as Paul understood it is emphatically not "a third race." Neither could he call it a state. It is not unified by the paying of taxes, and by the ceding of the right to coerce, to a particular leader. It is not a bureaucracy or empire. In fact, Paul's preferred terminology is, as we have already seen, familial, and we need to hold on to this. But we need other categories to understand what is going on here as well because in some important respects this growing and ultimately vast network is unlike any family we know. It is so much bigger, and it spreads through friendships as well as through healthy family relationships.

Three further analogies turn out to be especially important for Paul and they will deepen our understanding of what he is advocating.

The Temple[6]

First, Paul can describe this community as a temple.[7] This points metaphorically toward the purity and cleanliness of the community. Good and healthy relationships are pure; negative and destructive relationships are defiling. But a claim is also being made that the gathered community is a temple indwelt by the Holy Spirit and this has a radical edge. That God is fully present in a group gathering in a home suggests that God is not simply to be found in the Jerusalem temple, there to be approached by one person once a year, in the Holy of Holies, in a state of rigorous purity. An extraordinary geographical decentralization of God's presence has taken place. His followers no longer have to travel to Jerusalem to meet with him. They can travel out to those who do not yet know him, carrying his presence with them, rather as the children of Israel first carried God's presence with them through the wilderness of Sinai in the tabernacle. Moreover, if this is the case, communities no longer have to invest in capital-heavy projects to try to ensure that God will show up. Large buildings were redundant—a big change for Jews and pagans. God is traveling to where these small groups of people meet, and this is a religious as well as a cultural revolution.

The Polity

In some distinctive passages,[8] although most fully in Eph 5:22–6:9 and Col 3:18–4:1, Paul lays out regulations for the key relationships within the community: between husbands and wives, owners and slaves, and parents and children. He is reflecting longstanding Greek practice here, so we can find a very similar arrangement laid out in Aristotle's *Politics*. Luther called these tab-

---

6. I am reproducing some remarks from *Journey* in these three subsections.

7. See 1 Cor 3:16–17; 6:19–20; Eph 2:19–22; and 2 Cor 6:14–7:1. The authenticity of this last passage is much doubted, but I am unpersuaded by the theory of its pseudonymity and insertion; Gordon Fee's analysis is probative: "II Corinthians vi.14–vii.1 and Food Offered to Idols." *NTS* 23 (1977): 140–61.

8. Paul shows the imprint of this way of thinking in Rom 13:1–7; 1 Cor 6:9[–10], 12–20; 7:17–24; (possibly!) in Rom 1:18–32, especially vv. 24, 26–27; and in 1 Thess 4:3–7. The form is echoed in the rest of the NT more directly by 1 Pet 2:11–3:12; 1 Tim 2:1–15; 5:1–2; 6:1–2; Titus 2:1–10; 3:1. These texts are evaluated in more detail—and a particular navigation proposed—in two later chapters entirely devoted to these questions.

ulations the household codes or house-tables (*Haustafeln*) because they could be written up in a table of rules and hung on the wall of the kitchen to remind everyone of their roles in life. Originally, however, they were used to organize the ancient *polis* or city-state.[9] They described its correct arrangement, and this is significant. When Paul uses these rules to organize his communities, he is implying that the new network is a political entity too, and other passages support this imagery. So he exclaims rather shockingly to his Philippian converts, who came from a highly patriotic city,

> our citizenship is in heaven.
> And we eagerly await a Savior from there,
> the Lord Jesus Christ,
> who, by the power that enables him to bring everything under his
>   control,
> will transform our lowly bodies
> so that they will be like his glorious body. (Phil 3:20–21)

It follows from this that the new network writes its own rules and has its own rulers, ultimately being ruled by God. The church has its own politics—a politics of peace—and its members are citizens of another polity—another nation-state—from the one that they might think they occupy. Modern Christians accustomed to living in a society that separates church and state often forget this, but these texts, including the much-maligned household codes, instruct us to remember it.

Paul's most famous and useful image for his distinctive new network was probably, however, the image of the body.

The Body[10]

We must be a little careful here because Paul thought about bodies in an ancient way. We tend to think of bodies as occupying a distinct space, with a volume and some external boundary or barrier—our skin. Ancient people viewed bodies as rather less discrete than this. They were more dynamic and fluid.

---

9. Strictly speaking, in Paul's day the world was structured by empires and monarchies, although cities remained important political actors.

10. Romans 12:4–5; 1 Cor 6:15–17; 10:16–17; 12:12–31; Eph 1:22–23; 4:4–16, 25; 5:22–32; Col 1:18, 24; 2:16–19; 3:15.

Their boundary was less obvious. They were also more comfortable with tangible physical dimensions and more hidden spiritual dimensions interacting with one another to make them work.[11] This dynamic ancient notion of a body allows Paul to say several important things about his network of communities.

They are, precisely, a network, which is connected together. The communities are distinct, like the different parts of a body, but are irreducibly connected to one another as well—distinct but never separable then. This unity overrides local differences in status and cultural capital. However lowly or humble, everybody needs every part functioning well to function at all. Everybody needs everybody else. A basic equality is evident here. So the body speaks of a diverse and relational but utterly concrete unity. It is also animated throughout by spirit (especially if Stoic ideas are informing Paul at this moment).

In addition, the body metaphor speaks of the organic hierarchy in the community. Jesus is primary as the head is primary for the body. Everyone is connected to him and grows up into him; the connections here are quite concrete as well. But underneath him are other leaders who have matured more than their followers, and these leaders, gifted by the Holy Spirit, teach, encourage, and admonish the rest of the community. So the metaphor of the body nicely captures the elite, pedagogical arrangement of the community that we detected at Thessalonica, rooting it in Jesus himself.

Modern philosophers have a slightly more technical way of putting all this.

A Social Imaginary

Stepping back a little, we can see that Paul's account of the church—recalling that "church" denotes the entire early community spreading missionally to comprise both messianic Jews and various sorts of Christians—is a complete account of human communal life that supplies an appropriate explanation of acceptable difference, wrongdoing, accountability, and unity. It answers,

11. For this reason Paul can speak of several different bodies that seem to be in different places but assume that they all connect together—Jesus's ascended body, the body of Christ which is the church, and the body broken and shared in the Eucharist. Later theologians and scientists might speak of relational or "field" understanding of bodies here rather than a naive and ultimately incorrect understanding of a body as a displacement of space, fixed in one place, with discrete boundaries.

in short, all the key questions presupposed by any human organization that so many of our current constructions fail so dismally to understand and to deliver. It is a particular, distinct account—in modern parlance, a social imaginary (although some would speak of a paradigm or discourse)[12]—and it is the right one. So we should grasp it clearly, and continue to defend and to pursue it. *This is how we should live together.*

In essence, Paul's church, broadly conceived, affirms differences in the right way, not within an abstract and fronted account of certain differences *per se*, but in a process of diversification superintended by Trinitarian relationality. Certain differences are being recognized as valid. They are not fundamental—Jesus Christ is fundamental, and our resurrection in him—but neither are they erased. And this has the happy consequence that any accounts of difference are no longer derived out of differences themselves, which is to say from differences between groups and group identities that then inevitably devolve into competitive relationships, along with the negation of some of those differences. To begin an account of difference *with* difference entails that either I or you are superior as against negated, and such relationships are fractured from the outset, and also impervious to modification. (They are a foundation.) The pernicious consequences of playing this game are apparent in the church's treatment of Jews (which is something we discuss more shortly). Christian identity is not being rooted by Paul, however, in a particular negative account of Judaism in relation to which its differences must be parsed absolutely. Christianity is an appropriate diversification flowing out of Judaism, leaving both forms intact. And it follows from this that any other differences can be navigated constructively within the process of ecclesial diversification.

There is a sense then in which we can talk of a hybrid phenomenon. Christianity is informed by key Jewish insights and virtues, and includes a pedagogical structure learned from Judaism (although Judaism arguably learned much of this from ancient Hellenistic culture in turn). But Christianity is not Jewish all the way down, structurally, except in its original community—"at its root" (Rom 11:17). Furthermore, the Christianity flowing out of Judaism has diversified into different pagan locations, absorbing various pagan structures and forms, some of which have been adopted intact, and some of which have been modified. And many pagan structures have been abandoned, so although there is considerable overlap, there are still distinctive differences from most pagan cultures as well. In essence, healthy, relationally loving, pagan culture

---

12. The phrase social imagination is usefully canvassed at https://en.wikipedia .org/wiki/Imaginary_(sociology). I am using "paradigm" in the sense that Kuhn uses it.

has been adopted, and unhealthy, antirelational pagan culture has been rejected, which is hybridization at its best. And the church has spread into a thousand different expressions.

But we need now, almost at the end of our description, to face the fact that this process has not always gone smoothly, and that Paul himself was not a flawless practitioner of cultural navigation. Paul's imaginary must never be left in its original state. We must navigate onward to the *Pauline*.

From Paul to the Pauline

Paul did not get everything right. His imaginary, we might say, has significant internal tensions, although we have only really become aware of some of these in the last one hundred and fifty years, and of others in the last fifty. I nevertheless count us as extremely fortunate to possess these particular modern interpretative lenses, although I would also caution against plunging too enthusiastically into "presentism."[13] Few things are more foolish (as well as narcissistic in interpretative terms) than judging someone who wrote two *thousand* years ago for not being aware of issues that our culture discovered in the 1960s. It is nevertheless with the insights of the sixties to hand, along with the insights of the nineteenth century and the long struggle for abolition, that we now see where Paul's imaginary is internally unstable, and overlooks some of the key modes that he himself was so committed to. There are two key places where this happens.[14]

First, Paul is alert to the imposition of what we would denote as overtly Jewish *ethnic* forms on his converts. He correctly identifies these as structures that belong to a passing age that do not need to be transferred to Christians. But he does transfer a structure for sexual activity and the definition of gender to his converts, presumably in part because this seems to be rooted in creation. However, it is of course a *Jewish* account of creation, and thereby of sexual

13. Adequately defined and summarized at https://en.wikipedia.org/wiki/Pres entism_(literary_and_historical_analysis).

14. Strictly speaking, two further areas of conceptual incoherence and instability (by way of foundationalist intrusions) are being noted here. In part 1 we have already dealt with a vulnerability to Gnosticism caused by an overemphasis on "the intermediate state." And we have more recently addressed the potential problem caused by some of Paul's statements about the future—in particular, the possible loss of non-Christians to annihilation.

activity and gender, and so in many respects, one more Jewish ethnic structure. Moreover, as we will see in due course (see chs. 25 and 26), *it is not directly warranted christologically*, which is to say, this is a foundationalist moment in Paul. In fact we learn here especially clearly how foundationalism can set apart certain structures and forms that zealous missionary-apostles will effectively impose on their converts, in a process that is removed from christological correction, leading to what we might call a colonial moment. Local structures are overridden and modified here unnecessarily in the name of God, but in fact in the name of ethnic superiority. And a reflexive moment here has been resisted—by Paul himself.

As I just said, we are fortunate to be living after the sixties, when this type of unwarranted imposition began to be unavoidably exposed. (The warrants for this were not always christological either, however; so due account will have to be taken of the right way to critique, along with the right way to move forward.) The correction of this unwarranted imposition is consequently a further critical moment in our developing description of Paul's imaginary. We need to step here, guided by *Sachkritik*, from Paul to the Pauline, and we will in several chapters that follow.

If the imposition of a particular structure concerning sexual activity and gender construction is a key generator of internal instability within Paul's imaginary in the modern period, where he unjustifiably brings a Jewish structure into the Christian formation of his pagan converts, the second comes from the other direction. Christology and its revelation of triune relationality have *not* led in some cases to the necessary reform, and even to the condemnation, of local pagan structures, most especially of slavery.

To some degree this is the same problem as the imposition of a Jewish heteronormativity, as it is sometimes called. But what we would call a particular economic and class structure premised on the ownership of human beings is in play here, as against a binary, normed account of sexual activity and gender identity. Nevertheless at bottom, the presence of a vicious and unwarranted structure is detectable in both situations, whether this is being introduced or simply endorsed.

The abolitionists in the early modern period argued, quite rightly, that this arrangement was emphatically unwarranted by Christology—so much so that it warranted evaluative mode 4, not mode 3. A loving relationality demanded this. When someone owns someone else, a mature loving relationality is structurally occluded. That structure must go. It could not be reformed. It had to be condemned and to cease to exist.

The fact that it was not abolished—both Paul and many subsequent Christian leaders handling it with mode 2—and went on to endure for so long, with vigorous support from so many Christians, is explained, at least in part, by their capture by foundationalism at this point, in just the way that they were captured by heteronormativity.

Fortunately, abolition *has* happened—although its vast aftermath is still very much with us and still very much needs to be addressed—and so we can see here where the church has progressed from Paul's imaginary to the Pauline. *And it has to!* When loving relationality is obstructed by oppressive social structures and forms, these *must* be reformed or condemned. Paul's deepest commitments demand this. But as a result of this, there is not just some internal inconsistency in Paul's imaginary—some instability generated by occasional foundationalist endorsements of certain constructions of sex, gender, and class (and so on)—but a corresponding dynamism. The imaginary *demands its own reform*, in its own terms, ever upwards and onwards toward complete relational wholeness. The imaginary asks us to constantly self-correct, and this will happen, especially as we remain open to reflexive dynamics.

We can often learn from our new converts when we are engaging in a foundationalist moment—when we are too attached to a structure, and believe, mistakenly, that it is a universal ordinance. If our new converts do things differently, this is an opportunity for us to recognize our own cultural hubris. As they challenge us to justify the imposition of our structure christologically, and we see it begin to fall short, we are invited to reform ourselves. As we listen to their voices we ought to hear an articulation of our own shortcomings. To listen to the voices of enslaved Christians as Christians ought to have led to the realization that this structure of vast cruelty was wrong, and to repentance. But we resisted this challenge.

I would quickly add, before moving on, however, that there is something understandable about all this even if this does not make it acceptable (and this is why presentist posturing is doubly inappropriate). We are all located within inadequate and unstable Pauline imaginaries—even those of us who are prosecuting them with the most lucidity and vigor!

We are all given *tasks* to do by God, and we *focus* on those. Paul was an apostle, called to be an emissary to the pagan nations (Gal 1:15–16). And this means that ancillary matters tend to recede into the background.[15] Paul was focused on the task of including pagans as Christians within the original com-

---

15. The appreciation of focality is a particular strength of Polanyi's work; see his *Personal Knowledge: Towards a Post-critical Philosophy* (New York: Routledge & Kegan Paul, 1958) and *The Tacit Dimension* (New York: Doubleday, 1966).

munity of messianic Jews—a massive lift. He gave his life for this particular constituency. It is foolish to berate him for failing to include constituencies that the church only got around to addressing properly two millennia later. Moreover, the same applies to us all. We are all focused on the tasks that God has called us to—on the people and relationships and networks that we are being asked either to include or to form. There are many things on the periphery of these tasks, out of conscious purview, that we are not noticing that subsequent generations will be taught to see and will hopefully not judge us too harshly for overlooking. Human calling and the focal nature of human understanding (which Polanyi points out) combine to give us tunnel vision— something that is clear in retrospect. Indeed, we can immediately add that we are only detecting an earlier tunnel's occlusions because of the tunnel that we ourselves are now in.

In addition to the focality of tasks and of human understanding, as we ask for changes, we pursue those from where our communities are, subjecting our means to the end. Change itself must be relational. And this means that not everything can be done at once. Indeed, perhaps very little can be done at any given time (especially if some of the local churches I am familiar with are any indication). Intentional change is slow and difficult work, and especially if it is pursued properly, noncoercively and relationally.

Paul's emphasis at times on holding various structures in place is now more understandable. "Stay where you are," was one of his key instructions on arrival (see esp. 1 Cor 7:17, 20), something Albert Schweitzer perceptively dubbed "Paul's law of the *status quo*."[16] As we will see later, it was this instruction that created a lot of the difficulties at Corinth. Sexual and gender dynamics are never static, so fixing them in place, perhaps for years, generated significant tensions. (How would you feel if an apostle had asked you ten years ago to put your engagement on ice? Most modern engaged couples wouldn't last ten days!) And we can probably see that many customs will have to be placed under this rubric even now; everything can't be changed at once.

This command to remain static is not a universal law of church planting or of Christian ethics. It is a *judgment* that needs to be made for particular structures that need reform as relational considerations in a community dictate. "Can this thing change now, and in the appropriate way? Perhaps no, because we're all working on something else. So it needs to go on hold. I'll quote 1 Cor 7:20. We just can't handle the refugee crisis while we're dealing with a gender

---

16. See his classic treatment *The Mysticism of Paul the Apostle*, trans. W. Montgomery (Baltimore: Johns Hopkins University Press, 1998), 193.

issue. It's all going to be too much." We will need to have the courage to ask in due course when it is time to change something that we previously put on hold, but we don't have to change everything at once, and we don't need to feel condemned for not doing so. Prudential leadership will be the key—as usual.

With this said, we should turn now, at the end of this phase of our discussion, to reemphasize an absolutely critical dynamic within the entire navigational process, namely, the promptings of God, felt especially by way of the work of the Holy Spirit. And as we do so, it will be helpful to return to the scene of the crime, that is, the situation in Syrian Antioch where the disciples were first called Christians.

I am doing this partly because of the potentially misleading connotations of the signifier "imaginary" when we use it to describe Paul's system. Some scholars seem to suppose that we think our way through new forms of Christian community, whether on site or even in an office surrounded by suitably high piles of learned books. We use our minds, creatively, to envisage new possibilities for the church. We imagine our way into the future. But this is not at all what I see happening in Paul. The entire process of missional outreach into strange new spaces, with its consequent immersions and engagements and crafting of new forms of church, was, and so is, catalyzed and driven and oriented by the work of the Holy Spirit. *She* pulls her missionary-apostles, sometimes unwillingly, into engagement with people with whom *she* is already engaged, and *she* ratifies this engagement. Under the pressures of these shocking new engagements, our imaginations are *then* reshaped. It is a concrete, engaged, relational, and frequently surprising process, that unfolds as we follow the commands of the Lord who is the Spirit. And she is of course way out ahead of us. This is how the radical thing that is the Pauline mission began, along with the development of the imaginary that justified its existence. A Pauline imaginary develops by following on hard after the Spirit as she opens up surprising friendships in unexpected places. It is those friendships and those places that challenge us to navigate into new Christian forms and new imaginaries—the original lesson of Antioch.

Antioch

We saw earlier that Paul defended his radical approach to mission among the pagans against certain messianic Jews from Jerusalem determinedly from 49 through 52 CE, the crisis beginning in Syrian Antioch (Gal 2:11–14), and we will consider how exactly he defended himself in later chapters when we consider in detail his view of Judaism. But he himself had become convinced of this approach's legitimacy much earlier on, also at Antioch. By my calculations, he encountered an unprecedented situation in 36 CE in that city after he had been evangelizing pagans in quite conventional Jewish terms for two to three years.[17] Further reflection then led him nevertheless to affirm its legitimacy, to go on to practice it himself, and to defend it vociferously when it was attacked about twelve years later by other leaders in the early church who were suspicious of its diversity (all the while striving to preserve the church's unity). We need then to probe this early revolutionary situation a little more deeply to try to detect what might have prompted Paul's change of mind.

I say Paul "encountered" this new situation initially because this is what our evidence in Acts suggests happened (11:19–26). Apparently, a group of anonymous, messianic Jews, fleeing persecution in Jerusalem, ended up in Antioch, where they spoke to "Greeks," and some of those contacts seem to have "converted." (Friendship evangelism!) It seems fair to assume that these early amateur missionaries were speaking to their pagan friends who were probably "Godfearers" or "God-worshipers."[18] Barnabas and Paul arrived a little after this, at which point Acts tells us that this was when the disciples were first

---

17. The evidence is sparse, but what evidence we do have suggests that Paul himself did not practice a Torah-free mission until after his experience in Antioch toward the end of 36 CE. During the two to three years previous to this date, from his call to this revolutionary event, he called the pagans to convert to Jesus but seems to have asked them to convert fully to messianic Judaism. I say this because (1) he speaks in Gal 5:11 of a period of time during which he "preached circumcision," and this strange statement is best referenced to a period of evangelism on Jesus's behalf in this early part of his apostolic work; (2) his revolutionary ethical system was not discussed when he visited Jerusalem and met Peter and James just before he went to Antioch (Gal 1:18–19), suggesting that it did not yet exist; when it did exist it was discussed! (see Gal 2:1–10); and (3) Acts, as we know, tells us that the disciples were first called Christians in Antioch, which means that this was where and when they deviated ethically from a recognizably Jewish ethic, a claim that fits exactly with the evidence from Paul's letters. I discuss this evidence in more detail in a series of articles referenced below (although I would now articulate claim 2 more carefully than I do in those arguments because of some of the insights present within the scenario proposed by Paula Frederiksen; the Antioch crackdown in 49 CE seems to have been elicited to a significant degree by the conversion of later high-status and rigorous converts, who were probably Pharisees, and this factor must be taken into account).

18. This is a technical term Acts uses to denote Jewish sympathizers among the pagans who practiced many Jewish customs but had not quite made the full commitment to Judaism of proselytism, in the case of males, submitting to circumcision.

called Christians. So we know that at this time the practices of these disciples were developing in a diverse way, and many of the previously standard Jewish customs were not being followed by the new community. Moreover, Barnabas and Paul clearly signed off on this radical departure. But why?

I think there is a plausible initial explanation for Paul's confidence that this situation was an act of God, and we have already noted it when we described Paul's missionary practices. I suspect that during the worship of these odd new converts Paul and Barnabas observed the overt and unmistakable presence of the Holy Spirit among the Godfearers and the other worshiping pagans.

Imagine we are in a little house church meeting in Antioch. The new apostolic dignitaries authorized by the Jerusalem leadership have been invited—although they don't look that impressive—but otherwise things proceed as normal. The enthusiastic group gathers as usual in the evening for a communal meal. The sacrifice of Jesus is remembered and shared in the loaf of bread that begins the meal, and with the cup of wine that concludes it. These are blessed and passed around. Then speaking and singing begin. This mounts in excitement. Paul and Barnabas observe all the messianic Jews in the front row acting as they ought to. They are shouting out that Jesus is Lord, speaking in tongues, and prophesying and singing. They are laying hands on one another and praying for healing and deliverance. A few of those prayed for seem to fall over and then get up and declare that they feel healed. But now the two leaders notice something shocking. The Godfearers sitting in the back row of the gathering are doing the same things. They are shouting out that God has raised Jesus from the dead, and singing and expostulating in heavenly languages as well. They are laying hands on one another and praying for miracles. And some are even shaking and falling to the ground, such is the sense of the presence of God upon them.

This lively worship scene, reproduced countless times all over the world today, is, in this time and place, a theological and ethical crisis of the highest magnitude if one has the categories to recognize it.

As Paul and Barnabas well knew, this scenario signified that God had fully accepted these converts as pure. God was with them and even "in" them. However, if they were "Greeks," as Acts says, then they were not following the Jewish calendar or Jewish dietary practices, and the men were not circumcised. Technically, they were not Jews or under the instruction of the Torah, as Paul, the previous stickler for Jewish protocols, well knew. Yet the Spirit had personally indwelt them, so God clearly approved of them.

It was probably this phenomenon as well that seems in the first instance to have convinced the suspicious Jewish leaders of the early church in Jerusalem later on that this new missionary development ought to be acknowledged and affirmed, and that some sort of partnership was appropriate.

> The pillars of the church
> recognized that God was at work
> in my apostolic mission to the pagans,
> even as he was at work
> in Peter's work among the Jews. (Gal 2:7–9)

That is, the Holy Spirit was clearly at work in both these missions, and much of Acts tells a similar story. Hence the undeniable presence of God with these deviant converts convinced those experiencing it that God was in this entire situation—an event of revelation.

I imagine that this new situation also prompted some very hard praying and thinking by Barnabas and Paul at the time. If God had signed off on this radical inclusion, it did not follow immediately just why he had done so or what the appropriate explanation of all this was. Paul still had to articulate what was going on in terms that were persuasive both to him and to others. So I imagine that his great learning in the Scriptures would have been fully employed. And an important assist in this reflection was doubtless a positive attitude on his part toward these "Christians."

Paul had been called by God to the pagans. He had been living among them and reaching out to them for up to three years by now, possibly without a great deal of success, although we don't know this for certain. This contact had probably resulted in what scholars call "a hermeneutic of generosity" toward pagans on his part, as against what was arguably a more widespread hermeneutic of suspicion toward them among many other Jews (and perhaps especially many groups living in Judea). Paul viewed pagans sympathetically. He liked them (well, at least some of them). He wanted the best for them. So he was disposed to interpret what was happening as positively as he could, and not suspiciously and negatively. And the result was, in the end, the Pauline imaginary.

But with this important concluding emphasis on the work of the Spirit—on her occasionally surprising dynamics and interventions—it is worth taking some time to explore this more fully. We have uncovered here another major dimension within the Pauline imaginary. And, as it turns out, our use of Scripture will be bound up with this dimension as well.

Theses

‣ Several transformational missional modes need to be noted, in addition to the modes of missional engagement and evaluation already described. Again, there are four.

‣ (1) When any change is asked for, the means of that change is also subject to the appropriate relational considerations, which is to say that it must be fundamentally *respectful*. The means is the end.

‣ So change should not be coercive, or even rhetorically violent, which is counterintuitive to many modern advocates of social change. (The usual caveat on the use of force in a protective role, especially with respect to third parties, continues to apply.)

‣ Similarly, when cessation is asked for in the wake of condemnation, Christians should withdraw from participation in condemned structures, and not actively destroy them—the "ethical strike."

‣ (2) Christian relationality will need to be taught, entailing the introduction of a *pedagogy* and an associated teaching structure.

‣ But leaders who are already immersed and contextualized can do so with a minimum of inappropriate imposition.

‣ Moreover, most Christian pedagogy revolves around language.

‣ This should be *translated*, to further ease respect for local forms and structures.

‣ The church's Scriptures have always been translated, both instantiating and exemplifying an appropriate pedagogy, the first missionary-apostles, who were messianic Jews, using the Septuagint.

‣ A local liturgy can be crafted in appropriately contextualized terms.

‣ (3) Expressed needs should also be *resourced* if that is possible, while avoiding defining new converts in terms of their needs. (And resourcing need not be limited to converts; it can be extended to non-Christians in a way that corresponds to "the common good.")

‣ (4) Transformation includes a fourth, *reflexive* phase, when the parent culture of the missionary apostles is illuminated by the process of formation. The attempted introduction of some structures and forms can be revealed to be merely important, not mandatory, when this is not warranted in Trinitarian terms—often a humbling realization.

‣ The resulting community, spreading from messianic Jews through different Christian variations, was unique. This then presented Paul with the problems of what to call it, and how to describe it. He used familial metaphors basally, to which friendship has been added, as already noted.

But three further metaphors were highly suggestive: the church as a new temple; as a polity; and as a body.

> In more modern parlance, Paul's conception of the church amounts to an entire "social imaginary" (Charles Taylor's phrase), that is, a comprehensive account of how human life together should be organized, including a responsible account of difference within a process of diversification.

> Paul's imaginary has proved unstable in certain respects; his recommendations are not always christologically warranted but sometimes rest on foundationalist considerations.

> He imposed a structure of sex and gender on his pagan converts. This is based on a Jewish account of creation, and in certain respects lacks Trinitarian warrant. (We will examine this in much more detail later.)

> He also failed to ask for the reform and condemnation of the structure of slavery. This error rested on foundationalism too, and failed to be exposed by a sufficiently reflexive relationship with enslaved converts.

> It is important to avoid committing the fallacy of presentism, however. Most Christian leaders failed here, as Paul did, for millennia, which is not to excuse its shamefulness.

> Everyone working to further a Pauline imaginary is focused on a task at hand, and committed to changes with the appropriate relationality. Other things therefore tend not to be noticed and/or must be left temporarily in place.

> Nevertheless, Paul's imaginary demands, from its center, that structures be reformed and condemned as appropriate, as foundationalist moments are recognized and purged, and Trinitarian warrants are brought to bear increasingly clearly. It therefore generates internally its own progressive dynamic. We must, in terms of the imaginary itself, continue from Paul's imaginary to the Pauline.

> Paul himself seems to have been convinced initially of the legitimacy of his new, unprecedented community of Christians by the overt presence of the Holy Spirit, when he encountered it in Antioch, and this phenomenon seems to have played a key role in convincing the Jerusalem leadership of his mission's legitimacy as well.

> We learn from this that the Spirit prompts the creation of new Pauline imaginaries by leading missionary apostles into surprising friendships in unexpected places, in which locations they must "think things through," doubtless also with much prayer, fasting, and consultation. The imaginary and its imaginings follow on from concrete missional situations disclosed by the Spirit.

Key Scriptural References

Paul uses temple imagery to describe the church in 1 Cor 3:16–17; 6:19–20; 2 Cor 6:14–7:1; and Eph 2:19–22.

He uses polity imagery directly in Phil 3:20b–21; and presupposes it whenever he cites or appeals to elements within the household codes (which are listed and discussed in detail in later chapters).

He uses body imagery in Rom 12:4–5; 1 Cor 6:15–17; 10:16–17; 12:12–21; Eph 1:22–23; 4:4–16, 25; 5:22–32; Col 1:18, 24; 2:16–19; 3:15.

The importance of the Holy Spirit authenticating his missionary work through signs and wonders—a contention accepted by other leaders in the early church (Gal 2:8–9)—is evident in Rom 15:18–19; 1 Cor 2:1–5; and Gal 3:4.

Key Reading

Missional translation is discussed classically by Lamin Sanneh in *Translating the Message*.

Further Reading

The need for deep pedagogical formation is noted indirectly in a charming essay by Steinmetz, as he comments on the extraordinary capacity of an Amish community to forgive the murder of many of their children in Nickel Mine, Pennsylvania, in 2006, in "Forgiving the Unforgivable Wrong."

A widely recognized example of a beautifully contextualized liturgy is the New Zealand [Anglican] Prayer Book/*He Karakia Mihinare o Aotearoa* (although I'm not sure there is much point in non–New Zealanders immersing themselves in this; you have to live there to understand quite a bit of it).

A classic analysis of ancient conceptions of the body in conversation with Paul is Martin's *The Corinthian Body*.

The widely used phrase "social imaginary," along with much that underpins it, is developed in a particularly interesting way in relation to modernity by Taylor.

A superb application of this to New Testament analysis in relation to Acts (that is heavily informed by the work of Alasdair MacIntyre as well) is Rowe's treatment, *World Upside Down*. Rowe traces how Luke narratively both recounts and constructs a Christian social imaginary, detailing the comprehensiveness and challenges of this process to local paganism. The disruptive impact of church reformulations is evident in this story, and should not be underplayed in relation to Pauline missionary work either.

Hauerwas perceptively calls attention to the gift of the physically and mentally challenged, along with Lewis.

Polanyi's work on human understanding, truth, focality, and the tacit dimension, is always worth pondering. Another classic is Kuhn. (Throughout this book I have supplemented the insights of these thinkers into human cognition with the work of Kahneman, Lakoff, and those working on "the second personal.")

The biography assumed in this chapter is argued for in detail by my *Framing Paul*, especially in chapters two and three, and by my two articles, "Galatians 5:11," and "Beyond the Torah at Antioch." As noted, some of Paula Frederiksen's suggestions remain important as well.

Basic resources on the Holy Spirit were listed earlier (principally in ch. 7, and in relation to missional work, in ch. 19): specifically treating Paul see especially Fatehi, Fee, Levison, and Rabens; in more general terms, see Ekblad, Heron, Holmes, Rogers, Smail, and Thiselton, and two superb essay-length treatments by Hauerwas and Wainwright.

Bibliography

Anglican Church in Aotearoa, New Zealand, and Polynesia. *New Zealand Anglican Prayer Book / He Karakia Mihinare o Aotearoa*. New ed. Christchurch, N.Z.: Genesis Publications, 2005.

Campbell, Douglas. "Beyond the Torah at Antioch: The Probable Locus for Paul's Radical Transition." *JSPL* 4.2 (2014): 187–214.

———. *Framing Paul: An Epistolary Biography*. Grand Rapids: Eerdmans, 2014.

———. "Galatians 5:11: Evidence of an Early Law-observant Mission by Paul?" *NTS* 57 (2011): 325–47.

Frederiksen, Paula. "Judaism, the Circumcision of Gentiles, and Apocalyptic Hope: Another Look at Galatians 1 and 2." *JTS* 42 (1991): 532–69.

Hauerwas, Stanley. "Community and Diversity: The Tyranny of Normality." Pages 211–17 in *Suffering Presence: Theological Reflections on Medicine, the Mentally Handicapped, and the Church*. Notre Dame, IN: University of Notre Dame Press, 1986.

Kuhn, Thomas S. *The Structure of Scientific Revolutions*. 3rd ed.; London & Chicago: University of Chicago Press, 1996 (1962).

Lewis, Alan. "God as Cripple: Disability, Personhood, and the Reign of God." *Pacific Theological Review* 16 (1982): 13–18.

Martin, Dale B. *The Corinthian Body*. New Haven: Yale University Press, 1995.

Polanyi, Michael. *Personal Knowledge: Towards a Post-Critical Philosophy*. New York: Routledge and Kegan Paul, 1958.

———. *The Tacit Dimension*. New York: Doubleday, 1966.

Rowe, C. Kavin. *World Upside Down: Reading Acts in the Graeco-Roman Age*. Oxford: Oxford University Press, 2009.

Sanneh, Lamin. *Translating the Message: The Missionary Impact on Culture*. 2nd ed. Maryknoll, NY: Orbis, 1989.

Schweitzer, Albert. *The Mysticism of Paul the Apostle*. Translated by W. Montgomery. Baltimore: Johns Hopkins University Press, 1931.

Steinmetz, David C. "Forgiving the Unforgivable Wrong." Pages 79–80 in *Taking the Long View: Christian Theology in Historical Perspective*. Oxford: Oxford University Press, 2011.

Taylor, Charles. *Modern Social Imaginaries*. Durham, NC: Duke University Press, 2004.

———. "On Social Imaginary" (lecture in the course "Contemporary Sociological Theory," Spring 2000, NYU/Calhoun, 2004). https://web.archive.org/web/20041019043656/http://www.nyu.edu/classes/calhoun/Theory/Taylor-on-si.htm.

CHAPTER 23

Request Ethics

God's Commands

Paul's approach to ethics basically asks us to think constantly about the quality of our relationships. We are "to ponder whatever is true, reverenced, right, pure, lovely, admirable, excellent, and worthy of praise" (Phil 4:8), meaning, at bottom, to imitate people who mediate the character of Jesus (4:9; 2:5–8). But we are to imitate and mediate Jesus in different situations as communities are founded and formed in different social spaces. So ethics has a flexible, dynamic aspect as we constantly make judgments about what God is asking us to do. Moreover, it will clearly be helpful not just to think things through for ourselves, but to ask God about what is supposed to happen. But just how do we channel God as we navigate through all these diverse, challenging locations, sorting out what can stay, what needs to change, and what needs to go, as well as how? As usual, the answer to our question will come into focus as we return to first principles.

Any community is ultimately supposed to reflect the communion within God, and it is being drawn by God into that communion, which is relational, personal, and committed, so it is fundamentally familial in the best sense, or a community of friendship, again in the best sense. Its relationships are kind, loving, and enduring, drawing our own fractured families and friendships into conformity with its perfection. But while the persons within God are a single, unified God, they are distinct persons. The Father is constituted by his relationship with the Son, but is not reducible or collapsible into the Son. They are not the same. The Father and the Son are distinct from one another. Where we meet one, we meet the other, because they are constituted by their relationships, but we meet two distinct persons. And the same applies to the Spirit. She is the Spirit of the Father and of the Son, both identified with them and distinct from them. Consequently, the divine persons relate to one another and communicate with one another on a person-to-person basis (so Rom 8:26–27; 1 Cor 2:10–11). We learn from this model that at the heart of all appropriate behaving is communicating, which is to say, in our human case, *talking.* And it follows in turn that a critical part of our ongoing behavior will flow from what God tells us to do—and what we say back, although we will need to be careful about our responses. God will speak to us, frequently giving us instructions, and in those situations we, of course, ought *to obey.*

While this might seem a little unsettling—the thought that a significant part of our behavior is just listening to and doing what God tells us to do—when we think about it, it is also blindingly obvious. A personal God is at the heart of our reality so he is going to communicate with us constantly and, among other things, tell us what to do. The main initial obstacles to this approach can only be any doubt on our part that God is really there, coupled with the doubt that he can actually communicate with us. But these are obstacles of unbelief and so invalid. God is alive and thus can communicate with us whenever he wants to. We just need to be listening.

Let's think about our most important and intimate relationships. Here again I think again of my relationship with my spouse, Rachel, and how it works. We live our lives in constant relationship with one another. Indeed, in a sense, there is nothing but behaving in relation to one another. Relationships are powerful causes! And all this relating, as relating, is saturated with ethical content. This relating *is* ethics. But how do we work all this out? How do we figure out how to act and to act rightly? *We talk about it.* There was no book of marriage rules that we both read and signed off on when we got married and that we subsequently enforce when pressed. There are no regulations that we appeal to or read every morning to work out how to act toward one another that day. There are not even any overarching abstract principles that we apply to or interpret for individual situations.[1] There are critical relational dynamics that we navigate and negotiate through the complexities of life, generally by making quite specific suggestions. That is, we love one another, have made a covenant with one another, now have a history with one another, and talk with one another all the time. So, "can you make the marinade for the barbequed chicken this morning?" was an ethical event today. (For various relational

1. It can certainly be argued that there was a diffuse, complex tradition, partly shaped by culture, partly by a Christian subculture, that structured different options for activity. But it is so diffuse, diverse, and even contradictory that navigating through its options is by no means obvious.

reasons I said "Sure.") And it is basically no different with God. God talks to us and with us as we navigate our situations ethically.

This insight into the way God relates to us is sometimes called "command ethics," although this title is rather forbidding and might take us to a worrisome place. My wife doesn't usually command me to do anything. She makes requests, as do I, so perhaps we should call this "request ethics." It makes a difference when God is doing the requesting. We ought to obey divine requests, so they are analogous to commands. But God is not ordering us around in a way that violates our underlying relationship of mutual love, commitment, and respect. And we don't obey God just because we are being given a command. We should *want* to hear God's commands and to respond to them. They are liberating and nourishing. We look forward to responding joyfully to the one who is talking to us because of who he is. It is very important to grasp this connection, which is really to refuse to separate God's commands from the one who is commanding, whom we already know and trust as unconditionally committed to us. A command separated from a God revealed in Christ can be a terrifying thing, but that notion would be a false step into an untruth. The God who commands us is the loving God of Jesus, the God who dies for us. So his commands are acts of love, and we look forward to them eagerly and respond to them joyfully.

But another problem is usually gathering behind the furrowed brows of my students at this moment. They think back through their lives and sometimes struggle to recall moments when the voice of God has thundered from heaven giving them instructions in the unambiguous way that Moses was confronted by the burning bush or Paul by Jesus on the road to Damascus. They think, that is, that God's requests are direct, and even somewhat overpowering. And they don't necessarily have a large number of experiences of such encounters, sometimes even despite having asked for one repeatedly.

God's requests can be direct and unmistakable like this. We can't rule out this possibility. But like most things in his community, God's requesting and commanding activity is more often mediated. God uses things within our creaturely orbit and works through them, which is what he did by becoming human, and, as we already know, he particularly enjoys using other people. So God frequently speaks to us through those around us, even as we hopefully mediate some of God's communications to others in turn. We are all involved in the realization of God's plan for the cosmos, including its communication and ongoing daily navigation, which is a great joy and a great responsibility.

Complexity and Particularity

There is another reason why it is important to recognize this dynamic, personal, communicative approach to ethics on God's part. What I am calling a request ethics has the additional advantage that it can take account of the differences in detail that characterize each of our situations that we have just been discussing. This ethic matches our ongoing navigation of diverse situations, complementing the prudential judgments that we are constantly being asked to make.[2]

No one is ever occupying exactly the same place, situation, and journey, so it is never the case in ethics that one size fits all. The application of a rule to everyone is always going to have rough edges—places where a certain situation that it did not anticipate generates damaging consequences. We might, for example, think that it is right to observe the speed limit. Driving at a reasonable speed allows us to react to unforeseen situations like mistakes on the part of other drivers and deer crossing the road. Observing this rule, frustrating as it is at times, should allow us to drive more safely and thereby to avoid becoming one of the traffic statistics that tragically accumulate every year. (Around 33,000 deaths take place on US roads annually, the vast majority involving high speed.) But if our daughter is in anaphylactic shock from an unforeseen drug reaction we should not necessarily observe the speed limit as we rush her to the emergency room and a life-saving shot of adrenaline. Observing the speed limit in this situation may kill her, especially if we are in some distant rural location when she begins to spiral into asphyxia. Such situations abound in daily life, although they will hopefully be a little less dramatic.

As a result of such considerations, a request ethics can take account of the insight that lies at the heart of the ethical school known as situation ethics. Ethics isn't reducible to situation ethics, which would be to turn this insight into a rule, contradicting its nature at a fundamental level. But there is a truth here that we need to take account of. Our situations are always different, so

---

2. Such prudential judgments by us would correspond to the moments of initiative that take place in relationships of love. (John Gottman calls these "bids.") My hunch is that God delights in relationships that are a two-way street. There is a dominant direction, and this needs to be clearly and constantly recognized. God is God and we are frail creatures of flesh. But our God also loves us and desires a genuinely reciprocal relationship with us. And it seems that prudential judging is part of this reciprocity on our part, along with activities like praise and petition. We will return to Gottman's insights in our discussion of marriage in chs. 25 and 26.

the right action within them will always differ a bit as well. Certainly we can't just act the way we always do. Right behavior will shift around, sometime subtly, sometimes dramatically. I am going to drive around the speed limit on the freeway in general, but I'm going to put my foot to the floor when driving my dying daughter to hospital, and so on. The specificity of God's commands acknowledges the complexity of our cosmos, along with our detailed, irreplaceable, and irreplicable contributions to it—the feature of our existence best referred to as *particularity*.

Just as Jesus became a particular person and no other, complete in every detail, with certain hair, language, skin, and so on, we all exist in complex situations within which every detail is important. Every hair on our head matters, and every hair is different. Moreover, God's instructions to us reflect and respond to our complex and specific situations. Hence we can expect very detailed—and often very practical—requests from God as we navigate our communities and their diverse locations.

My favorite example of this principle comes from 1 Kings, the book that was the basis for my Hebrew prose instruction. "Leave here, turn eastward, and hide in the Kerith Ravine, east of the Jordan," God said to Elijah some unspecified time after the latter had informed Ahab of the beginning of a great drought (17:3). God added, "You will drink from the brook, and I have ordered the ravens to feed you there." Although Sunday School classes tend to major on the second set of instructions here, I am especially taken by the first.

It is quite specific. I don't imagine that anyone else in the history of Israel or even of Christianity has been commanded by God to turn eastward and to hide in the Kerith Ravine there to be fed by ravens. For a start, this instruction applies only to those standing to the west of the wadi, within traveling distance, and hungry. But this instruction made it into the Bible and was supremely important. Elijah needed to go and hide and survive, later to emerge for his climactic confrontation with the priests of Baal on Mount Carmel. Clearly, then, this word didn't endure as a law or principle or universalizable commandment. It is a command that is part of a quite specific story. The specificity of the command matches the specific circumstances of the story. Requests fit into particularity. But numerous examples of this sort can be plucked from Paul's life as well. "Collect this money." "Send A to me." "You, B, and you, C, get on with one another." "Expel D." "Welcome E." "Read F." "Do G." These types of instructions are all requests (or commands!) as well. Hence this is how the God of Jesus relates to us ethically for much of the time. He speaks to us in terms of our actual situations and tells us what to do. We just need to be listening carefully.

These commands can take full account of diversity as well. As God commands people to do things in terms of their specific situations—in their particular local contexts and networks of relations—he communicates diverse instructions. Diverse commands can respond to diverse particularities. And this can be supremely helpful, once we recognize what is going on.

Think momentarily of the current incarceration crisis in the United States—a country with around 4 percent of the world's population using its vast wealth and resources to incarcerate almost 25 percent of the world's imprisoned population. God is doubtless calling the church to engage with this situation and to remedy it. "Set my people free." But I am sure that different people are being called to diverse specific tasks. Different divine requests and commands are being issued to different people.

People are presumably being called to challenge the inequities of this situation publicly. They might point to the prison system's horrific size, its growth, its sinister partnerships with corporate America, to its overt racial biases and its discriminations against the poor, its punitive, grandstanding prosecutions, and its sinister logics, not to mention its frequent abuses. They might passionately inveigh against these evils and advocate change politically and socially, using social media and public protest. But such people will not get access to anyone who is imprisoned to support them directly through that trial (unless, that is, they are a lawyer, and in my experience lawyers tend not to offer a lot of personal and sustained support, because they are too busy to do so, although some saintly figures do).

So other people are presumably being called to visit prisons, and to get alongside those who are inside them, doing time, *but they must act rather differently from the public protestors in order to do so.* They must accept the restrictions of the current situation more placidly and navigate them carefully. If they are called to spend time regularly alongside those who are imprisoned, raging against the system's injustices publically may not be particularly helpful. Prisons are very sensitive to negative publicity. Moreover, teaching people doing time to rage against the system will probably just immerse them in a toxic stew of negative affect, further immiserating their experience, while overt public protest will lead, almost without fail, to a denial of access.

But I have seen those called to prophetic witness against the evils of the current system challenge the very legitimacy of those who have felt called to enter into the system to get alongside those suffering there. "That is cooperating with the powers; it is to endorse the evil status quo." And I have seen those who enter the system to work directly with the incarcerated become far too comfortable with the sinister dimensions of that system—with its flawed and occasionally harsh self-justifications, and with the messages it consequently sends to those in its custody. They sometimes need to listen to the prophets on the outside.

Both callings are of course right. We desperately need both prophets and pastorally minded teachers to engage the leviathan that is the current prison system in the United States. But it is destructive to force this engagement into one pattern and then to deny legitimacy to any others. We need both, and more types of engagement besides. We need the system engaged from every angle. And an accurate grasp of the requesting and commanding God, and of the specific nature of our relationship with him, will allow us to recognize the fundamental legitimacy of a diverse situation—and allow us to sit a little more lightly to our own importance. God might be commanding different people within a very large army to do different things. "You go here, you go there," as the centurion, who operated in an army, said (see Matt 8:5–13). If we are called to prophesy, prophesy; if we are called to teach, teach; and if we are called to show mercy, show mercy. But from this moment perhaps we should refrain from calling others to our tasks, also from assuming that they are the only tasks that matter.

In short, it seems that one size most definitely does not fit all. The important thing is to be attentive to what we think God is asking us to do. Happily, we are thereby liberated immediately from the burden of having to tell other people what to do. (Sometimes we do have to tell others what God is saying, but I suspect these situations are rather rarer than many of us would like to think.) We are free to respond to God as God is instructing us in all our details and particularity, and we are free at the same time from the burden of shaping others in our own image. As Paul well knew, "Where the Spirit of the Lord is, there is freedom," meaning here, at least in part, freedom from the need to be the same as one another (2 Cor 3:17).

Joining Hands

Note that this approach clearly does not exhaust Paul's ethics. We cannot reduce Paul's account of ethical behavior to obedience to God's requests and commands. This approach explains a lot, but it doesn't explain everything. As we have already seen at some length in part 2, we still need to learn things—to grow in our capacity to act rightly. A request from God will not do much if we are incapable of acting in obedience to it, and, in fact, if we are incapable of acting rightly, we will find it difficult even to hear certain requests from

God. If the rightness of certain actions hasn't entered our imaginative world yet, we won't be able to conceptualize what God is asking; it will be as if aliens have landed on the earth and started communicating with us in their own language. They will be incomprehensible until we have built up some overlap in conceptuality and metaphor—until we have learned more about what they are saying. A request ethics, putting things more technically, requires an underlying *language* and *grammar* of ethics to be intelligible and function at all. Requests ultimately make sense only in terms of stories, and so only a deep grounding in the story of Jesus will open up any possibility of a mediation of the ways of Jesus as God communicates with us in later navigational situations.

Moreover, given the specificity of God's commands, in response to the particular details of each situation, training in right or prudential judgment will also be essential. There are times when we just don't know what God is requesting us to do specifically, despite asking. We will need judgment here again. And we will need habits based on accumulated patterns of learning to structure a lot of our daily lives, because we can't spend every waking moment asking God what to do next. I know of a person who tried to live like this—a friend of a friend—and he walked around Oxford, in what seemed to me to be a rather random way, muttering prayerfully if a little strangely, achieving very little. Having said this, my hunch is that we err on the side of autonomy. We probably need to spend a lot more time acting like my Oxford example, seeking the will of God in all things and learning to hear it and to obey. "We should take every thought captive to obedience to Christ" (2 Cor 10:5), and "in everything, by prayer and petition, make [our] requests known to God" (Phil 4:6).

In sum, we should not think that a virtue ethic and a request ethic are in tension with one another. They interpenetrate and reinforce one another. We should press into both of these approaches as deeply as we can. They must join hands. The more virtue, the more obedience (which is the correlate to requests); and the more obedience, the more virtue; while underlying both, holding them together, is our sharing in the mind of Jesus.

Scripture

With this important clarification in place, we should now turn to think a bit more about the important dimension the need for attentiveness to divine requests has just foregrounded for us. Indeed, we will see here how divine commands are rooted in what is arguably the key resource within our pedagogy and its translated traditions that resource any new community, something we began to talk about earlier on but that now needs to be clarified considerably.

God's communications with us, and ours in return, along with our speaking with one another, will require language, and we have spent some time already reflecting on its relational tenor. It should, for example, be self-controlled and gentle. Even more importantly at this moment, however, we ought to recall that 95 percent of our acting is going to involve language. As we already know, ethics is all about relationships, and relationships are all about speaking, that is, the use of language. And language requires content as well as attention to its tenor, for which *the Scriptures* are the key resource. Scripture consequently lies at the heart of the church. But it needs to be handled very carefully, and Paul did.

God will speak to us frequently, and perhaps even predominantly, with language drawn from the Bible, and the Bible does talk about God a lot. It is packed with stories, phrases, songs, sayings, customs, oracles, and even argumentation, about God. Consequently, the Scriptures resource our language with God. They are a treasury from which things old and new are taken. It follows that as we learn the wording of the Scriptures more deeply, we will be the more capable of hearing God's words when he speaks with them to us. (Election creates freedom.) We see here, in short, the necessary interaction between the learning advocated by virtue ethicists and the insights from those emphasizing commands.

It might be helpful to recall at this moment that the Greek word *nomos*, usually translated "law," was informed for Paul by the Hebrew *torah*, and is better translated "sacred instruction" or "holy teaching."[3] Torah functioned for Paul and other Jews as the Bible does for many Christians today. It refers to the divine gift of the Scriptures and their role in the ethical instruction and formation of God's devotees (and it was broadened to include the Prophets and the Writings, which Christians know, rather unfortunately, as the Old Testament; here we have preferred the Jewish designation Tanakh). Their original form was a spoken word of God, whether direct or mediated, uttered into a particular situation. But these words were then written down, copied, and carefully passed on to posterity. As a result, this language can be taken up by God and spoken again into other relevant situations. God's further communications with us take place intelligibly within this universe of meaning.

But only as we learn the Scriptures, internalizing them so that they become part of our language, can God really use them effectively. Our modern Western culture tends to impede this process. We wealthy moderns generally fail to train our memories and rely instead on external archives of information

---

3. A couple of essays by W. D. Davies are an elegant reminder of this.

like libraries, computers, and the cloud. But language residing in storage devices is not language that God can take up and speak to us or through us very effectively. It is not, after all, in our heads as we think and act. When we rely on external devices for information storage, as against our own memories, we are a little like actors walking around on stage performing a play by reading the script off a manuscript in their hands. This is how things begin, in rehearsal, but we would ask for our money back if we showed up on opening night and experienced actors behaving in this way. Actors have to learn their lines. They have to internalize them—something they call being "off script." Only after they are off script can they really begin to act. Similarly, Jesus's followers need to be "off script" in the sense of being "off [written] Scripture" (at least to some degree) if they want to act. We need to know the Scriptures as actors know their lines so that we can recite them from memory and insert them into conversations at will—so that they shape our thinking at a very fundamental level. We haven't always got the time to find a book, leaf through it, and read it. This is not how people actually talk to one another. Training, then, and a rather traditional type of training, is vital. However, it is not wooden.

Recalling our emphasis earlier in this chapter on variations in every situation and circumstance, which is to say, on particularity, we must not simply insert memorized scriptural material into our advice on a rule-governed and rote-learned basis. This use of the Bible is likely to be insensitive and is unlikely to be mediating the actual words of God. Few things are more irritating than someone responding tritely to the sharing of a difficulty with a relevant "memory verse." As if that response will really fix things, and as if that suggests the reciter is really listening. God must take up the words of Scripture and speak them, adjusting them to the nuances and details of each situation. Our training in Scripture provides the basic resources for this engagement—the raw material of language, as it were—but then this resource must still be placed at the feet of God and caught up within his living purposes. And those purposes are creative and dynamic and individuated. So, writing to his Thessalonian converts around 40 CE, Paul gives thanks in 1 Thess 2:13 for the way that

> you received the word concerning God,
> which was heard from us,
> not as a word of a man,
> but as it is truly,
> a word of God,
> which is also working
> among you who are convinced by it.

Paul clearly distinguishes two agencies in play here within his words, the human and the divine, both of which are necessary. The Spirit has used the words of the missionaries, Paul, Silas, and Timothy, to create believing among the Thessalonians. And the same dynamic applies to his use of scriptural texts and motifs elsewhere.

I have heard people refer to this process as "traditioned innovation," which is a phrase worth remembering. It captures both aspects of the interaction between virtue and request nicely. Without the prior resourcing of our language, here through Scripture, and all the painstaking learning that presupposes, we have no material for God to take up. Without the practices we have learned we are contentless. God has nothing to work with. It is as if a carpenter has shown up on the job without a tool box or any idea how to use the tools. Such a worker is not really a carpenter. This learning is something that takes place within a "tradition," and this is a useful word to use. Tradition refers at its simplest to the transmission of a body of knowledge from teachers to students. It names the learning process that we have spent a lot of time talking about, and the particular habits and patterns of behavior that a specific learning process—here a training in virtue, and in the Scriptures—passes on. But this prior learning and resourcing, found within a tradition, must be taken up and used in response to a new situation as God speaks to us about it and calls us to engage with it. We must now innovate.

One of the further happy results of recognizing this usage is that our use of Scripture can be quite creative. The church has traditionally used Scripture in many different ways. Students of Scripture are often introduced to the "quadriga," which denotes four different ways of using texts as developed by the church through the centuries. They can be given their literal sense, an allegorical reading, a "tropological" (or moral) sense, and an "anagogical" meaning (this interpretation looks forward, in hope, to eschatology). And this is just to introduce in a very crude and programmatic fashion some of the ways in which the church through history has spoken the words of God through the scriptural texts.[4] Modern academic reading, with its "historical-critical approach," flattens out the reading of Scripture, judging only the original sense, painstakingly reconstructed through historical work, to be of value. This approach simplifies things, but at quite a cost. As Gadamer programmatically observes, great texts, like all great works of art, are not just *re*productive; they do not just repeat themselves. They are *productive*; new meanings emerge. They are creative and fresh. God's use of Scripture is then presumably the pinnacle of creative linguistic exuberance.[5]

---

4. The work of Henri de Lubac is a useful way into this interpretative cornucopia.

5. John Webster captures this dynamic in a delightful essay. We will briefly address

In sum, we will "innovate" as we follow God forward, using the resources provided by our tradition, but creating something that, while in continuity with that tradition, will change it into something partly new. In just this sense Scripture that is taken up and used by God clearly comes from tradition—the church created and sustains the Bible—but it is used in diverse, creative ways in various new situations. We see Paul doing just this when he cites Scripture among his communities.

Idols at Corinth

Paul begins one of his longer scriptural admonitions, in 1 Cor 10:1–14, on a positive note.

> I do not want you to be ignorant of the fact, brothers and sisters,
> that our ancestors were all under the cloud
> and that they all passed through the sea.
> They were all immersed into Moses in the cloud and in the sea.
> They all ate the same spiritual food
> and drank the same spiritual drink;
> for they drank from the spiritual rock that accompanied them,
> and that rock was Christ. (1 Cor 10:1–4)

Paul is referring here to the Israelites' exodus from Egypt, first referencing the Sea of Reeds, through which they escaped miraculously as God parted the waters, and then the cloud of God's presence that accompanied them through the desert. He goes on to reference the story of the rock that Moses split open so that the Israelites might have water. (This story occurs twice in the Torah in slightly different forms.) Some later rabbis then innovated this tradition surmising that the Israelites needed water every day, so the rock providing it must have accompanied them on their travels. Paul also references the story of God providing manna.

Paul has selected these four incidents—the sea, the cloud, the water flowing from the traveling rock, and the daily provision of manna—to correlate the story of the exodus with the situation in the Corinthian community. Like the ancient Hebrews, he says, the Corinthians have been baptized or immersed

---

at the end of this chapter the question arising at this point concerning how to judge the validity of different readings.

into water and into the cloud of God's presence (this presumably during their worship), and they drink and eat spiritual drink and food in the eucharistic meal when they pass around the cup and the bread that instantiate the blood and body of Jesus. But the similarity that Paul creates between these two communities has a bite to it. He continues,

> Nevertheless, God was not pleased with most of them;
> their bodies were scattered in the wilderness.
> Now these things occurred as examples
> to keep us from setting our hearts on evil things as they did.
> Do not be idolaters, as some of them were;
> as it is written:
> "The people sat down to eat and drink and got up to indulge in
> revelry."
> We should not commit sexual immorality, as some of them did—
> and in one day twenty-three thousand of them died.
> We should not test Christ, as some of them did—
> and were killed by snakes.
> And do not grumble, as some of them did—
> and were killed by the destroying angel.
> These things happened to them as examples
> and were written down as warnings for us,
> on whom the culmination of the ages has come. (1 Cor 10:5–11)

Paul is now referencing the story of the golden calf, recounted in Exod 32. While Moses was up on top of Mount Sinai receiving teachings from God, the Israelites pressured Aaron to make them an idol, a golden calf, and proceeded to worship it and to engage in the relevant cultic actions. They sacrificed animals, feasting on the meat, drinking during the banquet, then continuing the fun with singing and dancing. Of course, this was a heinous sin, and God was so angry that Moses organized a massacre to bring things under control, after which a plague struck the community, and the survivors of that calamity were then condemned to die in the desert just shy of the promised land. The Scriptures deemed this fate better than instant fiery annihilation and go on to speak of God relenting of his refusal to accompany them any more. (His presence, suitably accommodated in a new tabernacle, would continue in these chastened circumstances.) Nevertheless, it is a shocking story of betrayal by way of idolatry, followed by grim judgment. Paul's point, however, is that these stories contain warnings for the Corinthians. Some of them are involved with activity he regards as idolatrous, and so, in the same way, they are courting God's judgment. Like the good Jew he was, Paul wants them to have no direct part in pagan celebrations before statues and around temples.

Therefore, my dear friends, flee from idolatry. (1 Cor 10:14)

However, a scriptural pedant could now push back on Paul a little. Sure, there are similarities. But the worship of the golden calf was worship *of a golden calf*. Moreover, the cultic celebration the Israelites indulged in names only eating, drinking, and dancing. So, strictly speaking, the Corinthians could argue that they are not worshiping an animal image; they are not in fact worshiping images at all. They know that the gods their statues of people represent *do not exist*. Moreover, the scriptural text prohibits eating, drinking, and dancing, but it does not prohibit cultic sex or, less obviously, mere socializing.

I am of course "speaking in human terms" here, but the point is that the two situations do not match exactly, and our pedants could go on to question further correlations. Passing through the Sea of Reeds and following a cloud of God's presence are hardly the same thing as being immersed into the name of Jesus; and eating manna and drinking from water flowing from a rock have very little to do with eating the bread and drinking the cup of wine at the Eucharist. "This is all a huge stretch, Paul," we can hear the Corinthians saying. And it is quite a stretch. *But this doesn't stop the various instructions Paul is issuing from being valid instructions for the Corinthians from God.* Using the scriptural vehicle of this extended story, the legitimacy of his instructions does not stem primarily *from* the original story, which merely creates an intelligible set of connections. Their legitimacy stems from whether or not Paul is speaking a word from God, and whether his instructions are theologically plausible, and of course they are. The Corinthians should not engage in sexual immorality, and if they do, there will be consequences. Moreover, there is something very dangerous about attending worship events involving other "gods." This behavior risks betraying the one true God at a very fundamental level.

It would be nice to spend some more time unpacking this fascinating text. but the key insight for our present discussion should already be clear. This is all a nice example of traditioned innovation—of the necessary interaction between virtue and tradition, and divine commands, requests, and obedience. Using the story of the exodus and, in particular, the incident of the golden calf, which are drawn from scriptural tradition, and then assisted by subsequent Jewish tradition, Paul has innovated by applying them to a new situation, which is the risky and sinful behavior of some of the Corinthian

Christians. Paul is warning them, doubtless convinced that in doing so he is mediating the concerns of God. Some of their current behavior is horrifying, and the consequences of continuing to indulge in it will be grim. They were not living and acting exactly like the ancient Hebrews during the exodus, but stories from tradition about the Hebrews, in Paul's skillful hands, frame a set of commands that the formerly pagan Corinthians need to understand and to hear *and to obey*. They must flee from their Greco-Roman idolatry and from any associated practices like indiscriminate sex.

With this positive use of Scripture in front of us, we nevertheless need to consider a more sinister side to Paul's scriptural instructions. Paul's broader use of Scripture has frequently confused his interpreters, and if we are going to continue to use it positively in our communities today, we need to understand how things can become negative.

The Cooptation of Scripture

Paul obviously cites Scripture fairly frequently in an exhortatory way. As we have just seen, he threatens the Corinthians with plague and death if they do not desist from idolatry, as the Israelites failed to desist from worshiping the golden calf during the exodus (1 Cor 10:1–11). A little more positively, he exhorts the Roman Christians to attend to everything that has been written because it provides instruction and encouragement, thereby facilitating perseverance and hope (15:4).[6] But in other texts he calls Scripture *death-dealing!*

Here we pick up a thread that we left dangling back in part 1, chapter 5. There we learned that if the readers of Paul's letter to the Romans try to obey the tenth commandment in their own strength, that is, try not to covet in obedience to that command, they will lapse back into the enslaved and desperate condition of the Flesh (7:7–25). They will be coopted and will sin, repeatedly, so they need to avoid this way of serving God (8:2–3; 2 Cor 3:6). And this is not an isolated warning. If the Galatians undertake circumcision, as prescribed by the Torah, Christ will be of no use to them; they will also have to do everything in the entirety of the Torah (Gal 5:2–4), and Paul basically adds "good luck with that." The Mosaic Torah was a ministry that brought death, Paul says in 2 Cor 3. And it is the power behind sin that has a sting leading to

6. "For everything that was written in the past was written to teach us, so that through the endurance taught in the Scriptures and the encouragement they provide we might have hope" (NIV).

death (1 Cor 15:54–56). The Scriptures will kill you, Paul seems to be saying in all these places. What is going on?

Rather than ascribing a horrific confusion to Paul at a very basic level, it seems more coherent, and also ultimately rather more constructive, to suppose that he is working with the request/command approach that we have just outlined and specifying here the negative side of that dynamic. He is distinguishing between *the Spirit's* use of Scripture to mediate the commands of Jesus, and *other* uses of Scripture, which are presumably pretty much our own idea. This second, human use of Scripture is vulnerable to exploitation by the powers and by sinful lusts and leads ultimately to death. Hence it is clearer than ever at this moment that the words spoken in the past by God now treasured up in a written form as Scripture are *not* the word of God if they are not spoken again *by* God. Without the animation of the Spirit and the summons of Christ, they are just words that have been written down by human hands with pen and ink and parchment—treasured and valuable to be sure (Col 2:14; 2 Cor 3:3–11 speaks of engraving on stone tablets).[7] But words about God's former wishes drawn from the handwritten texts that record them are sadly open to exploitation, unless God reiterates them overtly and specifically.

Paul's template for this negative usage is the command that was manipulated by the forces of evil in the Garden of Eden to deceive Adam and Eve, as a result of which sin, suffering, and death were unleashed into the cosmos (Rom 5:12–14; 7:7–13). He then sees this dynamic at work in all subsequent uses of Scripture that are not taken up by God, and it is a sobering thought. Scripture in merely human hands is exploited by evil forces *and it kills people.*

I wonder whether the underlying experience that led Paul to this insight was not his persecution of the community of Jesus followers in Jerusalem prior to his dramatic call on the road to Damascus (something noted already in ch. 6, but contributing another explanatory layer as we recall it here). Paul undoubtedly learned a lot from this shameful episode.

Prior to the revelation of Christ on the road to Damascus, Paul was a deeply devout servant of God, but he understood that calling to mean being prepared to kill on his behalf. And doubtless he buttressed his persecutions of Jesus's followers with prayer, worship, exhortation, *and scriptural citation.* After all, he was a Bible-believing Pharisee. Perhaps he quoted the story of Phinehas, who impaled an immoral Israelite as he was sullying himself with a pagan

---

7. See also Paul's derogatory use of "hand-done" in relation to circumcision, either by way of implicit contrast to circumcision of the heart and its lusts by the Spirit, or with direct reference to fleshly circumcision: Rom 2:29; Eph 2:11; Phil 3:2; Col 2:11.

woman in his tent (see Num 25:1–9; Ps 106:28–31). But this activity in Paul's earlier life, along with this use of the Bible, was not godly. Damascus revealed that it was demonic. And it follows that the Scriptures themselves should not be used independently of an ethical location within God, guided by the Spirit, and they should certainly not be used independently of God, perhaps to verify God or to support other teaching and instruction. When used by the Flesh they serve the Flesh, and the Flesh serves the devil. This also means that they cannot be used through technique alone.

Learning in interpretative technique—and what we might even call great hermeneutical skill—could increase their potential use as we become more open to the semantic riches of the Scriptures. But this increased capacity should not be mistaken for increased access to the desires and instructions of God, who must still take up those resources and speak through them. Any ultimate reliance on our own interpretative technique would only unleash the horsemen of the foundationalist apocalypse. We would be asserting an independent check on truth again—here our own hermeneutical and interpretative expertise—and thereby undermining *the* truth, Jesus, revealed by Jesus, who is God. So this particular, technical use of Scripture is to be recognized and avoided. It is dangerous and ultimately death-dealing. The widespread use of highly sophisticated—and at times very accurate—exegesis by biblical scholars in the nineteenth-century US Confederacy to support the supposedly God-ordained institution of slavery springs to mind here as an excellent example of this sort of scriptural evil.[8]

This is not to abandon exegetical technique, any more than we should abandon flying because it can be used to drop explosives on people. (I am, after all, a professor of Bible.) But it is imperative that these interpretative actions be located within the right frame, which is to say, taken up and guided by the Spirit. The powers are far more sophisticated, capable, and subtle than we are, as are our fleshly desires, so we must remain vigilant.[9] Anything good, including the Bible—*anything*—can be manipulated by these evil entities that stalk our world as they further their destructive agenda, although presumably they especially enjoy working with sacred materials.

---

8. A useful collection of biblical texts debating slavery has been collected by Willard Swartley in "The Bible and Slavery," *Slavery, Sabbath, War, and Women*, 31–64. The exegesis of the pro-slavery camp is technically more precise than the anti-slavery interpreters of Paul. It wins the exegetical battle, in historical-critical terms.

9. This is another sustained motif in Paul. See Rom 13:11–14; Eph 5:8–14; 6:10–18 (and, in the light of this, probably also 1 Cor 16:13); and 1 Thess 5:1–11.

With this sobering realization about the possible exploitation of Scripture, we run into a further important question.

Discerning God's Use of Scripture

Paul can spend a great deal of time instructing his converts in what amounts to the paradoxical practice of Christian recognition. He constantly presses his converts to think through the revelation that is Jesus, and sometimes especially his acceptance of a fate of execution. In this shameful location that speaks, paradoxically, of God's limitless love for us, we receive the most pointed information about the sort of God that we are involved with, and we consequently learn how to discern when this God is speaking and when he probably isn't.

> Jews demand signs and Greeks look for wisdom,
> but we preach Christ crucified:
> a stumbling block to Jews and foolishness to Gentiles. . . .
> (1 Cor 1:22–23)

A more technical way of putting this issue would be to say that "a Christocentric hermeneutic" is often (if not always) discernable in a Spirit-led use of Scripture.[10] When Paul deploys scriptural stories and texts positively, *they basically speak about a God revealed in Jesus and working through that person.* "Whatever promises God has promised to us, they are 'Yes,' in him" Paul says at one point accurately about his own practice (2 Cor 1:20). In this sense, Paul can also speak of the "Torah that is Christ" (1 Cor 9:21; Gal 6:2), meaning the instruction that comes from his life and its activities that converts are now so powerfully shaped by, as we have already seen. *This* is now *the* instruction. And this makes sense in view of what we have already learned about God.

We know what the God who will be speaking through Scripture is like because he has definitively revealed himself through Jesus. So we must use our minds, tutored by our theological traditions—by what we have learned—to apply what we know about Jesus to any use of Scripture in his name. We must coolly analyze what is going on in terms of what we already know. Jesus doesn't

---

10. So—in a fairly technical setting—Richard B. Hays, "On the Rebound: A Response to Critiques of *Echoes of Scripture in the Letters of Paul,*" repr. in *The Conversion of the Imagination: Paul as Interpreter of Israel's Scripture* (Grand Rapids: Eerdmans, 2005), 163–89.

change in terms of who he is, and God is the God revealed definitively by Jesus. So the critical test for appropriate Scripture usage is *good theology*, which is why I have spent so much time setting out what I take to be good theology here, along with the many ways—sometimes in the name of exegesis—that we can wander from this narrow path and get thoroughly lost. We should, that is, basically insert the theological insights parts 1 and 2 pointed to into all our uses of Scripture. But we should supplement this primary test with other secondary tests as well.

When we reflect on missionaries more deeply, the character of the speaker is important as well. Those who reflect the astonishingly condescending life of Christ are more likely to be authentic mediators of God's words than those who don't. Moreover, we noted earlier that God's messengers can often be recognized by their struggles, vulnerability, and persecutions—what Paul terms "weakness"—rather than by their possession of key cultural markers of skill and intelligence.[11] This is an important truth mediated especially through Paul's struggles with the Corinthian community. But Paul, if asked, would also doubtless endorse the various spiritual practices that the church has subsequently emphasized when seeking the will of God.

It is obvious that communities seeking to hear God's voice must pray. They must be attentive to the Spirit. And they can doubtless increase their prayerful sensitivity by undertaking allied practices like fasting, silence, meditation, and retreat. Hence, when trying to discern the voice of God as against the voice of the Flesh and the devil, especially when they take up and use the words of Scripture, we should match the discipline of strenuous theological work with evaluations of character and with spiritual disciplines. These should intertwine and inform one another. Moreover, we should identify and listen to the voices of our prophets.

Certain people have been gifted with the knowledge of the mind of God. They will not be infallible, but they may also know a lot more than we do. Apostles need to navigate boldly into new spaces with a prophetic instinct for what God is doing (so, I would suggest, 2 Cor 12:1–9).[12] And ongoing commu-

---

11. This is a sustained theme especially in the letters written to Corinth: see especially 1 Cor 4:9–13; 2 Cor 4; 6:4–10; 11:23–29.

12. The interval named of thirteen years and a number of months prior to the composition of 2 Corinthians in 51 CE (see 2 Cor 12:2) suggests that this heavenly journey took place in late 36 or early 37 CE. This is exactly when Paul made the revolutionary breakthrough in his missionary praxis to a flexible resurrection ethic in Antioch, which took place in late 36 or early 37 CE. It was this breakthrough that opened up his ability

nity formation, especially in new ways that may shock and disrupt, can only benefit from further prophetic insight as well. This office is much neglected in the modern church (as, arguably, are all the more overtly charismatic roles in many traditions—while in others they are uncritically reified!). But God builds his community on a foundation of apostles and (then) prophets for a reason.

With this final insight in place, we are ready to face some of the deep challenges posed to the church by Paul's commitment to ethical navigation and ecclesial diversification—challenges that the church has not always handled well. But if we can recover some of this dynamism as we move from Paul to the Pauline, we will be able to face these challenges in highly constructive ways as they arise again in our own day.

Theses

- ‣ Ethical behavior derives from communion with God, whose nature is personal and therefore relational.
- ‣ A relational God and relationships with God are characterized by communication and, in the case of human beings, talking.
- ‣ Behavior within these relationships can often be shaped by commands, which might be better termed requests.
- ‣ When God commands/requests, we ought of course to obey.
- ‣ These commands/requests can, like everything else, be mediated through people around us.
- ‣ Divine commands or requests can be highly specific respecting the particularity of the recipient(s), a good thing because the details of their situations are always different from other situations. (This factor affirms an insight in "situation ethics," without endorsing that approach completely.)
- ‣ Commands/requests can be issued in diverse situations both reflecting and further creating diverse communities.
- ‣ Diverse commands/requests might also generate different activities and engagements by Jesus's followers, even within the same complex situation. This possibility liberates us from a certain sort of stultifying conformity, as well as from judging the appropriateness of (some of) the activities of others.

---

to enter different social spaces and to make strange friendships, although it was a very shocking innovation. Presumably then this journey confirmed the viability of that praxis despite the bodily struggles he was enduring.

▸ Ethics in the church needs both the training and approach of a virtue ethic and an openness to divine requests and commands. These two broad approaches complement one another. Training creates the capacity to hear specific commands/requests and to obey. Obedience results in further growth in virtue.

▸ Training, as noted earlier at length, takes place in a tradition—a body of teachings and practices taught and passed on. The church's tradition is primarily bound up with language.

▸ A key part of a tradition is Scripture. The Scriptures are the community's principal resource for language.

▸ We ought, however, to internalize them, and not merely to read them. We should also learn where to find texts and words. They must become part of our language and our thinking.

▸ To be a divine command or request, however, scriptural language must also be taken up and spoken by God.

▸ This inspiration results in "traditioned innovation," which is to say in new, creative uses of Scripture.

▸ It follows that Scripture can be read in a number of different ways, for example, literally, allegorically, tropologically/morally, and anagogically/eschatologically. Church tradition provides many examples of these different types of reading, as does Paul himself, for example, in 1 Cor 10:1–14. Such usage is diverse and creative (productive, in Gadamer's terminology).

▸ The divine appropriation of Scripture and of scriptural language will still need to be recognized or discerned, however, which is assisted by the use of theological and spiritual disciplines.

▸ Scripture can also be used without God's involvement, by the Flesh and/or at the behest of evil powers.

▸ When it is used in this way, it "kills," as Paul puts it.

▸ Paul probably learned about this evil use of Scripture when the revelation of Jesus to him near Damascus revealed his previous persecution of Jesus's followers to be evil. He doubtless cited Scripture in support of that activity, and this was now shown to be evil as well.

▸ Similarly, the Scriptures cannot be used aright through mere interpretative technique, which can lapse into foundationalism, and at this moment into complete and dangerous error.

▸ We must use theological discernment when evaluating when some use of Scripture is being offered as a command/request (i.e., a word of God), matching what is being said with what we already know about God as definitively revealed through Jesus.

> ‣ We can use secondary tests as well—the vulnerable character of the speaker, and prayer and other spiritual practices.
> ‣ The prophetic dimension of apostolicity and the prophets are helpful at these moments as well.

Key Scriptural References

Commands to and from Paul can be found throughout his letters, especially in the more practical sections occurring near the beginnings and the endings, which we tend to skip. A nice example of a specific divine request/command is Titus's eagerness to undertake a second visit to Corinth and to encourage the gathering of the collection; see 2 Cor 8:16–17.

Second Corinthians 10:5 and Phil 4:6 speak of the importance of every thought recognizing and obeying God acting in Jesus.

Paul's understanding of Scripture, used positively and in the Spirit, is noted pithily in 2 Cor 1:20, which points to the centrality of Jesus. See also Rom 15:3–4, which advocates it slightly more broadly. Similarly, 1 Cor 9:21 and Gal 6:2 both speak (probably!) of the Torah or teaching that is Jesus. First Thessalonians 2:13 is analogous but programmatic, that is, with the Spirit taking up and using human words. (First Corinthians 2 elaborates on this position much more fully.)

First Corinthians 10:1–14 is nice example of "traditioned innovation" when Scripture is used.

Romans 5:12–14; 7:7–25; 1 Cor 15:54–56; 2 Cor 3; and Gal 5:2–4 point to a converse, evil use of Scripture, when it takes place in the Flesh and under the influence of evil powers.

The handmade nature of Scripture is also evident especially in Col 2:14.

Prophets are noted programmatically in Eph 4:11 (and see also 2:20 and 3:5) and within broader discussions of community leadership in Rom 12:3–8; 1 Cor 11:4–6; 12; 13:1–3; 14; and 1 Thess 5:19–22.

Key Reading

Barth defines "law" perceptively in terms of "command," and he unfolds it—as he ought to—out of the gospel and as part of the gospel. His position is well summarized by Eberhard Busch in chapter 5 of part 2 in *The Great Passion* (especially toward the end of this analysis).

Hauerwas's essays on the importance of language and of learning "to talk right" are superb; see his "Speaking Christian" and "Why 'The Way Words Run' Matters."

John Webster's essay on Scripture cited below is also excellent.

Traditioned innovation is explored briefly but profoundly in a series of short essays by Kavin Rowe in *Faith and Leadership* (the online publication of LEADD: see http://leadership.divinity.duke.edu/).

Further Reading

Barth's basic approach to ethics is articulated in many places through the *Dogmatics* in dribs and drabs, but most extensively in III/4 (§§52–56, ch. 12, "The Command of God the Creator"). II/2 also makes an important extended statement in §§36–39 (ch. 8, "The Command of God").

A lucid primer on command ethics in general—but one that ought to be controlled by Barth's perspective—is Mouw's *The God Who Commands*.

One helpful aspect of this more Reformed, as against Lutheran, approach to the "law" as command and ethic is its obvious connection with Jewish accounts of the "law," spoken of as Torah, in terms of the same—a sacred set of instructions and commands. See in this relation two elegant essays by W. D. Davies below.

I have nodded briefly toward a particular account of Scripture here. It is summarized with great insight by John Webster in his essay "Resurrection and Scripture." (That account is not so clear in his book *Holy Scripture*.)

The resulting, more productive (to use Gadamer's word) or creative deployments from the text, as against merely reproductive deployments, are helpfully illuminated by de Lubac's analyses of the uses of the Scriptures by the fathers, which began with his famous description of Origen. What a relief it is to return to the way Scripture has been used by the church, as against the way the modern academy tells us it must be analyzed (and hence principally by the modern academy of course)!

Malpas is a useful introduction to Gadamer. Steinmetz has written a charming essay puckishly asserting the superiority of what he calls "precritical" exegesis to modern, historical-critical reading. His softer point is well made that the Reformers utilized what I am calling productive readings here, as they had to, and as church leaders have always had to.

A delightful modern variation on this approach is Sam Wells's *Improvisation*. Modern improvisation involves the careful learning of scripts, roles, and lines but then deploys these elements in new performances, undertaken without rehearsal, and often foregrounding humor. Similarly, comic performances, apparently unscripted, and certainly responding to audience feedback, are in fact based on the most careful prior learning of a script, *which gives good comics the freedom to move in and out of unscripted moments.* Knowledge and use of Scripture should be the same.

Having said this, the positive contributions from a historical-critical reading should not be overlooked. Such readings are attentive to the text, strongly affirm particularity, and resist presentism, which is a pervasive and arguably accelerating difficulty for modern readers of Scripture. It leads to engagement, through responsible reconstruction, with the voices of others. And it leads its practitioners deep into the details of the text. These are all good things. Green analyzes the method's positive and negative contributions helpfully.

Unsurprisingly, Barth's account of Scripture gets under way with some vigor in *CD* I/1. It is then articulated throughout the rest of the *Dogmatics* and not infrequently in his other writings. His account of inspiration as inclusive of the speaker, the text, and the recipient is especially important. He also resists equating the Bible with the actual Word of God, as he should.

This Fundamentalist move—well-intentioned but insufficiently thought through—is problematic because it erects a new, especially deceptive Foundationalism. In this respect, seeking to escape modernity's ethical and epistemological hubris, it recapitulates that hubris. Moreover, to suggest that the text of Scripture in the original autographs possesses inerrancy, being essentially coterminous with the word(s) of God, is to suggest a hypostatic union for these words. And this view is both incoherent, because words are not this stable, existing only as sign-functions (see, among others, Eco) and blasphemous, because only Jesus is fully God and fully part of creation. (Given the interpreted nature of sign-functions, infallibility must be ascribed to the authoritative human interpreter of Scripture as well, and not merely to the recipient, which is blasphemous again, as well as Foundationalist.) The emphasis on historical interpretation is also a modernizing error that Scripture itself does not bear out; Scripture does not interpret *itself* in univocally historicizing terms. So numerous deep difficulties are apparent in this paradigm.

Richard Hays has a nice account of Paul's uses of Scripture in 1 Cor 10 (which has its difficult side) in *Echoes*, chapter 3 (more generally), and in his commentary on 1 Corinthians, 159–73.

The slavery debate exposes the dark side to the Christian use of Scripture. In addition to the debate collected by Swartley, the essays below by Meeks and

Harrill articulate the different hermeneutics that Christian authors developed in relation to this issue.

Spiritual disciplines are introduced in a delightful way that has shaped my life profoundly by Richard Foster in his instant classic *Celebration of Discipline*.

The chronology used here is argued in several of my studies. See especially "An Anchor for Pauline Chronology," "Inscriptional Attestation," "Beyond the Torah," and *Framing*.

Bibliography

Barth, Karl. *Church Dogmatics*. I/1; II/2; III/4.

Busch, Eberhard. "Exacting Exhortation—Gospel and Law, Ethics." Pages 152–75 in *The Great Passion: An Introduction to Karl Barth's Theology*. Translated by Geoffrey Bromiley. Grand Rapids: Eerdmans, 2004.

Campbell, Douglas A. "An Anchor for Pauline Chronology: Paul's Flight from 'The Ethnarch of King Aretas' 2 Cor 11:32–33." *JBL* 121 (2002): 279–302.

———. "Beyond the Torah at Antioch: The Probable Locus for Paul's Radical Transition." *JSPL* 4, no. 2 (2014): 187–214.

———. *Framing Paul: An Epistolary Biography*. Grand Rapids: Eerdmans, 2014.

———. "Inscriptional Attestation to Sergius Paul[l]us (Acts 13.6–12) and the Implications for Pauline Chronology." *JTS* 56 (2005): 1–29.

Davies, W. D. "Law in First-Century Judaism" and "Reflections on Tradition: The 'Abot Revisited." Pages 3–48 in *Jewish and Pauline Studies*. London: SPCK, 1984.

Eco, Umberto. *A Theory of Semiotics*. Bloomington: Indiana University Press, 1976.

Foster, Richard. *Celebration of Discipline: The Path to Spiritual Growth*. San Francisco: HarperCollins, 1978.

Gadamer, Hans-Georg. *Truth and Method*. Translated by William Glen-Doepel. London: Sheed & Ward, 1975.

Green, Joel B., ed. *Hearing the New Testament: Strategies for Interpretation*. Grand Rapids: Eerdmans, 2010.

Harrill, J. Albert. "The Use of the New Testament in the American Slave Controversy: A Case History in the Hermeneutical Tension between Biblical Criticism and Christian Moral Debate." *Religion and American Culture* 10 (2000): 149–86.

Hauerwas, Stanley. "Speaking Christian: A Commencement Address." Pages 84–93 in *Working with Words: On Learning to Speak Christian*. Eugene, OR: Cascade Books, 2011.

————. *Unleashing the Scripture: Freeing the Bible from Captivity to America.* Nashville: Abingdon, 1993.

————. "Why 'The Way Words Run' Matters: Reflections on Becoming a 'Major Biblical Scholar.'" Pages 94–112 in *Working with Words.*

————. *With the Grain of the Universe: The Church's Witness and Natural Theology: Being the Gifford Lectures Delivered at the University of St Andrews in 2001.* Grand Rapids: Brazos, 2001.

Hays, Richard B. "Children of Promise." Pages 84–121 in *Echoes of Scripture in the Letters of Paul.* New Haven: Yale University Press, 1989.

————. *First Corinthians.* Interpretation: A Bible Commentary for Teaching and Preaching. Louisville: Westminster John Knox, 2011.

————. *The Moral Vision of the New Testament: Cross, Community, and New Creation; A Contemporary Introduction to New Testament Ethics.* San Francisco: HarperSanFrancisco, 1996.

————. "On the Rebound: A Response to Critiques of *Echoes of Scripture in the Letters of Paul.*" Pages 163–89 in *The Conversion of the Imagination: Paul as Interpreter of Israel's Scripture.* Grand Rapids: Eerdmans, 2005.

Leadership Education at Duke Divinity (LEADD). *Faith and Leadership.* https://www.faithandleadership.com/category/principles-practice-topics/traditioned-innovation.

Lubac, Henri de. *History and Spirit: The Understanding of Scripture according to Origen.* Translated by Anne Englund Nash and Juvenal Merriel. San Francisco: Ignatius Press, 1950.

Malpas, Jeff. "Hans-Georg Gadamer." *The Stanford Encyclopedia of Philosophy* (Winter 2016 Edition). Edited by Edward N. Zalta. https://plato.stanford.edu/archives/win2016/entries/gadamer/

Meeks, Wayne A. "The 'Haustafeln' and American Slavery: A Hermeneutical Challenge." Pages 245–52 in *Theology and Ethics in Paul and His Interpreters: Essays in Honor of Victor Paul Furnish.* Edited by Eugene H. Lovering Jr. and Jerry L. Sumney. Nashville: Abingdon, 1996.

————. "The Polyphonic Ethics of the Apostle Paul." *Annual of the Society of Christian Ethics* 8 (1988): 17–29.

Mouw, Richard J. *The God Who Commands.* Notre Dame, IN: University of Notre Dame Press, 1990.

Rowe, C. Kavin. "King Jesus." *Faith and Leadership*, January 4, 2010. https://www.faithandleadership.com/king-jesus.

————. "Navigating the Differences in the Gospels." *Faith and Leadership*, August 17, 2009. https://www.faithandleadership.com/navigating-differences-gospels.

————. "The New Testament as an Innovation of the Old." *Faith and Leader-*

ship, October 26, 2009. https://www.faithandleadership.com/new-testament
-innovation-old.

———. "Pentecost as Traditioned Innovation." *Faith and Leadership,* April 27, 2009. https://www.faithandleadership.com/pentecost-traditioned-innovation.

———. "Traditioned Innovation: A Biblical Way of Thinking." *Faith and Leadership*, March 16, 2009. https://www.faithandleadership.com/traditioned -innovation-biblical-way-thinking.

Steinmetz, David. "The Superiority of Pre-Critical Exegesis." *Theology Today* 37 (1980): 27–38.

Swartley, Williard. *Slavery, Sabbath, War, and Women: Case Issues in Biblical Interpretation*. Scottdale, PA: Herald Press, 1983.

Webster, John. "Resurrection and Scripture." Pages 138–55 in *Christology and Scripture: Interdisciplinary Perspectives*. Edited by Andrew T. Lincoln and Angus Paddison. London: T&T Clark, 2008.

Wells, Sam. *Improvisation: The Drama of Christian Ethics*. Grand Rapids: Zondervan, 2004.

CHAPTER 24

Rethinking Creation

A Trap

We need to appreciate at this moment that another trap is yawning before us, one that Paul himself has laid with some of the language he uses. Paul's theology is in fact internally unstable, and we must identify and address this issue if it is to guide us as we attempt to navigate our own modern locations in the terms he has laid down for us.

At the very basis of Paul's thought is salvation understood as a shift from an original creation of Flesh, which is deeply contaminated and corrupted, into a new creation, the world of the Spirit, which is resurrected, glorious, and perfected. We have passed from the old age to the new one, the age to come. As one of his most famous sayings declares, "If someone is in Christ, he is a new creation. The old has departed. Behold, he has become quite new" (2 Cor 5:17). Consequently, we tend to talk about this transition in terms of transcendence. But what is being transcended? A corrupt creation. And what are we entering in Christ? A new, better creation, that is, the age to come. We are leaving behind the template that is Adam and assuming the template that is the risen Jesus. We are leaving one image for the other (1 Cor 15:45–49), having been introduced to our origins in the initial image by the opening chapters of the book of Genesis, which recount the creation of the cosmos. "The first 'person,' Adam, 'became a living soul'; the last Adam [became] a life-giving spirit" (v. 45, the first half of the verse echoing Gen 2:7). But if we remain with this framework and stay with this basic sequence—with this broad underlying story of an old, fleshly, problematic creation being displaced by a new creation—we will eventually get ourselves into all sorts of trouble (and Paul did). So we need to rethink this narrative carefully. Note what happens if we continue to put things in terms of this sequence.

If something from our present created location is terminated and left behind and only certain parts of it are reconstituted and then transformed, there is a sense in which we are working with a Plan A–Plan B sequence, stretching these plans out over everything that exists. The technical theological term for this is "infralapsarianism," literally, the position that views Jesus as the solution to a problem that arrives *after* creation. He is the resolution of an unforeseen or unavoidable difficulty. He is Plan B arriving *after*—"infra" meaning below and hence, metaphorically, later (e.g., in a legal document)—a situation characterized by Plan A, the original creation, which has now been disrupted. And herein lies the problem. This way of putting things implies fairly directly that God is, at bottom, either slightly mean or a little stupid or perhaps both, and he is arguably somewhat incompetent to boot. Infralapsarian thinking inevitably pays these awful theological prices when we press on it.

Perhaps, knowing that Plan A would not work, God still inaugurated it, knowing as well that the real solution would come only later, through Plan B, which is his personally directed plan, in Jesus. But this whole arrangement makes God seem somewhat less than loving. Apologists for this approach sometimes respond by shifting God's character from love to justice, which is a disastrous move, although we will entertain it momentarily because even this change doesn't really save the scenario. This God is not loving, and he isn't really fair or just either![1] Why did even a just God launch Plan A in the first place? It's a one-way trip for most people to a horrid destination, and by virtue of their sinful construction, they have no way of avoiding it, which hardly seems fair. So we have ended up talking about a pretty unattractive God, and certainly one that is hard to square with Jesus.

But the main alternative to God knowing all this and persisting with its unfair and harsh outcomes is that God did not know all this but ended up with an unforeseen mess on his hands, and we certainly don't want to go there. A God who doesn't know where things are going and how they will end up? A God who is trapped in time and in ignorance?! Perish the thought!

1. That is, we can attempt to explain the large number of people created within Plan A, creation, who never get saved by Plan B, offered by the church, on the grounds of just deserts. They knew about God but turned away and therefore merit their harsh fates. However, any sense of debilitation within humanity within Plan A makes the condemnation of people who have no access to Plan B deeply unfair, to note just one problem here, and Paul thinks that this is very much the case; people are made of Flesh and struggle with vast evil powers that oppress them with deception, sin, and death.

One further possibility is that God could not construct creation in any other way. It just had to be this way. Apart from the fact that we have no basis for making this sort of judgment, this scenario makes him seem abysmally limited, which is to say, rather ungodlike again.[2] We sacrifice God's sovereignty and omnipotence once more. Besides all these difficulties, it is apparent, as we saw earlier in chapter 18, that Plan B doesn't work that well.

God's rescue attempt later on is surprisingly unsuccessful. Clearly not everyone is saved by Plan B, barring universalism. But Plan A–Plan B thinkers are not generally universalists, and they don't save God's integrity by uncharacteristically becoming one.[3] So Plan B doesn't fix everything, while many Christian traditions think that it doesn't come close to doing so, and this despite his own personal involvement. Is God this ineffective? His own attempt to right the difficulties in his wonderful plan makes only a minor and partially successful incursion, and this in spite of his arrival in person?! But our difficulties here are not yet over.

The alert will have noticed that a Plan A–Plan B sequence is also a foundationalist account of God's purposes in relation to broader reality. If Jesus is Plan B, then he is necessarily excluded from Plan A, creation, and all the problems of foundationalism are now set in motion, cloaked here with a misguided account of the doctrine of creation.

The account of creation in terms of Plan A must be founded on truth claims made before the arrival of God's particular and definitive revelation that is his Son, and so by way of some sort of natural theology. But as we have already seen, these sorts of claims inevitably prove false. They collapse. The investment of their advocates in this system nevertheless tends, with the best of intentions, to block any recourse to the special revelation that is Jesus. (Advocates of Plan A–Plan B theology usually defend this sequence because they think that their faith depends upon it. This means that the initial character of God, even if it is a little sinister, cannot be redefined by the definitive insight into that character provided by Jesus, who is God in person.) And the further

2. A free-will defense is usually detectable here in terms of a culturally constructed notion of freedom that we have already seen must be rejected.

3. Universalism would come from pressing God's benevolence through to its obvious end point. But if this is the case, then God's initial construction of a cosmos within which such serious problems would be unleashed on humanity in the meantime would be even harder to explain. This position seems deeply inconsistent, if not pernicious, and the defenses that God did not anticipate, or could not avoid, this outcome remain unsatisfactory.

result of this occlusion is a set of sinister social self-ratifications. Truth claims that are self-evident from reflection on nature turn out to be projections of privileged people reflecting on "nature," with a corresponding politics that tends to turn a blind eye to those who are not privileged enough to be doing any such reflecting. Alternatively—or complementarily—the Bible is wrapped in a flag. Disaster upon disaster follows.[4]

In short, it seems that we are in deep trouble if we tell the broad story of God's purposes for the cosmos in this way—with Plan A, which is creation, getting into difficulties, God then responding in person with Jesus as Plan B, although in rather a limited fashion. God's character is called radically into question in various ways, and foundationalism is unleashed, with all its destructive outriders.

But there are only so many ways that we can handle this challenge. And in fact there is one—a steep and narrow pathway threading its way beyond destruction. There are two other solutions, which Paul would say are not really solutions at all. But these fall off on either side of the pathway, so they are like two final abysses that we badly need to avoid. We will discuss them after we have first charted the narrow path through and beyond destruction.

Avoiding the Trap

We are navigating an apparent transition between two states, and there is a right way to do this—one that preserves God's integrity. But how exactly do we solve the conundrum present here, of thinking about a resurrection in Jesus in terms of Plan B, which transcends our current creation, but that seems thereby to necessarily supersede an original flawed Plan A? On one level the solution is very simple. On another, it's mind-bendingly subtle.

4. As I write these words, I have just finished reading an article reporting how evangelicals, which is to say, Bible-believing and diligently church-attending Christians, are generally lining up, to the tune of 94 percent, behind a candidate for the office of president of the United States who is, to mention just one problem, a serial liar, and besides, only dubiously Christian at all. (As I revise these words, I also ponder the fact that this support, finally at the level of 84 percent in the election, was decisive to his victory.) Only the powerful mental fusion that foundationalism effects between Christian thinking and local culture can explain this extraordinary phenomenon. See http://fivethirtyeight.com/features/evangelicals-have-rallied-to -trumps-side/.

Paul's gospel is utterly committed to resurrection and to our incorporation into a transcendent existence in Christ. We have seen this commitment
time and again in what precedes us. And we have learned to think about the
definitive truth of this resurrected location and to resist all manner of se-
duction away from it into foundationalism and the like. But what we need to
grasp now is that we must reconceptualize the very category of creation *itself*
to be faithful to these truths. If we do not do so—if we stay with the standard
sequence that even Paul himself uses (at least from time to time)—we will
ultimately disrupt and undermine his most basic insights. We will lapse back
into a form of foundationalism and thereby will blunt the radical edge of his
gospel. And we turn God into a bumbler or a monster. But how exactly does
this reconceptualization work? Equally important, is it warranted?

We have already laid the groundwork for this insight back in part 1 when
we talked about election. Appropriately, not harshly, understood, this doctrine denotes God's original plan for all that exists—a great gathering into
Trinitarian communion. Hence all we need to do now is to fold our account
of creation into this grasp of God's underlying purpose, which is to say, link
creation to election and then link both of those to Jesus. Fortunately for us,
Paul is quite specific about these connections. He knows well that creation is
ultimately christological (1 Cor 8:6; Col 1:15–17; see also 2 Cor 4:4; Eph 6:12).
This follows directly from his doctrine of God, as it ought to. And this book
has emphasized from the outset that Jesus is Lord, which is to say that Paul
is quite explicit that Jesus is the Lord *through whom all things were made.* He
was the creator:

> the Father,
> from whom all things came
> and for whom we live;
> and there is but one Lord,
> Jesus Christ,
> *through whom all things came*
> and for us there is but one God,
> through whom we live. (1 Cor 8:6)

It actually follows from this text that we now need to rethink creation
christologically, which means, *out of the place that we have been referring to
as transcendent.* Our "future" and "transcendent" dimension *is* our created
dimension in Jesus, the technical theological term for this approach being
"supralapsarianism." Literally this means that Jesus existed for us and with us

before—"supra" meaning above and hence metaphorically before—any problem arrived, and hence necessarily defined God's original created purposes. This is the reality that God intended for us and created us for, and into which he is now pulling us patiently and powerfully after we became entangled with evil through sin.

Creation understood in this dramatic sense will still feel and look transcendent to us, but it is the created purpose that existed for us from "before" the foundation of the world. Creation flows from Jesus and from Jesus's mediation of the triune communion to us. This *is* Plan A. *And there is no Plan B.* Hence, Paul states in a verse we know well but that has possibly just become even more important: "Those whom God foreknew he chose beforehand to be conformed to the image of his Son so that he would be the firstborn among many brothers" (Rom 8:29). This prior christological plan denotes creation, and Paul is quite clearly—at least in his best moments—supralapsarian, as he ought to be, although, with our more accurate grasp of time, we can probably see now how this plan and its purpose are operating on all of space-time "simultaneously," and continuously, as against being lost in a distant past. That is to say, this purpose is present now, and so is perhaps best conceptualized as pressing down on us constantly from above and/or without.

With these realizations we have resolved all the problems associated with Plan A–Plan B sequences without triggering foundationalism. We can now see clearly that God is no longer offering a prior, somewhat rudimentary plan, in "creation," and then intervening, somewhat ineffectively, with another one, enacted in Jesus, named "redemption." He is now offering a single, benevolent, and loving plan all along, and we are being pulled back into that plan through the resurrection and its transcendence of all the things that are currently troubling us. This transcendent life is God's creative plan for us that was established before the foundation of the world, as we saw back at the start of this book when thinking about election. Our election for resurrection life is Plan A. It is just that we are now caught up in the constant attack on Plan A by evil, and within God's struggle to pull us back into his original creative purposes.

Grasping this truth, however, entails reconceptualizing our reading of creation, also rereading and rethinking things that Paul—and not a few others—often call created, but which in fact are now revealed to be anything but. We must scrutinize everything that currently affects and structures us in the light of Jesus and his revelation of the Trinity and ask whether it is warranted and hence worthy of inclusion within what is really creation, which is God's purpose for us from before the foundation of the world. Our incorporation into the divine communion, in the image of the risen Jesus, is the map of our creation. So a lot of things we talk about as "created" are not really created in the correct sense of being our created destiny in Jesus existing from before the foundation of the world. But if this realization makes us nervous, we should recall that Paul does this himself quite overtly at times—and certainly we have just traced a lot of his missional navigations through in such terms. We can see this reconceptualization of what was previously thought to be created in more accurate terms as something less ideal and certainly not created when we consider his treatment of death, which is absolutely central to his thinking about God acting in Jesus.

Reconceptualizing Creation

We tend to think of death as part of the natural order. It seems to be created, and this view appeals to our unaided human reason because it is woven into the warp and woof of the structures that surround us.

Animal species spread and survive demographically by way of natural selection. Death is inextricably intertwined with birth and survival—something admittedly rather clearer since Darwin. (Soil ecosystems are arguably not quite so agonistic, but things still ceaselessly live and die.) Moreover, it is self-evident that *we* eat and survive on a daily basis because other things die, whether animal or vegetable. The death and even decomposition of the living make other living possible. And some entities (i.e., predators) depend on the ceaseless killing of others for life. Consequently, life apart from death is effectively inconceivable to us from our current human viewpoint, and our accounts of creation therefore tend to include it. (Imagine a world without cats and dogs?!) And yet Paul names death, on very solid christological grounds, as God's enemy who must be defeated, and who has been, through the resurrection and ascension of the Son. Death tries to fracture the very being of God, sucking the Son into nothingness and so breaking the relationships and the personhood of the Father and the Spirit, and it is thereby revealed to be the antithesis of the person and of the personal God. It is God's great enemy. Death is not then "natural" or "created" (and Gen 2–3 gives us a clue here). *People are not supposed to die.* They were created to live together eternally, in loving fellowship with God and with one another. It follows directly from Jesus's resurrection, then, that God's creation does not involve death. His original creation of humanity did not include this enemy, whom he went to such lengths to defeat. His creative purposes are purely and only for life. So Paul reconceptualizes his understanding of people in a way that does not involve death, in terms of the glorious resurrected body that does not die, distantly grasping that this is what we were created for, even though he tends to talk about it in terms of transcendence and eschatology (which is to say, as last things, within a second, superior creation).

These observations give us some idea both of the centrality of the reconceptualization of nature and creation that is already taking place within Paul's thinking—because life and death are such central dynamics within his account—and of its difficulty. It is small wonder that Paul himself did not always push through all the implications here. To conceive of our surroundings in ways that exclude death is deep and difficult work. It involves thinking about an entirely new sort of body for starters. Consequently, I don't think that Paul always pushed this new conceptualization as far as he could have, and I don't think we do either. We are all blind in certain, if not in many, respects to this radical reconceptualization of who we really are and what we were made to be. But Paul at least provides us with a direct warrant in his account of death for doing this reconceptualizing work concerning what is truly creation, so we need to continue this work, because frequently it has quite important consequences. In particular, it will directly affect our ethical recommendations within our missional navigations. Things created by God are nonnegotiable ethical *structures*, and Paul himself can issue instructions in these terms. So we need to think hard about how we should speak of all those things that we previously attributed to creation but that now, lacking Trinitarian warrant, we can see were not part of God's original creative purposes. Such structures are more navigable. And another brief consideration of time can help us further here.

Rethinking Time

Time, in Ray Cummings's famous saying noted earlier, is what keeps everything from happening at once, which would be destructive. Life as we know it is quite impossible without this field that prevents the collapse of everything "simultaneously" into nothing. It spreads events out from one another so that structures can unfold in terms of cause and effect. Without this temporal spread there would just be a horrendous big bang and a collapse of all that is into nothingness. "Boom," and all that exists and lives is here and gone in less than an instant—the entire cosmos, galaxies and all! So we certainly need it. But the field of time as it functions around us is still limited and imperfect. We also live in a tyranny of time, with the past behind us, inaccessible forever, and the future stretching anxiously before us, inaccessible again. We exist because we are a point on the field of time spread apart from everything else (although still in relationship with it), but we are also hampered by the fact that we are a point on the field of time.[5] Things can be lost and can fail to arrive. Meanwhile we live on what feels like the crawling knife-edge of the present, where we are effectively imprisoned. So, on the one hand, no life in the terms in which we currently live is possible without the spreading of events out through this field. But on the other hand, time is a harsh master. It confines us experientially in the present, on the razor edge of present existence, with many of the blessings of the past torn painfully away from us, and an uncertain and inaccessible future before us. The field of time is a mixed blessing, then, critical yet flawed.

It is therefore quite helpful to be able to suggest that time as we experience it is not part of God's original created intention. Authentic created time would involve us living in the perfection of time, as God does, neither losing the past tragically and irretrievably nor fearing an inaccessible future. All of time is "present" to God "all the time"! God's time is perfect time, and we are destined to enjoy it with him in due course. That is, time as God created it and enjoys it. But our time is something else—although what?

T. F. Torrance speaks very helpfully at this point of "ordering structures" (which also helpfully opens up our broader discussion to constructive contributions from science, a particular concern of his).[6] He is particularly concerned with the interacting fields of space and time, but there is no reason why these insights cannot be transferred to other structures. Ordering structures are temporary structures that help us in some way, often quite significantly, but they were not part of God's original created intention and so they are neither perfect nor permanent. But they serve to hold chaos in check—they stem the rush of existence into negativity, where evil's negations are sucking it—making life as we know it possible. Hence they are not written into the fabric of the cosmos from the very beginning. They resist the spiral of God's creation into annihilation as it is assaulted by evil. So they are supremely helpful. But they are not perfect and original to God's creation.

5. Strictly speaking, we are a set of space-time coordinates.

6. T. F. Torrance, *Space, Time, and Resurrection*, 185 and elsewhere. Colin Gunton, following Collingwood, speaks of transcendentals, but although the basic move seems right, I am not entirely comfortable with this suggestion. The term is worryingly abstract and vulnerable to Platonic misinterpretation. I don't think for a moment that Gunton himself made these mistakes. But I worry that those less able than he might.

The Story of Chaos

We already know that Paul speaks not infrequently of how the world of the Flesh is dominated by evil powers. We can go on to expand on this domination a little more now in a way that is potentially helpful.

Some scholars have discerned an ancient chaos story in the Jewish Scriptures, something that then becomes a staple of Jewish apocalyptic literature, as the book of Revelation in the Christian Scriptures dramatically emphasizes.[7] In this story, the God of Israel slays the monsters of the deep that plunge reality into disorder and establishes order over the chaotic floodwaters that underlie creation and threaten to overwhelm it. Creation is consequently the result of a victorious battle to draw order from destruction and disorder, and it appears at times like the ark floating on the surface of the flooded earth. It is something of a temporary, emergency measure. In just this sense, the world of the Flesh in Paul is the result of a winning but ongoing battle or contest between God and his supporters and the deadly forces of evil arrayed against him. These powers constantly threaten to pull that which is good into chaos, sin, and destruction. They war on God's plan.

We are given a certain permission here to think about our current fleshly location not so much as a creation that is flawed or broken and so needs healing and repair but as a contested area in which the forces of evil battle the order of God, inflicting damage and disorder on it. Our situation is a massive conflict between God's Trinitarian, life-giving order and evil's suction of this order by way of the powers into chaos and ultimately into annihilation.[8] And within this broader situation, we can now arguably detect various ordering structures that resist the spiral of God's creation into chaos and oblivion as it is attacked by the sheer negativity of evil. They arrest the spiral, then, although they were not necessarily part of God's original and perfect design. They prevent God's good creatures from being pulled into a vast black hole of evil and nothingness.

The field of time functions in the following way: it prevents everything from happening at once, which would simply be an instant annihilation. It holds back this awful collapse. But time as we know it is an imperfect structure

---

7. Gunkel was among the first to emphasize the creation myth of chaos in the OT. See overviews by Batto and Angel noted below. See Job 7:12; Pss 18:4–16; 29:10; 74:12–14; 104:1–4; Isa 13:9–13; 51:9–10; Jer 5:22; Nah 1:3–6; Hab 3:3–15; Rev 12:7–8; and see also T. Mos. 10:1–8a and Pr. Man. 3 (1Q5 26:9–10a).

8. Strictly speaking, the powers themselves are created entities that have been distorted and corrupted too.

that is clearly not part of God's original perfect intention for us either. God's experience of time is very different from ours. So time as we are structured by it performs an important "temporary" role, usefully but imperfectly arresting the further disintegration of what is until the "time" when all that is, is completely and perfectly reconstituted in a way that includes temporal perfection. Time as we know it was not created, then, but it is an interim ordering structure, upheld by God.

Now this account sounds plausible enough on theological grounds. We are surrounded and formed by temporary ordering structures that arrest our spiral into chaos and death. We often think of these as part of creation, and certainly God is involved with them, but they are not part of God's original perfect creation. They are temporary and provisional forms. But did Paul ever actually think in this way, apart from his radical reconceptualization of death as God's enemy?

Actually, there is some further warrant in his writings, at least arguably, for important entities and structures previously thought to be essential being reevaluated and reconceptualized in the light of Jesus, with the result that they remain important but are also subordinated as temporary ordering structures.

Interim Arrangements

In Gal 3:6–25—which we will expound in close connection with Rom 4—Paul ties various narrative strands together into an overarching story of salvation. Primarily, he wants to suggest that his unexpectedly inclusive gospel is in continuity with the origins of Israel in the call and life of Abraham. He argues for this continuity first by emphasizing how Abraham received life from the dead in the miraculous conception and birth of Isaac, going on to suggest that Israel will be consummated in the age to come with resurrection as well—with life from the dead. As a result of this, the famous promises made to Abraham long ago concerning land and seed can now be seen to be fulfilled in the resurrection of Jesus and his inauguration of the age to come. This is a whole new world, hence land with a capital "L" we might say, and one populated with a vast number of people who were technically Abraham's descendants, hence "seed" with a capital "S."[9] Paul goes on to argue, further, that the blessing to Abraham—not the promise, which we have just talked about—concerned the inclusion of pagans within this life. "All the nations

9. See also Rom 4:13.

will be blessed through you, the father of many nations," the Scripture says, as it denotes the gift to Abraham of his new name, which means just this (Gal 3:8 quoting Gen 12:3/18:18). So the pagan mission was always part of God's plan as well.

With this overarching story in place—a story apparent only in retrospect—Paul makes a secondary narrative move. The gift of the Torah, through Moses, does not alter this overarching arrangement, which basically "bookends" it, he suggests. Torah comes in the interlude between the time of Abraham and the coming of the promised seed, through whom the promise of life is fulfilled for everyone. And Moses did come in between these two figures. But Paul now suggests that, in view of this position, the Torah is shown to be an inferior, interim arrangement that confined Israel and "locked it up," "guarding" it until its age of majority was reached with the coming of Jesus (Gal 3:22–23). It is not bad (unless, that is, it is hijacked by sinful lusts), but neither is it utterly definitive for Israel, and so it is certainly not binding on pagans who are converting and entering the promised land that is the age to come. We see this limitation especially clearly from the fact that it could not bring life from the dead, the thing originally promised to Abraham and now effected by Jesus (3:21b).

Paul is obviously thinking here in terms of linear time. Abraham received promises, which are fulfilled much later, when Jesus comes, dies, and is resurrected. In between these two points on the time line, the Torah comes through Moses. Paul's key claim is that the patriarchal and messianic story enfolds and dominates the nomistic story, and the linear temporality conveys this notion nicely. The Mosaic dispensation is an interim arrangement. It is a holding measure. But as a result it also functions as an interim structure *ontologically*. Through its instruction and organization, it brings order to a situation that otherwise threatens to spill further into chaos. It is good and helpful, then, but it is not a part of God's elected created order, which is resurrection and eternal communion, promised to the patriarch and delivered through Jesus.[10]

Arguably, then, we are warranted by Paul here to consider those things that lie all around us in nature and society that we might previously have defined as created and perfect and ask whether they are instead imperfect but gracious interim arrangements that order our current existence and, like the

10. Strictly speaking, I am utilizing the semantic resource within this discussion of Torah of "interim-ness." I would not want to press this into a complete account of the Torah in Paul.

Jewish Torah, try to forestall any further spiral into decay and death. This is what we now know that the field of time is, along with, to a certain extent, the interim arrangement of the Torah. (We won't, after all, need regulations about food and time and sexual activity in the age to come.) And we have already reevaluated death. So clearly a great deal that is threaded through our current existence needs this scrutiny.

In short, if we are to avoid unleashing a spectrum of distortions and problems within Paul's thinking at the moment when we speak of eschatology and its transcendence of the imperfect state before it, we must follow Paul's lead in certain key respects and rethink creation christologically, and so, if necessary, against some of Paul's own explicit statements. The structures of the new, resurrected creation are in fact the indelible structures of creation, period; these are the same thing. And other things that we might previously have thought of as created are in fact temporary ordering structures and not part of God's enduring, perfect creation at all.

This programmatic reevaluation will involve some radical reconceptualizations on our part, but the repositioning of death by Paul has already pushed us in this direction, and it is closely followed by his radical instructions regarding food, clothing, ethnicity, and time. We tend to regard these things as "natural" and as part of our creation, but in theological terms, strictly speaking, they are not. They are interim ordering structures, as his treatment of the Mosaic Torah in Gal 3 also suggests.[11] It was Paul's grasp of these particular realities, however partial, that justified his original pagan mission, with all its distinctive inclusiveness and ethical variation. So it is a rather important move. Without the legitimacy of transcendence, Paul's suggestion that converts from paganism need not convert to Judaism is actually false! It is the transcendence of this location that makes this further position both legitimate and intelligible, while careful reflection suggests that, with due qualification, it is.

Assuming we have grasped all this, then, it is time to consider where other interpreters have arguably failed to grasp the problem, along with its appropriate resolution, and have advocated approaches that end up—with the best of intentions—undermining Paul's insights and gospel at a very fundamental level. Once again, it is so easy—and so destructive—to lose our way.

---

11. It might also be helpful to maintain the insights of the earlier chapter on time, namely, that these structures are not actually positioned on a time line for a limited period but exist within a space-time continuum, which is in its entirety subjected, on the one hand, to the pressures of the divine communion and, on the other, to negation by the powers and their evil "suction" of all that is into nothingness.

The Gnostic Abyss

There are generally two ways in which one can drive off a road: to the left or to the right. And so there seem to be two ways in which we can fall off the sides of the steep and narrow path that is appropriate Pauline thinking about creation. The first plunge that can take place, off to the left, we might say, is into the abyss of Gnosticism, although by now we have been identifying and avoiding this danger for some time.

As we already know, Gnostics press the transcendent aspect of Paul's gospel into an outright dualism that purports to leave our bodies behind. It is as if Christians have entered the new age completely (which is, in one sense, true; Jesus has, and we are connected to him and to the fullness of the Spirit here and now), by abandoning the present one fully (which is false). The *simultaneity* of Paul's thinking is lost, along with its emphasis on *embodiment*. A soul or spirit is all that matters, and as a result, ethics is eviscerated, which is the real problem. This dangerous exaggeration can be exposed and resisted, however, by holding on to certain key theological truths, most notably, to the incarnation, with its full affirmation of embodiment, along with every detail and tiny corner of our current lives, life's transience and inadequacy notwithstanding. (Detecting the non sequitur often at work in Gnosticism is also helpful—that is, the false conclusion that things that are transitory are unimportant.)

Gnosticism is a major theological problem—a perennial snare—and a particular temptation for Pauline interpreters. His claims about transcendence, which do overstep the mark a little at times in their rhetorical enthusiasm, make him vulnerable here (although, to reiterate, he is vulnerable rather than culpable). So the detection and refutation of Gnosticism are important, which is why it was identified back in part 1 and refuted there, this riposte being reinforced repeatedly in subsequent parts of the book that have emphasized bodiliness. Hence I suspect that we can press on now quickly, confident that Gnosticism has been laid to rest. We can see the abyss of Gnosticism to the left of the path, close by, but we know well to drive parallel to it and not into it. We must turn, however, to consider more carefully the second abyss that awaits the unwary to the right, an abyss I sometimes call Tertullianism. We have not been in a position until now to talk about this complementary, and equally dangerous, pitfall.

The Abyss of Tertullianism

Not infrequently, scholars choose a different way of responding to the challenges of Gnosticism from the orthodox christological defense I have just made. Appropriately concerned by Gnosticism's destructiveness, whether in legalistic asceticism or in libertine profligacy, they respond strongly; however, their strategy involves plunging into the abyss on the other side of the pathway. Overwhelmed by anxiety, we might say, they rush away from the abyss on the left and fall into the abyss on the right. The response to Marcion by Tertullian, at least at times, illustrates this tendency nicely.

We know Marcion only through his critics, and they were harsh, so we need to be a little cautious here, but basically, we are on reasonably safe ground supposing that Marcion had a problem with both Jews and the God of the Jews, and consequently with the Jewish Scriptures. He could detect only a vengeful God in this whole situation over against a fundamentally benevolent God revealed by Jesus—and he was not the last person to have this struggle. His solution, however, was rather too drastic. He suggested that this conundrum was caused by the presence of two gods. So he sliced the Jewish Scriptures off from the front of the Christian Scriptures (which were then most probably named by him the New Testament!) and purged them editorially of any connections with their predecessors; these false linkages, so he claimed, had been introduced by the evil retributive lesser god and his unattractive Jewish followers. The result was the relegation of creation and Israel to the rule of another god, in an essentially Gnostic move.

The church reacted powerfully against this radical step, and quite understandably. It realized viscerally that the God of Jesus Christ was irreducibly compromised if either creation or the concrete history of Israel was denied and jettisoned. *Quelle horreur!* But cogent answers to major problems seldom spring directly from anxiety.

Tertullian for much of the time (and he is, admittedly, more complex and constructive than this short summary will suggest) counters Marcion by affirming creation and Israel "up front." This is also a standard response by many subsequently to Gnostic anxieties, and hence the relevance of considering this particular debate here. That which Marcion abandons, Tertullian simply emphasizes, with copious evidence of the importance of creation and of Israel from parts of the Christian Scripture that Marcion himself affirms as well, that is, from Luke's gospel and Paul. This response does catch Marcion neatly in a Socratic move, although Tertullian also draws on all the Christian writings in a way that Marcion doesn't. But in his enthusiasm Tertullian sometimes detaches creation and Israel from the retrospective grounding in Christ that we have previously spent a lot of time detailing. Hence, he often loses a christological center to his accounts.[12] He simply starts his defense of Christian orthodoxy by affirming God as the self-evident creator and judge of the world. And the result is a particular anti-Marcionite program that has a lot of problems. In the name of combatting heresy it lapses into heresy.

Marcion (and the Gnostics)

Creation and Israel and the Jews: another inferior nasty god made them	Jesus and the Gospel: our God endorses them

Tertullian's reversal

Creation and Israel and the Jews: our God made them, self-evidently	Jesus and the Gospel: our God endorses them too, later

If we affirm God as the creator, along with his creation, prior to the coming of Christ in every sense, then we endorse infralapsarianism, and we fall back into Plan A–Plan B thinking, along with all the problems unleashed by that approach. But infralapsarianism is also a particular variation on foundationalism, and so this strategy unleashes all the additional problems of that approach, undercutting Paul's gospel at the most fundamental level. In particular, Paul's all-important emphases on transcendence are lost. So clearly by this point the cure is worse than the disease.

It is a supreme irony that by doing so, that is, by appealing to an infralapsarian foundationalism like Tertullian's in the name of avoiding Marcionism and the like, interpreters simply create a functional Marcionism of their own, this being one of T. F. Torrance's telling observations. Areas of "creation" have been removed by this approach from christological influence and hence from his lordship. And at this moment, God has been effectively bifurcated into separate spheres of operation, thereby threatening to fracture his very being. God is what he does and how he acts, so to endorse a great zone of operation, "creation," which is separate from Jesus's zone of operation, in redemption, is effectively to separate the creator God from the redeemer God. The God in control of creation is not the God of Jesus Christ, *which was*

---

12. I would emphasize that this is not always the case, and arguably these moments only constitute lapses in an otherwise Christocentric program.

Marcion's basic error. The Father is now effectively separate from the Son, as well as being rather larger and more influential. Hence the God acting here is no longer one—a collapse into the deepest heresy.[13]

It is vital, then, to stay on the steep and narrow pathway and to avoid falling either to the left or to the right into the abysses that flank the path on both sides. In fleeing from Marcionism and Gnosticism on the left, however, we must not run in fright into the abyss of Tertullianism on the right. That gorge is even harder to climb out of once we have fallen into it—and in large measure because everyone in it is hunkered down, thinking that they have to stay there to avoid Marcionism! As we put it earlier, we should not flee from the Marcionite lion only to be bitten by the foundationalist snake.[14]

However, if the correct way of conceptualizing creation has been grasped, in the light of Jesus, who is himself the creator, and if we have begun to learn how to reconceptualize structures in our surrounding locations in turn (i.e., when they lack appropriate Trinitarian warrant) as ordering structures rather than as indelible parts of creation—*and* if we have grasped how this approach, correctly prosecuted, is adamantly opposed to any form of Gnosticism—we are ready to address the further challenges that arise as Paul's missionary work, and the work of those like him, spreads into diversity. This diversity will be labeled heretical by those who are uncomfortable with it—it is violating God's created canons and ordinances—and hence the importance of knowing exactly where the heresy within this conversation lies. If the charges are coming from people cowering in the Tertullian ditch, there is nothing to fear. It is those fearful traditionalists who are in fact caught up in a heretical tangle.

---

13. A reprise of Alasdair Heron's elegant essay might be in order at this point; see ch. 1.

14. It is even more sobering to consider the fact that some Protestants seem to be able to occupy both ditches at the same time. I am thinking here of the sort of Protestantism exemplified by Douglas Hudgins. See the insightful analysis of his "gospel" by Charles Marsh. Hudgins was able to deploy a highly spiritualized, functionally Gnostic gospel to overlook the deformations of Jim Crow in the South and thereby leave an order ostensibly ratified by creation in place—the worst of both worlds. (My thanks to Curtis Freeman for this reference.)

Theses

- Paul argues frequently in terms of resurrection and our entrance, in some sense, into the age to come, and hence presupposes some notion of transcendence.
- The whole establishment of Christianity as distinct—although not separate—from Judaism is founded upon these claims.
- But this transcendence places a question mark over God's character if salvation is narrated as a sequence of progression between what seems to be a Plan A, creation, and Plan B, its transcendent redemption—an "infralapsarian" account.
- If God was originally committed to a Plan A–Plan B sequence, then he seems to be either unaccountably harsh (because Plan A fails, and possibly much of Plan B as well) or limited in knowledge or capacity (because he did not know that Plan A would fail, and fail so badly, or because he simply could not effect one that would work). This is also a foundationalist narrative.
- The solution to these conundrums is the realization that what we often refer to as Plan B is in fact God's creative plan and our original destiny. It is Plan A, and there is no Plan B, only a way of bringing Plan A back on track as it is assaulted by God's enemies—a "supralapsarianism" account. Our election for resurrection in Jesus is Plan A.
- However, what we previously often took to be "creation" must now be rethought in terms of transcendence. Only that which possesses Trinitarian warrant and christological attestation is in fact creation. Plan A is creation.
- Other structures frequently classified as created are not, and are in fact "interim ordering arrangements."
- Paul provides scriptural warrant for this reclassification as death is reclassified by him as unnatural and not part of God's created design in the light of the death and resurrection of Christ, despite its appearing to be natural, woven into the warp and woof of our current lives, operating there, to a degree, as an ordering structure.
- The reconceptualization of time undertaken in chapter 7 also provides an example of this reclassification. Time as we experience it is not perfect and created but an ordering structure that prevents the spiral of the cosmos deeper into chaos and disorder, and ultimately into nothingness.
- The biblical motifs of God's battle against chaos and the powers can be interpreted in terms of evil attacking God's good purpose and being held in check by ordering structures.

- Paul provides further scriptural warrant for this reconceptualization of created things as ordering structures in his treatment in Gal 3:19–25 of Torah as an interim structure. There it holds things in check, imperfectly, as the fulfillment of the promise of resurrection made originally to Abraham is awaited.
- An immediate and significant challenge arises at this moment, namely, whether this account is vulnerable to Gnosticism, which endorses a dangerous separation between the present body and a realm of spirit. This worldview tends to unleash either libertinism or horrific asceticism.
- The incarnation suggests directly, however, that God takes our present fleshly situation with complete seriousness in all its fullness and particularities. His lordship suggests the same, as do the many concrete activities undertaken by the church. That something temporary does not matter ethically is also a straightforward non sequitur. (The heresy of Gnosticism has been repeatedly refuted in previous chapters.)
- Those afraid of Gnosticism sometimes lapse into an opposite and even more serious error—Tertullianism, which posits an unchangeable creation prior to the arrival of the gospel, thereby ostensibly guaranteeing its ongoing presence, along with Israel, within Christian thinking.
- This is a grave error. It is actually to reintroduce foundationalism.
- Tertullianism also relaunches all the problems of Plan A–Plan B schemas, that is, the problems of infralapsarianism.
- Hence it is also—highly ironically—to introduce a functional Marcionism, with large parts of "nature" or "creation" taken away from the direct influence of Christ, who as Lord *is* the creator.
- It thereby subverts Paul's most basic theological commitments to revelation and its entailments, and so it is best recognized and avoided as even more destructive to Paul's gospel than Gnosticism. The cure here is worse than the disease.

Key Scriptural References

That Paul is committed to a resurrected and hence transcendent state solving our problems should be obvious by now. One of his most famous and compact assertions of this solution is Gal 3:28.

The problem of a Plan A–Plan B sequence, understanding Jesus in infralapsarian terms, is nicely posed by 2 Cor 5:17. A resurrected state of spirit in the new creation transcends the old creation, made of flesh. The story of Adam, both the first and the last, is stated in 1 Cor 15:45.

When we reorient our understanding of God's original creative purposes, election texts return to prominence, especially Rom 8:29. They should be supported by texts explicitly articulating the Son's role in creation, such as 1 Cor 8:6 and Col 1:15–17.

The negativity and inappropriateness of death are apparent in Rom 5:12–21 and 8:31–39. An underlying story of our current location as a battle or contest between God and the forces of disorder and chaos is apparent here as well. See also 2 Cor 10:3–6 and Eph 6:11–13.

The account of the Torah as an interim measure designed to hold chaos in check is in Gal 3:19–25.

Paul's response to proto-Gnosticism is most apparent in much of 1 Corinthians. Chapter 15 is particularly significant, but his challenge to sexual libertinism in 6:12–20 is also overtly embodied.

Key Reading

The supralapsarian account of creation that I am utilizing here is described in short studies by Wirzba and Van Driel, the latter in conversation with Pauline scholarship by way of Wright and Martyn.

Further Reading

Barth's account of creation is developed at length in part 3 of *CD*, but he constantly derives his claims about creation throughout all the *Dogmatics* from Christology. There are admittedly one or two famous lapses, most obviously in relation to gender. (This topic is discussed in detail shortly.) We have already touched on the correlative understanding of evil in terms of negation, which is developed by Barth in III/3, §50. Barth's account of the tyranny of time is superb; see III/2, §47.

An intriguing account of creation in terms of Coleridge's transcendentals is supplied by Colin Gunton in *The One, the Three, and the Many*. But I find more promising the hints supplied by T. F. Torrance in *Space, Time, and Resurrection*.

Van Driel's book-length study develops a supralapsarian account of creation in more depth.

A rich historical overview of the tradition is provided by Blowers. In-fra- and supralapsarian advocates are charted there, along with other de-bates that perplexed the fathers that we do not need to go into here. Some will recognize how the position I have developed out of Paul in this chapter resonates especially with the views of Irenaeus (and arguably also with Jus-tin, parts of Tertullian, and Melito), Pseudo-Dionysius, and Maximus the Confessor. Blowers argues for a refusal from very early on in the church's reflections by these thinkers to reduce creation to protology, that is, to the doctrine of origins, and a complementary determination to think the issues through with ultimate reference to Christ as the creator (67–100). The result for them is often an emphasis on "recapitulation" (Gk. *anakephalaiōsis*; see Eph 1:10).

The presence of a story of creation from chaos in the OT is debated. Not all scholars currently agree that it is significant, at least for creation, and others worry about its mode, namely, a violent subjugation of chaos and/or its monsters. But its exact origins and mode are not being deployed here. My interest is both simpler and more general—that God's activity can be under-stood over against dramatic cosmic tendencies toward chaos and disorder, which seems widely acknowledged. Akkadian, Babylonian, Canaanite, Hit-tite, and Egyptian sources speaking in this way all seem to have influenced the Bible. This discourse is usefully introduced by chapter 1 of Batto's *In the Beginning* (7–53) and by Angel's short introductory book *Playing with Drag-ons*. The latter draws on his longer scholarly treatment *Chaos and the Son of Man*. (My thanks to Thea Portier-Young for help with these references and this material.)

T. F. Torrance's concern about functional Marcionism remains relevant here.

A quick overview of Gnosticism can be found in Pearson's introductory treatment *Ancient Gnosticism*, especially "What Is Gnosticism?," 7–19. Help-ful remarks are also made by Blowers in *Drama*, 78–90, segueing into an analysis of Irenaeus. It is also important to recall that scholars like Williams dispute the very existence of the category "Gnosticism." I concede that the historical particulars are much more complicated than they are often pre-sented; as a theological error, however, recognition of the category seems unavoidable.

Marsh's essay on Douglas Hudgins is found in *God's Long Summer*, 82–115.

Bibliography

Angel, Andrew R. *Chaos and the Son of Man: The Hebrew Chaoskampf Tradition in the Period 515 BCE to 200 CE.* Library of Second Temple Studies 60. London: T&T Clark, 2006.

———. *Playing with Dragons: Living with Suffering and God.* Eugene, OR: Cascade, 2014.

Barth, Karl. *Church Dogmatics.* III.

Batto, Bernard F. *In the Beginning: Essays on Creation Motifs in the Ancient Near East and the Bible.* Siphrut 9. Winona Lake, IN: Eisenbrauns, 2013.

Blowers, Paul M. *Drama of the Divine Economy: Creator and Creation in Early Christian Theology and Piety.* Oxford: Oxford University Press, 2012.

Griffiths, Paul. *Decreation: The Last Things of All Creatures.* Waco, TX: Baylor University Press, 2014.

Gunton, Colin E. *The One, the Three, and the Many: God, Creation, and the Culture of Modernity; The 1992 Bampton Lectures.* Cambridge: Cambridge University Press, 1993.

Marsh, Charles. *God's Long Summer: Stories of Faith and Civil Rights.* Princeton: Princeton University Press, 1997.

Martyn. J. Louis (Lou). *Galatians: A New Translation, with Introduction and Commentary.* AB 33A. New York: Doubleday, 1997.

———. *Theological Issues in the Letters of Paul.* Edinburgh: T&T Clark, 1997.

Pearson, Birger A. *Ancient Gnosticism: Traditions and Literature.* Minneapolis: Fortress, 2007.

Torrance, Thomas F. *Space, Time, and Resurrection.* Edinburgh: Handsel Press, 1976.

Van Driel, Edwin C. "Climax of the Covenant vs Apocalyptic Invasion: A Theological Analysis of a Contemporary Debate in Pauline Exegesis." *IJST* 17 (2015): 6–25.

———. *Incarnation Anyway: Arguments for Supralapsarian Christology.* Oxford: Oxford University Press, 2008.

Williams, Michael Allen. *Rethinking "Gnosticism": An Argument for Dismantling a Dubious Category.* Princeton: Princeton University Press, 1996.

Wirzba, Norman. "Christian *Theoria Physike*: On Learning to See Creation." *Modern Theology* 32 (2016): 211–30.

Wright, N. T. *Christian Origins and the Question of God.* Vol. 4 (2 vols.): *Paul and the Faithfulness of God.* Minneapolis: Fortress, 2013.

———. *Justification: God's Plan and Paul's Vision.* Downers Grove, IL: InterVarsity Press, 2009.

CHAPTER 25

Navigating Sex and Marriage

From Paul to the Pauline

We now address a set of interrelated questions that Paul had to face frequently, and one that still challenges the church in all sorts of ways—questions about how to define appropriate sexual activity, gender construction, and marriage. This investigation will have the added virtue of showing how a Pauline navigation should unfold.

It begins with Paul's stated views, which must be summarized accurately and fairly. This is done in an explicitly historical—although not historicizing—mode. But the analysis does not stop here, as though this is the end of the matter—far from it. The conversation is just beginning. We then interrogate Paul's stated opinions in the light of his deepest assumptions about God acting in Jesus in an act of *Sachkritik*, or sense-criticism. This is an explicitly theological analysis, reading Paul in terms of Paul. And if this analysis finds his own particular opinions to be inconsistent in any way, we infer from his deepest convictions what a Paul*ine* opinion on the question today should sound like, taking due account of our own locations and what God might be requesting of us now. We move from Paul's position, then, to a Pauline recommendation. This development prompts complementary discussions about how to handle his texts appropriately, which are now Scripture, and how to navigate forward with and through the church in tactical terms. Moreover, these later realizations are as important as the first analytic discoveries because, as Paul has taught us, the how is as important as the what; navigation of an issue is an ethical process every bit as important as the substantive goal of that navigation, and Paul has provided both a theological framework and a powerful exemplification for us in these respects. The result of this entire process should be a compelling and dynamic statement in Pauline terms of

God's calling vis-à-vis this set of issues and their potential resolution for the church today.

We begin, then, with Paul's stated opinions, which occur, as always, in highly circumstantial texts.

The Data in Paul

The clearest formal instructions in Paul about sex, in the sense of appropriate sexual activity, about gender, and about marriage occur in passages scholars have dubbed "the household codes," which can be found in his letters to the "Ephesians" and the Colossians (see Eph 5:21–6:9; Col 3:18–4:1).[1] These instructions mirror codes that were developed many hundreds of years prior to Paul in the Greek intellectual tradition, extending in different subtle variations down to his own time, although Jews like Paul developed them with biblical warrants. One of my favorite examples is in Aristotle's *Politics*. There the sage asks how the ideal city should be structured, and he develops a beautiful if somewhat frightening command-and-control model. If the smartest people— educated Greek men of course—are at the top of a pyramid of social arrangements and everyone else is neatly arranged in strict subordination under them, then the polity should function smoothly, if not with maximum intelligence, much as an army maneuvers successfully when it obeys the orders of a clever general. (Ancients did not put things quite this way; they tended to speak of a body functioning smoothly if all its parts and organs obey its rational head.) Hence the city should be structured relationally, in a stack of vertical binary oppositions. The ancient household begins the stack at the bottom. There, children should obey their parents, wives should obey their husbands, and slaves should obey their owners. (Recall that the ancient household was usually a larger and more diverse grouping than the modern nuclear family.) This pattern covers all eventualities. As these neatly organized households combine like stacking Lego blocks into cities, the ruled should obey their rulers, and humans should obey the gods. Moreover, superior races like the Greeks should

---

1. These instructions are then echoed in various other places in the Apostolic Writings; see 1 Pet 2:11–3:12; 1 Tim 2:1–15; 5:1–2; 6:1–2; Titus 2:1–10; 3:1.The circumstances eliciting Ephesians and Colossians encourage quite a generalized statement from Paul. The former is a programmatic summary. The latter often abbreviates this summary because it was written to a group that had not been personally taught by Paul. For more details, see my *Framing*, ch. 5, 260–338.

conquer and enslave inferior races like the barbarians found to the north of the Black Sea known as Scythians (see Col 3:11). Such muscular but stupid people, Aristotle suggests, make the ideal slaves.

Paul issues instructions in these general terms in Ephesians and Colossians, so at this moment he judges that a particular form or structure should be imposed on his converts, although they probably already shared it to some degree. In his communities of converts wives are to obey their (hopefully loving) husbands, children to obey their parents—a command I have some sympathy for—and slaves are to obey their (hopefully fair) owners.

Later on we will consider the important question of just how to handle these texts constructively, since they so grate against modern Western sensibilities. But for now we simply need to observe that quite a lot that Paul says in 1 Corinthians, in particular, makes sense in terms of this binary scheme, suggesting that it was a significant structure within his broader thinking. However, we need to realize, further, that the basic binary model we see operating in both him and Aristotle is realized socially with a myriad of gender codes—rules and general practices concerning how men or women dress, move, and speak; what social spaces they are allowed to occupy; the roles they undertake appropriately; and so on. We see these codes at work in 1 Corinthians.

In chapter 11 Paul instructs women speaking in the assembly to do so respectfully in relation to their husbands, maintaining appropriate modesty in their dress.

> Every man who prays or prophesies with his head covered
> dishonors his head.
> But every woman who prays or prophesies with her head uncovered
> dishonors her head—
> it is the same as having her head shaved. (11:4–5)

The precise details of the situation are difficult to detect, but it might have involved something like the following. Women in Paul's day were supposed to have neatly gathered hair, the hair of upper-class Roman women being elaborately coiffed. Keeping it braided and pinned up and covered at the top with a head scarf, the *pulla*, which extended down the back of the neck and over the shoulders, signaled due modesty and propriety—although without completely obscuring the glories of an elaborate hairdo if one had the money to afford one. Conversely, exposing the full hairdo, and perhaps also the shoulders and the back of the neck, was socially shameful and even erotically charged. Some of the Corinthian wives seem, nevertheless, to have been gyrating their heads during charismatic worship and causing their head scarves to slip off—think of rockers at a death metal concert. This resulted in the ancient equivalent of woman exposing their breasts during vigorous hymn singing. Furthermore, the resulting disheveled hair was a cultural signal for drunkenness and abandon—the equivalent of women today doing pole dances during worship by the altar. It took people culturally to the wrong place.

Paul tries to take this situation in hand in 1 Cor 11:2–16 by insisting that the male husband is the "head" of his wife, and so she should act respectfully toward him, maintaining due modesty and not embarrassing him during worship, especially by letting her head covering and her hair get out of control. His argument is difficult and much-debated, but perhaps something like the following is going on.

It is fine for men to pray and speak in the worship meeting with uncovered heads, Paul says, because they are, as Gen 1 says, the image and glory of God.[2] Why cover that up?! Let it shine! However, women were created from and for men, Gen 2 says, from the body of the first male. Consequently they function like bodies, which, as everyone knows, need to be covered up! What man wants his body exposed?![3]

It's not a great argument, so Paul intertwines it with something a little different. If women lose their head scarves, it is as if they have shaved their heads—something that is only just achieving cultural acceptability in our own day, and even then still gives people a bit of a fright. But this is still not an especially compelling contention. Moreover, Paul has to concede some good counterarguments—that apart from the first female, everyone else who has been born has come from a woman.[4] By implication, then, should every man be covered up so he doesn't shame his mother? Moreover, neither man nor woman is "separate from one another in the Lord," 1 Cor 11:11 observes. The key relationship here, in other words, is with the one head, Jesus, so, by implication, either we all cover up or we all let it shine.

As his argument begins to spiral, Paul appeals finally to universal practice in the community, and to "nature" dictating something that is simply obvious—short hair for men and long hair for women (1 Cor 11:13–16).[5] "This is

---

2. Gen 1:27, echoed by 1 Cor 11:7.

3. Gen 2:21–23; 1 Cor 12:14–31; see also Eph 5:22–33, especially 5:28–29.

4. "For as woman came from man, so also man is born of woman" (11:12).

5. I am reminded here of the climactic scene from the classic film *Easy Rider* (dir. Dennis Hopper, 1969). As the two protagonists ride through the US South, they are gunned down from their bikes for being long-haired hippies. (They had previously escaped a beating for the same.)

just what we all do," he states a little desperately at the end of this subsection. "If anyone wants to be contentious about this, we have no other practice—nor do the [other] gatherings of God."

In like manner, he states a little later on, in 1 Cor 14, women are not to interrogate male speakers in the communal assembly but are to hold their questions for their husbands at home.

> Women should be quiet in the gatherings.
> They are not allowed to speak out, but must be in submission, as the
>   Torah says.
> If they want to inquire about something,
> they should ask their own husbands at home;
> for it is disgraceful for a woman to speak in the gathering [in this way].
>
> (14:34–35)

Another potential source of disruption during worship is addressed, then, again hopefully to be controlled by the relevant husbands in the room. Women interjecting and interrogating male speakers during a meeting would be disruptive, disrespectful, and shameful.

We can see from all this that when Paul thought about the organization of the community, he thought in binary Hellenistic terms, which is to say that he basically thought like Aristotle. The Christian community was a stack of vertical relationships, one of which was marriage. This was a heterosexual hierarchy in which female wives also obeyed their male husbands. But as in all societies, this simple system was developed by a constellation of coded and deeply embedded practices. Disrupting this model by transgressing some of these gender codes in terms of clothing or public speech shamed the relevant authority figures (i.e., the married men) and was to be stringently avoided.

Now Paul said all this a *long* time ago, so it might seem hard to take some of his instructions seriously now. But I sometimes remind my students that we do in fact still take equivalent gender codes today very seriously—codes that others, two thousand years from now, will doubtless regard as quaint.

Imagine a group of young teenagers from southern states in the United States undertaking a summer beach mission in Europe. They have done the appropriate missionary training and so are fully apprised of the need to contextualize as thoroughly as they can. But what do they do when they arrive on the beaches of Europe and see that their young women must remove their tops? And what sorts of letters would they receive from their parents and pastors back home in Georgia and Texas as pictures of their shapely evangelism begin to spread across Facebook, the chests of only the fortunate shielded by their songbooks? The sensibilities expressed would, I suggest, be strikingly parallel to some of Paul's in 1 Corinthians. This is not to suggest that they would be strongly justified theologically in terms of permanent norms of culture and dress. But they would be understandable. The violation of gender codes tends to elicit strong reactions, especially when male or parental shame is activated, and the Corinthian situation is no exception. (We could add that this is an example not just of the social disruption that results when gender codes are suddenly violated but of the double standard that tends to inform those codes; there is no fuss over bare-chested men, whether in France or in jogging around running tracks in the United States.)

In 1 Corinthians Paul also evidences a commitment to a strong marital boundary around sexual activity. First Corinthians 6 assumes that the binary opposition of a man and a woman norms sexual activity and marriage. Appropriate sex takes place within this relationship, although, as in all cultures, such liaisons should not take place between close relatives, as the outrage of 5:1 signals ("I hear that a man has his father's wife!"). Sexual activity with a member of the same sex and gender-flouting practices like effeminacy are unacceptable for Paul and result in exclusion from the age to come.

> Do you not know that
> the unrighteous will not inherit the kingdom of God?
> Do not deceive yourselves.
> Neither the sexually immoral, idolaters, adulterers,
> the effeminate [*malakoi*, lit. "soft ones"],
> [or] those who have sex with males [*arsenokoitai*, lit. "man-bedders"][6]
> . . . will inherit the kingdom of God." (1 Cor 6:9–10)[7]

Chapter 6 goes on to warn the Corinthian men, quite consistently, that the visiting of prostitutes, presumably of any variety, is wrong. Then in chapter 7 Paul urges some Corinthian males to get married to the virgins they are

---

6. Dale Martin's elegant arguments notwithstanding (*Sex and the Single Savior*, 37–50), this word does look to me like a compound drawing on Lev 18:22 and 20:13.

7. Consequently, although I am not convinced that Paul is personally committed to the categories described in Rom 1:18–32, and hence to the scathing condemnation *in self-evident terms* of same-sex love and relations articulated there in vv. 24 and 26–27, the brief statements in 1 Corinthians suggest that he would have endorsed its heteronormative account of appropriate and implicitly deviant sexual activity and gender construction.

currently pledged to (i.e., engaged to) because this is better than "burning with lust," a state that will doubtless result in something really bad (i.e., visiting a prostitute). It is worth emphasizing that this last stance, inherited from Jewish antecedents, was countercultural in its day in relation to paganism. So here local cultural practices were *not* being affirmed.

As we saw earlier, Greco-Roman society generally operated with the proverbial double standard, and in spades. Women were supposed to be under male control. They were answerable to their fathers until their marriage, then they were answerable to their husbands. They were, furthermore, supposed to be chaste and modest. There were exceptions, like elite Spartan women, who were famously independent, but a double standard was the norm, as it was just up the road from Sparta at Athens. Men were allowed to have sex fairly indiscriminately, as long as they did not humiliate their wives by sleeping with women of similar rank. Certainly they could have constant access to low-status women—or men, if that was preferable—and even to the children of low-status people like slaves, as well as to prostitutes. Paul's insistence on sex within the parameters of heterosexual monogamous marriage, then—his stress on monogamy being implicit rather than overtly stated—was significantly countercultural, paralleling the extraordinary Jewish and Christian rejection of temple culture revolving around statues and images. But certain complications flowing from this stance are now worth quickly noting.

Like all accounts of reality in terms of a simple, clear-cut binary opposition, this one tends to fray as it encounters social realities. Human relationships are far too complicated to fit into neat boxed pairs, and so we see Paul navigating some of these complications in 1 Corinthians.[8]

In chapter 7 Paul addresses mixed marriages between Christians and non-Christians, and he argues boldly, despite the instruction in one strand within the Jesus tradition that the married must not divorce, that this teaching does not apply in these circumstances. His rabbinic training, essentially in religious lawyering, shows through clearly here. The members of such marriages are "called to peace" (v. 15), so they must negotiate the best way forward, perhaps staying together, perhaps separating, and this allowance is interesting.

---

8. A further problem for Paul here that need not hold us up at this moment is his evident command to "stay as you are" when conversion takes place, leading to pressures over time (7:17–24). People tend to transition between these boxes, for example, progressing from childhood through betrothal to marriage. So Paul's static advice concerning these binary categories tends to run into difficulties at Corinth too, most notably, in the case of betrothals.

Marriages between a man and a woman often do not last, so the question of divorce inevitably arises, and we see here that Paul's response is, in certain respects, shockingly flexible. Moreover, we have already seen him urge the betrothed who are burning with passion to marry, although by way of a concession, which is another essentially flexible stipulation. A similar flexibility is evident when he considers the category of the widow, that is, the slightly worrying situation that arose when a woman passed from the control of her father and her husband into a state of relative independence after the death of her spouse. This was not an uncommon phenomenon in the ancient world, with its frequent marriages between women just after (or even just before) puberty and older men who had lost their first wives to events such as childbirth. The older men often then died, leaving their young brides as widows (and this situation might lie behind 5:1–5, 13). Paul briefly urges a sensitive and flexible navigation of this situation (7:39–40). And a final important aspect of Paul's thinking in all this is now coming into view.

When instructing the betrothed, widows, and a curious situation of apparent deliberate asceticism within a marriage (7:1–7), Paul consistently urges the superiority of celibacy. He himself was a celibate, apparently under no compulsion to have sex and hence able to carry on happily in an unmarried state (7:8–9). Consequently, part of the flexibility he counsels in each of these situations derives from his exhortation to adopt this posture if it is possible, although to marry if sexual urges cannot be resisted (7:26–28, 32–35, 37–38). Asceticism or abstinence within a marriage should be temporary and by mutual consent. Those who are beginning to act improperly toward their betrothed should marry them. Widows in a similar situation should marry too. But those who do not need to follow through on a betrothal and those who can remain widowed without slipping into sexual activity, possessing the gift of celibacy, should do so. This state is better—and on a practical level, it probably is.

Celibates can go places and do things that married people struggle to (although this flexibility applies to single adults not called to celibacy as well). They are less encumbered by "the concerns of the world," as he puts it. They do not "need to please a spouse" in addition to pleasing God.[9] Missionary work is hard and dangerous, so celibates have advantages. They are not encumbered by families and their needs. Have you noticed any soldiers on the front lines

9. We can recall here, as noted earlier, that Catholic missionary work in Africa has often been more effective than Protestant efforts because its protagonists have been celibates. This point is made by Paul Johnson in *A History of Christianity* (New York: Simon & Schuster, 1976).

recently who have marched off into action with their spouses and children trailing behind? Do people arrange going into combat in relation to the needs of their children? "This is a really bad area for us to be deployed in just at the moment because we need a good high school next year for our eldest daughter." And so on. Paul has a point, and we will return to it shortly, because its theological implications are so significant.

To summarize our first navigational phase, then, namely, Paul's stated opinions on these issues: when Paul thinks about the social organization of sex and gender in the Christian community, he operates out of a common Hellenistic worldview that arranges society into neat binary oppositions, although it overlaps with biblical opinions. At the base of this system is a monogamous and hierarchical account of marriage, between a man and a woman. This is where sexual activity is appropriate and not elsewhere, in any terms, this being a more countercultural stance for pagans that he enjoins on them if necessary. Outside of this arrangement, one is either single or a celibate and in both cases abstinent. But when this neat schema fails to map complicated social realities—in borderline cases like betrothals, mixed marriages, and widows, and these arise all the time—Paul navigates the situations arising fairly flexibly. And navigating gender codes is usually a complex matter.

It is now time to subject all these issues to theological scrutiny, although we will of course use theology Paul himself supplies. And it is critical now to recall that Paul's fundamental viewpoint on reality is supralapsarian.

Supralapsarianism

As we have just seen, an infralapsarian approach understands salvation as unfolding in a Plan A–Plan B sequence. Plan A, established with Adam, fails, and so Jesus is sent as Plan B to effect a rescue operation, although—a little strangely—this effort is not entirely successful. Those converting and entering the church will be plucked from the fire, but everyone else who resists Plan B will, under the terms of Plan A, be consigned to perdition. Plan A defines the problem, then, to which Plan B is the corresponding solution, and the whole arrangement thinks and works "forward." Stating this (unhealthy) dynamic in slightly different terms: it builds upward from the foundation that is Plan A, *where the contours of creation are defined.*

As a result of this procedure, infralapsarians view heterosexual monogamy as being written into the fabric of creation—into Plan A—and hence as normative and nonnegotiable. Cultural variations and differences here simply cannot be affirmed. Messing with these structures is blurring a "line in the sand" that must not be crossed, partly because any messing with Plan A fouls up the model in its entirety. So those who are not heterosexual are just deviant, and any denial of this judgment will call Christian salvation into question. A great deal of opposition to discussions of nonmajority approaches to sex and gender stems from this underlying stance, and so it is quite understandable.

But we have learned well by now that infralapsarian arguments are deeply flawed, being foundationalist and inherently unstable.[10] The correct approach, and Paul's approach at his best moments, is supralapsarian, which opens up a rather different conversation about sex and gender. It begins with the realization that Jesus is the creator, so his work on our behalf *is* Plan A; Trinitarian communion is God's plan for us, which was established "before the foundation of the world" (Eph 1:4) and is the only form or structure (if these terms are even appropriate) that is nonnegotiable. Hence supralapsarians view the stakes as somewhat lower in the debate over appropriate gender construction and its acceptable sexual expression than infralapsarians do. Moreover, we can enter into a deeper conversation with science. We can ask what our current "location" is, informed by science and other scholarly disciplines—although not limiting what informs us to these insights—and then ask what arrangements enjoy theological warrant. We do not need to assume that what we seem to be now was created this way as God's eternal plan (Plan A), which is consequently indelible. Sex and gender might, rather, be part of an interim ordering structure, and hence malleable and adaptable, if relational concerns demand modifications.

When thinking about all these topics, I have been helpfully informed by anthropologist Helen Fisher's recent work *Anatomy of Love*.[11] Fisher describes three biological systems that link together to keep our species viable and that are universally recognized with some notion of marriage. She identifies the sex drive, what we can call the infatuation system, and the system of attachment. The sex drive is fairly self-explanatory. It is a compelling urge, like urges for water and food. It is a key part of our species' adaptation to survival. The infatuation system is the high associated with falling in love that is analogous to

10. This is not to say that Paul does not on occasion talk like an infralapsarian when discussing gender, but such arguments are not well integrated into his most important convictions and moves, which were rooted in the resurrection and lordship of Christ.

11. Helen Fisher, *Anatomy of Love: A Natural History of Mating, Marriage, and Why We Stray*, rev. ed. (New York: Norton, 2016 [1992]).

other highs caused by drugs. It is associated with a shower of dopamine in the brain, and in the case of some fortunates, can affect a relationship for years. The attachment system is a calmer but still very powerful sense of connection with a partner reinforced by different neurotransmitters—vasopressin and oxyto-cin—and is linked with sexual activity. After sex, lying together in contact—postcoital cuddling—releases these hormones that reinforce attachment. All three systems operate out of the limbic part of the brain, which is commonly viewed as one of the more "primitive," or earlier, components of the brain's development. So we share large parts of these systems with other mammals and even with other species. Fisher argues that all three systems combine to ensure—among other things—the continued viability of our species, which is faced with both common and peculiar challenges.

The individual members of all species living in our cosmos—thinking here of the world Paul denotes as the Flesh—age and die. So ongoing life in the world of the Flesh requires reproduction. Hence, as the Bible well knows, for the human species to survive, males and females need to have sex to-gether, and women need to conceive and to give birth, from which moment the human baby needs to be nurtured and raised through to viability and its ability to procreate and parent in turn. This is a fairly standard scenario for a lot of species occupying the earth, and especially for mammals like us. Fisher observes, however, that of all species, humans face the greatest challenge in terms of "altriciality," that is to say, of the vulnerability of their young.

The huge cranium of the human, with its extraordinarily large brain, must fit through a pelvis narrowed dramatically by a uniquely bipedal gait. So birth must take place very early on in the developmental process, which results in a deeply vulnerable baby who must be nursed, nurtured, and carried *for many years*. Hence we must picture carrying around a baby while gathering and hunting food on the Serengeti Plain with just a few tools and with a pride of hungry lions living four hundred yards away. A woman carrying a child on her hip just might need a spear-wielding man in order to survive the daily round of food-gathering, cooking, and eating. And she needs him *for at least four years*. Children are only remotely viable around the age of four, when they can walk long distances for themselves as against having to be carried, although parenting does not stop then either, as most of us know. Human children must learn enormously complex social codes rooted in language, and they themselves must learn to survive, to procreate, and to parent—things taking at least another ten years, being completed at puberty.

The three systems in the brain that we have just noted are wonderfully adapted to encourage the ongoing success of this complex and demanding life cycle. Fisher opines that they can take place in any sequence but that all three ideally combine in due course to create a bond between parents that leads to the conception and raising of children, despite the length and difficulty of this process. Sex, infatuation, and attachment draw and hold males and females together, result in children, and then contribute to years of parenting together, and even to years of grandparenting. And most people are programmed on a very deep level to seek out such relationships, which are happy when they work well. There is something quite wonderful about sex, conception, and parenting, then, which is so universally recognized in some sort of marriage arrangement—granting that they have their hard as well as their enjoyable aspects. However, they do not seem to be mystical, sacred, or even fundamentally indelible. It is a bit like drinking, then, which involves participation in the water cycle and a functioning digestion system, circulatory system, and kidneys; or eating, which involves participation in systems of food production and involves many of the same organs. The sex-conception-parenting sequence too is just part of fleshly life as we know it, and arguably we can even see much of Paul's advice dimly recognizing these systems.[12] But we can also

12. Paul acknowledges the compulsion of sex that we would now speak of as the sex drive. He uses the term "lusts" (Gk. *epithymiai*), often with a slightly pejorative connotation, because he favors the state of celibacy so strongly over sexual activity: see Rom 1:24 (although this is not in my view directly relevant to Paul's understanding); 6:12; 7:7–8 (much more indicative); 13:14; Gal 5:16, 24; Eph 2:3; 4:22; Col 3:5; 1 Thess 4:5. Philippians 1:23 and 1 Thess 2:17 are positive. But he is quite practical in recognizing the urgency of sexual desires in many people. It is "better to marry than to burn" he observes famously (1 Cor 7:9). Couples, then, should not part in ascetic terms for a long time without mutual consent, and those who are betrothed should marry if they cannot restrain themselves and behave appropriately, as should widows.

The bonding and attachment generated by sexual activity might also be dimly apparent in some of his advice. He notes that married men and women are partly disadvantaged because they are concerned about one another and many related worldly things. This might just be the practical burden of marriage and all its responsibilities; indeed, doubtless it includes this. But it might also extend, a little more positively, to the attachment of married men and women to one another. "A married man is *concerned about* . . . how he can please his wife. . . . A married woman is *concerned about* . . . how she can please her husband"; see 1 Cor 7:33–34, which uses the Greek verb *areskō*, meaning to please, accommodate, give pleasure. And one wonders whether the experience of infatuation does not also lie behind the struggling betrothals that Paul addresses in 7:25–38. Indeed, it would be strange if it didn't lie behind at least some of them. Moreover, an infatuation clearly lies behind the union named in

see him navigating the two main ways in which Fisher sees this arrangement breaking down.

A large minority of people are unfaithful to the monogamous pair bond, although exact percentages are difficult to ascertain. However, males are almost certainly more promiscuous than females.[13] This infidelity can play out in polygamy but more frequently in adultery. Closely related to these practices, many marriages fail, resulting in divorce, these two problems being connected, although not precisely correlated. Marriages don't always fail because of adultery, but that is named by most modern people as a principal cause of marital dissolution.[14] Fisher notes, moreover, that there is a marked statistical tendency for marriages to fail at the four-year mark—the four-year itch we might say—and this time might be significant. Biologically, as we just saw, this is the time when an infant reaches viability, and mothers living the vigorous life of a hunter-gatherer become fertile again. (Research into existing hunter-gatherer societies suggests that breast-feeding, a low-fat diet, and extreme exercise limit fertility sharply up to this time, although they do not curtail it altogether.)

What should we make of all these data in view of the challenges and confusions of our own day? We can begin by asking what a marriage is, and our discussion now needs to take a theological turn, although it will do so in stages.

5:1, although obviously Paul does not approve of that situation. (It is technically incestuous.)

Hence he recognizes these three key processes, which would have operated as vigorously in the brains of those around him as they do in the brains of those surrounding us today, and as they did in the 99 percent of our ancestors, millennia past, who felt a sex drive strongly, along with infatuation for a mate and attachment to a fellow parent. Fisher suggests that 1 percent of the population does not experience a compulsive sex drive.

13. A survey of American sexual behavior in the 1970s by Morton Hunt estimated that 41 percent of men and 25 percent of women had philandered, percentages that did not differ significantly from Kinsey's famous and very large survey in the late 1940s and early 1950s, which recorded the adultery of over a third of men and 26 percent of women (*Anatomy*, 68). Other surveys place the range of unfaithfulness by men between 20 and 40 percent, and for women between 15 and 25 percent, ranges that do not seem to differ significantly cross-culturally, insofar as such things can be ascertained.

14. In modern terms, and especially from a female point of view, adultery can be emotional and social—"coffee cup adultery"—as against physical.

Marriage?

I suggest that we begin our evaluation with the fact of heterosexual and largely monogamous marriage. And I would suggest that this is—to use T. F. Torrance's nice phrase again—an *interim ordering structure* ensuring ongoing (fleshly) life, despite the mortality of individuals. Like time (which is the subject of Torrance's claim), it resists the descent of humanity into annihilation.[15] In spite of the death of the individual, humanity lives on, and so human life as a whole, in this manner, endures. Sex, procreation, and parenting keep us all going in this world. But this structure is not how we were created or what we were created for. We read the parameters of our creation in supralapsarian terms, out of the reality into which we are being resurrected by Jesus, and this reality transcends death, and hence transcends all the interim ordering structures that cope with—but do not defeat—death within the world of the Flesh. Procreation and parenting endure despite death, but they do not pass beyond it or triumph over it like resurrection. Indeed, they are inextricably intertwined with it. Their victory is gained always with bitterness and pain (as the Bible again well knows). Our loved ones die. Women die in childbirth. Children die. The species lives on, but we, in all our wondrous relationality, do not. It is supremely comforting, then, to recall that this is not what God made us for.

From before the foundation of the world we were destined for an unbreakable fellowship of love—one that transcends our existence here in numerous critical ways.

> Those he knew beforehand
> he also appointed beforehand
> to be conformed to the image of his Son,
> so that he might be the firstborn among many "brothers." (Rom 8:29)

This is what we were made for: the delights of Trinitarian communion. And as we are rescued—at great cost—and God's majestic plan is brought back on course, we learn that we will not die. (Hallelujah!) We will not sin. (Hallelujah!) We will live in unbroken fellowship with our community and with our God. (Hallelujah!) But we see at this moment that our resurrected, transcendent existence lies beyond death and so beyond many of our other fleshly parameters as well: beyond ethnicity and race, beyond class and social status, *and beyond*

---

15. See Torrance, *Space, Time, and Resurrection*.

sex, gender, and procreation, and so also beyond marriage. Consequently, Paul says quite correctly in Gal 3:28:

> There is no Jew or pagan [lit. "Greek"],
> no slave or free, no "male and female";
> for you are all one and the same in Christ Jesus.

We know this text well by now, for it summarizes a great deal that is going on in the rest of Paul's writings. This resurrected state is what we were created for. Moreover, we have already assembled much of the data in Paul that point toward this critical position—the transcendence of circumcision in favor of baptism, and of the Jewish calendar, cultus, and Jewish food rules, as well as of death, along with Paul's expectation that that resurrected body will be spiritual. But we have not yet noted how his treatments of sex and gender often make exactly the same move. Nevertheless, numerous clues and statements in Paul point toward the way the resurrected state transcends gender and sex in the way he states explicitly just this once in Gal 3:28.

Women who possess the Spirit transcend the world of the Flesh, with all its gender expectations, *and so speak in the assembly* in prayer, prophecy, tongues, and by direct implication, with inspired teaching, exhortation, discernment, and deliverance. In the midst of its infamous restrictions, people can miss the way that 1 Cor 11 explicitly allows women to pray and to prophesy when Christians meet together. Moreover, they can bring spiritual songs of their own composition to sing (1 Cor 11:2–16; 14; Col 3:16). And Paul himself transcends gender categories in his ministry in the Spirit, suggesting again that the new age for which we have always been destined lies beyond sex and gender. He *gives birth* to the Galatians, and he *suckles* the Thessalonians.[16] The mirror image of this language is women occasionally occupying leadership roles in Paul's communities that would have ordinarily been filled by men. Phoebe was the *patron* and *deacon* of the gathering in Cenchrea (Rom 16:1). Junia was *an apostle*, no less (Rom 16:7). Moreover, Paul's emphasis on celibacy affirms this transcendence directly as well. Those who possess this gift and resulting lifestyle witness to the way that resurrected personhood lies beyond current fleshly structures, which include sex and gender (see 1 Cor 7:25–40; 9:5).[17]

---

16. See especially 1 Thess 2:7 (although see also 1 Cor 3:1–2) and Gal 4:19 (although see also Rom 8:22 and 1 Cor 15:8)—texts first noticed and discussed by Gaventa.

17. The implicit account he supplies of his own masculinity arguably supports this trajectory as well; see the studies by Larson, by Kahl, and by Wilson.

But none of these gender-flouting examples should be remotely surprising. We have already seen at some length how Paul's entire mission to the pagans, with all its shocking departures from Jewish markers, is premised on the entry of his pagan converts directly into the age to come. That reality must transcend race and ethnicity if this approach is to stand, and these are embodied biological forms and structures, at least to some degree. It simply follows that a Pauline mission can sit lightly to the structures of sex and to gender as well.

Given that we have always been destined for a life beyond sex and gender and, further, given that, as I am arguing, there is nothing especially sacred or fixed about their practices and structures, we need to ask now how to navigate them ethically in the world of the Flesh. These structures and sets of practices are not normative, but they are not irrelevant either, which would be Gnostic. We must ask the key ethical question, then: how is the relational reality that is the Trinity, in which we participate, acting on the sex and gender of our locations? What sort of behavior is God warranting in this whole cluster of structures and practices, which is to say, what deeper reality are we being pulled into and asked to conform to? And there is a surprisingly obvious answer to this question once we notice it. This reality is characterized by *covenant*, a word we should inscribe on our doorposts and wrap around our wrists and foreheads.

When males and females have sex, conceive, and raise children, bonding together to ensure the success of this difficult process, along with the ongoing life of the human race as a whole, Trinitarian realities attest that these relationships should be committed, unconditional, and faithful. They illuminate the key relational dynamics in play within this form. Marriage is a covenant, although a particular covenant oriented toward children, along with all that such a relationship entails. Furthermore, a complementary consideration of consequences, which is to say, of destructive practices, corroborates this primary account of marriage in terms of a covenant. It points the finger immediately to certain ubiquitous practices that Fisher has noted often corrode this arrangement painfully, damaging its relationships of love, namely, adultery and divorce.

The erosion of the marriage covenant through unfaithfulness is clearly a bad thing in general. There is widespread cross-cultural attestation to the damage that adultery typically does, along with its obvious precursors. (As Jesus well knew, sheer infatuation with people outside a marriage, when coupled with a desire for sex, will almost certainly elicit jealousy, something that corrodes relationality deeply; see Matt 5:27–30.) Adultery and jealousy are primary causes of domestic violence, Fisher notes,[18] and even, in terrible but widely attested circumstances, result in the killing of nonbiological children. These practices are obvious sins that the Christian community must continue to name and to work against, and they can do so in the light of a positive covenantal account of marriage. Equally clearly, the breaking of this covenant through divorce is often a bad thing. The dissolution of a marriage involving children, especially young children, is widely attested as being a supremely painful and difficult process—and divorces apart from young children can be awful processes as well.

So these two sins further reinforce our developing account of marriage in terms of a covenant. They are widely acknowledged to be destructive and to have deeply painful consequences, which confirms that marriage is a covenant best characterized by relational integrity and fidelity. *But none of this is rule-governed.*

The marriage covenant is a particular relational reality characterized by commitment and faithfulness. So every specific marriage covenant must be *navigated.* It is held within the cradle of the Trinity, but it is also assaulted by the evils of Adam. Hence it is entirely possible that other relational dynamics are in play, and marriage covenants can be distorted and damaged by many other destructive practices apart from acts of betrayal. A partner might, for example, be an inveterate substance abuser. And in these circumstances a marriage might be better dissolved because the relational damage will be less extensive than the damage that would result from continuing this covenant. The standard example of domestic abuse arises here, although this too must be navigated and not rule-governed.[19] We must always ask what action will be most constructive for the specific relationship in view. And I would suggest that Paul is quite helpful here in an analogous way.

In 1 Cor 7 he does not treat the Jesus saying concerning divorce as a universal rule. He does apply it in this way to Christians, but he allows members of mixed marriages to navigate the difficulties involved. Such people are "called to peace," which is a critical gesture toward the profoundly peaceful and life-giving dynamics of the Trinity into which we are all being drawn. Adultery is not necessarily present here, especially if a marriage between a Christian man

---

18. http://www.nzherald.co.nz/nz/news/article.cfm?c_id=1&objectid=11623865. In 2010 Brad Callaghan murdered and dismembered his partner, Carmen Thomas, in New Zealand, having learned that he was not the father of their son.

19. See the important work of Julia Perilla (http://womensenews.org/2001/05/latinas-create-own-domestic-violence-strategies/).

and a pagan woman is in view. Hence a door is opened by Paul in this text for us to think about when marriage covenants are becoming so relationally damaged and damaging that dissolution is the right action—when dissolution will lead to a more peaceful family.

To be sure, Paul is no advocate of cheap divorce, and neither am I. The deepest reality into which we are being drawn is unconditionally committed in relational terms. This is what the covenant of marriage is meant to be. But this is the reality of the Spirit, and we lapse constantly, this side of eternity, into the world of the Flesh. At times particular sins are so intertwined with our marriages that the distortions and distress arising from them are worse than our continued commitment to them. A divorce is then the proverbial lesser of two evils.

In short, it would seem that the primary marital reality is covenantal. It is a particular covenant involving sex and, in many cases, conception and parenting. However, sometimes a covenant can be eroded by deeply destructive practices like adultery or violence. A dissolution is understandable in these circumstances. But in between these two realities lies a zone of cheap divorce, where the church will ask some people to press more deeply into the relational fidelity of God and will hopefully help them to do so (which we will momentarily talk more about).

With this initial account of marriage in place, we now need to ask some further important but difficult questions. In particular, we need to ask, like the Corinthians, whether sexual activity can be detached from the marriage covenant.

Sex?

Modern culture agrees emphatically with some of Paul's ancient Corinthian converts that sexual activity can indeed be detached from the marriage covenant. As the Corinthians put it pithily, "Food for the stomach, and the stomach for food" (1 Cor 6:13), which is really to say (at least in addition), "sex for the genitals, and the genitals for sex." And doubtless a quick romp in the brothel down the road sometimes followed the bold proclamation of this adage during church. But this argument is surprisingly strong, once one thinks about it, especially in the modern period. Contraception has allowed people to detach sexual activity much more reliably (although not infallibly) from conception, and from all the resulting entanglements of parenting. So perhaps the covenantal ideal of sex within marriage should just be dispensed with as well as somewhat dated? We should be able to have sex the way that we might wander into McDonalds and order a burger. Eating and sex are parallel appetitive acts and nothing more. I'm not so sure.

Most of us are still driven to get married and to make and raise children—and we need to if the human race is to survive in its fleshly sense. This is still the majority position, and the consequences of abandoning it are quite serious in entirely practical ways. Societies simply require vigorous populations in order to survive. And happy children really need happy, united parents, as much as that is possible. But if we concede that sex needs to stay within marriage *for married people having children*, then it seems that admitting a radically different account of sexual activity outside of marriage cannot but erode that already fragile covenant. As long as married people regard sexual infidelity as problematic—and to my knowledge most still do—then we really need to regard all sexual infidelity as problematic. Marital betrayals are widespread, but I imagine that most of us agree that they are generally sad disruptions to a relational phenomenon that needs to endure in spite of them. So advocating indiscriminate sexual activity just seems incompatible with the way sex needs to take place within a marriage if that marriage is to endure and stable, effective parenting is to result.[20] It can erode marriages indirectly, as partners might have been habituated prior to marriage into infidelity, and directly, as nonmarried people practice and pursue a promiscuous ethic with the married. In short, sexual activity has a critical covenantal location in relation to conception and child-rearing for vast numbers of people, which entails that profoundly anticovenantal accounts of sexual activity should be resisted. The latter cannot but undermine the former, and the former needs all the help it can get.

But maintaining this position will also help sexual activity to be "safe," not so much in the sense that unplanned pregnancies are usually best avoided (although it seems that they are), but in the sense that sexual activity should take place between people who are old enough to handle it. The modern liberal definition of this concern, which is vaguely usable here, is that sex needs to be consensual. The sin correlative to the virtue of safety is the sexual abuse of minors, the consequences of which show clearly that this is deeply

---

20. The only alternative here seems to be the advocacy of open marriages, but I don't think, as things currently stand, that these have much plausibility. Sexual activity not with a covenanted sexual partner is widely regarded as a betrayal and seems obviously and usually to result in great pain and relational destruction, and this position does not seem likely to change soon. It seems written into our DNA.

traumatizing and destructive, a discussion that strays onto tragic territory for the church.

We have already noted the profoundly countercultural stance of Jews and Christians in the ancient world in their sexual ethics. Modern interpreters tend to hold their noses as they look back at the early community's hierarchical and rigidly binary account of marriage. But buried within this basic definition is an important positive feature. By confining sexual activity within this relationship, both Jews and Christians created a safe zone within their communities for many people who were otherwise exposed to the essentially predatory sexual culture of surrounding Greco-Roman society.

Men in the Roman Empire could, as a rule of thumb, have sexual relations with anyone of a lower status whom they chose, and clearly these relations did not need to be consensual because lower-status people did not need to be consulted about anything; their role was to obey. When this approach was combined with the difficulties women faced finding employment in the ancient city, positions as domestic servants being sharply limited, given the small percentage of wealthy households, a thriving sex industry resulted. And doubtless this practice did not extend respectful treatment and a living wage to its workers as a result of shrewd collective bargaining, as is the case in New Zealand today. But men also had access to the lower-class slaves and clients of their own households, as well as to those of their friends and hosts, access that included *access to their children, should they so desire.* It would not be untoward, then, to be invited to a person's house for a banquet, to notice an attractive child, and to be allowed by the owner to have immediate sexual access to that child—indeed, to be positively encouraged to do so as part of the evening's entertainment. These elastic boundaries resulted in a fundamentally predatory culture and a deeply traumatizing one for many of the low-status people living in it. As a result, Jewish and Christian communities were a relatively safe haven from this culture; people were more secure there. Sex was limited to married men and women there—at least in theory.

Sadly, Christian communities have not always been safe sexual spaces. Abuses have taken place, as we all know, in part because of the difficulty that priests have had managing their sex drive and the requirement of celibacy (although this is not the only problem). And I doubt that ancient Christians were able to insulate themselves fully from pagan habits of predation. We must not romanticize the situation. But I suspect that a differential in terms of sexual predation did still exist between broader society and local communities of Christians. What communities publicly regard as licit and illicit makes a difference. And this may go some way toward explaining an intriguing fact.

Christianity was extraordinarily popular in the ancient world with women.[21] Why? It wasn't exactly liberal. But women are often in certain respects, I would hazard, simply more sensible than men. Child-bearing and child-rearing tend to lead to quite practical judgments about a lot of matters. And many unmarried and lower-status women seem to have realized that, among other benefits, Christian communities provided a safer sexual zone for them and their children than surrounding pagan society.[22]

How tragic, then, that we have betrayed this legacy so often and so profoundly. Clearly we badly need to pursue the sexual safety of our communities, in part by talking about our problems honestly and addressing them practically. And I wonder whether two initiatives would not be especially helpful.

First: research on the sex drive noted by Fisher suggests that only 1 percent of the population does not feel an overwhelming urge to have sexual activity. In view of this, it seems to be inviting deception and abuse if we make celibacy mandatory for Christian leaders (only 0.5 percent of whom would be "natural" celibates if leadership is restricted to males). Of course, we ought not to abandon the importance of celibacy in a rush of enthusiasm for marital bliss. If people can be celibates, they should be, says Paul. "You will save yourselves a lot of trouble and can be mightily used of God," he says in effect. This state *must* be honored. I even dare to think of bands of celibate female apostles moving out into the world to make strange friendships and found flourishing new congregations—leaders like Thecla. But equally clearly, those who are not called to celibacy should be allowed to marry. I dream of the day when professional church hierarchies will have a nice balanced mixture of the single and the married.

Second: I wonder whether the church doesn't need to be far more intentional about resisting a surrounding culture that in many respects has descended again into paganism, one that needs its antirelational practices here judged and repented of. I am particularly concerned about its pornographic dimensions. If women are to feel safe in churches, we need to

21. Hard data supporting this claim are scarce—as most hard statistical data from the ancient world—but useful evidence from a slightly later period has already been noted: the court proceedings related to the Diocletian persecution of Christians in North Africa, in Cirta (present-day Tunisia), on December 13, 320. See ch. 12, n. 29.

22. Lynn Davidman's fascinating account of her recent conversion to Orthodox Judaism is apposite here: *Tradition in a Rootless World: Women Turn to Orthodox Judaism* (Berkeley & Los Angeles: University of California Press, 1991).

create and to foster an internal culture that resists the broader messaging concerning their bodies, their roles, and their valuation in fundamentally sexual terms. And we need to provide the appropriate support for those addicted to pornography—principally men. We know now that those regularly viewing pornography have the structures of their brains altered by this activity. This change cannot but impact healthy and happy marriages. Are our Christian communities spaces where both men and women can find rest from sexual stereotyping and imagery? And find healing from sexual trauma and addiction? I hope so. However, it seems that the clear and vigilant association of sexual activity with a covenanted relationship is part and parcel of this restorative communal ethic.

So we have ended up at this point in our investigation with the familiar alternative of marriage or celibacy, marriage at this point denoting a heterosexual, monogamous covenant. Those not married and those gifted with celibacy stand outside this particular covenant and are called to abstinence. And maintaining this covenantal boundary around sexual activity is both faithful and safe. This is what a relational analysis of this interim ordering structure has led us to. But some further important concerns must now be registered (and I need to ask those passionately concerned about the inclusion of gender minorities to be patient and to wait for the next chapter).

Support

If the church is going to continue to urge this ethic, then it needs to recognize the pressures that modern society places on unmarried Christians, whom it asks to remain celibate. It needs, furthermore, to act concretely and not merely rhetorically to support them.[23] Our rich modern diet leads to young women reaching puberty rapidly, at which point they are essentially programmed to seek out sexual activity and partners, as are our young men. But at the same time, modernity has greatly extended the period of cultural immaturity assigned to young adults—"teenagehood"—lengthening the process of formation and education well into a person's twenties. This change is understandable, given the complexity of modern society, but it greatly increases the period of singleness within a young adult's life, when the sex drive is operative. The biological mechanisms are popping, and yet marriage is culturally regarded

---

23. And similar considerations arguably apply to some sex workers, although I will not consider that constituency in detail here.

as premature. Increasing the pressures on this biologically fraught zone is a constant sensory assault from a hypercommunicative culture that is also hypersexualized, which, for all sorts of reasons, encourages the commodification of sex. (The sexualization of youth in the United States is palpable in things like child models and youth pageants.) The same culture then reinforces the postponement of marriage and further pressures its very viability by advocating life goals in essentially liberal, individualist, and careerist terms. It holds out that happiness, wealth, and success are key correlative goals that can be attained only by postponing attachment and childrearing for as long as possible. However, while directly challenging the validity of early marriage and postponing it an agonizing distance into the future, and then filling the interim with highly sexualized imagery and commodities, modernity somehow also endorses the importance of constant infatuation. Think just of the latest hit singles. They are almost always about falling in love, that is, experiencing the high associated with infatuation. So the expectations of those marrying—in due course—are often quite inflated, and marriages can collapse under this weight alone.

Evolution has gifted parents with sexual activity and a period of infatuation to enhance their capacity to stay attached, and to endure through the stresses and strains of child-rearing. However, it did not have to compete with the cheap alternative enticements of modernity. And that same modernity often suggests that relationships should be abandoned when the period of infatuation has worn off, on the assumption that this is the only love that matters. To cap things off, we live in small, nuclear families—if we are that fortunate—and so often lack the relational resources of the ancient village when raising our children. Uncles, aunts, and grandparents no longer live just next door to help us as we struggle through all challenges presented by the pitterpatter of little feet.

It is critical, then, that we recognize clearly the heavy additional burden that a teaching of "marriage or celibacy" places on young unattached Christians in our modern world, and that we craft church communities to support them. To slip momentarily from Paul to Matthew: we must not bind heavy burdens and lay them on our younger brothers and sisters but then not lift a finger to help them (Matt 23:4); Paul makes much the same point (Rom 15:1–3; Gal 6:1–2).

Do our communities support young, single Christians with things like less sexualized environments, honest discussion groups, and opportunities for confession and healing? Do they support young married couples with things like appropriate counseling about marital expectations and appropriate teaching about sexual activity? Do they support couples having children with cheap child-care? (And there are of course many other related constituencies that our churches should support as well.)[24]

Clearly the church has a major battle on its hands here—a *major* battle. Its position is powerfully countercultural.

Now, we should not necessarily be afraid of this challenge. The original community, following in the footsteps of its Jewish progenitors, consistently repudiated idolatry, which stood at the very center of the spaces and rhythms of the ancient city. It also stood against many of the sexual practices of the ancient city, which were equally widespread, and so must we. But we must be prepared to offer a community of support and not just information and moralizing rules—deeds in addition to mere words—although we should note another theological insight here that might slightly lessen this burden.

Even as the church endorses the importance of marriage and its covenantal account of sexual activity, it must refuse to *fetishize* marriage.

Supralapsarians know that personhood is not to be equated with either gender or sex. Deep down, these are negotiable realities, and a life of full personhood is entirely possible, here and now, with no sexual or reproductive activities. Supralapsarians must consequently consistently refuse to over-elevate the importance of marriage in an anxious attempt to safeguard the appropriate location of sexual activity (which is what infralapsarians tend to do) and must emphasize instead that numerous other deeply fulfilling and important relationships and roles are possible—relationships of friendship equally important to marriages and procreative relationships. Deep infatuation and attachment—that is, love—are clearly possible in these friendships. And the gift of celibacy (provided it is authentic) attests to this possibility for the long term. Those who get married do well; those who do not—being under no compulsion to do so—*do better*. So part of the church's pivot to support the young unmarried Christian, as well as the young married couple raising children, must include the ongoing endorsement of celibacy as an important and *valued* posture that can be underwritten by deep friendships. (And perhaps a liturgical acknowledgment of covenants of friendship would be useful.) This should be part of the warp and woof of the entire situation.

24. Given the demographics of most Western Christian communities today, many women cannot find an appropriate Christian man to marry. Do we support these faithful figures helpfully? Do we allow them to navigate this situation, or do we impose rules on them, citing Paul? My personal preference would be to encourage them to live into their possible divine callings to apostleship.

But we have as yet left some key aspects of ancient marriage as Paul describes it unexamined. Marriage between a male and a female should be understood in covenantal terms, and this is where sexual activity takes place appropriately, and not elsewhere. Appropriate relationality suggests this account of this structure, which is dedicated in most instances to child-rearing. But we must now evaluate whether the female wife should pledge to obey her male husband as a body should obey its head. This is, after all, what Paul says. We turn now, that is, to place theological pressure on Paul's conventional constructions that we have yet to examine—the patriarchy in his account of marriage and its underlying account of appropriate gender construction. So we are about to navigate here from Paul to the Pauline.

Theses

> We address now the related questions of sex, gender construction, and marriage.

> This navigation will eventually take us from Paul's stated opinions to a Pauline position, as his own reasoning is found to be inconsistent with his deepest convictions, in an act of *Sachkritik*, or "sense-criticism." Paul is read here against Paul, resulting in a Pauline account, although any further navigation on the ground to reflect this account must itself possess relational integrity.

> We begin, however, with Paul's own position: he organizes the community for much of the time in a pyramid of vertical binary oppositions summarized in texts known as the household codes: husbands govern wives; owners govern slaves; parents govern children.

> This is a standard rationalistic Hellenistic scheme for organizing ancient society; it can be found, for example, in Aristotle's *Politics*.

> It endorses a heterosexual, monogamous, and hierarchical account of marriage.

> Sexual activity is appropriate within this arrangement and *not* elsewhere, that is, with anyone to whom one is not married, whether of the same or another gender or orientation. (These last are Jewish, not typically pagan, emphases.)

> This arrangement extends to other gendered practices of clothing and public decorum, the flouting of which by women shames their husbands—letting modest head scarves slip during charismatic worship or interrupting and questioning speakers.

> Paul generally urges conformity to these standard arrangements, but he counsels flexibility (1) in mixed marriages between a Christian and a pagan, (2) in engagements, and (3) with respect both to widows and to temporary asceticism within a marriage.

> Celibacy is invariably a superior state for those who can cope with it, given the challenges facing Christian leadership.

> This general stance with respect to sex and gender is in certain respects countercultural. Greco-Roman custom generally endorsed widespread sexual access to low-status partners for men, and it was not always concerned about sexual relations with people of the same orientation and gender. It was basically binary in gender construction, however, and patriarchal.

> As we think about this arrangement in Paul theologically, an infralapsarian approach is to be rejected, even though he is utilizing one here. His account of the structure norming sex and gender is in terms of creation—humanity made originally as male then also female as in Gen 2, resulting in monogamy as in Gen 2:24—but this structure is part of the old cosmos, which the new creation transcends. Indeed, we have just seen, in chapter 24, that Paul is ambivalent with respect to creation and that his emphases, direct and indirect, on a supralapsarian account should be preferred.

> This realization weakens some of the warrants in his recommendations concerning sex and gender and their introduction to, or affirmation within, pagan missional contexts.

> This perspective also opens up a conversation with science to gain further knowledge about our current structures of sex and gender, which are not necessarily created and indelible.

> Human beings currently possess three interrelated systems that ensure the survival of the species—the sex drive, the infatuation system (associated with dopamine), and the attachment system (associated with oxytocin and vasopressin). These facilitate male-female bonding, procreation, and parenting, despite the unique challenges to human beings of altriciality, this issue being brought on principally by our bipedal gait, narrow pelvises, and large brains.

> Moreover, married people often commit adultery, men more than women; and marriages often end in divorce, adultery being named as a principal cause of divorce. These common events clearly damage marital relationality.

> Marriage seems to be an interim ordering structure (analogous to time) for the majority of our population (i.e., heterosexuals), imperfectly allow-

ing our species to survive despite death, including reproducing and raising children to the age of viability, if not independence.

> Our resurrected state reflects God's original purposes and hence does not include these corruptible structures. Paul's key data strongly confirm this conclusion. The resurrected state lies beyond sex and gender.

> Theologically, we can affirm strongly the covenantal nature of marriage. It should be characterized by fidelity. This view is relationally warranted. Child-rearing seems best in this type of covenantal marriage.

> This situation, though, is not rule-governed but relational, one that must be navigated. It might be wise for a marriage to dissolve if other forces are acting on it even more destructively than dissolution itself.

> Sexual activity takes place most appropriately for the heterosexual and procreating population within marriage. In many other situations it is clearly traumatic.

> Relational evaluation suggests that restricting sexual activity to marriages should create a safe space for others, free from sexual predation.

> In modern society the basic alternative of marriage or celibacy places great burdens on teenagers, who are placed in a difficult position. They are biologically ready for procreation but socially and culturally encouraged not to marry. Nevertheless, during this culturally constructed period of time they must navigate a cultural space characterized by widespread sexual commodification, and perhaps also by overly high expectations of love in terms of infatuation. The churches need to be concretely supportive and restorative here (as they should also be for any others burdened by these structures and their function).

Key Scriptural References

The most pristine instances of the household codes in Paul can be found in Eph 5:21–6:9 and Col 3:18–4:1. It is a fairly widespread structure. In the rest of the Apostolic Writings, see also 1 Pet 2:11–3:12; 1 Tim 2:1–15; 5:1–2; 6:1–2; and Titus 2:1–10; 3:1.

This form structures Paul's sexual ethics, which is apparent especially in 1 Corinthians, where much of his advice is informed by it: see 5:1–13; 6:9–11, 12–20; 7 (vv. 1–40); 10:8; 11:2–16; 14:33b–36; 15:33–34. But see also 1 Thess 4:1–8, as well as, to a degree, verses 9–12.

I will argue shortly, in chapter 26, that Rom 1:24–27 is not a direct statement of Paul's views of sex and gender. Nevertheless, his broad agreement with this account is apparent from texts like 1 Cor 6:9–11 and 1 Thess 4:1–8. Paul's account is not, I would suggest, self-evident from the contemplation of nature, as Rom 1 suggests, but informed by the scriptural story found in Gen 2 that recounts God's creation of Adam and Eve.

Key Reading

Fisher's *Anatomy of Love* is superbly researched and written.

Further Reading

Basic background to the household codes is provided by David Balch's entry in *ABD*.

An excellent broader treatment of the dynamics in play here can be found in Cartledge, *The Greeks: A Portrait of Self and Others*. It is well worth reading Aristotle's arguments in his *Politics*.

Pomeroy's classic *Goddesses, Whores, Wives, and Slaves* supplies useful background information concerning some roles for women in surrounding pagan culture; see especially "Sovereign Isis," 217–26; and "Women of the Roman Lower Classes," 190–204.

Horrell gives a nice account of some of the dynamics in the Corinthians texts in chapter 5 of *Solidarity and Difference*: "Purity, Boundaries, and Identity: The Rhetoric of Distinction" (133–65). He is especially alert to the important way in which Paul utilizes discourses of purity and pollution and of relationship. Paul's use of purity discourses can support relational considerations. They should also, if necessary, be subject to relational *Sachkritik*. The classic early anthropological account of Douglas remains helpful here as well: *Purity and Danger: An Analysis of Concepts of Purity and Taboo*.

Barclay's insights into 1 Cor 7 need to be noted. My favorite commentary on 1 Corinthians is by Thiselton, although his overarching enthusiasm for "inaugurated eschatology" as the problem at Corinth is unfortunate. Some further especially useful analyses of 1 Cor 11:1–16 include Peppiat and the relevant parts of Hays's commentary on 1 Corinthians.

Analysts attuned to brain science, reproductive biology, evolution, and related topics, such as Diamond and Fisher, are alert to the embodied structural issues, although obviously they are not warranting sexual ethics in theological terms. We insert this important information into a Pauline navigation here.

Leys discusses commodification helpfully (my thanks to Jonathan Wilson-Hartgrove for this reference).

Bibliography

Aristotle. *The Politics*. Translated by T. A. Sinclair. Revised by Trevor J. Saunders. London: Penguin, 1992.

Balch, David. "Household Codes." *ABD* 3:318–20.

Barclay, John M. G. "Apocalyptic Allegiance and Disinvestment in the World." Pages 257–74 in *Paul and the Apocalyptic Imagination*. Edited by Ben C. Blackwell, John K. Goodrich, and Jaston Maston. Minneapolis: Fortress, 2016.

Cartledge, Paul. *The Greeks: A Portrait of Self and Others*. New York: Oxford University Press, 2002.

"The Commodification of Everything," *The Hedgehog Review: Critical Reflections on Contemporary Culture* 5 (Summer 2003). https://hedgehogreview.com/issues/the-commodification-of-everything.

Diamond, Jared. *The Third Chimpanzee: The Evolution and Future of the Human Animal*. New York: HarperCollins, 1992.

Douglas, Mary. *Purity and Danger: An Analysis of Concepts of Purity and Taboo*. London: Routledge & Kegan Paul, 1966.

Fisher, Helen. *Anatomy of Love: A Natural History of Mating, Marriage, and Why We Stray*. Rev. ed. New York: Norton, 2016.

Hays, Richard B. *First Corinthians*. Interpretation. Louisville: Westminster John Knox, 1997.

Horrell, David. *Solidarity and Difference: A Contemporary Reading of Paul's Ethics*. London: T&T Clark, 2005.

Leys, Colin. "Commodification: The Essence of Our Time." *OpenDemocracy*, April 2, 2012. https://www.opendemocracy.net/en/opendemocracyuk/commodification-essence-of-our-time/.

Peppiat, Lucy. *Women and Worship at Corinth: Paul's Rhetorical Arguments in 1 Corinthians*. Eugene, OR: Cascade, 2015.

Pomeroy, Sarah B. *Goddesses, Whores, Wives, and Slaves: Women in Classical Antiquity*. New York: Schocken Books, 1995 (1975).

Thiselton, Anthony. *The First Epistle to the Corinthians: A Commentary on the Greek Text*. NIGTC. Grand Rapids: Eerdmans, 2000.

CHAPTER 26

Navigating Gender

Patriarchy?

It is worth reminding ourselves at this moment that the static marriage hierarchy affirmed by the household codes has seemed blindingly obvious for much of human history, an arrangement frequently denoted by the word "patriarchy."[1] The suggestion that men and women covenanting within a marriage are of equal stature, agency, and dignity, is a comparatively new perspective, and remains a minority even in the world today, existing largely where that recognition has been fought for in post-European societies through the twentieth century. Elsewhere and earlier the suggestion that a wife should obey and publicly respect her husband would be as obvious as the suggestion that a horse ought to wear a bridle. Nevertheless we now need to consider carefully here just what to do with patriarchy.

The biblical view of marriage as attested by Paul is that a wife ought to

---

1. Arguably, it has only seemed obvious for much of recorded history, meaning the relatively recent history of organized agricultural societies and their descendants. But we won't pursue this provocative line of thought here. Fisher complains that the subordination of women was a function of agricultural society and, in particular, the invention of the iron plough. This associated farm work with muscular labor and hence with men, confining women to the domestic sphere, a dynamic that then combined with private property to create patrilineal cultures and to further disempower women. Plough-oriented agricultural society is a relative newcomer in terms of human reproductive history. Millennia preceded this eight-thousand-year span during which women were (supposedly) much more equal and independent within hunter-gatherer societies ("'Till Death Us Do Part': Birth of Sexual Double Standards," *Anatomy*, 281–94). I am sure there is some truth to this, but it is also a very bold and programmatic thesis.

obey her husband. We see this arrangement being endorsed in Paul's letters in various places, for example, in Eph 5:21–33. Verses 22–24 are explicit:

> Wives, submit yourselves to your own husbands
> as you do to the Lord.
> For the husband is the head of the wife
> as Christ is the head of the church,
> his body,
> of which he is the Savior.
> Now as the church submits to Christ,
> so also wives should submit to their husbands
> in everything.

Here Paul elaborates a male-female marriage in a compelling analogy with Christ's relationship with the church as his body. Husbands should love their wives as Christ loved the church, recalling that he went as far as to die for her cleansing. To press the metaphor, husbands thereby love their own bodies, and obviously should nourish and care for them; in doing so they love themselves (a point where I cannot help thinking about the gymnasium I visit regularly, and the bevy of young bodies there—primarily male—assiduously sculpting themselves with weights in the mirror). Wives, conversely, should obey and respect their husbands as the church obeys its loving and self-sacrificial husband and lord.

This was probably a rather countercultural softening of ancient patriarchy by Paul—an act, in other words, of admonition. That wives should obey their husbands was obvious. That husbands should *love* their wives, and even as they love themselves, was not. It is significant then that Paul is inserting an appropriate relationality into this structure, and there can be little question that a kind, loving patriarchy is vastly superior to an indifferent, disrespectful, and/or tyrannical one. This difference must not be overlooked. But from our modern point of view Paul is not yet off the hook. The *structure* of patriarchy is still in place. Is this form *itself* warranted?

The key difficulty underlying the basic analogy Paul draws here is probably apparent to most of us modern readers attuned to gender-driven anomalies. Paul has structured the relationship between Christ and his church in terms of a male-female binary. Males have been precisely correlated with Christ, and females with the church. And this pairing is clearly inappropriate theologically, once one notices it.[2]

2. It is inappropriate, moreover, because it is an overt act of foundationalism. A

Paul cannot limit participation in Christ to males, or participation in the church to females, as he does momentarily here in Eph 5, and in 1 Cor 11 as well. This makes no sense. The two genders cannot be divided up and distributed neatly into either Christ or the church. These two locations overlap and exist within one another. We are in the church *because* we are in Christ, and to be in Christ *is* to be the church. We are *all* in Christ, and we are *all* in the church.[3] So Paul is right in what he affirms here—males are in Christ and females are in the church—but wrong in what he fails to affirm and therefore implies—that females are not in Christ and that males are not in the church.

The difficulties here have been tragically hard to detect. People don't like disagreeing with Scripture, especially when it sounds so christological, and here for the half of the time it does. And people don't like placing critical pressure on arguments in the Bible that endorse favored cultural arrangements.[4] Moreover, what Paul affirms here positively is absolutely right. Women are part of the church and so ought to willingly obey Christ; and men are in Christ and so lead when he leads through them, although they ought to do so, as he goes on to say, in a loving fashion. This is all true. It is what Paul leaves out that is problematic. Men are part of the church as well and so ought willingly to obey Christ; and women are in Christ and so ought to lead in love when he leads through them. There is a subtle set of absences in this text resulting in a culturally endorsed silence. In fact, we can see here emerging into view a nice example of the attempted theological justification of an existing social arrangement—a moment when Paul lapses into cultural foundationalism, partly by way of appeal to an infralapsarian account of creation.

"natural" "created" structure has *overridden* the information we have received from our relationship with Christ about personhood (where we learn that true personhood transcends biological categories), and this is not how Paul usually argues, and certainly not in relation to anything he really seems to care about. If we applied this reasoning to the race binary, we would end up with all pagan converts adopting full Jewish customs! Our movement into the realm of eschatology seems to have been temporarily lost sight of then, although the Corinthian text actually acknowledges this problem when it states that no one is separate in the Lord (1 Cor 11:11).

3. Moreover, to break these roles down strictly in terms of gender would be to insert the biological gender binary into the relationship between God and humanity with the former controlling and dictating the latter—an egregious instance of foundationalism and an utterly inappropriate intrusion of created categories into the actions of the creator. It would also be to ignore all of Paul's arguments about transcendence!

4. That is, for certain readers, a male-dominated marriage.

The argument is not for this reason entirely wrong. It may have been an important posture to urge to the audience of Ephesians (as well as, later, to the audience of 1 Corinthians); the Lord might have been commanding Paul to send these instructions to these communities in 50 and 51 CE. But it is a significant error to suppose that these localized exhortations norm a universal arrangement within marriage. The participation of all within Jesus, resurrected in him, suggests, conversely, that marriages should be *equal*—and these *are* universal "norms." A static hierarchy is inappropriate for people who have been raised in Jesus, whether male or female. God must be able to speak through both, as Paul's argument in 1 Cor 11 concedes. Consequently, the modern church should endorse the (sadly only recent) movement of Western societies toward a general equality of dignity, respect, and agency within marriages between men and women. This move has rock-solid christological underpinnings.[5] Everyone is in Christ, whether Jewish or pagan, and everyone is in the church, and Paul, if pressed, is never going to deny these truths. But once acknowledged, these insights subvert his patriarchal account of marriage. His differentiation of roles in terms of a gender binary must be *reformed*.

This important realization has some further important ramifications. Here for the first time we have broken with explicit statements by Paul when evaluating the appropriateness of his accounts of marriage, sex, and gender. Up to this point we have signed off on the basic alternative of sex within the covenant of marriage over against celibacy and abstinence. These moves have been strongly warranted theologically, being underpinned by the relational dynamics of the Trinity, especially in terms of covenant. However, we have just rejected the claim that the male-female relationship within this marriage should be arranged universally in a fixed, hierarchical fashion, which is to say, in terms of patriarchy, with the ancient cultural construction of males as dominant ruling over the ancient cultural construction of women as subordi-

5. The only powerful counter-argument I know of at this point would appeal to a hierarchical or monarchical account of the Trinity. Although common in various traditions, I would nevertheless suggest that this cannot but fracture the *homo[i]-ousion*, and tends to import into the Trinity inappropriate notions like causality. For example, the Father is the head of the Son because the Son proceeds from him in the sense of being caused by him, and so on. The debate between John Zizioulas and the Torrances is instructive here (T. F., J. B., and A. J.). The latter have convinced me that the egalitarian account of the Trinity is the correct one. See especially A. J. Torrance, *Persons in Communion: An Essay on Trinitarian Description and Human Participation with Special Reference to Volume One of Karl Barth's "Church Dogmatics"* (Edinburgh: T & T Clark, 1996).

nate. This understanding is not warranted, and is in fact challenged by good theological contentions. All those in Christ are equally resourced by him and therefore equal.

But this conclusion immediately raises a question concerning what we should now do with Scripture. Paul's statements here to the contrary are in the Bible. On any given Sunday anywhere in the world today we might hear these patriarchal texts preached and taught. If we need to limit the implications of his teachings here, how can we do this appropriately and respectfully? Fortunately, we have a lot of options here, including those suggested by Scripture itself.[6]

Scripture

Up to this point I have been treating Paul's texts in the Bible in a very modern fashion, using them to reconstruct his thinking in his own context—an essentially historical use of his texts. But this is not the way Paul used Scripture. If we attend to his mode of interpretation, along with its basic rationale, it seems that we can still use biblical texts that we disagree with in strictly historical terms in a different but constructive way within our later discussions in the church. We will just need to apply different ways of reading to them—different "hermeneutics," to use the technical parlance of scholars. And I have collected quite a few different reading strategies over the years in relation to these particular texts—sixteen at present, and counting—some of which allow us to say a number of helpful things with these texts that so fundamentally challenge modern readers, although, admittedly, not all the strategies are helpful.

I don't recommend either simply *affirming* or *avoiding* these discussions (hermeneutic 1 and 2). The former has done untold damage, something plainly apparent when we think about the endorsement of slavery that takes place right next to the marriage texts. And we can't just avoid the parts of the Scriptures we don't like (as the lectionary does here)—although this is a useful tactic on occasion. Nevertheless other preachers might use these texts destructively, and we won't know what to do about it. But various other strategies are only marginally better.

Some would continue *to historicize*, suggesting that these texts were written a *very* long time ago (hermeneutic 3) and so can be safely ignored. Advice about marriage given two thousand years ago in the Roman Empire is simply

---

6. And we resume here the conversation about scriptural usage begun in ch. 23.

not relevant to the twenty-first century, and obviously there is some truth in this claim. But if we distance the material in this way we make it irrelevant, and by implication, make all scriptural texts irrelevant, which is probably not going to convince the many Jews or Christians who think that these texts as Scripture *are* relevant *in some sense*. Nevertheless it is still common to encounter this basic type of rereading strategy in more specific variations, and these can sometimes play a useful supplementary role.

We can *historically reconstruct a specific narrative* that enfolds some arguments, explaining them plausibly, although in terms that no longer apply (hermeneutic 4). So earlier on we painted a rather lurid picture of the excesses of the Corinthian women during worship. They are shouting and screeching on top of one another and gyrating under the power of the Spirit so that their breasts are spilling out (or the ancient equivalent) and so on. Clearly Paul needs to bring this congregational mayhem under control. Given the specificity of the situation, however, his arguments clearly do not apply to us in detail, although his overarching goal was good. But Paul's arguments are not rendered any better by this hermeneutic, although a bad argument made in support of a good end—and one that usually no longer applies—is more palatable than a bad argument applied universally through time and space.

An apologetic move rooted in *historical comparison* can be equally helpful (hermeneutic 5). Other household codes from Paul's day frequently fail to address the inferior agent within the overall scheme, viewing their agency as so constricted and irrelevant that it was not even worthy of appeal. However, not so with Paul. Not only are the agents in the weaker position all addressed, but they are frequently addressed in extensive and highly persuasive terms. In comparative terms, then, they are greatly dignified, and in general cultural terms, this reading is a significant step forward in terms of respect and the attribution of agency. But the hierarchy is not abolished by this hermeneutic; it is merely mitigated.

Complementing this argument, the pressure Paul places on the superior agents in the binary relationships can be emphasized as well. These figures are to rule like Jesus, in self-sacrificial love—what some scholars have called *love patriarchy* (hermeneutic 6). The ethical demand of ruling in Jesus-like love is arguably more challenging than the instruction for all subordinate figures to obey and should result in a highly mitigated social arrangement. Again, however, this strategy does not abolish the vertical binary relationships as a whole, which is what the Jesus-like analogy really requires. Jesus entered fully into the constituency he ruled, gathered it all to himself, and raised it into a new existence. This is not what Paul's texts suggest for husbands, parents, and owners. Husbands do not become their wives and then lift them back into a transformed husband-like location of fundamental equality. However, there can be no question that if hierarchical rule exists—and it does in most places—it is a good thing to place pressure on those with power to act, like Jesus, with kindness and compassion.

We can also gain interpretative leverage on the codes from Paul's instructions to "stay where you are"—the rule already noted that Albert Schweitzer perceptively dubbed Paul's "law of the status quo" (1 Cor 7:17–24; hermeneutic 7). If converted pagans and Jews stay where they are, then Paul's mission to the pagans is effectively legitimized. Pagans do not need to move across that ethnic boundary into "favored nation status" with Jews and could thereby retain many of their own cherished customs and practices. This maxim thereby reinforces Paul's missional affirmation of pagan legitimacy. But there is no further disruption to the household or to broader social relations, beyond these ethnic claims, which in and of themselves do not require change by way of conversion, so much as resist it, which is presumably what Paul really wanted when it came to his converts from paganism. Paul was possibly just being astute here, then, arguing—quite properly—for change that his communities could cope with. Pagan inclusion was sufficient trouble for the day. But that day has passed, so this expedient position no longer applies.

Having said this, we don't know whether Paul argued in this way because he was also a *fundamentally conservative* figure, perhaps a little like Martin Luther (heremeneutic 8). Religious emancipation was enough and should certainly not be extended to the "murdering, robbing, bands of peasants" or their ancient equivalent. But this reading is unlikely to move Paul's interpretation forward persuasively in the modern period.

A little more palatable is the development of this argument in combination with *an urgently imminent eschatology* (hermeneutic 9). Paul expected the return of Jesus imminently, in his own lifetime, if not quite soon, in a matter of months, and this sense of urgency made him focus on quick and primary actions like conversion, ignoring the work of slow transformation (see 1 Cor 7:29–31). In view of the closeness of the end, patient advocacy of social change would have seemed like insisting on redecorating the dining hall of the Titanic after it had struck the iceberg. So this inattention seems entirely understandable. And it could even be surmised, in complement to this, that such a posture made Paul's gospel *more politically palatable* to his conservative Jewish critics in Jerusalem (see hermeneutic 7 above, also Gal 2:1–10).

However, this hermeneutic does, like most modern historicizing strategies, marginalize the texts even more into the temporal distance, here on the basis of a primitive expectation that we now supposedly no longer share, rendering them largely useless for modern discussion. We are probably not sitting around putting all social work on hold because Jesus is going to return before Christmas. Once again, in this reading Scripture no longer speaks at all.

Yoder offers a rather different angle, arguing famously for *revolutionary subordination* (hermeneutic 10). Raised within the Peace Church tradition, his suggestion is that social transformation comes through essentially martyrological behavior that does not coerce or violently enforce change but summons people to do the right thing, even as the wrong thing is being steadfastly and heroically resisted. Slavery is wrong, but overthrowing it violently is even more wrong. So some more peaceful and less coercive way forward needs to be found that will thereby involve enduring wrong arrangements, and possibly for some time.

Yoder's arguments have not endeared him to many constituencies who fear brutal and calloused moral agents who never change, while they run the risk of holding exploited people in an oppressive location (and further grounds for suspicion could be mentioned). Moreover, he does not deal with the problem that the text does seem to argue for these hierarchical arrangements indefinitely. His is not a global and utterly convincing solution, then, but it is a further useful supplementary point. We do *at times* need to endure, turning the other cheek. Christians can be far too quick to abandon this fundamentally christological trajectory, and Yoder's reading provides a way for it to be reintroduced with these texts, suitably qualified. But it is not a fully satisfying reading.

Other reading strategies are more conscious of the reader's modern location. The softest of these is what I sometimes call mere *acknowledgment* (hermeneutic 11).

Some people just cannot see a way around the difficulties in the text, so one way of at least moving discussion forward is to describe clearly just what the difficulties are without trying to solve them. Paradoxically, by clearly acknowledging the problems that the arguments of the text raise in terms of theological warrant, this frank exposition leads its auditors through a short process of responsible theological reflection. The actual text operates negatively, the theology being learned in relief as it were, but theological movement does take place, which is arguably what ultimately matters.

A variation develops this perception with slightly more edge. Many just condemn Paul for being *inconsistent* (hermeneutic 12), and, again, there is a truth in this.

We have detected inconsistency in the application of resurrection in Paul's texts as it applies to marriage. Only husbands seem to be fully and genuinely resurrected, able to lead and to rule. But I would counsel refraining from condemning Paul for this. The underlying assumption is often that Paul and we are all liberals in the sense that we live in a world of obvious universal rules, where Kant's categorical imperative is again the prime example. So we extrapolate commands and instructions, universalizing them, and then condemn everyone who does not extrapolate everything perfectly as we have just done. But few escape condemnation in these terms—and neither will we. So it would be wise to avoid casting the first stone here. Even more problematically, we thereby endorse a liberal account of ethics, which is conspicuously modern and fundamentally flawed—and we are involved in an egregious act of presentism! Ethics derives from participation in a particular relational reality. It is *navigated* through different contexts and particularities. It is simply not rule-governed or legally imposed. So we must deal with the inconsistencies evident to us now in another fashion.

We could make a case for these instructions in terms of Paul's fragile location in the repressive Roman Empire. In this way we could apologize for an arguably deliberate inconsistency on *practical political and cultural grounds* (hermeneutic 13). Paul worked in a trenchantly and monolithically masculinist culture, at the head of a tiny movement making such radical moves on race that it was already perceived to be subversive. Paul was arrested and jailed in every region he entered. Wholesale reconstruction of gender codes and economic arrangements in this situation was just not feasible. So there seems to be explicit scriptural warrant for *proceeding on an issue at the right pace*, not too quickly—although hopefully also not too slowly. It is relationally irresponsible to upend all key existing forms and structures, not to mention, tactically naive, and there is some truth in this strategy. The how matters as much as the what, and this consideration placed significant constraints on this particular renegotiation. Indeed, its difficulty is clearly evident even as we navigate it today. But this is a not a fully satisfactory solution because Paul's position is not obviously argued in this way. There is no need to try to warrant a patriarchal arrangement christologically if the only reason for endorsing it is tactical expediency, and yet this is what the text does.

We could argue equally constructively in terms of *commands* (hermeneutic 14). It was arguably appropriate for Paul to issue commands in the form of instructions that conformed momentarily to hierarchical cultural codes. However, there is no need to universalize these instructions beyond these settings and suppose they are mandatory everywhere now—although even today we can still conceive of contexts where the same commands to respect a hierarchical order might be appropriate.

Think for a moment of the challenges missionaries from the post-European West to a conservative Islamic state face. Such figures are under the most profound suspicions, in part because they come from a culture widely perceived to be profligate in terms of sexual activity. It is viewed as comprehensively promiscuous and disgusting. It is difficult enough simply to be a Christian in this sort of setting. Some pockets of Islamic culture might demand the murder of a brother if a Muslim male converts to Christianity. For missionaries to arrive and to cheerfully advocate the immediate abandonment of hierarchical dress codes and gender roles—to ban the veil or discard the dupatta—would be contextual suicide. It would be far smarter to arrive and *to affirm* those codes, reassuring any potential converts of the sexual propriety of the resulting communities, and then, if any conversions ensue, to work gently and quietly—and safely—to move those communities, as the Spirit leads, beyond androcentrism. But this is clearly a highly localized strategy.

We come now to one of my favorite rereading strategies, which opens up *role flexibility on the grounds of participation* (hermeneutic 15).

The difficulties with Paul's instructions derive primarily from the way he has defined the roles in the text statically. Married men are always to love and to be obeyed; married women are always to obey. It is the structuring of these injunctions within a fixed gender-coded binary that is problematic in theological terms. So let's just relax that expectation, as we should in view of the participation of all in Jesus, and let people position themselves more flexibly, at which point something quite interesting happens. *People flow between both categories and become subject to both sets of instructions.*

People are constellations of relationships, all of which differ in degrees of status, intimacy, power, and so on. We are fundamentally intersubjective. Hence, the actions within these relationships are constantly "modulating." How often do I rule or lead my wife? Not very often in overt formal terms, if at all. But I frequently *initiate* and hence lead her in relation to any number of particular things—what John Gottman calls making a "bid."[7] And she frequently does the same.

I initiate an activity or an observation—something Gottman contends that happy couples do dozens of times a day. "Let's have a cup of coffee." "Let's get together with Mary and Kay for a game of Catan tomorrow night." "Let's go to Ocracoke Island for a week in the summer." And a good relationship responds positively to these bids. In this moment, the person "obeys." "A cup of coffee would be perfect. Thanks." "A game with Mary and Kay tomorrow would be

---

7. http://highline.huffingtonpost.com/articles/en/love-in-the-age-of-big-data/.

great fun; let me buy a nice bottle of New Zealand wine for the occasion." "Ocracoke for a week in summer? Awesome!" But these bids, which are moments of initiative and hence leading or rule, which elicit acts of obedient response in turn, *come from both sides of the relationship*. So when my wife makes a bid and suggests something, I tend to respond positively, following her lead and in effect obeying her. (She actually makes a lot of suggestions, generally giving these things more thought than I do, so one could say that I spend more of my time responding and obeying than initiating, which I am quite happy about.) Gottman goes on to point out that a key to healthy relationships is to accept bids, even when we can't actually do them, that is, we need to find a way of responding positively—of obeying—even if the underlying answer is "no." The key point is that in all our relationships, we initiate and lead and rule in some instances, and we obey and follow in others. And in all these rapidly interchanging moments we can benefit from learning to initiate in the sense of initiating like Jesus, in kindness, love, and self-sacrificial concern for the other, and to respond in the sense of obeying like the church, in sincere, wholehearted gratitude and obedience. This is how all relationships tend to work, and possessing these dynamics should help them to work well. So explicating the texts in these terms, with their instructions applying to everyone at the appropriate moment, seems to me to be a supremely constructive reading.

Interpretation of the household codes can thereby slip into a highly constructive mode with the greatest of ease. "Are you a church leader (whether male or female)? Cherish your flock as Christ nourished his own body. Are you a Christian (whether male or female)? Faithfully obey the words of Christ as they are being mediated to you through your reading of Scripture, your worship in the assembly, and the wisdom of your friends." Alternatively (reflecting here on 1 Cor 11), "Are you behaving badly in worship (whether male or female), under the supposed inspiration of the Spirit, shaming your family and shouting down those worshiping around you? Get it together! The Spirit is peaceful and orderly as well as joyful." And so on.

Finally, the vast repository of readings in the church offers us a treasury of *nonliteral methods* of textual interpretation (hermeneutic 16). Allegory, typology, symbolism, figural readings, and so on are all richly productive interpretative techniques long despised by modern critical scholars but in fact beautifully designed to let biblical texts speak constructively to later contexts and situations, and as we have just seen in chapter 23, Paul himself frequently reads Scripture this way. "The rock was Christ" Paul says boldly in 1 Cor 10:4. "We are all children, like Isaac, of the promise . . . [being] born of the Spirit" he analogizes in Gal 4:28–29. (When does Paul *not* read Scripture like this? David Bentley Hart observes, with a degree of exaggeration.)[8] A recovery of the rich diversity of scriptural interpretation present within the tradition is taking place in many academic circles these days, and we should avail ourselves of it.

We have ended, then, with two particularly constructive readings of these difficult texts, readings that should greatly benefit their community auditors. In these terms the Spirit can prompt us to say various helpful things to Jesus's followers today through these supposed "texts of terror."[9] Consequently, while we have placed considerable pressure on a strictly historical construal of the text, rejecting its account of marriage in terms of an inflexible hierarchy between a man and a woman, I hope it is apparent that the reading of Scripture, and even of these parts of Scripture, remains important, relevant,[10] and dynamic. And with these important realizations in place—concerning the need at times to press beyond Paul's stated instructions (on Pauline grounds of course), and to reinterpret Scripture he wrote accordingly—we are ready to tackle a final important question.

I said earlier that the church must resist binding heavy burdens and laying them on the backs of people without lifting a finger to help them, referring then to teenagers and young adults trying to navigate through the fraught cultural space that modernity has created between (1) the onset of sexual activity and (2) marriage. But if we advocate the alternative of celibacy or marriage and expound the marriage covenant solely with reference to sexual activity between a male and a female that results in children, we risk imposing a grievous set of burdens on other minority populations that we must now carefully consider.

Heteronormativity?

My account of marriage has focused up to this point on the heterosexual and procreative majority, although we have just moved past any necessary structuring of that male-female marriage in terms of hierarchy. And the further questions now arise: Is this heterosexual population a *norm* or *rule* that excludes

---

8. David Bentley Hart, "The Spiritual Was More Substantial than the Material for the Ancients," *Church Life Journal*, July 26, 2018; http://churchlife.nd.edu/2018/07/26/the-spiritual-was-more-substantial-than-the-fleshly-for-the-ancients/# (accessed Oct 28, 2018).

9. Phyllis Trible's useful phrase: *Texts of Terror* (Philadelphia: Fortress, 1984).

10. Relevant, that is, in the best sense of this word.

all other types of marriage as illegitimate? or Does this group function more like an original population—a community—in relation to which the marriages of other similar, but not identical, communities can be included, under the prompting of the Spirit? Can we extend a covenantal account of procreative heterosexual marriage to include other minority groups, for example, to those who cannot have children or do not want to, and to those whose sexual orientation is toward members of the same basic gender?

It is vital to recall at this moment that the Pauline gospel works in a concrete, missional way as it extends through apostles to include populations that are initially perceived to be problematic but turn out, following the lead of the Spirit, to be welcome and, to some degree, on their own terms, although with the appropriate ethical navigations. It is a concrete navigation from community to community, utilizing evaluative and transformational modes, and not a vision or ideal or rule. The church community began with an extension from messianic Judaism to include various pagans, enjoying the lead of the Spirit as it did so, and we know well by now that the pagans continued to live, in certain respects, as pagan. This diversity turned out to be warranted (although parts of it were admonished, reformed, or erased). We need to ask at this moment, then: is God summoning the church to include minority populations in terms of sexual orientation and gender construction within the covenant of marriage as that is practiced by heterosexual procreating couples? This would be an analogous move. New groups would be included within marriage without adopting all the practices of the current majority population, provided their own practices enjoyed theological warrant. Is marriage something that can diversify?

The answer to this question should flow directly out of what has already been said about God's purposes within the cosmos and Paul's resulting ethic. An eschatological account of marriage is a relational account, which is why we have derived its definition so directly and firmly in terms of a covenant. (It is also a safe space.) And a covenantal account of a marriage is clearly not as interested in the form or structure of the marriage—whether it is procreative and/or gendered—as it is in the relational tenor of the marriage. Is it a covenant? Are the adults pledged unconditionally and faithfully to one another in perpetuity? Do they love one another and commit to one another in this way, thereby reflecting the relational dynamics of the Trinity? If so, it seems fair to recognize that they can marry, which seems to lead fairly quickly to the conclusion that nonnormative populations can marry, in addition to the majority heterosexual population. This is the right form for their love and their sexual activity with one another. On one level the answer would seem to be as simple as this. But someone might object that we need to untangle an important set of considerations here more clearly.

Everyone agrees that heterosexual couples involved with conception and child-rearing are an acceptable account of marriage. This is our "base" population. But doesn't this link sex *and procreation* together in what amounts to a classic Catholic account of marriage? Can even heterosexual couples who are infertile marry? And in the concomitant practice that most people are really worried about, can any couple use birth control? A strict linkage between sex, procreation, and marriage would say "no." All three things must be present, as suggested by the existing dominant population of married people, for a marriage to be valid.

This challenge actually introduces the first and all-important inclusive step in the entire marriage debate. And I would suggest that there are no good *Trinitarian* or *relational* reasons for insisting that, while sex is *often* linked directly to procreation, it *has* to be, in all instances, in what amounts to a universal binding rule. And to suppose that this linkage exists on Trinitarian grounds is to generate the most outrageous consequences immediately for our understanding of God! (We would be projecting biological categories and structures into God—reproductive organs and activities and the like.) Sex should be viewed from a supralapsarian point of view as part of an interim ordering structure. It is not an indelible structure written into the fabric of creation—a misguided infralapsarian claim. It is biologically linked with procreation, and it needs to be for the ongoing viability of the human species. So it is clearly not a part of God's original created order, which is revealed in Trinitarian communion, and we are entitled to navigate the exact form of marriage in the light of the relational pressures of the Trinity. Sex is like death and eating and drinking and the organization of time—important, something we need to do (well, most of us), and yet, something cultures can play with and enjoy in multiple variations. We need to eat something to survive; but beyond this commonplace, we can enjoy quite a lot of variation, and God seems comfortable with most of them. And the same seems to apply to sexual activity.

These considerations all suggest that marriages do not need procreation to be marriages. Essentially, this claim is *not* warranted relationally. So we can affirm the inclusion of both planned parenthood and nonprocreative marriages alongside the dominant population of procreative marriages.[11] Hence Protes-

---

11. And perhaps we can add one more consideration here. The existing connections between sex and procreation do need to be protected by the covenant of marriage. Parents need one another and children need parents. This is clearly relationally

tant churches have long affirmed nonprocreative sex within marriage as a good thing. And it can also be managed responsibly through the use of birth control (provided the birth control used is ultimately relational). Planned parenthood can be highly relational! It follows that infertile couples can marry, and any couple can have sex without necessarily intending to have a child immediately. However, this inclusion of infertile heterosexual couples within marriage, along with temporarily and deliberately infertile couples, so to speak, shows that sexual activity in marriage can be detached from procreation, and the implications of this admission are far-reaching.

When we combine these recognitions with the affirmation of nonpatriarchal marriage that we developed earlier on, it is apparent that the definition of marriage as it was advocated in Paul's day has already undergone some significant reforms, while the populations included under its umbrella have significantly diversified. New inclusions have already pushed its boundaries outwards in several ways, introducing subtly but ultimately significantly new structures, although these inclusions are all soundly warranted and are ratified, further, by constructive consequences.

A covenantal account of marriage allows us to affirm today that marriage should be between equal partners—moving here beyond patriarchy—and that sexual activity does not need to be oriented constantly toward procreation—moving beyond necessary fertility to planned parenthood. Having said this, we have not lost sight of our original constituency. The covenant of marriage holds together and protects those heterosexual couples who still have sex with one another and have children together. So sex still takes place within a safe space, and covenantal relationships between parents are encouraged.

Concomitantly, destructive sexual practices that would erode this population are discouraged. Our covenantal account of marriage turns its face away from adultery, frivolous divorce, general promiscuity, and sexual relations with minors. All these practices erode marriage in all its forms and are exposed thereby as sinful. They are to be condemned, and any participation in them by Jesus's followers must cease.

---

critical. But this rationale would seem to endorse the marriage of infertile couples, and other couples like them, on further, pragmatic grounds. This inclusion upholds those who are married by throwing a marital cordon around *all* sexual activity. It sends the message that sex takes place within marriage, and marriage is a covenant between adults; this is the right space, so to speak, for sexual activity. Moreover, this position encourages adults who want to be sexually active to get married, thereby reducing pressure from unmarried sexual activity *on* marriage.

At this moment we are well positioned to place the $64,000 question about marriage that many churches are grappling with today. Can couples who are not heterosexual marry? Is the community characterized by a marriage covenant of lifelong commitment and sexual fidelity—already somewhat diverse—open to this group too?[12]

A covenantal account of marriage, which embraces sexual activity but does not connect it automatically to procreation, provides no good reasons for resisting the inclusion of these communities. This move does not violate the basic relational dynamics in play in any way and merely supplies a new form, which seems unobjectionable in and of itself in theological terms. The pagans can be included here within God's people, so to speak, and attached to the Jewish people, and at this precise point, to a degree, on their own terms. Gay populations can have their form of gender construction endorsed, but their sexual activity should be located within the covenant of marriage, like everyone else's, although it might also be helpful to include some further secondary warrants for this suggested embrace.

Any failure to extend our account of marriage to include those minority groups asking to be affirmed is to generate destructive relational consequences, and in a variety of ways, further suggesting that any continued refusal is probably wrong. Exclusion is relationally damaging.

Sex is, as Fisher reminds us, a drive. And minority populations are not gifted with celibacy any more than majority ones. Only 1 percent will be comfortably celibate, so most people of a minority disposition have drives too. Moreover, we have already seen that the appropriate location for drives in the heterosexual population is marriage. It has this covenantal relational setting. It is framed by faithfulness. So the most obvious course of action would seem to be to ask our minority populations, if they have a strong sex drive, and are infatuated and/or attached to someone, to express that attachment within marriage as well, that is, to have sex within covenantal bounds. Not to do so

---

12. It is not necessary for my argument to provide precise definitions. So let it suffice to say that I mainly have lesbians, gays, bisexuals, transsexuals, and intersexuals in view—LGBTTI (assuming here that transsexual journeys can take place in two very different directions). I'm not sure an engagement with the adoption of atypical expressions of gender construction—applying "queer" here primarily to this practice—should bother the Pauline interpreter too much. Any queer behavior would simply need to avoid being too disruptive or shaming to other community members (so 1 Cor 11) and fold into a loving relationality. This is, in other words, a different question from the foregoing challenges that can generate profound dysphoria.

would be—at the least—to risk undermining the marriages of our existing population of heterosexuals in various ways.

It would be to ask our minority populations not gifted with celibacy to resist their sex drive inappropriately, which is not a good thing and is not something that Paul actually endorses. "It is better to marry than to burn with passion," he says realistically in 1 Cor 7:9, unwittingly contributing to the case for gay marriage by inference. To encourage sheer abstinence, by forbidding marriage, would be to invite promiscuity within minority populations, even as it would ask those populations to bear a burden that married heterosexuals were not being asked to carry—the burden of celibacy for those not gifted to be celibates. It would basically unleash sexual immorality and general promiscuity.

Conversely, to ask minority populations to have sex with one another within marriage covenants would be to maintain with complete consistency a general ethic of sexual fidelity. We would still be saying, "sex within marriage," which is an approach possessing a deep relational integrity. To affirm minority marriages is therefore, it seems to me, to affirm marriage, period. (This would also reduce the risk of members of a sexual minority trying to enter into a heterosexual marriage—in some contexts still the main option for sexual activity available—and failing, leaving relational pain and mayhem in their wake—a sadly frequent phenomenon.) To fail to affirm minority marriages, however, is to place further quite practical pressures *on* marriages, principally by placing the demand for abstinence on populations who are not called to celibacy but are enjoined to live that way, unleashing promiscuity. The consequences of this decision seem frequently to be destructive.

In light of these considerations, I am confident that, with two thousand years of hindsight, and all the navigations by the church of different questions of gender during this period already, most notably of patriarchy and fertility, not to mention with many recent scientific insights into the nature of the human brain and of the survival of the species, Paul would approve of what I am now saying. We are called to peace, not to burn with passion. He would doubtless ask for evidence that the Holy Spirit was operating fully within these populations at the margins of the heterosexual community who nevertheless are claiming "the full rights of citizens." But once any homophobia has been repented of, there is plenty of evidence that God *is* at work within godly people of a minority disposition. Think in our time just of the example of Lonnie Frisbee, who was so critical to the births of both Calvary Chapel and the Vineyard Movement. Frisbee was nakedly and deeply involved with signs and wonders—God used him overtly and powerfully—and he was gay.[13] But there is plenty of additional evidence besides Frisbee of God's love for populations who can be so marginalized and despised, and who face such painful specific challenges.[14]

Some human beings are attracted to members of the same basic sex, and some are attracted to both, which is to say that the sex drive is not invariably oriented toward a heterosexual opposite. Some do not identify strongly with a culture's construction in gendered terms of one of the two main options of male and female, while others are an intriguing mixture or a colorful crossover. And some heterosexual people cannot have children. In short, *spectrums* of characteristics seem to be in view, which should hardly surprise us. Biological populations always exist in bell curves of variations, as a great Christian scientist of yesteryear, Gregor Mendel (1822–84), first pointed out.[15] It seems fine, then, for variations on heterosexuality to exist, and here, as in relation to all other biological phenomena, there are some delightful minority positions. God's community is, to borrow Nelson Mandela's poetic phrase, a rainbow nation.

In sum: these are, it seems to me, the main considerations in favor of an inclusive account of marriage, and they are Pauline all the way down. The judgment that this inclusion is valid is based, as it must be, primarily on positive theological warrants.[16] A covenantal account of marriage, which is a relational

---

13. See "Frisbee: The Life and Death of a Hippie Preacher" (dir. David de Sabatino, 2005).

14. We have just noted the need for the church to support young heterosexual couples who face acute challenges during the child-bearing years, and especially in the modern period. Perhaps then we have been quite foolish to stigmatize as promiscuous and deviant, and to go on to ignore, a sensitive and caring population that has much to offer, including here. I still remember a deeply loving young man whose eyes filled with tears as I shared the story of one of the medical challenges that one of my young children had had to face, who went on to say how in his life "some things were just not meant to be." I had not fully realized until that moment just how painful the impossibility of biological child-rearing could be for people with a minority sexual orientation. But an appropriately diverse community could do much to help its young heterosexual couples navigate the exhausting challenge of child-rearing, and to heal some of the pain experienced by infertile minorities.

15. Noting the presence of a bell curve is a constructive, not a destructive, contention here. For a mature use of the bell curve in a profoundly progressive way see James R. Flynn, *Race, IQ, and Jensen* (London: Routledge & Kegan Paul, 1980).

16. I have also invariably found arguments to the contrary to be infralapsarian, and hence foundationalist, and so unpersuasive. "Complementarianism" is an obvi-

account of marriage, has no objections to adults of any sexual orientation or gender construction covenanting with one another in marriage.[17] But this judgment strengthens as it responds to the concrete leading of the Spirit in her blessing of Christian leaders from the minority populations in question, also as it considers, in an act of wisdom, the consequences of failing to do so (i.e., an intensification of the pressures toward promiscuity). And note how this is an exemplary Pauline navigation.

We have evaluated various new populations of people—people who are different, and in some respects, disturbingly so. In so doing, we have distinguished between the structures and forms that they are indwelling and their relationality. Moreover, in a step beyond Paul, we have identified some of *his* advice as rooted in infralapsarian claims about creation (i.e., his endorsement of patriarchy), advice that now enjoys only tactical, not universal, force. His endorsement of heteronormativity because of its ostensibly created nature is actually unwarranted. We have concluded, then, that heterosexual structures do not need to be enjoined on any new, different populations we are relating to—evaluations in modes 1 and 2 of affirmation and, if necessary, of admonition. The inclusion of all in Christ does, however, place pressure on patriarchy, suggesting reformation in evaluative mode 3. Furthermore, an insistence on a loving, covenantal relationality does challenge people of any gender construction to marry; this is the safe and relationally constructive space where sexual activity is appropriately located, as our heterosexual parent (and parenting)

---

ous case in point, writing a particular binary *form*—drawn from a particular Jewish narrative—indelibly into God's created purposes. The mandatoriness of this form is unwarranted in Trinitarian terms, and it is mistaken in any case about its indelibility, being sub-Christian in its account of creation. This is of course not to deny that this is the form for some, and even for many. But, just as the messianic Jews in the early church were not to impose the teachings of Moses on Paul's converts from paganism, current Christians should not impose this particular structure on their converts and friends. This would be an instance of colonizing overreach.

17. Someone might ask if marriage is even still necessarily binary, between just two adults. I cannot consistently make binary marriage a rule because Pauline ethics is not rule-governed. But I would say in response that marriage must certainly begin here! So any navigation into plurality, so to speak, would have to satisfy the criterion of loving relationality, and hence of complete, equal, uncoerced admission of another person by the two people already married. And my superficial study of polygamy has only ever found a patriarchal structure behind this decision, which would be unacceptable. (Missionary encounters with contexts characterized by patriarchal polygamy are a slightly different matter, raising transformational as well as evaluative challenges.)

population makes clear. So promiscuity, which is defined as sexual activity outside of a covenantal arrangement, continues to be challenged, along with predation—condemnations in terms of mode 4.

Hence, although Paul had a lot to say about marriage, sex, and gender, some of his most constructive insights come to us now, not atypically, indirectly rather than directly, as we think, out of his deepest supralapsarian and transcendent convictions. We have undertaken here, in other words, a Pauline navigation after the time of Paul and have ended up endorsing the two main alternatives that he lays out of celibate singleness or sexual activity within marriage. But we have reformed his affirmations of a gendered hierarchy and, in a similar vein, have allowed adults from different minority populations and orientations to covenant with one another in marriage. We have abandoned, that is, his imposition of the Jewish heteronormative construction of gender on his converts and any related condemnation of nonheterosexual marriages. The latter turns out to be an inappropriate imposition of a structure from Paul's own parent context on his converts. Put slightly differently, we have affirmed alternative, nonreproductive marriage structures, including nonheterosexual forms that Paul condemned, judging his condemnation to be poorly warranted.

If the appropriate evaluations seem clear, however, we still have much work to do. The "what" has been clarified, but we still need to manage the "how." Transformative work almost certainly lies ahead of us, and Paul continues to help us here in various further, quite specific ways.

Navigating Forward 1: Strange Friendships

One of the biggest impediments to the endorsement of same-sex unions is visceral rather than theological. The contemplation of such unions can evoke horror, fear, and disgust—the phenomenon of homophobia. The association of these powerful negative affects with a minority population undoubtedly plays an important part in deliberations between various church traditions and groups over the definition of marriage. It is hard to embrace an extension of marriage when it evokes revulsion. But such revulsion is merely cultural coding. Certain practices and groups have been associated with negative affects by the stories that our cultures tell and the stereotypes they evoke. These associations are programmed into our brains. So the way forward is *to recode* these practices and groups with positive affects, which is best done *face-to-face*. Sustained relationships with people from the group that is feared or reviled will result in neural recoding so that negative affects fall away to be replaced by normal, warm patterns of friendship. Consequently, Paul's missionary strategy of forming strange friendships in unexpected places is the perfect solution to the practical obstacle to endorsing an inclusive account of marriage caused by the presence of pockets of homophobia in the church. The making of these strange friendships will be a key part of any movement forward, and it has the added bonus of bringing the voices of those most affected by this discussion directly into the conversation.[18]

Navigating Forward 2: Peacemaking

We have already seen how one of Paul's key apostolic skill-sets was diplomatic. Within the virtue of peace he was a peacemaker and a reconciler, despite how he is often portrayed. He was in fact extraordinarily committed to ecumenical practices and processes, traveling long distances to meetings, negotiating, and even raising significant sums of money as gifts to his opposition. This involvement eventually led to his long incarceration and the cessation of his missionary ministry, and it cost him his life. So he models for us here the virtue of peacemaking within the church, including its connections with fidelity, its patience, its effort, its generosity, its encouragement, and its value. I expect that his speech ethics was critical in these negotiations as well. Hopefully he used, whenever possible, self-controlled and even gentle speech, not language and argument designed to evoke conflict (although his letters don't *always* evidence this quality). Navigating forward in relation to marriage today will require leaders with similar dedication, reconciling in Paul's costly mode. The virtues will need to be married here to the appropriately respectful transformational mode (1).

Navigating Forward 3: Defending the Gospel

Having just noted Paul's diplomatic skills and effort, it is nevertheless both obvious and important to note his trenchant defense of what he took to be primary issues. He would not compromise his "gospel," traveling twice to Jerusalem not merely to negotiate with the leaders there and to maintain the unity of the church, but also to convince them of the correctness of his position and of the danger and deceptiveness of the opposition to it. In Gal 2:4–5 he says,

---

18. And contact theory will again shed light on this process.

This matter arose because some false brothers had infiltrated our ranks
to spy on the freedom we have in Christ Jesus
and to make us slaves.
We did not give in to them for a moment,
so that the truth of the gospel might be preserved for you.

Similarly, it is important for us to maintain the key issues with charity but also with clarity, and Paul identifies for us fairly clearly what those are. The identity of God must not be compromised, and for him that was revealed definitively through Jesus and by the power of the Holy Spirit. Consequently, those walking in Paul's determined footsteps today must maintain the truths attested by the creeds, which encapsulate the key claims implicit within the critical but compressed confession "Jesus is Lord." Quite apart from the issue of basic loyalty to the truth about the God we love, if this position is not maintained, *there is no possibility of achieving communal clarity on any other question.* These are the truths in the light of which all other truths are discerned. Without holding on to this truth, then—and in this position, up front, as revealed to us *by* the truth—we ultimately lose all evangelical truth. So this line must be held with blood and tears, which was something Paul clearly did.

As we have just seen, however, this conservative theology does not necessarily mean a conservative ethic when it is faced with a new population asking for inclusion and affirmation. New constituencies can even reflexively reveal insufficiently Trinitarian and christological practices within *our* existing tradition—remaining vestiges of foundationalism that continue their corrosive work. They might not, but they might, in which case, the defense of orthodoxy, somewhat counterintuitively, is located in the ethically progressive camp. Gospel orthodoxy is frequently ethically radical, we might say. It follows that all talk of "holding the line" must be scrutinized carefully to see whether the right line is being drawn, and whether it is being held in the right way. Orthodoxy is the line that really counts, and when other lines are drawn, they often rub the orthodox line out—the line that really matters!

With this particular Pauline navigation complete, we can turn to the second key modern navigation that will be addressed here—a Pauline account of Jews and of Judaism. The description of Paul can go tragically astray at this point as well, which is doubly ironic, since a clear grasp of his views has such constructive things to say.

Theses

> An indelibly hierarchical account of marriage is not theologically warranted in supralapsarian terms; no coherent or plausible Trinitarian or christological warrant exists for this marriage arrangement, but cogent relational warrant exists for reforming it (evaluative mode 3).

> The problem is somewhat disguised in Eph 5:22–24 because Paul is right in what he affirms, although wrong in what he fails to affirm and so implicitly denies. A heterosexual gender binary is laid over our relationship with Christ and our membership in the church. The former is attributed to husbands, who are then enjoined (correctly) to love; the latter to wives, who are then enjoined (correctly) to obey. But these affirmations do not exclude their parallel affirmations, which are left unstated: wives also participate in Christ and should therefore, as Christ leads, lead in love; and husbands are members of the church and therefore ought to obey Christ when he leads through men or women. To state these last two relationships overtly, however, would undermine the surrounding household code.

> We must therefore recognize Paul's deficient arguments here (except perhaps in terms of a command in his day), in the light of his more strongly warranted arguments made elsewhere, and must remove any patriarchal account from marriage.

> We ought nevertheless to read Scripture constructively where it endorses patriarchy, as well as related potentially oppressive forms; numerous reading strategies lie to hand for making good use of his technically incorrect arguments, most powerfully, the "interchanging" and allegorical approaches (hermeneutics 15 and 16 from strategies 1–16).

> In hermeneutic 15, everyone interchanges moments and roles of initiative and response in a relationship. (Gottman calls moments of initiative "bids.") Bids should be offered in love; they should be responded to positively, in what we could call loving obedience.

> Hermeneutic 16 utilizes nonhistorical reading strategies such as allegory, as church tradition has developed and exemplified them.

> If Paul's patriarchal account of marriage is to be superseded and any texts making that recommendation reread, we need now to evaluate forms of marriage that are not procreative, and not even heterosexual.

> Is reproduction a normative feature of marriage or merely a majority feature?

> Strictly speaking, this query includes evaluating the legitimacy of barren marriages and marriages using birth control. Protestants have long accepted these minority populations as included within marriage. These judgments detach sexual activity from a strict association with procreation. But no good warrants are evident for forbidding infertile couples from covenanting in marriage, whether by circumstance or by choice. Appropriate new forms of marriage are therefore recognizable here—evaluative modes 1 and 2 of affirmation and, if necessary, admonition.

> The question now arises whether nonheterosexual (i.e., LGBTTI) couples who wish to covenant together in marriage could also be so affirmed. But, again, there are no good relational or Trinitarian warrants suggesting that nonheterosexual couples should be forbidden this possibility. It is a thoroughly relational contention, suggesting evaluative judgments concerning this new form of marriage in modes 1 and 2 again.

> The consequences of forbidding nonmajority groups in terms of sexual activity and gender to marry would also be relationally destructive, for it would place pressure on all those not gifted with celibacy to engage in promiscuous and unfaithful sexual activity, thereby indirectly, and perhaps at times directly, undermining faithful sexual activity within heterosexual marriages.

> Conversely, allowing these nonmajority marriages would seem to endorse consistently and in general the position that sexual activity takes place appropriately only within marriage. (This last practice is strongly warranted in relational terms and must continue to be affirmed; sexual activity outside of marriage is destructive and to be condemned in mode 4.)

> Exclusive contentions invariably rest on infralapsarian warrants and are therefore invalid. (Infralapsarianism is foundationalist.)

> Paul makes such arguments himself, so we step here beyond Paul's stated position concerning these questions by appealing to key warrants he himself affirms elsewhere—Trinitarian, christological, *and pneumatological*.

> This is an act of *Sachkritik*, as we develop from Paul's position to a Pauline judgment.

> The leading of the Spirit within the minority populations seeking inclusion should also be expected.

> However, the Spirit *is* apparently working through LGBTTI Christian leaders (e.g., Lonnie Frisbee).

> Any endorsement of this inclusion must be navigated on the ground, in specific communities, preferably in relationships of friendship with those being included.

‣ This approach should undermine any homophobia in play, through consistent friendly contact.

‣ Community leaders advocating inclusion should also act as peacemakers in relation to communities who are resisting this recommendation, doing so faithfully and strenuously as necessary. They should act relationally, with integrity, speaking accordingly.

‣ Nevertheless, while doing so, they must also uphold the heart of the gospel, namely, the truth that Jesus is Lord, which unpacks very quickly into the truths of the incarnation and the triune God as stated by the creeds. Any arguments made against inclusion on the basis of foundationalism should be identified and opposed *as* foundationalist, that is, as detrimental to these primary truths.

Key Scriptural References

Patriarchy is explicit within Paul's account of marriage especially in Eph 5:22–24. See also Col 3:18–4:1; 1 Cor 11:2–16; 14:33b–36; and 1 Thess 4:1–8 (which androcentrically addresses only husbands).

Paul's "law of the *status quo*," identified by Schweitzer, is evident especially in 1 Cor 7:17–24.

Paul's most imaginative, allegorical, or figural readings of passages in the Tanakh can be found in 1 Cor 10:1–22; and Gal 4:21–5:1.

Key Reading

Gaventa's important study emphasizes frequently overlooked supralapsarian data in Paul in relation to sex and gender.

Gottman's work on relational bids is helpfully introduced by Emily Esfahani Smith's essay "Masters of Love." I recommend reading this carefully, irrespective of any engagement with debates over gender construction. For an overview of Gottman's contribution, see the online article by Eve Fairbanks.

Further Reading

Barth was famously corrected by Paul Jewett in his account of gender. As a learned friend of mine put it once: "He just got that wrong," although it is only fair to note that, given when he was actually writing, his emphasis on the importance of a woman's voice in theology was considerably ahead of its time.

Rogers provides a difficult but theologically insightful analysis of the issues in essentially Barthian terms. He is close to the position I am developing here.

Data in various texts contemporary to Paul concerning the suprasexual nongendered view of angels are also indirectly pertinent; see Newsom's summary. They confirm the supralapsarian nature of the new creation. Barth analyzes angels carefully and appositely in *CD* III/4.

More technical studies by Kahl and Larson detect a subversive dimension in Paul's self-depiction as a male, and Wilson detects the same in Luke's depiction of Paul ("An Out-of-Control Convert: Paul on the Way to Damascus [Acts 9]," pages 153–89 in *Unmanly Men*.

Martin's collection of essays on this set of questions, *Sex and the Single Savior*, is widely influential, and at times highly informative.

Hauerwas's essay addressing some of the key arguments against the legitimacy of gay Christians is a masterpiece of comic subversion.

McClintock Fulkerson offers a thorough education into the way gender and gender coding is constructed (along with Foucault, although he is not infallible).

Rubin is extremely difficult but is a classic instance of feminist theory that describes superbly how three dominant accounts of gender and sex—by leading white male theorists—have supplied fundamentally negative accounts of women and related constructions of gender. It is vital to go beyond such essentially foundationalist reifications. Paul's orthodox position that personhood is distinguishable from sexual activity and gender construction ultimately offers a much more positive potential account of nonnormative genders.

Having said this, there is an embodied, biological, and reproductive dimension within the situation that must not be lost sight of, as emphasized in the previous chapter, especially by Fisher and Diamond. (Food is not just a constructed phenomenon; we need to eat food, and the right types and amount, or we die.) Volf is alert to this issue and elegantly combines embodied and constructed dimensions, although the distinction between infra- and supralapsarianism is not always sharply drawn in his analysis.

Many of the texts discussing Scripture and its interpretation listed in chapter 23 are also usefully consulted here, especially those describing interpretative struggles concerning Scripture in relation to slavery, which often engaged with the household codes. Dawson and Radner canvas figural reading strategies insightfully. Brownson is a highly constructive account, while Keen's personally limned analysis is especially informative.

When considering how to read the sex and gender texts in Paul, it is worth recalling that his advice concerning slaves has long been universally abandoned, and the relevant texts reinterpreted (or, more commonly, avoided).

General background on ancient slavery is supplied by Wiedemann in *Slavery* and in *Adults and Children in the Roman Empire*. See also Glancy, *Slavery in Early Christianity*.

Williams helpfully links liberation from slavery to liberation from gender construction in conversation, especially with his African American tradition; see *An End to This Strife*.

An innovative development of this material in relation to Pauline theology is Martin's *Slavery as Salvation*.

Bibliography

Barth, Karl. *Church Dogmatics*. III/2.

Brownson, James V. *Bible, Gender, Sexuality: Reframing the Church's Debate on Same-Sex Relationships*. Grand Rapids: Eerdmans, 2013.

Dawson, John David. *Christian Figural Reading and the Fashioning of Identity*. Berkeley and Los Angeles: University of California Press, 2001.

DeFranza, Megan K. *Sex Difference in Christian Theology: Male, Female, and Intersex in the Image of God*. Grand Rapids: Eerdmans, 2015.

Diamond, Jared. *The Third Chimpanzee: The Evolution and Future of the Human Animal*. New York: HarperCollins, 1992.

Fairbanks, Eve. "Love in the Age of Big Data: Scientists Believe They've Discovered a Simple Formula for Happy Relationships; Reader, I Tried It." http://highline.huffingtonpost.com/articles/en/love-in-the-age-of-big-data/.

Fisher, Helen. *Anatomy of Love: A Natural History of Mating, Marriage, and Why We Stray*. Rev. ed. New York: Norton, 2016.

Foucault, Michel. *The History of Sexuality*. 3 vols. Translated by Robert Hurley. New York: Random House, 1976–86.

Gaventa, Beverly. *Our Mother Saint Paul*. Louisville: Westminster John Knox, 2007.

Glancy, Jennifer. *Slavery in Early Christianity*. Minneapolis: Fortress, 2006.

Graham, Elaine. *Making the Difference: Gender, Personhood and Theology*. London: Mowbray, 1995.

Hauerwas, Stanley. "Gay Friendship: A Thought Experiment in Catholic Moral

Theology." Pages 105–21 in *Sanctify Them in the Truth. Holiness Exemplified.* Edinburgh: T&T Clark; Nashville: Abingdon, 1998.

Hays, Richard B. *First Corinthians.* Interpretation. Louisville: Westminster John Knox, 1997.

———. *Moral Vision of the New Testament: Community, Cross, New Creation. A Contemporary Introduction to New Testament Ethics.* New York: HarperCollins, 1996.

Hill, Wesley. *Washed and Waiting: Reflections on Christian Faithfulness and Homosexuality.* Grand Rapids: Zondervan, 2010.

Jewett, Paul K. *Man as Male and Female. A Study in Sexual Relationships from a Theological Point of View.* Grand Rapids: Eerdmans, 1975.

Kahl, Brigitte. "No Longer Male: Masculinity Struggles behind Galatians 3.28?" *JSNT* 79 (2000): 37–49.

Keen, Karen R. *Scripture, Ethics and the Possibility of Same-Sex Relationships.* Grand Rapids: Eerdmans, 2018.

Larson, Jennifer. "Paul's Masculinity." *JBL* 123 (2004): 85–97.

Martin, Dale B. *Sex and the Single Savior: Gender and Sexuality in Biblical Interpretation.* Louisville: Westminster John Knox, 2006.

———. *Slavery as Salvation: The Metaphor of Slavery in Pauline Christianity.* New Haven: Yale University Press, 1990.

McClintock Fulkerson, Mary. *Changing the Subject: Women's Discourses and Feminist Theology.* Minneapolis: Fortress, 1994.

Newsom, Carol A. "Angels." *ABD* 1:248–53.

Radner, Ephraim. *Time and the Word: Figural Reading of the Christian Scriptures.* Grand Rapids: Eerdmans, 2016.

Rogers, Eugene F. *Sexuality and the Christian Body: Their Way into the Triune God.* Oxford: Blackwell, 1999.

Rubin, Gayle. "The Traffic in Women: Notes on the 'Political Economy' of Sex." Pages 74–113 in *Women, Class, and the Feminist Imagination.* Edited by Karen Hansen and Ilene Philipson. Philadelphia: Temple, 1975.

Schweitzer, Albert. *The Mysticism of Paul the Apostle.* New York, Seabury, 1931.

Smith, Emily Esfahani. "Masters of Love." *The Atlantic* Jun 12, 2014. https://www .theatlantic.com/health/archive/2014/06/happily-ever-after/372573/.

Trible, Phyllis. *Texts of Terror.* Philadelphia: Fortress, 1984.

Volf, Miroslav. "Gender Identity." Pages 167–91 in *Exclusion and Embrace: A Theological Exploration of Identity, Otherness, and Reconciliation.* Nashville: Abingdon, 1996.

Wiedemann, Thomas E. J. *Adults and Children in the Roman Empire.* New Haven: Yale University Press, 1989.

————. *Slavery*. Oxford: Clarendon, 1987.

Williams, Demetrius. *An End to This Strife: The Politics of Gender in African American Churches*. Minneapolis: Fortress, 2004.

Wilson, B. *Unmanly Men: Refigurations of Masculinity in Luke-Acts*. Oxford: Oxford University Press, 2015.

Yoder, John Howard. *The Politics of Jesus: Vicit Agnus Noster*. 3rd ed. Grand Rapids: Eerdmans, 1994.

CHAPTER 27

Beyond Colonialism

The Teaching of Contempt

For most of its history the church has viewed Jews with contempt. It has denigrated, ostracized, and periodically violently persecuted them. It has consistently taught the most appalling racial stereotypes about Jews, without which a horror such as the Holocaust would have been impossible. Hitler's racial anti-Semitism flourished in European soil that had been poisoned for millennia by Christian anti-Judaism. Moreover, readings of Paul are deeply intertwined with these abuses. Hence few questions are more important when interpreting Paul than getting his views about Jews right. Now more than ever we ought to be sensitive to the implications of how we read him for Jews and for Judaism.

Sadly, the recognition of this critical interpretative imperative is a minority tradition within the guild of Pauline interpreters, and even when it is recognized, scholars have not always known how to proceed. The most promising debate of these issues in recent times, sparked by the publication in 1977 of E. P. Sanders's epochal *Paul and Palestinian Judaism*,[1] involved limited positions and ran quickly into a cul-de-sac. Exchanges continue between the "old" and the "new" perspectives on Paul, but the moniker "new" is now rather misleading, since most of the perspective's original advocates are currently drawing their pensions. Arguably, nothing new has been said on this front since the 1980s. Even more sadly, some scholars use the sterility of this debate to block the exploration of further, more creative exchanges, and scholarly retrenchments appear by the year.

There are reasons for all this deadlock and misdirection, however, and it has been one of the main agendas of this book to put the positions in place

1. E. P. Sanders, *Paul and Palestinian Judaism* (Philadelphia: Fortress, 1977).

that will allow us to clearly illuminate both the basic problem and its resolution. The initial key to unlocking this situation is the recognition that the destruction is being wrought *largely by a foundationalist account of the Christian difference from Judaism.*

Foundationalism explains the damage that many Christian readings of Paul do to Jews, along with the inadequacy of most Christian responses to the Jewish questions—because they do not recognize this underlying causality and fail to purge their positions of foundationalism. It follows, however, that as we free Paul's interpretation from foundationalism—on the assumption that he did not support this view and that to hold this position leads to a significant misreading of some of his texts—we open up the possibility of a vastly more constructive account. Paul's most important insights into the nature of Judaism in the Christian era are ultimately astonishingly inclusive and constructive. He explains difference not in terms of *displacement* but in terms of *diversification.* But before we can grasp Paul's positive contributions, we must free him from his negative readings; the ground must be cleared of its foundationalist debris.

Beyond Foundationalism

I have been identifying and avoiding foundationalism through the entirety of this book, and the treatment of Jews by Christians has been one of the most important reasons for doing so. I have constantly distinguished between a theology grounded in God's revelation and a theology (which is really unworthy of that name) grounded in some other foundation for the truth—some other set of overarching truth criteria—that we have built for ourselves, hence the name "foundationalism." A revealed theology grounds the truth appropriately in the truth, namely, the God revealed in Jesus, and hence *by* the truth. A foundationalist theology of our own making, mirroring the way we are made of Flesh, will falter, obscure, and ultimately kill. Of particular note to us now is that it will poison our description of Jews and of Judaism.[2]

The damage is done by the way that Christian foundationalism works forward. When this intrinsic methodological tendency is combined with the diversity of the early community, which embraced pagan converts acting eth-

---

2. It is important to recall here that rejecting foundationalism is important first and foremost as a matter of basic loyalty to God. It is then important, second, for ethical reasons.

ically but in many respects very differently from messianic Jews, the poison of *supersessionism* is concocted. A reverse derogation of Judaism must take place.

If the account of Christianity supplied, often by way of a reading of Paul, proceeds forward, then by definition Christianity grows out of something that preceded it, and in Paul (as well as in the rest of the Apostolic Writings) this is Judaism. Christianity emerged historically from Judaism. This relation is undeniable. It is as if we are dealing with two boxes again, Box A and Box B, and a great historical progress between them. But here we need to see clearly that Box A is Jewish and Box B is Christianity. However, if Christianity is not like Judaism in key particulars, for example, abandoning full Torah-observance, then its reasons for doing so—for being different from Judaism—need, in a foundationalist analysis, *to be found in the state that precedes it*, which is Jewish. The reason for Box B and all its differences must lie in Box A, and, in a forward-moving analysis, the reason can only be that Box A is inferior to Box B in some way and needs to be improved on. The truth of Christianity thereby grows directly out of the inadequacies of Judaism, inadequacies that are intrinsic and self-evident to the occupants of Box A, as well as to any later analysts.[3] Christianity is a later, superior version of whatever Judaism was originally, growing out of the obviously inferior state of Judaism, and so supersessionism must result. In short, Christian identity, when it is constructed within an overarching foundationalist schema and is also understood, as it must be, as something different from traditional Judaism, *invariably constructs Jewish identity in deficient terms both intrinsically and self-evidently*—a more sinister othering schema is hard to imagine. But this is also a principal reason why those operating within this schema find it so hard to address anti-Judaism effectively.

This perspective will be deeply entrenched for any occupants of Box B who think that the basic relationship between A and B is constructed in these terms. If the people occupying Box B, who are Christians and who are thinking forward in this way (i.e., from A to B), *don't* attribute fundamental inadequacies to Box A, then there is no good reason for Christianity to exist in Box B! Box B is unnecessary (or, God forbid, inferior or even some sort of mistake). Everyone should still be Jewish. Box A should be fine in and of itself. Hence, even though the consequences of living in Box B, on the

---

3. This progression can be softened from Judaism-bad/Christianity-good to Judaism-good/Christianity-better, and this is a step forward. But it is much more difficult, if not impossible, to justify coherently in relation to Paul, *and* it is still supersessionist. Judaism should still be erased.

backs of those laboring in Box A, are appalling, they are appalling for other people. But if the appalling consequences are recognized and addressed, Christianity *itself* is called into question. Box B risks being undermined, and unfortunately Christians, like most people, will generally sacrifice someone else's identity if by doing so they can preserve their own. As a result of this, Christians thinking in this way, foundationally, are caught in a nasty conundrum. To hold on to their account of Christianity, they must continue to denigrate the Jews, while to reverse this judgment is to invalidate Christianity. At bottom, Christians who think in this way are trapped in a classic othering schema, but the damage is being compounded by its combination with a foundationalist methodology that locks in the negative identity of the other in the basis of its own.

Fortunately, this conundrum is ultimately unnecessary because it arises from a fundamentally false account of Christian truth that can happily be abandoned, and once this insight has been grasped, Paul's texts can be interpreted from a very different point of view. But a hard road still lies ahead of us. Anti-Jewish foundationalism exists in multiple forms, and all of them need to be identified and avoided if the demon of anti-Judaism is to be exorcised from the interpretation of Paul. There are in fact three variations of anti-Jewish foundationalism within the interpretation of Paul that need to be confronted: (1) soteriological, (2) historicizing, and (3) salvation-historical. Each of these schemas unleashes virulent anti-Judaism and so ought to be identified and purged from Paul's description—if it is possible, but I think that it is.

In my experience, soteriological foundationalism is the variant that does the most damage. This is the place—which is to say, the set of texts—where foundationalism is introduced into Paul's interpretation in an especially intractable form. So it will be particularly important to address it carefully. It will be described and repudiated in the rest of this chapter. Historicizing foundationalism and salvation-historical foundationalism are addressed in the chapter that follows.

The Usual Reading of Galatians 2:15–16

The misguided reading of Paul in terms of soteriological foundationalism that unleashes an especially nasty form of anti-Judaism can be identified quickly by looking at how Gal 2:15–16 is often read. Here is how the New International Version understands Paul's underlying Greek:

> We who are Jews by birth and not sinful Gentiles
> know that a person is not justified by the works of the law,
> but by faith in Jesus Christ.
> So we, too, have put our faith in Christ Jesus
> that we may be justified by faith in[4] Christ
> and not by the works of the law,
> because by the works of the law no one will be justified.

Most scholars read Paul here as having a discussion with Jews and Judaism about getting saved, and this view has some truth to it. But they tend to assume further that the text discusses salvation in terms of how someone gets from Box A to Box B, and this assumption, as we have just noted, has momentous and very damaging consequences. Those occupying Box A are assumed to be unsaved and in a sense presaved, and in this text its occupants are clearly Jewish. People start their journey to salvation from this place, which is characterized by something called justification "by the works of the law." Law obviously means the laws of Moses found in the first five books of the Bible, which contained the key instructions to guide Jewish lives. So Box A, the unsaved condition, looks very much like a Jewish condition. However, unsaved Jews are clearly not supposed to stay there. The smart thing to do is to transfer from Box A to Box B, the Christian box, and thereby to get "justified" and to inherit eternal life. Box B is where salvation is found. But the overarching argument—the construction of how these two boxes relate to one another, in a sequence that runs from A to B—is clearly working forward. A foundationalist account of salvation is therefore being supplied, unfolding from a definition of a plight facing Jews before coming to Christ, to its solution through the Christian gospel, when that eventually arrives. The reasons for transferring to Box B to get saved therefore lie within Box A, and so Paul is held to be setting up Box A to place pressure on its occupants to commit to Jesus and thereby to jump across to Box B. (It is this feature of the reading that seems to make it useful for evangelism.) In fact, Jews are set up in Box A for this jump with the theological equivalent of a pressure cooker—a pressure cooker that technically boils us all until we are ready to embrace the gospel.

The pressure is generated as people first try to be righteous by observing the demands of the law for themselves or, in the usual translation, to be "justified." Paul uses this word instead of the word "saved" because he is supposedly

4. Significantly, the NIV adds here in a footnote "Or *but through the faithfulness of . . . justified on the basis of the faithfulness of*" thereby attributing the faith to Jesus.

envisioning a crucial future moment when everyone stands before God's throne on the day of judgment. God pronounces a verdict then over all of us, whether righteous and so saved, at which point we can, like the rest of the sheep, enter into the delights of heaven, or unrighteous, sinful, and guilty, at which moment we head off with the goats to hell. To be "justified" at this moment is to be "judged just" or "judged righteous" by God.[5] (Technically, it is to be judged innocent of all wrongdoing.) To fail to be justified is to be condemned to annihilation or worse.

But Paul argues (supposedly) that no one from Box A will be pronounced innocent, and so saved, on that day by being a perfectly righteous person for the simple reason that we aren't. Everyone sins for some of the time, however trivially, including Jews. Everyone gets parking tickets and exceeds the speed limit, and Jews all do the Jewish equivalent, perhaps lapsing into occasional moments of covetousness like the benighted sinner of Rom 7 (vv. 7–25). So we will all show up on the day of judgment and God will say, quite truly, "This is not a fully righteous person," therefore "You will not inherit eternal life." This judgment seems like very bad news, and on one level it is. We are heading for hell.

But we do learn something important if we go through this analysis before we get to the day of judgment, which is to say, while we are still in Box A. We realize that we are sinful right now and in desperate need of help from God. The flames of hell are flickering in our future. So when help from God arrives, we should grab it. This is the offer of the gospel, which we grasp on to by believing in its good news, assuming preachers or missionaries have visited to tell us about it. This vastly easier act gets us into Box B. If we believe in Jesus, then we are saved, although Paul continues to use the word "justified."

But, someone might ask, what happened to the stern God judging everyone for their deeds on the last day and pronouncing them guilty and punishing them? People haven't either suddenly become perfect or been appropriately punished, right?

---

5. "Just" and "righteous" mean the same thing. But "just" comes into English originally from the Latin *iustus*, by way of French, and "righteous" comes into English from Germanic languages and the root *recht*. Unfortunately, although the German "righteous" is probably a slightly better translation than the Latin/French "just," the German verb corresponding to the noun "righteous" has been lost. So when we need to translate Paul's Greek "just/right" words with a verb, thereby holding on to his use of these cognate words in Greek, we have to go to the Latin/French "justify," which can be a little archaic and/or mystifying.

This is where Jesus comes in.

His death on the cross (which isn't mentioned in Gal 2:15–16 but comes into view, at least in some sense, in v. 20) is a payment for the punishment of everyone, at least potentially. His death "satisfies" God's just anger with sin, which demands some sort of equivalent recompense.[6] This event consequently balances out the scales of justice, or in a slightly different picture, it pays for the debt that has been accumulated when sinners have injured others. So Jesus's death, understood in these terms, is very important. He steps into the place of punishment and bears that burden for us, vicariously (this being an act of divine generosity rather than justice). But we have to grasp on to this solution that God is offering us or it isn't applied to us, and we do so by believing in it. We are saved by faith. We should place our entire hope in Jesus and trust that he will pay off the punishment accumulating in store for us. In addition, his perfect life will be "credited" to us so that when we stand before God on the day of judgment God will pronounce a verdict over us as if we are Jesus, and not as we actually are ourselves. It will be as if we are clothed with Jesus, and so we will receive the verdict "You are indeed perfectly righteous; enter into your owner's joy in heaven."

Now we would be stupid not to believe, since if we don't grab onto Jesus's work, we will end up going to hell. It is in our own interests to believe. But failing to do so would be a moral and not merely a rational failure. We would be resisting the lessons of Box A about our sinfulness. On some level, we would be denying that we were sinful, which is obviously a very bad idea. Moreover, we might be still trying to make it on our own in spite of our sinfulness, and such pride and self-deception should be judged as well, and not affirmed.

This whole sequence of learning about our own sinfulness by striving to obey the law, getting appropriately anxious and fearful, then hearing the good news that Jesus has paid for our sins on our behalf should end up with us enthusiastically and gratefully grasping the offer of salvation by faith. Consequently, the entire process is the gospel according to many scholars who read Paul in this fashion, with the preaching of the gospel necessarily prefaced by the proclamation of the law. The basic underlying sequence, then, is "law first, then gospel," and clearly this progression works forward and can only work forward. It is our experience of the law that drives us to the gospel.

6. A process that many modern societies can pursue for themselves as the state inflicts pain on perpetrators in amounts (supposedly) equal to the pain that perpetrators have inflicted on others.

Read in these terms, Gal 2:15–16 looks like a compact summary of Paul's preaching about salvation. The two motifs in the text of works of law and faith denote the two boxes or states that encompass everyone. The motifs or boxes are arranged in a sequence, one after the other, and together they tell the story of salvation, here termed justification. And this story clearly needs both of them to work *and in this exact order*. The first box is the foundation for the story. The story starts here, with the non-Christian, and if this box is taken away or its terms are significantly altered, the whole story falls apart. Salvation loses its rationale. There would be no reason to become a Christian and no explanation of how to do so or of what exactly God accomplishes in Jesus to make salvation happen. In addition, however, and as we have already seen, this box is Jewish. So Jews must represent the generic non-Christian. (Paul supposedly addresses in Rom 2 the obvious question that non-Jews do not necessarily possess the law of Moses and so can't be held accountable for their wrongdoing. Romans 2, following on from implications stated in chapter 1, suggests that everyone naturally possesses an internal moral law by which they too can be judged.[7])

But this schema also neatly explains why Box B is ethically so different from Box A, recalling that the law seems to have been left behind and that Christians act rather differently from Jews in many respects. Works of law, which is to say, acting like a Jew, must stop once a person realizes how futile life in Box A is and has made a decision for Jesus. We must not continue to rely on works of law once we have been justified by faith, while any such reliance would suggest that we have slipped back into Box A and are trying to be justified by ourselves again through our own efforts—the quintessential sin of Box A. So Judaism must be left behind by this story of salvation. It is the story of the failure that sets up the success that is Christianity.

It is easy to see at this moment why Christian scholars reading Paul's argument in Gal 2:15–16 in this way think that they are on the right track. When Paul wrote this letter originally, people were trying to persuade Paul's Christian converts in Galatia to act like orthopractic Jews, if not simply to convert to Judaism (see 1:7; 3:1; 5:7–12). Pressure was being placed on the men,

7. See Rom 2:12–16, 26–29—although this argument only goes some way toward resolving this problem. To have two very different but equally valid laws in play at any one time is problematic. It is also awkward affirming universal self-evident culpability, but limiting the offer of salvation to particular visits by missionaries or preachers. Everyone experiences the former and will be judged and condemned; not everyone experiences the latter, and will have the chance to be saved.

in particular, to get circumcised, which was a key Jewish practice (see 5:2–3; 6:13, 15). If Paul is saying what these scholars think he is saying in Galatians, then he is reminding his converts in texts like 2:15–16 of the very basic reasons why they left all this stuff behind, although there is a slightly counterintuitive side to this story.

The Galatians were not Jews originally but pagans (Gal 4:8). So Paul's point seems to be that to adopt Judaism is in effect to return to paganism and to abandon salvation by faith because Jews are the quintessential non-Christians. There is no fundamental difference between Jews and pagans, except that Jews present the basic salvific issues especially clearly. So any pagans who have become Christians and then decided to convert to Judaism have in effect gone back to Box A. This movement might look different on the ground—it might look like another forward step in piety, which is what seems to be confusing the Galatians—but underneath all the superficial religious flim-flam, it's a drastic step backward, from justification to its abandonment, and hence (ostensibly) Paul's passion as he writes to them. "Don't become a Jew; it's the same thing as losing your faith and returning to paganism!"

The law-faith sequence comes up again briefly in Philippians, principally in chapter 3, because the same problem seems to have recurred in relation to those converts, and it comes up extensively in Romans. According to many scholars, Romans provides an account of Paul's gospel in full, with him leading with the two boxes of works of law and faith in chapters 1–4 and then building everything in the rest of the letter on top of this. Moreover, this sequence arguably fits Paul's life as the book of Acts recounts it as well. Paul has a dramatic conversion, as the model prescribes, turning from legalistic law-observance to a life of freedom and salvation by faith alone. Acts describes this event three times (although, the careful reader will note, not in these exact terms; a former life of tortured legalism is never mentioned, nor is a specific decision of faith that alone justifies).[8] The story goes on to recount how Paul's converts no longer obey the law and how Paul defends his position determinedly against other misguided Jewish leaders in the early church like James, rather as Paul's later disciple, Martin Luther, stood up to the misguided legalism of Catholicism. (There are again some further details that don't fit this overarching narrative particularly well, especially the moments we have already noted when Paul, journeying through Jewish spaces, adopts Jewish practices, but these small data points are easily overlooked or explained away.) We know from this entire

8. See Acts 9:1–9; 22:3–11; 26:12–18.

story, in short, why Christianity is not Judaism—and, I am tempted to add, why Protestantism is not like Catholicism.

Most of us will have heard this account of Paul's gospel at some point, and many of us know it like the backs of our hands. Some congregations talk of little else. But less well-known is the fact that we are touching here on one of the most poisonous roots of the teaching of contempt.

This account of Paul's gospel builds, as we have just seen, on a foundation that is a description of Jews attempting to be justified by works of law, a foundation that is entirely negative. Jews are basically supposed to realize that Judaism sucks, and self-evidently so! It is supposed to collapse because it is, in and of itself, unworkable. No one can get saved by doing works of law perfectly, which is to say that Judaism saves no one. And so those Jews who grasp this "truth" become Christians saved by faith alone and leave Judaism behind. It is the moral and rational thing to become a Christian, then, and the immoral and irrational thing to remain Jewish. As a result, the heart of Jewish identity is the realization that Jewish identity is inadequate and should be abandoned! It is a negative identity—an identity that rejects itself, and if it does not do so, it should be condemned.

It should be clear by this point in our analysis, then, that this particular soteriological reading of Gal 2:15–16, along with any related passages in Paul, must release a particularly virulent form of anti-Judaism into Paul's theological description. Jews *must* be defined in this negative way on an ongoing basis because this is what grounds Christianity.

Fortunately, further critical scrutiny suggests that the reading from which this definitional hostility springs is questionable. It is very good news that in the growing thicket of difficulties that we see here, it is ultimately our assumptions that are the problem, and not Paul's account of salvation.

Authentic Judaism

There is a spread of more technical problems that we could talk about—principally objections that this understanding of Paul's overarching argument and its accompanying model of salvation do not enjoy an especially tight fit with the text that supposedly outlines it in the most detail, Rom 1:16–4:25, although the other texts where he is supposedly arguing in this way all have their problems of fit too.[9] But these are highly technical discussions about the precise nuances

9. Someone might object that vast numbers of readers of Paul have not spotted

of Paul's Greek, so any interested readers will need to check out my more detailed treatments elsewhere if they want this information.[10] I will concentrate here on just one of the big problems: the baffling and sinister implications of the reading for Jews and for Judaism. That is, at this moment, we will turn the damaging implications of this reading back on its own head. The reading's virulent account of Jews turns out to be one of its greatest weaknesses.

As we have already seen, the generic occupants of Box A and the unsaved condition are Jews, and they are Jews characterized above all, according to this reading, by the attempt to gain salvation by doing works of law. It is as if salvation is a brownie point system. Each good deed earns points, and when Jews show up before God on judgment day, they expect the verdict "Well done, my good and faithful servant; you have earned enough brownie points to get into heaven; enter into your master's joy." This approach is often called legalism, and its advocates legalists (although we will recharacterize things more accurately in a moment). And there is a very basic problem here: *Jews in Paul's day were just not like this.*

This observation has been made many times,[11] but E. P. Sanders made an especially compelling case in *Paul and Palestinian Judaism.* Doubtless some Jews were legalists (here softening Sanders's overly programmatic claim), much as some Christians are legalistic when they are not supposed to be. But many if not most Jews were not (and are not) legalists, just as many Christians are not legalists either. Would we want all Christians to be categorized as legalists when just a minority are? Probably not. And the same applies to Jews. Even if some are legalists, why characterize the majority in this way? Moreover, even

---

these mistakes before or have worried about them, so aren't these problems exaggerated? But there are two good reasons for thinking there *are* problems: (1) Christians were unlikely to pick up major problems in relation to Jews until very recently—essentially after World War II and the *Shoah*; and (2) people occupying a paradigm—and a reading undergirding an account of a gospel is a paradigm—don't like to ask critical questions of their own position, precisely because it is so important. This sort of blindness is very common. This is why Max Planck famously quipped that the progress of science can be measured by its funerals. For those who want more details concerning this resistance, see the justly famous analysis by Thomas Kuhn in *The Structure of Scientific Revolutions.*

10. My suspicions are introduced in *Quest*, developed in detail in *Deliverance*, and then summarized and defended in *Beyond*. The key biographical issues are addressed in *Framing*. A summary and overview that blends together the biographical and the theological issues can be found in *Journey*, chs 10–11, 127–50.

11. By the great rabbinic scholar George Foot Moore, and then later by Sanders's teacher, W. D. Davies and by my Doctorvater, Richard N. Longenecker.

if some were legalists, they were not necessarily *unreasonable* legalists, in the manner that this argument requires in order to continue. Neither God nor they necessarily demanded absolute perfection.

When we read what Jews themselves wrote in Paul's day about God, as Sanders did, we find a very dedicated group of teachers who followed the instructions of Moses scrupulously because God had given these teachings to them to guide their lives. When God gives instructions, handing them down personally to one of your great leaders in an extraordinary event on a mountaintop, you take very careful consideration of what they say. So, just as many Christians are dedicated to studying and obeying the Bible today, Jews were (and are) dedicated to studying and to obeying the Torah. Most Christians don't obey the Bible because by obeying it they hope to accumulate brownie points and thereby to get to heaven. They obey it because it contains critical instructions for living life. It is Scripture. It lies at the heart of pious living and obedience—of ethics. Christians know that they can't do everything instructed by the Bible. But we still read it and study it and try to do what it says (suitably interpreted). Just so, most Jews obey the Torah for ethical reasons, not for self-interested reasons of salvation. Torah is a gift from God that shapes the Jewish way of life. Putting things a little more technically here, we could say that a careful analysis of the Jewish sources reveals a critical inaccuracy in this reading; the dogmatic location of Torah for most Jews is within ethics, not within soteriology.

Complementing this insight is the belated realization that Jews are saved by election, which is to say, by God. God chose the Jews' ancestors a long time ago and promised to save both them and their descendants. He called the Jewish people into existence by summoning and blessing Abraham and Sarah, Isaac and Rebekah, and Jacob and Leah and Rachel. The resulting people, whom we know now as the Jews, are consequently his chosen people. God loves them and has a wonderful plan for their lives, which includes saving them. What sort of God would dump a people he called into being, having stayed in relationship with them through all sorts of ups and downs? It would be like deserting a beloved marriage partner on his or her deathbed!

But someone might say, What about sin? Doesn't sin break apart this cozy arrangement and separate the Jews from God?

By no means. Like any good parent, God knows his people sin and has made a lot of arrangements to deal with it. Moreover, like any good parent again, God does not cut off his people—his children—because they step out of line. His relationship with them is not dependent on a mere contract. He is Israel's *parent*, and so he stays committed to the Jews *in spite of* and *through* any wrongdoing. And Jews in Paul's day could be equally mature. They were often quite realistic about their transgressions.

They knew they sinned, but as anyone reading the Torah knows, God had made careful arrangements to deal with all this sin, and Jews were deeply dedicated to continuing those arrangements. They supported and in some cases ran a highly expensive and complex temple system that, among other things, atoned for sins. It did this every day and local Jews defended its purity to the death. Even if they lived thousands of miles away, Jews would send large sums of money for its upkeep annually and would travel and visit it in pilgrimage as often as they could. That is, most of the Torah is taken up with instructions for building and running the tabernacle, instructions that were taken to apply in turn to the temple in Jerusalem. And the temple, among other things, atoned for sins (see esp. Lev 16–17). So everyone Jewish knew that sin existed and that it was a problem that had to be dealt with, but they faithfully continued one of God's solutions to this problem located in the temple.

But Jews relied on the many other ways the Bible speaks of attaining forgiveness as well, a forgiveness grounded in the deeply generous and forgiving character of God. God cared about those who were kind to others, perhaps by giving alms self-sacrificially to the poor and burying the dead. Those who had shown kindness would be shown kindness—for example, Tobit. And like David after his awful sin committed with Bathsheba, Jews knew that honest confession and deep repentance could elicit God's forgiveness. Furthermore, God simply cared about the descendants of the patriarchs and matriarchs whom he loved so much. The sons and daughters of Jacob, renamed Israel, would not be judged harshly but would be blessed and nurtured because of God's deep commitment to their original parents. So the exquisitely penitent Prayer of Manasseh says,

> You, Lord,
> according to your gentle grace,
> promised forgiveness to those who are sorry for their sins.
> In your great mercy,
> you allowed sinners to turn from their sins and find salvation.
> Therefore, Lord,
> God of those who do what is right,
> you didn't offer Abraham, Isaac, and Jacob,
> who didn't sin against you,
> a chance to change their hearts and lives.
> But you offer me,

the sinner,

the chance to change my heart and life,

because my sins outnumbered the grains of sand by the sea. (7–9 CEB)

So when scholars read Paul's claim "You are [not] justified by works of Law" in places like Gal 2:16 and suggest that this reflects a definitive account of Judaism in Paul's day in legalistic terms, they are misguided. "Jews think that they can be justified by works of Torah; they work away and expect God to pronounce them righteous on the day of judgment, in which they will fail because God will condemn them for not being perfect," they opine. But most Jews in Paul's days would have said "What?!" (and they still do). This just isn't an accurate or fair description of Judaism.[12]

The reading of Paul's argument in texts like Gal 2:15–16 in soteriological terms—as the definitive story of Christian salvation—is now in deep trouble. The challenging Jewish arrangement in Box A is the foundation for his whole position. It sets the entire account of salvation in motion by placing pressure on its occupants to learn that they are sinful and thereby need to move on to become Christians, *and it just seems untrue*. It is in fact an absurd and rather nasty generalization that cannot stand up to close scrutiny. Jews were not legalists, or at least many of them weren't. However, without this claim holding good, in its entirety, for all Jews and then everyone else besides, Paul's account of Christian salvation in terms of faith alone has no rationale. We are supposed to get saved by faith alone, which is nice and easy,[13] *because* we fail so badly at

12. Some Jews might have added, "Of course we aren't justified by doing works of Torah. We are justified by our loving and gracious God, as the Scriptures say quite clearly. He saves us in the very same way that he called us into existence in the first place, through our father Abraham, and then through Moses and the exodus, by giving life to us, and ultimately by resurrecting us, as a gift. We are his chosen people, and he chose us before we chose him! However, he has also gifted us with these precious instructions about how to live our lives before him in a way that pleases him, and we are deeply dedicated to doing that as best we can. He is our God after all and has given us these instructions because he cares about us. In fact, I would never use the translation 'law' for them but would speak only of 'Torah,' meaning, as the underlying Hebrew suggests, our sacred teachings and instructions. I do expect to give an account of myself to God on the day of judgment. But I expect God to treat me like his child and to save me in and of himself, since this is what he has always intended and always said that he will do."

13. Ostensibly! Our earlier discussion of belief-voluntarism in ch. 13 suggests that choosing to believe things that we don't believe, and also that we may have no access to

attempted justification through works, as Jews do. Faith is manageable for us, we learn. And we want to get saved *because* God is going to punish us harshly if we don't grasp onto Jesus by faith. But the first stage in this argument now seems to be false. Jews aren't like this, and neither is God. God doesn't expect us to observe the law perfectly, as any reasonable Jew will tell us. So there is now no reason to progress out of the first box into the second. In fact, there is no need to enter into Box A in the first place. Its account of Judaism is too extreme and unreasonable.

But if this reading is so badly mistaken in its most basic claims, our suspicions should be gathering that Paul didn't actually argue in this manner. Would he be this unfair about his fellow Jews? He says on one occasion that he loves them enough to sacrifice himself for them (Rom 9:1–3). And would he be this rhetorically ineffective, beginning his account of the gospel with a description that anyone with half a Jewish brain could evade? Would he be this stupid?

These are admittedly not knock-down arguments. People can say all sorts of terrible things when they are placed under enough pressure, and some people say horrible things all the time. Perhaps Paul was under pressure. Or perhaps he was just a horrible person. But I don't think so. Some important evidence suggests that this account of Paul's argument in Gal 2:15–16 and similar passages is just plain wrong. It is time to lower the boom on this particular reading of Paul, along with its vicious anti-Judaism.

Paul's Signature Issue

As we already know well by this stage in our book's discussion, Paul's teaching was ethically challenging for any pagans who converted to the Jesus movement, but he did not ask them to convert fully to Jewish ways. The men did not have to be circumcised, and the communities did not have to observe the Jewish calendar, to eat Jewish food, and so on. This teaching caused a lot of controversy. It was shockingly innovative and felt very lax to Jewish conservatives in the Jesus movement, and this controversy confirms that Paul was doing something rather new and different. The traditionalists were offended. However, Paul defended his position successfully at the big Jerusalem meeting

---

verifying, is anything but easy. How do we find out whether Jesus's death has actually paid for the sins of humanity? Where do we go to verify this assertion, especially if we are just not sure whether it is true? How do we simply choose to believe these things if we don't think that they are true?

that was dedicated to discussing it (Gal 2:1–10), and the early church, at least for a time, evidenced a commendable commitment to diversity. It pursued a Jewish mission under the leadership of Peter, which was conducted in standard Jewish terms, and a pagan mission conducted in terms of Paul's more flexible, relational ethic, which allowed various aspects of local pagan identity to be maintained within the new Christian communities that formed (see esp. Gal 2:8–9). And the reading we are currently discussing of texts like Gal 2:15–16 in terms of justification not by works of law but by faith alone *cannot explain either this situation or its rationale.*

The argument cannot account for this spread of different ethical approaches within the church, and *it cannot actually explain why Paul's converts sat so lightly to the demands of the Jewish Torah.* It cannot explain, that is, the signature feature of Paul's mission, because when we read the argument about justification very carefully, we notice that the Torah is *not* abolished in relation to Christian behavior. It is abolished only salvifically, or as the texts say, in terms of justification. Christians are not justified and saved by observing the law. Fair enough (although who ever really thought they were, apart from a few foolish Jewish proto-Pelagians?!). But Christians *should still be living in terms of the law's instructions* (which is what reasonable Jews did). Its *ethical* relevance is *undisturbed!*

Now the advocates of this reading tend not to notice this implication. It is considered one of justification's greatest strengths that it can explain why Paul's converts largely left the law behind, even if one of the prices paid for this explanation is that Judaism is left behind as well. People in Box A will not be saved by observing the demands of the Torah largely because they can't observe them perfectly, so they are saved by believing alone. So clearly they have left a lifestyle of attempted works of law behind. We will grant these claims for the sake of argument, even though they are false. We just need to observe now, however, that this contention does not prove that the demands *themselves* are wrong, which is a fairly blatant non sequitur.

When the Torah says, "Do not covet," it is true that no one can fully observe this commandment. We won't be saved by fulfilling this demand perfectly if that is the way we get saved. But just because we won't be saved this way, it does not follow that we don't have to worry about covetousness any more. The ethical challenge named here remains. It is still the right thing not to covet, as the Torah says. Just because we can't do it perfectly doesn't mean it no longer applies. We should continue to work on our covetousness as hard as we can, meaning, we should try to resist it. In like manner, I am not a perfect father. But I'm not going to stop trying to be a good father, even though

I know I'm not perfect. It's still the right thing to try to do. And so, pursuing the line of inference further, everything in the Jewish Scriptures should still theoretically be the right thing for Christians to do as well: circumcising male children on the eighth day, resting on the Sabbath, avoiding impure forms of meat, refraining from adultery and false witness, and so on.

Hence we can imagine the Galatians objecting to Paul as follows if he was arguing as the justification advocates say he was: "Paul, we know we get saved through faith alone—and, again, we're very grateful that you came and told us this. It feels great to be saved. But we're wanting to move on in a serious way now with right living. We are disciples of Jesus and we're seeking guidance for this life from the Scriptures, which he knew intimately and quoted himself quite a lot. Moreover, they are, as you yourself say, the words of God preserved and written down to instruct us, so they are very precious texts. And they say quite clearly that we must be circumcised if we are males, and we should all be obeying the purity instructions and following the Jewish calendar. The Sabbath is, after all, one of the Ten Commandments. We don't see any reason why we shouldn't be doing any of this, as these visitors from Jerusalem have helpfully pointed out to us. We understand fully that we won't be saved by this. But we're not worried about salvation any more. We're worried about how to be good people and how to please the God of the Bible."

This objection is entirely fair and, more to the point, quite valid. Paul doesn't have a leg to stand on. His argument—if he is arguing as the justification advocates say he is—does not give the Galatians any good reasons for not doing what he seems to be saying in his entire letter to them that they should not do, that is, get circumcised and convert to Judaism (on ethical grounds of course)!

Hence, the construal of Gal 2:15–16 (along with any analogous texts) in terms of a journey to salvation—to justification—tells us nothing about relaxing the Jewish demands that should be placed on a convert (let us say, a woman) once she has committed to Christ. Her sins are forgiven. (Yay.) She is saved by faith alone. (Phew.) But she now has to try to live like a good person, because this is what God wants. (Yikes.) And there is absolutely no reason within this schema why she would not try to observe all the things that are written in the Bible, including in its first five books, known to many as the law. What else would she do? It was handed down to God's people in a fiery cloud, by God in person, to answer precisely these questions. Who is going to stop observing the Ten Commandments after they have been saved? Heck, some American politicians want vast versions of them engraved on hillsides.

In short, once we grasp this conundrum, we clearly have a major problem with what actually happened in Paul's mission. Everyone who converts, according to this reading, should still look like a Jew, not because they get saved in this way, but because this is the right way to live. *And this is clearly not what happened.* Paul's converts became Christians, not Jews—and he defended this position to the death. So this is a massive explanatory failure on the part of this reading. It doesn't explain the one key thing about Paul that we need explained, especially in Galatia—why Paul's converts from paganism are not living like Jews. So this reading just cannot be right. In view of this problem then, I think we can safely say that this was not Paul's argument in Gal 2:15–16 to begin with.

But can we save Paul's argument in these terms with some qualifications? Can we get his signature ethical freedom out of the traditional justification sequence in some clever way?[14] In fact, there is no solution to this dilemma, and neither can there be by the very nature of the case. The demands of the law, to which God holds us accountable, must remain in place as the fundamental structure of Box A.[15] Without them, the entire progression makes no sense. The story of the individual's salvation never gets started, a story generated by our culpability to future retributive judgment for not fulfilling the demands of the law. If the correctness and validity of these demands is negotiated away, then the entire model collapses. Its foundation is broken apart, which clearly cannot happen. And yet, if this is the right way to read Paul's argument in his justification texts, forward, and with reference to salvation, Christians should

---

14. There is a "free-rider" argument that I sometimes entertain, but it is immediately implausible. "Leave the law behind salvifically *and* ethically and live however you like, doing whatever you want, however sinful, assured that you will be saved through faith alone." This rejoinder's condemnation is deserved.

Others appeal to something in Paul called "sanctification," a model that does explain his ethical flexibility. But this move reduces justification to redundancy. Sanctification explains everything important in Paul that needs to be explained, as Schweitzer and Sanders have both famously observed. Moreover, attention to the fundamental differences between covenantal and contractual schemas suggests that justification and sanctification are fundamentally different accounts of both God and the gospel. So endorsing this sequence introduces contradictions into Paul's thinking at its most basic level. He is then deeply confused—the thesis of Räisänen.

15. In my experience, advocates of justification love the law and are ardent supports of "law-enforcement" and of "law-and-order" agendas in politics. Lutheran theology acknowledges this issue in part by speaking of *tertium usus legis*, the "third use of the law."

all still be Jews. Christianity, as a different ethical form from Judaism, should not exist. It remains a more likely conclusion that this reading is badly wrong.[16]

However, a few more pieces need to be set in place before soteriological foundationalism and its virulent anti-Judaism are removed from Paul's description. We need to supply a convincing alternative reading of the texts in question that solves our anti-Jewish conundrum. We need to be sure, that is, that Paul was not actually saying any of this. Fortunately, all the pieces are already assembled that will allow us to do this, and this book has been gathering them, carefully and deliberately, up to this moment, largely to make this alternative and non-foundationalist construal possible. These texts remain important, but they counsel us about different issues from salvation; they speak, rather, about the issue of missionary colonialism.

The Enemies

The basic problem, as we know well by now, is caused by foundationalism, which is to say, by reading forward Paul's argument in texts such as Gal 2:15–16. The text contains two "boxes," which we have been referring to from time to time as Box A and Box B. A foundationalist reader supposes that Box A is the foundation for Christian salvation in Box B. But let us suppose for a moment that Paul is not thinking like a foundationalist and thereby arguing forward. Another reading of these two important boxes might then be possible. Galatians 2:15–16 is, after all, simply an opposition—a straight-out antithesis. There are a Box A and a Box B in the text to be sure, but nothing says that they have to be connected together into some sort of overarching story of salvation, and it is this connection that does the damage. Nothing in the text actually says that Paul is arguing *from* A *to* B. Can we read this text, then, as a simple opposition between two states, one wrong and one right, which would solve a lot of our problems? Absolutely!

Earlier on in Galatians, in chapter 1, Paul details the reason why he wrote this letter. Verses 6–8 read:

16. A more sophisticated rejoinder could be made here—that Rom 2 reduces the Jewish Torah to a simpler "natural" law, and that this is the basis of Paul's pagan ethic. Sometimes we hear this position operating in terms of a distinction between the ceremonial and the moral law. But this move effectively erases Jewish history, as well as Jewish identity, and Paul overtly, and most obviously later in Romans (in chs. 9–11), affirms these things unequivocally.

I am astonished
that you are so quickly deserting
the one [i.e., me!] who called you to live in the grace of Christ
and are turning to a different gospel—
which is really no gospel at all.
Evidently some people are throwing you into confusion
and are trying to pervert the gospel of Christ.
But even if we or an angel from heaven
should preach a gospel other than the one we preached to you,
let them be under God's curse!

We learn here that certain figures have arrived in Galatia who are subverting Paul's gospel, displacing his teaching with another proclamation, that is, a "gospel," that he regards as unworthy of the name. Recognizing Paul's engagements with this group of counter-missionaries is a key move as we try to purge these passages of their anti-Judaism. We need to realize that he is debating in Galatians specifically with the agenda of these countermissionaries and nothing more.

We have already seen how Paul had to negotiate his shockingly radical new missionary approach with the other Jewish leaders of the early church. This process culminated in a gathering in Jerusalem over the winter of 49–50 CE, during which an important deal was made. Peter would lead a mission to the Judeans, which would proceed in conventional Jewish terms; Paul would lead a mission to the pagan nations, which would continue in a more diverse way, and he would also send a great deal of money to Jerusalem to assist their ministry to the poor. But not everyone accepted the Jerusalem deal. As is common in deep conflicts, a small, militant faction did not accept the decision of the majority at the meeting and set out to undermine it. We will call them "the enemies," since this is what Paul calls them once in an uncharitable moment.[17]

In 51 CE the enemies began to travel through Paul's communities, insisting that his converts from paganism adopt Judaism fully. The men had to be circumcised and to join the local synagogue.[18] Everyone had to start

---

17. Phil 3:18: "I have said to you many times and now say to you in tears that many walk [and ask you to imitate them] who are enemies of the cross of Christ."

18. They probably had a more technical reason for insisting on circumcision. Like the ancient Jewish philosopher Philo, they thought that circumcision of the foreskin of the penis literally cut "the evil impulse" off from people as well. This was the impulse living within that prompted people to sin. (It is a male-oriented argument.) So without

reading Torah assiduously (which is not a bad thing if it is done for the right reasons, but here it isn't), eating the right food, avoiding contaminated wine and idols, avoiding sexual immorality (which they were already supposed to be doing although, again, it needs to be for the right reasons), and following the Jewish calendar, lighting the Sabbath lights, resting on Saturdays, and observing the Jewish feasts. Reading between the lines, the enemies thought that only circumcision and complete commitment to the Torah would generate right behavior. If people did all this and lived righteous lives, they would show up before God's throne on the day of judgment and be pronounced righteous, which was pretty important. Only the righteous entered the kingdom of heaven.

This identification of the enemies and their agenda is highly significant. We can see now that they perfectly exemplify a *colonial* mentality. Moreover, they illustrate how colonialism frequently operates in a sinister alliance with foundationalism. Critical lessons lie for us here, then, as we parse their destructive "gospel," which Paul references in "Box A" (while critical errors lie in wait for us here if we fail to understand that Paul is opposing this position, not describing the first phase in his story of salvation).

A Colonial Gospel

Paul's enemies actually take us deeper into a key problem in relation to Pauline navigation that we began to address in previous chapters. There we saw that Paul's own advice concerning the construction of gender imposed an unwarranted form on his pagan converts—entirely understandably in certain respects, but in a way that should not be followed today. He justified the imposition of this structure with a particular account of creation, which was ultimately a mistake. His infralapsarian assumptions concerning creation needed to be reformulated in supralapsarian terms, at which point any warrant for his heteronormative construction evaporates (and we have since learned that terrible prices are ultimately paid if we resist this act of *Sachkritik* vis-à-vis creation). This was presumably a largely unwitting instance of colonialism, however; the introduction of this structure from Paul's parent context was not sufficiently thought through, we might say. He was impressively flexible and

---

circumcision, people had no way of resisting sinful behavior. They would spiral inevitably into deeper and deeper sins at the behest of the evil impulse and would be judged unrighteous on the day of judgment and sentenced to death and/or hell.

672

relational in many other respects, so generally he provides us with a missionary strategy that is anything but colonial.

The enemies, however, are much more aggressive colonizers. They want Paul's converts to embrace Judaism in toto! There will be no careful adoption of local pagan forms but a comprehensive introduction of Jewish structures alongside the introduction of an appropriate relationality. Pagan culture, except where it fortuitously overlaps with Judaism, must be erased, and Paul's Christian converts will become messianic Jews. And most significantly, in support of this agenda, the enemies seem to have done something that Christians through the ages have done as well.

They took the practices that they cared about ethically *and built them into salvation*. Becoming a Jew and doing all the deeds prescribed by Torah are how you get saved, they claimed. "Do them or go to hell!—but do them well and you go to heaven!" We know well by now that this move conditionalizes salvation and shifts it into a contractual form. Moreover, by refusing to renegotiate any of these claims christologically, the enemies necessarily endorse foundationalism as well. These cherished practices and claims are now the truth about the nature of God and God's will for humanity, overriding any additional insights that might come from Christ. So presumably their foundationalism was something of a Mosaic- and Torah-centric foundationalism—the sort of aggressive pro-Jewish agenda we see in a text like the Wisdom of Solomon (and hence not necessarily representative of the views of many other Jews in Paul's day, who wrote and read very different books). It probably contained what we could call messianic elements as well. The enemies seem to have believed that Jesus was the Messiah, resurrected on the third day, and that his death, with its shed blood, had atoning value, although to just what extent is hard to say. But this embrace of Jesus and his significance was far too limited. He might have been confessed as Lord, but he was not operating as Lord over the enemies' understandings of the truth and ethics!

In short, we learn from the gospel of Paul's enemies that colonizers are foundationalists and foundationalists are colonizers, although it is historically somewhat ironic to see this playing out first in relation to a view of Judaism. But we should quickly recall that Judaism was the dominant, powerful partner when the church first got going; the converting pagans were a marginal and dubious minority. We learn from the enemies, then, that colonizers reify parts of their culture as God-given—as a foundation—which makes them nonnegotiable forms that must be imposed on any converts.[19] Christological

---

19. The causality might have run the other way, with prejudices about cherished

scrutiny is thereby also blocked, which means that any structures endorsed fundamentally—here Jewish—along with any inappropriate relationality embedded in those (perhaps the legitimacy of violence in their defense) will not be subject to the overarching challenge of a loving triune relationality either. Moreover, any differences from these nonnegotiable forms are to be condemned. Such differences are sinful and wrong. So the colonial project operative here has a certain impermeability built into it, along with a characteristic self-righteousness. Everyone must look the same. Disaster!

Fortunately for us, Paul was having none of it. He opposed these enemies of the cross, as he termed them, in person when he could, but he couldn't be everywhere at once. So he sent volleys of letters to his communities when he thought that the enemies were either there or were about to arrive, and three of these are preserved in the Apostolic Writings—in historical order: Galatians, Philippians, and Romans. And it follows that a certain sort of messianic Jewish foundationalism is present in Paul's texts when he talks about the gospel of his enemies in these letters, although, of course, as he remarks caustically in Gal 1:7, it doesn't deserve the title of gospel at all.

The phrase "You will be justified by doing works as instructed by the law" is a summary of the gospel of the enemies, and it captures their conditionality nicely, beneath which we can detect a Jewish colonialism as well. "If you do works as taught by the divinely revealed lawbook, then you will be saved on the day of judgment. You will be pronounced righteous by God because you are! You will receive a verdict of 'righteous' in that court because a court is what decides these sorts of things. And you should get going as fast and as hard as you can now, beginning [addressing males] with circumcision, and following that up with a comprehensive abandonment of your disgusting pagan ways and a comprehensive adoption of our Jewish customs."

Of course, Paul adds in the fairly crucial little word "not" here. He has absolutely no confidence that this system will work. You will "not" be saved or justified by doing all the deeds prescribed by the Torah. You are too sinful, for starters. So it is a "gospel" that is just plain wrong, all the way through and all the way down. It doesn't know God, it doesn't understand what Jesus has revealed about God and what God has done for us through Jesus, and it doesn't even understand Judaism properly. This is what is going on in Box A in Gal 2:15–16, as well as in any related texts.[20]

---

structures and forms—traditions—leading to the unwitting unleashing of a foundationalist theology; but the results are the same.

20. The realization that Paul is engaging with another "gospel" in much of Gala-

Box A does not address Judaism directly at all. It describes a particular group of messianic Jews who have a debased view of God and of salvation—a messianic Jewish colonialism intertwined with foundationalism. And understood as such, we have broken the all-important progression between Box A and Box B. Paul is not describing a soteriological progression here at all. Box A is not a description of the unsaved state where we all begin our journey to the gospel from. Paul is contrasting two versions of the gospel, one of which—a messianic Jewish colonizing foundationalism—is wrong (and horribly so). The other version, Paul's, emphasizing resurrection through Jesus, is right, although this last claim leads to an important part of the situation that we still need to address. How should we now read Box B?

Faith

People reading these texts as a foundationalist story of salvation might point to Paul's repeated use of faith language in relation to Box B and go on to suggest that this clearly links the two boxes together in a single progression and story. The faith in question is the faith of the individual (here picture a man)—his decision for Jesus, by which he has been saved—and it follows that the texts *must* be speaking of his journey from unbelief to belief, and of salvation more broadly. If there is a moment when he believes, then there is a part of his journey before he believed. And presumably he had to be given reasons in that part of the journey to believe, which points toward Box A and Box B being linked together and telling the story of an individual's journey from unbelief and possible damnation to belief and salvation. It is clearly the story of one person's journey to faith. It focuses on him and his crucial moment of decision. The emphasis, we might say, is anthropocentric throughout.

---

tians, Phil 3, and Romans opens up a very different view of Paul's argument in his key anti-Jewish and foundationalist text: Rom 1:18–3:20. From this viewpoint, it becomes apparent that this is not a foundationalist account of the gospel at all, but a masterful Socratic subversion of the opening preaching gambit of the enemies, which seems to have been based on the account of pagans supplied by Wisdom. Reading Paul's argument in this Socratic fashion eliminates several nagging exegetical and argumentative problems that the usual, foundationalist reading cannot deal with, and so seems more plausible. Read in this way, any foundationalism is also eliminated. Paul identifies and exploits this commitment within his enemies' gospel. This Socratic reading is briefly described in *Quest*, argued in detail primarily in *Deliverance*, and then debated, clarified, and defended in *Beyond*.

But this possible objection was anticipated and dealt with some time ago. In chapter 13 we discussed the virtue of faith, including a careful description of the way it involves, but is not reducible to, believing.[21] We spent some time there exploring how Paul grounds our faith in Jesus's faith. We saw then that Paul loves to use the terminology of Hab 2:4, although assisted by texts like Gen 15:6 and Isa 28:16, to link the faith of his converts to the foundational faith of Jesus himself, arguing that the presence of this faith within us is a guarantee that God is at work within us by his Spirit and that we are on track for glory. We are part of the difficult part of Jesus's life now, when he journeyed faithfully and obediently to the cross, but precisely because of this action, we know that we are on track to enjoy the resurrection and ascension that came after this for him. It is consequently an argument intended to assure us, not to tell us how to become Christians in the first place. We believe in fact only because we have become Christians already; our believing is a part of the character of Jesus that we now dimly reflect. And this argument for assurance fits the situation like a hand in a glove.

Box B texts now speak of the importance of participation in Jesus as the basis of our discipleship and our growth in the key virtues. Moreover, they gesture toward the way in which these virtues and our relationship with Jesus himself are rooted in a future age, accessible through his resurrection, which is now breaking into our tawdry present but which we are nevertheless one day certain to enjoy. The risen and living Jesus is the source of our faith—and of our love, our giving, our obeying, our believing, our peacemaking, our joy—and hence of our future life in glory together with him. Furthermore, we have been set free, released from the need to repay the debt generated by sin *now* (which is death) and so "justified," right where we are. So we do not have to wait nervously and uncertainly for a verdict on the day of judgment. God is for us because God is in us, now. And the threats of the enemies can be ignored, and on all counts.

Understanding Paul's argument in this way, there is no need to connect Box A and Box B together on the basis of Box B's repeated references to faith. In fact, they really belong more firmly apart, as distinctly contrasting accounts of salvation. The enemies, thinking foundationally, want Christians to earn their way to heaven, basically by becoming Jews. If all goes well, they will be granted entry into the blessings of the age to come after the day of judgment. So resurrection is all about us and how we earn it, and an aggressive messianic

---

21. Our faith, derived from Jesus's faith, involves obeying and being faithful, trust, and believing, as well as believing and trusting in relation to the future, hence hope.

colonizing project will meanwhile unfold on the ground. But Paul is investing heavily in God's plan for resurrection, which involved the sending of his Son, who died bearing our humanity and was resurrected carrying a new humanity for us into heaven. If we are connected to him, through the Spirit, we will be resurrected. And our faith is evidence that we are part of him now and that the completion of our journey is guaranteed.

Paul's repeated use of revelation elsewhere in Galatians now reinforces the sense in which there is no human journey to salvation from an unsaved to a saved state that is oriented primarily by human considerations—that is to say, a journey that we control and think through for ourselves. God brings us to the realization of his Son and of his truth and importance by revealing these things to us, as they were first revealed to Paul. So a key text from Galatians noted earlier bears repeating here:

But when God,
who set me apart from my mother's womb
and called me by his grace,
was pleased *to reveal* his Son to me
so that I might preach him among the pagans,
my immediate response was not to consult any human being. (1:15–16)

Paul repeatedly emphasizes in Galatians, as well as in other letters, that God breaks into our lives, interrupting them, whether dramatically, as he broke into Paul's, or gently, quietly, and gradually into ours, perhaps mediated by other Christians or messianic Jews. It doesn't matter. The key point is that underlying whatever process took place God was in charge revealing himself. We know that Jesus is the Lord because the Lord has revealed it to us. So we are certainly involved in this event and are summoned to respond to the resulting relationship. God loves us and respects us as people, treating us with more dignity than we deserve. But the initiative and the effectiveness within this whole process lie with God. We don't work our way out of Box A into Box B. (We could say that we are located in some sort of Box A, which takes its distinctive contours from our specific situation—so every Box A is different!—and that God locates us in Box B, which we are duly invited to respond to.)

Drawing all these insights together—the presence of the enemies at Galatia peddling their foundationalist gospel, Paul's emphasis on the faith of Jesus, and our inclusion within him by way of God's revelation and divine intervention—I would translate Gal 2:15–16 as follows, and our problems with soteriological anti-Judaism are solved.

We who were born Judeans and not pagan sinners,
who know that a person is not released [from the debt of sin]
through works instructed by Torah only
but through the faith of Jesus Christ as well,
even we believed concerning Christ Jesus
that we are released through the faith of Christ
and not through works instructed by Torah,
[and understood further] that [as Scripture says]
"all flesh will not be released through works as instructed by Torah."

This is no longer a foundationalist text or a story of salvation in two stages. And it no longer boxes Jews and Judaism irrevocably and negatively into Box A, to supersede them as individuals journey across to the Christian state in Box B. It is a compare-and-contrast exercise. It juxtaposes a gospel that is not really a gospel at all but a colonizing program, one that views resurrection as something that people might be able to earn in the future, with the real gospel of God effected through Jesus, which views resurrection as a gift given through Christ and the Spirit now.[22]

With these realizations we also learn more deeply why people can be so offended by Paul and can resist the diversifications flowing from his flexible missional engagements. We see here the humbling *reflexive* dimension in the navigations he pioneered that can challenge members of their parent communities—transformational mode 4. Paul's enemies have recurred through much of church history, probably for much the same reason that they occurred in the first place. Taking reflexivity on board is difficult.

Missional Reflexivity

A Pauline navigation, as we have seen repeatedly in what precedes this point, should enter any new context in an incarnational mode, freely adopting the healthy relationality operative there already, along with any structures or forms that are not overtly offensive in relational terms. It is a noncolonial venture and a diversification inevitably results—a flourishing of God's community into

22. Stating things a little more technically, the argument runs: "We were in state A, and after B was added, received C; *therefore* C results from B *and not* from A, and C does *not* result from A in isolation." Note, arguably this argument also subtly suggests that Jews should be messianic, something we will probe more in the next chapter.

new, different expressions. Much still needs to be navigated locally, whether the introduction of a translated pedagogy or the reform or even abandonment of any sinful practices and structures. A transformation still needs to take place, and it can be quite dramatic. But much in the original context can be left in place as well, or at least remains recognizable after its relational modification. So a legitimate diversification in the church as a whole slowly takes place. And it is important to recall now, with the example of Paul's enemies fresh in our minds, that one feature of this situation is a *reflexive* impact on the group and the parent culture that sent out the missionaries in the first place. In Paul's day, however, this parent culture was of course Judaism.

When what we can call the parent culture's forms and structures are not imposed in toto on the evangelized people, something of a downgrade in their significance is experienced. When pagan converts become Christians and not Jews, the structures and forms of Judaism—the cherished customs and practices underwritten by the teachings of Moses—are necessarily revealed to be important but not mandatory, which is to say that they matter to Jews precisely as their historical and traditioned forms but do not have to matter to other people in the same way. I have taken pains to point out that they are neither trivial nor erasable. Jews are embodied, like everyone else, and the structures and forms that they act through count; they are the vehicles of their relationality and key components of their identity. They matter. God cares about them. But they matter *only to this degree*, which can be a humbling realization. Previously some Jews might have thought that their customs were rather more important than this. They might have thought that Jewish practices were *the* practices, superior to all others, and, if possible, necessarily to be adopted by all others. They should be universalized.

But Paul's mission revealed that such conclusions would be in fact to overvalue Jewish practices. They were important. They were no less, but they were also no more than this, and this implication was clearly rather galling to his messianic enemies. Indeed, they rejected this position and inserted their cultural affections into the basis of their theological program, producing a certain sort of early colonizing foundationalism. And presumably other non-messianic Jews felt the same way if 1 Thess 2:14–16 is any indication. Indeed, we can assume that this was a common reaction to a Pauline navigation because it still is.

It is irritating to be told that our particularities are merely important, and important largely to us and so not that special, and certainly not superior to all others. *But it is imperative that we hear this correction.* We must grow up in Christ and, if necessary, become adults at this moment. *If we resist this lesson, we resist Paul's constructive account of differences in terms of diversification and return to an account of difference in terms of superiority and inferiority, to a colonial mentality, and to attendant practices of inappropriate negation and erasure.* It is vital, then, to accept the implication of Paul's diversifying missionary work, namely, that our own structures and forms, which we might be very fond of, are merely important. Furthermore, we do not need to feel insecure about this reassessment.

Forms do not need to be mandatory to guarantee their importance, and to push for this further legitimation can be profoundly counterproductive. It is to enter a less secure space because, on the one hand, it is to unleash foundationalism, which inevitably collapses. On the other, the claim that our own structures are fundamentally superior issues a challenge to other forms as well, unleashing a never-ending struggle in zero-sum terms for survival. To make this claim is automatically to insist on some form of erasure. Valued as merely important to us, however, within our current embodied communal expression, our structures and traditions are unassailably important, and we do not need to undervalue or to override any others. Our practices are part of the way we are responding together, where we are, as we are, uniquely, to God. What could be more important than this?[23]

The preceding discussion has been a little technical at times, but it had to be. So many people go so badly astray at this moment in these distinctive texts that we had to grasp clearly just how this happens and how we can avoid it. I hope this is all quite clear by now. A great deal is at stake. Paul's interpretation will be shipwrecked if we read these texts in their usual fashion, an approach that has very little to commend it and much that should be said against it. In particular, we have learned that a vicious anti-Judaism will be written by this into the very foundation of Paul's gospel. And his gospel will in turn be cast in irreducibly foundationalist terms—terms that were actually being promul-

---

23. I actually know of no other account besides Paul's that can plausibly affirm differences, without merely ratifying differences per se (which would be to overlook sin), within an overarching arrangement that gives differences due weight but affirms them in a noncompetitive way—an account of difference within a process of ecclesial diversification. Every other account I am familiar with loses its way at some point. To its credit, classical political liberalism is at least aware of the importance of differences and tries to accommodate them in relation to an affirmation of the things that need to be held in common to facilitate a diverse life together, but it generates various distortions, partly because of its legal mentality, along with its predilection for abstractions and its ultimate reification of the nation-state.

gated by his deadly opponents! Few misreadings in the history of Pauline interpretation have been more ironic or more momentously destructive than this. It is time to rid ourselves of it, root and branch.

Theses

> For most of its history the church has described Jews negatively and hostilely and has frequently treated them poorly and even horrifically and has abetted the same by other actors.
> Without this prior history of contempt, the Holocaust would have been impossible.
> It is therefore especially important in a post-Holocaust era to be sensitive to the implications of any reading of Paul for Jews and for Judaism.
> The presence of any foundationalism within a description of Paul's thinking will generate anti-Jewish implications automatically. Recognizing the nature of foundationalism, along with its sinister role in generating anti-Judaism and supersessionism, is critical.
> The analysis in foundationalism works forward (A → B). The state preceding Christianity (B) is Jewish (A). Christianity (B) emerged from A as something different and later. It emerged, therefore, out of the *deficiencies* of state A (Judaism). Christianity (B) was the solution to the problems perceived self-evidently in Judaism (A). Its differences are superiorities to the self-evident problems in A. The rationale for later Christian difference from Judaism consequently lies in the inferiority of the previous state, which is Judaism (A− → B+). That rationale must be evident in state A, so it can lead to state B. So Judaism must be self-evidently insufficient, inadequate, and even immoral, incoherent, and irrational. A correct understanding of Judaism should entail the abandonment of Judaism for Christianity.
> This basic anti-Jewish dynamic operates in Paul's interpretation in three ways: in terms of (1) soteriological, (2) historicizing, and (3) salvation-historical, foundationalism.
> Soteriological foundationalism is the most important influence. It contributes significantly to a trenchant, definitional anti-Judaism in Paul, and the texts it relies on are the key texts for reading him in foundationalist terms. Foundationalism and anti-Judaism coincide exactly in these texts.
> A foundationalist and anti-Jewish account of Paul's gospel occurs when his antithetical "justification" texts are understood to be accounts of the

individual's journey to salvation, where justification is not by works of law but by faith. A woman (let us say) first learns from the attempt to do works of law (Box A) that she is under God's punitive judgment. Suitably anxious, she then grasps the offer made by the gospel of salvation by faith alone, thereby entering Box B. The punishment we justly deserve for our debt of sin is paid for by Jesus on our behalf. Box A is Jewish; Box B is Christian.

> Clearly in this schema, Jews are generically representative of unbelievers.
> This state in Box A is supposed to be abandoned because of its inherent inadequacy and because of anxiety about future judgment. This evaluation should prompt eager acceptance of the offer of salvation made by the gospel in terms of faith alone.
> The inadequacy of Judaism is self-evident. Those who resist these conclusions are irrational and/or immoral.
> This model seems to fit historically with the situation in Galatia. It purportedly explains why Paul's converts from paganism there should not convert to Judaism. That would be to return to Box A and to deny the validity of salvation by faith alone, which achieved entry to salvation in Box B.
> This reading can be challenged.
> This is a deeply inaccurate portrait of Jews and of Judaism in Paul's day, as E. P. Sanders and others have argued. Some Jews were covenantal, not contractual; others were reasonable, as against unreasonable legalists. (The model needs unreasonable legalism to work.) Jews had multiple biblical and theological solutions to transgression and sin, especially the temple, but also almsgiving, suffering, and repentance. The Bible also speaks of a forgiving God, especially in view of his commitment to Israel's founding ancestors.
> Paul is therefore being unfair, stereotypical, and reductionist, about Jews, if he is arguing in this way in his texts addressing Box A. He is also being argumentatively ineffective.
> Alternatively, this is not what Paul was arguing.
> We can confirm that this was not what Paul was arguing because this reading cannot explain Paul's flexible Christian ethic, which was his "signature issue." (Salvation, or justification by faith, actually requires the law to stay entirely in place ethically. That the law is to be abandoned ethically after it has been abandoned soteriologically is a non sequitur. Moreover, to suggest that it should be abandoned would be fatal to the entire construction,

which depends on its validity as it operates in Box A placing pressure on its occupants to move on to Box B. But Paul's converts did not observe the law as disciples, as they should have, if this was what he was arguing. This fact suggests that this particular construal of his argument is false.)

- An alternative construal of Paul's justification texts can be offered that avoids their anti-Jewish construal and these problems.
- This approach is more sensitive to his historical circumstances.
- Paul is engaging with "another gospel" in these texts—the teaching of people he calls his "enemies" (see Gal 1:6–7; Phil 3:18).
- They were messianic Jews hostile to Paul, with a fundamentally colonial attitude toward his pagan converts. They expected pagans to convert comprehensively to Judaism.
- This agenda was combined with a foundationalist emphasis on Jewish customs and practices as detailed by the books of the law.
- This led to a conditional and contractual account of salvation.
- "Justification by works of law" was their gospel, as well as their method of achieving resurrection.
- "Justification by works of law" does not therefore refer to Judaism in general or to a generic state prior to Christianity where a journey to salvation should begin in self-evident terms. Box A is simply a false messianic Jewish gospel. It is untrue.
- The enemies traveled through Paul's communities in 51 CE trying to subvert his teaching.
- Paul wrote Galatians, Phil 3:2–4:3, and Romans to oppose them—a more plausible account of their composition in historical terms than the alternative.
- Paul opposes the essentially colonial approach of his enemies to salvation by emphasizing Jesus's faithfulness to the point of death, followed by his resurrection and ascension. He uses scriptural language to warrant this emphasis, especially Hab 2:4. Those who believe are evidencing their connection to Jesus and are thereby guaranteed resurrection ("life," in Hab 2:4). This is God's chosen method of providing resurrection to sinful people. It is effective now to a significant degree. There is no need to wait until the day of judgment to learn whether we are saved. The presence of the faith of Jesus in Paul's argument has been discussed earlier, in chapter 13, when loving as faithfulness was analyzed. Participation in Jesus is central to Paul's ethics, as we learned earlier in part 2 as a whole.
- The "gospel" of the enemies is a useful lesson. It demonstrates how re-

sistance to a Pauline navigation into, and affirmation of, differences, can arise out of an overcommitment to the traditions, customs, and practices of a parent body.

> A Pauline navigation that sits lightly on structures and forms necessarily reveals many of the structures and forms in a missionaries' parent body to be merely important, not mandatory or universalizable. In this way colonization is resisted. But the price paid for this approach is the designation of Jewish structures and forms as merely important. This teaching offended some Jews both inside and outside the early church.

> But this Pauline account of difference, in terms we might say of mere importance, allows a constructive account of difference, and a secure one. Differences are explained in terms of missional and ecclesial diversification. They matter ultimately as particular expressions of communities before God.

> If differences are reified more strongly, they combine with foundationalism. This linkage creates vulnerability, not security, because that foundationalism will collapse under closer scrutiny. Moreover, it will engender a competitive account of difference, leading necessarily to attempted negations and erasures. So an attempt to increase the importance of certain structures and forms by elevating them is misguided and counterproductive.

> The reading of Paul's justification texts in terms of soteriological foundationalism needs to be repented of, not the least because it generates a virulent anti-Judaism.

Key Scriptural References

The construal of Gal 2:15–16 is central to the discussion of anti-Judaism in Paul, especially as it can be representative of more or less constructive readings of a family of similar passages in Paul, texts frequently understood in some sense to be about "justification." See Gal 2:15–3:29; 5:5–6; Rom 1:18–5:1; 9:30–10:17; and Phil 3:2–11; also Eph 2:8–10. Ultimately, the key text is Rom 1:18–3:20. Vestiges of righteousness terminology can also be found in 1 Cor 1:30; 6:11; and 2 Cor 5:21.

Paul speaks of "enemies of the cross" in Phil 3:18.

Galatians 1:15–16 recounts his call/conversion/commission, emphasizing that it took place through revelation (see also 1:12; and 3:23).

Key Reading

An important set of essays stating the issues, their solution in these terms, and their attempted defense against critics is gathered together neatly by Tilling in *Beyond*. (I wrote four essays and respond to the rest.) Chapter 6 should prove especially helpful: "Connecting the Dots: One Problem, One Text, and the Way Ahead." Several helpful introductory essays can also be found in chs. 7–11 of my *Quest*: 132–261. *Journey* blends together the biographical and the theological issues in chs. 10–11, 127–50.

Further Reading

The contentions of this chapter build directly on the affirmation of revelation and critique of foundationalism found in chs. 1 and 2, which rested ultimately on Barth, especially *CD* I/1, a position restated and nuanced in I/2, although it is also ably articulated by the Torrances. They also build on the critique of conditional and contractual accounts of God's relationship with humanity found earlier in several places, especially chs. 3 and 18 (leaning there on J. B. Torrance and ultimately John Macmurray); on the interpretation of some of Paul's believing language with reference to Jesus, argued in chapter 13 (see the literature referenced there, especially by Richard Hays); and on the diversity of the early church, comprising both messianic Jewish and formerly pagan, now Christian, members, argued especially in chs. 20–21.

Barth's account of Israel and of Judaism is contentious and has been sharply criticized. He wrote an astonishingly far-sighted account of Israel in *CD* II/2, which circulated, in an awful irony, in 1943. It does have its harsh side, however. An overtly post-Holocaust account of Barth on Israel probably needs to soften his views still further.

The diversity of Jews in Paul's day is nicely captured by (among others) Barclay and Cohen (in the Diaspora), and Neusner (principally in Judea, and extending beyond the first century).

Important forerunners to Sanders's challenge were W. D. Davies, his teacher, and G. F. Moore, who in 1921 wrote an astonishingly prescient essay addressing anti-Judaism in Paul and his New Testament interpreters. Richard N. Longenecker is an early Evangelical champion of this view as well. Few have pressed the resulting contradictions harder than Heikki Räisänen.

The basic way to avoid the anti-Jewish trap when reading Paul is indicated by Martyn's magisterial scholarship. He emphasizes revelation and its unconditionality, the importance of Paul's opponents to the interpretation of Galatians and related texts, and the centrality of the faith of Jesus to Paul's arguments. We also link hands here with the great founder of the modern biblical analysis of Paul, F. C. Baur, who discerned that the Paul of the letters, as against the Paul of Acts, had a real fight on his hands with a more orthopractic, Jewish wing of the church.

In addition to the shorter, more introductory treatments noted above, I provide a more detailed account of the situation and its solution in *Deliverance* and provide details of the biographical issues and solutions in *Framing*.

Bibliography

Barclay, J. M. G. *Jews in the Mediterranean Diaspora from Alexander to Trajan (323 BCE–117 CE)*. Edinburgh: T&T Clark, 1996.

Barth, Karl. *Church Dogmatics*. I/1; II/2.

Baur, F. C. *Paul the Apostle of Jesus Christ. His Life and Works, His Epistles and Teachings*. 2 vols. London: Williams & Norgate, 1873.

Campbell, Douglas A. *The Deliverance of God: An Apocalyptic Rereading of Justification in Paul*. Grand Rapids: Eerdmans, 2009.

———. *Framing Paul: An Epistolary Biography*. Grand Rapids: Eerdmans, 2014.

———. *Paul: An Apostle's Journey*. Grand Rapids: Eerdmans, 2018.

———. *The Quest for Paul's Gospel: A Suggested Strategy*. London: T&T Clark, 2005.

Cohen, Shaye J. D. *The Beginnings of Jewishness: Boundaries, Varieties, Uncertainties*. London, Los Angeles, and Berkeley: University of California Press, 1999.

Davies, W. D. "Law in First-Century Judaism," and "Reflections on Tradition: The 'Abot Revisited." Pages 3–48 in *Jewish and Pauline Studies*. London: SPCK, 1984.

———. *Paul and Palestinian Judaism: Some Rabbinic Elements in Pauline Theology*. 4th ed. London: SPCK, 1980.

Longenecker, Richard N. *Paul, Apostle of Liberty*. 2nd ed. Grand Rapids: Eerdmans, 2015.

Martyn, J. Louis (Lou). *Galatians: A New Translation with Introduction and Commentary*. AB 33A. New York: Doubleday, 1997.

———. *Theological Issues in the Letters of Paul*. Edinburgh: T&T Clark, 1997.

Moore, G. F. "Christian Writers on Judaism." *HTR* 14 (1921): 197–254.

———. *Judaism in the First Centuries of the Christian Era*. New York: Schocken, 1927–1930.

Neusner, J. *From Politics to Piety: The Emergence of Pharisaic Judaism.* Englewood Cliffs, NJ: Prentice-Hall, 1973.

Räisänen, Heikki. *Paul and the Law.* Tübingen: Mohr Siebeck, 1987 (1983).

Sanders, E. P. *Paul and Palestinian Judaism: A Comparison of Patterns of Religion.* Philadelphia: Fortress, 1977.

Soulen, R. Kendall. *The God of Israel and Christian Theology.* Minneapolis: Fortress, 1996.

Tilling, Chris, ed. *Beyond Old and New Perspectives on Paul: Reflections on the Work of Douglas Campbell.* Eugene, OR: Cascade, 2014.

CHAPTER 28

Beyond Supersessionism

Interpreting Judaism in Paul

The previous chapter charted how easy it is to make a critical mistake when reading some of Paul's arguments in Galatians, Philippians, and Romans, taking them to be his account of salvation in two steps, from works to faith, and hence from Judaism to Christianity. It changes things considerably when we grasp that Paul wrote these letters to deal with the enemies. Salvation was at stake in this engagement, not to mention resurrection, but the texts are *not* speaking about an individual's journey from an unstable Jewish state to a superior Christian existence. Paul was opposing a misguided messianic Jewish gospel that had lapsed into foundationalism and colonialism, countering it with his gospel, which centered on participation in the death and resurrection of Jesus. The recognition that this is the argument that was going on—an opposition of two different gospels, one wrong and one right—removes the virulent anti-Jewishness generated when Paul's justification arguments are misunderstood. All the textual data in Paul that ostensibly describe Judaism legalistically in terms of attempted justification through works of law as the basis of Christianity—the terms of Box A—can now be sidelined. This characterization summarizes a misguided messianic Jewish gospel and is just plain wrong. So we can now jettison Rom 1:18–3:9a, and any other texts that sound like it, for the purposes of describing Paul's view of Judaism, although there aren't that many of them. (Gal 2:15–16 is a nice summary of this group of passages.) This material looks Jewish, and in a certain sense it is, but it is not Paul's account of Judaism.[1] It is a distorted and inadequate account of

---

1. We can still use it to describe Judaism in Paul's day "phenomenologically," in terms of what various Jews at the time thought about God and salvation, although

salvation by contemporary competitors that he rejected, and we would be wise to follow him here.

Unfortunately, however, the anti-Jewish demon in Paul is not slain by this single stroke of the sword, although it is quite a stroke. If soteriological foundationalism and its anti-Jewish implications can be eliminated by reading texts like Gal 2:15–16 and Rom 1:18–3:20 more accurately in their original historical settings, it can still rear its dreadful head in two other ways: methodological and salvation-historical.

Historicism

The second form in which we encounter foundationalism and its characteristic forward thinking—which is what really does the damage to the Christian interpretation of Judaism—is *historicism.*

Historicism is not history or sheer historical analysis. Far from it. It is an underlying set of presuppositions, themselves closed off to historical analysis, holding that observable history and its causalities are all that exist. It is the assumption that reality is entirely immanent. These premises about the nature of history cannot be established by history. We do not observe or reconstruct them from the available evidence. They are really a prior metaphysics in the light of which certain types of derivative "historical" interpretation are then undertaken. Nevertheless, they are held by many modern secular scholars, and even by theistic scholars who accept the secular parameters of analysis within the modern university. Moreover, there is some truth in this viewpoint. God's incarnation, in particular, reveals that our embodied world is significant, and action within it is valid and meaningful. To a degree, history does proceed forward in this way. Much causality is immanent. However, this is a half-truth and, as such, dangerous. Divine action *on* our world, as well as *within* it and *through* it, is also rather important!

If we reify the importance of our own actions and those actions we can observe around us into an exhaustive account of reality, then history must proceed forward, and we will do history by histori*cizing*, which is to say, by assuming that history is a closed causal process. Everything happens because of something that happened before it. Reality moves in one direction. The

---

here messianic Jews. The speeches by the angel Uriel in 4 Ezra and, to a degree, the program underlying 4 Maccabees, along with part of Wisdom, are points of contact with contemporary Jewish texts.

present arises directly out of the past, making the study of a phenomenon's origins the key to much of its later development. Moreover, biological analogies will beckon.

The assumption of historical immanence has often been combined with an equally strong commitment to historical progress. A great impetus to this entire way of thinking was given by Darwin's theory of evolution, which burst onto the intellectual scene in 1859 with the publication of his *Origin of Species*. This theory combined in interesting ways with the rise of the modern capitalist and democratic nation-state in Europe. The astonishing success of capitalist economies—their massive increases in productivity and population as they industrialized from the late 1700s onward—and the emergence of complex and very powerful bureaucratic states led to a widespread and deeply rooted belief among the Western intellectuals funded and teaching in their universities that history is progressive. Immanent reality was also, then, we might say, fundamentally optimistic; it had a high opinion of itself.[2] History moves and evolves and develops upward, frequently culminating, a little predictably, in the culture and politics of the philosopher writing the large book about history and politics that people are reading at the time. So one of the greatest exponents of this viewpoint, Georg W. F. Hegel, argued from 1812 to 1831 that history was God on a great quest for conscious self-discovery, spiraling upward from lower to higher stages, until history and God culminated in nineteenth-century Prussia, with a little help from Napoleon.

This myth of progress is far from dead. It lives on where I currently reside, in the United States, many of whose residents are deeply convinced of its own developmental superiority to every other nation on earth—of its "manifest destiny"—and are equally deeply convinced that things have to move forward and upward, to progress. A nice marker of this historical optimism is provided by the campaign slogans of recent successful presidential campaigns. Reagan campaigned in 1980 with the slogan, "Are you better off than you were four years ago?" (The answer was No, making it an effective slogan because it should have been Yes.) Clinton campaigned in 1992 with "Don't stop thinking about tomorrow" (which also used a jaunty theme song of the same title by pop band Fleetwood Mac). Obama campaigned in 2008 with the mantras "Change we can believe in," "Hope," "Yes we can!", and "Forward"—a plethora of upward-moving tropes. Trump's campaign slogan in 2016, "Make America great again" clearly also implied that things should move upward and onward.

2. This is Barth's jocund opening observation about the Enlightenment in *Protestant Theology in the Nineteenth Century: Its Background and History*.

But this worldview, when it is secularized, will, as we saw in the very first chapter of this book, cut us off from a great deal that Paul says about actors such as God, and it will lead us to supply a reductionist account of his thought, and probably to question his sanity as well. And even if Paul's analysts do not overtly embrace these drastically narrowed parameters, when they proceed in this way tacitly, analyzing events in history like the emergence of Christianity from Judaism in terms that are accessible only within history, then historicism will dominate and a methodological foundationalism will be unleashed. And this in turn will release a second form of supersessionism.

If history works forward, immanently, and also evolves upward, the emergence of Christianity from Judaism must again be rooted in some prior deficiency within Judaism, and we will thereby return to all the problems of soteriological supersessionism, although these will play in a new key, so to speak, in grand historical mode. The new form that is Christianity emerges out of Judaism, although it is different from Judaism in many respects; consequently, it improves on Judaism, progresses beyond it, and must displace it. Jews who resist this movement resist progress, and maybe even resist "freedom" and "modernity" as well. Hegel's terminology for this shift was a movement from "the particular" to "the universal." God in history needed to move from the narrow details of existence to the great universal abstractions of modernity and the nation-state. So the cramped details of Judaism needed to be discarded and left behind for the massive and greatly purified reach of Christianity.

This claim turns out to be almost complete nonsense once it is pressed. All historical peoples are irreducibly and permanently caught up in details and particulars. So Christianity is entirely particular. It is not an abstraction, Hegel's hopes notwithstanding. It is not just a great idea, universally applicable like Kant's categorical imperative. Christians are real people caught up in all the messy details of specific lives—eating, working, reproducing, and so on. Moreover, Judaism is as committed to universalism, in the healthy sense, as Christianity is. As soon as the affirmation is made that God is the Lord, a significant universal claim is in play (although this is not abstract). So Hegel's distinction doesn't make much sense. But it still recurs within our scholarship, staggering through our analyses like a zombie, in part because the great father of modern critical Pauline studies, F. C. Baur, was a devout Hegelian.[3]

Moreover, a tacit cultural alliance is often present here with anti-Judaism. Many cultured Europeans were embarrassed by Christianity's Jewish roots and

---

3. It was noted earlier that F. C. Baur had some insightful things to say about Paul—but not everything he said was insightful.

so were happy to grasp on to a theory that allowed Judaism to be abandoned as a primitive and early form to be discarded for the higher evolution that was Christianity. The bizarre tumult of the eastern European synagogue could be left behind for the elegant liturgical, architectural, and musical refinements of the German church. So this theory often mapped the social locations of the viewpoint's advocates nicely.

In short, if the changes that history itself delivers from within are in any sense a step forward, which is to say, a moment of progress—and both evolution and much modern Western cultural thought would say "Yes, they are"—then Christianity must supersede Judaism as *Homo sapiens* succeeded the dinosaur and capitalism succeeded feudalism. This worldview and its progressive outworkings resonated nicely, moreover, with widespread anti-Jewishness in Europe. And at the heart of this progress was Paul (and this even if some of the categories he used to express the point were quaintly superstitious). He was the great apostle of progress, who pioneered, enacted, and justified the emergence of Christianity, the highest form of religion, and the abandonment of its Jewish precursor as a primitive form that must now be firmly repudiated, along with all its inadequacies.

What should be done about this derogation and ultimate erasure of the Jews?!

The problem here is again initially methodological. So the only way to prevent the emergence of this demonic supersessionist variant within the analysis of Paul is by insisting that history is an open process, not a closed one. This approach still allows us to undertake sober historical analysis, but it will not be pursued in historicizing terms, which would in any case, if I am right, be reductionist. God is involved in history, and so good historical analysis needs to take this factor into account, and I have tried to do so throughout this book. Moreover, as election indicates, God's plan for history is the real key to the ultimate direction of history, however complicated and opaque its detailed outworking might be (Rom 8:28), and we grasp this truth only after it has grasped us, through revelation. So history does not *itself* contain an internal upward momentum—far from it. It stands always on the edge of chaos and evil, being held against complete disintegration by a good God acting on it faithfully "from above." The truth about history holds history in the palm of its hand. If we let go of these insights we inevitably fall back into a closed historical process, and then it is very difficult to resist building anti-Jewishness into the heart of Christianity. Moreover, any Christian commitments on the part of this type of analyst will, somewhat ironically, make supersessionism nigh on unavoidable.

Fortunately, an open, elective view of history—which is really just to say an eschatological view of history—is undergirded by deeply Pauline claims. Almost everything he wrote makes sense only on the assumption that God exists and acts definitively through Jesus, and that our gathering in him into the triune communion is the destiny of the cosmos. This is as important and as real as it gets. It is a difficult stance to maintain within the modern academy. But if we are followers of Jesus in the terms that Paul describes, then we have no choice. We simply hold this to be true, and it is true because it has been revealed to us, so we can no more deny this reality than deny that the sun rises. Moreover, the heart of our ethic calls us to maintain these convictions with as much courage as we need to resist their erosion, if necessary to the point of death!

But at least this stance, which is to say, the faintly ridiculous claim that God is in charge of history, now has the added bonus that we do not need to engage in a historicizing reduction of Judaism to a primitive historical antecedent to the development of Christianity. Christianity did not evolve from and transcend its historical antecedent, the Jewish people, in the way that higher species like primates evolved from lower forms like fish. Humankind has to be gathered into the ultimate purpose of God, which is communion. The development of Christianity was clearly part of God's great plan. It need not follow, however, that the Judaism that preceded it was in any way inferior to it or needed to be abandoned. God's plan was for the church to *diversify* outward from Judaism as all things are gathered back into communion, which is a rather different thing.

With this set of important realizations in place, along with their critical counter to methodological supersessionism, we must turn to consider the third principal way in which anti-Jewishness can slip into Pauline interpretation, by way of salvation history, although as we do so we will need to address the problem that various important scholars of Paul don't want him to have a salvation history at all. This dimension within his thinking can be rejected, and attempts to introduce it have been hotly disputed. We see here, in fact, that the elimination of supersessionism from any salvation-historical dimension in Paul is caught up with foundationalism in an especially complex way.

Sacred-Nation Theology

Much history as it is described by the Jewish Scriptures revolves around a divinely constituted people who colonize a divinely gifted area of land, driving out, enslaving, or assimilating the original inhabitants, and then developing political institutions that are divinely ratified in turn. Monarchies ensue with taxation, armies, and capital cities complete with palaces and a temple, which is all the outworking of God's great plan within history. Hence, the vehicle within which all God's purposes are concentrated is, at bottom, *a sacred nation*. And it is privileged over its ethnic neighbors, divinely entitled to its territory, and justified in appropriating and defending itself with lethal and even genocidal force.

When we take a step back from this construct, it is a truly frightening thing. A group of people is entitled by God to occupy a particular area of land, resisting all ethnic assimilation or inclusion, and blessed, if necessary, in its bloody acquisition and defense. I suspect that people need no encouragement to form such essentially tribal allegiances. When they do so in these theological terms, however, they are removed from all moral restraints as they further the perceived interests of their people, and the results have been quite horrifying as they have played out in subsequent history.

Just this ideology, for example, informed the appropriation of the upland territory now organized as the Transvaal and Orange Free State in South Africa by Dutch settlers in the early 1800s—the Voortrekkers. (They also colonized Natal.) December 16 is still commemorated annually as the day a covenant was formed between God and the Dutch settlers, when a vastly outnumbered force of settlers defeated a huge Zulu *impi* (army) at the Battle of Blood River in 1838. On December 9 the settlers had prayed,

> If the Lord might give us victory, we hereby deem to found a house as a memorial of his Great Name at a place where it shall please him, and that they also implore the help and assistance of God in accomplishing this Vow and that they write down this Day of Victory in a book and disclose this event to our very last posterities in order that this will forever be celebrated in the honor of God.[4]

On December 16 the Zulu attacked, hoping to drive the migrating Voortrekkers from their land. About three thousand Zulu warriors were killed assaulting the Voortrekker laager of wagons, which was defended by muskets

---

4. https://en.wikipedia.org/wiki/Battle_of_Blood_River. See also https://en.wikipedia.org/wiki/Voortrekkers; https://en.wikipedia.org/wiki/Orange_Free_State; https://en.wikipedia.org/wiki/Transvaal_Colony; and https://en.wikipedia.org/wiki/Colony_of_Natal.

and two small cannons, and only three defenders were wounded. (In other words, it was a massacre.) The battle was a turning point, and colonization of the new territories followed—territories that were then defended against later British absorption and, still later, organized on racial lines. (It is only fair to note that the original Dutch invasion was not completely one-sided in moral terms. The Zulu king Dingane had invited an initially peaceful party of settler leaders to his kraal, ostensibly for a celebratory beer-drinking feast after making a treaty with them, only to have them massacred.)

Further examples of horrific violence perpetrated in the name of a sacred nation are easy to find. The breakup of Yugoslavia from 1991 to 2001 witnessed ghastly incidents of ethnic cleansing. Many Serbian atrocities were justified by the conviction on the part of the Serb perpetrators that Serbia was a sacred nation, with particular holy sites and territory, surrounded by ethnic and religious others who needed to be expelled or exterminated—a group including Catholic Croats, Slovenes, and Albanians and Muslim Bosnians and Albanians. (The intellectual center for this ideology was the University of Belgrade.) The same basic stance can be detected in militant Zionism. It recurs again centrally to much of the trouble that has unfolded in Northern Ireland, in both Catholic and Protestant militant groups. But the most notable example of this way of thinking is of course German National Socialism, the cradle within which some of the most important Pauline scholars of a previous generation were raised and formed. Hence when these scholars and their pupils see the phrase "salvation history," they think immediately of a sacred nation and its appalling legitimization of the Nazi reign of terror, and so they quite understandably just say No.

Complicating this situation is the fact that this sinister legacy tends not to be noticed by many other Christian scholars who are situated in liberal and democratic cultures. It is unthinkable in this context that naked tribal dynamics would be fanned into flame by what is initially just a hermeneutical program—a reading strategy—that builds from the Jewish Scriptures continuously through to the Apostolic texts. But this is merely fortuitous. Such a program contains no automatic political safeguards. A careless account of the history of Israel can endorse a sacred nation clearly and continually, and have a powerful resonance with later political projects in just the same terms, however unintentionally. The aggressive and genocidal political implications latent within this particular approach to salvation history need to be faced and dealt with directly—*but not by refusing to undertake salvation history at all.* This is a mistake, and a big one, for reasons that now need to be fully appreciated.

Salvation-Historical Foundationalism

If God is a faithful and ultimately also an all-powerful God—bearing in mind the critical insights into the nature and operation of God's power revealed by the crucified Jesus[5]—then his original plan for the cosmos needs to work out within the cosmos. And this plan began in earnest within human history with the creation of his people, a people that Paul descends from directly, whom he refers to as Jews or Judeans.[6] God's involvement with us did not begin with Jesus. It began long before this central moment. To deny this involvement was Marcion's great error. Moreover, Paul is no Gnostic. He believes in a fully embodied life and so believes in a fully embodied history within which God is involved using, as usual, people to convey his purposes. It follows that there are (so to speak) concrete antecedents to the new communities that formed around Jesus, namely, the Jews. And any responsible account of Paul—and simply any responsible theology, period—*must* contain a story about these Jewish antecedents. So we must include a salvation-historical dimension in our account of Paul—and he certainly did.

However, many traps lurk here as we do so, including of course the great trap that underlies almost all others, foundationalism. If the response offered to the rejection of salvation history by scholars traumatized by the horrors of the Nazi regime is a knee-jerk affirmation of salvation history undertaken in foundationalist terms by well-intentioned anti-Marcionites, then the cure is as bad as the disease, and the debate will be driven, moreover, into an intractable impasse.

It is very easy, that is, for Tertullianism to rear its ugly head again within any account of salvation history. We should recall that Tertullianism—which is not, to reiterate, a complete description of Tertullian himself—is prompted principally by canonical and historical anxieties involving Jews and creation, anxieties first raised by Marcion. Marcion argued that the God of the Jews, the Jewish Scriptures, and the Jewish people could have nothing to do with the God of Jesus, the Christian Scriptures (which he defined narrowly, around Paul), and the Christian church. He denied any need, then, for salvation history, as well as denying any need for an account of creation.

5. See especially 1 Cor 1:18–31.

6. The Greek *Ioudaioi* can denote either of these referents, suggesting either what a modern person would call an ethnic group or someone from a particular place, in this case, Judea. There is a concrete connection between these two notions, but they are not the same thing.

Tertullian, along with many others, realized that this was a disaster on multiple levels. God's integrity is called into question; the scriptural basis that the church rests on is compromised, and ethics is ultimately placed in jeopardy by the flight of the church from the gritty, embodied realities of creation and history. However, if the response to these anxieties is the assertion up front of the truth and significance of God, of creation, of the history of the Jews, and of the Jewish Scriptures, without due attention being paid to the careful derivation of these truths from the primary truth that is Jesus, then the result is an endorsement of foundationalism in salvation-historical guise. And at this moment the baby has gone out with the bathwater. This posture—the telling of the story of salvation history like a quest—will ultimately and somewhat ironically erode all the key claims about God and reality that Tertullianists ultimately hold dear, because as foundationalist claims they will not stand up to further scrutiny. Moreover, this well-intentioned but badly founded strategy will pay the further price of supersessionism, which is our principal concern here. It may even, in addition, unleash the radioactive salvation-historical form of sacred-nation theology.

The key truths about God, creation, and history, including Jewish history, might be affirmed up front, as was just said, in advance of the coming of Jesus and his definitive revelation, as the foundation for all further Christian thinking. This assertion of the basal role of ancient Israel is supposed to safeguard its importance (although it will ultimately do anything but). The overarching schema works forward, from Israel and its history to Christianity and its somewhat different history. Hence, given that the thrust of the schema is forward, the differences that Christianity embodies will, once again, as in the soteriological schema, have to arise out of the prior deficiencies of Israel. In a schema that works forward, a later state that is different entails an explanation in terms of the deficiencies of the first state from which it arises, and supersessionism must result.

It is actually quite difficult to build a broad, salvation-historical story that accounts coherently for this fundamental shift at all. So one of the most important contemporary representatives of this view, N. T. Wright, although preferring the broader, salvation-historical canvas, retreats to good old-fashioned soteriological categories to make this case; the deficiencies of trying to be justified by works of law are writ large across Israel's history, to be succeeded by a new dispensation based on faith. As a result, true Jews in the new era of Jesus, arising out of the great story of Israel that precedes him, look suspiciously like Protestants who have learned that law-observance demonstrates only the presence of sin and of a deep problem with a God who judges, although they have also now been disobedient to their divine calling to evangelize the nations.[7] Other advocates of the New Perspective try to offer a alternative, nuanced version of this progression, but the price they pay for this modification is a collapse into frequent argumentative incoherence and exegetical implausibility. A somewhat different, promise-fulfillment schema, which seems initially to be rather more kind-hearted, is sometimes affirmed by scholars like Krister Stendahl and Oscar Cullmann. Judaism here is not in and of itself necessarily intrinsically negative; it is the bearer of the promises in its precious Scriptures, which Jesus will come and fulfill. However, this schema struggles to explain the radical divergences between Christianity and Judaism, and when it does so, burying the explanation of that coming divergence in the promises, a harsh side again emerges within the explanation, not to mention, within God. Soteriological supersessionism tends to emerge again, although with a new sting in its tail.

It follows from this particular rationale that the coming of Jesus should have been anticipated by Jews. After all, they possessed the Scriptures that sketch out their current promissory state and the hope of a perfected future, which is realized in their coming Messiah. So when Jesus arrived, fulfilling all their promises, Jews should have embraced him—and when they did not, they therefore failed to understand their own history and their own Scriptures. As a result of this failure, Christians, who did accept Jesus, now understand Jewish history, Jewish hope, the Jewish Scriptures, and their all-important promises better than the Jews do. Hence Christians effectively colonize all these dimensions of Jewish life, and judge nonmessianic Jews with customary harshness to be deficient, resistant, and foolish. So we are not really much further ahead when we promulgate this promise-fulfillment schema (and we still often struggle to explain coherently why Christianity is so different from Judaism).[8]

In short, we can see that whatever particular rationale we choose to run, a harsh form of Jewish accountability is again necessarily generated by any broad

---

7. I call this position "panoramic Lutheranism"; see my essay-length review "Panoramic Lutheranism and Apocalyptic Ambivalence: An Appreciative Critique of N. T. Wright's *Paul and the Faithfulness of God,*" *SJT* 69 (2016): 453–73.

8. The claim that God intended this change all along, and built it into the promises, has challenges of basic scriptural plausibility, because the Jewish Scriptures emphasize the Torah so strongly; it raises insurmountable questions about God's integrity. These match the problems raised if God intends a two-stage creational schema, a preliminary inferior form being succeeded by a later superior version.

account of salvation history that works forward, from Judaism to Christianity. Christianity inevitably goes on to displace Judaism, moving beyond its prior deficiencies. And the Torah will be left behind somehow, for some reason, so Jewish forms and structures will ultimately be erased. It seems, then, that any forward-moving account of salvation history is inevitably supersessionist (i.e., where it is not either unorthodox or completely incoherent). Tertullianism is a Jewish poison pill, then, which is not a little ironic when it arises from anxieties that Marcion dangerously cut the Jews off from the gospel. But why reaffirm them in such a way that they are negated, judged, and erased?[9]

Moreover, all the dangers of foundationalism have been unleashed again, which we know well by now, except that in this instance they link hands with sacred-nation theology!

One of the great problems generated by foundationalism that we have noted repeatedly is its inability to criticize its own favored cultural and political commitments. When these are built into the foundation of the system being advocated, they are removed from Trinitarian and christological challenge. And one of the reasons for this constant attention is to prepare us for this very moment, where we see that a foundationalist salvation history either offers absolutely no defense against sacred-nation theology or it *is* sacred-nation theology! Sacred-nation theology is really nothing more than a peculiarly self-righteous and ultimately vicious form of foundationalism, whose virulence is repeatedly attested to by history. And with this realization we can probably grasp why so much contemporary debate is caught in a bitter and intractable impasse.

Paul *must* have a salvation history or his interpretation risks collapsing into Marcionism. The critics of overly disjunctive approaches to Paul are right to point to this necessity. But when salvation history is introduced by such critics, a comprehensive supersessionism *and* a sacred-nation theology are unleashed! And it is entirely correct for this construct to be firmly rejected as well. Moreover, these positions seem to be a straightforward either/or; it is one or the other—*although both these alternatives are fatal*. What is to be done?

The way ahead lies—as usual—with the recognition that the damage is being done in all these constructs, whether in terms of supersessionism or sacred-nation theology, by foundationalism, and with the complementary

---

9. What this dynamic exposes, sadly, is a Christian concern that is actually canonical, worried about the sundering apart of the two testaments of the Bible, and a lack of much concern for the Jews themselves.

realization that the problems unleashed can be dealt with as we learn to tell Paul's salvation-historical story in the right way, backward. Never has it been more important than here to hold all these methodological insights together.

Salvation History as Memoir

We can articulate a salvation history in Paul, as we must, and in fact kill all our supersessionist birds with one stone, including any sacred-nation theology, if we cleave to our original insight about storytelling, articulated first in chapter 3, and tell this story retrospectively, or backward, like a memoir. This approach will prevent the unleashing of foundationalism. It will free us from the foundationalist need to describe Judaism as innately and self-evidently deficient, evolving into the higher, and very different, state of Christianity. In other words, it will free us from supersessionism. And it will allow us to criticize and to reformulate, if not simply to expunge, any sacred-nation theology from our account, resisting the suggestion that this political form needs to be carried on. Only a loving relationality needs to be carried on, as God's goal for the cosmos, and all other social and political arrangements are to be subjected to the lordship of the one who was crucified before he was resurrected and enthroned. Hence it is to our great good fortune that this is exactly what Paul does, once we notice it (although the following will necessarily be a very brief sketch).

Paul narrates the pre-messianic history of Israel as a smoothly continuous and coherent story, *now that the figure to which everything has slowly been building has been revealed.*

> Theirs [Israel's] is the adoption to sonship;
> theirs the divine glory,
> the testaments,
> the receiving of the sacred teachings,
> the temple worship [in the presence of God],
> and the promises.
> Theirs are the patriarchs,
> *and from them is traced the human ancestry of the Messiah,*
> *who is God over all, forever praised!*
> Amen.[10] (Rom 9:4–5)

10. The syntax is, strictly speaking, capable of being read in different ways from

The Holy Scriptures [made promises]
regarding his [God's] Son,
who as to his earthly life was a descendant of David,
and who through the Spirit of holiness
was appointed the Son of God in power
by his resurrection from the dead:
Jesus Christ our Lord. (Rom 1:2–4)

So,

The Son of God, Jesus Christ,
who was preached among you by us—by me and Silas and Timothy—
was not "Yes" and "No,"
but in him it has always been "Yes."
For no matter how many promises God has made,
they are "Yes" in Christ.
And so through him the "Amen" is spoken by us
to the glory of God. (2 Cor 1:19–20)

In the light of Jesus's climactic arrival, death, resurrection, and ascension to lordship on high, Paul looks backward and now sees faithfulness and resurrection inscribed into Israel from its very beginnings and attested to by the Jewish Scriptures. Israel began when it was called into being through the household of Abraham. Abraham, known as Abram at the time, was promised seed and land by God:

I will make you into a great nation and I will bless you;
I will make your name great, and you will be a blessing.
I will bless those who bless you,
and whoever curses you I will curse;
and all peoples of the earth will be blessed through you. (Gen 12:2–3)

God reiterated these promises in a subsequent chapter:

---

this translation. But this construal is, given the available evidence, most likely. See Robert Jewett, with Roy D. Kotansky, *Romans: A Commentary*, Hermeneia (Minneapolis: Fortress, 2006), 566–69; and Richard N. Longenecker, *The Epistle to the Romans: A Commentary on the Greek Text*, NIGTC (Grand Rapids: Eerdmans, 2017), 779–95.

> Look up at the heavens and count the stars—
> if indeed you can count them. . . .
> So shall your offspring be. (Gen 15:5)

These promises had translated by Paul's day into entry by Abraham and
his seed into the life of the age to come through resurrection, and the inheritance of that perfect world forever (so most clearly Rom 4:13). But there was a
technical problem. Abraham had no direct heir with Sarah, his wife. Nevertheless, at an extraordinarily advanced age, having soldiered on in faith for sixteen
years or so after receiving the last iteration of the promises, God miraculously
gifted the couple with Isaac, an heir through whom Abraham's seed would
descend and the promises be fulfilled. Paul describes both Abraham's old loins
and Sarah's barren womb as "dead," so the conception and birth of Isaac was
literally an event of life from the dead, like a resurrection.

> He [Abraham] is our father in the sight of God, in whom he believed—
> the God who gives life to the dead and calls into being things that were
>   not.
> Against all hope, Abraham in hope believed
> and so became the father of many nations,
> just as it had been said to him, "So shall your offspring be."
> Without weakening in his faith,
> he faced the fact that his body was as good as dead—
> since he was about a hundred years old—
> and that Sarah's womb was also dead.
> Yet he did not waver through unbelief regarding the promise of God,
> but was strengthened in his faith and gave glory to God,
> being fully persuaded that God had power to do what he had prom-
>   ised. (Rom 4:17–21)

We need now to note carefully just what account of past Judaism Paul has
created. The story has God placed centrally as the key actor, as is appropriate.
God calls Judaism into being through its original ancestors, then promises
future life to them. They will have land and posterity and will ultimately inherit the world to come. In this fashion they are "elected," or chosen. So God
initiates this relationship and gifts Israel with existence and purpose. Abraham
responds faithfully to this relationship after his call, trusting God. God then
begins to fulfill his original promise almost immediately through an act of resurrection in Isaac that opens up new life, which foreshadows the main event,

which will come much later, at the end of the age. The generation of Israel is also effected, the people who will inherit this new world, although God is again at work explicitly in this genealogy, calling and creating. So in just the same way as he called Abraham, God calls Isaac and then Jacob, the younger son of Isaac, over Esau, gifting them with seed and inheritance.

In view of these origins in the patriarchs and matriarchs, it now seems like the most natural thing in the world that Jesus has come—God in person—and opened the doorway into the promised new life through his resurrection. Another faithful figure has arrived who has endured suffering obediently and then been gifted with resurrection, although this time life has been given in the age to come and not merely anticipated. The promises have been fulfilled! The original intimations of resurrection and inheritance promised to Israel at its inception have flowered into full bloom. Death has been defeated!

Paul is even able to ingeniously slip his mission to the pagans into this overarching narrative arc. God did not just *promise* Abraham seed, which is to say descendants, and land, meaning in its later, expanded sense, the age to come. He promised *to bless* Abraham as the father *of many nations*—the pagan nations. Abraham was told repeatedly, "All the nations of the earth will be blessed through you" (Gen 12:3; 18:18; 22:18). Consequently, Paul's mission to the pagan nations is just the outworking of this original blessing. The pagans gain entry into the life of the age to come through Abraham's most important descendant, Jesus, although the way they live now, without fully adopting Jewish customs, is unexpected. But this inclusion by God of the pagans into his original chosen people who will be gifted life in the age to come is in continuity with these foreshadowings in Abraham's very name and with sundry other Scriptures.[11]

Paul then adds in Rom 9 that God is obviously free to include whomsoever he wants into his people as long as he doesn't turn his back on his original people—and he doesn't—which is an argument anticipated by Rom 4:11–12.

> [Abraham] is the father of all who believe but have not been
>   circumcised,
> in order that deliverance might be credited to them.
> And he is then also the father of the circumcised,
> *and* of those who not only are circumcised
> but who also follow in the footsteps of the faith
> that our father Abraham had before he was circumcised.

---

11. Romans 9:24–26, citing Hos 2:23 and 1:10; and Rom 15:9–12, citing 2 Sam 22:50/ Ps 18:49; Deut 32:43; Ps 117:1; and Isa 11:10 (LXX).

This is a controversial retelling of Jewish origins and subsequent history. Although Paul knows the Mosaic stories well and appeals to them from time to time as he needs to,[12] he has defined Israel in terms of its origins using the stories of the patriarchs and matriarchs. This marginalizes the story of the exodus and the giving of the Torah on Mount Sinai more than many other Jews in his day would have been happy with. Those great events become an interlude. They are far from constitutive. Moreover, the gift of the Torah is, as we have seen, a double-edged sword. It is not just a treasured repository of God's instructions about right living, although it is this. It is an opportunity at the same moment for the evil powers working on human nature and the sinful lusts present within, to seduce and to deceive Jews into sinning—a position informed by other aspects of Jewish tradition, principally by the tragic story of Adam and Eve, but underlined by the universal human experience of death. New information in the Torah about right living is also new information about wrong living, and wrong living takes people onto the pathway to death; this is the "payment" that we must all make for the accumulating debt that is our sin (Rom 6:23). So Paul's history of Israel reduces the gift of the Torah—which remains a good gift—to an interlude between the patriarchal origins of Israel, with all their anticipations of resurrection, and their later fulfillment in Jesus's arrival, death, and resurrection. The Torah cannot resolve the conundrum of mortality and death. Indeed, it exacerbates this situation.

At bottom, then, past Israel is depicted by Paul as having a *telos*, or goal, the overarching goal that is the resurrected Messiah (Rom 10:4).[13] With the arrival of that goal, Paul sees the previous history of Israel as building toward it. This is a plausible narration only for those who believe in the goal, but he, along with all the other Jewish followers of Jesus, did. God has come to Israel in person, and as a result of this definitive insight, revealed to him on the road to Damascus, Paul tells the story of Israel backward, like a memoir. The significance of Israel becomes apparent in retrospect. Moreover, by telling the story of the Jews prior to Jesus in this way, Paul has avoided some very nasty traps. In particular, there is now no need to erase Judaism, including many of its precious forms and structures, when Jesus comes and Christianity emerges shortly after. It is possible to tell a story of subsequent diversification instead, and one that by this point we know well. Which is also to observe that in order

---

12. See Rom 5:19; 9:16–18; 1 Cor 10:1–13; 2 Cor 3:7–18; Gal 3:15–25.

13. There is no need to press this motif in the direction of termination. It is possible on lexicographical grounds, but nothing in the context necessitates this understanding—setting aside presuppositional pressures from soteriological foundationalism!

to exorcise the demon of supersessionism from Pauline interpretation completely, we must press on to consider what Paul does with Jews in the present and in the future, and not merely in the past.

Beyond Supersessionism

Jews in Paul's day were divided—and still are—between those who confessed Jesus's lordship and those who didn't, and how Paul treats both these groups is significant.

The former were in the minority, so he uses the biblical motif of a remnant to describe them in Rom 9 and 11, and this is another positive sign. Remnants were small groups of things left behind, often after a devastating experience, from which new life could later flourish. The prophet Isaiah speaks of a tree that has been cut down, with only a stump left.[14] Fresh growth and another tree will eventually spring from it, evoking the way a small group of Jews returned to Jerusalem after their seventy-year exile in Babylon and flourished again. So messianic Jews like Paul exist, even if there aren't very many of them, and their presence suggests that a great future flourishing could take place. Moreover, it is important to recall that messianic Jews within the present remnant are still Jews.

They are not Christians. Paul expects them to live like Jews. We can detect moments when messianic Jews are called to Paul's mission among the pagans and so live to a degree like pagans.[15] But otherwise we see that messianic Jews in the early church, and even Paul when he moves through Jewish spaces, lived in full obedience to the Torah's instructions. In Acts Paul takes a Nazirite vow twice during two trips to Jerusalem. He shaves his head, avoids corpse impurity, avoids alcohol, then shaves his head of its unkempt hair again and makes an offering of it when he arrives in the temple in Jerusalem. This behavior is pretty Jewish. He circumcises Timothy, who was technically a Jew, being born of a Jewish mother, but who had not been circumcised. Paul observes the Passover in Philippi. He debates from the Jewish Scriptures in synagogues on the Sabbath. And such is his commitment to his own people he himself

---

14. See Isa 6:13b: "And though a tenth remains in the land, it will again be laid waste. But as the terebinth and oak leave stumps when they are cut down, so the holy seed will be the stump in the land" (NIV; the original text quoting from the MT, not the LXX).

15. See Col 4:11, where Paul says he is comforted by the assistance in the pagan mission of fellow-Jews Aristarchus, Mark, and Jesus/Justus. Their lifestyle during this missionary work is best summarized by 1 Cor 9:19–23, especially v. 21.

tells us that on five occasions he endured the frightful community discipline of thirty-nine lashes from them.[16]

Similarly, we get no sense at any time from Paul that he expects the missionaries to the Jews in the early church, led by Peter, to abandon the Torah or to teach the same to their Jewish converts. They are not to universalize that lifestyle into the Christian mission when pagans convert. Pagans can stay where they are, with some adjustments. But Jews are to stay where they are when they were called, with only messianic adjustments, which means living as good Torah-observant Jews.

Christians now exist, as we have taken some pains to emphasize, as a valid missional and ethical diversification from Judaism. Christianity exists, that is, because God pushed his Jewish community, especially by means of the Spirit, out into non-Jewish, pagan groups and networks to gather them up into the great plan at the heart of the cosmos. However, as this missional inclusion took place—this great outreach—at the behest especially of those people chosen as apostles and set apart for missionary work, it became apparent that they could live, to a degree, on their own terms. These converts were ethical, but they were not ethnically Jewish.

The rationale for this liberty, to reiterate a claim made repeatedly up to this point, was essentially eschatological, although this realization had to be coupled with several others. In drawing people into the age to come, God was drawing them into the play of divine communion, whose dynamics are primarily relational. This communion is the original plan for creation (although Paul does not press this insight to its fullest extent), and is the basis for the entire process that follows. That everyone is one in Christ is fundamental. But it follows from this that where we are located now is structured by interim forms that are impermanent—things like ethnicity, class, and gender, not to mention death and time. These are helpful and embodied structures—or at least they are related to embodiment—but they are also imperfect, fallible, and impermanent. So God presses into these forms, gently inserting the relational dynamics of the coming age through Jesus and the Spirit into the details and patterns of life that we currently occupy, without either affirming them universally or overthrowing and abolishing them.

The result is a diversifying ethic, with missionaries like Paul being called to navigate the differences that emerged within the church. Some pagan practices could be affirmed, some had to be practiced better, while others had to be reformed or abandoned, the result being a particular form of Christianity. And

16. See Acts 13:14–43; 16:3; 18:18, 22; 20:6; 21:24, 26; and 2 Cor 11:24.

it follows that neither Judaism nor Christianity needed to be displaced. The ongoing existence of Judaism does not entail the erasure of Christianity, and the ongoing existence of Christianity—which rapidly becomes different forms of Christianity—does not erase Judaism. In fact, Judaism remains historically prior. The root of the tree is Jewish. Jesus was Jewish. The original Scriptures were Jewish, and the new Scriptures are mainly Jewish as well. The patriarchs and matriarchs were Jewish. So Judaism comes first. But it does not overwhelm Christianity, even as Christianity must not later overwhelm Judaism.

Hence a narrative of appropriate diversification is another important part of the solution to our overarching problem of supersessionism (although it arises out of a shared Trinitarian reality). We explain the Christian difference coherently without negating Judaism by doing so, which is a very important realization for additional reasons. A Christianity that can avoid erasing Judaism can also avoid erasing non-Christian cultures inappropriately when it comes into contact with them through mission. It clearly has an account of itself in place that can recognize a healthy diversity. A Christianity that erases Judaism, however, most likely contains an internal colonial program and so will also erase any non-Christian cultures it encounters. To be insensitive to Judaism is automatically to be insensitive to other non-Christians as well, because such insensitivity is driven by foundationalism, and foundationalism imposes aspects of its originating culture uncritically on its converts (the third horseman). Hence if Judaism dies, like the canary in the coal-mine dying as a gas leak begins, thereby warning any coal-miners that death is on its way, other cultures will be threatened with erasure and death as a Christian church that is insensitive to Jews, now made immensely powerful by its reach and wealth, spreads to eagerly grasp those who are not yet made in its image.

In short, any trace of supersessionism is a profoundly bad sign. Supersessionism is the death of Judaism, which is clearly an awful thing in and of itself. But it is also the death of the canary, which means that it is the death of all the local cultures sucked up into the maw of a foundationalist church as it spreads its stultifying influence. So it is vital to purge it from our readings of Paul—if that is possible, of course, but I hope that it is clear by now that it is. Having said this, however, we must nevertheless insert a quick caveat.

Critiquing Judaism

We must recognize that Paul does not endorse Judaism in toto, and in every form. We noted earlier the horrific dangers of sacred-nation theology. If some

Jews understand themselves as a sacred nation, formed in this way, occupying this structure, is this thinking left alone? Does Paul's gospel leave *this* construction undisturbed?

Here the critical evaluative distinction between structure and relationality that is followed during appropriate mission work takes on a more searching aspect, if necessary in its reflexive mode. As we well know by now, Paul does not ask us to treat forms and structures uncritically. They are not just endorsed happily and automatically as diverse but neutral cultural expressions. They might be neutral, but they might not be. Structures must be treated sensitively, with due respect. But they are subject to divine pressure and subsequent evaluation. Jesus is Lord over any structures and forms, which means including over the forms operating in the parent culture of the missionary-apostles themselves, which in Paul's day, was Judaism. And the loving relationality that Jesus reveals must reform even those Jewish forms that do not channel it effectively, or eliminate those that stand directly in the way of it.

In this light we can see that Paul criticizes his fellow Jews, even as he affirms their importance and states that he loves them deeply. He is not afraid to suggest that they are making some very serious mistakes—rejecting Jesus, the incarnation of their God, being one of them, something he holds them fully responsible for (Rom 10:5–21). On one occasion he also angrily notes how Judeans resist the proclamation of salvation to pagans (1 Thess 2:13–16), thereby eliciting an appropriate parental chastisement. (Moments of admonition, reform, and condemnation will all be appropriate here.) It follows, then, that any sacred-nation theology, even within Judaism, will fall under judgment as well and be radically reformed or eliminated.

With these clarifications made, we must tie off the final remaining supersessionist vulnerability within Paul's thinking.

The Future

One last final anxiety about supersessionism might still remain—concerning the future of the Jews who continue to resist Jesus. Does God ultimately throw them under the bus? If this is the case, we risk introducing a conditionality into God's relationship with Israel at the last and cast doubt on the strength and reach of his love, suggesting limits to our love for Jews as well. Are there any Jews who are ultimately beyond the reach of God, which might suggest in turn that the church does not need to care about them either?

But we have already seen that Paul argues extensively for the eventual inclusion of "all Israel" in the cosmos's final salvation, a phrase that at least includes all of ethnic Israel alongside believing pagans, although I suspect that Rom 11:26 simply means all of ethnic Israel.[17] And this is just as it should be. There are no ultimate constraints on the final execution of God's great plan, and no limits on his love. So Israel will eventually be gathered back to the God revealed in Jesus in its completeness, just as humankind will be. The love of God will finally win, and win, most significantly, over his own recalcitrant people. Having said this, however, perhaps we can add, at the last, one final flourish in terms of *Sachkritik*.

We discussed the nature of time earlier on, in chapter 6, because the introduction of a more accurate viewpoint unavailable to Paul allowed us to resolve one of the great tensions in his thinking as he presents our resurrection in Jesus. Do the spirits of those who have died in Jesus go to be with him immediately after death, in an intermediate state, where they await the receipt of a body later on the last day? Or is the person annihilated for a time and then resurrected completely, soul and body, when Jesus returns? Both of these options are deeply problematic. The first implies a fundamental dualism within human nature, undermining the significance of bodiliness, and the second implies that our relationship with God, established through Jesus, is breakable, making death a power temporarily but still scandalously greater than God.

A modern view of time, realized since the seminal work of Einstein, resolves this conundrum. The conundrum is caused by treating time as a fixed constant that even God is subject to. Once we grasp that time is a field that shifts and bends relative to space, a field that God is positioned outside of and is lord "over," we can see that resurrection denotes *a different time*, just as it denotes a different space and a different body. After death the person experiences a complete resurrection immediately, so to speak, in God's time, and this realization solves our problem. There is no dualism and no waiting period.

This demythologization of Paul's view of time, essentially updating it to a more modern account, was warranted because it was theologically responsible and constructive (and Paul himself was already taking explicit steps in this direction). But with this introduction, we are also warranted to introduce it here in relation to salvation history, which tends to operate in terms of a con-

---

17. Paul can speak of an eschatological Israel inclusive of Jews and Christians (so in all probability one of the instances of "Israel" in 9:6), but the immediate context of 11:26, and the actual thrust of the argument, suggest this meaning here. Note that he is referring to a group that is not currently saved but that he is asserting will be; not to a future group already included and glorified.

stant time line as well. What happens if we introduce Einstein's more accurate understanding of time as a field that engages relationally with other fields to structure our current existence specifically to salvation history and Israel? I think two helpful insights result that reinforce our movement beyond any sense of Jewish supersessionism in Paul's thinking to full Jewish inclusion.

We need to begin by thinking about time as a field that is laid out before God in the way that space is. It is as if the combination together of space and time—the "space-time manifold"—is a great beach ball of existence floating in the presence of God, space-time being the surface of the ball. We experience this as the past, present, and future, but from the point of view of God, there is no past, present, and future. All of space-time is "present" to God all of the time. And we can perhaps see now that the entry of the Son *into* space-time as Jesus must ripple through *all* of space-time, and hence, in a rather counterintuitive way, into the past as well as into the future. We don't need to get into all the technical details here. But the takeaway is quite simple. Jesus comes to a certain point on the surface of the beach ball that is space-time, and when he touches it, the entire surface of the beach ball changes. It follows, however, that Jesus was present to Israel, in our past. He is present to all of space-time. Both the past and the future are not inaccessible to God, who is the Lord of time, whether he is presiding over it from "outside" or entering it—as the scientists would say—mapped by a specific set of space-time coordinates.

It is extraordinary to think about the possibility that on some level Paul knew this. He wrote a much-maligned comment to the Corinthians that we have already briefly discussed, picking up an episode from the ancient Hebrews' wilderness wanderings that turns out to be impeccably precise in Einsteinian terms (well, almost):

> For I do not want you to be ignorant of the fact, brothers and sisters,
> that our ancestors were all under the cloud
> and that they all passed through the sea.
> They were all baptized into Moses in the cloud and in the sea.
> They all ate the same spiritual food
> and drank the same spiritual drink;
> for they drank from the spiritual rock that accompanied them,
> and that rock was Christ! (1 Cor 10:1–4)

At the very least, we have a direct warrant here from Paul for reading the history of the Jews prior to Jesus's arrival in resolutely christological terms. Jesus might not have been known then in his incarnate form, but he was there, all the time, *and this presence infuses that history with a powerful validity.* God loved Israel and loves Israel. It is clearly an arrangement that he is particularly fond of and a people he cares for deeply. We should therefore banish forever from our minds the thought that it might need to change drastically. It just needs Jesus acknowledged in its center, and he is there in any case, even if he is unacknowledged, as he is the center of every life and structure, acknowledged or not. He follows Israel, perhaps unseen, through its past, present, and future, as the rock followed Israel through the wilderness. Hence it can and should continue much as it is—although we are entitled to read the Jewish Scriptures rooted in that history in an overtly christological way, as Paul does here.[18]

A second insight flowing from this deeper account of space-time resumes our earlier discussion of the future of disobedient Israel and the eventual triumph of God in chapter 18. There we briefly noted that God's victory over suffering, sin, and death, which we have just affirmed includes his triumphant gathering of his people up in all their fullness, reaches into all of time. There is no state existing at the end of a time line that gets resurrected and perfected by itself. Space, time, and existence are all rolled up together, around a ball, and space-time *itself* is resurrected, including all its suffering, *which means that all of Israel in the past will be resurrected too. History itself* is resurrected, from which it follows that *salvation* history is resurrected. What an amazing prospect to contemplate!

Jesus is present to all of Israel's history, from its inception to its last steps (phenomenologically speaking), and Jesus will resurrect all of Israel's history. Every tear will be wiped from every Jewish eye—and many have been shed. As Paul prayed in Eph 3:14–19, and as we have had frequent cause to note before now,

> I bend my knees to the Father . . .
> so that he might give to you from his glorious riches
> the capacity to be grasped by the Spirit in your inner person;
> and that Christ might dwell through a right understanding in your
>   hearts,
> so that you might be rooted and founded in love;
> and that you—together with all the saints—
> might be able to grasp and to know
> the knowledge that surpasses knowing, namely,
> what the width and length and height and depth of the love of Christ is.

18. Stephen Chapman's commentary on 1 Samuel is an excellent example of this approach.

The love of God grasps time. It is present to it, and eventually reaches into it, takes it up, and heals it. And folded into this love is his original people, the Jews, to whom he has always been present, and to whom he will always reach out, eventually to perfectly restore them through all of their history, including their sufferings.

Summation

In sum, supersessionism can be avoided in Paul's thought when we describe his salvation-historical dimension, but only if:

1. we first take a nonfoundationalist, nonhistoricizing approach to salvation history, reading Israel's past retrospectively, like a memoir (having already jettisoned the passages that describe Judaism as an attempt to be justified by doing works of law);
2. if we realize that in the present pagans are included within God's explicit community as a diversification, so Judaism is not displaced (the rationale for this being eschatological, supralapsarian, and relational); and
3. if future Israel is included within God's good and final purposes in toto and saved.

We can't drop the ball at any one of these moments. But Paul didn't, so why should we? Furthermore, a reintroduction of Einstein's view of time, as a field in relation to the other dimensions structuring our current existence, presses these inclusive insights to their christological limit—a limit that has no limits. The Jews were called into being as the overt bearers of Plan A within history, and that has never changed. They remain at the center of God's plan, and God's plan is definitively realized through their greatest representative and climactic moment, Jesus. And it is now clear, moreover, that Jesus was always present to them, and that he will gather them from every corner of space *and time* at the last, in his resurrection. There is nothing unknown or mysterious about God's plan, then. It is a wondrous thing well worth praising and celebrating.

> Oh, the depth of the riches of the wisdom and knowledge of God!
> How unsearchable his judgments,
> and his paths beyond tracing out!
> "Who has known the mind of the Lord?
> Or who has been his counselor?"

"Who has ever given to God,
that God should repay them?"
For from him and through him and for him are all things.
To him be the glory forever! Amen. (Rom 11:33–36)

Theses

> Supersessionism can be present in Pauline description, first, by way of his justification passages when they are read soteriologically and in terms of foundationalism. However, reading these passages more circumstantially, with reference to his enemies, removes the characterization "justification through works of law" from his Jewish description—the subject of ch. 27.

> The second way that supersessionism is present in Pauline description is by way of historicism, a philosophy of history that holds history to be a closed causal process that works forward through time from antecedents and causes to results.

> This view of history is often coupled with a belief that history progresses "upward," from lower to higher forms. This view is encouraged both by evolutionary thinking, and by the rise of modern liberal, democratic, and industrialized states.

> The application of this view to salvation history leads to the view that Christianity emerges from Judaism as a higher form from a lower precursor.

> This view neatly mapped the social location of much European anti-Jewishness.

> The founder of modern Pauline studies, F. C. Baur, a Hegelian, consequently argued, in a widely influential view, that Judaism was a particular religion from which Christianity evolved as a higher, more universal religion, even though this distinction collapses into incoherence on closer examination.

> The antidote to historicism's necessary supersessionism is an open view of history, hence an eschatological account. All "history" teeters on the brink of chaos and annihilation, ordered and saved only by the action of a good God and his gifts.

> The third way that supersessionism is present in Pauline description is by way of salvation history, although the dangers here are especially acute.

> Some scholars reject the suggestion that Paul has a salvation history at all, fearing any endorsement by him of "sacred-nation theology."

713

> Sacred-nation thinking has done untold damage in human history, for example, legitimizing the origins of apartheid in South Africa, ethnic cleansing in former Yugoslavia, persistent terrorism in Northern Ireland, militant Zionist expropriation of Palestinian land, and, most important, the German National Socialist project.

> So visceral rejections of the very notion of salvation history are understandable.

> However, we always have to supply an account—a story—of the history of God's dealings with humankind prior to the coming of Jesus, and this history revolves around Israel and the Jews, hence the rubric "salvation history." This is unavoidable or the theological consequences are crippling—the original great error of Marcion.

> But the response to the rejection of salvation history should not be an anxious endorsement of salvation history in a foundational location. Unfortunately, such foundationalism is not uncommon in relation to salvation history when scholars, pressed by Marcionite anxieties, reproduce the error of Tertullianism. By affirming God, creation, and here Israel, up front, foundationalism is endorsed (so the claims responding to these anxieties will ultimately collapse in any case), and supersessionism is now inevitable, and in a harsh form.

> The soteriological progression from works to faith can be redeployed here, with supersessionist results.

> The New Perspective is not a plausible alternative explanation, being argumentatively incoherent and exegetically unsupported.

> Insofar as prior Judaism is preparatory and promissory, any rejection of Jesus by Jews entails, in addition to the standard criticisms, that they do not understand their own Scriptures, promises, or history. In all these locations, Christians will still displace Judaism.

> The solution to all these challenges and problems is the construction of salvation history retrospectively, or backward, in the form of a memoir (as outlined in ch. 3). This approach will avoid foundationalism in a salvation historical form—salvation historical Tertullianism—along with its innate supersessionism in general, and any unleashing of sacred-nation theology in particular (because this last will be subject to christological critique).

> In fact, Paul does give an account of Israel that looks backward, seeing everything as building toward Jesus, from the patriarchs onward. It is the story of promised life and resurrection fulfilled in Jesus. But the pagan mission is also anticipated in the blessing to Abraham, "the father of many nations." This retrospective account reduces Moses and the giving of the

Torah to an interlude, one with mixed potential. Informed by the deception of Adam and Eve by the commandment, the Torah can give life but
also kill, a fact attested by the universality of death.

- This (brief) account of salvation history avoids foundationalism and
any necessary displacement of Judaism with the arrival of Jesus and the
church.
- The continued avoidance of supersessionism can be reinforced by realizing that Paul never expected Judaism to be erased.
- He himself lived like a Jew on occasion and never expected the mission
to Jews to abandon Jewish practices.
- He argues that a small group of messianic Jews functioning like a remnant indicate God's commitment to the rest of his original people and his
intention to bring a future flourishing to them.
- He justified the differences evident within the church between Christian communities and messianic Jews on eschatological and relational
grounds. Forms and structures are relationally transformed but not necessarily abolished. So Jews and different types of Christian community can
all legitimately flourish alongside one another. The Jewish community is
at the center, as the community to which God came in the incarnation,
the original community from which all the others spring. The basic narrative emerging from Paul is, in short, not supersession, but legitimate
diversification.
- Jews also function in relation to Christianity as "the canary in the coal-
mine." If they are erased, then a Christian colonialism is being endorsed
that will erase non-Christians as well; if they are not erased, then an
account of Christianity is being supplied that will be sensitive to non-
Christians during any encounters with them. In other words, the death
of the canary, which is to say, the erasure of Judaism, reveals the presence
of Christian foundationalism.
- This understanding does not remove Jews from all theological challenge,
however. All structure and forms, including Jewish forms and structures,
are subject to pressure from the Trinity's loving relationality and should
be reformed or even abandoned, if necessary—the reflexive mode in any
navigation.
- Hence, Jewish endorsement of militant sacred-nation theology should
be abandoned.
- A final vulnerability arguably remains, however: will any Jews remain
unsaved in the end, thereby casting doubt on God's relationship with his
people, and inviting a concomitant insensitivity from Christians?

> Paul is convinced that God will eventually gather all Jews into salvation and resurrection, so God's love will win, and his covenant with Jews will be unbroken.
> The introduction of a demythologized account of time reinforces this realization.
> When time is understood as a field, not a line, operating relative to space, and as a structure to which God is not subject, then we can grasp that the Son is present to all of time and hence to all of history, including to what we call the past, as Paul intimates in 1 Cor 10:4. The pre-messianic history of Israel is consequently fraught with christological significance and is a fully legitimate form.
> Furthermore, all of time and hence all of Israel, past, present, and future, will ultimately be resurrected, and its sufferings addressed and healed, a remarkable hope that Paul praises extravagantly in Rom 11:33–36.

Key Scriptural References

Paul's most important accounts of the origins of Israel in the patriarchs appear in Rom 4, especially vv. 16b–23 (not forgetting v. 1); Rom 9:6–26 (shading here into an account of pagan inclusion); and Gal 3:4–4:7 (again, including comment toward the end of this section on pagan inclusion).

The key statement of Jesus as the *telos* of Israel is Rom 9:4–5; and of the Torah, in 10:4.

The remnant is introduced in Rom 9:27–29 and is developed in chapter 11.

The future inclusion of "all Israel" is affirmed in 11:26–27.

Jesus's presence with past Israel is affirmed in 1 Cor 10:1–4.

Convincing arguments can be made that, in their mention of "Israel," Rom 11:26 and Gal 6:16 are referring to the concrete historical community of Jews. This is not to deny that Paul views what we might call eschatological Israel, the community of the age to come, in terms inclusive of Jews and Christians; see here Eph 2:11–22 and probably also Rom 9:6, supported by vv. 25–26 and more indirectly by Rom 4:1, 9–11; 1 Cor 10:1; and Gal 4:21–31.

Key Reading

Most of the key issues detailed here in relation to Paul are laid out programmatically in chapter 7 of *Quest*, "Paul's Gospel, Judaism, and the Law," 132–45.

An alternative account of much the same position is Richard B. Hays, "The Conversion of the Imagination." Few have captured the broader issues and their solution better than Mark Kinzer, a "postmissionary" messianic Jew.

Further Reading

Barth constantly affirms and articulates salvation history, which is explicitly oriented by Jesus and constructed retrospectively. He uses the category "covenant" a great deal in these discussions. Its clearest presentation is probably at the beginning of *CD* III/1. He discusses and clearly refutes presuppositional philosophies of history in III/3, when discussing providence.

The appropriate conception of history over against historicism is discussed by Kerr, Adams, and Rae, as noted in chapter 1.

Famous attacks on the very possibility of salvation history in Paul have been made by Käsemann and echoed by his later English-speaking disciples Martyn, and Cousar, in a hyperallergic—although entirely understandable—reaction against German National Socialism and its resonances with sacred-nation theology. Käsemann was initially concerned with the overly sunny salvation history of Stendahl, but Cullmann's famous account of history and time is arguably also susceptible to his concerns as well. But the possibility of salvation history should not be rejected. To fail to supply one is to slip into Marcionism. Instead, a correct account of salvation history ought to be supplied—an explicitly retrospective account, which will eliminate the constructs that concern Käsemann and his pupils.

Wright has a strong salvation-historical agenda but fails to distinguish clearly between a prospective and a retrospective viewpoint. So he deploys soteriological supersessionism at the crucial moment to explain Christian differences from Judaism. Israel then becomes something of a cipher for a reading of the Jewish Scriptures and not for the Jewish community—and a hermeneutical program is then evident in his work as against an actual concrete concern for Jews. See my article "Panoramic Lutheranism and Apocalyptic Ambivalence."

The New Perspective is unhelpful. The reasons for this judgment are laid out in my article "The ΔΙΑΘΗΚΗ from Durham" and in *Deliverance*.

The links between erasure or supersession in relation to Israel and the Jews and later Christian colonial distortions are articulated eloquently by Jennings, as we have already seen. He was anticipated by Boyarin's concerns about Jewish erasure. Soulen has written a deeply sensitive analysis of the key underlying issues, as has, more recently, W. S. Campbell.

Goldman's work probes the relationship between Christianity and Judaism insightfully. He also offers a powerful Jewish critique of Zionism, tracing its distorting influence through intellectual work.

The demythologization of time used here was, as was said earlier, pioneered by T. F. Torrance, especially in his *Space, Time, and Incarnation* (further details in ch. 6).

Longenecker is helpful on Rom 9:5, as is Jewett.

Eastman is very insightful on Gal 6:16.

Wagner should be consulted on Rom 11:26.

Bibliography

Barth, Karl. *Church Dogmatics.* III.3.

———. *Protestant Theology in the Nineteenth Century: Its Background and History.* Translated by Brian Cozens and John Bowden. Grand Rapids: Eerdmans, 2002 (1947, 1952).

Baur, F. C. *Paul, the Apostle of Jesus Christ, His Life and Works, His Epistles and Teachings: A Contribution to a Critical History of Primitive Christianity.* 2 vols. London: Williams & Norgate, 1873–75.

Boyarin, Daniel. *A Radical Jew: Paul and the Politics of Identity.* Berkeley: University of California Press, 1994.

Campbell, Douglas A. "The ΔΙΑΘΗΚΗ from Durham: Professor Dunn's *The Theology of the Apostle Paul.*" *JSNT* 72 (1998): 91–111.

———. "Panoramic Lutheranism and Apocalyptic Ambivalence: An Appreciative Critique of N. T. Wright's *Paul and the Faithfulness of God.*" *SJT* 69, no. 4 (2016): 453–73.

Campbell, W. S. *The Nations in the Divine Economy: Paul's Covenantal Hermeneutics and Participation in Christ.* Lanham, MD: Fortress Academic/Lexington Books, 2018.

Chapman, Stephen B. *1 Samuel as Christian Scripture: A Theological Commentary.* Grand Rapids: Eerdmans, 2016.

Cousar, C. B. "Continuity and Discontinuity: Reflections on Romans 5–8 (in Conversation with Frank Thielman)." Pages 196–210 in *Pauline Theology.* Vol. 3: *Romans.* Edited by D. M. Hay and E. E. Johnson. Minneapolis: Fortress, 1995.

Cullmann, O. *Christ and Time. The Primitive Christian Conception of Time and History.* Philadelphia: Westminster, 1946.

Eastman, Susan G. "Israel and the Mercy of God: A Re-reading of Galatians 6.16 and Romans 9–11." *NTS* 56 (2010): 367–95.

Goldman, Shalom. *Jewish-Christian Difference and Modern Jewish Identity: Seven Twentieth-Century Converts.* Lanham, MD: Lexington Books, 2015.

———. *Zeal for Zion: Christians, Jews, and the Idea of the Promised Land.* Chapel Hill: University of North Carolina Press, 2014.

Hays, Richard B. "The Conversion of the Imagination: Scripture and Eschatology in 1 Corinthians." Pages 1–24 in *The Conversion of the Imagination: Paul as Interpreter of Israel's Scripture.* Grand Rapids: Eerdmans, 2005.

Jennings, Willie J. *The Christian Imagination: Theology and the Origins of Race.* New Haven: Yale University Press, 2010.

Jewett, Robert, with Roy D. Kotansky. *Romans: A Commentary.* Hermeneia. Minneapolis: Fortress, 2006.

Käsemann, Ernst. "Justification and Salvation History in the Epistle to the Romans." Pages 60–78 in *Perspectives on Paul.* Translated by Margaret Kohl. London: SCM, 1971.

Kinzer, Mark S. *Israel's Messiah and the People of God: A Vision for Messianic Jewish Covenant Fidelity.* Edited by Jennifer M. Rosner. Eugene, OR: Wipf & Stock, 2011.

———. *Postmissionary Messianic Judaism: Redefining Christian Engagement with the Jewish People.* Grand Rapids: Brazos, 2005.

———. *Searching Her Own Mystery: Nostra Aetate, the Jewish People, and the Identity of the Church.* Eugene, OR: Wipf & Stock, 2015.

Kwon, Yon-Gyong. *Eschatology in Galatians: Rethinking Paul's Response to the Crisis in Galatia.* WUNT 2.183. Tübingen: Mohr Siebeck, 2004.

Longenecker, Richard N. *The Epistle to the Romans: A Commentary on the Greek Text.* NIGTC. Grand Rapids: Eerdmans, 2017.

Martyn, J. Louis. *Galatians: A New Translation, with Introduction and Commentary.* AB 33A. New York: Doubleday, 1997.

———. *Theological Issues in the Letters of Paul.* Nashville: Abingdon, 1997.

Soulen, R. Kendall. *The God of Israel and Christian Theology.* Minneapolis: Fortress, 1996.

Stendahl, Krister. "Paul among Jews and Gentiles." In *Paul among Jews and Gentiles, and Other Essays.* Philadelphia: Fortress, 1976.

Wagner, Ross. J. *Heralds of the Good News: Isaiah and Paul in Concert in the Letter to the Romans.* Leiden: Brill, 2002.

Wright, N. T. *Christian Origins and the Question of God.* Vol. 4 (2 vols.): *Paul and the Faithfulness of God.* Minneapolis: Fortress, 2013.

———. *Justification: God's Plan and Paul's Vision.* Downers Grove, IL: InterVarsity Press, 2009.

CHAPTER 29

The Pastor's Wisdom

The First Edition

The initial controversy surrounding Paul was caused by his actual missionary work and his powerful advocacy of this work when it was challenged by other, more conservative leaders in the early church.[1] As we saw in chapter 20, a fragile consensus seems to have formed over the winter of 49–50 CE that signed off with quite extraordinary courage on a diverse church and its spread of missions. On one side, Paul's radical mission to the pagans went ahead, and on the other, a more orthopractic mission was led by James and Peter to Jews. But strains within this alliance were beginning to be felt as early as 51 CE, when the enemies arrived in Paul's mission territory claiming to have the support of the Jerusalem leaders.

Paul's death around 57 CE would have had a significant impact on this situation. There could be no doubting his commitment to the cause. He was a martyr. But his death removed his powerful personality and intellect from the scene. He had recruited quite a network of followers, and they doubtless continued his

1. He advocated a radical mission that not only extended salvation to the despised pagans but folded them into a diverse community, as many of his converts sat lightly to revered Jewish practices or completely ignored them. If we think again of our radical mission to Utah and the Mormons and its abandonment of the sacraments and its endorsement of polygamy, we feel again something of the shock and horror this new approach must have caused other leaders within the early church in Judea. There would have been enormous controversy. "You're abandoning most of the Bible, Paul—and you, a Bible scholar! This just can't be right!" "How can we trust these pagans not to lapse into their disgusting practices of drug-taking and indiscriminate fornication without serious tutoring in our Jewish ways!?"

work, although their efforts were probably also opposed. Then someone had a brilliant idea. He (or, less likely, she) collected and published a short edition of some of Paul's letters, which created an ongoing presence for Paul's voice among his communities and those founded by them in turn, well after his death—and we see here an immediate reinforcement of the importance of language for Jesus's followers, its scriptural resourcing, and the centrality of speaking to formation and the virtues. Unfortunately, we don't know exactly when this critical IT innovation happened, although we do have some indicators.[2]

We can detect a dim echo of this first edition of Paul's letters in the opening chapters of the book of Revelation, so we know that it predated the final form of that text. Unfortunately, the book of Revelation is almost certainly a composite document, and we are uncertain of the date of its final edition. Revelation is a fairly typical apocalypse—a dramatic, highly symbolic literature of crisis written and read by Jews in Jesus's day.[3] The kernel of this particular apocalypse seems to have been written by a messianic Jew after the horrifying persecution of the Christians by Nero in 64 CE and the destruction of Jerusalem in 70—two deeply traumatic events.[4] But very unusually for an apocalypse, its second and third chapters contain a series of seven letters to seven churches. The number seven is coded quite explicitly by the Apocalypse with universal implications. So we have a collection of seven letters interrupting an apocalypse written to seven particular churches—Ephesus, Smyrna, and so on—but also thereby written to the church universal, all of which seems rather curious. We can explain these anomalies, however, when we realize that the earliest edition of Paul's letters probably comprised ten letters to seven churches.

Ten was an important number for Greek culture, and seven was a perfect number for Jews, so this pattern sends the same basic signal as the letter col-

2. There are some suggestions that this publication might have been in the revolutionary new form of a book—a format that subsequently proved wildly popular. Gamble introduces the issues, and the broader technical questions surrounding ancient books and scrolls are explicated beautifully by Johnson.

3. Strictly speaking, the book of Revelation supplies this name for the broader genre of Jewish texts that scholars have recognized it belongs to. As we saw in ch. 1, the Latin "revelation" in Greek is *apokalypsis*, from which scholars derived the word "apocalypse," helped by the fact that the book of Revelation describes itself as an *apokalypsis* with its opening word.

4. So the origin of this document is probably during the reign of Vespasian (69–79 CE), who would be the tenth imperial horn if we begin the count with Julius Caesar. But because it was probably added to, we don't know when the final version, including the small letter collection, was produced.

lection in Revelation. Hence, although Paul's letters were originally written to particular communities in various quite specific cities originally—to Rome, Corinth, and so on—a collection of those letters addressed to seven congregations suggests that they also address the rest of the church. We, who are very different from the letters' original recipients, should therefore reread them for what they can tell us about the church—which is why we are reading this book an astonishing two thousand years later.

But the sharp-eyed among my readers will have noticed that I just committed to ten letters in this first edition. How do I know this? And why did I do this? There are, after all, thirteen letters bearing Paul's name in the anthology usually known—arguably somewhat unfortunately—as the New Testament, although I have used only ten in my preceding analysis. We will need to do some sleuthing here.

I suspect this ten-letter collection in part because the earliest explicit evidence we have concerning the original edition of Paul's letters comes from Marcion, who was active around the middle of the second century (150-ish CE), and Marcion worked with a ten-letter edition of Paul's letters:

Galatians
1 and 2 Corinthians
Romans
1 and 2 Thessalonians
"Laodiceans" (i.e., some form of our Ephesians)
Colossians and Philemon
Philippians

This order probably represents a missionary journey by Paul around the Aegean Sea that circles out from Ephesus counterclockwise and back, and then heads to Rome (the typically insightful thesis of the great Scandinavian scholar Nils Dahl). But the evidence of the book of Revelation, which does not seem to know about Marcion and also seems rather earlier than him, suggests that a letter collection by Paul was already in circulation well before Marcion's career in the middle of the second century. So it seems that Marcion inherited this collection of texts by his hero and went to work editing, popularizing, and interpreting it.

First, we should note that Marcion and the original Pauline letter collector seem to have had more conservative views concerning Pauline authorship than many modern scholars.

In the modern period, doubts have been voiced for a very long time about the authenticity of the so-called Pastorals: 1 and 2 Timothy and Titus. They were not part of Marcion's collection, so we will set them to one side for the moment. But after doubts gathered in the modern period concerning the Pastorals, they spread to Ephesians, Colossians, and 2 Thessalonians, and then even to 1 Thessalonians, Philippians, and Philemon. So F. C. Baur thought that only four letters were actually originally by Paul: Romans, 1 and 2 Corinthians, and Galatians. The pendulum swung even more firmly in the skeptical direction after him for a while, so a few scholars thought that only Galatians was genuine, and someone even cleverer eventually went the whole hog and decided that that letter had to be fake as well. But clearly this is all getting a bit silly, so most modern scholars have recovered their confidence in Baur's original four, along with Philippians, 1 Thessalonians, and Philemon, and consequently work with what we call a seven-letter canon. However, I worry that the methods underlying most of this discussion are deeply flawed and believe that we need to take a fresh look at all these questions. We need to begin by discarding the false arguments littering these debates, which are surprisingly common—things like circular claims and false appeals to methodological doubt.

For example, scholars in the past have often said that a given letter is authentic or fake because it is like or unlike Galatians, which we know to be authentic. But how do we know Galatians is authentic and also the benchmark for what an authentic Pauline letter usually looks like? We don't. People say such things only because Luther liked Galatians a lot, and what if he was wrong? (The scholars having these authorship discussions are usually Protestants, and in the early years, Lutherans.) Galatians could be quite anomalous. It is, after all, very unlike the letters Paul wrote to Thessalonica and to Corinth. Irenaeus liked Ephesians, and modern scholars don't take that as the benchmark of authenticity (although perhaps they should). So this entire argument is in fact fundamentally circular and invalid. But scholars tend to make similarly invalid, circular claims in terms of Paul's biography and also his thought. Before we know which letters he wrote, we are not in a position to know much about his biography or his thought either.

If we reject all these sorts of bad arguments, we end up with a much simpler situation. We have to press hard on all the texts bearing Paul's name in the Scriptures (and eventually on all the texts we can find bearing his name, because there are a few more lying around outside the Bible, but we won't worry about those for now), and see whether they carry the marks of forgery. More neutral, technical characterizations of this scenario would call such a letter pseudepigraphic or pseudonymous.

Forgers tend to make mistakes. So if we can find a mistake in a letter's self-presentation or in the way it fits together with other letters that we are confident about, we can judge it to be a forgery, but not otherwise. If we can detect significant statistical differences in its Greek style, we can add this argument to the mix. But we need to use the latest statistical sampling packages and techniques, and this evidence needs to be used as a supplementary consideration and never in its own right, as the authors of the latest sampling software invariably remind us. And we must give any letter the benefit of the doubt; letters are innocent until proven guilty. (Modern scholars tend to work in reverse here, from doubt to certainty, but this approach is self-defeating. We can't get anywhere if we assume from the outset that Paul didn't write any letters bearing his name.) Finally, we should take the external evidence into account concerning the earliest historical edition of Paul's letters that we can detect, which is the ten-letter edition Marcion inherited, as we have just seen.

After all the dust settles and we have investigated everything carefully from the ground up—which I do in another book—I would suggest that Marcion's edition is basically correct. Modern scholarly doubts over Ephesians, Colossians, and 2 Thessalonians are too scrupulous, and possibly also too biased. (These letters are too Catholic to be by Paul?!) I find all the arguments against their authenticity lack cogency and conclude that these letters are authentic, along with the seven that most modern scholars already trust. So we have presupposed this judgment in this book. But what about the Pastorals, namely, 1 and 2 Timothy and Titus?

The Pastorals

The Pastorals were obviously not part of the edition of letters that Marcion inherited and worked with, which does not mean that they are automatically fake, but it does raise a small question mark in our minds. Marcion, whatever we make of his theology, was much closer to Paul than we are, and he inherited a letter collection that was much closer to Paul again. So the Pastorals, at the very least, can't profit from their grouping with other authentic letters in this first edition.[5] And when we examine their texts carefully, I think we find some little anomalies that betray the hand of an author other than Paul.

5. There are some other indications from Marcion's period casting doubt on the authenticity of the Pastorals, whether because they were unknown or because they were regarded as fake. Clement of Alexandria (ca. 200 CE) says that various Gnostics rejected them. Jerome says that Basilides rejected Titus (ca. 130s), along with Marcion, but that Tatian (d. 170) rejected 1 and 2 Timothy, although not Titus. These testimonies seem partly garbled but also indicative.

1 Timothy

In 5:18 the author of 1 Timothy is trying to justify the payment of a wage to church leaders, which is clearly a departure from Paul's practice, since he refused to be paid by a community during his missionary work among them. To make his point the author quotes "the Scripture" Deut 25:4 (which Paul quotes in 1 Cor 9:9), "Do not muzzle an ox while it is treading out the grain," and the author also quotes Luke 10:7, "The worker deserves his wages." It is difficult to avoid the observation that Luke 10:7 is being quoted here as Scripture as well.

> The elders who direct the affairs of the church well are worthy of double honor,
> especially those whose work is preaching and teaching.
> For Scripture says,
> "Do not muzzle an ox while it is treading out the grain," and
> "The worker deserves his wages." (1 Tim 5:17–18)

This appeal presupposes the existence of the Gospel of Luke, as well as its wider acceptance as Scripture, which were true only long after Paul's day.[6] The author has made a mistake here.

---

6. Luke and Acts were probably written in the same basic period by the same person. If one of Paul's later companions lies behind the first-person material in Acts (16:10–17; 20:5–28:31), as seems likely, then we can't affirm a date too late in the first century. But if Acts betrays some knowledge of Josephus, as also seems likely (see Mason), we can't place its composition before 93 CE, which was roughly when Josephus's *Jewish Antiquities* was published. If the gospel was written around 95, then it still would have taken some time for it to be accepted as Scripture. So 1 Timothy would be written, on these grounds, at least in the second century. But the allusions to Marcion provide more precision.

The dating of Acts might also shed light on when Paul's letter collection was published. Acts probably presupposes the existence of the letter collection—the story of the founding of each congregation that receives a letter is told, and not many others—and effects "a bridging operation" between Paul and Peter. This suggests that the collection was produced before 95 CE. Acts seems to be creating an environment for this collection's reception during the Julio-Flavian period, when relations between the Christian and the Jewish wings of the church seem to have been especially strained. (Sadly, there is evidence of this rupture even in Paul's lifetime, from 51 CE.)

Others could be mentioned, although they do not really need to be. The basic scenario the letter presupposes is a probable return by Paul from Macedonia to Timothy, who is waiting behind in Ephesus. So Paul has made some journey there and is sending a letter in case he is delayed (1:3; 3:14–15).

The Greek describing this journey is suspiciously close to Acts 20:1. But Paul did not leave Timothy behind when he made that journey. So if the journey presupposed by 1 Timothy is real, then it has to be another journey, made after Paul has left the area for many years—his departure probably being in 52 CE—and returned after his long imprisonments in Caesarea and Rome described in Acts, so perhaps as late as 56 or 57 CE, and at least this would explain a thriving Ephesian mission, with several generations of converts present. But it is hard to understand how Timothy could still be a "young person" then (4:12) or, alternatively, "youthfully inexperienced," or need formal instruction from Paul concerning the basics of missionary and church work at this time. He may have been working with Paul at this point for as many as twenty years. He is a mature adult and missionary.

In the light of these further discrepancies, the letter's last verses are especially telling. There the author warns Timothy to turn away from "godless babble," that is to say, from "the *antitheses* of falsely called knowledge [Gk. *gnōsis*]." Apparently some, by proclaiming these things concerning the faith, have suffered shipwreck.

> Timothy, guard what has been entrusted to your care.
> Turn away from godless chatter
> and the antitheses of what is falsely called knowledge,
> which some have professed and in so doing
> have departed from [lit. "suffered shipwreck from"] the faith.
> (1 Tim 6:20–21)

Marcion was a wealthy shipowner, and the title of his key work was "The Antitheses." So this looks like a deliberate signal to later readers of the letter to read between the lines and to detect a critique of Marcion's views concerning Paul in the name of Paul. Paul's true followers, like the carefully authorized and instructed Timothy addressed in the letter, proclaim an authentic Pauline gospel as this letter interprets it. So not only is 1 Timothy pseudepigraphic, but we know why the pseudepigrapher wrote it—to combat Marcion.[7]

---

7. This clue was first pointed out in the modern period by F. C. Baur. I still find it

Titus

A careful examination of Titus suggests similar problems to those found in
1 Timothy, and therefore that the same author wrote them for much the same
reasons. Things are not quite as clear-cut, but the basic scenario that the letter
assumes is again problematic.

"Paul" is writing to his follower, Titus, who is wrapping up an extraordinarily successful mission on Crete. It has gone so well that he has to appoint
elders in every town (1:5). Paul has been there himself but is now in a city called
Nicopolis, meaning "city of victory." Several cities had this name, although two
candidates are most likely: one in western Achaia, near where Augustus (then
Octavian) triumphed over Anthony in the naval battle of Actium, and one in
Pontus. However, these missions must again postdate Paul's earlier work in the
area, in the fashion that 1 Timothy, if genuine, necessitates a later return visit
after his imprisonment in Rome. (There are too many of Paul's old opponents
from that era being mentioned for the letter to predate his engagement with
them.) But at this moment one wonders why Paul has returned to evangelize
two more regions in an area he pronounced fully evangelized some five years
earlier at the end of his letter to the Romans (15:19).[8] So this location seems
dubious. Moreover, in just this instance, the stylistic differences begin to cross
the threshold of statistical significance. All the key studies of style in Paul raise
questions about it.[9]

So there seem to be good reasons for supposing that the author of 1 Timothy also wrote Titus and characteristically made some small errors that betray
a rather later time of composition. But what of 2 Timothy?

2 Timothy

There are no obvious mistakes in 2 Timothy as there are in 1 Timothy and, to
a lesser extent, in Titus. But there are several small problems that accumulate

---

to be one of the most powerful contentions in the entire discussion. It is worth adding
here that the letter combats other perceived heresies at the time as well.

8. "So from Jerusalem all the way around to Illyricum, I have fully proclaimed
the gospel of Christ" (NIV).

9. This is the only Pauline letter the highly cautious Kenny questions on grounds
of style. My own recent statistical researches, using John Burrows's "Delta" procedure,
confirm this judgment. For more details, see my *Framing*.

to suggest that 2 Timothy was composed by the same author as 1 Timothy and Titus, and for much the same reasons. It is a wonderful and powerful letter written from a dramatic location. Paul is in prison on the eve of his execution and, like many followers of Jesus through history, writes a last will and testament to his most faithful disciple. But some historical glitches are present.

The places mentioned in the letter seem strangely out of order. Paul, an experienced traveler, usually lists places in the sequence in which he would visit them, which is how ancient travelers thought—not unlike strings of markers and destinations in Google directions today. But the strings of locations in 2 Timothy are literally all over the map (Thessalonica–Galatia–Dalmatia; Ephesus–Troas–Corinth–Miletus–Inner Asia[?]–Rome). The individuals named also overlap significantly with those present when Colossians and Philemon were written, which were other imprisonment letters (Mark, Demas, Luke, Tychicus, and possibly Onesimus reappearing as Onesiphorus[10]).

> Epaphras, my fellow prisoner in Christ Jesus, sends you greetings.
> And so do **Mark**, Aristarchus, **Demas** and **Luke**, my fellow workers.
>   (Phlm 23–24)

> **Tychicus** will tell you all the news about me.
> He is a dear brother, a faithful minister and fellow servant in the Lord.
> I am sending him to you for the express purpose that you may know
>   about our circumstances
> and that he may encourage your hearts.
> He is coming with **Onesimus**,
> our faithful and dear brother, who is one of you.
> They will tell you everything that is happening here. (Col 4:7–9)

> Do your best to come to me quickly,
> for **Demas**, because he loved this world,
> has deserted me and has gone to Thessalonica.
> Crescens has gone to Galatia,
> and Titus to Dalmatia.
> Only **Luke** is with me.
> Get **Mark** and bring him with you, because he is helpful to me in my
>   ministry.
> I sent **Tychicus** to Ephesus.

10. These two names mean basically the same thing.

When you come, bring the cloak that I left with Carpus at Troas,
and my scrolls, especially the parchments. . . .
Greet Priscilla and Aquila and the household of **Onesiphorus**.
Erastus stayed in Corinth,
and I left Trophimus sick in Miletus.
Do your best to get here before winter.
Eubulus greets you,
and so do Pudens, Linus, Claudia and all the brothers and sisters.

(2 Tim 4:9–13, 19–21)

But Colossians and Philemon were written many years earlier—by my reckoning, in 50 CE, as against 58, and near the Lycus Valley in the province of Asia, present-day Turkey, not in Rome. Are all five companions and visitors from the earlier mission in Asia with Paul again, eight years later, in Rome? This seems unlikely.

In 2 Timothy Paul also recalls sufferings that he experienced to bolster Timothy's courage. But he never mentions any of the sufferings they suffered together, during twenty or so years of ministry with one another (see 2 Cor 11:23–28). He mentions a list we know of only through the book of Acts involving sufferings that took place before he reaches Timothy in the story (3:11; see Acts 13–14). This seems odd, although later readers of Acts would be more familiar with these sufferings than those Paul and Timothy went through together that Acts does not talk about.

You, however, know all about my teaching,
my way of life, my purpose,
faith, patience, love, endurance,
persecutions, sufferings—
what kinds of things happened to me in Antioch, Iconium and Lystra,
the persecutions I endured.
Yet the Lord rescued me from all of them. (2 Tim 3:10–11)

I have worked much harder,
been in prison more frequently,
been flogged more severely,
and been exposed to death again and again.
Five times I received from the Jews the forty lashes minus one.
Three times I was beaten with rods,
once I was pelted with stones,
three times I was shipwrecked,

I spent a night and a day in the open sea,
I have been constantly on the move.
I have been in danger from rivers,
in danger from bandits,
in danger from my fellow Jews,
in danger from Gentiles;
in danger in the city,
in danger in the country,
in danger at sea;
and in danger from false believers.
I have labored and toiled and have often gone without sleep;
I have known hunger and thirst and have often gone without food;
I have been cold and naked. (2 Cor 11:23–27)

Moreover, the faith that Paul and Timothy proclaim has somehow had time to spread down to Timothy generationally, from his grandmother Lois to his mother Eunice and then finally to him. (This emphasis on generational transmission is an important emphasis in all these letters for reasons we will note shortly.)

I am reminded of your sincere faith,
which first lived in your grandmother Lois
and in your mother Eunice
and, I am persuaded, now lives in you also. (2 Tim 1:5)

But Timothy and his family were converts during a mission by Paul, and so presumably all converted together.

Finally, the concluding grace wish in the letter blesses a plural audience:

The Lord be with your [sing.] spirit. Grace be with you [pl.] all.

(2 Tim 4:22)

The grammar in the letter is otherwise strictly singular, as we would expect. Paul is writing to Timothy. So why does a broader audience come into view in the letter's last four words, although almost identically here to the final words of 1 Timothy and Titus? It is another slip.[11]

11. This was first brought to my attention by Richard Pervo in *The Making of Paul: Constructions of Paul in Early Christianity* (Minneapolis: Fortress, 2010), 314n268.

These suspicions are enough to make me include 2 Timothy with 1 Timothy and Titus as the work of a later, rather gifted author writing in the name of Paul (and applying Burrows's Delta procedure confirms this conclusion). Marcion was right! (although he only makes this point implicitly). The Pastorals were not by the original apostle. But why were they written?

The Role of the Pastorals

The Pastorals were written for the very reason we just noted. For much of their time these letters oppose Marcionism. They also oppose Gnosticism and Montanism, three of the most significant challenges facing the early church in the second century. And in so doing they push back on one of the key vulnerabilities that we have identified within Paul's gospel.

Marcionites, many Gnostics, and even the early Montanists—who were an extremely charismatic and ascetic movement based in ancient Phrygia[12]—all emphasized transcendence to the extent that important connections with the community's current embodied location were lost. This is not to affirm this location too strongly (i.e., in the foundationalist manner of a Tertullianist) but merely to observe that God's presence there was lost sight of, which is also to say that Jesus's presence there was underemphasized. And this deficiency seems to have led in due course to all sorts of problems. Marcion, in particular, as we have already seen, abandoned God's presence in creation, in history, and in the particular life of the Jews, so he even jettisoned the Jewish Scriptures.

To their credit, all these movements are grasping the importance of the new age in Paul. His accent was on transcendence. But plainly something has gone badly wrong at this moment. Such communities will find it difficult to live! They won't know how to navigate the myriad practical issues of everyday life, and they certainly won't know how to bring christological and Trinitarian thinking to bear on them, so excesses could take hold, which is what happened to the Montanists. They were rather ferocious ascetics. Marriage, sexual activity, and certain types of eating and drinking, along with all their intertwined cultural customs and codes—which are very important to most normal folk—were challenged if not erased, which was just too much. Paul could sit lightly to these customs himself, and we need to hold on to this dimension in his approach, but he never erased them from his communities entirely. He navigated them.

12. A somewhat mountainous region in the southwest of modern Turkey.

These extreme second-century movements nevertheless seem to have been very popular, especially in their home regions. So the early church faced a big challenge at this moment. If we drop into the language of networks and hubs for a moment, we could say that the early church was flourishing relationally, and certain key cities and regions lay at the heart of a rapidly growing network. Like all networks, however, it was oriented by key clusters or "hubs"—great spirals and clumps of relationships flowing in and out from key nodes that dominated the network's connectivity, in the way that Facebook dominates social media today and Google dominates web searches, wiping out competitors like AOL. It seems that in the second century, a number of new Christian hubs were developing that threatened the existing hubs in extent and influence. Moreover, these new hubs were advocating troubling new product innovations. Innovations were nothing new for Pauline hubs, so this was not automatically bad. These new hubs, however, had made some significant mistakes, cutting themselves off from the Jewish network that the authentic Pauline hubs were still in contact with, however tenuously, and overstating some of Paul's key insights. So the main Pauline network faced a significant challenge here. It was facing pressure from innovative new Pauline hubs that were nevertheless misappropriating the apostle's dynamic but subtle gospel. And it was still probably facing pressure from certain messianic Jews and perhaps from other Jews as well, all of which led—to switch metaphors—to the dreaded phenomenon of a war on two fronts. What was it to do?

One of the key ways it sought to meet this challenge was by institutionalizing. An intergenerational transfer of leaders was organized. Leaders in different levels were to be assessed in terms of certain criteria, principally in terms of virtues. They were to authorize one another in orderly transfers of power that reached in their origin all the way back to Paul and his immediate circle. They were to be paid. And they were to guard and to pass on a particular body of teaching, if necessary holding fast to this with their lives. False teachers were to be excluded and avoided. The authorized teaching was, moreover, essentially Pauline. It is nicely summarized in a short section in Titus:

> But when the goodness and loving kindness of God our Savior
>   appeared,
> he saved us,
> not because of any works of righteousness that we had done,
> but according to his mercy,
> through the washing of rebirth and renewal by the Holy Spirit,

whom he poured out on us richly through Jesus Christ our Savior,
so that, having been released[13] [from our debt of sin]
by this benefaction,
we might become heirs according to the hope of eternal life.
This saying is trustworthy. (3:4–8a NRSV modified)

This compact summary tells us how the author of the Pastorals and his tradition read Paul, and it is a trustworthy reading! God is fundamentally merciful. He intervenes to save sinners, of whom Paul is the worst. The transfer into the community is understood baptismally, but at this and subsequent moments, the presence and activity of the Holy Spirit are acknowledged overtly. Something still lies ahead—eternal life. In the meantime, leaders and converts are to live hopeful and virtuous lives ordered by their communities.

These communities, however, now possess further ordering structures in addition to the simple binaries employed by Paul's ancient household codes. Widows compose a particular category and are the object of special concern. (Androcentric cultures are often anxious about widows, who are legitimately released from the control of either fathers or husbands.) Leaders have two levels: overseers and deacons. Leadership is restricted to men, and a body of elders is more clearly discernable. Moreover, they are steeped in the Jewish Scriptures (and in the Gospel of Luke!). They are not to love money. They are not to be too fussy about food or to reject marriages. Leaders are to have well-controlled families, not to lack them, as celibates—points where the excesses of the writer's opponents become apparent. Above all, however, these are communities of virtue. They are to evidence all sorts of considerate and righteous behavior—kindness, self-control, modesty, uncontentious speech, and respect for elders. I find all these requirements incredibly interesting.

Scholars can spend an inordinate amount of time writing about how Paul was heard and interpreted by his contemporaries, developing some impressively subtle accounts of this thought as a result (and I am the worst of such sinners). Yet here we have an early devotee of Paul and a leader within at least one of his traditions interpreting him quite clearly for us. And his reading seems to confirm strongly Paul's gospel as we have already outlined it here. As I read this summary, I find myself thinking of chapters 5–8 in Romans, which speak of baptism and the Holy Spirit facilitating lives of virtue and hope, followed by the particularly overt ethical material in Rom 12 and following,

13. *Dikaiothentes*, normally translated, in my view a little opaquely, as "justified."

which speak of the virtues that nourish the community. And this all suggests that the analysis of Paul that I have been supplying through much of this book is on the right track.

Additionally, it seems that it was clearly not the right time during this period to revise certain hierarchical structures that our modern location now regards negatively. There is no explicit christological warrant for the development of the household codes that these letters evidence. Their development generally continues Paul's mitigation of their relationships; any leadership or dominance is to be kind, and so on. As is typical of institutions, "charismatic" and somewhat unpredictable leadership is curtailed, which is a step backward. So women are overtly prohibited from teaching. They spoke when inspired in the original Pauline gatherings and thus taught in this way. Hence there is as yet no sense that these structures and forms within the church need to be reshaped or even to go. So, going forward, we need to interpret these instructions constructively, using some of the hermeneutics that were identified earlier to deal with the same material in Paul.

In certain contexts we probably ought to continue with practices that in Western locations would be inappropriate. I would, to repeat myself, endorse this hierarchical approach to community organization (at least initially) in any mission to a conservative Islamic region. God might command these practices in circumstances like these. Moreover, navigating out of any such community will take time and sensitivity. Relationships must be reoriented, not torn, and communities reshaped and not dismembered. In a fundamentally relational situation, the how matters as much as the what "to both the Holy Spirit and to us" (Acts 15:28).

Nevertheless, we can now add that if a second-century provenance for the Pastorals is right, then we might be entitled to see a further command element in the restrictions on women teaching. This, and the prohibitions of asceticism in relation to food and marriage, seem to target Montanism, which famously followed two female prophets, Priscilla and Maximilla, as well as the male Montanus. Hence, in the absence of Montanism, we are entitled to reconsider this command.

More important than these perceived deficiencies, however, is the positive insight supplied by the Pastorals that a process of institutionalization has begun, as it had to. Modern people—partly encouraged by a dubious liberal notion of freedom—tend to cavil against institutions. But while they have their weaknesses and their frustrating sides, institutionalization is a powerful force without which small personal movements will sputter and die. Paul's missionary outlook and his personal control over the communities he succeeded in establishing had to be institutionalized if they were to survive challenges after his death, whether from a hostile pagan environment, from new hybrid Christian challenges, or from a retrenching messianic Judaism. The institutionalization we see here was a positive step forward—although the community that the Pauline material in the Apostolic Writings depicts is now formed like a cake, and we need to attend to this arrangement carefully as we close. This is the great lesson we learn from the Pastorals.

The base—the cake proper—is the original authentic networking effected through missionary work done by unpaid figures like Paul, who inserted themselves sensitively and carefully into their contexts. These apostolic figures call and establish and shape small communities of converts, largely through personal friendship and imitation; they bake the cake! They are hard-core missionaries and generally nonstipendiary, at least in some sense (and this last feature is frequently critical to the formation of the strange friendships that then lead to the genesis of small communities).

But once these communities have been established—once this cake has been baked—these small communities need to be linked together, preserved, and strengthened by a paid, professional, organized, and orderly set of leaders who are rooted in a tradition that they have been taught, and taught how to interpret over against false developments. This tradition needs to guard the position of its founder but also to enhance it as necessary. All this is the icing on the cake—the later, institutional layer of Pauline development evident in the Pastorals.

It is critical to appreciate, at the end, that in order to survive, the church needs the cake *and* its icing, and so it is rather fascinating to see both these two critical dimensions in play within the canon. People like Paul bake the cake—something that arguably needs to be happening a lot more than it does these days.[14] These are dedicated bivocational missionary-apostles, arriving unnoticed and working alongside their potential friends. Then, as things unfold and grow, a professional clergy puts the icing on the cake. And we need both. The church needs both of these layers—both of these types of leaders—to function as it should, growing and enduring. Fortunately, the result of combining these intergenerational dynamics together should be nothing short of a delicious Pauline ecclesiology—a suitably embodied and joyful analogy with which to end our main discussion.

14. See some of my comments in "Paul and the Mission to America," *Divinity*, Spring 2018, 4–9.

Theses

> Most probably after Paul's death someone within his movement collected some of his letters and published them.
> This activity further indicates the importance of texts, Scripture, and language for the church.
> The publication of this collection predated the final edition of the book of Revelation, which contains seven letters to seven churches in a probable response to the publication of Paul's letters (Rev 2–3). So the collection was almost certainly published in the first century, and it could have been published during the reign of Vespasian (69–79 CE). (It also probably predated the publication of Luke and Acts ca. 95 CE.)
> When we press hard on all the letters in the Apostolic Writings bearing Paul's name to try to detect the sorts of mistakes that forgers make—and also discount invalid and question-begging argumentation like biased denominational or circular claims—we are not justified in rejecting Ephesians, Colossians, or 2 Thessalonians.
> These judgments in terms of the internal evidence of each letter correlate exactly with the external indication of the ten-letter edition attested to by Marcion.
> The ten-letter edition of Paul's letters to which Marcion attests was written before 140 CE to seven churches. It contained Ephesians (known to Marcion, more plausibly, as Laodiceans), Colossians, and 2 Thessalonians, along with the letters widely accepted in the modern period: Romans, 1 and 2 Corinthians, Galatians, Philippians, 1 Thessalonians, and Philemon.
> The situation is different with respect to 1 and 2 Timothy and Titus. These letters were either excluded by or—more likely—unknown to the author of the original edition of Paul's letters, also to Marcion.
> Mistakes in 1 Timothy suggest that it was composed later by someone other than Paul. In particular, 1 Timothy 5:18 anachronistically quotes Luke 10:7 as Scripture.
> Titus contains similar small slips on the part of its later author.
> Second Timothy contains no obvious mistakes, but about half a dozen problems together suggest its forgery as well.
> First Timothy 6:20–21 alludes to Marcion and his (in)famous *Antitheses*, suggesting the composition of all three letters in the middle of the second century to try to rescue Paul's interpretation from his heretical advocacy by Marcion, Gnosticism, and Montanism.

> These movements discounted present fleshly embodiment too much in view of transcendence. They lapsed into dualism, generating a destructive spiritualizing piety.

> The church from which the Pastorals came met these challenges partly by institutionalizing. It created a paid, hence professional, male leadership, with two main levels: overseers and deacons.

> It also emphasized an orderly patriarchal family structure and the exercise of virtues.

> The continued emphasis on the subordination of slaves and women should be dealt with by *Sachkritik* and the application of constructive hermeneutical strategies, as outlined in ch. 26.

> The Pastorals provide critical information about how Paul was being interpreted by the mainstream church in the middle of the second century and about the nature of the church.

> Their canonical role suggests that the church is founded by teams of nonstipendiary apostle-missionaries and then nurtured initially by home-grown teachers, evangelists, and prophets.

> But perhaps the most important canonical lesson contained in the Pastorals is that in due course *any Pauline network needs to institutionalize*; it needs a paid leadership, an orderly transmission of doctrine, and Scriptures.

> Presumably both dimensions within the church—nonstipendiary missionaries and institutionalized and ordered clergy—ultimately need to remain in play. To lose one or the other dimension is detrimental if not disastrous. To maintain both is to maintain a dynamic ecclesiology—a well-baked cake with delicious icing!

Key Scriptural References

First Timothy 5:18 and 6:20–21 are important indicators that this letter, and the two other letters in the AW rather like it, 2 Timothy and Titus, are forgeries. They were forged, furthermore, to counter Marcion in the middle of the second century.

Revelation 2–3 seems to react to a collection of Pauline letters.

An excellent summary of how Paul's theology was understood at this time is Titus 3:4–8a, which accords very much with how he has been described in this book (i.e., not in a foundationalist, contractual fashion)—an impression confirmed strongly by James.

Key Reading

The evidence in favor of these authorship decisions is collated and argued in my *Framing*, chapter 6, 339–403. References to a great deal of additional literature, both primary and secondary, can be found there. Note that it is especially important to engage closely with the evidence of Ignatius and Polycarp in this relation, usefully collected in *The Apostolic Fathers*.

Further Reading

Excellent background on the origin of apocalyptic literature is provided by Portier-Young, as already noted in chapter 5. She argues persuasively that it is indeed a literature of trauma and crisis.

Mason provides an excellent introduction to the possible connections between the author of Acts and Josephus. I am confident that his case is correct, and thus that the author of Luke and Acts betrays a knowledge of Josephus's publications, including of *Jewish Antiquities*, published 93 CE. So the publication of Luke and Acts must be after this date.

A classic, powerful, but also overtly prejudicial case against the Pauline authorship of Ephesians and Colossians, as instances of "early Catholicism," is made by Käsemann in "Ministry and Community in the New Testament," *Essays on New Testament Themes*, 63–94, exemplifying this point of view.

The thesis that the Pastorals were anti-Marcionite and rescued Paul for the orthodox church was first promulgated by F. C. Baur and elaborated by von Harnack. It has been challenged lately but not, to my mind, convincingly. We have already described and engaged with Gnosticism in chapter 7. This vulnerability recurs in relation to creation, as described by chapter 24. Chadwick provides a useful brief overview of the challenges faced by the church in the second century in "Faith and Order," chapter 2 of his *The Early Church*, 32–53. Barabási was first used to describe networks and hubs in chapter 3; his insights are especially relevant here as well. A learned recent treatment of Marcion is Lieu. A classic collection of prison literature written on the cusp of martyrdom is *The Bloody Theater* (ed. Van Braght). Second Timothy could belong to this genre, but I would argue ultimately mimics it. The case for forgery has recently been prosecuted vigorously, if a little imprecisely, by Ehrman.

In a classic analysis, W. Bauer has pointed out that the use of the categories of "orthodox" and "heretical" during this period is somewhat anachronistic.

The network that later became Pauline orthodoxy, which was knitted in turn into a broader catholic and apostolic orthodoxy, gave rise to the Pastorals. But at their time of composition things were not so clear-cut.

The key claims about the importance of institutionalization are as old as the father of modern sociology, Weber, but they remain well made. A very readable application of these important sociological dynamics to a recent church movement is Walker.

A brilliant analysis of the genesis of the Pauline letter collection prior to Marcion is supplied by Dahl.

A more recent and highly innovative overview of the contest for Paul's description during the second century is supplied by White.

Bibliography

Bauer, W. *Orthodoxy and Heresy in Earliest Christianity*. Edited by Robert A. Kraft and Gerhard Krodel. Translated from 2nd German ed. (1964) by the Philadelphia Seminar on Christian Origins. Philadelphia: Fortress, 1971.

Burrows, John F. "Delta: A Measure of Stylistic Difference and a Guide to Like Authorship." *Literary and Linguistic Computing* 17 (2002): 267–87.

———. "Questions of Authorship: Attribution and Beyond." *Computers and the Humanities* 37 (2003): 5–32.

Campbell, Douglas A. *Framing Paul: An Epistolary Biography*. Grand Rapids: Eerdmans, 2014.

———. "Paul and the Mission to America." *Divinity*, Spring 2018, 4–9.

Chadwick, Henry. *The Early Church*. Grand Rapids: Eerdmans, 1969.

Dahl, Nils A. "The Origin of the Earliest Prologues to the Pauline Letters." *Semeia* 12 (1978): 233–77. Reprinted, pages 179–209, in *Studies in Ephesians: Introductory Questions, Text- and Edition-Critical Issues, Interpretation of Texts and Themes*. Edited by D. Hellholm, V. Blomkvist, and T. Fornberg. Tübingen: Mohr Siebeck, 2000.

Ehrman, Bart D., ed. *The Apostolic Fathers*. 2 vols. LCL. Cambridge: Harvard University Press, 2003.

———. *Forgery and Counterforgery: The Use of Literary Deceit in Early Christian Polemics*. Oxford: Oxford University Press, 2013.

Gamble, Harry F. *Books and Readers in the Early Church: A History of Early Christian Texts*. New Haven: Yale University Press, 1995.

Johnson, William. *Readers and Reading Culture in the High Roman Empire: A Study of Elite Communities*. Oxford: Oxford University Press, 2010.

Käsemann, E. *Essays on New Testament Themes*. Translated by W. J. Montague. London: SCM, 1964.

Kenny, Anthony. *A Stylometric Study of the New Testament*. Oxford: Clarendon, 1986.

Lieu, Judith M. *Marcion and the Making of a Heretic: God and Scripture in the Second Century*. New York: Cambridge University Press, 2015.

Mason, Steve. *Josephus and the New Testament*. 2nd ed. Peabody, MA: Hendrickson, 2005.

Pervo, Richard. *The Making of Paul: Constructions of Paul in Early Christianity*. Minneapolis: Fortress, 2010.

Van Braght, Thieleman J., ed. *The Bloody Theater; or, Martyr's Mirror of the Defenseless Christians Who Baptized Only upon Confession of Faith, and Suffered and Died for the Testimony of Jesus, Their Saviour, from the Time of Christ to the Year A.D. 1660*. Translated by Joseph F. Sohm. Scottdale, PA: Mennonite Publishing House, 1951.

Walker, Andrew. *Restoring the Kingdom: The Radical Christianity of the House Church Movement*. London: Hodder & Stoughton, 1985.

Weber, Max. *Economy and Society*. Edited by G. Roth and C. Wittich. 2 vols. Based on the 4th German ed., edited by J. Winckelmann. Berkeley: University of California Press, 1978 (1956).

White, Benjamin L. *Remembering Paul: Ancient and Modern Contests over the Image of the Apostle*. Oxford: Oxford University Press, 2014.

A BRIEF RETROSPECTIVE CONCLUSION

This book is basically my A to Z of Pauline theology, hence it is thoroughly theological, but like Paul's thinking, it shows how theology properly understood is also highly practical.[1] Theology is a series of disciplined acts and practices that is caught up in actual relationships and that expects relationships to be formed and to flourish as a result. This is where it is located and what it is supposed to contribute to, as Paul would certainly have pointed out, were he with us. The end point of a proper Pauline theology, then, is a practical manual instructing leaders how to plant and to nurture communities of Jesus followers, and to do so navigating the challenges of any context, including the especially astringent challenges offered by modernity. So you have before you a Pauline dogmatics in outline that at the same time is, as it should be, a manual of Pauline church planting.

Like most projects, it is motivated in part by what it is not. I am concerned—to put it mildly—that Paul's theology is at present enduring a Babylonian captivity, widely imprisoned by a false framework that overrides and subverts many of the most important things he has to tell us. So I am deliberately trying to set out an alternative to this regnant but distorted account. My readers will know well by this point that I do not read Paul in "Lutheran" terms, as Stendahl defined them. Which is to say, I do not read him in terms of a fundamentally legalistic and retributive God, and in terms of a punitive atonement and contractual salvific dynamics.[2] Indeed, I contend that these

---

1. If a reader is doing at this moment what I myself increasingly do—picking up this book and reading the conclusion first to see whether it is worth reading anything else in it—may I direct you to the introduction as well, which lays out the goals and structure of this project in more detail.

2. Stendahl's intuitive concerns still need to be clarified; see my *Deliverance*, es-

are some of the most debilitating challenges that the church faces today, and they come in large measure from a deep misreading of Paul's gospel in foundationalist terms, assisted by an unwitting insertion of cultural and political commitments. The destructive ramifications of false accounts of the gospel are far-reaching—think just of the current crisis of mass incarceration in the United States—and hence my concern to trace through the exact commitments of the true Pauline gospel here and to show how and where some of Paul's interpreters have lost their way.

Part of my correction to this false account is by way of a broader Pauline canon. The letter we know as Ephesians, along with Colossians and 2 Thessalonians, ought to be included in any account of what Paul thought and otherwise did because there are no really cogent reasons for supposing he didn't write them. If we had dutifully followed Irenaeus's lead some time ago and placed Ephesians at the heart of Paul's theology, many of his most destructive interpretations in later church history might have been avoided. But we did not. It is well past time, however, to correct this mistake, and I have tried to do so here, showing how these letters deepen a plausible account of Paul's thought throughout without obviously distorting it into something it is not.

Moreover, I have also shown how we must push past the thought-act dualism that characterizes so much Western thinking and that tacitly dogs so much work on Paul, and how we must intercalate Paul's discursive thoughts and recommendations with his other acts on the ground—his relationships, movements, and missionary work. Any account of his theology must be a biographically integrated theology because biography *is* theology. I have not structured this account biographically; it is structured dogmatically. But a biography is presupposed, and biographical data have been used throughout, as they should be, to thicken the description of Paul's theology. Paul's biography is a theological text.

I have explicated Paul with the help of Karl Barth, but have also brought Barth into conversation with all the questions and figures that I have been

---

pecially ch. 6, "Beyond Old and New Perspectives," 172–76. At this point it becomes obvious that the real culprit is a certain theological structure, in a typical foundationalist alliance with a certain culture and a particular politics. Luther and Lutherans are vulnerable at times to criticisms in these terms, but no more so than most other Christian leaders and traditions. Unfortunately, however, Stendahl's article and term still orient most discussions of this question, so the term still needs to be used, even as it is immediately qualified. Luther's work contributes brilliant solutions to my concerns, as well as contributing to the problem.

challenged by since arriving at Duke Divinity School in 2003. I am now more firmly convinced than ever that we must begin with Barth. He helps me to see the way that Paul began, with revelation, and with the reality of the triune God, thereby rejecting all forms of foundationalism. (This is known among Pauline scholars as an apocalyptic starting point.) But it is equally clear we must go beyond Barth as we face questions of formation and virtue—a discussion where Hauerwas has been especially important—and then face the challenges of colonialism and of navigating race and gender, a point at which Jennings has often placed the issues with particular elegance.[3]

But my primary conversation partner throughout has been Paul, and hence much of this discussion has been a historical, although not a historicist, reconstruction of his dogmatics. Paul thought and taught as if God was real, and I actually don't think there's much point reconstructing his dogmatics if this isn't true. He appeals so strongly and consistently to another reality inaugurated by God the Father through the Son and the Spirit that he is either giving us the key to the cosmos or he is insane (or, at least, deeply deluded). But if it is the former, then it's very important to grasp what he was saying about this reality, and it seems pointless to disguise that these are the underlying terms of the situation.

I have ended up articulating his theology in four broad phases, beginning in the first with revelation and resurrection; a following phase analyzes the subsequent nature of the church in terms of a certain virtue ethic learned through imitation; the third then asks us to explore how the church gets outside of itself, so to speak, in mission, and in an appropriately noncolonial way; and then the fourth part explains what I call Pauline navigations. This last process draws together all the previous phases of discussion to present Paul's profoundly insightful explanation of how God's people can be diverse without merely reifying local differences, which would mean abandoning any account of sin, or imposing structures and forms unnecessarily on a given people, which would be colonial. We have seen here finally, then, a full social imaginary—a vision of what humanity can be, although one grounded in what it is like now and connected concretely to how we can get there.

3. If my reader is getting nervous about the emphasis on Barth, may I point out (again) that Paul is best read as a Barthian because Barth got most of his good stuff *from* Paul. Barth was a Paulinist. A sustained reading with Romans was, we should recall, the activity that led to the great breakthrough in Barth's theology and life. Ephesians 1:4 was then central to his reformulation of the doctrine of election against Calvin. And so on.

Paul's theology is also deeply interwoven with particularity, and so any application of Paul's dogmatics today must also take due account of how our particularities are different from his. We must step, that is, from Paul's dogmatics to a Pauline dogmatics, and so, in acts of *Sachkritik*, I have probed for the seams and tensions in his thought that need to be demythologized, or even corrected by things he said elsewhere. We have asked how God is at work where we are now, informed by the way Paul understood God's working in his day, but aware that things are not exactly the same. And this has led us to navigate into diverse forms of community in relation to various questions of gender, while affirming vigorously the importance of the messianic Jewish voice within Paul's conception of the church.

I hope it is apparent at this final moment, then, that to grasp all these discussions entails following in the footsteps of Paul in quite a practical sense. It is not really enough just to describe him; we must enact that description with a degree of imitation. The truth he attests to is a matter of obedience and not merely of doctrinal fussiness or even precision. It is to participate more faithfully in the church, speaking about God more accurately, and contributing to its loving tenor more helpfully. The main goal of every project, is, after all, as Paul defined it so accurately some time ago (to paraphrase just a little), that we might be conformed more nearly to the image of God's Son so that he would be the firstborn among many siblings. As we pursue this goal, even as it pursues us, we are participating in something that Paul himself was entirely caught up in, and I am sure he would be delighted to think that two thousand years later his writings, in the broader context of his life, carefully studied and applied, are still contributing to this all-important goal.

BIBLIOGRAPHY

Adams, Samuel V. *The Reality of God and Historical Method: Apocalyptic Theology in Conversation with N. T. Wright.* Downers Grove, IL: InterVarsity, 2015.

Aelred of Rievaulx. *Spiritual Friendship.* Edited by Marsha L. Dutton. Translated by Lawrence C. Braceland. Collegeville, MN: Cistercian Publications/Liturgical Press, 2010.

Anderson, Gary A. *Sin: A History.* New Haven: Yale University Press, 2009.

Anglican Church in Aotearoa, New Zealand, and Polynesia. *New Zealand Anglican Prayer Book / He Karakia Mihinare o Aotearoa.* New ed. Christchurch, N.Z.: Genesis Publications, 2005.

Aristotle. *The Politics.* Translated by T. A. Sinclair. Revised by Trevor J. Saunders. London: Penguin, 1992.

Ascough, Richard S. *Lydia: Paul's Cosmopolitan Hostess.* Collegeville, MN: Liturgical Press, 2009.

Augustine. *The Confessions.* Translated by H. Chadwick. Oxford: Oxford University Press, 1992.

Aulén, Gustaf. *Christus Victor.* London: SPCK, 1953.

Aune, David. "Anthropological Duality in the Eschatology of 2 Cor 4:16–5:10." Pages 215–39 in *Paul: Beyond the Judaism/Hellenism Divide.* Edited by Troels Engberg-Pedersen. Louisville: Westminster John Knox, 2001.

Balch, David. "Household Codes." *ABD* 3:318–20.

Banner, Michael. *The Ethics of Everyday Life: Moral Theology, Social Anthropology, and the Imagination of the Human.* Oxford: Oxford University Press, 2014.

Barabási, Albert-László. *Linked: How Everything Is Connected to Everything Else and What It Means for Business, Science, and Everyday Life.* New York: Penguin/Plume, 2003.

Barclay, John M. G. "Apocalyptic Allegiance and Disinvestment in the World."

Pages 257–74 in *Paul and the Apocalyptic Imagination*. Edited by Ben C. Black-well, John K. Goodrich, and Jaston Maston. Minneapolis: Fortress, 2016.

———. *Colossians and Philemon*. New Testament Guides. Sheffield: Sheffield Academic Press, 1997.

———. "Do We Undermine the Law? A Study of Romans 14:1–15:6." Pages 287–308 in *Paul and the Mosaic Law*. Edited by James D. G. Dunn. Tübingen: Mohr Siebeck, 1996.

———. *Jews in the Mediterranean Diaspora from Alexander to Trajan (323 BCE–117 CE)*. Edinburgh: T&T Clark, 1996.

———. "Manna and the Circulation of Grace: A Study of 2 Corinthians 8:1–15." Pages 409–26 in *The Word Leaps the Gap: Essays on Scripture and Theology in Honor of Richard B. Hays*. Edited by J. Ross Wagner, C. Kavin Rowe, and A. Katherine Grieb. Grand Rapids: Eerdmans, 2008.

———. *Paul and the Gift*. Grand Rapids: Eerdmans, 2015.

———. "Paul, Philemon, and the Dilemma of Christian Slave-Ownership." *NTS* 37 (1991): 161–86.

Barr, James. "'Abba, Father' and the Familiarity of Jesus' Speech." *Theology* 91 (1988): 173–79.

———. "Abbâ Isn't 'Daddy.'" *JTS* 39 (1988): 28–47.

Barth, Fredrik. *Ethnic Groups and Boundaries: The Social Organisation of Cultural Difference*. London: Allen & Unwin, 1969.

Barth, Karl. *Christ and Adam: Man and Humanity in Romans 5*. Translated by Tom A. Smail. New York: Collier, 1962.

———. *Church Dogmatics*. Edited by T. F. Torrance and G. W. Bromiley. 4 vols. in 13 parts. Edinburgh: T&T Clark, 1956–1996 (1932–1967).

———. "No!" Pages 67–128 in *Natural Theology: Comprising "Nature and Grace" by Professor Dr. Emil Brunner and the Reply "No!" by Dr. Karl Barth*. Translated by Peter Fraenkel. Eugene, OR: Wipf & Stock, 2002.

———. *Protestant Theology in the Nineteenth Century: Its Background and History*. Translated by Brian Cozens and John Bowden. London: SCM Press, 1959.

Barth, Karl, and Carl Zuckmayer. *A Late Friendship: The Letters of Karl Barth and Carl Zuckmayer*. Translated by Geoffrey W. Bromiley. Grand Rapids: Eerdmans, 1982.

Barth, Markus. *Ephesians: A New Translation, with Introduction and Commentary*. 2 vols. AB 34. New Haven: Yale University Press, 1974.

Bauckham, Richard. "Freedom in Contemporary Context." Pages 26–49 in *God and the Crisis of Freedom: Biblical and Contemporary Perspectives*. Louisville: Westminster John Knox, 2002.

————. *Jesus and the God of Israel: God Crucified and Other Studies on the New Testament's Christology of Divine Identity*. Grand Rapids: Eerdmans, 2008.

Baur, F. C. *Paul, the Apostle of Jesus Christ, His Life and Works, His Epistles and Teachings: A Contribution to a Critical History of Primitive Christianity*. 2 vols. London: Williams & Norgate, 1873–75.

Beeley, Christopher A., and Mark E. Weedman, eds. *The Bible in Early Trinitarian Theology*. Studies in Early Christianity. Washington, DC: Catholic University of America Press, 2018.

Begbie, Jeremy. *Music, Modernity, and God: Essays in Listening*. Oxford: Oxford University Press, 2014.

————. *A Peculiar Orthodoxy: Reflections on Theology and the Arts*. Grand Rapids: Baker Academic, 2018.

————. *Resounding Truth: Christian Wisdom in the World of Music*. Grand Rapids: Baker, 2007.

————. "Room of One's Own? Music, Space, and Freedom." Pages 141–75 in *Music, Modernity, and God: Essays in Listening*. Oxford: Oxford University Press, 2014.

————. *Theology, Music, and Time*. Cambridge: Cambridge University Press, 2000.

Beker, J.-C. *Paul the Apostle: The Triumph of God in Life and Thought*. Philadelphia: Fortress, 1980.

Bell, Rob. "God, Creation, and Evil: The Moral Meaning of *creatio ex nihilo*." *Radical Orthodoxy: Theology, Philosophy, Politics* 3, no. 1 (2015): 1–17.

————. *Love Wins*. New York: HarperOne, 2011.

Berlin, Isaiah. *Two Concepts of Liberty*. Oxford: Clarendon, 1958.

Bird, Michael F., and Preston M. Sprinkle, eds. *The Faith of Jesus Christ: Exegetical, Biblical, and Theological Studies*. Peabody, MA: Hendrickson, 2009.

Birkerts, Sven. *The Art of Time in Memoir: Then, Again*. St. Paul: Graywolf Press, 2008.

Blackwell, Ben C. *Christosis: Pauline Soteriology in Light of Deification in Irenaeus and Cyril of Alexandria*. WUNT 2.314. Tübingen: Mohr (Siebeck), 2011.

Blowers, Paul M. *Drama of the Divine Economy: Creator and Creation in Early Christian Theology and Piety*. Oxford: Oxford University Press, 2012.

Boer, Martinus de. "Paul and Apocalyptic Eschatology." Pages 345–83 in vol. 1 of *The Encyclopedia of Apocalypticism*. Edited by John J. Collins. New York: Continuum, 1998.

Boyarin, Daniel. *Border Lines: The Partition of Judaeo-Christianity*. Philadelphia: University of Pennsylvania Press, 2004.

————. *A Radical Jew: Paul and the Politics of Identity*. Berkeley: University of California Press, 1994.

Brown, Peter. *The Body and Society: Men, Women, and Sexual Renunciation in Early Christianity*. 2nd ed. New York: Columbia University Press, 2008.

Brownson, James V. *Bible, Gender, Sexuality: Reframing the Church's Debate on Same-Sex Relationships*. Grand Rapids: Eerdmans, 2013.

Bruce, F. F. *The Pauline Circle*. Exeter: Paternoster Press, 1985.

Buber, Martin. *I and Thou*. 2nd ed. Translated by R. G. Smith. New York: Scribners, 1958.

Buckley, Michael J. *At the Origins of Modern Atheism*. New Haven: Yale University Press, 1987.

———. *Denying and Disclosing God: The Ambiguous Progress of Modern Atheism*. New Haven: Yale University Press, 2004.

Bultmann, Rudolf. *Existence and Faith*. Translated by Schubert M. Ogden. New York: Living Age Books, 1960.

———. "Jesus and Paul." Pages 183–201 in *Existence and Faith*. Translated by Schubert M. Ogden. New York: Living Age Books, 1960.

———. *Jesus Christ and Mythology*. New York: Charles Scribner's Sons, 1958.

———. *New Testament and Mythology and Other Basic Writings*. Translated and edited by Schubert M. Ogden. Minneapolis: Fortress, 1984.

———. "The Significance of the Historical Jesus for the Theology of Paul." Pages 220–46 in *Faith and Understanding*. Edited by R. W. Funk. Translated by L. P. Smith. Vol. 1. London: SCM Press, 1969.

Buren, Paul M. van. *Discerning the Way: A Theology of Jewish-Christian Reality*. New York: Seabury, 1980.

Busch, Eberhard. "Exacting Exhortation—Gospel and Law, Ethics." Pages 152–75 in *The Great Passion: An Introduction to Karl Barth's Theology*. Translated by Geoffrey Bromiley. Grand Rapids: Eerdmans, 2004.

———. *The Great Passion: An Introduction to Karl Barth's Theology*. Translated by Geoffrey Bromiley. Grand Rapids: Eerdmans, 2004.

———. *Karl Barth: His Life from Letters and Autobiographical Texts*. Translated by J. Bowden. 2nd rev. ed. London: SCM, 1976.

Campbell, Charles. *The Word before the Powers: An Ethic of Preaching*. Louisville: Westminster John Knox, 2002.

Campbell, Constantine R. *Paul and Union with Christ: An Exegetical and Theological Study*. Grand Rapids: Zondervan, 2012.

Campbell, Douglas A. "2 Corinthians 4:13: Evidence in Paul That Christ Believes." *JBL* 128 (2009): 337–56.

———. "An Anchor for Pauline Chronology: Paul's Flight from 'The Ethnarch of King Aretas' 2 Cor 11:32–33." *JBL* 121 (2002): 279–302.

———. "Beyond the Torah at Antioch: The Probable Locus for Paul's Radical Transition." *JSPL* 4, no. 2 (2014): 187–214.

———. *The Deliverance of God: An Apocalyptic Rereading of Justification in Paul.* Grand Rapids: Eerdmans, 2009.

———. "The ΔΙΑΘΗΚΗ from Durham: Professor Dunn's *The Theology of the Apostle Paul*." *JSNT* 72 (1998): 91–111.

———. "Faith." Pages 327–36 in *The Oxford Encyclopedia of the Bible and Theology.* Vol. 1: *ABR–JUS.* Edited by Samuel E. Balentine. Oxford: Oxford University Press, 2015.

———. "The Faithfulness of Jesus Christ in Romans 3:22." Pages 57–71 in *The Faith of Jesus Christ: Exegetical, Biblical, and Theological Studies.* Edited by Michael Bird and Preston M. Sprinkle. Peabody, MA: Hendrickson, 2009.

———. *Framing Paul: An Epistolary Biography.* Grand Rapids: Eerdmans, 2014.

———. "Galatians." In *The New Oxford Bible Commentary.* Edited by David Lincicum et al. Oxford: University Press, 2020.

———. "Galatians 5:11: Evidence of an Early Law-Observant Mission by Paul?" *NTS* 57 (2011): 325–47.

———. "Inscriptional Attestation to Sergius Paul[l]us (Acts 13.6–12) and the Implications for Pauline Chronology." *JTS* 56 (2005): 1–29.

———. "The Issue of Shame in Robert Jewett's Commentary on Romans." Pages 255–66 in *From Rome to Beijing: Symposia on Robert Jewett's Commentary on Romans.* Edited by K. K. Yeo. Lincoln, NE: Prairie Muse, 2012.

———. "Mass Incarceration: Pauline Problems and Pauline Solutions." *Int* 72 (2018): 282–92.

———. "Panoramic Lutheranism and Apocalyptic Ambivalence: An Appreciative Critique of N. T. Wright's *Paul and the Faithfulness of God*." *SJT* 69, no. 4 (2016): 453–73.

———. "Participation and Faith in Paul." Pages 37–60 in *"In Christ" in Paul: Explorations in Paul's Theology of Union and Participation.* Edited by Michael J. Thate, Kevin J. Vanhoozer, and Constantine R. Campbell. WUNT 2.384. Tübingen: Mohr Siebeck, 2015.

———. *Paul: An Apostle's Journey.* Grand Rapids: Eerdmans, 2018.

———. *The Quest for Paul's Gospel: A Suggested Strategy.* London: T&T Clark, 2005.

———. "The Story of Jesus in Romans and Galatians." Pages 97–124 in *Narrative Dynamics in Paul: A Critical Assessment.* Edited by Bruce W. Longenecker. Louisville: Westminster John Knox, 2002.

———. "Strange Friendships." *Divinity* 14, no. 1 (Fall 2014): 4–9.

———. "The Trinity in Paul: From Confession to Ethics." Pages 193–217 in *Essays on the Trinity.* Edited by Lincoln Harvey. Eugene, OR: Wipf & Stock, 2018.

————. "Unravelling Colossians 3.11b." *NTS* 42 (1996): 120–32.

Carcopino, Jerome. *Daily Life in Ancient Rome*. Edited by Henry T. Rowell. Translated by E. O. Lorimer. London: Penguin, 1941.

Cartledge, Paul. *The Greeks: A Portrait of Self and Others*. New York: Oxford University Press, 2002.

Chancellor, Joseph, Seth Margolis, Katherine Jacobs Bao, and Sonja Lyubomirsky, "Everyday Prosociality in the Workplace: The Reinforcing Benefits of Giving, Getting, and Glimpsing." *Emotion* June 5 (2017): 1–11. http://dx.doi .org/10.1037/emo0000321.

Chapman, Stephen. "God's Reconciling Work: Atonement in the Old Testament." Pages 95–114 in *T&T Clark Companion on the Atonement*. Edited by Adam J. Johnson. New York: T&T Clark, 2019.

Claiborne, Shane. *The Irresistible Revolution: Living as an Ordinary Radical*. Grand Rapids: Zondervan, 2006.

Cleveland, Christena. *Disunity in Christ: Uncovering the Hidden Forces That Keep Us Apart*. Downers Grove, IL: InterVarsity, 2012.

Cohen, Shaye J. D. *The Beginnings of Jewishness: Boundaries, Varieties, Uncertainties*. Los Angeles and Berkeley: University of California Press, 1999.

————. *From the Maccabees to the Mishnah*. 3rd ed. Louisville: Westminster John Knox, 2014.

"The Commodification of Everything." *Hedgehog Review: Critical Reflections on Contemporary Culture* 5 (Summer 2003). http://www.iasc-culture.org/THR /hedgehog_review_2003-Summer.php.

Cone, James. *The Spirituals and the Blues: An Interpretation*. New York: Seabury Press, 1972.

Cotterell, Peter. *Mission and Meaninglessness: The Good News in a World of Suffering and Disorder*. London: SPCK, 1990.

Cousar, C. B. "Continuity and Discontinuity: Reflections on Romans 5–8 (in conversation with Frank Thielman)." Pages 196–210 in *Pauline Theology*. Vol. 3: *Romans*. Edited by David M. Hay and E. Elizabeth Johnson. Minneapolis: Fortress, 1995.

Cullmann, O. *Christ and Time: The Primitive Christian Conception of Time and History*. Philadelphia: Westminster, 1946.

Cummings, Ray. "The Time Professor." *Argosy All-Story Weekly*, January 8, 1921.

Darwin, Charles. *The Expression of the Emotions in Man and Animals*. Chicago: University of Chicago Press, 1965 (1872).

Davidman, Lynn. *Tradition in a Rootless World: Women Turn to Orthodox Judaism*. Berkeley & Los Angeles: University of California Press, 1991.

Davidson, Allan. *Christianity in Aotearoa: A History of Church and Society in New Zealand.* 3rd ed. Wellington, N.Z.: Education for Ministry, 2004.

Davidson, Osha Gray. *The Best of Enemies: Race and Redemption in the New South.* Chapel Hill: University of North Carolina Press, 1996.

Davies, W. D. "Law in First-Century Judaism" and "Reflections on Tradition: The 'Abot Revisited." Pages 3–48 in *Jewish and Pauline Studies.* London: SPCK, 1984.

———. *Paul and Palestinian Judaism: Some Rabbinic Elements in Pauline Theology.* 4th ed. London: SPCK, 1980.

———. *Paul and Rabbinic Judaism: Some Rabbinic Elements in Pauline Theology.* 4th ed. Philadelphia: Fortress, 1980 (1948).

Dawson, John David. *Christian Figural Reading and the Fashioning of Identity.* Berkeley and Los Angeles: University of California Press, 2001.

DeFranza, Megan K. *Sex Difference in Christian Theology: Male, Female, and Intersex in the Image of God.* Grand Rapids: Eerdmans, 2015.

Deissmann, G. A. *Saint Paul: A Study in Social and Religious History.* London: Hodder & Stoughton, 1912.

Diamond, Jared. *Guns, Germs, and Steel: The Fates of Human Societies.* New York: Norton, 1999.

———. *The Third Chimpanzee: The Evolution and Future of the Human Animal.* New York: HarperCollins, 1992.

———. *The World until Yesterday: What Can We Learn from Traditional Societies?* New York: Penguin, 2012.

Douglas, Mary. *Purity and Danger: An Analysis of Concepts of Purity and Taboo.* London: Routledge & Kegan Paul, 1966.

Duncan, Mick. *Alongsiders: Sitting with Those Who Sit Alone.* Dandendong, Victoria: Urban Neighbors of Hope, 2013.

Dunn, James D. G. *Baptism in the Holy Spirit: A Re-examination of the New Testament Teaching on the Gift of the Spirit in relation to Pentecostalism Today.* London: SCM, 1970.

———. "The Justice of God. A Renewed Perspective on Justification by Faith." *JTS* 43 (1992): 1–22.

———. "The New Perspective on Paul." Pages 183–206 in *Jesus, Paul, and the Law.* London: SPCK, 1990.

Eastman, Susan Grove. "Israel and the Mercy of God: A Re-reading of Galatians 6.16 and Romans 9–11." *NTS* 56 (2010): 367–95.

———. *Paul and the Person: Reframing Paul's Anthropology.* Grand Rapids: Eerdmans, 2017.

————. "Philippians 2:6–11: Incarnation as Mimetic Participation." *JSPL* 1 (2010): 1–22.

————. "The Shadow Side of Second-Person Engagement: Sin in Paul's Letter to the Romans." *EJPR* 5 (2013): 125–44.

Eco, Umberto. *A Theory of Semiotics*. Bloomington: Indiana University Press, 1976.

Ekblad, Eugene Robert. *A New Christian Manifesto: Pledging Allegiance to the Kingdom of God*. Louisville: Westminster John Knox, 2008.

Engberg-Pedersen, Troels. *Cosmology and Self in the Apostle Paul: The Material Spirit*. Oxford: Oxford University Press, 2010.

Fatehi, Mehrdad. *The Spirit's Relation to the Risen Lord in Paul: An Examination of Its Christological Implications*. Tübingen: Mohr Siebeck, 2000.

Fee, Gordon. *God's Empowering Presence: The Holy Spirit in the Letters of Paul*. Peabody, MA: Hendrickson, 1994.

————. *Paul, the Spirit, and the People of God*. Peabody, MA: Hendrickson, 1996.

————. "II Corinthians vi.14–vii.1 and Food Offered to Idols." *NTS* 23 (1977): 140–61.

Feuerbach, Ludwig. *Principles of the Philosophy of the Future*. Translated by Manfred H. Vogel. Indianapolis: Bobbs-Merrill, 1966.

Fiddes, Paul S. *Participating in God: A Pastoral Doctrine of the Trinity*. London: Dartman, Longman & Todd, 2000.

Fisher, Helen. *Anatomy of Love: A Natural History of Mating, Marriage, and Why We Stray*. Rev. ed. New York: Norton, 2016.

Fitzgerald, John T. *Cracks in an Earthen Vessel: An Examination of Catalogues of Hardship in the Corinthian Correspondence*. SBLDS 99. Atlanta: Scholars Press, 1988.

Flett, John. *The Witness of God: The Trinity,* Missio Dei, *Karl Barth, and the Nature of Christian Community*. Grand Rapids: Eerdmans, 2010.

Flynn, James R. *Race, IQ, and Jensen*. London: Routledge & Kegan Paul, 1980.

Folsom, Marty. *Face to Face*. Vol. 1: *Missing Love*; vol. 2: *Discovering Relational*; vol. 3: *Sharing God's Life*. Eugene, OR: Wipf & Stock, 2013–16.

Foster, Richard. *Celebration of Discipline: The Path to Spiritual Growth*. San Francisco: HarperCollins, 1978.

Foucault, Michel. *The History of Sexuality*. 3 vols. Translated by Robert Hurley. New York: Random House, 1976–86.

Fowl, Stephen E. *The Story of Christ in the Ethics of Paul: An Analysis of the Function of the Hymnic Material in the Pauline Corpus*. Sheffield: JSOT Press, 1990.

Fowler, James H., and Nicholas A. Christakis. "Dynamic Spread of Happiness in a Large Social Network: Longitudinal Analysis over Twenty Years in the

Framingham Heart Study." *British Medical Journal*, December 4, 2008 (*BMJ* 2008;337:a2338), available at http://www.bmj.com/content/bmj/337/bmj.a2338 .full.pdf.

Freeman, Curtis. *Contesting Catholicity: Theology for Other Baptists*. Waco, TX: Baylor University Press, 2014.

Frei, Hans. *The Eclipse of Biblical Narrative: A Study of Eighteenth and Nineteenth Century Hermeneutics*. New Haven: Yale University Press, 1974.

Gadamer, Hans-Georg. *Truth and Method*. Translated by William Glen-Doepel. London: Sheed & Ward, 1975.

Galinksy, Ellen. "Trusting Relationships Are Central to Children's Learning—Lessons from Edward Tronick." *HuffingtonPost* 12/01/2011. https://www.huffing tonpost.com/ellen-galinsky/trusting-relationships-ar_b_1123524.html.

Garrels, Scott R., ed. *Mimesis and Science: Empirical Research on Imitation and the Mimetic Theory of Culture and Religion*. East Lansing: Michigan State University Press, 2011.

Gaventa, Beverly. *Our Mother Saint Paul*. Louisville: Westminster John Knox, 2007.

Gibson, James L. "On Legitimacy Theory and the Effectiveness of Truth Commissions." *Law and Contemporary Problems* 72 (Spring 2009): 123–41.

Giddens, Anthony. "Elites in the British Class Structure." Pages 1–21 in *Elites and Powers in British Society*. Edited by A. Giddens and P. Stanworth. Cambridge: Cambridge University Press, 1974.

Gilbert, Daniel. *Stumbling on Happiness*. New York: Vintage (Random House), 2005.

Gladwell, Malcolm. *Blink: The Power of Thinking without Thinking*. New York: Little, Brown, 2005.

Glancy, Jennifer. *Slavery in Early Christianity*. Minneapolis: Fortress, 2006.

Goldman, Shalom. *Jewish-Christian Difference and Modern Jewish Identity: Seven Twentieth-Century Converts*. Lanham, MD: Lexington Books, 2015.

———. *Zeal for Zion: Christians, Jews, and the Idea of the Promised Land*. Chapel Hill: University of North Carolina Press, 2014.

Gordon, Benjamin D. "On the Sanctity of Mixtures and Branches: Two Halakic Sayings in Romans 11:16–24." *JBL* 135 (2016): 355–68.

Gordon, Richard. "*Superstitio*, Superstition, and Religious Repression in the Late Roman Republic and Principate (100 BCE–300 CE)." *Past and Present* 199, supp. 3 (2008): 72–94.

Gordon, Wayne, and John Perkins. *Making Neighborhoods Whole: A Handbook for Community Development*. Downers Grove, IL: InterVarsity, 2013.

Gorman, Michael J. *Becoming the Gospel: Paul, Participation, and Mission*. Grand Rapids: Eerdmans, 2015.

———. *Cruciformity: Paul's Narrative Spirituality of the Cross*. Grand Rapids: Eerdmans, 2001.

———. *The Death of the Messiah and the Birth of the New Covenant: A (Not So) New Model of the Atonement*. Eugene, OR: Cascade, 2014.

———. *Inhabiting the Cruciform God: Kenosis, Justification, and Theosis in Paul's Narrative Soteriology*. Grand Rapids: Eerdmans, 2009.

———. "Paul and the Cruciform Way of God in Christ." *Journal of Moral Theology* 2 (2013): 64–83.

———. "Romans: The First Christian Treatise on Theosis." *JTI* 5 (2011): 13–34.

Graham, Elaine. *Making the Difference: Gender, Personhood, and Theology*. London: Mowbray, 1995.

Granovetter, Mark S. "The Strength of Weak Ties." *American Journal of Sociology* 78 (1973): 1360–80.

Green, Joel B., ed. *Hearing the New Testament: Strategies for Interpretation*. Grand Rapids: Eerdmans, 2010.

Greenberg, Irving. "Cloud of Smoke, Pillar of Fire: Judaism, Christianity and Modernity after the Holocaust." Pages 7–55 in *Auschwitz: Beginning of a New Era?* Edited by E. Fleischner. New York: Ktav, 1977.

Gunton, Colin. *Act and Being: Towards a Theology of the Divine Attributes*. London: SCM, 2002.

———. *The Actuality of the Atonement: A Study of Metaphor, Rationality, and the Christian Tradition*. Edinburgh: T&T Clark, 1998.

———. *Enlightenment and Alienation: An Essay toward a Trinitarian Theology*. Eugene, OR: Cascade, 2006.

———. *The One, the Three and the Many: God, Creation and the Culture of Modernity*. Cambridge: Cambridge University Press, 1993.

Gutiérrez, Gustavo. *A Theology of Liberation*. 15th ann. ed. Maryknoll, NY: Orbis Books, 1988.

Hadot, Pierre. *Philosophy as a Way of Life*. Translated by Michael Chase. Oxford: Blackwell, 1995.

Harink, Douglas. *Paul among the Postliberals. Pauline Theology beyond Christendom and Modernity*. Grand Rapids: Brazos, 2003.

Harrill, J. Albert. "The Use of the New Testament in the American Slave Controversy: A Case History in the Hermeneutical Tension between Biblical Criticism and Christian Moral Debate." *Religion and American Culture* 10 (2000): 149–86.

Harrington, Daniel, and James Keenan. *Paul and Virtue Ethics*. Lanham, MD: Rowman & Littlefield, 2010.

Harris, Robert. *Dictator*. London: Penguin Random House, 2015.

————. *Imperium: A Novel of Ancient Rome*. New York: Pocket, 2006.

————. *Lustrum*. London: Hutchinson, 2009.

————. *Pompeii*. New York: Ballantine, 2003.

Harrison, James R. *Paul's Language of Grace in Its Graeco-Roman Context*. Tübingen: Mohr Siebeck, 2003.

Hart, David Bentley. "God, Creation, and Evil: The Moral Meaning of *creatio ex nihilo*." *Radical Orthodoxy: Theology, Philosophy, Politics* 3, no. 1 (2015): 1–17.

————. "The Spiritual Was More Substantial than the Material for the Ancients." *Church Life Journal*, July 26, 2018. http://churchlife.nd.edu/2018/07/26/the-spiritual-was-more-substantial-than-the-fleshly-for-the-ancients/.

Harvey, Lincoln. *A Brief Theology of Sport*. Eugene, OR: Cascade, 2014.

Hasan, Ali, and Richard Fumerton. "Foundationalist Theories of Epistemic Justification." In *The Stanford Encyclopedia of Philosophy* (Winter 2016 Edition). Edited by Edward N. Zalta. https://plato.stanford.edu/cgi-bin/encyclopedia/archinfo.cgi?entry=justep-foundational.

Hauerwas, Stanley. *After Christendom: How the Church Is to Behave If Freedom, Justice, and a Christian Nation Are Bad Ideas*. Nashville: Abingdon, 1991.

————. "Community and Diversity: The Tyranny of Normality." Pages 211–17 in *Suffering Presence: Theological Reflections on Medicine, the Mentally Handicapped, and the Church*. Notre Dame, IN: University of Notre Dame Press, 1986.

————. *A Community of Character: Toward a Constructive Christian Social Ethic*. Notre Dame, IN: University of Notre Dame Press, 1981.

————. "Gay Friendship: A Thought Experiment in Catholic Moral Theology." Pages 105–21 in *Sanctify Them in the Truth: Holiness Exemplified*. Edinburgh and Nashville: T&T Clark and Abingdon, 1998.

————. *Hannah's Child: A Theologian's Memoir*. Grand Rapids: Eerdmans, 2012.

————. "How to Be Caught by the Holy Spirit." In *ABC Religion and Theology*, November 14, 2013. https://www.abc.net.au/religion/how-to-be-caught-by-the-holy-spirit/10099524.

————. "Love's Not All You Need." Pages 111–26 in *Vision and Virtue: Essays in Christian Ethical Reflection*. Notre Dame, IN: University of Notre Dame Press, 1981 (1974).

————. *The Peaceable Kingdom: A Primer in Christian Ethics*. Notre Dame, IN: University of Notre Dame Press, 1983.

————. "Seeing Darkness, Hearing Silence: Augustine's Account of Evil." Pages 8–32 in *Working with Words*. Eugene, OR: Cascade, 2011.

————. "Speaking Christian." Pages 84–93 in *Working with Words*. Eugene, OR: Wipf & Stock, 2011.

———. *Unleashing the Scripture: Freeing the Bible from Captivity to America.* Nashville: Abingdon, 1993.

———. "Why 'The Way Words Run' Matters: Reflections on Becoming a 'Major Biblical Scholar.'" Pages 94–112 in *Working with Words.* Eugene, OR: Cascade, 2011.

———. *With the Grain of the Universe: The Church's Witness and Natural Theology; Being the Gifford Lectures Delivered at the University of St Andrews in 2001.* Grand Rapids: Brazos, 2001.

Hauerwas, Stanley, with Charles Pinches. *Christians among the Virtues: Theological Conversations with Ancient and Modern Ethics.* Notre Dame, IN: University of Notre Dame Press, 1997.

———. "Witness." Pages 37–63 in *Approaching the End: Eschatological Reflections on Church, Politics, and Life.* Grand Rapids: Eerdmans, 2013.

Hauerwas, Stanley, with Jean Vanier. *Living Gently in a Violent World: The Prophetic Witness of Weakness.* Downers Grove, IL: InterVarsity, 2008.

Hauerwas, Stanley, with Will Willimon. *Resident Aliens: Life in the Christian Colony.* Nashville: Abingdon, 1989.

Hays, Richard B. "Children of Promise." Pages 84–121 in *Echoes of Scripture in the Letters of Paul.* New Haven: Yale University Press, 1989.

———. "Christology and Ethics in Galatians: The Law of Christ." *CBQ* 49 (1987): 268–90.

———. "Christ Prays the Psalms: Israel's Psalter as Matrix of Early Christianity." Pages 101–18 in *The Conversion of the Imagination: Paul as Interpreter of Israel's Scripture.* Grand Rapids: Eerdmans, 2005.

———. "The Conversion of the Imagination: Scripture and Eschatology in 1 Corinthians." Pages 1–24 in *The Conversion of the Imagination: Paul as Interpreter of Israel's Scripture.* Grand Rapids: Eerdmans, 2005.

———. *Echoes of Scripture in the Letters of Paul.* New Haven: Yale University Press, 1989.

———. *The Faith of Jesus Christ: The Narrative Substructure of Galatians 3:1–4:11.* 2nd ed. Grand Rapids: Eerdmans, 2002.

———. *First Corinthians.* Interpretation: A Bible Commentary for Teaching and Preaching. Louisville: Westminster John Knox, 2011.

———. *The Moral Vision of the New Testament: Cross, Community, and New Creation; A Contemporary Introduction to New Testament Ethics.* San Francisco: HarperSanFrancisco, 1996.

———. "On the Rebound: A Response to Critiques of *Echoes of Scripture in the Letters of Paul.*" Pages 163–89 in *The Conversion of the Imagination: Paul as Interpreter of Israel's Scripture.* Grand Rapids: Eerdmans, 2005.

———. "The Story of God's Son: The Identity of Jesus in the Letters of Paul." Pages 180–99 in *Seeking the Identity of Jesus: A Pilgrimage*. Edited by Richard B. Hays and Beverly R. Gaventa. Grand Rapids: Eerdmans, 2008.

Hengel, M. *Judaism and Hellenism: Studies in Palestine during the Early Hellenistic Period*. London: SCM, 1974.

Herdt, Jennifer A. *Putting On Virtue: The Legacy of the Splendid Vices*. Chicago: University of Chicago Press, 2008.

Heron, A. I. C. *The Holy Spirit: The Holy Spirit in the Bible, in the History of Christian Thought, and in Recent Theology*. London: Marshall, Morgan & Scott, 1983.

———. "*Homoousios* with the Father." Pages 58–87 in *The Incarnation: Ecumenical Studies in the Nicene-Constantinopolitan Creed, A.D. 381*. Edited by Thomas F. Torrance. Edinburgh: Handsel Press, 1981.

Heuertz, Chris, and Christine Pohl. *Friendship at the Margins: Discovering Mutuality in Service and Mission*. Downers Grove, IL: InterVarsity, 2010.

Hill, Wesley. *Washed and Waiting: Reflections on Christian Faithfulness and Homosexuality*. Grand Rapids: Zondervan, 2010.

Holmes, Christopher R. J. *The Holy Spirit*. Grand Rapids: Zondervan, 2015.

Hooker, Morna D. "Interchange and Atonement." *BJRL* 60 (1978): 462–81.

———. "Interchange in Christ." *JTS* 22 (1971): 349–61.

———. "ΠΙΣΤΙΣ ΧΡΙΣΤΟΥ." *NTS* 35 (1989): 321–42.

Horrell, David. *The Social Ethos of the Corinthian Correspondence: Interests and Ideology from 1 Corinthians to 1 Clement*. Edinburgh: T&T Clark, 1996.

———. *Solidarity and Difference: A Contemporary Reading of Paul's Ethics*. London: T&T Clark, 2005.

Hunsicker, David B. *The Making of Stanley Hauerwas: Bridging Barth and Postliberalism*. Downers Grove, IL: IVP Academic, 2019.

Hursthouse, Rosalind, and Glen Pettigrove. "Virtue Ethics." *The Stanford Encyclopedia of Philosophy* (Winter 2016 Edition). Edited by Edward N. Zalta. https://plato.stanford.edu/archives/win2016/entries/ethics-virtue/.

Hurtado, Larry W. *One God, One Lord: Early Christian Devotion and Ancient Jewish Monotheism*. 2nd ed. London: T&T Clark, 1998.

Jacobson, Matthew Frye. *Whiteness of a Different Color: European Immigrants and the Alchemy of Race*. Cambridge: Harvard University Press, 1998.

Jennings, Willie. *The Christian Imagination: Theology and the Origins of Race*. New Haven: Yale University Press, 2010.

———. "The Fuller Difference: To Be a Christian Intellectual." *Fuller Magazine* 4.

Jewett, Paul K. *Man as Male and Female. A Study in Sexual Relationships from a Theological Point of View*. Grand Rapids: Eerdmans, 1975.

Jewett, Robert, with Roy D. Kotansky. *Romans: A Commentary*. Hermeneia. Minneapolis: Fortress, 2006.

Johnson, Paul. *A History of Christianity*. New York: Simon & Schuster, 1976.

Jones, L. Gregory. "Truth and Consequences in South Africa." *Christianity Today* 43, no. 4 (1991): 59–63.

Kahl, Brigitte. "No Longer Male: Masculinity Struggles behind Galatians 3.28?" *JSNT* 79 (2000): 37–49.

Käsemann, E. *Essays on New Testament Themes*. Translated by W. J. Montague. London: SCM, 1964.

———. "Justification and Salvation History in the Epistle to the Romans." Pages 60–78 in *Perspectives on Paul*. Translated by Margaret Kohl. London: SCM, 1971.

Katongole, Emmanuel. "Greeting: Beyond Racial Reconciliation." Pages 68–81 in *The Blackwell Companion to Christian Ethics*. Edited by Stanley Hauerwas and Samuel Wells. Oxford: Blackwell, 2006.

Keen, Karen R. *Scripture, Ethics and the Possibility of Same-Sex Relationships*. Grand Rapids: Eerdmans, 2018.

Kerr, Nathan. *Christ, History, and Apocalyptic: The Politics of Christian Mission*. London: SCM, 2009.

Kinzer, Mark S. *Israel's Messiah and the People of God: A Vision for Messianic Jewish Covenant Fidelity*. Edited by Jennifer M. Rosner. Eugene, OR: Wipf & Stock, 2011.

———. *Postmissionary Messianic Judaism: Redefining Christian Engagement with the Jewish People*. Grand Rapids: Brazos, 2005.

———. *Searching Her Own Mystery: Nostra Aetate, the Jewish People, and the Identity of the Church*. Eugene, OR: Wipf & Stock, 2015.

Kinzig, Wolfgang. "Καινὴ διαθήκη: The Title of the New Testament in the Second and Third Centuries." *JTS* 45 (1994): 519–44.

Kirk, Daniel J. R. *The Faith of Jesus Christ: The Narrative Substructure of Galatians 3:1–4:11*. 2nd ed. Grand Rapids: Eerdmans, 2002.

———. *Unlocking Romans: Resurrection and the Justification of God*. Grand Rapids: Eerdmans, 2008.

Kruger, C. Baxter. *The Great Dance: The Christian Vision Revisited*. Jackson, MS: Perichoresis Press, 2000.

Kwon, Yon-Gyong. *Eschatology in Galatians: Rethinking Paul's Response to the Crisis in Galatia*. WUNT 2.183. Tübingen: Mohr Siebeck, 2004.

Lakoff, George. *Moral Politics: How Liberals and Conservatives Think*. 3rd ed. Chicago: University of Chicago Press, 2016.

———. *Whose Freedom? The Battle over America's Most Important Idea*. New York: Farrar, Straus & Giroux, 2006.

Lang, T. J. "Disbursing the Account of God: Fiscal Terminology and the Economy of God in Colossians 1,24–25." *ZNW* 107 (2016): 116–36.

Larson, Jennifer. "Paul's Masculinity." *JBL* 123 (2004): 85–97.

Leadership Education at Duke Divinity (LEADD). *Faith and Leadership.* https://www.faithandleadership.com/category/principles-practice-topics/traditioned-innovation.

Levison, John R. *Filled with the Spirit.* Grand Rapids: Eerdmans, 2009.

———. *Inspired: The Holy Spirit and the Mind of Faith.* Grand Rapids: Eerdmans, 2013.

Lewis, C. S. *Beyond Personality: The Christian Idea of God.* London: Macmillan, 1945.

———. *The Great Divorce.* New York: HarperCollins, 2001 (1946).

Leys, Colin, and Barbara Harriss-White. "Commodification: The Essence of Our Time." *OpenDemocracy*, April 2, 2012. https://www.opendemocracy.net/ourkingdom/colin-leys-barbara-harriss-white/commodification-essence-of-our-time.

Litwa, M. David. "2 Cor 3:18 and Its Implications for *Theosis*." *JTI* 2 (2008): 117–34.

———. *We Are Being Transformed: Deification in Paul's Soteriology.* BZNW 187. Berlin: de Gruyter, 2012.

Lockwood O'Donovan, Joan. "The Poverty of Christ and Non-Proprietary Community." Pages 191–200 in *The Doctrine of God and Theological Ethics.* Edited by Alan J. Torrance and Michael Banner. London: T&T Clark, 2006.

Longenecker, Bruce W., ed. *Narrative Dynamics in Paul: A Critical Assessment.* Louisville: Westminster John Knox, 2002.

Longenecker, Richard N. *The Epistle to the Romans: A Commentary on the Greek Text.* NIGTC. Grand Rapids: Eerdmans, 2017.

———. *Paul, Apostle of Liberty.* 2nd ed. Grand Rapids: Eerdmans, 2015.

Lubac, Henri de. *History and Spirit: The Understanding of Scripture, according to Origen.* Translated by Anne Englund Nash and Juvenal Merriel. San Francisco: Ignatius Press, 1950.

MacDonald, Gregory. *"All Shall Be Well": Explorations in Universalism and Christian Theology from Origen to Moltmann.* Cambridge: James Clarke, 2011.

MacIntyre, Alasdair C. *After Virtue: A Study in Moral Theory.* 3rd ed. Notre Dame, IN: University of Notre Dame Press, 2007.

———. "Genealogies and Subversions." Pages 284–305 in *Nietzsche, Genealogy, Morality: Essays on Nietzsche's Genealogy of Morals.* Edited by Richard Schacht. Berkeley: University of California Press, 1994.

———. *Three Rival Versions of Moral Enquiry: Encyclopaedia, Genealogy, and Tradition.* Notre Dame, IN: University of Notre Dame Press, 1990.

———. *Whose Justice? Which Rationality?* Notre Dame, IN: University of Notre Dame Press, 1989.

MacMullen, Ramsay, and Eugene N. Lane, eds. *Paganism and Christianity 100–425 C.E.: A Sourcebook.* Minneapolis: Fortress, 1992.

Macmurray, John. *Persons in Relation.* London: Faber & Faber, 1961.

———. *The Self as Agent.* London: Faber & Faber, 1957.

Maddox, Randy L. "A Change of Affections: The Development, Dynamics, and Dethronement of John Wesley's 'Heart Religion.'" Pages 3–31 in *"Heart Religion" in the Methodist Tradition and Related Movements.* Edited by Richard Steele. Metuchen, NJ: Scarecrow Press, 2001.

———. *Responsible Grace: John Wesley's Practical Theology.* Nashville: Abingdon, 1994.

———. "Shaping the Virtuous Heart: The Abiding Mission of the Wesleys." *Circuit Rider* 29 (July/August 2005): 27–28.

Maddox, Randy L., with Paul Chilcote. Introduction to *A Plain Account of Christian Perfection,* by John Wesley. Kansas City, MO: Beacon Hill, 2015.

Malpas, Jeff. "Hans-Georg Gadamer." *The Stanford Encyclopedia of Philosophy* (Winter 2016 Edition). Edited by Edward N. Zalta. https://plato.stanford.edu/archives/win2016/entries/gadamer/

Marcus, Joel. "The Evil Inclination in the Epistle of James." *CBQ* 44 (1982): 606–21.

Marsden, Samuel. *The Letters and Journals of Samuel Marsden, 1765–1838.* Edited by John Rawson Elder. Dunedin, N.Z.: University of Otago, 1932.

Marshall, Christopher. *Beyond Retribution: A New Testament Vision for Justice, Crime, and Punishment.* Grand Rapids: Eerdmans, 2001.

———. *Compassionate Justice: An Interdisciplinary Dialogue with Two Gospel Parables on Law, Crime, and Restorative Justice.* Eugene, OR: Cascade, 2012.

Martin, Dale B. *The Corinthian Body.* New Haven: Yale University Press, 1995.

———. "Paul without Passion: On Paul's Rejection of Desire in Sex and Marriage." Pages 65–76 in *Sex and the Single Savior: Gender and Sexuality in Biblical Interpretation.* Louisville: Westminster John Knox, 2006.

———. *Sex and the Single Savior: Gender and Sexuality in Biblical Interpretation.* Louisville: Westminster John Knox, 2006.

———. *Slavery as Salvation: The Metaphor of Slavery in Pauline Christianity.* New Haven: Yale University Press, 1990.

Martin, Ralph P. *Reconciliation: A Study of Paul's Theology.* Atlanta: John Knox, 1981.

Martyn, J. Louis. "Epistemology at the Turn of the Ages." Pages 89–110 in *Theological Issues in the Letters of Paul.* Nashville: Abingdon, 1997.

————. *Galatians: A New Translation, with Introduction and Commentary.* AB 33A. New York: Doubleday, 1997.

————. *Theological Issues in the Letters of Paul.* Nashville: Abingdon, 1997.

May, Stephen. *Stardust and Ashes: Science Fiction in Christian Perspective.* London: SPCK, 1998.

McClintock Fulkerson, Mary. *Changing the Subject: Women's Discourses and Feminist Theology.* Minneapolis: Fortress, 1994.

McGlothlin, Thomas D. *Resurrection as Salvation: Development and Conflict in Pre-Nicene Paulinism.* Cambridge: Cambridge University Press, 2018.

McSwain, Jeff. *Movements of Grace: The Dynamic Christo-realism of Barth, Bonhoeffer, and the Torrances.* Eugene, OR: Wipf & Stock, 2010.

————. *"Simul" Sanctification: Barth's Hidden Vision for Human Transformation.* Eugene, OR: Pickwick, 2018.

Meeks, Wayne A. "The 'Haustafeln' and American Slavery: A Hermeneutical Challenge." Pages 245–52 in *Theology and Ethics in Paul and His Interpreters: Essays in Honor of Victor Paul Furnish.* Edited by Eugene H. Lovering Jr. and Jerry L. Sumney. Nashville: Abingdon, 1996.

————. "The Polyphonic Ethics of the Apostle Paul." *Annual of the Society of Christian Ethics* 8 (1988): 17–29.

Miller, Colin. *The Practice of the Body of Christ: Human Agency in Pauline Theology after MacIntyre.* Princeton Theological Monograph Series 200. Eugene, OR: Pickwick, 2014.

Minamiki, George. *The Chinese Rites Controversy from Its Beginning to Modern Times.* Chicago: Loyola University Press, 1985.

Moltmann, Jürgen. *The Trinity and the Kingdom of God.* London: SCM, 1981.

Monks of New Skete. *The Art of Raising a Puppy.* Rev. ed. New York: Little, Brown, 2011.

Moore, David B., and John M. McDonald. *Transforming Conflict in Workplaces and Other Communities.* Sydney: Transformative Justice Australia, 2000.

Moore, G. F. "Christian Writers on Judaism." *HTR* 14 (1921): 197–254.

————. *Judaism in the First Centuries of the Christian Era.* 3 vols. New York: Schocken, 1927–30.

Morrison, Karl F. *The Mimetic Tradition of Reform in the West.* Princeton: Princeton University Press, 1982.

Moses, Robert Ewusie. *Practices of Power: Revisiting the Principalities and Powers in the Pauline Letters.* Minneapolis: Fortress, 2014.

Mouw, Richard J. *The God Who Commands.* Notre Dame, IN: University of Notre Dame Press, 1990.

Nahin, Paul J. *Time Machines: Time Travel in Physics, Metaphysics, and Science Fiction*. 2nd ed. New York: Springer-Verlag, 1999.

Nathanson, Donald L. *Shame and Pride: Affect, Sex, and the Birth of the Self*. New York: Norton, 1992.

Neusner, J. *From Politics to Piety: The Emergence of Pharisaic Judaism*. Englewood Cliffs, NJ: Prentice-Hall, 1973.

Newsom, Carol A. "Angels." *ABD* 1:248–53.

Noakes-Duncan, Thomas. *Communities of Restoration: Ecclesial Ethics and Restorative Justice*. London: Bloomsbury, 2017.

Oates, Stephen B. *Let the Trumpet Sound: A Life of Martin Luther King, Jr.* New York: HarperCollins, 1982.

O'Donovan, Oliver. *Finding and Seeking: Ethics as Theology 2*. Grand Rapids: Eerdmans, 2014.

———. *The Problem of Self-Love in St. Augustine*. New Haven: Yale University Press, 1980.

———. *Self, World, and Time: Ethics as Theology 1; An Induction*. Grand Rapids: Eerdmans, 2013.

Pappas, George. "Internalist vs. Externalist Conceptions of Epistemic Justification." In *The Stanford Encyclopedia of Philosophy* (Fall 2017 Edition). Edited by Edward N. Zalta. https://plato.stanford.edu/cgi-bin/encyclopedia/archinfo.cgi?entry=justep-intext.

Parry, Robin A., and Christopher H. Partridge. *Universal Salvation? The Current Debate*. Grand Rapids: Eerdmans, 2003.

Pearson, Birger A. *Ancient Gnosticism: Traditions and Literature*. Minneapolis: Fortress, 2007.

Peppiat, Lucy. *Women and Worship at Corinth: Paul's Rhetorical Arguments in 1 Corinthians*. Eugene, OR: Cascade, 2015.

Perkins, John. *Beyond Charity: The Call to Christian Community Development*. Grand Rapids: Baker Books, 1993.

———. *Let Justice Roll Down*. Grand Rapids: Baker, 2014.

———. *With Justice for All: A Strategy for Community Development*. 3rd ed. Ventura, CA: Regal Books, 2007.

Perkins, John, and Wayne Gordon, with Randall Frame. *Leadership Revolution: Developing the Vision and Practice of Freedom and Justice*. Ventura, CA: Regal Books, 2012.

Pervo, Richard. *The Making of Paul: Constructions of Paul in Early Christianity*. Minneapolis: Fortress, 2010.

Pinsent, Andrew. "The Non-Aristotelean Virtue of Truth from the Second-Person Perspective." *EJPR* 5 (2013): 87–104.

———. *The Second-Person Perspective in Aquinas's Ethics: Virtues and Gifts*. London: Routledge, 2012.

Pinsent, Andrew, with Eleanore Stump, ed. *The Second Personal in the Philosophy of Religion*. Special issue: *EJPR* 5 (2013).

Pisani, Jacobus A. Du, and Kwang-Su Kim. "Establishing the Truth about the Apartheid Past: Historians and the South African Truth and Reconciliation Commission." *African Studies Quarterly* 8, no. 1 (2004): 77–95. http://www.africa.ufl.edu.proxy.lib.duke.edu/asq/.

Placher, William C. *The Domestication of Transcendence: How Modern Thinking about God Went Wrong*. Louisville: Westminster John Knox, 1996.

Polanyi, Michael. *Personal Knowledge: Towards a Post-Critical Philosophy*. New York: Routledge & Kegan Paul, 1958.

———. *The Tacit Dimension*. New York: Doubleday, 1966.

Pomeroy, Sarah B. *Goddesses, Whores, Wives, and Slaves: Women in Classical Antiquity*. New York: Schocken Books, 1995 (1975).

Postman, Neil. *Amusing Ourselves to Death: Public Discourse in the Age of Show Business*. New York: Penguin Group, 2005.

Poston, Ted. "Foundationalism." *Internet Encyclopedia of Philosophy*. http://www.iep.utm.edu/found-ep/.

———. "Internalism and Externalism in Epistemology." *Internet Encyclopedia of Philosophy*. http://www.iep.utm.edu/int-ext/.

Pranis, Kay. *The Little Book of Circle Processes: A New/Old Approach to Peacemaking*. Intercourse, PA: Good Books, 2005.

Pranis, Kay, Barry Stuart, and Mark Wedge. *Peacemaking Circles: From Crime to Community*. St. Paul: Living Justice Press, 2003.

Rabens, Volker. *The Holy Spirit and Ethics in Paul: Transformation and Empowering for Religious-Ethical Life*. 2nd rev. ed. Minneapolis: Fortress, 2014.

———. "*Pneuma* and the Beholding of God: Reading Paul in the Context of Philonic Mystical Traditions." Pages 293–329 in *The Holy Spirit, Inspiration, and the Cultures of Antiquity*. Edited by Jörg Frey and John R. Levison. Berlin: de Gruyter, 2014.

Radner, Ephraim. *Time and the Word: Figural Reading of the Christian Scriptures*. Grand Rapids: Eerdmans, 2016.

Rae, Murray A. *History and Hermeneutics*. London: T&T Clark, 2005.

Räisänen, Heikki. *Paul and the Law*. Tübingen: Mohr Siebeck, 1987 (1983).

Reed, A. H. *Marsden of Māoriland: Pioneer and Peacemaker*. Dunedin, N.Z.: A. H. & A. W. Reed, 1938.

Rogers, Eugene F. *After the Spirit: A Constructive Pneumatology from Resources outside the Modern West*. Grand Rapids: Eerdmans, 2005.

———. *Sexuality and the Christian Body: Their Way into the Triune God.* Oxford: Blackwell, 1999.

Rorty, Richard. *Philosophy and the Mirror of Nature.* Princeton: Princeton University Press, 1979.

Ross, Rupert. *Returning to the Teachings: Exploring Aboriginal Justice.* Rev. ed. Toronto: Penguin, 2006.

Rowe, C. Kavin. "Biblical Pressure and Trinitarian Hermeneutics." *ProEccl* 11 (2002): 295–312.

———. "For Future Generations: Worshiping Jesus and the Integration of the Theological Disciplines." *ProEccl* 17, no. 2 (2008): 186–209.

———. "The Grammar of Life: The Areopagus Speech and Pagan Tradition." *NTS* 57 (2011): 69–80.

———. "King Jesus." *Faith and Leadership,* January 4, 2010. https://www.faithand leadership.com/king-jesus.

———. "Navigating the Differences in the Gospels." *Faith and Leadership,* August 17, 2009. https://www.faithandleadership.com/navigating-differences-gospels.

———. "The New Testament as an Innovation of the Old." *Faith and Leadership,* October 26, 2009. https://www.faithandleadership.com/new-testament -innovation-old.

———. *One True Life: The Stoics and Early Christians as Rival Traditions.* New Haven: Yale University Press, 2016.

———. "Pentecost as Traditioned Innovation." *Faith and Leadership,* April 27, 2009. https://www.faithandleadership.com/pentecost-traditioned-innova tion.

———. "Romans 10:13: What Is the Name of the Lord?" *HBT* 22 (2000): 135–73.

———. "Traditioned Innovation: A Biblical Way of Thinking." *Faith and Leadership,* March 16, 2009. https://www.faithandleadership.com/traditioned -innovation-biblical-way-thinking.

———. *World Upside Down: Reading Acts in the Graeco-Roman Age.* Oxford: Oxford University Press, 2009.

Rubin, Gayle. "The Traffic in Women: Notes on the 'Political Economy' of Sex." Pages 74–113 in *Women, Class, and the Feminist Imagination.* Edited by Karen Hansen and Ilene Philipson. Philadelphia: Temple University Press, 1975.

Sanders, E. P. *Paul and Palestinian Judaism: A Comparison of Patterns of Religion.* Philadelphia: Fortress, 1977.

Sanneh, Lamin. *Translating the Message: The Missionary Impact on Culture.* 2nd ed. Maryknoll, NY: Orbis Books, 1989.

Schweitzer, Albert. *The Mysticism of Paul the Apostle.* Translated by W. Montgomery. Baltimore: Johns Hopkins University Press, 1998 (1931).

———. *Paul and His Interpreters*. Translated by W. Montgomery. New York: Schocken, 1964 (1912).

Scott, James C. *Domination and the Arts of Resistance: Hidden Transcripts*. New Haven: Yale University Press, 1990.

Sechrest, Love L. *A Former Jew: Paul and the Dialectics of Race*. London: T&T Clark, 2009.

Smail, Thomas A. *The Giving Gift: The Holy Spirit in Person*. London: Hodder & Stoughton, 1988.

Smith, Christian. *What Is a Person? Rethinking Humanity, Social Life, and the Moral Good from the Person Up*. Chicago: University of Chicago Press, 2010.

Smith, Emily Esfahani. "Masters of Love." *The Atlantic*, June 12, 2014. https://www.theatlantic.com/health/archive/2014/06/happily-ever-after/372573/.

Smith, J. Warren. "'Arian' Foundationalism or 'Athanasian' Apocalypticism: A Patristic Assessment." Pages 78–95 in *Beyond Old and New Perspectives in Paul*. Edited by Chris Tilling. Eugene, OR: Cascade, 2014.

Soulen, R. Kendall. *The God of Israel and Christian Theology*. Minneapolis: Fortress, 1996.

Stambaugh, John E., and David L. Balch. *The New Testament in Its Social Environment*. Philadelphia: Westminster, 1986.

Stanley, Brian. *The Bible and the Flag: Protestant Missions and British Imperialism in the Nineteenth and Twentieth Centuries*. Trowbridge, Eng.: Apollos, 1990.

Stark, Rodney. *The Rise of Christianity: A Sociologist Reconsiders History*. Princeton: Princeton University Press, 1996.

Steinmetz, David. "Forgiving the Unforgivable Wrong." Pages 79–80 in *Taking the Long View: Christian Theology in Historical Perspective*. Oxford: Oxford University Press, 2011.

———. "The Superiority of Pre-critical Exegesis." *Theology Today* 37 (1980): 27–38.

Stendahl, Krister. "The Apostle Paul and the Introspective Conscience of the West." *HTR* 56, no. 3 (1963): 199–215.

———. "Paul among Jews and Gentiles." Pages 1–77 in *Paul among Jews and Gentiles, and Other Essays*. Philadelphia: Fortress, 1976.

Stewart, James. *A Man in Christ: The Vital Elements of St. Paul's Religion*. London: Hodder & Stoughton, 1935.

Storey, Peter. "A Different Kind of Justice: Truth and Reconciliation in South Africa." *Christian Century* 114, no. 25 (1997): 788–93.

Stringfellow, William. *An Ethic for Christians and Other Aliens in a Strange Land*. Waco, TX: Word, 1973.

Stump, Eleanore. "Omnipresence, Indwelling, and the Second-Personal." *EJPR* 5 (2013): 29–54.

———. *Wandering in Darkness: Narrative and the Problem of Suffering*. Oxford: Oxford University Press, 2010.

Swartley, Williard. *Slavery, Sabbath, War, and Women: Case Issues in Biblical Interpretation*. Scottdale, PA: Herald Press, 1983.

Tallon, Luke B. "Our Being Is in Becoming: The Nature of Human Transformation in the Theology of Karl Barth, Joseph Ratzinger, and John Zizioulas." PhD. diss., University of St Andrews, 2011. https://research-repository.st-andrews.ac.uk/bitstream/handle/10023/2572/LukeTallonPhDThesis.pdf?sequence=6&isAllowed=y.

Tannehill, Robert C. "Participation in Christ: A Central Theme in Pauline Soteriology." Pages 223–37 in *The Shape of the Gospel: New Testament Essays*. Eugene, OR: Cascade, 2007.

Taussig, Hal. *In the Beginning Was the Meal: Social Experimentation and Early Christian Identity*. Minneapolis: Fortress, 2009.

Taylor, Charles. *Modern Social Imaginaries*. Durham, NC: Duke University Press, 2004.

———. "On Social Imaginary." Lecture in the course "Contemporary Sociological Theory," Spring 2000, NYU/Calhoun, 2004. https://web.archive.org/web/20041019043656/http://www.nyu.edu/classes/calhoun/Theory/Taylor-on-si.htm.

Thiselton, Anthony C. *The First Epistle to the Corinthians: A Commentary on the Greek Text*. NIGTC. Grand Rapids: Eerdmans, 2000.

———. *A Shorter Guide to the Holy Spirit: Bible, Doctrine, Experience*. Grand Rapids: Eerdmans, 2016.

Tilling, Chris, ed. *Beyond Old and New Perspectives on Paul: Reflections on the Work of Douglas Campbell*. Eugene, OR: Cascade, 2014.

———. *Paul's Divine Christology*. WUNT 2.232. Tübingen: Mohr Siebeck, 2012.

Tomkins, Silvan S. *Affect Imagery Consciousness: The Complete Edition*. 4 vols. Philadelphia: Springer, 1962–1992.

Torrance, Alan J. "*Auditus Fidei:* Where and How Does God Speak? Faith, Reason, and the Question of Criteria." Pages 27–52 in *Reason and the Reasons of Faith*. Edited by Paul J. Griffiths and Reinhardt Hütter. New York: T&T Clark, 2005.

———. "Is Love the Essence of God?" Pages 114–37 in *Nothing Greater, Nothing Better: Theological Essays on the Love of God*. Edited by Kevin J. Vanhoozer. Grand Rapids: Eerdmans, 2001.

———. "Jesus in Christian Doctrine." Pages 200–219 in *The Cambridge Companion to Jesus*. Edited by Markus Bockmuehl. Cambridge: Cambridge University Press, 2001.

———. *Persons in Communion: An Essay on Trinitarian Description and Human*

Participation with Special Reference to Volume One of Karl Barth's "Church Dogmatics." Edinburgh: T & T Clark, 1996.

———. "The Self-Relation, Narcissism, and the Gospel of Grace." *SJT* 40 (1987): 481–510.

———. "The Trinity." Pages 72–91 in *The Cambridge Companion to Karl Barth.* Edited by John Webster. Cambridge: Cambridge University Press, 2000.

Torrance, James B. "The Contribution of McLeod Campbell to Scottish Theology." *SJT* 26 (1973): 295–311.

———. "Covenant or Contract: A Study of the Theological Background of Worship in Seventeenth-Century Scotland." *SJT* 23 (1970): 51–76.

———. "The Vicarious Humanity of Christ." Pages 127–47 in *The Incarnation: Ecumenical Studies in the Nicene-Constantinopolitan Creed, A.D. 381.* Edited by T. F. Torrance. Edinburgh: Handsel Press, 1981.

Torrance, Thomas F. *The Christian Doctrine of God: One Being, Three Persons.* Edinburgh: T&T Clark, 1996.

———. *Space, Time, and Resurrection.* Edinburgh: Handsel Press, 1976.

Travis, Stephen H. *Christ and the Judgment of God: The Limits of Divine Retribution in New Testament Thought.* Peabody, MA: Hendrickson, 2009.

Trible, Phyllis. *Texts of Terror.* Philadelphia: Fortress, 1984.

Tutu, Desmond Mpilo. *No Future without Forgiveness.* New York: Doubleday, 1999.

Vanhoozer, Kevin J., Constantine R. Campbell, and Michael J. Thate, eds. *"In Christ" in Paul: Explorations in Paul's Theology of Union and Participation.* WUNT 2.384. Tübingen: Mohr Siebeck, 2015.

Volf, Miroslav. *Exclusion and Embrace: A Theological Exploration of Identity, Otherness, and Reconciliation.* Nashville: Abingdon, 1996.

———. *Free of Charge: Giving and Forgiving in a Culture Stripped of Grace.* Grand Rapids: Zondervan, 2009.

———. "Gender Identity." Pages 167–91 in *Exclusion and Embrace: A Theological Exploration of Identity, Otherness, and Reconciliation.* Nashville: Abingdon, 1996.

———. "'The Trinity Is Our Social Program': The Doctrine of the Trinity and the Shape of Social Engagement." *Modern Theology* 14 (1998): 403–23.

———. "Worship as Adoration and Action: Reflections on a Christian Way of Being-in-the-World." Pages 30–41 in *Worship at the Next Level: Insight from Contemporary Voices.* Edited by Tim A. Dearborn and Scott Coil. Grand Rapids: Baker Books, 2004.

Wagner, Ross J. *Heralds of the Good News: Isaiah and Paul in Concert in the Letter to the Romans.* Leiden: Brill, 2002.

Wainwright, Geoffrey. "The Holy Spirit." Pages 273–96 in *The Cambridge Compan-*

ion to Christian Doctrine. Edited by Colin E. Gunton. Cambridge: Cambridge University Press, 1997.

Walls, Andrew. "The Multiple Conversions of Timothy Richards: A Paradigm of Missionary Experience." Pages 271–94 in *The Gospel in the World: International Baptist Studies*. Edited by David Bebbington. Carlisle: Paternoster, 2002.

Watson, Francis B. "Resurrection and the Limits of Paulinism." Pages 452–71 in *The Word Leaps the Gap: Essays on Scripture and Theology in Honor of Richard B. Hays*. Edited by J. Ross Wagner, C. Kavin Rowe, and A. Katherine Grieb. Grand Rapids: Eerdmans, 2008.

———. *Text and Truth: Redefining Biblical Theology*. Edinburgh: T&T Clark, 1997.

———. *Text, Church, and World: Biblical Interpretation in Theological Perspective*. Edinburgh: T&T Clark, 1994.

Webster, John. "Resurrection and Scripture." Pages 138–55 in *Christology and Scripture: Interdisciplinary Perspectives*. Edited by Andrew T. Lincoln and Angus Paddison. London: T&T Clark, 2008.

Wells, Samuel. *Improvisation: The Drama of Christian Ethics*. Grand Rapids: Zondervan, 2004.

Wells, Samuel, and Marcia A. Owen. *Living without Enemies: Being Present in the Midst of Violence*. Downers Grove, IL: InterVarsity Press, 2011.

Wiedemann, Thomas E. J. *Adults and Children in the Roman Empire*. New Haven: Yale University Press, 1989.

———. *Slavery*. Oxford: Clarendon, 1987.

Williams, Demetrius. *An End to This Strife: The Politics of Gender in African American Churches*. Minneapolis: Fortress, 2004.

Williams, Michael Allen. *Rethinking "Gnosticism": An Argument for Dismantling a Dubious Category*. Princeton: Princeton University Press, 1996.

Wilson, B. *Unmanly Men: Refigurations of Masculinity in Luke-Acts*. Oxford: Oxford University Press, 2015.

Wilson-Hartgrove, Jonathan. *New Monasticism: What It Has to Say to Today's Church*. Grand Rapids: Brazos Press, 2008.

———. *Reconstructing the Gospel: Finding Freedom from Slaveholder Religion*. Downers Grove, IL: InterVarsity Press, 2018.

———. *The Rule of Saint Benedict: A Contemporary Paraphrase*. Brewster, MA: Paraclete Press, 2012.

Wink, Walter. *Engaging the Powers: Discernment and Resistance in a World of Domination*. Philadelphia: Fortress, 1992.

———. *Naming the Powers: The Language of Power in the New Testament*. Philadelphia: Fortress, 1984.

———. *Unmasking the Powers: The Invisible Forces That Determine Human Existence.* Philadelphia: Fortress, 1986.

Winner, Lauren. *Girl Meets God: On the Path to a Spiritual Life.* Chapel Hill, NC: Algonquin Books, 2002.

———. *Mudhouse Sabbath: An Invitation to a Life of Spiritual Discipline.* Brewster, MA: Paraclete Press, 2003.

———. *Still: Notes on a Mid-Faith Crisis.* New York: HarperCollins, 2012.

Wirzba, Norman. *Way of Love: Recovering the Heart of Christianity.* New York: HarperOne, 2016.

Wrede, W. *Paul.* Translated by Edward Lummis. Boston: American Unitarian Association, 1908.

Wright, N. T. *Christian Origins and the Question of God.* (With N. Perrin) Vol. 3: *The Resurrection of the Son of God.* Vol. 4 (2 vols.): *Paul and the Faithfulness of God.* Minneapolis: Fortress, 2003–13.

———. *The Climax of the Covenant: Christ and the Law in Pauline Theology.* Edinburgh: T&T Clark, 1991.

———. *Justification: God's Plan and Paul's Vision.* Downers Grove, IL: InterVarsity Press, 2009.

Yeago, David S. "The New Testament and the Nicene Dogma: A Contribution to the Recovery of Theological Exegesis." *ProEccl* 3 (1994): 152–64.

Yoder, John Howard. *The Politics of Jesus: Vicit Agnus Noster.* 3rd ed. Grand Rapids: Eerdmans, 1994.

Young, William P. *The Shack.* Newbury Park, CA: Windblown Media, 2007.

Zehr, Howard. *The Little Book of Restorative Justice.* Intercourse, PA: Good Books, 2002.

Zizioulas, John D. *Being as Communion: Studies in Personhood and the Church.* New York: St. Vladimir's Seminary Press, 1985.

———. *Communion and Otherness: Further Studies in Personhood and the Church.* Edited by Paul McPartlan. London: T&T Clark, 2006.

INDEX OF AUTHORS

INDEX OF SUBJECTS

sion of, 427, 432–34, 438, 708–14. *See also* supersessionism; universalism

Jesus Christ: faith of, 298–300, 302–5; incarnation, 23n16, 61, 65, 81–83, 88, 98n6; presence of, to Israel, even in the past, 708–11, 715, 716. *See also* atonement; resurrection

Jews. *See* Israel

joy, 355–61

Judaism. *See* Israel

judgment, 420–26; annihilation of unbelievers, 425–26; prudential, when navigating local contexts and community formation, 511; restorative, 327–28, 332–35, 340–41, 348–52, 437. *See also* resurrection: limited resurrection (in Paul); universalism

justice: not punitively retributive, 188, 258, 319, 323, 348, 350, 400, 417–18, 420–26, 437–39, 741; as restorative, 332–35, 340–42, 348, 352

kindness, 339–40, 490, 495

language: importance of ethically, 346–48, 350, 503, 513, 520, 551, 553, 567; during missional immersion, 451. *See also* teachers, teaching

leaders, 223–51; indigenous, 522; institutionalization in the Pastorals, 732–35, 737, 739; making prudential judgments, 536. *See also* apostleship, apostles; evangelists; peace, peacemaking; prophets; teachers, teaching

learning, 198–205

liberal, liberalism, 616, 631, 680; contributions to supersessionism through the myth of progress, 690,

713; indifference to dangerous sacred nation theology, 695; partly useful notion of consent, 612; problematic account of freedom, 119n8, 201n4, 204, 205–15, 217, 218, 219, 221, 316–17, 323; problematic account of identity, 383, 395

liturgy, 521–22, 540, 542. *See also* modes of transformation: translation; teachers, teaching

Lord's Supper, 283, 414, 481, 530n11

love: as instantiated in different subordinate virtues, 264–69; as the key overarching virtue, 257–64, 267–70; key to the divine relationality, 51–56, 61–62, 65–69; relation to faith, 315–16. *See also* agapeism; Augustine, Augustinianism

Marcionism, 724, 732; functional Marcionism, 151n23, 413, 432n21, 485, 486n7, 587, 592; Pastorals as against Marcion, 724, 725n6, 726, 731–35

marriage: appropriate and inappropriate sexual activity and gender construction, 594–649; covenantal definition of, 635–37; demythologized account of sexual activity and, 602–6, 607–11; different hermeneutical strategies, 627–34; false liberal account of, 211–13; as an interim ordering structure, 607–11; marriage by gender and sexual minorities, 634–42, 646; patriarchal dimension in Paul, 623–27; Paul's account of, 595–602, 618–21; sexual activity, account of, 611–15; situation at Corinth, 93. *See also* covenant; inclusion

INDEX OF SCRIPTURE AND OTHER ANCIENT TEXTS